Henrietta Green's

FOOD LOVERS'

GUIDE TO BRITAIN

BBC BOOKS

*To the late Jane Grigson who
is an inspiration to all food lovers,
and whose personal encouragement
I much miss.*

The Author and Publishers would like to thank
the Rural Development Commission for their
assistance with this book.

Published by BBC Books,
A division of BBC Enterprises Ltd
Woodlands, 80 Wood Lane,
London W12 0TT

First Published in 1993
© Henrietta Green 1993

Reprinted 1993 (twice)

ISBN 0 563 36792 X

Edited by Lewis Esson
Designed by David Robinson
Base map © Bartholomew

Set in ITC Berkeley Oldstyle
Printed in England by Clays Ltd, St Ives plc
Cover printed by Clays Ltd, St Ives plc

Contents

FOREWORD

For fifteen years BBC Radio 4's *The Food Programme* has been singing the praises of good food and campaigning on behalf of the enthusiasts who produce and sell it. Battered by the recession and harassed by a tidal wave of directives from Brussels and Whitehall, far too many have been put out of business. As Henrietta Green discovered on her journey round the British Isles, however, the commitment to providing produce of integrity has never been higher.

The people you will meet in the pages of this book are defenders of our regional tradition and preservers of the nation's culinary heritage. They remind us that there is still a healthy living food culture not obsessed with long shelf-life, skilful packaging and cosmetic appeal. Their success is built on the growing market for food which is full of taste and flavour – food produced with concern for the environment, sound husbandry and a respect for animal life.

This book can be enjoyed on several levels. It is a comprehensive guide to food of character and individuality as essential for any traveller who cares about what they eat as a road map. It is also a good read, a chance to experience a real taste of Britain without picking up a knife and fork. Moreover, if you can't get to where all this wonderful food is being produced a lot of it can be enjoyed by means of mail order.

However you use *Henrietta Green's Food Lovers' Guide to Britain*, I hope it will kindle a renewed respect for the dedicated band of British food-makers whose refusal to compromise their principles puts us permanently in their debt.

Derek Cooper

INTRODUCTION

For good food you must have good ingredients – it makes cooking so much easier and eating far more enjoyable. Years ago I heard the late great Jane Grigson on the radio talking about the essence of her cooking. She said that it was about buying the best produce and cooking it as simply as possible to emphasize its inherent flavour, and I have never forgotten that.

But where do you buy such produce? You can try the supermarkets, but so often they disappoint with their mass-produced food. Far more satisfying is to seek out the smaller speciality producers – the craftspeople of the food world. They include the farmers and growers who raise old-fashioned breeds of animals known for their richness and depth of flavour or choose vegetables and fruit varieties for taste rather than appearance and yield; or the cheese-makers who still make by hand in the time-honoured way; or the preserve-makers who boil up whole fruit in small batches.

To discover them all and many more, my dog Violet and I have travelled the length and breadth of Britain. This has meant years of work and most of it has been pleasurable. If anyone tries to tell you that Britain suffers from a dearth of quality producers of either raw or processed foods, just don't believe them – there are hundreds. However, trying to define 'quality' is never easy; it is more than a pretty label or old-fashioned image. For me it means food produced with a commitment to taste and texture, made with the proper ingredients in the proper way with no short cuts; for example a true shortbread is made with flour, the rights fats, sugar and nothing else, and for the traditional texture it must be carefully mixed and rolled out.

In compiling my *Food Lovers' Guide to Britain*, I have included the most interesting shops and only the best producers who deal directly with customers either through their own outlets or by mail order.

Shopping is the essence of good food. I hope by using my book you will find new suppliers and rediscover all that is good in food from Britain.

Henrietta Green

HOW TO USE THIS BOOK

STRUCTURE
As you can see, I have divided the book first of all into sections on England, Wales and Scotland (Food Lovers interested in Ireland should use *The Bridgestone Irish Food Guide* by John and Sally McKenna, Estragon Press). These sections are divided by counties – keen geographers may well be irritated by my somewhat whimsical combination of the old and new county boundaries, but I make no apologies for it. Within the counties, the main entries are arranged alphabetically by place-name – be it city, town or hamlet. London, as usual, is the exception as it is arranged by postal district. At the top of each entry is a map reference keying it to the appropriate map at the end of the book.

THE MAPS
These show all the place-names of the main entries. The maps are, however, really only meant as a rough guide to location or to help you plan a trip to the various producers within the counties. When on the road I do recommend that they should only be used in conjunction with a good road atlas.

THE ENTRIES
At the top of each main entry you will find the full name and address of each producer. Alongside that appear the map reference and the products for which I particularly recommend them. You will also see any number of the following symbols:

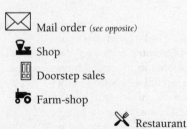

Mail order *(see opposite)*

Shop

Doorstep sales

Farm-shop

Pick-Your-Own

Market Stall

Scenic

Organic *(ie producing to a verified organic standard)*

Restaurant

Apart from these main entries, the book is peppered with boxed features on certain producers, restaurants, hotels and shops, the occasional recipe and rather opinionated comment. At the end of each county, I have also put together an '*And Also…*' section in which I round up all those other places worthy of mention.

MAIL ORDER ✉

As so many of the producers are in isolated spots, mail order is a vital part of their business. However, I would like to stress that mail order does not necessarily mean sending food by post, it can mean dispatch by overnight courier or even delivery by their own van; each supplier has their own arrangements. Please also note that not all producers with a mail-order service are prepared to mail-order their entire range: when this is the case, l have indicated the available mail-order range at the end of the entry,

VISITING SUPPLIERS

Where appropriate, I have given opening hours in the main entries. I have gone to great pains to get the latest information in each case, but hours can vary at little or no notice. The same is obviously true of PYO availability, and indeed the seasonality of all fruit and vegetables. Where I have asked you to telephone ahead before visiting, it means that there are no regular and guaranteed opening hours; often there will be someone there, but you should check first to avoid any disappointment.

INDEXES

At the end of the book there is a general index listing all the producers mentioned in the book. Following that there is a second more detailed index of the products for which I have recommended each producer – say, for example, you want to scan all the Cheddar-makers, you can find them all listed together under cheese. Mail-order producers are also clearly indicated in both indexes.

Although I have gone to great lengths to ensure all the information in the book is correct at time of going to press, I do apologize in advance to any reader or producer if there are any inaccuracies, but I cannot accept responsibility for them.

READERS' REPORTS

If you have any comments – good or bad – on any of the products or services provided by any of the places listed in the book I would love to hear from you. Similarly, if you would like to recommend anyone not listed for future editions, please send full details (including the complete name and exact postal address and telephone number with full prefix). Please make your comments as full as possible, to include your opinions of the taste and quality of the produce, the service, value for money and the efficiency of the mail-order service, if appropriate, as well as some idea of the date of your purchase. Address your letters as follows:

The Food Lovers' Guide to Britain,
Room A3144, BBC Books,
Woodlands, 80 Wood Lane, London W12 OTT

England

AVON

Hobbs House Bakery 🍞

BREAD

39 High Street, Chipping Sodbury, Bristol, Avon BS17 6BA
TEL *0454 321629*   **CONTACT** *Sam Wells*   **HOURS** *Mon-Sat 9.00-17.30*
DIRECTIONS *In town centre*

If it wasn't for the queue outside, you could almost walk straight past Hobbs House Bakery in the High Street of the busy Cotswold town of Chipping Sodbury, as its shop frontage is very discreet. The shop, with the bakery behind, is in half a large Georgian stone house that dates back to the 1700s. Inside, the shelves are tightly packed with their remarkable range, freshly baked daily. A family business, Hobbs set up about 10 years ago as bakers of ordinary breads but, as Sam Wells told me, 'We soon started experimenting to relieve the boredom. The last thing we wanted was to get into a rut and we had seen all sorts of different breads when we'd been away and customers would bring us loaves they'd brought back from their holidays. So we thought – why not give it a whirl?'

The result is not what you would expect from a small country bakery. Here you will find gloriously flavoured breads: sun-dried tomato, generously studded with thick pieces; a rich nutty walnut that not only contains chunks of nut, but is also basted and kneaded with walnut oil; black olive; basil and green olive; and onion. With a soft, moist texture, these breads are certainly made with great flair and imagination. Then there is 'tiger' bread, based on a Cornish idea of painting fermented rice paste on an overnight dough to give it a creamy crunchy crust. 'Quern', made only for Saturdays, is a coarse wholemeal mixed with black treacle; 'soft', with a sharp-sweet taste, has good keeping qualities and is delightful with a mature cheese. They also bake a German-style sour dough; organic and three-seed (poppy, sesame and sunflower) wholemeals, both with flour from Shipton Mill (see page 100); and a good dense, full-bodied 'overnight' white bread in which the dough is left to ferment overnight.

Although they see themselves as 'essentially bread-makers', the shop also stocks plenty of cakes, buns and slices, as well as their own pork pies (with meat from Nelsons the butchers next door) and Sodbury cake, a date and walnut sponge. What struck me particularly about Hobbs House Bakery was their flair and the quality of their products (there is certainly no stinting with the ingredients). When I asked why most other small bakers do not follow their example, Sam could not give me the answer, 'All it needs is a bit of imagination. Anyone can do it – but we're glad they don't'. Perhaps they should; it might give the small bakeries the shot-in-the-arm they obviously seem to need.

As history would have it, Sally Lunn – a Huguenot escaping persecution in France – came to Bath to work for a baker in Lilliput Alley and started baking the eponymous bun. The 'secret' recipe – based on the French brioche – calls for butter, eggs, milk, sugar, plain flour and yeast with, apparently, four provings of the dough. Difficult to describe, it is not rich enough for a brioche, but is too yeasty and light for a bun – and it looks like a large, puffed-up bap. **Sally Lunn's, 4 North Parade Passage, Bath (tel 0225 461634)** is the oldest house in Bath, with the bakery on the second floor, a teashop on the first and ground floor and a museum in the basement. Either buy the buns to take away or try them in the tearooms, where they serve them cut in half, toasted and spread with a variety of sweet or savoury toppings.

TIMSBURY   MAP 2

Sleight Farm   CHEESE

Sleight Farm, Timsbury, Bath, Avon BA3 1HN
TEL *0761 470620* CONTACT *Mary Holbrook – telephone ahead*

Mary Holbrook makes some of the best goats'- and ewes'-milk cheeses in England. You do not just have to take my word for it; the numerous prizes she has won at Nantwich and The Specialist Cheesemakers' Association Shows testify to it. The farm, in the rolling Mendip Hills, offers excellent pasture for her goats and sheep and they graze extensively with the minimum use of fertilizers.

Her cheeses, made in the dairy by the farmyard, are all unpasteurized and offer such depth of flavour and smoothness of texture that they knock spots off several French equivalents. (Without wishing to appear too chauvinistic, I take great pleasure in serving them to my French friends. They can't believe they're made here – and by an Englishwoman!) They can be bought from Neal's Yard Dairy in Covent Garden, London (see page 164) and several other specialist cheese shops throughout the country.

Dealing with the goats' cheeses first: Mary makes Sleight, a lightly salted young creamy and moist cheese with a mild but pronounced flavour, in 115 g (4 oz) rounds. This is either plain or coated in coarsely ground black pepper, rosemary or crushed garlic and herbs. Ash Pyramid is a more compact, creamier cheese with a flavour described by cheese specialist Juliet Harbutt as 'fermenting fruit'; moulded into 200 g (7 oz) pyramids, it is coated with charcoal. Tymsboro' is a semi-soft, mould-induced pyramid with a hint of sweetness; and Mendip, a hard cheese with a pliant texture and a taste of fresh pastures, can be eaten when young and mild at 3 months or when harder at 6 months.

Her ewes'-milk cheeses include a soft, crumbly but mild Feta that is matured for up to 6 months; mould-ripened Emlett with a smooth creamy interior that softens and mellows with age; Little Rydings, a 200 g (7 oz) mould-ripened Coulommiers shape that has a nutty sweet fullness; and Tyning, a superb hard cheese that is matured for 6-12 months; reminiscent of Pecorino it has a deeply satisfying sheep's tang. Eat it cut in slivers with fresh pears; or grate it over pasta.

One cautionary note: as I write, Mary Holbrook's future is uncertain due to the current food legislation issued both from here and the EC. Mary's hygiene is exemplary but, even so, it may not be good enough for the 'powers that be'. Currently she matures her hard cheeses in a special barn off the farmyard. Obviously they have to be transported there from the dairy, and the only way is to cover and carry them through the open air. However, the Authorities do not like this as they claim that, even though it takes a few seconds, it is not good practice. It seems ridiculous that cheeses as good as Mary's may be under threat.

TOCKINGTON
MAP 2

The Kitchen Garden 🐾 🍵 🍨
FRUIT & ICE-CREAM

Oldown Estate, Tockington, Bristol, Avon BS12 4PG

TEL *0454 413605* FAX *0454 413955* CONTACT *Robert Bernays* HOURS *Apr to end-Oct: Tues-Sun 10.00-18.00; Nov to end-Mar: Tues-Sun 10.00-16.00 (open bank holidays)* CARDS *Access, Visa, Mastercard, Eurocard* DIRECTIONS *From Bristol take A38 towards Gloucester. From the junction with M5, follow Oldown Estate signs. If on M5, come off at junction 16 and follow signs.*

Oldown Estate covers 400 acres of wood and farmland overlooking the river Severn. There is plenty to do here for all the family as there are walks, rides, farm visits, a 'forest challenge' that boasts 'probably the longest rope slide in the world', as well as the more leisurely activities of picking, shopping or merely eating in their restaurant. Entry is £3.00 for adults and £2.00 for children and OAPs. However, if all you want to do is pick, shop or eat, entry is free.

As you come up the drive, you pass the high mellow brick walls of the kitchen garden on your left. It is a fine example of the scale of an old-fashioned kitchen garden, well protected by its walls and an indication of how self-sufficient country estates once were. Now it is full of fruit and vegetables to pick-your-own. You will find asparagus, runner and broad beans, sugar snap peas, courgettes, carrots, various lettuces and other salad crops, as well as several varieties of strawberries and raspberries (both main and autumn crops), tayberries, gooseberries, blackcurrants and redcurrants, blackberries, apples and pears.

Round the corner, in the large farm-shop converted from an out-building, you can buy the vegetables ready-picked. They also sell jams, jellies, marmalades and chutneys made by Rita the gardener from surplus fruit and vegetables. Not all of them are always in stock but there are usually tayberry, raspberry and mixed berry jams; crab apple and redcurrant jelly (plain or with brandy) or ginger Seville orange marmalade. There is also a huge range of chutneys, including pumpkin, green bean, pear, plum, and a cucumber and celery relish. They also make their own ice-cream with milk from the farm in about 15 flavours. The tayberry, again made with their own fruit, was fresh-tasting and very fruity (it even had the tiny pips) and the blackcurrant had a markedly deep flavour. However, as I was unable to get any technical details, I am afraid I cannot tell you any more. There are also various cakes and meringues, all made by local ladies (the broken meringue bits invariably end up in the ginger and meringue ice-cream), Hobbs House bread (see page 8) on Wednesdays and Saturdays; their own potatoes; cider, apple juice and sparkling perry from Long Ashton; cream from Cricket Malherbie (see page 221) and various cheeses and sausages.

And also...

- Bath boasts two cheese shops, *Paxton & Whitfield Fine Cheeses* at 1 John Street (tel 0225 466403) and *The Fine Cheese Company*, 29 Walcot Street (tel 0225 483407). The latter stocks well over a 100 on-farm British cheeses, own-made fresh cream truffles flavoured with liqueur and Hobbs House Bakery bread (see page 8)
- Steve Downey of *Heritage Foods* ✉, Lakeside, Bridgewater Road, Barrow Gurney, nr Bristol (tel 0275 393979) deals in fish for the 'environmentally aware'. Glenarm salmon, farmed in Northern Ireland, is free of chemicals, sea-bass is line-caught, scallops are dived – nothing is dredged or trawled as this harms both fish and environment. Delivery within 24 hours is promised throughout the UK.
- Open to the public, *Norwood Farm*, Bath Road, Norton St Philip, nr Bath (tel 0373 834356) is one of the few approved Rare Breed Survival Trust centres in the country and organically reared rare-breed meat is on sale at their farm-shop.

BEDFORDSHIRE

Springwell 🔳   NATURAL SPRING WATER

*The Barn, Butchers Wick, Sewell, Dunstable, Bedfordshire
LU6 1RP*

TEL *0582 608895* FAX *0582 665236* CONTACT *Ian Gridley – telephone
ahead*

We drink a fair amount of bottled water in this country, last year we
swallowed 550 million litres (about 1 billion pints) of the stuff; with
two-thirds imported, mainly from France, Switzerland and Italy.

We tend to call all bottled water 'mineral water'. In fact, according to
the EC, mineral water must be bottled at source from underground
water; untreated other than filtration to remove solid particles; and it
must contain naturally occurring minerals and benign micro-organisms.
Spring water, on the other hand, can be drawn from one or more
sources, including both underground or surface water, and can be
treated or processed.

Springwell water is a natural spring water and one of the few that you
can buy directly. The water rises up through the sweeping chalk
escarpment of Bedfordshire into a sealed culvert on Ian Gridley's land,
which is in a conservation area. A naturally hard water, it has a high
calcium content because it has risen through the chalk hills. Filtered
and bottled at source, it is either sold still or lightly carbonated (carbon
dioxide is injected into the water to make it fizzy); either way it has a
sharp clean taste.

And Also...

• *Clophill Fruit Farm* in Shefford Road, Clophill (tel 0525 861456) has
a good range of pick-your-own and ready-picked soft fruit, including 10
varieties of strawberries, 7 different raspberries, and redcurrants, blackcurrants and white currants.

• *Hill House Beef* ✉ at Hill House Farm, Pavenham Road, Carlton (tel
023482 5910) rear Limousin Friesian cross heifers for beef. Slaughtered
between 15 and 18 months and hung for 10 days, they butcher the beef
and sell it in 11.5 kg (25 lb) boxes. Each box contains a good cross-
section of cuts: for example, a joint each of topside, silverside, rib and
brisket; 6 sirloin or rump steaks; and trays of mince, chuck and stewing
steak.

BERKSHIRE

Doves Farm Foods 📖 🌾   ORGANIC FLOUR

Salisbury Road, Hungerford, Berkshire RG17 ORF

TEL *0488 684880* **FAX** *0488 685235* **CONTACT** *Clare Marriage* **HOURS** *Mon-Fri 9.00-17.00* **DIRECTIONS** *From Hungerford, take A338 towards Salisbury. Follow the road about 2½ miles. Farm is on the left, about 500 yards after the county sign for Wiltshire.*

Doves Farm is an interesting company. They have managed to combine running a successful and commercial business with an unquestionable commitment to the Organic movement – something cynics thought was impossible to achieve.

They started stone-grinding organic (to Soil Association standards) flour in 1978 and have built up their range over the years. Although their produce is widely distributed throughout the UK, they make a point of selling to the public direct from the mill. If you are a keen baker it is useful, as from here you can also buy their large sacks that normally are only sold to commercial bakers.

Their flour is divided into 3 categories: Organic, Premium (non-organic) and Specialist. The Organic range includes several 100% wholemeal flours: Strong, from hard wheat that is ideal for bread-making; Extra fine that is particularly finely ground for pastry-making; and Self-raising. They also mill spelt (*Triticum spelta*), which comes from the same genus as common wheat (*T. aestivium*) but has a different genetic structure: a higher protein content, and a greater concentration of vitamins and minerals. By all accounts, it bakes well, to produce a nutty wheaty-flavoured bread that does not crumble when sliced. For the past 4 years they have also milled by rollers and they now produce a 'Bio bake' range using organic flour, but roller-milled rather than stone-ground and only available in a minimum weight sack of 32 kg (5 stones).

The Non-organic range includes 100% strong wholemeal and self-raising flours and a Malthouse (a blend of brown flour, soft malted grains and rye flour). The Specialist range includes rye flour; barley flour for a creamy, close-textured loaf; three gluten-free flours; buck-wheat for noodles and crêpes; maize (cornmeal), and brown rice flour. They also sell their own organic whole-wheat crackers and peanut, chocolate chip and digestive biscuits made with their conventional flour and baked for them by a manufacturer.

✕ **The Harrow** ✉, *opposite the village pond and cricket field in* **West Ilsley, nr Newbury RG16 0AR (tel 0635 281260)** *is a popular pub with walkers. From here you can sup on Moorland beer and enjoy on-farm British cheeses and their own-made pies. Depending on the time of year, they make a lemony wild rabbit pie; a well-seasoned game pie, with locally shot pheasant, hare, and partridge or whatever else may be in season; venison pie, with rosemary, juniper berries and stout; and steak and mushroom pie. All are topped with a flaky pastry and baked in foil dishes. Weighing 675 g and 1 kg ($1\frac{1}{2}$ and $2\frac{1}{4}$ lb), they have proved so popular that landlady Heather Humphreys will send them anywhere in the country.*

RISELEY MAP 3

Village Maid ✉ ▥ SPENWOOD CHEESE

The Cottage, Basingstoke Road, Riseley, Reading, Berkshire RG7 1QD

TEL *0734 884564* CONTACT *Anne Wigmore – telephone ahead*

Matthew Fort, food editor of *The Guardian*, was obviously rather taken with cheese-maker Anne Wigmore. 'If I had to conjure up a picture of what a cheese maid should look like, Anne Wigmore is just about as close as you could come – tanned, merry, glowing with health, in bonnet, apron, shorts and wellies'. Evidently, at The Specialist Cheesemakers' Association Show in 1991, he was also taken by her cheese Spenwood: made from unpasteurized sheep's milk, it was described as, 'balanced, full of flavour,' and having a 'delightful woody aroma' and a 'stunning flavour of nuts and herbs', and was promptly awarded *The Guardian* 'Big Cheese'.

Anne, formerly a microbiologist for 10 years at the National Institute for Research in Dairying, started cheese-making for herself about seven years ago, 'messing around with soft cheeses'. Her ambition always was to make a mature sheep's-milk cheese, which is how Spenwood started. She spent two months researching in Corsica and several months back home (then Spencers Wood – hence the name), until she felt she had cracked it. A lightly pressed cheese, Anne matures it for 6 months until it develops its nutty flavour. Fresh from judging the hard-pressed ewes'-milk cheeses at the International Food Exhibition's cheese show, I must add that there I found Spenwood to have a deep – almost caramel – taste that, although delightful, was dissimilar to past cheeses I have tried. From the same milk she also makes Wigmore: a washed-curd cheese, it is matured for 6-8 weeks. With a spongy texture, smooth rind and rich mild tang, its deep nuances remind me of a good Reblochon.

Anne also makes two cows'-milk cheeses; Wellington and Waterloo, using the unpasteurized Guernsey milk from the Duke of Wellington's herd at Stratfield Saye. Wellington, a clear Monet yellow that Anne insists is natural and is a sign of the milk's richness, is made according to a recipe 'we've messed around with'. Working with milk with such a high fat content is not easy, and most people do not believe that you can make a good Guernsey-milk cheese – that is, until they have tasted Anne's. Hard-pressed and matured for about 6 months, it is finely textured with a warm – again almost caramel – afterglow. Waterloo is still at its development stage: like Wigmore, it is curd-washed and matured for 6-8 weeks until is ripens to a mild creamy softness; but, for a perfectionist like Anne, it is still not quite right.

All her cheeses are made in her converted dairy next to the house. Wellington is then taken back to Stratfield Saye for maturing in the Duke's cellars; the others Anne keeps in her cheese store. Sold in 2.3 kg (5 lb) truckles, Anne makes them in smaller sizes at Christmas; if anyone sent me one for a present I'd be thrilled.

And Also...

• For a thick buttery Guernsey cream sold straight from the farm, visit **Prosperous Home Farm**, Salisbury Road, Hungerford (tel 0488 684557). Sold either as whipping or double in 150 and 300 ml ($\frac{1}{4}$ and $\frac{1}{2}$ pt) cartons with both pasteurized and unpasteurized available, it is so thick you can stand the pot upside down and nothing moves.

• *Brunning Hams* at Heath Ride, Wokingham (tel 0734 733287) brine-cured hams, bacon and chicken in brown sugar, salt, herbs and spices; they also marinate saddle of pork in mustard.

• *Garlands Farm Shop* at Gardeners Lane, Upper Basildon (tel 0491 671556) sells organic (to Soil Association standards) fruit and vegetables throughout the year. In summer they have 2 acres of PYO organic strawberries and raspberries. Apart from bread and various whole-foods, they also sell The HOF Shop meat (see page 204) and Rachel's Dairy yoghurts (see page 308).

• The bread from *Cold Ash Bakery*, Cold Ash, near Newbury (tel 0635 863297) comes highly recommended for 'a good old-fashioned bake'.

• Local game, well hung, is the speciality of **Wm. Vicars & Sons**, 20 West Street, Reading (tel 0734 572904) and they are also licensed to sell pure-bred Aberdeen Angus beef.

BUCKINGHAMSHIRE

R. Waller 🔲   AYLESBURY DUCK

Long Grove Wood Farm, 234 Chartridge Lane, Chesham, Buckinghamshire HP5 2SG

TEL *0494 772744* CONTACT *Richard Waller – telephone ahead*

I have food writer Michael Raffael to thank for tracking down the only remaining commercial producer of the pure-bred Aylesbury ducks. 'Our family has been rearing them since 1775 and the unbroken bloodline dates back to then,' Richard Waller proudly asserted. A true Aylesbury can be recognized by its white feathers, its flattened shape and flattened keel and its beak 'pink as a lady's thumbnail'.

It was not so long ago that in and around Aylesbury there were plenty of small-scale 'duckers'. 'It was a cottage industry and every farm-worker would keep a small flock. After the First World War, however, no one could be bothered; they wanted easy money in their pockets.'

By the '50s, Richard's father and Bill 'Ducky' Weston, a well-known Aylesbury breeder, were the only full-timers left. 'Ducky' had all but dropped out of commercial production, as he was concentrating on breeding for showing; he may have wiped the board in the duck classes at the Thame show but, according to Richard, their eating quality suffered. 'The ducks he sent up to London were known as tennis rackets – long and flat. They won prizes for colour of bill, length of neck or depth of keel – but bore no resemblance to the true Aylesbury.'

Cherry Valley was already mass-producing Aylesbury-crosses and the future for pure-breds looked pretty grim. They were not popular for all sorts of reasons: the Aylesbury had acquired an unjustified reputation for being rather fatty; it was difficult to compete with the big producers and their 'improved' cross-breeds; and 'restaurants stopped carving at the table and started serving half-birds. The Aylesbury was far too big for their needs'. None the less, father and then son kept on going.

Nowadays Richard tends a flock of 2,000 ducks, killing around 300 a week. 'I match, hatch and dispatch within 8 weeks.' The ducklings are kept indoors for the first 2 weeks, hardened off during the following week and then spend the rest of their lives outdoors in pens (with a bit of judicious 'cheating', by increasing the hours of daylight, Richard manages an all-year-round supply). Fed a broiler ration with plenty of protein to build up their flesh, while still keeping them lean, and – Richard insisted – 'definitely no drugs', they are slaughtered in the time-honoured way by having their necks wrung. Dry-plucked, waxed and stripped, they are hung in the chiller for 48 hours, then eviscerated and sold oven-ready with the giblets. They weigh between 2.3-3.5 kg (5-7½ lb) 'to feed 4 people well'.

If you've never had a true Aylesbury, you have a treat in store. They are well fleshed, with a thin layer of fine-flavoured fat that is 'hard like beef fat'; if the fat is soft and lardy then, according to Richard, it is not a true Aylesbury. The flesh is significantly pale (almost the colour of pork), soft and remarkably tender, with virtually no grain and with a pronounced gamy flavour.

Apparently, for the best of all ducks you should try a stock duck. Killed at 14 months, they can weigh up to 6.4 kg (14 lb) and you have to cook them slowly otherwise they are tough; but, I am told, their flavour is 'incomparable'. No one buys them nowadays so, when they have outlived their egg-laying usefulness, Richard buries them in the field. Another sad example of how we neglect our national delicacies.

And Also...

• Peter Clarke (see page 201) also owns **Denham PYO Farm** at Holly Bush Lane, Denham (tel 0895 834707) and I am told that this one is as good. Reports please from anyone who has picked the vegetables.
• Local butchers **W.J. Morris & Sons**, 4 High Street, Princes Risborough, (tel 0844 343927) and **Mayo Bros**, Bois Lane, Chesham Bois, Amersham (tel 0494 726357) both sell Aylesbury Duck from R. Waller (see page 16).

CAMBRIDGESHIRE

BOTTISHAM   MAP 5

River Farm Smokery ✉ ▦   SMOKED MEAT & FISH

Junction Wilbraham Road & A1303, Bottisham,
Cambridgeshire CB5 9BU

TEL *0223 811382* CONTACT *Roger Enoch – telephone ahead*

If the name River Farm Smokery suggests a picturesque old smokehouse nestling on the banks of a clear fast-flowing river, be prepared for a shock. The reality is a collection of pre-fabricated buildings on the edge of a disused runway. You should also be warned that Roger Enoch admits neither liking nor being terribly good at dealing with the public. None the less, I was delighted to discover River Farm Smokery because they offer something that I have not come across before – smoked pike.

Pike, easily recognized by their elongated jaws full of sharp teeth, live in the slow-flowing rivers and chalk streams of North Europe. Their flesh is white, firm-textured and scattered with literally hundreds of tiny little bones – but that does not put off the Continentals. In Switzerland, *eglifilet* (fillet of pike) and, in France, *quenelle de brochet* (a light melt-in-the-mouth poached mousse of pike, egg white and cream) are highly prized. Needless to say, here we usually ignore pike.

Roger gets his pike from Rutland and Grafham Waters. Once filleted and cured in salt, he cold-smokes it over Fenland peat mixed with oak chippings for an earthier flavour. Sold as sliced whole sides (the weight varies according to the size of the pike), it has a slightly rubbery consistency and a taste that reminded me of sucking on marrow bones – but not nearly so rich. He has three kilns that he built himself, loosely based on the Torrey smoker (their advantages are the vented smoke-boxes that allow for easier control of the heat and smoke). Roger also oak-smokes salmon, halibut, kippers, the occasional yellow-fin tuna, pheasant, chicken, pigeon, duck breasts and Suffolk-cure hams.

CAMBRIDGE   MAP 5

Pretzels Continental Bakery   BREAD

22 Cheddars Lane, Cambridge, Cambridgeshire CB5 8LD

TEL *0223 352146*   CONTACT *Tina Magdalinski – telephone ahead*

A small bakery on an industrial estate off the Cambridge-to-Newmarket road, Pretzels is not easy to find. Primarily wholesalers (they supply several Budgen stores in East Anglia), they do welcome retail customers. It is run by miniature human-dynamo Tina Magdalinski, an Englishwoman married to a Pole. Together they lived in Germany and there she discovered the glories of good bread. On her return to England she never meant to become a baker but, somehow, just fell into it.

With an emphasis on flavoured breads and rolls, Tina offers a most unusual range. The texture of her white bread is a little spongy – possibly a result of not proving the dough long enough – but the flavours are interesting. These include: herb and onion; green pepper-corn and tomato; garlic, cheese and chives; walnut; and tomato and rosemary. The wholemeal combinations I found far more satisfactory – probably because of their denser texture. These were: three peppercorn (black, white and pink), walnut, mustard, and onion. She also makes a yeasty sour-dough using raw potato as a starter, and a suitably Germanic rye that comes flavoured with caraway, or spinach and nutmeg, or cranberries, or marbled (a mixture of black and white doughs).

Always inventing new combinations, self-taught Tina is ever-ready with suggestions for what should be served with what. The moist spinach and nutmeg she recommends eating with a ripe Chaumes cheese, whereas the plain sour-dough sets off a sweeter one like Emmental. Dinner rolls are sold in mixed packs to allow everyone to have a chance to try-out her novel flavours.

A. Waller & Son 🔨   FRESH MEAT

15 Victoria Avenue, Cambridge, Cambridgeshire CB4 1EG

TEL *0223 350972* **CONTACT** *Peter Welton* **HOURS** *Mon 7.30-13.00 Tues-Fri 7.30-17.30 Sat 7.30-14.00* **DIRECTIONS** *Off Mitchams Corner, close to river.*

Mr Welton, by his own admission, is an old-fashioned butcher. As he has been at Waller – man and boy – for the last 52 years, this is perfectly understandable. 'God,' he likes to tell his customers, 'made the animals: boffins interfered with them and made them larger.' Clearly he does not approve of modern 'improvements' in livestock breeding.

The days have long since gone when Waller slaughtered at the back of the shop; but he still chooses carefully from local sources as 'I was brought up that way'. A couple of years ago several customers were regularily asking for 'real' meat. Mr Welton, ever eager to please, bought in some stock from the Real Meat Company (see page 272). 'But it didn't work out...anyway what does it mean? "Real" meat is what I sell.'

Now all his meat is reared with an emphasis on good finishing. Breed of beef is all-important, 'there's nothing like a good Hereford crossed with a Continental to give it a bit of size. But if you introduce too much Continental blood, it's far too lean'. The current concern with leanness is obviously something else with which he does not hold much truck. 'There's no flavour in the lean. For good eating, it must have a covering finish,' he told me, proudly showing off a piece of prime rump steak. Not only was it surrounded by a generous layer of creamy-yellow fat, but the flesh was also delicately marbled. This is beef for dedicated carnivores: well hung with plenty of oomph, it has a rich meaty taste with a good length of flavour.

His lamb comes from Lincolnshire and is always hung for a minimum of 4 days when it is still Spring lamb; but as the season progresses he hangs for longer 'to relax the meat'. Apart from fresh pork, Waller sell own-cooked haslet (savoury loaf made with pigs' fry and sweetbreads) and a moist substantial ham on the bone – both are powerfully salted. There is a range of sausages called Royale Cambridge (invented in Jubilee Year) with a 75% meat content and a 'secret' seasoning; pork and herb for a 'Lincolnshire flavour'; a juicy long-linked coarse Cumberland with a robust flavour and again, well salted. For Burns' Night they make their own well-spiced haggis. The own-made coarse pâté, made with pigs' liver, eggs, sherry and anchovy sauce, was quite powerful and they also cure salt beef, salt pork and pickle tongue. At Christmas they sell Traditional Farm Fresh Turkeys and geese. Ducks are reared locally for them and there is always a choice of plump free-range and conventionally reared chickens. Game, at one time hung and plucked on-site, is now bought in oven-ready from C. E. Brown (see page 21) because of the new hygiene regulations.

Chivers Farm Shop 🚜 ⊖   PRESERVES & APPLE JUICE

Impington, Cambridge, Cambridgeshire CB4 4PJ

TEL *0223 237799* CONTACT *Sally Manning* HOURS *May to end-Sept: 9.00-
19.00; Oct to end-Apr: 10.00-17.00* DIRECTIONS *From Cambridge take A45
towards St Neots. About 3 miles from the centre of Cambridge, turn right on
to B1049 signposted Histon and Cottenham. Turn first right into New Road
and first right again on to a track. Follow the track for about $^1/_3$ mile to shop.*

Chivers' Jams are still being made, but the Chivers family no longer have
anything to do with it – they sold out to Schweppes in the early '60s.
Jam-making started on the farm in a barn in 1873 and by the turn of the
century had moved to larger premises in Histon. The irony is that the
family has now come full circle. Once again jam is being made from
their fruit, on and around the farm, only this time it is exclusively for
their farm-shop.

Caroline Chivers converted an old barn about two years ago. Before
that they did sell eggs and apples to the public, but it was 'through a
hatch in a barn'. She is still adding to her range, with the promise of a
British cheese counter sometime this year. Meanwhile there are the jams
that are made with their own fruit by a team of local ladies. Each lady
makes a particular variety to ensure consistency of product to a recipe
laid down by Caroline. With a high fruit content of between 60-65%
(legally classified as extra-jam), they are very spreadable with a clear
clean fruity-fresh flavour. The varieties are strawberry, raspberry,
rhubarb, blackberry, blackcurrant, Victoria plum and a heady gooseberry. There are also various fruit jellies and chutneys.

Caroline's great-grandfather, by way of being a fruit breeder and
improver, developed the apple Chivers Delight which has a fresh
intense, slightly nutty flavour. This is juiced for them by Copella and
blended with Bramley apples (the amount varies each year according to
the sweetness of the Chivers Delight). The result is a very good juice –
finely balanced with a full apple taste and a refreshing but full flavour.
They sell fruit ready picked, pick-your-own and frozen throughout the
year. The varieties of their strawberries, raspberries, gooseberries,
blackberries, redcurrants and blackcurrants are, as Caroline admits,
'commercial ones because we grow for a dual purpose – to supply the
supermarkets as well as for the public'.

Apples, conventionally grown, include Worcester, Fiesta, Royal Gala
(a red-skinned Gala) and Egremont Russet as well as Chivers Delight.
Pears are Conference, Comice, Williams and a sweet, juicy and grainy
Beurré-Hardy. Then there are greengages, damsons and Victoria plums,
as well as another of great-grandfather's successes Chivers Seedlings.
This is not the easiest plum to grow as it blossoms very late, so
pollinating it can be a problem. It does, however, ripen very late, after all

the other plums, so it extends the season and it has a meaty taste similar to the Victoria.

They sell lots of fruit tarts and pies, made by the same local ladies who make their jams. They also produce Christmas cakes and puddings. With an emphasis on East Anglian products, the shop also stocks Mrs Elizabeth King's pork products (see page 197) and Les Fines Herbes flavoured vinegars and jellies (see page 156).

> *If plums are your favourite fruit, then it is probably worth your while visiting* **J.M. & E. Handley, 100 Stretham Road, Wilburton (tel 0353 649318)***. Mary Holmes of Garden of Suffolk Preserves (see page 247) relies on them for her jam and she tells me they are always in prime condition as they are picked on a daily basis. With 7 acres of plums ripe from about mid-August to early September, their varieties include Early Rivers, Black Prince, Marjorie Seedlings, Cambridge Gage, Burbanks and, of course, Victorias.*

SHUDY CAMPS   MAP 5

C.E. Brown 🎲   GAME

Southlawns, Main Street, Shudy Camps, Cambridgeshire CB1 6RA

TEL *0799 584461* CONTACT *Colin Brown – telephone ahead*

Colin Brown, game dealer *par excellence*, is, according to his wife, 'a law unto himself and very fussy with his game'. Dealing from portakabins behind his cottage, Colin supplies A. Waller (see page 19), Cambridge colleges and good restaurants in the area. Most of his game comes from local-ish estates – Audley End, the Vestey's shoots, Thetford in Norfolk (for wild venison). Grouse is a different matter: it is brought halfway south by a Yorkshire game-dealer friend and they meet *en route*.

The eating quality of game depends on many factors: age, sex and condition of the bird or animal, temperature and length of time hung, and plucking and dressing. Colin picks over everything he is offered and his experience allows him to distinguish immediately between old and young game. Young birds he recommends roasting, whereas older game generally gets sold for casseroles and stews. (One pointer for us novices is to look at the spurs of a cock pheasant: if they are small, sharp and hooked it is a young bird; the older it gets the rounder and blunter they become.) Hanging is done to his customers' preferences: some like a milder-flavoured bird, but others request it 'so it walks out the door'.

Everything is superbly dressed and, in season, Colin sells grouse, pheasants, partridges – young English (Grey) or the commoner French (red-legged) partridge, woodcock, wood pigeon (either breasts only or whole birds), mallard, widgeon, teal and snipe. Golden plover is a very rare treat which Colin 'used to have...when it was wetter'. Hares weigh about 3 kg ($6\frac{1}{2}$ lb); under that, Colin dismisses them as leverets (immature hares) or just 'very poor hares'. He also has rabbits, venison in a variety of cuts – haunch, on bone or boneless or in steaks, saddle, shoulder and stewing cuts.

He also sells own-made juicy game sausages from mixed game, eggs and a bit of rusk, and a chunkily cut game-pie mixture – again from a selection of mixed game. Whatever is not sold Colin freezes while still in prime condition. As a result, out of season, he can be relied on to have some game birds in his massive freezers.

SOHAM   MAP 5

Downfield Windmill ✉ 🏠 🖋   FLOUR

Fordham Road, Soham, Ely, Cambridgeshire CB7 5BG

TEL *0353 720333* CONTACT *Nigel Moon* HOURS *Sun 11.00-17.00*
DIRECTIONS *From Ely take A142 towards Newmarket. After about 12 miles, at the junction with A1123, take the 3rd exit off the roundabout, signposted Downfield Mill. Mill is about 100 yards along on the left.*

Mills were once a feature of the Fens. In the 1850s Soham had seven windmills and one water-mill – now only Nigel Moon's remains in working order. The first mill on this site was built in 1726 and was a smock mill (the tower was made of wood instead of the more common brick). It underwent several changes and improvements until, in 1887, it was wrecked by a gale. Eventually it was restored and grinding started again in April 1980. Downfield, a charming glistening white windmill, suffers from one serious disadvantage – it is plum in the middle of a modern housing estate. This, as you can imagine, causes Nigel a lot of grief. The local authorities do not make life easy for him; they would rather he converted it into a residence; but he resists the pressure and carries on regardless.

Around Britain there are several mills producing stone-ground flours (see 'stone-ground flours' in the product index); but for really excellent flour the secret is 'heat and speed'. The very fact of using stones (as oppose to rollers) is not enough, the stones must not be allowed to run too fast. If they do, they over-heat and destroy some of the goodness in the flour. Nigel must have got it right, as he supplies Innes (see page 234) and The Better Bread Bakery in Leicester (tel 0533 540019) – companies with good reputations for the quality of their bread. Nigel produces two ranges of organic (Organic Farmers and Growers verified) flour. One is made with 100% English wheat, the other is a mixture of two-thirds English and one-third North-American strong wheats. These both come as 100% wholemeal, 85% brown, and 75% white. He also produces a 100% conventionally grown wholemeal, organic oatmeal, barley and rye and a non-organic maize.

Although he will send flour by post, it is not very cost-effective. If you cannot visit him on a Sunday, he suggests ringing Naturally Yours in Witcham Toll (see below). They are not far away and can be relied on to keep supplies of his products.

WITCHAM TOLL   MAP 5

Naturally Yours ✉ ▦   FRESH MEAT & POULTRY

The Horse & Gate, Witcham Toll, Ely, Cambridgeshire CB6 2AB

TEL *0353 778723* CONTACT *Pam Finn – telephone ahead*

It was with certain reservations in mind (see page 273) that I went to meet Pam and Roland Finn of Naturally Yours. I spent several hours with them, questioning them (as far as I was able) about their standards, as they do not belong to any recognized group nor do they publish the standards to which they farm. They do, however, print a chatty newsletter/price list. In it they write, 'We are more convinced than ever that animals should be kept as ours are, in an extensive system where they can behave in a natural way and enjoy their life'. Admirable intentions, but what, in real hard terms, do they mean? In a follow-up letter to me, they wrote that '...(having) given considerable thought to your questions about standards and confusion in the mind of the public. We feel that it comes down to three main points – a clear explanation of what we do, trust and customer satisfaction'. Fair enough – they do seem to have an extensive list of satisfied customers.

They currently produce a wide range of meat and poultry from traditional or rare breeds. Several local farmers rear to their speci-fications, although some of the meat is their own. Everything is butchered on site and Pam, a former cookery teacher, makes the stuffings. Beef, hung from 2-3 weeks, is mainly Hereford, Irish Moil crossed. Jack Lang – former partner in Midsummer House, Cambridge's leading restaurant – and I together tried a piece of rump steak. This was excellent – tender, juicy, nicely aged and with a good length of flavour. Jack subsequently roasted a piece of sirloin: this time the report was less favourable. The meat, though soft and buttery, had very little texture and pizzazz – the result, Jack thought, either of being killed when too immature or not being hung long enough or possibly both.

The chicken, however, was very satisfactory. Adamant that they want birds 'that behave like birds rather than just sit around in a heap of white feathers', they use an Ixworth, Legbar cross. A meaty bird, its dressed weight is around 1.8-2.7 kg (4-6 lb) – although they are often larger – and it is hung for a week. The flavour was deep and mellow, with a hint of game, and it had an unusually resilient texture.

They make a range of natural-skin sausages, including Witcham with a 100% pork content flavoured with fresh sage; the others have a meat content of about 80% – Fenland pork was meaty, if slightly under-seasoned. Their list is very extensive (if a little complicated to order from) and they do deliver within their area and as far south as Kent. They also sell lamb and kid (leg, shoulder, casserole and in sausages mixed with lamb). Dog lovers may be interested to know that my dog Violet wolfed down the pet mince, made with minced meat and offal, and 20% organic 'middlings' (bran and small particles of flour) from Downfield Mill (see page 22). They also keep most of Downfield Mill's flours and a selection of Rosebud jams and preserves (see page 295).

And also....

• *The Herbary Prickwillow* ✉, Mile End, Prickwillow, nr Ely (tel 0353 88456) are the country's major growers of organic (Soil Association standard) herbs. They post fresh-cut herbs, edible flowers and herb plants.
• One of the few butchers in Britain still running a small slaughter-house is F.W. *Brown* at 7-8 Church Street, off Cathedral Square, Peterborough (tel 0733 62104). Their meat has a local reputation for flavour and texture. Also on offer are enticing own-made French *ballotines* and pâtés (son Thomas trained in France as a *charcutier*), spicy haslet loaves and stuffed breast of lamb.

CHESHIRE

HALE   MAP 4

Durig Swiss Patisserie 🏆   BREADS & CHOCOLATES

4 Broomfield Lane, Hale, Altrincham, Cheshire WA15 9AQ

TEL *061 928 1143* CONTACT *Mrs Durig* HOURS *Tues-Sat 9.00-17.00*
DIRECTIONS *Turn off M56 at Junction 6, signposted Hale. Follow signs into Hale for 2 miles. Where road divides at Cenotaph, take left fork into Broomfield Lane. Shop is on the left at the end of the lane.*

When I first discovered Durig, tucked around the corner of Hale's smart high street several years ago, my immediate reaction to this obviously foreign and very chic *chocolatier/confiserie/boulangerie* was one of utter amazement. To find a shop like this anywhere at all in Britain was pretty stunning, but in Hale of all places (and no offence meant to Hale) it was incredible. Since then a few others have sprung up, but this does not make Durig any less extraordinary. The formidable Mrs Durig rules the shop and she makes sure standards never slip.

> In the county, and bordering land of North Shropshire, there are several on-farm Cheshire cheese-makers. **Appleby's** in Shropshire (see page 214) are the only makers of unpasteurized Cheshire, but makers of pasteurized cheese include **Hares & Son, Millenheath, Higher Heath, nr Whitchurch, Shropshire (tel 0948 840288)** and **H. S. Bourne** ✉, **The Bank, Malpas, SY14 7AL (tel 0948 81214)**. Both give guided tours around the dairy (ring in advance for details of times) and both sell own-made cheese and whey-butter. **Henry Barnett** ✉ at **Overton Hall, Malpas, SY14 7DG (tel 0948 860519)** will not allow you around his dairy, but it is worth visiting him just to see his stunning black-and-white half-timbered farmhouse that dates back to pre-Tudor times.

Mr Durig came originally from Switzerland and he makes traditional hand-made chocolates. With the current craze for Belgian, I think we tend to overlook the merits of Swiss chocolates. They tend to be smaller and, like the Swiss themselves, less flashy and quietly rich; more of a subdued, subtler chocolate but when they are good, they can be very good indeed. They do not exactly come cheap, but then they are – as Mrs Durig is at pains to point out – 'made with the best-quality ingredients and the best expertise. If kirsch is used, it is kirsch – the real thing. We use the best possible couverture and, apart from the mints, we never use a fondant filling'. The range will vary: at Christmas they go in for things like a 2-foot-high moulded Santa Claus; but you can expect to find some splendid dark, milk and Cognac (made with Cognac and cream) truffles, smooth pralines, and bitter-sweet mint crisps.

Everything is made on the premises; and local cookery writer Evelyn Rose told me that all the apprentices are hand-picked by Mr Durig. He chooses them from homes where food is really appreciated, rather than from a bakery college; and they make far better bakers. There are some excellent-looking rolls and breads, including a very Swiss muesli bread which is 'beautiful toasted'. Buttery, if a little bready, croissants are baked daily, as are Linzertorte, Sachertorte and a Forest cake of hazelnut sponge with praline and fresh cream. For the more parochially inclined, there are moist carrot cakes, sausage rolls, crisp meringues, various cream cakes and gleamingly glazed apple slices. At Christmas, the Swiss in Mr Durig gives rise to immense and carefully constructed honey-dough houses, but you will also find own-made figgy and ginger puddings and Christmas puddings.

The bakery leads through to an adjoining shop in which there are freezer cabinets filled with various cooked dishes, including plaice Mornay, chilli con carne (and a vegetarian version), mini savouries, frozen croissants and own-made sorbets. In rows above are jars and packets of an imaginative range of own-made preparations such as: dried herbs, including herbes de Provence 'with a bit of lavender to give it taste'; a horseradish sauce mix of finely ground breadcrumbs and dried horseradish, to blend with cream for a pungent sauce; own-blended curry powder; sharp syrupy *mostarda di frutta*; coarse honey and green peppercorn mustards; various chutneys; dried stuffings, including a tasty mixture of French bread, apricots and chestnuts; fruit vinegars; and flavoured rices, made with an American long-grain rice combined with herbs, dried apricots, onion, celery and thyme, mushroom and bay leaf, and spiced biryani. It is a shop to delight all lovers of good food.

> **Haworth's Fruit Farm** at **Eddisbury Farm, Yeld Lane, Kelsall (tel 0829 51188)**, *on the edge of the Delamere Forest, has fields of pick-your-own fruit or sells it ready-picked from their shop. They have no less than 6 varieties of strawberries, including the plumptious sweet Gorella, and raspberries in season from July right through to the first frosts. There are also various plums, such as Early Rivers 'a good jammer', Victorias and damsons. They make a feature of their various apple varieties that you can pick-your-own if you feel inclined to a day out, but it is a good idea to check when they are being harvested. Some, such as Discovery, Katy, James Grieve and the cooker Grenadier can be eaten straight off the trees; others like Cox's, Russet, Sunset, Chivers Delight and Kidd's Orange Red should be stored (their nifty leaflet gives you explicit instructions). From the shop they also sell own-made jams which use their own fruit and various fruit crumbles and pies.*

TABLEY   MAP 4

Holly Tree Farm Shop ✉ 🦽   GEESE & DUCKS

Chester Road, Tabley, Knutsford, Cheshire WA16 OEU

TEL *0565 651835* **CONTACT** *Karol Bailey* **HOURS** *Tues-Sat 9.00-19.00 Sun 10.00-18.00* **DIRECTIONS** *Turn off M6 at junction 19, signposted Knutsford/A556. At roundabout, take exit signposted Knutsford. After about 50 yards, farm is signposted on the left.*

Over the last 2½ years, since Karol opened her small farm-shop, 'business has been building up very nicely'. Wisely, she concentrates on poultry and lamb, although she does grow some vegetables and fruit – but 'they're a bit haphazard and there are hundreds of farm-shops along the road to fill in that gap'. 'Just several sorts but mainly Peking cross' ducks are reared all year round out in the fields. She brings them on slowly, so they are less fatty, and she also has a few Muscovy, with their darker, leaner and more gamy flesh. 'They're bigger and, I think, coarser. A drake will make 6-9 pounds, enough to feed 4-5 people'. Hung on-farm for about a week, there is certain to be a stock of them in the freezer; if you want one fresh, however, it is wise to ring Karol in advance, if possible.

She also rears around 600 geese for Michaelmas right through to the New Year, but again she can be relied on to keep some in the freezer throughout the year. Her Danish hybrid stock are kept out in the fields, grass-fed with a ration of corn up to 8 weeks of age; they have to be brought in at nights as 'foxes are a major problem. People catch them in the middle of Manchester, drive them down the motorway and let them out round here'. There is a degree of good-natured rivalry between all the free-range goose producers, so it was amusing to hear from Karol about 'the bones of contention' between her and Judy Goodman (see page 282) about colour of flesh and finish.

Apparently Karol's grass-fed geese are paler-fleshed. Judy thinks it is because of their diet as a whole; Karol believes it is just due to the quality of grass. Whatever the reason, Karol's birds do have a mild gamy flavour and moist creamy texture. Then there is the tricky question of trussing. Once the birds are hung for between 7-10 days, hand-plucked, then wax-dipped for a smooth finish, they are dressed with the livers, gizzard, heart and neck and a bag of goose fat stuffed inside the cavity. So far, so good: but from here on Karol deviates from Judy's practices. She does not sew or tie up her birds but leaves them open 'to make stuffing easier'. Judy disagrees with this practice, as she thinks stuffing is more likely to fall out. This might not seem of major importance to you, but believe me goose producers take their birds very seriously.

Karol also sells own-lamb. Again there is a variety of breeds to provide a range of carcass size and leanness. 'It may sound a bit higgledy-piggledy, but I do offer a good personal service. People can ask for the amount of fat cover they want and all the lamb is hung for a week to 10 days to make it really tender.'

A keen cook, Karol has won several cookery prizes in the local shows and prepares a goose roll made with a boned goose rolled around a boned turkey, rolled around a boned pheasant stuffed with an apricot and parsley stuffing. She also makes her lamb and mint sausages 'with a tiny bit of rusk and preservative, this I'd like to take out as soon as trade builds up enough'. She also buys in pork from a 'reputable source' and makes a separate range of sausages, including pork and leek, pork and apple, a mild Gloucestershire, and a turkey, pork and chives mixture. Apart from her apricot stuffing, she prepares a rosemary and orange mix and an apple (using fruit from her orchard) with celery, almonds and bread. Made with fresh ingredients she sells these frozen in packs.

Also on sale in the shop are her husband's intensively grown turkeys; quite a big producer, he keeps about 25,000 birds.

And Also...

• *Cheshire Herbs* ✉ at Fourfields, Forest Road, nr Tarporley CW6 9EF (tel 0829 760578) has won gold medals at the Chelsea Flower Show for their display of herbs. With over 200 varieties of herb plants, here you can buy white borage, garlic chives and 13 different basils, including the more astringent anise basil and the charming Green and Purple Ruffles.

• *Snugbury's*, Hurleston, Nantwich (tel 0270 624830) make a Jersey milk ice-cream with a 12% fat content and quite a high over-run (added air) of between 70-80%. Flavours are mostly bought-in. 'Yum-yum', a toffee biscuit fudge flavour, is imported from the USA and if you're feeling seriously self-indulgent you can have it topped with their own-made Friesian-milk clotted cream.

• Following the success of the Spitalfields Organic Market in London, Elizabeth Taylor has decided to open an *organic market in Altrincham*. For details she can be reached on 071 625 8056. The market is on Thursdays between 10.00-16.00 at The Market Hall, Greenwood Street, Altrincham. Producers regularly to be found there include The Village Bakery (see page 44) and the inimitable Arthur Hollins of Fordhall Farm (see page 212).

• Every year, on the last Wednesday of July, the Nantwich Agricultural Society hold the *International Cheese Show* at Dorfold Hall in Nantwich. I've judged there for a few years and it is fascinating seeing all the different cheeses piled on the trestle tables. If you are at all interested in cheese, I urge you to go.

• Cookery writer Evelyn Rose recommends three shops in the Greater Manchester area: *Evans* at 1 Barlow Moor Road, Didsbury (tel 061 445 2404) has fish 'of superb quality meticulously prepared to one's specifications'; down the road is Axons at 5 & 7 Barlow Moor Road (tel 061 445 1795), an 'old-style butcher who often buys prize-winning carcasses'; also in Didsbury is The Cheese Hamlet at 706 Wilmslow Road (tel 061 434 4781), where 'cheeses are cosseted like wine, there's a vast choice of both Continental and home-produced cheeses with many from named makers'.

• Inside the city walls of Chester, *The Cheese Shop* ✉ at 116 Northgate Street (tel 0244 346240) specializes in British cheeses and stocks at least 100. With customers' choice in mind, they always try to sell both a pasteurized and unpasteurized version of each cheese, so you will find Cheshires from both Appleby's (see page 214) and Bourne's (see page 25), three Lancashires including Mrs Kirkham's unpasteurized (see page 142) and as many Welsh cheeses as possible. To go with the cheese, they sell The Village Bakery bread (see page 44).

• *The Mid-Cheshire Gooseberry Shows Association* runs 8 shows in the area, held on the last Saturday in July and the first in August, plus one on the first Sunday in August this year. Gooseberries are judged by weight rather than taste: the 1978 overall champion, grown by Albert Dingle, weighed 37 pennyweights and 15 grains – 58 g (2.06 oz) – and still holds the world record. For details, contact Gordon Cragg at 7 Hulme Lane, Lower Peover (tel 0565 722574).

CLEVELAND

MAP 6

Mr Twizell's ✉ 🔳

SAUSAGES & BACON

*Gilly Flatts Farm, Bishopton, Stockton-on-Tees, Cleveland
TS21 1HH*

TEL *0740 30111* **CONTACT** *Philip Twizell – telephone ahead*

By the turning to the farm of Philip Twizell (yes, it is his real name), there is a large intimidating sign telling everyone to keep away. Not very welcoming, I thought, but how wrong I was. When I arrived at the farmhouse, I was ushered into the kitchen and given a cup of tea and a good talking to about sausages. The forbidding sign, by the way, is to keep away agricultural salesmen not potential buyers.

Philip has his own breeding unit of Large White, Landrace cross pigs kept semi-intensively in straw yards. He had two options: either to expand the herd, or to start marketing and adding value to the pigs. He chose the latter. Pigs are notoriously economical animals, not so long ago every bit – from their heads to their tails – was eaten. Now we are far more fastidious but, even so, there is very little wastage. By that, I do not mean to suggest that Philip uses up every bit, rather that he has a clever business using the various cuts to their best advantage.

He sells some fresh pork cuts to order: such as leg, loin chops, spare rib, barbecue spare rib and fillet. Legs are also brined for gammon, gammon steaks and bacon joints. Belly and middle are dry-cured in salt and Demerara sugar for about 2 weeks, hung for about 1 week and sliced into a gently sweet, firmly textured bacon. The shoulders go into his sausages: he makes two types, Low-fat and Not-so-Low-fat. Low-fat have a fat content of under 15%. The meat content on the packs is labelled at 65% (the minimum requirement), but in reality it varies between 70-80%. Made in small batches in natural skins with a medium-coarse texture, the flavours include: spicy with herbs; tomato; garlic; leek; and apple (Low-fat); Cumberland; and breakfast (Not-so-low-fat).

Currently buying in seasoning mixes, he is thinking of going back to making up his own; and when Philip started making sausages he also made them preservative-free. 'Up here, there was no demand', but given the slightest encouragement, he hopes to make them that way again.

CORNWALL

Cornish Smoked Fish Co ✉ 🐟 🦪

SMOKED MACKEREL

Charlestown, St Austell, Cornwall PL25 3NY

TEL *0726 72356* CONTACT *Martin Pumphrey* HOURS *Mon-Fri 8.00-17.00 (Whit to end-Sept also open Sat 10.00-12.00)* DIRECTIONS *From St Austell, take A390 towards St Blazey. Follow the road about 1 mile to the third roundabout just off the by-pass and take the third exit off the roundabout, signposted Charlestown. After about ½ mile, take the first exit off the mini-roundabout and smokery is on the left.*

The old port of Charlestown is a tourist trap: thousands flock here every year to visit the atmospheric setting of *Poldark*, *The Onedin Line* and other such favourites. Wandering by its deep quays, I was lucky enough to catch it on a grey blowy day when most everyone had gone home. It was easy then to imagine it when the harbour was bustling with rigged boats unloading precious cargoes and barrels of mackerel or pilchards.

The Cornish Smoked Fish Company faces the narrow harbour; sad to say, however, no fish is landed here any more. In fact none of their mackerel comes from Cornwall, as they cannot get the right-sized fish with the right oil content they need for smoking. As Martin Pumphrey explained, 'Buying is an imprecise art, but we need quite large mackerel, between 1½ and 2 lb, the ones caught around here are much smaller, about 10 oz. And the oil content must be right; around here in summer they're not oily enough and after spawning, they're not worth the eating. You'd never eat a cow after it's calved, neither should you touch a fish.' So Martin buys mackerel that fit his specifications caught off the coast of Scotland; filleted and frozen at sea, he draws off his stock of frozen fish as and when he needs it throughout the year.

He does hot-smoke whole and fillets of mackerel; but it is for his cold-smoked mackerel that he excels. Treated exactly as you would salmon, the fillets are dry-cured in salt for 1½-2 hours, cold-smoked over oak sawdust for between 4 and 6 hours, then thinly sliced. Sold in 225 g (8 oz) packets, the finely textured moist slices of pearly-grey have a full, meaty flavour lightly cut with salt. They also smoke salmon and, when they can get them, eels from the local rivers.

B. A. Lake 🏠

CLOTTED CREAM & BUTTER

Priors, Coads Green, Launceston, Cornwall PL15 7LT

TEL *0566 82547* CONTACT *Barbara Lake – telephone ahead*

Barbara Lake and her mother live in a stone cottage running at right angles to the steep lane. Out back are the vegetable plot and their 8 Guernsey cows, Gloria, Snowdrop, Goldie, Clover, Rosie, Dandy, Candy, Mary and the heifer Briony, and their pigs. Barbara runs the small-holding single-handedly, as her mother is confined to a chair. Every day she milks the cows, separates the milk, clots it into cream and feeds the skimmed milk to the pigs.

Her clotted cream is made in the traditional way by scalding it in a basin set in a big pan full of water on top of the Rayburn (see also A. & M. Pigott, page 31) 'for real taste, it has to be 3 days old' before you eat it. If there is any spare cream, Barbara will make a full-cream butter; and, if there is any clotted cream left over at the end of the week, she will turn that – crust and all – into a clotted cream butter. Now I knew about full-cream and whey butters and had even heard that years ago in Cornwall clotted cream was used instead of butter; until I met Barbara, however, I must admit I had never even heard of clotted cream butter. Barbara must be one of the few people left in this country who still makes it and by hand. Or, as she said disarmingly, 'Real old-fashioned. Not many do that'; indeed they don't.

To make the clotted cream butter, first she whips it with a hand-held whisk until it goes 'crumbly', then she works it with her hands squeezing it hard to get rid of as much moisture as possible, then washing it with fresh water until it runs clear. She puts a large knob at a time on a round wooden patter (which looks like a darning mushroom) and beats it with a boiled cloth to get yet more water out. Then twisting the stem so it whizzes round, she works it into a circular pat, 'that can be difficult as, in the hot weather, it gets sticky'. Finally, using a wooden butter stamp carved with a Guernsey cow, she stamps the butter into a perfect round mould.

In summer it is a bright, bright yellow; in winter it is paler but, compared to what most of us are used to, it is still a pretty dazzling colour. As for its taste – it is far richer and far creamier than ordinary butter and has a lingering aftertaste of sweet milkiness. It has to be tried to be believed.

LEZANT   MAP 1

A. & M. Pigott ✉ ▦   CLOTTED CREAM

East Penrest, Lezant, Launceston, Cornwall PL15 9NR

TEL 0579 370270 CONTACT *Mary Pigott – telephone ahead*

Clotted cream is a bit of a cliché. When in Cornwall, everyone has to try at least one teaspoonful. Be warned, however, there is clotted cream and good clotted cream. Mary Pigott's is one of the best.

She makes hers from the unpasteurized milk of her 30-strong Jersey herd that graze on unsprayed mixed pastures. 'You can make it from

Friesian milk,' she told me doubtfully, 'but Jersey milk is better'. A richer milk with a higher butterfat content, it follows that it should make a fuller cream, and for the best of all clotted cream Mary uses the evening's milk 'as it's even richer'. This goes straight through the separator and the cream is kept in stainless-steel jugs overnight. Apparently whether you age (ripen) the cream or not is an 'irrelevance', the technique for making – according to Mary – is all about 'timing and temperature'.

Commercially made clotted cream is either baked in the oven or in steam cabinets. Needless to say, Mary dismisses these and sticks to the proper traditional way of gently 'cooking' it on top of the Aga. The cream is poured into enamel pans and placed in a *bain-marie*; then it is carefully heated (scalded), taking 'about 2 hours from birth to maturity. If you overdo the heat the cream is gritty; if you under-do it, it's bland'. At first nothing seems to be happening; then, as the cream slowly condenses, minute bubbles start breaking to the top, pitting it like the surface of the moon. Suddenly it turns golden and forms a thick honeycomb crust – it has clotted. Left to cool and set overnight in Mary's immaculate dairy, it is then refrigerated. A well-clotted cream will last about a fortnight in the fridge.

To pot it, Mary puts a knob of the crust in the bottom, spoons the cream on top and covers it with a generous wedge of crust. Her clotted cream has a fat content of between 55-60%, 'If it's too high, the cream'll set rock solid. It'll be too thick and buttery, the right consistency is spreadable'. Round here, one way of taking the cream is to smear a Cornish split (bun) with the crust, cover it with a dollop of jam and then, yet more clotted cream. 'But', warns Mary, 'you must never eat it straight out of the fridge. You'll lose its full creamy sweet flavour' and that would be a tragedy.

Worth a visit is **Oughs The Unicorn Grocer, 10 Market Street, Liskeard (tel 0579 343253).** *One of the best-preserved grocery shops in the country, the original wooden counters, shelves and glass fronted cabinets date back 130 years. Inside Mrs Parker, the manager, tries to sell as much Cornish produce as possible; but she is, by her own admission, 'scratching around a bit' for a full range. From the county you will find cheeses like Cornish Yarg (see page 38) and Tala (see page 36), an excellent Saffron cake (a sweet yeast bread) made with proper saffron by the Chapel Bakery in St Keyne, clotted cream and clotted cream butter from Barbara Lake (see page 30), Phillimore Fine Foods' mustards and chutneys (see page 40), Callestick Farm ice-cream (see page 39), meaty Cornish pasties and local honey, fudge and marzipan. From out of the county come sausages made at Brick Yard Farm in North Devon, Crowdy Mill flour (see page 58), and lots more.*

MAP 1

Stein's Delicatessen ✉ 🏺

PRESERVES & COOKED SEAFOOD DISHES

8 Middle Street, Padstow, Cornwall PL28 8AR

TEL *0841 532221* FAX *0841 533344* CONTACT *Mrs Gard* HOURS *Mon-Sat 9.00-18.00* CARDS *Access, Barclaycard, Mastercard* DIRECTIONS *In town centre.*

I have long been an admirer of Rick Stein. His book *English Seafood Cookery* is full of delightful simple-to-follow recipes and it is a joy to eat in his Seafood Restaurant. Ever since I surprised him in the kitchen, elbow-deep in his vivier, trapping a one-clawed lobster to return to sea in the vain hope it might grow another, I became a total fan.

You might surmise then that I am biased in his favour, but I would defy anyone not to be completely won over by his delicatessen. Tucked away in one of the old back streets of Padstow, it is total joy for every food lover. It is rare to be able to rave about a food shop in this country, but Stein's is an exception: packed to the gunnels with goodies of great distinction, the bliss of it is that it sells The Seafood Restaurant food-to-go and at to-go prices.

Oils, vinegars and local clotted cream apart, virtually everything else in the shop is own-made. From the bakery in the back come loaves of walnut, granary, rye and crusty white bread; buttery croissants and pastries and cakes aplenty: glazed individual fruit tarts; feather-light millefeuilles; tea cakes; sticky treacle tart; pear & almond tart; bread & butter pudding; a glorious Dorset apple cake; and a gooey chocolate fudge cake.

From the restaurant kitchens come the savouries: pasties bulging with pork, apples onion & sage; cheese & leek; fish with leek dressed in a buttery emulsion with a hint of tarragon; and hearty chunks of steak mixed with peppery potato, onion and swede for the best Cornish filling I have ever tasted. You can also buy some of Rick Stein's 'signature' dishes – a light velvety terrine of lemon sole with prawns; a full-blown gutsy fish soup with a pot of fiery rouille; superb fish or bubble & squeak cakes; moist salmon baked in a buttery croûte; and seafood thermidor, a cunning mixture of white fish, prawns and mustard dressed in a white-wine sauce topped with cheese and breadcrumbs. There are always plenty of fresh salads – tomato & basil, three bean, penne with tomatoes, waxy potatoes dressed in a proper mayonnaise – as well as slices of rare roast sirloin or topside, a glistening glazed ham, potted ham with lentils, and a vibrant duck liver parfait. After a trip here you need never cook again.

Last, but by no means least, are the jars of own-made pickles, preserves, various jams, such as redcurrant, strawberry and gooseberry, and marmalades. On my first trip here I bought a pot of their chilli paste, a fiery blend of chopped chillies with spices and oil; it proved to be a stalwart of the kitchen, pepping up many a soup or stew. Other favourites include tiny onions sweet-pickled with tarragon, allspice and cloves; chillies marinated in oil; a fruity pear chutney with a hint of poppy seeds; and slivers of ginger preserved in a sweet pickle for adding to duck.

The inventiveness of Rick Stein's kitchen shines through; everything is stamped with his sure touch and his innovative use of fresh quality ingredients – long may he continue to go from strength to strength. While there, don't forget to pop upstairs, you'll find a selection of reasonably prices wines gathered from all over the world. (⊠ Preserves, jams and pickles only.)

---

*Trevose Seafoods at **Old Fish Market, South Quay, Padstow** (tel 0841 532973) keep an interesting collection of fish and shellfish in tanks – spider and velvet crabs, lobsters, langoustines, conger eels. Out front in the shop they sell dressed crab, live or cooked lobsters, locally dredged scallops and a good selection of locally caught fish, including John Dory 'when its cheap enough to put out on the counter', turbot, skate, red mullet and the little-known weever (a British substitute for wrasse, essential for a proper bouillabaisse).*

PORT NAVAS MAP 1

The Duchy of Cornwall Oyster Farm ⊠ ▦ ▲
NATIVE OYSTERS

Port Navas, Falmouth, Cornwall TR11 5RJ

TEL *0326 40210* **CONTACT** *Len Hodges* **HOURS** *Mon-Fri 8.00-16.00 Sat 8.00-12.30* **DIRECTIONS** *From Falmouth, take road signposted Constantine/Helston. After about 5 miles, turn left signposted Port Navas. Follow the road about 1 mile into the village and join the private road at the end of the creek. Oyster farm is on the second quay.*

To call this a 'farm' is perhaps, a little misleading. The word summons up visions of regimented beds of oysters seeded in regular rows with tractors ploughing through the mud; nothing could be further from the truth. When you finally get to the 'farm', all you see is an oyster shed that looks more like an Edwardian boathouse and, flowing past it tranquilly, the river Helford. The only hint of industry is an oyster dredger moored up alongside.

Len Hodges and his merry band of helpers have the lease for dredging oysters in both the Helford and the Percuil that flows out at St Mawes. A still clean river (graded category A, the top in cleanliness) the Helford is a salt river full of plankton (ideal for oysters) and there have been naturally seeded oyster beds downstream for as long as anyone can remember. In fact, Len does a little 'farming' by scattering empty shells on the beds to encourage the spats (baby oysters) to settle on them as they grow, and also relays spats from the rivers Fal and Truro.

Native oysters were nearly wiped out in this country in 1982-3. The problem was *bonamia*, a parasite that feeds off them. Stocks are still lower than they were before the disaster, but they are building up nicely. Although, as Len told me philosophically, 'It's like myxomatosis, it might recur any time'. According to him (and most oyster aficionados), natives are far superior in taste and texture to Pacifics. Generously he opened several for me as we sat chatting by the river bank. A first whiff of sea breezes, and as I tipped one in my mouth chewing gently and swallowing, a burst of biting saltiness mingled with a sweet aftertaste.

Graded into four sizes (the smallest ones get put back), all the oysters are put through ultraviolet purifying tanks for 36 hours. Natives are available from September through to April and – dispelling the myth that you can only eat them when there is an 'r' in the month – Len told me, 'You can eat them any time, they're still plump in May or June, but we have to protect the breeding stock. And they're not too pleasant when spawning, as they go milky'. Sold in most of the best restaurants, such as Bentleys, Sweetings, and Green's of St James, Len will also send a minimum of 25 packed in seaweed to anywhere in the country. If you visit him, you are welcome to take a picnic of bread, lemon, chilled white wine and sit by the river. Len promises to open as many oysters as you can manage 'as long as you don't hinder us working'.

'*A sort of turnover with meat and potatoes inside, instead of fruit or preserve,*' *is how the Reverend Francis Kilvert described a Cornish pasty in the late 1800s. A meal in itself, the 'pastry parcel' was the traditional dinner taken from home by miners and farm labourers. It was filled with anything from meat, fish, bacon and cheese, to vegetables or eggs; and when times were hard, it could be no more than a few wild herbs. What I look for in a good pasty is a light, crisp pastry, good quality meat with a good filling-to-pastry ratio. Finding one in Cornwall, however, is no easy matter. Journalist Jo Fairley pointed me in the direction of Ann's Pasties,* **The Lizard Pasty Shop, Beacon Terrace, The Lizard (tel 0326 290889)** *and for that I am eternally grateful. Ann makes her own pastry, which she describes as 'halfway between a puff and a short pastry'. Beef is skirt or chuck and is mixed with the traditional filling of potato, onion, swede (which is what the Cornish call turnip), salt and pepper. Everything is wrapped in the parcel raw, then baked off for about an hour until it emerges, crisp, golden and full of flavour. I have also heard good things of* **Pentillie Pasties, Unit 14, Windsor Lane, Saltash (tel 0752 840953)**...*more reports please.*

TREVERVA   MAP 1

Menallack ✉ 🚜 ⚓   CHEESE

Menallack Farm, Treverva, Penryn, Cornwall TR10 9BP

TEL *0326 40333* **CONTACT** *Caryl Minson* **HOURS** *10.00-16.00* **DIRECTIONS**
*From Falmouth, take unclassified road to Gweek (seal sanctuary). Go
through Treverva and, after ½ mile, farm is signposted on the left.*

John and Caryl Minson are very busy people – running a camping site,
riding stables and a farm-shop – yet they still find time to make
Menallack cheese. Their farm is very sheltered, so the cows can stay out
most of the year grazing on the rich Cornish grass. The land has an
underlying granite seam with an acid soil and this, says Caryl, must
contribute to Menallack's interesting sharpness and faint lemon tang.

With only 22 Friesian cows to milk, Caryl makes the cheese in 45
litre (100 gallon) batches, using 2 days unpasteurized milk as and when
the holding tank is filled. Once the milk has been started and renneted,
the curds are broken by hand in a method similar to a Cheshire, and
she works on them for about 1½ hours, until the acidity level is right;
then she 'mills like mad'. The
cheese is pressed for 3 days,
turned daily for 2 weeks, then
every 4 to 5 days. Sold at a
minimum of 6 weeks, when it is
fresh, quite crumbly and
pleasantly sharp, it will mature
on; if you try it at 5-6 months, it
is much stronger and denser.

Menallack is sold from the
farm-shop. There you can also
buy Caryl's own-made bread
from granary and Crowdy Mill
flour (see page 58), and
Nanterrow, an interesting ewes'-
milk cheese similar to a Feta
both in flavour and texture,
which is made by the Cheethams
in Connor Downs near St Ives.
She is building up a collection of
local foods to sell: Devon Blue
cheese (see page 67), Merrivale
(see page 37) sausages, pâtés and
hams; Trewithen ice-cream,
yoghurt, fromage frais and
clotted cream; Cornish lamb, and
locally made preserves.

> 📖 *Tala, made by* **Heather
> White** ✉ *at* **North Beer
> Farm, Boyton, Launceston
> PL15 8NR (tel 0566 85607)**, *is
> an unpasteurized hard-pressed
> washed-rind ewes'-milk cheese
> made in 400 g and 2 kg (14 oz
> and 4½ lb) truckles. Heather
> works in the old farmhouse dairy
> on a very small scale using a 140
> litre (30 gallon) vat. Once the
> curds are cut, they are washed in
> warm water to remove the whey
> and to reduce the acidity of the
> cheese. They are then moulded,
> pressed for about 20 hours, dried
> for a day, brined for about a day,
> dried again, and finally rubbed
> all over with vegetable oil, before
> being left to mature. The small
> cheese matures for about 8
> weeks, the larger 5 months; until
> they have developed a compressed
> texture, with a mild light finish
> not unlike a young Pecorino.*

MAP 1

Merrivale Charcuterie CHARCUTERIE

1 Coombes Lane, Truro, Cornwall TR1 2BJ

TEL *0872 222227* CONTACT *Sally Jones* HOURS *Mon-Fri 9.00-17.00 Sat 9.00-16.30* DIRECTIONS *In town centre, off Pydar Street.*

Huw Jones has simple enough tastes. Ask him what he likes to eat best of all and he does not hesitate, 'A plate of charcuterie, with good bread and olives'. Now that he is a producer of charcuterie, it must be very satisfying to make your own favourite food.

Huw came to it in a roundabout way: training he acquired as a chef in the RAF, 'we bought in primal cuts so I learnt butchery'; then he and his wife Sally ran the Trengilly Wartha, a hotel/pub in Nancenoy, until they both felt their children were of an age when best out of a pub. By then, his own-made pies, sausages and pâtés had acquired a certain reputation locally, so he made them privately. Success – in the form of winning the 1991 Guardian Sausage Competition – swiftly followed, and orders flooded in. Thus encouraged, they opened their shop.

And what a shop...all the more extraordinary for being tucked away down a narrow side street in Truro. Believe it or not, it is probably the nearest we get in the entire country to a proper *boucherie/charcuterie*. Almost everything is own-made (Huw works from the farmhouse a few miles away while Sally runs the shop). You will still find the prize-winning garlic & herb sausage, together with a couple more in the English style, but almost everything else has a distinct Continental bias. There is a subtly flavoured *jambon persillé*, with the shredded ham floating in a translucent jelly; coarse, robust Toulouse sausages, flavoured with red wine and garlic; fat chorizos studded with red and green peppers, which you can buy fresh or dried and smoked. Bratwurst come tinged with lemon; turkey and ham frankfurters hot-smoked; Hog's pudding, a mixture of pork, thyme, parsley, white pepper and rusk, is made in the Devonian style, stuffed in runners as opposed to the Cornish preference for the large fatter ox middles; and chicken liver pâté laced with brandy was rich and grainy. Huw even mixes and cures his own salamis: on offer were a meaty, mildly garlicky Italian-style with a good tang, and a denser fragrantly spiced German-style.

Recently he has taken to producing a Parma-style ham; perhaps he lacks the delicate touch of the Italians, but it is still a worthy attempt. Wet-cured and cooked ham is sold on the bone; I loved it for its plainness of unadulterated meat, and it was moist and fresh with a good biting texture. He also cures a Spingo ham, named after a local beer: initially dry-cured, it is basted for a month in the beer mixed with molasses and Muscovado sugar until it turns a mahogany black; then it is hung and dried for 2-3 weeks.

All the meat is bought from a local abattoir, then hung and

butchered by Huw. He does sell it fresh, but again you will notice a Continental influence: veal is flattened to make wafer-thin escalopes; noisettes, cut from the loin, are boned-out, rolled and carefully trimmed; and there is usually 'something' marinating. When I was there it was saddle of wild venison in red wine, onion and juniper berries.

UPTON CROSS   MAP 1

Lynher Valley Dairy ✉ 🚚 ⚓   CORNISH YARG

Netheron Farm, Upton Cross, Liskeard, Cornwall PL14 5BD

TEL *0579 62244* FAX *0579 62666* CONTACT *Michael Horrell* HOURS *Easter to end-Oct: 10.00-16.00* DIRECTIONS *From Liskeard, take B3254 towards Upton Cross. At Upton Cross, turn right signposted Rilla Mill and Cheese Farm. Follow the signs for about 1 mile to the farm.*

A name like Cornish Yarg suggests a cheese as old as the hills that has been made in the county for centuries. In fact it was only invented about 13 odd years ago by a Mr and Mrs Gray – and Yarg is their surname spelt backwards.

Mike Horrell bought the recipe from them 10 years ago and moved its production to his farm in the Lynher Valley. From his farmhouse window you can see the Cheese Ring high up on the edge of the Cornish moors; rather fittingly the rounded boulders, stacked one on top of the other on the edge of the quarry, look like huge farmhouse cheeses wrapped in cloth to drain. It was from this very quarry that granite was taken for building the Thames Embankment.

Mike's Friesian herd graze on the escarpment that plunges down to the valley and up to the moors. The milk is pasteurized and, depending on demand (Safeway have recently started selling Yarg), he makes cheese most days. It is quite a fast cheese to make, similar to a Caerphilly: the curds are cut and turned, and cut and turned again until the acidity level is right; they are milled, lightly pressed overnight, brined for a few hours and then 'nettled'. It is the nettle coating that makes Yarg so distinctive: nettle leaves, frozen so they go like limp lettuce for easier handling, are spread all over the cheese and brushed with a sterilized water – a deep dark green, they glisten like leaves after a rainstorm.

Locals do a roaring trade selling Mike nettles, but because of the demand he has actually started a nettle plantation. Odd though it may seem to add nettles to cheese, there are good precedents for it. Although I have never had an exact scientific explanation, I think it has something to do with the leaves' properties to turn – or sour – milk. I have come across several recipes in old country craft books, where cottage cheeses (soft plate cheeses) were wrapped in nettles to sour and/or ripen the milk; and in Holland you can still buy on-farm Gouda with chopped nettles mixed in.

A relatively young cheese, Yarg is kept for a minimum of 2 weeks; by which time the nettle coating has turned a pale spidery grey. I prefer it matured a bit longer, between 4-6 weeks, when it is creamier and has mellowed out to give an almost grassy honey flavour. They also make Cornish Pepper and Cornish Herb & Garlic: both soft full-fat cream cheeses with pepper or herb coatings. If you visit the farm, you can watch the cheese being made from a viewing gallery, have a snack in the tearoom and, of course, buy the cheeses.

And Also...

• You can buy *Callestick Farm* ice-cream at several tourist spots: the beach at Hemmick, on the quay at Falmouth and in the centre of Truro. Made at the farm in Callestick, near Truro (tel 0872 573126 fax 0872 571450), it has a fat content between 10-12%, an over-run (added air) of 80% and comes in various flavours bought in from a flavour-house.

• *Atlantis Smoked Fish* ⊠ , The Smokehouse Shop, Fore Street, Grampound, nr Truro (tel 0726 883201) smoke salmon, trout (both hot and cold), cod and chunky pork sausages from a local butcher. They have a small selection of locally caught wet fish, dressed crabs and make the most generously filled crab sandwiches I've eaten in years.

• *Sainsbury Brothers* at 5 Newbridge Street, Truro (tel 0872 41446) stock several of the local cheeses. These include Menallack (see page 36), Cornish Yarg (see page 38), Tala (see page 36), Ticklemore cheeses (see page 67) and Kes, a new one to me.

• *Roskilly's Ice Cream* ⊠ , Tregellast, Barton, St Keverne (tel 0326 280479) will mail-order their clotted cream and clotted cream fudge. From the farm-shop, they also sell own-made chutneys, mustards, and ice-cream made with their Jersey milk in a range of about 20 flavours.

• Once Lady Mayoress of Truro and then Mayor in her own right, *Armorel Carlyon* makes superb clotted cream and clotted cream butter from her Jersey herd, which you can buy on every Friday at Perranporth W.I. market. Nancassick Farm Shop, King Harry Ferry Road, Feock (tel 0872 8622224) sells her cream only.

• *Di's Dairy and Pantry*, Rock (tel 0208 863531) bake all sorts of pies, cakes and puddings, with Treacle Tart the most popular. They sell Helsett Farm ice-cream and Trevone clotted cream from Jersey milk.

• Huw Jones of Merrivale Charcuterie (see page 37) rates *Hodges Butchers* of 1 Fore Street, Constantine (tel 0326 40225) very highly for his properly hung meat and game that he shoots himself.

• Strange though it might seem, *Constantine Stores and Post Office* ⊠ , 30 Fore Street, Constantine, Falmouth (tel 0326 40226) stock 350 different whiskies – malt, rare and aged and blended – one of the largest selections in the country.

• With a harbour-side fish shop, *Quayside Fish Centre* ⊠ ,

Porthleven, nr Helston (tel 0326 562008) buys most of its fish from Newlyn Fish market on a daily basis or from boats that fish for them. Salmon apart, all the fish is locally caught and they have local shark (porbeagle), weever, cod, plaice, pollack, ling, crabs, lobsters and crawfish. They also smoke salmon, prawns and scallops. (✉ Smoked salmon only.)

• **Trevaskis Fruit Farm** at Gwinear Road, Hayle (tel 0209 713931) have PYO fruit and ready-picked vegetables, and also sell their own South Devon beef and Cornish potatoes.

• **Phillimore Fine Foods** ✉ coarse-grain garlic and horseradish mustards and their chutneys, including an 'overwhelmingly gingery' Peach & Ginger, a tart Lemon, and Spiced Tomato made with green chillies and fennel seed, are sold where they are made at The Lugger, Harbourhead, Porthleven (tel 0326 562761).

CUMBRIA

BROUGHAM   MAP 6

The Old Smokehouse & Truffles ✉ 🏬
SMOKED PRODUCTS & CHOCOLATE TRUFFLES

Brougham Hall, Brougham, Penrith, Cumbria CA10 2DE

TEL *0768 67772* **CONTACT** *Rona Newsom* **HOURS** *Easter to 24 December 10.00-17.30* **DIRECTIONS** *From Penrith, take A6 towards Shap. Follow the road through Eamont Bridge and turn left at the signpost for Brougham. Shop is ½ mile along on the left.*

Brougham Hall, a residential castle re-built in the 19th century, was known in Victorian times as the 'Windsor of the North'. In the 1930s 'it fell on hard times' and in 1985 it was rescued from decay to become home to several small craft workshops. In among the jeweller, wood-turner, art-metalworker, upholstery workshops and café are two enterprising food units: The Old Smokehouse and Truffles.

Let me deal with The Old Smokehouse first. Their products have a noticeably mild cure and mild smoke: eels from Scotland, ranging from 225-425 g (8-15 oz) were small in size and delicate in taste; local chickens were moistly succulent, with just the merest hint of a smoky haze; smoked Cumberland sausages, made for them by Richard Woodall (see page 46), had the lightest smoky touch. Smoked Herd-wick lamb was of stronger stuff: brined then larded with rosemary, it had a deeper woody flavour punched with the pungent bitterness that the herb sometimes brings to food. They also lightly smoke various cheeses, some game, loin of pork, goose, and salmon, and will make up gift packs to order.

Truffles, housed in a separate unit, make a range that is sold in London's Fortnum & Mason. Using a good quality couverture, fresh cream, fresh fruit and real alcohol, their truffles had an immediate freshness unsullied by 'essences or flavourings' that mar so many British-made chocolates. Made by piping the rich mixture into round shells, then closing them with a layer of couverture, rolling them in yet more couverture and then in a dusting of cocoa or even coconut, I was particularly impressed by the coffee & cream. Strong, dark and thickly coffee-flavoured, it was sophisticatedly bitter. Apricot, cream & Cointreau was fruity but sparingly sweet, with a strong alcoholic glow; and peppermint was superbly bitter, as good as a Bendicks bittermint.

As I do not have a serious sweet tooth, I opted to try the plain chocolate truffles although, as far as I could work out, almost everything is also made with a milk or white couverture. Personal shoppers can have the opportunity to pick and choose; if ordering by mail, however, expect to receive a box of mixed truffles weighing 200 or 370 g (7 or 13 oz). They send them out gift-wrapped with a card and they suggest that, once opened, the box should be kept in the fridge.

CORNEY   MAP 6

Ashdown Smokers ✉ 🏭 SMOKED HERDWICK MACON

Skellerah Farm, Corney, Cumbria LA19 5TW

TEL *0229 718324* FAX *0229 718339* CONTACT *Harry Fellows* HOURS *Mon-Fri 10.00-16.00 Sat-Sun telephone ahead* CARDS *Visa, Mastercard* DIRECTIONS *From Broughton-in-Furness, take A595 towards Whicham. Follow the road over the river Duddon and turn immediately right, signposted Bootle/Corney. After about 7 miles, take the first turning left after the cattle grid at sign for Bootle/Corney. Smokery is on left after about 400 yards.*

In the heart of the Cumberland Fells, Harry Fellows has run Ashdown Smokers for the past 10 years. Not for him modern smoking cabinets: 'We smoke in a traditional way in smoke holes contained in a wooden smokehouse, with the product suspended over the heat source'. He regards smoking as an exacting craft; not only does the quality of the produce count, but the cure, the temperature, the time, even the woods are all critical. Each plays a vital part in the ultimate taste and texture of the end-product and for each product it will be different.

Harry is a curious mix of innovative and traditional: he claims he was the first to smoke – amongst other things – quails' eggs, and he has built up a successful side-line in smoking many of the on-farm cheeses. However, he also has revived Smoked Herdwick Macon (Mutton Ham), a local speciality that dates back centuries. Herdwick is the local breed of fell-ranging sheep that feed on heather and scrub, supplemented in the autumn with the crop of wild bilberries. Harry uses the ham (back leg) from the 2-3-year-olds. Those from pure-breeds weigh about 4.5 kg (9 lb) when he starts the process, but reduce to around 3 kg (6 lb) bone-in, or 1.8 kg (4 lb) boned by the time he has finished the process. For larger hams he cures cross-breeds.

The hams are dry-cured in a blend of salt and spices for about 3 weeks, cold-smoked over oak mixed with juniper wood for about 4 weeks and then matured for about 8 months. Sold as whole hams bone-in or boned, or thinly sliced in 225 g (8 oz) packets, the closely textured meat packs a powerful punch. I have tried it several times and to be perfectly honest, I really cannot decide whether or not I like its florid gamy flavour.

However, I have no such misgivings about his rich and slightly gelatinous Buttermere eel or the juicy sirloin of beef that he cures in a spiced brine and then cold-smokes for hours, until the outer edges darken while the centre remains a rosy pink. Harry smokes various other cuts of beef: using a plain dry cure, he prepares fillet of Aberdeen Angus, then lightly smokes it over oak and beech so it retains its grassy complexity; for Shropshire Sirloin he also uses a dry cure, but then rubs the meat all over with treacle and smokes it over a mixture of beech, peat and oak – the result is surprisingly light, a good meaty flavour gently tinged with a salty sweetness.

Harry's list is very long: there is a variety of smoked sausages; kippers; haddock smoked over peat; Windermere char, a delicate fish similar to trout; various game birds, including pheasant, partridge and

> ❝ At the time of writing, the continued existence of Harry Fellows of Ashdown Smokers – and, indeed, all traditional smokers – is threatened by possible EC regulations.
>
> The directives are still up for consultation, but the real fear is they will impose certain restrictions: only stainless steel kilns will be allowed; each kiln must be product-dedicated (ie a different one for each type of meat, fish, game, etc); each product must have its own dedicated curing room; and the heat source must be separated from the actual product. This will change the entire basis of traditional smoking, as no longer will it be allowed to smoke in smoke-holes. The smoke will have to be tunnelled through to the food from a separate source and will lose, as Harry states categorically, 'all its taste-enhancing properties. Character and interest would be lost'. The effect of this proposed legislation will probably be to put most traditional smokers out of business. They will not be able to afford the costs of converting nor, probably, will most of them be interested in so doing. They love their craft and they are doing a good job, so why should they be subject to such interference?
>
> We must make sure, while there is still time, that the EC is not allowed to threaten one of our great culinary traditions. ❞

pigeon, with a fruity nuttiness; venison, including a venison ham that is dry cured in spice and garlic and smoked over oak and bracken for a lively soft-textured meat; ox tongue; rabbit; ham and bacon; even whole smoked suckling pig. Each of his products does have individuality, unlike those of the larger industrial smokers whom Harry accuses of doing 'no more than a cosmetic job'. That is certainly something of which no one could accuse Harry.

GRASMERE   MAP 6

Sarah Nelson's Grasmere Gingerbread Shop

✉ 🏭   GINGERBREAD

Grasmere, Cumbria LA22 9SW

TEL 05394 35428   CONTACT Christine Batey   HOURS Mon-Sat 9.30-17.30 Sun 12.30-17.30   DIRECTIONS In town centre.

Well over 130 years ago, Sarah Nelson began baking gingerbread in what was once the old schoolhouse tucked by the lych-gate of St Oswald's where no less a personage than William Wordsworth is buried. Such was her reputation that business thrived and in the fullness of time Grasmere gingerbread became well known both in and out of the county.

Interestingly enough, there is quite a tradition of using spices in the area, as they were brought by sea direct to the small ports along the Cumbrian coast and no doubt Sarah would have benefited from this trade. Much is made of her in the old-fashioned bakery: there is a photograph of her and she looks far too mean-mouthed and forbidding ever to have – as history has it – spent time in genial pursuits like making gingerbread alphabets in order to tempt the local children to read.

Grasmere is a thriving tourist town and the gingerbread shop certainly does capitalize on the tourist trade. However, they have not compromised on the quality of their gingerbread and they still use the same 'secret' recipe to which only 3 families have been privy, and it is superb. Made daily, if you time your visit right you can buy it while still warm and soft. More like a biscuit than a parkin or bread, the thin oblongs harden to a firm chewiness, with a texture of melting sand and a glorious afterglow of ginger that fires the throat. Sold wrapped in old-fashioned vegetable parchment in packets of 6 or 12 pieces, the fruity-spiced gingerbread is a deep warm brown. They also make a grainy-textured rum butter, well laced with alcohol.

Let me give you one word of advice. As you hit Grasmere, you will notice various shops claiming to sell 'real' or 'original' gingerbread. In general they do not, so do not be taken in. Theirs are no more than poor imitations: thick, floury, bland, looking like low-grade flapjacks, and to be avoided at all costs.

For a most unusual drink, drop into the **Masons Arms, Strawberry Bank, Cartmel Fell (tel 05395 68486)** for a glass of Damson beer. The Lyth Valley is famous for its damsons and landlord Nigel Stevenson got the idea of brewing them for beer from a visit to Belgium, where apparently fruit beers are very popular. Nigel uses whole fruit mashed up, stones and all, and a reduced hop level for a deep rich-red colour, a creamy head and a strong fruit taste. He also makes a dry but fruity Damson wine, ginger beer and a flinty cider. **Lyth Valley Farmshop at Dawson Fold (tel 05395 68248)**, right by the side of the A5074, sells damsons 'come the second week of September' through to the end of the month, although one year they were still cropping as late as the end of October.

MELMERBY   MAP 6

The Village Bakery ✉ 🫖 🌿 🍺   BREAD

Melmerby, Penrith, Cumbria CA10 1HE

TEL 0768 881515 FAX 0768 881848 CONTACT Andrew Whitley HOURS Mon 8.30-17.00 Tues-Sat 8.30-17.00 Sun 9.30-17.00 CARDS Access, Visa, Mastercard, Diners DIRECTIONS From Penrith, take A686 towards Melmerby. At Melmerby, turn left immediately after the sharp left bend in the road at sign for bakery. Bakery is 100 yards along on the right.

Andrew Whitley was probably born to bake. Even when he was working as a full-time producer for the BBC Russian Service he still found time to make rye bread that 'was jumped on by Russian expatriates. They'd sniff the dough and tears formed in their eyes'. Encouraged by its success and longing for a simple life, he decamped up North to bake full-time.

Fast-forward 15 years to November 1991... Already a well-established baker, running a shop and restaurant that won Egon Ronay's Tea Place of the Year, he expanded and opened a spanking new bakery with a state-of-the-art wood-burning brick oven imported from France – a *four à gueulard*. A good oven is essential to good bread and Andrew is immensely proud of his. The very fact that he uses it immediately qualifies him to join the select band of traditional French bakers that '*cuit au four à bois*' (bake in a wood-fired oven).

The wood burns in the fire-box underneath the oven and heats the brick sole (floor). There is a hole in the floor and flames burn up through it and are directed to the back by a metal *gueulard* (throat). Using wood is cheaper and more ecologically sound – an important point to Andrew – and the oven gives superior baking quality. 'The brick floor gives a great solidity of heat and allows the heat to penetrate the bread so it bakes more evenly and faster with a greater moisture retention – so you get a satisfying crust,' he explained. 'The flame going through the oven is a brilliant compromise as you get all the flame heat but none of the mess of charcoal, as you would in a traditional oven. There's no wood flavour, but we're not barbecuing bread.'

Using organic (to Soil Association standards) flour from the Watermill at near-by Little Salkeld (see below) and Shipton Mill (see page 100), Andrew bakes superb bread. His French country bread is naturally leavened (ie without yeast), with a creamy moist inside (wonderful to tear apart) and a thick crusty exterior. 'Essential,' as Andrew remarked, 'crust is like the skin of a fruit, it often has the best flavour that permeates right through the dough'. He makes two splendid flavoured breads: tomato and olive. For these the yeast is added and left for 24 hours until it has 'gone tired, meaning it rises, collapses and then, when you touch it, it seems almost to give out a yawn'. The doughs are mixed with olive oil (Italian for the tomato and Greek for the olive) and then vast quantities of tomato purée and sun-dried tomatoes or olive paste and green stuffed olives are mixed in. The dough is rolled, cut and twisted to give a shaft of flavour streaking through the bread.

Andrew's pride is his sour-dough Russian rye. He even went to Kostroma on the Volga to collect the starter and, fearful that its power might be diminishing, went back last spring for more. Made over 24 hours to give it a chance to mature, it is full of body and tinged with sharpness. Then there are his biscuits, oatcakes, Borrowdale tea bread made with tea-soaked fruit, gingerbread, Christmas puddings and cakes, and Rum Nicky (a date, ginger, rum and butter tart). Everything is first-rate. Last year he started supplying Waitrose with his breads. You will be pleased to hear he now also runs week-end courses for professional or amateur bakers.

> *The Watermill [⌧] at Little Salkeld, Penrith, CA10 1NN (tel 0768 881523) sells a vast range of own-milled flours, oat meal and flakes, and animal feeds (my dog Violet particularly appreciated the dog meal of flaked maize with bran, soya meal, rolled oats, wheat and barley). Vegetarians will be interested in their Special Blend, wheat and soya flour, sesame and sunflower seeds with a protein level of 20%. Everything conforms to one of three existing organic standards: viz Soil Association, Bio-dynamic (Demeter) or Organic Farmers and Growers.*

PENRITH   MAP 6

BEST SWEETS

The Toffee Shop ⌧   FUDGE & TOFFEE

7 Brunswick Road, Penrith, Cumbria CA11 7LU

TEL 0768 62008   **CONTACT** Mr Boustead   **HOURS** Mon-Sat 9.00-17.00 **DIRECTIONS** In town centre.

The Toffee Shop has made it into *Courvoisier's Book of the Best*. And quite right too, as they make the best fudge in England.

You could almost walk straight past the plain white shop without realizing that this is where it all happens. Its window is full of blue-and-white china, more in keeping with an antique shop than England's finest sweet shop. Once inside, however, the rich sweet aroma of melting butter and boiling sugar give the game away. Everything is made out in the tiny kitchen in the back. Neat and trim, the 8 brass pans are kept well-polished and always ready for use.

The keys to any good product are the right ingredients, the right recipe and the right techniques. The Bousteads do not deviate from any of these precepts. Fudge is made from butter, sugar and milk to a simple recipe and in small batches, so it cooks evenly and thoroughly. There are always plenty of people to fuss over it, stirring it when it needs stirring and checking it never boils over or catches in the pan. They have been using the same recipe for 90 years 'and haven't changed it one iota'. Why should they when it is so good? Once cooked, it is poured into cooling trays and then cut by hand into slabs, making it more like Scottish tablet in shape (though not in texture) than an English fudge. It is so extra-specially good, with a honeyed freshness and a rich and buttery fullness, it makes you want never to stop eating it. As it is neither too sweet nor too cloying, you can nibble away for hours.

As well as plain fudge, they do make two flavours: mint, using the same mint oil as in Kendal mint cake; and chocolate, using a dark plain chocolate. As a bit of a purist, however, I prefer it unadulterated so its full glory shines through. In my enthusiasm for the fudge, I must not forget their seriously good toffee. Made with butter, sugar and black treacle, it packs a powerful punch. Again it is made by hand and, once cooled in the trays and broken up with a hammer, the irregularly shaped pieces are then individually wrapped in plain paper.

Both fudge and toffee can be sent by post anywhere in the country in 225, 450, 675 or 900 g ($\frac{1}{2}$, 1, $1\frac{1}{2}$ or 2 lb) boxes. As Mr Boustead Junior told me firmly, don't ask for a mixed box of fudge that includes mint: they will just not send it, as the danger is the mint will overpower the other flavours. Believe me, that would be a disaster.

WABERTHWAITE MAP 6

Richard Woodall ✉ ☎ HAM & BACON

Lane End, Waberthwaite, nr Millom, Cumbria LA19 5YJ

TEL *0229 717237 & 717386* CONTACT *Bar Woodall* HOURS *Mon-Fri 8.30-12.15 & 13.15-17.30 Sat 8.30-12.00* DIRECTIONS *From Broughton-in-Furness, take A595 towards Ravenglass. Drive through Bootle and follow road for about 3 miles past Brown Cow Inn on right. About 100 yards after pub, bear left and shop is 200 yards along on left.*

Ancient Recipes ✉, Unit 3B&C, Longtown Industrial Estate, Longtown, Carlisle, CA6 5TJ (tel 0228 792062) use old English recipes to produce a range of jams, pickles and chutneys. The pity is they were unwilling – or unable – to give chapter and verse of their sources. Not that it makes any difference to the taste, but as they make such a thing of it and claim they are 'preserving the past with ancient recipes', I think it is only reasonable to be told. Using a brewed malt vinegar for all their pickles, they produce a wide range: including powerful Olde English pickled onions; Chow-Chow (a chopped piccalilli); Cumberland pickle; a gentle well-textured mixture of sliced cucumber and onions known as a 'bread and butter pickle', presumably because it is eaten spread on a slice of bread; pickled red cabbage, and pickled beetroot. In the jam and marmalade line, there is Jamaican Lime, Tudor and Appledore Jam, the latter a blend of Bramley apples and sweet oranges.

The Queen and British Airways' first-class passengers are familiar with Bar (Richard) Woodall's juicy Cumberland sausages. Supplying such high flyers has not changed the business one jot, it is still run from the local village shop that doubles as a general store and sub-post office. Students of the finances of The Royal Mail may also be interested to know that Waberthwaite is the only sub-office to have shown a consistent increase in turnover because, as Bar points out with a certain satisfaction, 'We are our own best customers'. Throughout the year they are pretty busy, but at Christmas-time the number of orders soars into the hundreds and a special collection van has to be sent daily.

Bar (a seventh-generation Woodall) and his wife June run the business, and nephew Colin is being carefully groomed to take over. It was started in 1828, when the then recently widowed Hannah Woodall set about curing her neighbours' pigs in order to provide for her family. In those days nobody would think anything of a ham weighing in at a massive 13.5 kg (30 lb); pigs were a lot larger and fatter then. Now his Cumberland hams top the scales at a mere 7.7 kg (17 lb), with the average weight somewhere between that and 6.4 kg (14 lb).

Most of their meat comes from the pig farm run by Bar's brother. Since 1976 it has been a closed herd (they do not buy in stock and only breed from within) of Landrace and Large White pigs. Reared on a semi-intensive system, they are fed an antibiotic-free diet of cereal and vegetable proteins. 'Control of the raw material is essential, we aim for a consistency of size and obviously it gives us the great advantage of being able to process when the meat is really fresh'.

Bar's range may be limited, but it is outstanding. His Cumberland ham, traditionally cured in salt and saltpetre for 1 month, washed and dried then matured for 3 months, has a rasping full-bodied flavour; its texture, similar to a York ham, is resilient with plenty of bite. He supplies them as whole or half hams, bone-in or boned, rolled and vacuum-packed, and either smoked or unsmoked. For the smaller appetites he also sells ham steaks in a pack of 2 slices.

The first time I ever met Bar was when he was contemplating an air-dried ham along a similar line to the Italian Parma ham. Several samples and several comments went flying back and forth from Cumbria to London until he perfected the technique. I was amongst its first customers, we served it daily at the British Harvest restaurant at The Hilton in Park Lane when I worked there as a consultant and I must admit to claiming full responsibility for its name, Cumbria Air-dried Ham. It is gorgeous – harsher perhaps than a Parma ham, but all the more interesting for that. Dry-cured for 1 month in salt, saltpetre, herbs and a few spices (Bar has always been reticent about the exact ingredients), the hams are air-dried (matured) for 12 months.

He has since introduced a Cumbria Mature Royal that is pickled in beer, treacle, sugar vinegar and salt for 1 month, then matured for 12 months. Both are sold thinly sliced and eaten like a Parma ham, that is to say in their raw state. It is only fair to say that, although others in Britain have copied, only Bar's have that rich mellowness, that warm meatiness and succulence that makes them worthy rivals to the Italians.

His bacon also has his sure touch. Dry-cured for about 14 days, washed, dried and matured for a month, it is lean and sweet, has a superb length of flavour and certainly never shrinks or splutters in the pan. Finally there are his sausages, made from shoulder, belly and a few trimmings, 'Only good goes in it to get good out' is his motto. His Cumberland, a long continuous link of pure meat pungently spiced with pepper, is satisfyingly chunky and coarsely ground.

If you visit Bar (and I warn you he is miles from anywhere), ask him if he will take you up to the ham loft. The wooden rafters are crowded with hooks from which hang the hams in varying stages of maturity. The air is fragrant with a sweet meatiness, and there is not a fly to be seen, 'A sign of properly cured meat,' Bar told me proudly.

Two miles from Devil's Bridge is **Adamson** ⊠ *at* **The Barn, Tearnside Hall, Kirby Lonsdale, LA6 2PU (tel & fax 05242 72530)**. *Piers Adamson wholesales the best of Cumbrian produce to the South and the shop, run by his mother, is guaranteed to stock the best from the area. Here you will find a range of smoked foods from Ashdown Smokers (see page 41), The Village Bakery (see page 44) bread, honey from the Lakes, Slack's sausages (see page 49), and interesting cheeses made by* **Carolyn Fairbairn** *of* **Thornby Moor Dairy** ⊠**, Aikton, Wigton CA7 0JZ (tel 06973 43160)**. *These include brine-washed Crofton, made with a mixture of cows' and goats' milk; Bewcastle, a crisp fresh ewes'-milk cheese sold wrapped in vine leaves; and Cumberland, a Cheddar-style cheese that Caroline also smokes herself.*

And Also...

- To catch their Morecambe Bay shrimps, **Flookburgh Fishermen** ⊠ of Moor Lane, Flookburgh, nr Grange-over-Sands (tel 0539 558353) trawl for them from tractors when the tide is out. Once washed, boiled and hand-picked, they are frozen until needed for potting (see also James Baxter, page 00).

- **Cumberland Mustard** ⊠ at Sharon Cottage, 16 Hillhouse Lane, Alston, Carlisle (tel 0434 381135) produces Original, Garlic, Green Peppercorn, and Horseradish coarse-grain mustards. Brown and white mustard seeds, which she grinds herself, are mixed with a local spring water, honey cider vinegar, nutmeg and sea salt for a sweet but pungent condiment.

- A brother and sister team, David and Alison, former pâtisserie chef at Sharrow Bay, set up **Kennedys** ⊠. With a factory shop at Silver Yard, Orton (tel 05396 24 781) and a shop at 5 St Alban's Walk, Carlisle (tel 0228 819875), they make luscious chocolates using 55% cocoa-solids Belgian couverture 'based on Swiss recipes and English know-how'.

- You can reach **Muncaster Mill**, Ravenglass (tel 0229 717232) either by road or rail, as the old Ravenglass & Eskdale Railway (starting from Ravenglass) takes you right to the door. At the mill you can buy 100% wholemeal, coarse 85% brown, and unbleached semolina milled from grain grown to Soil Association approved organic standards.

- Contact **Armathwaite Herbs** ⊠, Kilchoman, Armathwaite (tel 06974 72 265) for organic herb plants grown to Soil Association standards, plus a few salad annuals such as rocket, green purslane and nasturtium.

- **Slack's** ⊠ of Newland's Farm, Raisbeck, Orton, Penrith (tel 05396 24667) produce a range of meaty sausages that are subtly flavoured with unusual blends of spices. Their coarse-cut long-linked Cumberland, in a choice of 93% or 75% meat content, is seasoned with salt, pepper and sage; chunky Toulouse (93%) is spiked with a mixture of ginger, nutmeg, cinnamon and cloves; and their chipolatas (93%) have pepper, coriander, pimento, nutmeg, thyme and cayenne to give them plenty of punch. Cooked hams are also available by mail order.

- Visit **The Barn Shop** at Lower Sizergh Farm, Sizergh (tel 05395 60426) for pick-your-own strawberries. They also sell Village Bakery bread (see page 44), a fruity tea loaf from Bentham Home Bakery, local free-range chickens, herb jellies from The Herb Farm, Levens Hall Honey (see over) and flavoured honeys from Lancaster. There is also a good selection of bacon, ham and sausages from Richard Woodall (see page 46), and smoked produce from Ashdown Smokers (see page 41).

- **Burbush's**, Unit 3, Gilwilly Industrial Estate, Penrith (tel 0768 63841), make open game pies topped with fruit. Try their cunning mixtures of chicken, pheasant and apricot or guinea fowl, turkey and cranberries, both sold as $\frac{1}{2}$, 1, 2 or 3 kg ($1\frac{1}{4}$, $2\frac{1}{4}$, $4\frac{1}{2}$ or $6\frac{1}{2}$ lb) pies.

• *Levens Hall*, nr Kendal (tel 05395 60321) is famous for its topiary, but did you know that you can now buy honey collected by the Head Gardener from hives in and around the garden? Spring/summer honey is gently fruited from a mixture of blossoms and flowers; late summer honey, collected when the bees take their holiday up on the Yorkshire moors, is denser and heavier – just what you would expect when they have been busying themselves around heather.

DERBYSHIRE

BAKEWELL   MAP 4

Holdsworth Chocolates ✉ ☕   CHOCOLATES

Station Road, Bakewell, Derbyshire DE4 1GE

TEL *0629 813573* FAX *0629 813850* CONTACT *Barbara Holdsworth* HOURS *Mon-Sat 9.00-17.00* DIRECTIONS *From Bakewell, take A619 towards Chesterfield. On the outskirts of the town, bear right off the main road immediately after the old bridge. Follow signs for Holdsworth to the industrial estate at the top of the road.*

Bakewell has long since lost its local railway line, but the station and yard have been put to good use as an industrial estate. Holdsworth's rent one of the units and from this very English set-up, Barbara Holdsworth makes Continental-style chocolates. They are, to use the technical term, 'filled chocolates', which means – as Barbara puts it – 'chocolate coated with something inside'. The 'something inside' is either a ganache (chocolate, butter and cream) for truffles, praline base (ganache mixed with a nut purée) for the pralines, or a cream (chocolate, butter and fruit purée) for the chocolate creams.

Using a good Belgian couverture (with 60% cocoa solids), unsalted butter and 'proper' spirits and liqueurs, fruit purées and essences, Barbara's chocolates are crisp and terse, neither too sweet nor too rich but satisfyingly moreish. She produces 60 or so varieties in all. The truffles include a light champagne, a sultry dark chocolate rum and a vibrant poire Williams with a deep fruitiness. Pralines I'm a sucker for and was pleased to find that each one – almond, cashew, hazel, pecan & walnut – had a nicely developed taste of the individual nut.

Barbara also makes terrific mint crisps, with dark chocolate couverture flavoured with peppermint oil and mildly sweetened with raw cane sugar. Crisp to the bite, they are minty in the mouth but leave a good afterglow of plain chocolate. If, like the Duchess of Devonshire (see Chatsworth Farm Shop, page 52), you would like them embossed with your crest or more likely initialed, Barbara will happily oblige.

Has it ever struck you just how many of our traditional recipes are the result of an 'accident'. Many a misguided (and no doubt under-paid) kitchen maid has burnt this, added that and – hey presto – a new dish is born. Bakewell Pudding is just such an accident; this time Cook put strawberry jam into a puff pastry case before, instead of after, an egg mixture. The result met with universal approval in 1860; I wish the same were true today.

In the town of Bakewell, there are three pudding-makers all with some claim to the 'original' recipe, and I had the misfortune to try them all. **The Old Original Bakewell Pudding Shop** ⊠, **The Square, DE45 1BT (tel 0629 812193)** *makes the most of the historic connection, but its puddings are a disgrace; the pastry is flabby and greasy, the filling lumpy and the whole confection reeked of cheap essence and cheap jam.* **The Bakewell Pudding Parlour** ⊠, **Water Street, DE1 4EW (tel 0629 815107)** *was equally vile and synthetic. Only* **Bloomer's Original Bakewell Puddings** ⊠ *in* **Matlock Street, DE45 1EE (tel 0629 813724)** *have any merit. Their own-made pastry was passable, their filling – if a little solid and rubbery – at least had a pleasant fresh flavour that hinted of almonds and the jam did actually taste of fruit.*

BUXTON MAP 4

St Ann's Well

SPRING WATER

The Crescent, Buxton, Derbyshire

HOURS 00.00-24.00 **DIRECTIONS** *In town centre.*

Buxton mineral water is sold throughout Britain, but are you aware that in Buxton you can get it for free? The stone fountain of St Ann's Well, opposite the scandalously decaying Crescent, spews it out at the rate of 7,000 litres an hour – all day and night. Canny locals know to come laden with bottles for filling.

Buxton's water is 'thermal' water. This means that at the point of emergence it has the same or a greater temperature than the mean average for the surrounding air. According to Mike Langham and Colin Wells in their booklet *Buxton Water*, 'The water emerges from the springs at a constant temperature of 81.5°F regardless of the season and has not varied since reliable temperature measurements were started 200 years ago'. There are several springs in Buxton; some are capped and diverted into the river Wye, a group emerges in the bath house where you can still take the waters, and another comes up at St Ann's.

Just as the television adverts claim, the waters are pure. The water, 'first fell on the ground at least 20 years ago, but possibly much earlier, on to a catchment area of about 20 square miles to the south and east of the town...From here it goes underground, seeping through layers of limestone to a depth of about $1\frac{1}{2}$ km (5,000 ft). At this point the water meets a geological fault in the limestone and rises, under hydraulic pressure to the surface. Mixed with the water are bubbles of gas, mostly of nitrogen and carbon dioxide, but also of argon and helium. Both the water and the gas are slightly radioactive and when seen in quantity, the water is of a clear, light blue colour...Due to the continuous filtration it has received during its long underground passage, the water emerges quite sterile, containing no bacteria'.

And very good it tastes too; crystal clear, clean tasting and very refreshing, if perhaps a little warm... and it doesn't cost a penny.

Pugsons of Buxton ✉, *Cliff House, Terrace Road, Buxton SK17 6DR (tel 0298 77696, fax 0298 72381) is run by the pugnacious Peter Pugson. He makes much of his cheeses; here you can buy Buxton Blue, orange-marbled and softer than Stilton; a well-matured creamy Stilton from J.M. Nutall; Mrs Kirkham's Lancashire; Deaville's Staffordshire Organic (see page 231); a creamy, smooth-textured fresh goats' cheese from Jumble Farm and much, much more. It is a jolly friendly shop, with a good balance of imported and own-produced foods. Their own-made cakes and tarts are splendid:* tarte Normande *is a caramely affair with the crisp pastry base tinged with* rum; tarte aux fruits *is 'made properly enriched with brandy' and the almond tart, loosely based on the Bakewell pudding, beats it handsdown with its buttery* pâte brisée, *creamy custard flavoured with powdered almonds, and fruity apricot jam topping. Hams, from Maynard Davies (see page 216) are baked off generously washed in a marmalade glaze; pâtés are freshly made and French bread is baked throughout the day. Fresh every day are Derbyshire oatcakes, a thicker version of their better-known relations from Staffordshire (see page 232), pikelets and jam tartlets. There are also chocolates hand-made by Peter Thornton (a cousin of the Thornton's chocolate family) and an excellent range of wines. (✉Cheeses, hampers and wine only.)*

PILSLEY   MAP 4

Chatsworth Farm Shop ✉ 🚜 ⚱

SAUSAGES & CHEESE

Stud Farm, Pilsley, Bakewell, Derbyshire DE4S 1UF

TEL 0246 583392 **FAX** 0246 583464 **CONTACT** *Sandy Boyd* **HOURS** *Apr to Oct: Mon-Sat 9.00-17.30 (Tues 9.30-17.30); Nov to Mar: Mon-Sat 9.00-17.00 (Tues 9.30-17.00)* **CARDS** *Access, Visa* **DIRECTIONS** *From junction 29 on the M1, follow signs to Chatsworth House. Drive through Baslow and turn left at roundabout on to B6012, signposted Edensor. After about 1 mile, turn right signposted Pilsley. Shop is on left.*

More a food hall than a farm-shop, Chatsworth Farm Shop is one in a million. To cite it as a role model to which all other farm-shops could aspire would not be fair, as Chatsworth has tremendous advantages: its position near one of our best-known stately homes and the visitors that attracts; a duchess for a proprietor, with great style, taste and flair; and a sound capital investment.

What is heartening is that these advantages have not been squandered. The easy option would have been to 'label-appeal but never mind the contents' food that seems to attract gift-buying tourists in their thousands; this they have avoided. Instead, under the ever-watchful eye of manager Sandy Boyd, it has become a Mecca for farmhouse produce. His philosophy is 'to source from the farm, primarily Chatsworth, tenant or local farms and then to spread our wings and buy from elsewhere with an emphasis on quality British foods'.

The shop itself is a delight; pedimented pine shelving, fired-tile floors, stencils around the walls, and stunning animal tiles hand-painted by Bobby Jones (who also decorated Prince Charles's loos at Highgrove) set off the food. At one end is the butcher's counter which sells own-farm beef hung for 14 days; lamb from the estate, including the Duchess's Jacobs; pork; free-range maize-fed chickens "reared for 81 days for a firm texture'; ducks from the Hereford Duck Company (see page 117); game from the estate; free-range geese and turkeys for Christmas; and a good range of sausages, including the Duke's Favourite, with a 90% meat content and made with pork, pork liver, white wine and seasonings to give it a unique deep robust flavour.

Cheese is one of Sandy's pride and joys. The 80-odd on-farm cheeses are all British or Irish and here you will find some of the perennial favourites: Mary Holbrook (see page 9), Bonchester (see page 328), as well as few lesser-known locals, such as a tangy semi-hard sheep's milk from Ram Hall Dairy. There is a rich unpasteurized double cream made from their Friesian herd, with a few Jerseys 'for good measure'. Chocolates come from Holdsworth (see page 50) and I loaded myself up with the dark bitter-mint wafers embossed with the Duchess's crest – so smart for the supper table. Les Fines Herbes (see page 156) is well represented, as are James White apple juices (see page 237). There are also Derbyshire oatcakes, Bakewell puddings from Bloomers (see page 51) and a heather honey from the moors above the house.

A fair proportion of the produce is made in the shop's own kitchen, often to the recipes of André, the Duchess's chef. Bread is baked daily, and there are pies (the game pie is sold with the warning 'this pie may contain lead shot'), pâtés, biscuits and cakes. Occasionally you may find grapes from the hot-house and vegetables and salads from the garden; otherwise they are bought in. You could spend hours here – I did – as everything is cooked and/or chosen with great care and commitment to quality. If only more shops would follow Chatsworth's example and dedicate themselves to stocking the finest of British produce.

George Stafford 🎖   BLACK PUDDING

130 Belper Road, Stanley Common, Derbyshire DE7 6FQ

TEL *0602 325751* **CONTACT** *George Stafford* **HOURS** *Mon-Fri 7.30-18.00 (-14.00 Wed) Sat 7.30-15.00* **DIRECTIONS** *From Ilkeston, take A609 into the centre of Stanley Common. Shop is on the right, just opposite the recreation ground.*

At an age when lesser men would have willingly retired, George Stafford is up every morning at 4.00, devotedly making his black puddings. As he flaps around the factory out back of the shop, he ruefully describes himself as a 'bionic man'. This refers not to the incredible man hours he puts in, but to his hip replacements; he has already worn out 4 and now his doctors have decided to call it a day – hence the flapping penguin walk.

Happily this state of affairs does not affect the black pudding. George had been making them for years in his uncle's shop, but was never really satisfied with the taste until, 'one night I changed the recipe and realized I was on to a winner'. What those changes were, he is far to canny to admit; I can only suspect that George lightened it, using less oatmeal or barley or flour in order to make it lighter and creamier – more in line with the French (see also Morris's Gold Medal Black Pudding, page 139). Should anyone even attempt to find out, let me warn them that the recipe is deposited under lock and key in the bank.

Since that fateful night in 1948, George's black puddings have won 6 gold, 4 silver and 2 bronze medals at the annual French black pudding championships at Mortagne-au-Perche; there's nothing like beating the French at their own game. Friend and colleague, Marie-Pierre Moine – a French cookery writer living in London – could quite see why; she pronounced his by far the best she had tried of those made in this country. With the texture of velvet, they are quite strong but not overly so, with a well-rounded flavour gently punctuated with spice, George eats them cold with a glass of beer. His final test for a good pudding is that it is moist and moves when you press it.

And Also...

• Made redundant in the last wave of pit closures, miner **Eldred Grocock** of 10 Valley Road, Bolsover (tel 0246 824512) now makes chocolate truffles and a teeth-crunching Bonfire toffee from butter, sugar and black treacle.
• **The Herb Garden** at Hall View Cottage, Hardstoft, nr Pilsley (tel 0246 854268) sells a good range of potted herbs.
• In the late-summer, **Derbyshire Beekeeping Centre** at Nether

Cottage, Nether Lane, Hazelwood, nr Duffield (tel 0773 550513) take their hives up to the moors for a thick ling-heather honey. Buy it direct from them or from Chatsworth Farm Shop (see page 52).

• Hugh Lillington of Innes (see page 234) recommends *The Cheeseboard Delicatessen* ✉. With two shops in the county at 4 Hebden Court, Matlock Street, Bakewell (tel 0629 814814, fax 0629 814090) and 22 Market Place, Ashbourne (tel 0335 342631) they sell Hartington's Stilton and several British on-farm cheeses.

DEVON

ASHPRINGTON   MAP 1

Sharpham Creamery 🏠 ♣   SHARPHAM CHEESE

Sharpham House, Ashprington, Totnes, Devon TQ9 7UT

TEL *0803 732203* CONTACT *Mark Sharman* HOURS *Easter to end-Sept: Mon-Fri 14.00-18.00* DIRECTIONS *From Totnes, take A381 towards Kingsbridge. After about 1 mile turn left signposted Ashprington. Follow the road about 2½ miles into village centre. At the War Memorial, turn left uphill into dead-end road. Follow the road 1 mile on to the estate and follow signs to Sharpham Vineyard.*

Converted from a stable block, Sharpham Dairy is on the Sharpham estate that covers 500 acres in an area designated as of outstanding natural beauty. Quite right too, as it is stunning countryside and if, like me, you manage to miss the turning to the dairy, you drive through a dappled wood right down to the plunging banks of the river Dart. I've never been so happy to be lost before.

When I finally did find the dairy, I was greeted by the cheese-maker Debbie Mumford. Although Debbie was far too discreet to mention it, Sharpham has had a slightly chequered history. It was devised by Isabella Carroll and she made it for several years. Then it hit various problems and production ceased until Debbie came on the scene. Incidentally, she used to work for Robin Congdon (see page 67) and it strikes me that almost everyone in the area is inter-connected in one way or another... but back to the cheese.

Sharpham is a Coulommiers-type cheese made with milk from the estate's Jersey herd. In the good old days Isabella used unpasteurized milk and, at its best, it would ripen and ooze in a meltingly rich buttery stream; admittedly it was variable and, at its worst, it could remain rock-hard and taste of nothing. For a more consistent cheese, the milk is now flash-heated, which is a less stringent treatment than pasteurization.

So, although it may not hit the high spots any longer as it no longer ripens and runs, it never dips into the lows. For all that, Sharpham is still an interesting cheese; made over 4 days, the curds are cut, moulded, drained and brined, then left at a comparatively warm temperature – 9-10°C (48-50°F) – for about 4 weeks to allow the mould to develop so it makes a thick white coating. By then the cheese has developed an interesting grassy richness and a soft creaminess, whilst still remaining firm enough to cut with a knife.

*In a county with pastures as rich as Devon, you would expect to find good cheese. Worth trying is Vulscombe, made by **Graham Townsend** ✉ at **Higher Vulscombe, Cruwys Morchard, nr Tiverton EX16 8NB (tel 0884 252505)**. A full-fat dense soft cheese, it is made with the unpasteurized milk from his British Saanen herd and sold within 3 weeks of making. What is unusual is the recipe: Graham starts the milk, leaves it to ripen, strains it through muslin for 24 hours, ladles it into moulds and lightly presses it; he then leaves it to ripen, and sells it plain, peppered or decorated with fresh herbs from the garden. Aiming for a creamy mild cheese, Graham eschews rennet, as he believes it makes for a drier 'clarty' texture. Rachel Stephens makes the black-waxed Curworthy Cheese at **Stockbeare Farm, Jacobstowe, nr Okehampton (tel 0837 810587)**. Mild and 'almost spreadable' when young, as it matures it firms and dries. Meldon is flavoured with Chiltern Ale mustard for a sweeter finish and Rachel also produces Belstone, made in a similar way to Curworthy but with unpasteurized milk and a natural rind.*

CAPTON   MAP 1

Dittisham Fruit Farm 🚜 🥣   VEGETABLES & HERBS

Capton, Dartmouth, Devon TQ6 0JE

TEL *0804 21452*   CONTACT *Edward Kain*   HOURS *Mar to end-Oct: 10.00-17.00*   DIRECTIONS *From Dartmouth, take A3122 towards Halwell. After about 2½ miles, follow signs for the Prehistoric Hill Settlement Museum (part of the farm), which start at The Sportsmans Arms.*

Every so often I come across a pick-your-own that reinforces my belief that they are a good thing. In principle I'm for them as they are a useful source of fresh-from-the-field produce and you can choose the size, condition and variety you want. In practice, they often turn out to be unimaginative little numbers offering uninteresting varieties of run-of-the-mill vegetables; with nothing to tempt you out of the car, let alone into a muddy field.

Happily, Dittisham Fruit Farm is one such pick-your-own that does confirm my belief. It has a seriously good selection of unusual vegetables and salads all grown with flavour in mind. The list they put out is 'no more than a taster' for, as Edward Kain says, 'if you want something else, do ask; as we've plenty more veg that don't get written down'. 'Written down' are salad leaves, such as sorrel, rocket (in more or less continuous supply as they have 12 sowings a year), mizuna, gold and green purslane (I recently heard it called 'miner's lettuce'); edible flowers, like courgettes (from late-June to the end of August), chives, borage, pinks, marigolds and nasturtium; lettuces, including red Continuity, pinky-red frilly Rossa fruilliana, oak leaf in both red and green, Tom Thumb and Little Gem; and baby vegetables, like leeks the size of a biro, Ping-Pong ball (or smaller) turnips and beetroot, mange-tout peas that measure no more than 2.5 cm (1 in), Yellow Currant tomatoes the size of a large pea, with a piercingly sweet flavour and Pink Fir Apples.

Off the list and worth asking for are La Ratte, an early waxy salad potato, and two unusually coloured potatoes: Purple Congo, with its blue flesh, and Pentland Blue, with a blue skin. They also grow patty pans (nutty round courgettes), baby broad and runner beans, tiny garden peas, a good selection of culinary herbs including flat-leaf parsley and various basils, and a good range of soft fruit from which they make fruit liqueurs.

Various local restaurants, including Joyce Molyneux at the Carved Angel who is famous for buying the best, flock for their produce and the Kains are always willing to try something new, last year it was seakale 'but it's not for the general public – yet'. They are in constant touch with Frances Smith, the doyenne of growing-for-restaurants (see page 126), and they meet up every year to exchange seeds, vegetable gossip and new ideas.

CHITTLEHAMPTON   MAP 1

Melchior ✉ ☕   CHOCOLATES

Chittlehampton, Devon EX37 9QL

TEL *0769 540643* **CONTACT** *Linda Melchior* **HOURS** *Mon-Fri 9.30 -17.30 weekend – telephone ahead* **CARDS** *Access, Visa, Mastercard* **DIRECTIONS** *In village centre.*

Scratch most good *chocolatiers* and you'll usually find some Swiss blood flowing in their veins. Carlo Melchior is no exception; he came over from Switzerland in 1977 'for the longest 6 months of my life – as I'm still here'. Like every true Swiss he missed his chocolates, so he set about making them and serving them to the customers in the tea-room/restaurant he ran with his, then, newly acquired wife Linda, a local girl. 'I made a few, then a few more, started selling them for Christmas and Easter, orders built up and then we had to decide – chocolates or restaurant'. Luckily for us, they choose the chocolates.

That was 6 years ago, since then the Melchiors moved and converted the stables into the chocolate factory where Carlo toils away. Using a good Swiss couverture (with 60% cocoa solids) and local cream, he specializes in truffles, pralines and fruit liqueurs. Finish is important, 'they must look right with a high shine,' but so obviously is the taste. Carlo likes them rich and creamy, but 'they must leave the palate fresh' – presumably to make us go on and on eating more and more; and what is so extraordinary is that you do want to. Yes, they are rich and creamy, but they are also incredibly light. Without wanting to give too many of his secrets away, Carlo told me it is because, unlike most *chocolatiers*, he never uses butter in his ganache; and for his pralines he uses a nut oil extract instead of a nut paste or nut butter.

Soft and luscious truffles come in white, milk or dark chocolate. If Carlo has a heavy hand at all, it is with the liberal doses of liqueurs, spirits and *eaux-de-vie* he generously applies. Champagne was soft and silky; Amaretto, with an icing-sugar finish, was creamily orange; and Marc had a deep resonance. Each and every one was vibrant and zingy. The light almost airy pralines had a pure nutty intensity and as for the liquid liqueurs – one bite and they burst open in your mouth oozing with a grabbing headiness. New on the market – and just in time for me to try them – were gritty strong peppermint creams covered with a bitter dark chocolate and mini Christmas puddings, decorated with a red sugar holly berry, a green marzipan leaf and a lick of white chocolate 'custard'. These looked adorable and tasted magnificent, a sharp fruity mousse laced with brandy that lingered long in the mouth.

Carlo also makes various hollow 'novelties', including Father Christmas in different sizes, a snowman and a Hansel and Gretel house; at Easter, there are eggs, hens and bunnies. What I will remember him for is the clarity of his chocolates, the fine balance of sweet with bitter; until I tried Carlo's, I never realized that chocolates could be so fresh and so clear in flavour, or that I could eat so many in one go.

HARBERTONFORD   MAP 1

Crowdy Mill 🚜 🌿 ♟   STONE-GROUND FLOUR

Bow Road, Harbertonford, Totnes, Devon TQ9 7HU

TEL *0803 732340* CONTACT *Ann Benton* HOURS *10.00-17.00* DIRECTIONS
From Totnes, take A381 towards Kingsbridge. Follow the road about 3 miles into Harbertonford and turn sharp left at The Maltsters Arms into Old Road. After about 500 yards, turn right into Bow Road. Mill is ½ mile along on the right.

Pretty as a picture, nestling by the banks of a mill stream, Crowdy Mill stone-grinds organic (Soil Association standards) wheat grown in this country.

The wheat we grow tends to be softer (containing less gluten); but it

> **Treloar's** at **38 High Street, Crediton (tel 0363 772332)** is an airy uncluttered shop full of surprises. As Min Raismin, researcher for Radio 4's Food Programme remarked, 'It sells a few really good things rather than lots of mediocre ones'. Owner Guy Treloar Garrett used to run Food for Thought in London's Covent Garden; when he returned to Crediton he determined to stock as much local produce as possible and in order 'to arrest the trend towards over-processed, over-packaged foods' to make as much as possible. To that end he has a kitchen at the back and from it comes a range of first-class pâtés, pies, quiches, savoury dishes, cakes, puddings and, of course, pasties. His are succulent and hearty, made with chuck steak, ox kidney, onion, swede and potato, and sell out as fast as they come from the kitchen. The cheese counter stocks the better known local on-farm cheeses and a few really unusual ones, such as Colespark (tiny mild-flavoured goats' cheeses wrapped in vine leaves) or Langley Meadow (a ewes'-milk cheese with 'real bite'). A Mrs Helliwell bakes him buttery hazelnut and ginger shortbread, walnut crisps and crumbly deeply cheesy Parmesan biscuits; mustard comes from Highfield Vineyards (see page 00); herbs are grown in Guy's garden; and vegetables are especially grown in a poly-tunnel. You will find various lettuces, radicchio, ridge cucumbers, garlic, shallots and, in late summer, I noticed at least 4 different beans: Speckled French, bobby, Haricot blanc and Black Hunter. In season he sells wild mushrooms – chanterelles, ceps and other varieties of edible boletus – collected by the locals.

is generally thought that for good bread you need a hard (strong) wheat. Tom Jaine, one-time bread-maker and now editor of *The Good Food Guide*, is not totally convinced, 'In fact, I like a reasonably soft flour – the softer the better, up to a point as you don't have to work so hard when kneading. The gluten doesn't stretch so far, so there is the danger that the dough over-proves and collapses, but as long as you watch it you're OK. Softer flour will makes a cakier bread, but that's the fashion at the moment.' Tom lives near Crowdy Mill and buys their flour. 'It's reliable and fresh – the keys to a good flour'.

For the flour, Ann Benton favours two varieties: Flanders because it is easy to mill, and Maris Widgeon for its nutty good flavour. These are milled into a 100% wholemeal, plain or self-raising; 85% brown, with some of the bran sifted out, in plain or self-raising; and an unbleached white with the bran and middlings (the coarser elements of the flour) removed, also in plain or self-raising. They also mill organic rye, and malted grain, a granary flour made with wheat, rye and malted wheat flakes.

From the mill, either to take-away or eat in the café, Ann bakes various breads, including cheese & onion, sour-dough and seeded wholemeal, as well as spiced fruit loaf, carrot, sponge and fruit cakes, and scones – all made from their flour. Sometimes she bakes them in the faggot-fired oven that was loosely copied from Tom Jaine's. The fire is lit, is left to burn out and the ashes are brushed to one side; the bread is baked first (for the full benefit it should be put straight on the oven floor), and as the heat dies, the biscuits go in.

> *Pipers Farm* ⊠ *at* **Langford, Cullompton EX15 1SD (tel 0392 881380, fax 0392 881600)** *is run by the enterprising Peter and Henrietta Greig. On their 50 acres, they rear beef and lamb 'the natural way'. Pigs, chickens, ducks, bronze turkeys and venison are reared for them by their neighbours to their specifications. Meat is hung on-farm and butchered; you can buy it traditionally prepared, but it is for their boning, trimming and stuffings that they are building a reputation. Boned shoulder, leg, or gigot of lamb come with a choice of stuffings: apricot, peach, fresh mint & cumin; coriander & garlic; pesto; and rosemary & garlic. Chickens are filled with pesto & brown breadcrumbs or apricots, hazelnuts & fresh herbs; or prepared for a stir-fry with tarragon & ginger. More reports please.*

KINGS NYMPTON   MAP 1

Heal Farm ⊠ 🚜 ⚓   RARE-BREED MEATS

Kings Nympton, Umberleigh, Devon EX37 9TB

TEL *0769 574341* **FAX** *0769 572839* **CONTACT** *Anne Petch* **HOURS** *Mon-Fri 9.00-17.00 Sat 10.00-16.00* **CARDS** *Access, Visa* **DIRECTIONS** *From South Molton, follow the road signposted George Nympton. Follow the road out of George Nympton and take the first turning on the right, signposted Sampson Barton Guesthouse. Follow the road straight over Sampson Cross and take the first turning right at Sletchcott Cross, signposted Heal/Yeotown. Farm is signposted on the left.*

Anne Petch runs a highly successful business from Heal Farm, set in the rolling hills of North Devon. Anne's first love is for rare-breed pigs; a moving force in the Rare Breeds Survival Trust (Heal Farm is one of their approved breeding centres), she rears Gloucester Old Spot, Middle Whites, russet-red Tamworth, Berkshire, Large Black, Saddleback with their distinctive stripe, and British Lop – the rarest of the rare breeds.

Anne farms to her own principles, they are (and I quote) 'based on humane animal husbandry, an appreciation of the natural behavioural needs of domestic livestock, common-sense approach to medications and an abhorrence of the chemicals and methods used in modern food production'. If you visit the farm, you cannot miss the fat, jolly and extremely old-fashioned sows and their piglets snuffling around the fields or lazing contentedly in their pens. Apart from their appeal in the field of genetic conservation, Anne fell in love with them because 'they are intelligent, down-to-earth and you can't bullshit with them' I know what she means.

Anne believes there is an inherent difference in eating qualities between rare and modern 'improved' breeds, 'Rare breeds have a very distinctive flavour due to the conformation of their carcasses and the distribution of the intra-muscular fat. They develop much more slowly and are slaughtered at a greater age – our pigs get sent off between 5 and 6 months – so their flavour is more highly developed.' When it comes to differences of flavour between the actual breeds of her pigs, Anne is not convinced it is sufficiently marked to justify promoting the differences. 'All our pigs get fed the same feed and drink the same water, so the flavour will be more or less the same. Where there are differences, they tend to be in the conformation. A Middle White makes little round chubby hams, whereas a Tamworth's ham is far more streamlined, elongated with a fine texture.' So, although Anne does not specify from which breed her pork comes, she is delighted to provide the information and should anyone request a particular breed she is more than happy to provide it.

Originally she raised the pigs and just sent them off to the abattoir; but when she saw the return was less than the feed bill, she started processing on-farm 'out of bare necessity' and now runs her own butchery with a total of 8 employees. From her pigs, she sells fresh pork, butchered into a variety of cuts; succulent and stunningly deeply intense hams that are brine-cured (immersed in salt, saltpetre and water), 'because the flavour of the meat is so outstanding that this is the best way to bring it out,' and then hung for 3-4 weeks to age. Bacon is cured similarly, and both are available unsmoked or smoked over oak, beech and apple-wood, 'when we can get it'. Sausages are a speciality, coarsely ground 'so you can see what goes into them, and we only use shoulder meat, hard back fat and occasionally belly', they have a full-bodied flavour and a meat content of 85%, generously filled into natural casings. Flavours include plain, a spiky pork, tomato & chilli, and a lingering smoked garlic.

Anne also sells North Devon 'Ruby Red' beef, reared to her speci-fications and hung for 3 weeks; as well as conventional and primitive rare-breed lamb, including Shetland, Soay, Hebridean, Manx Loughton (used to great effect by a regional winner of this year's *Masterchef*), Portland, Ryeland and Southdown. These are all finished by shepherd Richard Wear, another stalwart of the Rare Breed Survival Trust. Every autumn he also produces for Anne superb deeply grained mutton. This is the real thing with all the intensity of the 'days of yore'; slaughtered at 24 months, it comes from a Shetland Wensleydale cross, 'so it's neither too fat nor too lean'.

Anne is one inventive producer. She packs original hampers at Christmas with the best of local produce, has turkeys, geese and ducks reared to her specifications, produces seasonal packs of ready-to-cook dishes that include pork casserole with own-made *cotechino* or beef casserole with plump Kalamata olives. Her stance on quality is reflected as much in her products as in her animal husbandry. If you have not tried them, you should.

KINGSBRIDGE   MAP 1

Salcombe Smokers ✉ ⚖   SALCOMBE SMOKIES

54 Fore Street, Kingsbridge, Devon TQ7 1NY

TEL *0548 852006* **FAX** *0548 852612* **CONTACT** *Jeff Benson* **HOURS** *Mon and Thurs 8.00-16.00 Tues, Wed & Fri 8.00-17.00 (-13.00 Sat)* **CARDS** *Visa, Mastercard* **DIRECTIONS** *In town centre.*

Much is made by Mr and Mrs Benson of their 'secret' recipe for Salcombe Smokies. Much is probably needed as, when it comes down to it, smokies are no more than mackerel hot-smoked over oak.

In fact they are different from the common-or-garden smoked mackerel, they have a firmer texture and denser, meatier flesh. Quite how this is achieved, the Benson's 'wouldn't tell'; I suspect the fact that they only smoke winter fish as 'summer's mackerel are too oily' must have something to do with it, and I also venture that they either brine the fish for longer than normal or possibly dry cure it – which would account for its compact texture. On first bite it is relatively mild, with a slight sharpness almost as if it has been lightly soused; then wham...the salt overwhelms.

The Bensons smoke a fair amount of fish: farmed salmon from Scotland, trout, cod's roe, haddock and halibut, which was also well textured and salty. They have a good range of wet-fish, mostly bought from Looe and Plymouth, and they also sell Avon oysters and mussels (see page 69), dressed crab and samphire.

LAPFORD   MAP 1

Best of The West ⚖   SAUSAGES

Unit 4B, Lapford Cross Industrial Estate, Lapford, Devon EX17 5LE

TEL *0363 83794* **CONTACT** *Nigel Schofield* **HOURS** *Mon-Thurs 9.00-16.00 Fri & Sat 9.00-13.00* **DIRECTIONS** *From Copplestone, take A377 towards Eggesford. After about 4 miles, turn right signposted Lapford Cross Industrial Estate. Take first turning on the left into the estate and unit is signposted on the left.*

Under the brand name of 'Bangers', Nigel Schofield makes some very good sausages – you may have tried them if you ever visited his now defunct sausage restaurant in Edinburgh. Nigel's mission is to produce

> ✕ **Joyce Molyneux** at **The Carved Angel, 2 South Embankment, Dartmouth (tel 0803 832465)** has a well-deserved reputation for her food. With an accent on the finest local ingredients, she cooks with simplicity in a well-judged balance of the traditional with the individual. If you can eat there, you should; if not console yourself by buying a jar of her own-made jam, marmalade or pickles from the restaurant. She makes 'whatever I feel like, with whatever is in season'; but at Christmas she is certain to have her rich dark puddings for sale.

high quality affordable food for the middle market that, according to him, exists between 'cheap supermarket trade and the exclusive producers like Ann Petch (see page 60)'.

His coarsely cut bangers are made with a varying meat content (to give him his due he prints it on his list) and of that a good proportion is lean. Beef, with 80% meat and blended with pork fat to 'beef up' its flavour, was good and robust and I also particularly enjoyed his very coarse 100% Toulouse sausage which cooks well in a cassoulet. Others include: a Peri-peri, 80% pork with the Portuguese chilli spice sharpened with lemon juice; and tomato, pork, garlic & oregano; and Herb Garden, made with a mixture of fresh herbs.

Nigel also makes good cutting pies in 1.25, 1.5, 2.3 and 3.2 kg (2½, 3½, 5, and 7 lb) rounds, either plain pork; chicken & ham; chicken & apricot, which has a bright orange strip of apricots running through the centre; turkey & chestnut; turkey & cranberry; duck & orange; and game. He is developing a range of French-style charcuterie, that includes liver sausage, pâtés, garlic sausage and a *saucisson Lyonnais*.

Highfield Preserves ✉ 🏭 🌳   MUSTARDS

Highfield Vineyard, Longdrag Hill, Tiverton, Devon EX16 5NF

TEL 0884 256362   **CONTACT** Jennifer Fraser   **HOURS** Apr to end-Dec: Mon-Sat 10.00-18.00   **CARDS** Access, Visa, Mastercard   **DIRECTIONS** From Tiverton, take B3137 towards Nomansland. Follow the road up Longdrag Hill and vineyard is on the right.

Ian and Jennifer Fraser started planting the vineyard at Highfield in 1981. Now they have over 6,000 vines of Seyval Blanc, Siegerrebe, Madeleine Angevine, Kernling, Gewürztraminer and Scheurebe grapes growing on the well drained south-facing slope. If you wander up to the top vineyard you can look out over the Exe Valley towards the Black Downs and Taunton Dean; it is a magnificent view and on a clear day, you can see the Wellington Monument. Most of the wine they make is single-variety white, but as they planted their sunny conservatory with two red grapes, Cabernet Sauvignon and Merlot, they do produce a small quantity of red.

Mustard-making began as a side-line, but now Jennifer is busier than ever, producing somewhere in the region of 48,000 pots a year. A blend of yellow and brown whole seeds and yellow mustard powder (the quantities and balance depend on which mustard she is making), her mustards are relatively smooth. As a rule, she grinds the seeds quite fine, but for some of the flavours she does mix in a few whole grains, 'to give it detail'. The danger is, she told me, 'if you soak lightly crushed seeds in alcohol, they swell up and it ends up like eating tapioca'.

The first mustard she ever made was the white wine: mild but quite sharp, a blend of ground yellow seeds with a little brown are soaked overnight in their Madeleine Angevine wine and mixed with honey and a little olive oil 'to give it polish'. The red wine has a larger amount of brown mustard seeds and is therefore more mellow. The Devon cider, made with their own cider, is lighter and creamier and quite sweet, 'as I use a lot of honey'. Jennifer also makes mustards flavoured with dill, garlic and gherkin, and a hot and fiery green peppercorn mustard. Although mustards are her first love, she produces various chutneys, including a grape 'not made with ours as you've no idea how long it would take to seed them' and tomato & ginger, as well as conserves.

TIVERTON   MAP 1

Mrs Gill's Country Cakes ✉ ▦   FRUIT CAKES

Unit 1 & 5, Link House, Leat Street, Tiverton,
Devon EX16 5LG

TEL *0884 242744* FAX *0884 257440* CONTACT *Jacqueline Gill –*
telephone ahead

Jacqueline Gill has been baking her rich dark fruit cake in a small way for several years. Recently she moved from her farmhouse kitchen to a small industrial unit in the centre of Tiverton and from here things have really taken off – last heard of she was supplying Waitrose. Nevertheless, Mrs Gill's is still a small-scale operation and Jacqueline intends to keep it that way. Most foods, and cakes in particular, suffer when they are made in large batches. Once you start scaling up, it is so much easier to start cutting corners, to compromise on the quality of the ingredients; but that is something Jacqueline vows she will never do.

Her cakes are very old-fashioned; rich and dark with just a smidgen of spice. The ingredients are all of the best quality: plump currants, raisins and sultanas, juicy mixed peel, a dark Muscovado sugar, black treacle, unbleached white flour, butter, fresh eggs, fat glossy undyed morello cherries (a dark – almost black – red, Jacqueline is understandably very proud of these) and brandy, although she will add whisky if you prefer. The smallest cake is 10 cm (4 in) in diameter, weighing 350 g (12 oz), and they graduate up in size inch by inch to a generous 17.5 cm (7 in), weighing 1.35 kg (3 lb). The only square cake she makes is a 12.5 cm (5 in). Her cakes come plain or neatly decorated with rows of whole nuts and cherries. She will also make wedding cakes to order from 'an even richer mixture – with more fruit and more brandy' and can arrange to have these royal-iced.

Next door to the tiny kitchen is the store-room, stacked ceiling high with tightly wrapped cakes; everything is matured for at least 2 months before is it sent out. Dense, moist and splendidly rich, the cakes will keep for years and, like a good wine, they develop with the years.

Riverford Farm Shop at *Riverford Farm, Staverton, Totnes (tel 0803 762 523) is a family concern. Mr Watson rears the pigs semi-intensively, son Ben processes them into 10 different types of sausages: including a vibrant Thai sausage, made with fresh coriander, garlic, ginger and chilli. Brother Guy grows organic vegetables for the farm-shop and Mrs Watson turns some of them into pickles and chutneys. Ben also cures ham, makes pies and pâtés, and he butchers locally reared organic (to Soil Association Standards) beef and lamb. They sell free-range chickens, ducks, game in season and a selection of on-farm local cheeses and ciders.*

TORQUAY   MAP 1

Rocombe Farm Fresh Ice-Cream 🍴   ICE-CREAM

123 Union Street, Castle Circus, Torquay, Devon TQ1 3DW

TEL *0803 293996* **FAX** *0626 873645* **CONTACT** *Peter Redstone* **HOURS** *Sep to end-Jun: Mon-Sat 10.00-17.30 Sun 14.00-17.30; 1st Jul to end-Aug: Mon-Sat 10.00-17.30 & 19.00-23.00 Sun 14.00-17.30 & 19.00-23.00* **CARDS** *Access, Visa* **DIRECTIONS** *In town centre, near town hall.*

Rich, luscious, creamy, pure and infinitely moreish, this is ice-cream at its most magnificent. Containing the best – and only the best – ingredients, the basic mix is made with organic (to Soil Association standards) full-cream Jersey milk, double cream, unrefined cane sugar and organic free-range eggs. In other words, everything you'd hope for in an ice-cream.

Peter and Suzanne Redstone have been running a Jersey herd in Devon for nearly 20 years. They had always had a dream to make the 'best-ever ice-cream' but it was not until 1987 that it came to fruition. Making on the farm was impossible (then they could not afford to install the necessary 3-phase electricity), so they rented a shop in Torquay. 'We made it like it is made in a kitchen. What you'd throw in is what we'd throw in. One of our first flavours was banana, so we thought let's throw in bananas – and out came nectar'. The holiday-

---

makers obviously agreed as it was a sell-out. Everything was freshly made every day in the shop, and each day they 'invented' a new flavour. Some, like Cinnamon'n Biscuit, Thunder & Lightning (treacle and clotted cream), Honey & Toblerone, and Sparkling Cyanide (champagne, brandy and toasted almonds) sound scrumptious; others, including Marmite & Peanut Butter, Peter is the first to admit were not exactly triumphs.

The quest for new combinations still continues in the shop and every day they launch a new one. To date they have come up with over 1,500 flavours. Sean Hill of Gidleigh Park contributed Prunes in Armagnac and Joyce Molyneux of the Carved Angel gave them Orange Cardamom. It is the freshness, the home-madeness, the 'real' ingredients of Rocombe ice-cream that makes it stand out a mile. If they want to add caramel, then they make the caramel, 'a lot of extra work, but worth it' and 'because it is difficult to incorporate whole fruit into a continuous machine, we make in batches'.

Since that auspicious start, the Redstones have gone from strength to strength. They run another shop at 7 Torbay Road, Paignton, and they now wholesale their ice-cream all over the country as well as in such top shops as Harrods, Harvey Nichols and Selfridges. Manufacturing has returned to the farm but – and it is a very important but – they have not compromised the standards one iota. Everything is still fresh; no flavour-house ingredients are used, so there are no cloying or synthetic aftertastes; the clarity and purity are startling. With a minimum butterfat content of 16.5% and an over-run (added air) somewhere between 35 and 40%, this a super-premium ice-cream in a class of its own, way up there with Häagen-Dazs. Moreover, when I recently blind-tasted it with Häagen-Dazs for a Radio 4 *Farming Today* programme, Rocombe won hands-down.

Now you may have noticed that no mention has been made of emulsifiers and stabilizers. This is because the Redstones do not use any, 'People don't believe us' Peter told me, 'but it's rather like Roger Bannister. No one thought a 4-minute mile was possible until he came along'. Emulsifiers and stabilizers are generally put in to hold the mix together and to give it texture and shelf-life; but if you have as high a fat content 'and for the right texture it must be cream' and use eggs as Rocombe ice-cream does, you just don't need them. The fact that these additives are not there not only makes Rocombe a purer product but also means it has a purer, cleaner, fresher flavour.

Their wholesale range includes such miracles of delight as Lemon Meringue, a sharp lemon base softened with melting meringue; Bananas'n Cream with the taste of the fruit shining through; Bailey's Toasted Almonds, which succeeds in a nutty, alcoholic haze; and a Super Chocolate Chocolate Chip that is densely deeply chocolatey; and lots more – about 20 in total. Believe me, if you are an ice-cream freak, you have to taste them. Enjoy, I'm certain you will.

> ❝ Seemingly hundreds of farms make and sell ice-cream. The reason why is simple: farmers want to 'add value' to their milk and we, the general public, are only too happy to buy a 'farmhouse' product. Closer inspection reveals that these ice-creams are not any different from those made in a factory. Granted some do have a higher dairy-fat content, but most contain the same stabilizers and emulsifiers added to prolong shelf-life and to make the ice-cream hold together – not a very 'farmhouse' approach. Equally, most are not as you might hope, flavoured with the real thing – be it fruit or nuts or whatever. Instead tins bought in from flavour-houses are used. Yes, I know the farmers proudly claim 'No artificial flavourings or colourings', but don't be fooled. Because of a quirk in our food labelling laws, if a flavouring is human-made but chemically identical to the real thing, it does not have to be called 'artificial'. Now I am not necessarily suggesting that these chemically identical flavours are harmful, but they are misleading; and, more to the point, they taste synthetic. If I buy a farmhouse ice-cream, I want it to taste fresh and to be made with fresh ingredients that come from a farm not a laboratory. When you've tried as many as I have, you'll realize that – with few exceptions – it is an impossible dream. ❞

TOTNES   MAP 1

Ticklemore Cheese ✉ 📠   BEENLEIGH BLUE

l Ticklemore Street, Totnes, Devon TQ9 5EJ

TEL 0803 865926 CONTACT Sarie Cooper HOURS Mon-Fri 9.30-17.00 Sat 9.15-14.00 DIRECTIONS In town centre.

To avoid any confusion, I had better explain that Ticklemore Cheese at 1 Ticklemore Street is both a cheese shop and the headquarters for Robin Congdon's incomparable cheeses – Beenleigh Blue, Harbourne Blue and Devon Blue. Robin makes his cheeses a few miles up the road, deep in the countryside, while Sarie, his partner in every sense of the word, runs the cheese shop in the centre of Totnes.

Robin is a cheese-maker *par excellence*. He has been making for the last 14 years, starting with Beenleigh Blue made from ewes' milk. About 7 years ago he launched the goats'-milk Harbourne Blue and finally added the Ayrshire cows'-milk Devon Blue to the range about 2 years ago. Although he once farmed, he now buys in all his milk. All 3 cheeses are made more or less in the same way: the milk is flash-heated, started, renneted and the mould *penicillium roquefortii* is added. At this point Robin deviates from the norm, 'as I cut the curds early – that's how the French do it. And I stir frequently for the feel of the curd'.

His cheese is far more French in style of making than British. 'British blue cheeses are first matured to allow a hard crust to form, then spiked to encourage the blueing; the French spike them after a matter of days, allow them to blue, then wrap them in foil to stop the rind'. These subtle but important differences in technique, result in different cheeses. Devon Blue, while rich and creamy, has a crumblier, shorter texture than Stilton's creamy paste; Beenleigh, for my money stands up to any Roquefort with no traditional British equivalent. It has that glorious velvety texture and cutting briskness of a well-blued cheese, while avoiding the sharp saltiness that so often blights a Roquefort.

Robin ripens his cheese for at least 3 months, although he prefers them even older; the shop usually stocks them at about 5 months. Unlike Roquefort, which is made from late November to June 30th when production stops dead, he only makes Beenleigh between March to July, 'they (the French) have a different climate to us'. Robin thinks his best cheeses are made with the early summer's milk, when 'the herbs are up and the grass still fresh'. The early cheeses still have a good flavour, 'but they ripen quicker and lack the subtlety of the later cheeses'. Blue cheeses apart, Robin also makes Ticklemore goat: hard-pressed and dry-salted, it is recognizable by its distinctive ridge shape. For the shop only, he makes a fresh curd cheese with Ayrshire milk and Ticorino, a hard-pressed ewes'-milk cheese based on a Pecorino and with a similar resonance of sheep.

As well as Robin's cheeses, The Ticklemore Cheese Shop sells an excellent range of on-farm British cheeses. Several of the favourites are here, including Bonchester (see page 328), Chris Duckett's Caerphilly (see page 224), Keen's Cheddar (see page 229), Blue Vinney (see page 77) and Golden Cross (see page 260).

UMBERLEIGH   MAP 1

Head Mill Trout Farm ✉ 🏆 ♣   SMOKED TROUT

Head Mill, Umberleigh, Devon EX37 9HA

TEL *0769 80862* CONTACT *Caroline Boa* HOURS *9.30-17.30* CARDS *Access, Visa* DIRECTIONS *From South Molton, take B3226 towards Exeter. After about 8 miles, farm is signposted on the right.*

Farmed trout usually turns out to be a disappointment. To be honest, I find there is very little difference between the taste of fish from one farm or another. 'Not so', says Caroline Boa, 'for really good farmed trout, you have to have exceptional waters. Our farm is fed by the river Mole, which flows off Exmoor running over mostly granite, so the water is particularly clear and clean. And all our rearing tanks and ponds are solid-based, which means the fish never come into contact with mud'.

The trout are fed a proprietary fish food and, yes, it does contain dye to turn the flesh pink, but apparently we like it that way. 'No one,' Caroline insists, 'would buy trout if it was grey-fleshed, so we have to use a colorant in the food'. Ranging in size from 285 g (10 oz) to as large as 2.3 kg (5 lb), to make sure they are really extra fresh the trout will be netted for you to order while you wait.

It is for hot-smoked trout, however, that they excel. Sold either as whole trout weighing 170-200 g (6-7 oz) or as fillets, they are brined and oak-smoked for several hours until they are 'cooked' right through. Moist, succulent and with a clear flavour lightly dusted with a smoky haze, these are the very same that grace the table of London's Connaught Hotel. Caroline also makes a smoked trout pâté with cottage cheese, a hint of tomato purée and paprika, and a potted smoked trout sharpened with a purée of sorrel and lemon. (✉ Smoked trout fillets, trout pâté and potted trout only.)

TROUT IN NEWSPAPER

Wrap each trout neatly in 3 sheets of newspaper and soak the parcel under cold running water. Place in an oven preheated to 180°C/350°F/gas 4 for 25-30 minutes, or until the newspaper is dry. Cut open the paper and the skin will come away with it. (Supplied by Caroline Boa.)

And Also...

• *Coombe Fisheries*, 5A Marlborough Road, Ilfracombe (tel 0271 862900) sell scallops dredged from the coasts around Devon and Cornwall.

• *Langage Farm* ✉ at Plympton, nr Plymouth (tel 0752 337723, fax 0752 339712) will send its clotted cream by post. If you visit, you should try their creamy cottage cheese and thick nutty sour cream, which reminded me of crème fraîche.

• For Pacific oysters and mussels farmed in the river Avon, contact Peter Lewis of *Avon Oysters* ✉, Bigbury Cottage, Bigbury, Kingsbridge (tel 0548 810392, and 0548 810876). He also has bunches of samphire in season, from mid-June to August.

• *Blackdown Goat Centre* on Blackdown Farm, Loddiswell, Kingsbridge (tel 0548 82387) is really more a visitors' centre than a dairy farm, but they do make an unpasteurized mellow creamy soft goats' cheese which Joyce Molyneux insists on serving at her glorious restaurant.

• *Welcombe Country Fayre* ✉, Darracott Farm, Welcombe, nr Bideford (tel 028883 322) grows an interesting range of culinary herbs and edible flowers, including chive, borage and viola. They also sell bags of mixed garnish that could include bronze fennel, chervil, nasturtium leaves and variegated mints & balm; and bags of salad leaves made up with endives, land cress, red and green lettuces, corn salad, purslane and rocket.

• As well as Devon and Somerset honey, *Quince Honey Farm* ✉, North Road, South Molton (tel 0769 572401) sells complete combs of

Exmoor honey weighing 900 g (2 lb) and cut comb sections.

• The **Devonshire Apple Sanctuary**, at Redhill Farm, Burlescombe, Tiverton (tel 0823 672244) welcome visitors at weekends by appointment only. Run by Everard O'Donnell, it has 36 acres of unusual apples, including a graft taken from Sir Isaac Newton's celebrated tree; Red Astrachan an early Russian apple with pure ivory-coloured flesh; a good collection of Pearmains and Devonshire Quarrenden.

• For farmed venison, own-made venison pasties and venison or chicken, ham & orange raised pies, plus various pâtés and quiches, visit **Moorland Larder's** ✉ shop at 113 East Street, South Molton (tel 0769 573554).

• In Salcombe, you can watch the ice-cream being made at **Salcombe Dairy**, Shadycombe Road (tel 0548 843228, fax 0548 843096) through huge glass windows, while licking on a cone. Strawberry, raspberry and blackcurrant flavours are made with real fruit, and all the flavours have Devon double cream as a base. They also make various ice-cream puddings, including a Christmas Pudding that a *Sunday Times* tasting pronounced as having a 'good smell and taste of spirit in fine ice-cream'.

• Sally Dimbleby runs the **Post Office** in the idyllic village of Dittisham (tel 080 422 214). She stocks plenty of local products and, in season, genuine Dittisham plums.

DORSET

Bridfish ✉ 🏪   SMOKED FISH

Unit 1, Sea Road North, Bridport, Dorset DT6 3BD

TEL 0308 56306   **CONTACT** Patrick Gibb   **HOURS** Mon-Fri 9.00-17.00 Sat 9.00-16.00   **CARDS** Access, Visa   **DIRECTIONS** On the outskirts of Bridport, on the A3066 Beaminster road.

From a smokery/shop on the Old Laundry Estate on the outskirts of Bridport, Bridfish sell fresh and smoked fish. As far as supplies go, it is the same old story – fresh local fish is hard to come by. They do buy some from the boats at West Bay and Lyme Regis, but the bulk of the wet fish comes from Cornish or North Sea fishing ports. Although they keep a wide selection (shark, halibut, etc), quite a large proportion is frozen, including – somewhat surprisingly – lobsters. As for the fish they use for smoking, both the trout (from Wessex Fish Farms) and silver eels are local, otherwise they are bought from all over the country and abroad. All the preparation, curing and smoking is done behind the shop and they use a modern Afos kiln and oak sawdust.

The smoked salmon comes from Scottish salmon farmed on the west coast (they will use wild if they can get it; and they will smoke customers' fish for them). With a mild cure contrasting with a strong smoke, it had a soft pliant texture and was pleasantly juicy. Also with a strong smoke was their rich and punchy cod's roe: imported from Iceland, it is dry-cured and smoked for about 8 hours at a temperature mid-way between hot- and cold-smoking. Their herrings come (or, perhaps – since the disastrous wrecking of the oil-tanker *Braer* – I should say 'came') from the Shetlands and by all accounts have a loyal local following. They also smoke mackerel (whole and plain or peppered fillets), cod, pollack, prawns and haddock.

If the colour of the haddock strikes you as being markedly vibrant do not be alarmed. I was assured they use absolutely no dyes or colourings – no more than I would expect from a craft smokery. Look out for their smoked sardines; eating them may be a bit of a chore as they are not very meaty, but their flavour is far more interesting than the ubiquitous smoked mackerel.

In the shop they also sell a few local products, plus a small but interesting selection of white wines especially chosen for the fish-eater.

BROADOAK   MAP 2

Denhay Farms ✉ 🚜   CHEDDAR CHEESE & HAMS

Broadoak, Bridport, Dorset DT6 5NP

TEL *0308 22770 Fax 0308 24846* CONTACT *Amanda Streatfeild*
HOURS *Mon & Thurs 9.00-17.00* CARDS *Access, Visa* DIRECTIONS *From Bridport take the B3162 towards Chard. After about 2 miles, turn left at sign for Broadoak. Drive through the village and turn left at sign for Denhay on to a farm track.*

Denhay Farm lies in the lush Marshwood Vale, referred to as the 'vale of small dairies' by Thomas Hardy. Home to the Streatfeilds, Denhay is one of the few dairy farms left in the area still making cheese, in this case a Cheddar using milk exclusively from their own Friesian herd.

The cheese is pleasant and mellow enough, but perhaps lacks a distinctive personality (often the consequence of pasteurizing milk). Made as block (see page 230), traditional 25 kg (56 lb) rinded wheels or Dorset Drums – 2 kg (4½ lb) truckle – you can buy them from their small shop at the bottom of the yard. There they also sell their own mild salted whey cream butter and a small selection of Dorset produce, including Dorset REal ALe Chutney and the local Field Honey Farms Heather Honey.

George and Amanda Streatfeild have always kept pigs to feed on whey, a by-product of cheese- and butter-making. A couple of years ago, like many go-ahead farmers, they decided to 'add value' to their produce by processing their pigs. After several months' experimentation they came up with a new product – Denhay Air Dried Ham. Its production involves several lengthy techniques: the hams are first cured in a salt brine flavoured with Dorset apple juice, honey and herbs, then they are lightly smoked over oak chippings before finally being air-dried for several months.

The result is like a cross between a Parma and a Westphalian ham. It has a more fibrous texture than a Parma ham and, for some tastes, the ham is a little too salty. The Streatfeilds are aware of this, however, and are still trying to perfect the cure. Sold in wafer-thin slices in 115 g (4 oz) and 350 g (12 oz) packs, Denhay Ham is best served with slices of fresh melon or pear, or snipped into a creamy pasta sauce.

FERRY BRIDGE   **MAP 2**

Abbotsbury Oyster Farm ✉ 🏪   OYSTERS

Ferry Bridge, Weymouth, Dorset DT4 9YU

TEL *0305 788867* **CONTACT** *Neville Copperthwaite* **HOURS** *Easter to end-Sept: Mon-Sat 9.00-17.00 Sun 12.00-15.00; Oct to Easter: Mon-Fri 9.00-17.00* **CARDS** *Access, Visa* **DIRECTIONS** *From Weymouth take A353 towards Portland. The oyster farm is on the right, just before the causeway.*

Abbotsbury oysters are grown in the Fleet Lagoon, a natural estuary that runs from the Island of Portland as far up as the village of Abbotsbury. In *Moonfleet*, J. Meade Falkner mentions the Lagoon (or 'lake', as it is known locally) as 'good for nothing except sea-fowl, herons and oysters'. Today it is a nature reserve and the Swannery at nearby Abbotsbury is enchanting, with clean, mineral- and plankton-rich waters – essential elements for oysters.

Although they do farm a few Natives, the bulk of their 1 million oysters a year is Pacifics. Graded and sold by weight – 80, 90, 100 and 110 g (3, $3\frac{1}{4}$, $3\frac{1}{2}$ and $3\frac{3}{4}$ oz) – they are markedly salty, with plenty of meat and a firm texture. As they are so meaty, they are also very good for cooking. Abbotsbury purify their oysters in UV tanks for about 48 hours, and keep them in aerated holding tanks until they are sold. This, they claim, is necessary 'to maintain public confidence in the quality of our oysters' even though they are grown in such pure waters. Are we really that fastidious a nation?

Sold from the farm off the causeway that links the Isle of Portland to the mainland, you can either take-away (they will pack them for your journey) or sit by the Lagoon and be served them ready opened with French bread and a glass of wine. Prices are kept very low as the policy is 'to encourage everyone to try'.

James Trehane & Sons ✉ 🍲   BLUEBERRIES

Trehane Camellia Nursery, Stapehill Road, Hampreston, Wimborne, Dorset BH21 7NE

TEL 0202 873490   **CONTACT** Jennifer Trehane   **HOURS** mid-Aug to early-Sept 10.00-17.00   **DIRECTIONS** From Wimborne, take A31 towards Ringwood. Turn right into Ham Lane (B3073) and first left into Stapehill Road. Nursery is signposted on the right.

To the north of Bournemouth, around Ferndown, the land is heathland. The sandy soil with a high acid level of ph4.5-5.5 makes ideal growing conditions for blueberries. When, in 1949, David Trehane (Jennifer's father) saw an advert in a trade journal looking for possible growers, he needed no further encouragement. It took 10 years before they harvested their first commercial crop and now they are the country's leading growers.

Blueberries (*Vaccinium corymbosum*) are blueish-black with a soft bloom and about the size of the old 5p piece. Sweet, juicy and tight-skinned, with a flavour of their own that is best described as like a cross between a cherry and a grape, they are closely related to the bilberry (aka blaeberry or whortleberry). At Trehane the blueberries are all North-American Highbush, giving good large fruit that grows at an easy-to-pick height. These, according to Jennifer, are vastly superior to the German varieties which produce smaller fruit that lacks flavour.

Commercial picking starts towards the end of July, but Jennifer likes to wait until whole clusters of fruit are ripe before launching the PYO season. She starts off the first weekend with a Blueberry Bonanza (telephone to check date first). There are blueberry talks, tastings and hundreds of blueberry pies and crumbles to buy. From then until the end of season – usually early-September – you can pick from the PYO section, which is not normally sprayed (unless disaster, in the shape of caterpillars, threatens). Picking the fruit is easy enough: if the whole berry is blue all over, it is ripe; then you gently grasp the berry between your fingers rolling it over to avoid spoiling the bloom. Blueberries stay fresh for a long time, they will keep in the fridge for well

BLUEBERRY PANCAKES
(makes 14-16)
Mix 2 eggs, with 115 g (4 oz) plain flour. Gradually add 300 ml ($\frac{1}{2}$ pt) milk, beating thoroughly until the batter is smooth (the Americans add 2 tablespoons of vegetable shortening). Fold 450 g (1 lb) of blueberries into the batter. Drop 1 tablespoon portions of the batter on to a hot greased frying pan. Fry on both sides until golden brown. Serve with butter and syrup, or sprinkle with cinnamon and sugar. (From *Dorset Blues*, a leaflet published by Trehane Nurseries.)

over a week and they also freeze well.

Jennifer also sells blueberry bushes for growing in the garden (provided your acidity level is right) or for growing in tubs. There are various varieties that ripen either early or later in the season and she is happy to answer any queries. (✉ Blueberry bushes only.)

LEIGH   MAP 2

Fudges Bakery ✉ 🏆   DORSET CHEDDAR WAFERS

Bridge Bakery, Leigh, Sherborne, Dorset DT9 6HJ

TEL *0935 872253* **CONTACT** *Stephen Fudge* **HOURS** *Mon-Sat 8.30-12.30*
DIRECTIONS *From Sherborne, take the A352 towards Dorchester. After about 2 miles, turn right at sign for Leigh. Follow the road into the village and bakery is on the right.*

From a small family bakery in the quiet village of Leigh, Fudges now runs 380 lines and supplies such top shops as Harrods and the new(ish) food market in Harvey Nichols. This turn-around happened a mere 2 years ago, when Stephen joined the family business. Apprenticed as a baker in Germany, he returned to England and for 9 years happily taught at the Salisbury College of Bakery. The only way to tempt him back was to give him *carte blanche* – the freedom to develop and to experiment – and this is one baker who is buzzing with ideas.

Among his first products were Dorset Cheddar Wafers: crisp and light, with a lingering deep intense cheesiness. They are so moreish I ate an entire packet in one go. The idea came about because Stephen wanted a product with a local identity to capitalize on local products. As this is serious dairy country, such a product had to include cream and cheese. Made with local cream, local (whenever possible) flour, local milk and Cheddar, eggs, cornflour, salt and spices, and baked almost on a daily basis, they are very special indeed. He also makes garlic- and curry-flavoured wafers, but my heart (and stomach) belongs to the cheese.

Influenced by his stay in Germany, he makes moist fruity *Weihn-achtsstollen* (traditional Christmas bread). Stephen's version is more elaborate than you usually find in Britain: the yeast-based dough, enriched with butter and fruit, is wrapped round a generous cylinder of marzipan. 'It's the marzipan that makes or breaks it', Stephen believes, and I could not fault his creation: densely made with a smooth finish, it had an obvious bitter-sweet taste of almonds. There are also ordinary and 'toasting' (rich tea) breads; chunky flavoured breads (cheese, cheese & garlic, walnut, onion, and six seed); lardy cakes; a range of elegantly scalloped biscuits – I particularly liked the sharp Lemon Butters with a crisp short texture. Everything is made with real ingredients: if eggs or butter are needed, then fresh eggs or butter are used.

Freshly caught, freshly cooked shrimps are in a class of their own. Try buying them, however, and you will find it is almost impossible. Even though our coasts are alive with them, no one seems to catch them. The fishermen claim 'there isn't a demand and anyway no-one would be prepared to pay the price'. Is that the real reason? Or is it that they just cannot be bothered? Whatever the answer, the result is the same. We end up ignoring our own produce in favour of imported foreign alternatives – in this case deep-frozen Mediterranean or Asian shrimps and prawns. Granted these may be larger, meatier and less fiddly to peel but they are certainly not cheap and, by the time they reach our tables, they have virtually no flavour whatsoever. Time and time again, I come across such examples of us not valuing our own produce. Why this is, I cannot begin to imagine.

With their shop alongside the quay, **Weyfish, Old Fish Market, Customs House Quay, Weymouth (tel 0305 761277)** is one fishmonger that insists on local shrimps. Pale pink and etched with fine brown veins, they are caught in Portland Harbour during a season that extends from August until 'the first frost, when they're off'. With an immediate fresh sea flavour punched with a sweet nuttiness, sensible people gorge themselves straight out of the bag. If you manage to save a few until you get home, eat with fresh bread liberally spread with butter.

MILTON-ON-STOUR · MAP 2

Whistley Crayfish ✉ ▦ · CRAYFISH

Whistley Waters, Milton-on-Stour, Gillingham, Dorset SP8 5PT

TEL *0747 840666* **CONTACT** *Christopher Campbell – telephone ahead*

When I lived in 'twixt and 'tween land by the Oxfordshire-Gloucestershire border, between the foot of the Cotswolds and the banks of the Thames, I once went crayfish fishing with my next-door-neighbours. Once was enough. I spent the entire day wading in and out of streams, water pouring down my wellies, doing fiddly things with hair-nets and sticks. I only caught 3 and they had to be thrown back as they were far too small to eat.

Freshwater crayfish look like miniature lobsters and are native to our streams; but they are very small and their population was decimated around the turn of the century by the equivalent of rabbits' myxomatosis. Farmed freshwater crayfish are a different species, the Signal (*Pacifastacus eloniusculus*): they are bigger, grow faster and are more resistant to disease. Originally they came from the West coast of America, but were brought into this country via Sweden. By law they can only be introduced into enclosed waters (to protect the native population). For this reason Christopher Campbell farms – or 'ranches', as he prefers to call it – in a series of ponds. The crayfish will eat anything, including weeds and other fish, and prefer acidic water. Nocturnal creatures, they live near the banks in burrows, tend to go out at night to forage (which explains why I had such little luck) and are then trapped in a contraption similar to a lobster pot.

Before eating, crayfish have to be cleansed to clear out their gut. This is done by starving them in tanks of clear spring water for about 48 hours. Christopher always has some in stock ready for sale, but it is advisable to ring first just in case. In season between May to October (they semi-hibernate in winter when the water is cold), Signal Crayfish take about 3 years to reach 'restaurant' size, ie 5-10 cm (4-5 in) long and weighing around 55 g (2 oz), so you get between 8-10 per 450 g (1 lb).

Christopher advises cooking them in the Swedish style: for each 450 g (1 lb) of crayfish, boil up 2 litres (3½ pints) of water with a small can of lager or light ale, 3 tablespoons of rock salt, 1 teaspoon of sugar and as much dill as possible. When the water is at a good rolling boil, drop in the live crayfish and boil for 3 minutes. Then remove them from the heat and leave to cool. Drain about an hour before eating and serve with ice-cold Aquavit. About one-third of their weight is succulent flesh; the rest is shell that can be turned into stock or soup.

Like all good ranchers, Christopher sends his livestock live – kept cool and damp in boxes – by overnight courier. If kept cool, they will remain alive for 2 weeks. Never *ever* even think of cooking them once dead. There are about 80 producers of Signal Crayfish in Britain. Christopher Campbell is one, but for details of the others contact Mo Richards at Riversdale Farm, Stour Provost (tel 0747 838495).

MORCOMBELAKE   MAP 2

S. Moores ✉ 🏰   DORSET KNOBS

The Biscuit Bakery, Morcombelake, Bridport, Dorset DT6 6ES

TEL *0297 89253* FAX *0297 89753* CONTACT *David Winship* HOURS *Mon-Fri 9.00-17.00* DIRECTIONS *From Bridport take A35 towards Honiton. After about 4 miles the bakery is on the left.*

'With early morning tea', so Moores Bakery claim in a publicity hand-out, 'Dorset Knobs were the traditional meal for local farm workers at the start of the day'. As if that was not enough, they go on, 'They were, incidentally, a favourite food of Thomas Hardy who, we are told, had them in the evening with Blue Vinney cheese'. Apparently the Moores Family have been baking Dorset Knobs 'to a secret recipe' for almost 150 years. Originally they were baked in the dying embers of 'the faggot-heated oven' after the day's baking was done. Shortly after the Second World War, making Dorset Knobs had become the main function of the firm, but times and tastes change – sweet biscuits being the current thing. Now production of Knobs is relegated to a brief period between January and March. Yes, I know Dorset Knobs are old-fashioned, but I like them.

Similar to Norfolk Knobs (see Merv's Hot Bread Kitchen, page 187), they are larger in size, sweeter in taste and have a drier texture. Try twisting a Dorset Knob in your hand to break it in half and it will disintegrate into a mass of crumbs. As they were altogether less forthcoming than Mr Ashworth at Merv's about ingredients and techniques, I am afraid I cannot give you chapter and verse on the differences. The best I can do is to quote from the hand-out, 'Each biscuit is individually moulded by hand and has three separate bakings lasting a total of 4 hours, the whole process taking 8 to 10 hours'. Still, as the bakery is open all year and welcomes visitors, I will try and nip down some time between January and March. I will report back if I find out anything.

STOCK GAYLARD

MAP 2

Dorset Blue Vinney Cheese ✉ 🔳 BLUE VINNEY

Woodbridge Farm, Stock Gaylard, Sturminster Newton, Dorset DT10 2BD

TEL *0963 23216* **CONTACT** *Michael Davies – telephone ahead*

Blue Vinney was once made all over Dorset, now there is only that from Michael Davies. 'It is,' as he explains, 'a real farmer's wife cheese. She would make it from left-over milk, after she had skimmed the cream for butter-making. As a result it had a very low fat content – around the 1.8% mark'. Vinney comes from vinew, an old English word for mould, and Blue Vinney was traditionally a blue cheese. 'But a skimmed milk cheese is difficult to blue, there's very little medium for the moulds to work with. So it often was a hit-and-miss affair.'

Cheeses would spoil, turn as hard as cart-wheels, with a wastage rate often as high as three out of four. Moreover, in the days when blueing was a natural phenomenon – before controlled mould spores were added to milk – there was also no guarantee that they would ever develop their blue veins. That is why rumours were legion of cheese-makers dipping old horse harnesses into the vats, or storing the cheese on damp flagstones covered with hessian bags or next to mouldy boots, to encourage the growth of the moulds. Michael Davies, you will be relieved to hear, resorts to none of these practices; but he still makes his cheese in the time-honoured way.

The morning's milk from his Friesian herd (Vinney was originally made from Shorthorns) is hand-skimmed: 'skimming by a machine makes a terrible cheese. And morning's milk is far lower in fat because of its sheer volume, compared to the evening's milk.' Once skimmed, they actually add skimmed milk powder to bring the fat content up to about 3.3%. This is because the original cheese was very dry and hard and not at all suited to our modern tastes. Blue Vinney takes 24 hours to make. Starter is added to the unpasteurized skimmed milk, then vegetarian rennet and a penicillin mould (to ensure blueing). Once the milk has coagulated, it is cut into 'small pieces the size of walnuts' and left to settle overnight. The following morning the whey is drained off, the curds are cut into blocks, milled, salted and packed into moulds. They stay in the moulds in the warm dairy for 5 days to encourage blueing and are turned regularly. When taken out, they are coated with a paste of flour and blue mould and stored in the ripening rooms for anything from $2\frac{1}{2}$ to 5 months. After about 1 month, they are pierced so the mould can develop and spread through the cheese. After this they are carefully monitored, and may be spiked a couple more times, 'but it's very exciting, they're quite unpredictable and sometimes we don't need to spike them at all'.

From the farm, Michael sells only whole cheese, weighing 1.35-2.3 kg (3-5 lb) or 5.9-6 kg (12-14 lb), but Sabins in Sherborne and Farmer Bailey's Cheese Shop in Shaftesbury sell it by weight. A good blue Vinney, although unpressed, is quite a hard, crumbly cheese. Paler, with lighter finer veins than a Stilton, it is drier and tighter with a subtle but lingering aftertaste. I once heard it described as a man's cheese – that no man with a strong relishing palate should die without tasting it. As a mere woman, I think of it as an interesting – rather than a great – cheese, but certainly one with good curiosity value.

TARRANT KEYNSTON MAP 2

Keynston Mill Shop 🝱 🍴 🥣 FRUIT & VEGETABLES

Keynston Mill, Tarrant Keynston, Blandford,
Dorset DT11 9HZ

TEL *0258 452596* CONTACT *Anni Partridge* HOURS *May to Dec: 10.00-17.30; Jan to end-Apr: Tues-Sun 10.00-17.30* CARDS *Access, Visa, Mastercard* DIRECTIONS *From Blandford, take B3082 towards Wimborne into Tarrant Keynston. At cross-roads, turn right at sign for Keynston Mill Fruit Farm and follow road for about $1\frac{3}{4}$ miles.*

Shopping with American cookery writer Martina Nicolls is never easy as she is such a 'taste queen', but even she was pleased with Keynston Mill. The minute we arrived, we both had the same instinctive reaction that we had come to an interesting place. On closer inspection, we were proved right.

Outside, before you even enter the wooden framed shop, you are greeted with stands and tables stacked with own-grown unusual salads, fruit and vegetables – all in the pink of freshness. A family business (Mr Partridge grows, Mrs Partridge runs the PYO, daughter Anni runs the shop and tearooms), their philosophy is to 'satisfy anyone who cares about food and to grow anything you can't easily buy'.

Here we found small Pink Fir Apple potatoes (the best for salads) and Golden Wonder (the best for roasting); glossy baby artichokes tinged with purple; the last of the juicy figs picked from their garden; fiery chillies; several different squashes; and a glorious selection of endives, lettuces and cut herbs, including frisée, lollo rosso, radicchio, Little Gems, Webbs, cos, coriander, flat and curly leaf parsley, basil, sage, mint and tarragon. In season they also sell their own asparagus, melons, peppers, aubergines, courgette flowers (by special order) and lemon cucumbers (a rich yellow, they are the size of a tomato with a peppery lemon flavour). You can either buy or pick-your-own sugar snap peas with their edible peas and pods, pea-less mange-tout, courgettes, broad beans and tomatoes. There is also a good range of fruit, such as strawberries (that last through to the end of October); raspberries; gooseberries; white currants, redcurrants and blackcurrants; Merton Gem, Marjorie Seedling and Victoria plums; greengages; damsons; and various apples.

Inside, the shop has a welcoming cluttered atmosphere. Everything has been chosen with the cook in mind. Apart from a selection of well-designed but practical utensils, a carefully chosen selection of cookery books and some charming Dorset delft pottery, there are plenty of local and regional foods. To name but a few: mint chocolates by Mr Ungaretti of Dorchester, Denhay cheese and ham (see page 71), Mrs Montgomery's Cheddar (see page 221), smoked fish from Mere Fish Farm (see page 274), boar meat and sausages from Barrow Boar (see page 228), Childhay Manor ice-cream, Thursday Cottage jams and preserves, local honey and honeycombs, fresh and frozen oven-ready game from the local shoots, and various cakes baked by Sue, who also runs the tea-rooms next door (her lemon cake is light and airy and the almond shortbread, buttery and rich). Incidentally the family also sell their own wine, made by North Wotton Vineyard from their own grapes.

Serious seekers of organic (certified to Soil Association standards) vegetables and salads, might be interested to hear about **Gold Hill Organic Farm, Childe Okeford, nr Blandford (tel 0258 860293)**. *They grow an amazing range on their $4\frac{1}{2}$-acre holding which is sold from a barn that is open during daylight hours (but it is probably best to telephone first). Apart from the usual root vegetables, there are cauliflower, aubergines, peppers, sweetcorn, globe artichokes, bunched beetroot with their tops, spinach, leeks and cabbages. There are also several different varieties of tomato including Alicante, beef and Gardener's Delight and a wide range of salad leaves such as Green Salad Bowl, lollo rosso, Little Gem, oak leaf, cos and red cos lettuces; and Gallia melons which were surprisingly sweet and juicy. With everything looking fresh and in good condition, prices are unexpectedly reasonable as part of their mission 'to serve the local community'.*

And also....

- **The Sausage Shop**, Dairy House, Wigbeth Farm, Horton, Wimborne (tel 0258 840723) has Dorset Scrumpies sausages (made with cider) and good faggots with chopped bacon.
- From Thursday to Sunday Fiona Idda sells own-made pasta (made with eggs and Italian semolina flour) from a shop called Saporito at **Bere Marsh Farm**, Shillingstone, nr Blandford (tel 0258 860284).
- Carol Trewin, producer of Radio 4's On Your Farm, was impressed by **The Dragons Village Bakery**, The Square, Corfe Castle (tel 0929 480400). White bread is proved overnight and there are various Continental breads made from German pre-mixes: herb, six-grain, sunflower, *korn knacker*, dark and light rye.
- For a creamy, Greek-style, live sheep's milk yoghurt, try **Woodlands Park Dairy**, Woodlands, nr Wimborne (tel 0202 822687).
- Noelle Campbell of **Coach House Herbs** ⊠, Lewell Lodge, West Knighton (tel 0305 853779) supplies several of London's top hotels and restaurants, including Claridge's, The Connaught, The Berkeley and Le Caprice, with her fresh-cut herbs. She also does bed and breakfast in her 18th-century manor house and you may well bump into a chef as they often stay the night after inspecting the herbs.

DURHAM

BARNARD CASTLE   MAP 6

The Teesdale Trencherman ⊠ ▦ SMOKED GROUSE

Startforth Hall, Barnard Castle, Co Durham DL12 9RA

TEL *0833 38370* CONTACT *Johnny Cooke-Hurle – telephone ahead*

Johnny Cooke-Hurle describes his method of smoking as 'loosely based on the London smoke-hole, a cupboard with smoke dribbling through'. He opted for this kind of equipment because it works best for him and as he bluntly said, 'it was the cheapest'. He works from a converted farm building and concentrates on poultry and game (his list does include salmon and other fish, but this he buys in from Loch Fyne Oysters, see page 357).

With the exception of quail, everything is smoked over oak chips and sawdust bought from Yorkshire furniture-makers. Grouse from the local moors are first brined in a plain salt solution, the whole birds are cold-smoked to give them flavour, then hot-smoked to cook them through and finally the breasts are sliced off for sale, while the legs are thrown away ('fit for the birds'). This was the first time I had ever tried smoked grouse breasts: densely fleshed with a nutty gaminess accentuated by a light veil of woodiness, they are certainly very interesting and possibly best served thinly sliced with a fruit sauce.

Whole chickens are also subtly cold-smoked, then cooked off with a hot-smoke. Johnny also marinates the smoked breasts in a light mixture of lemon and pepper for a sharper flavour and sells them in vacuum packs of two per packet weighing 225 g (8 oz). Pheasants, hung for just a few days to soften the texture rather than to develop the taste, are smoked in the same way as the grouse and sold either as a pair of breasts or whole birds. Venison, mainly from the silverside ('the thin bit of the thigh muscle') of the Red deer, comes thinly sliced. Quail is smoked over hickory to give a smoky flavour in as short a time as possible to prevent the birds from drying out. Johnny also smokes wood pigeon breasts, Barbary duck breasts imported from France, and wild boar hams from Prince Bishop Boar Breeders (see page 83).

Partners ✉, *26 Horsemarket, Barnard Castle, D12 8LZ (tel 0833 38072) is a stylish departmental store with a well-stocked food department which over the years, just like Topsy, 'has grown and grown'. Cheeses are a speciality, with a concentration on locally made small farmhouse cheeses, so you will find the best from the Dales, including Wensleydale, Swaledale, Coverdale, Ribblesdale (see page 290), Cotherstone (see page 82), Bonchester (see page 328) and Thornby Moor Dairy. Other local products include smoked game from The Teesdale Trencherman (see opposite), bacon from Richard Woodall (see page 46), Mr Twizell's sausages (see page 29), Egglestone Post Office cakes (see below), flour from the Watermill at Little Salkeld (see page 45) and game pies by Pepper Arden. Mrs Gray, the Managing Director, ran the cookery school at Egglestone Hall and the food for Partners is still cooked in their kitchens; there is an ever-changing range of pâtés, quiches and fresh or frozen cooked dishes. ('✉ Cheese and fruit cakes only.)*

EGGLESTON   MAP 6

H.D. & R. Bainbridge ✉ 🏪 ⚱   Fruit Cakes

The Post Office & Stores, Eggleston, Barnard Castle, Co Durham DL12 0AA

TEL *0833 50250* CONTACT *Rhona Bainbridge* HOURS *Mon-Fri 9.00-17.30 (-13.00 Thurs and Sat)* DIRECTIONS *From Barnard Castle, take B6278 towards Eggleston. In village, turn left opposite the Methodist chapel. Post office is 100 yards along on the left.*

Travelling around Britain I've almost come to expect the unexpected from country sub-post offices, and Eggleston's did not let me down. On the outside it may look like any other small village store facing the village green, but inside it is a different story.

Nestling among the packets of this and the rows of that are some of the best fruit cakes you are likely to find, made by Rhona Bainbridge. What started with 2 cakes for a church bazaar has now become a full-time occupation and she has stuck to more or less the same recipe for the last 31 years. Made with 'all the best stuff – butter but no brandy, as I try to keep the price realistic', she modestly describes her cakes as 'just as you would make yourself in your own kitchen' (obviously she has not seen what I get up to in mine).

Her kitchen has expanded and now houses one of those professional cake-mixing machines. However, she still keeps her batches to a small but manageable size, and the fruit is still picked over and sorted by hand with everything neatly weighed up for the morning's baking. In the narrow corridor outside are tightly shut cupboards: behind their closed doors lie hundreds of Rhona's cakes stacked on shelf upon purpose-built shelf, just the right depth for the cakes. They are left to mature for at least 3 months 'as that's the earliest we like to sell them'. With customers coming from miles around to buy her cakes, it is surprising she manages to build up any back-stock at all.

Rhona makes two grades of fruit cake: farmhouse and wedding/celebration, 'although there's not that much difference, just more of everything, more cherries and more ground almonds'. Sold plain and undecorated, either round or square in graduated sizes from 15-32.5 cm (6-13 in), you can buy them singly or as a set for a graduated wedding tiered construction. Rhona's cakes have a good reputation among cake-icers, as it is essential for them that they have straight sides and a level top. Needless to say, hers look almost geometrical in their precision. Biting into a slice of the celebration version, I found it light with a moist crumbly texture and fruity with just the merest whiff of spice. Apparently the longer it is left to mature, the more it acquires a rich tang of honey.

Rhona also bakes a good old-fashioned tea loaf cake (with the fruit soaked overnight in tea) 'to cut and butter', and a succulent gingerbread cake made from flour, lashings of syrup, milk and eggs. Based in a post office, Rhona will now mail-order her cakes.

MARWOOD   MAP 6

Cotherstone Cheese 🔲   COTHERSTONE CHEESE

Quarry House, Marwood, Barnard Castle, Co Durham DL12 9QL

TEL *0833 50351* CONTACT *Joan Cross – telephone ahead*

As far as she knows, Joan Cross is the only remaining maker of on-farm Cotherstone cheese, 'but you can never be too sure, there may be someone else in the Dale'.

The Dale, in this case Teesdale, was once full of farmers' wives making cheese, 'It was always the women who made it, my mother did. It was strictly a family cheese'. That is until Peggy Birkett starting making it earlier in the century on the family farm just outside Cotherstone. She soon became renowned for it and started selling it out of the county, even putting it on the train for London. The curious thing is that, although Joan's cheese is also known as Cotherstone, she does not know whether the two are even made to the same recipe, 'I never tasted Mrs Birkett's, so I can't be certain'.

In fact Joan thinks that all Dales cheeses are slightly different, but 'not tremendously so'; hers she makes with the unpasteurized milk from her Friesian herd. Remarkably reticent to give details about the method, other than it is pressed for about 12 hours and dried salted, she excused herself with the explanation, 'I'm Dales-bred, we're very cautious and don't give away anything willingly'. She did, however, give me a huge piece of her Cotherstone.

She sells it fairly young, at about 2-3 weeks, although Randolph at Neal's Yard Dairy (see page 164) matures it very successfully. Eaten here in Teesdale, it had a freshness, a mild acidity not unlike crème fraîche, and an open-textured crumbliness with a springy texture. The cheese is made in 450 g, 900 g and 2.7 kg (1, 2, and 6 lb) flattish rounds, because 'it's a soft cheese and if you make it flat, it can't flatten out any further'...

Prince Bishop Boar Breeders ✉ *of **Wilbor Farm, Newfield, Bishop Auckland, DL14 8DG (tel 0388 602944)** achieved a certain notoriety when one of their wild boar sows, Bonnie escaped into the wild (to date she still has not been captured). You can buy wild boar from them either as whole or half animals, in various cuts or as a ham smoked for them by The Teesdale Trencherman (see page 80). Stock is bred from imported Danish and Polish wild boar, slaughtered between 12-15 months and hung for at least 7 days to develop both the flavour and texture.*

And Also...

- Until recently butchers **J. Allinson** at 8 Market Street, Ferryhill (tel 0740 651370) used to run their own slaughterhouse. Although they now buy from the abattoir, they still make brawn, black pudding, pork pies, various sausages and pease pudding cooked up with ham bones.
- 'Pork Purveyors' **Zisslers** at 104 Bondgate, Darlington (tel 0325 462590) produce all things pig. As well as the obvious sausages and pork pies, they also have pickled pork, black pudding, polony (a finely textured boiled sausage), brawn, pease pudding, cooked shanks, pigs' cheeks (Bath chaps), cooked tails and brined trotters. They also sell Mr Twizell's dry-cured bacon (see page 29).

ESSEX

Crapes Fruit Farm ✉ 🚜 APPLES

Rectory Road, Aldham, Colchester, Essex CO6 3RR

TEL *0206 212375* **CONTACT** *Andrew Tann* **HOURS** *Mon-Sat 8.00-17.00*
DIRECTIONS *From Colchester, take A12 towards Chelmsford. Turn off at signpost for Marks Tey. At roundabout take A120, direction Puckeridge. At next roundabout, follow the sign to Aldham. After about 1 mile, turn left on to Rectory Road and orchard is on the left.*

Andrew is one of the third generation of Tanns to grow apples. His grandfather planted the first trees in 1922, now the farm grows somewhere in the region of 150 varieties. Of these, only about 15-18 are grown in commercial quantities; the rest are measured in pounds, coming from 1 or 2 trees. A few even exist as 'no more than a branch grafted on to a tree bearing 15 apples a season'. Andrew guards them all because, like his father and grandfather before him, he is an apple fanatic – they are his passion. He wants to develop and preserve the richness of their differences, the wealth of their colours and shapes, tastes and textures.

With orchards on what is known as 'hot land' (light, sandy, a bit on the acid side, quite shallow, and free-draining), he claims his trees give 'slightly smaller fruit but with a deeper colour and flavour'. (Curiously it also means that cookers do not keep that well after January.) Starting with Andrew's personal favourite varieties: Kidd's Orange Red for eating between mid-October to mid-February, 'a rich red with a russet over the red, it's lovely to look at...its texture is like a Cox's, but it is stronger-flavoured and sweeter...'; Orléans Reinette, with a season from mid-November to mid-January, 'has a very strong distinct flavour and is for eating with a Stilton or strong Cheddar'; and Adam's Pearmain, an old Norfolk apple with 'a pointy shape with a brick red flush, smooth and russety...it has an old-fashioned taste, not extra-sweet...It's dense in flavour and texture and similar to a russet'. He grows one of my favourites, Pitmaston Pineapple, but sadly only has 1 tree so its fruit is in very short supply. A tiny pale-yellow apple, it is full of surprises, with its extraordinary pineapple taste and aroma.

Andrew makes a point of growing local varieties. These include D'Arcy Spice, juicy, sharp and fruity with a hot pungent taste, and Sturmer Pippin, crisp with a large core. When first picked this is quite sharp, but by December it has developed a rounded sweetness. Also ripe in December is Gray Pippin, a smallish pointed apple with a yellow skin splattered with brown lenticels (spots).

Recently he was given a chance seedling – a new variety from a pip.

(Most apple pips, when planted, will grow into trees; but sometimes they do not fruit, nor will they be the same variety as the apple from which the pips were taken. If you do want to reproduce the same variety, you have to graft buds from that variety on to root-stock. If, however, you want to breed a new variety, it is safer to put the pollen from one variety on to the blossom of another. Then you plant the subsequent pip.) This chance seedling produced rather good apples, so Andrew has named Hadfield Pippin (pippin means a variety created from a chance seedling) after the couple from Maldon who gave it to him. Last year was the first year he grew it, only as one branch grafted on to a tree – but he has high hopes for the future.

Andrew sends out apples carefully packed in boxes of 2.3 kg (5 lb) – about 20-25 apples – and 4.5 kg (10 lb) – up to 50 apples. Varieties also worth looking out for include: Baker's Delicious, a juicy apple similar to James Grieve; St Edmunds Russet, the first russet of the season with a rich flavour that tastes of pears; Laxton's Fortune with a fruity straw-berry taste; Red Ellison, a red-skinned Ellison's Orange with a stunning flavour of aniseed; and Ribston Pippin, an old English apple that was probably the parent of Cox's and tastes of pear drops.

He also sells apple juice. Juiced locally, it is a blend of 'whatever is available to make a well-rounded crisp and dry juice. At the moment it's Sturmer Pippin, Crispin and Cox's, but it varies'. He runs the occasional day course on 'Making the most of your garden apple trees' and 'Tree planting and pruning', allowing plenty of time to inspect the trees.

> *If you are interested in growing your own vegetables, salads and herbs you should send for the Suffolk Herb catalogue from* **E.W. King** ✉, **Monks Farm, Pantlings Lane, Kelvedon, Essex CO5 9PG (tel 0376 572456)** *who deal only with mail order. Just reading their seed list makes you hungry. They sell everything from Early Jade Pagoda, one of several Chinese cabbages, peppery Greek cress, sugary-sweet Tiny Tim tomatoes, 7 varieties of radicchio including red-speckled with white Variegata di Sottomarina Precoce, crisp reddish-leaved Rougette du Midi lettuce, to clary sage – the leaves of which can be fried in fritters.*

DANBURY   MAP 3

Kelly Turkey Farms ✉ ▦   BRONZE TURKEYS

Springate Farm, Bicknacre Road, Danbury, Essex CM3 4EP

TEL 0245 223581 FAX 0245 226124 CONTACT Paul Kelly HOURS Mon-Fri 8.00-17.00 DIRECTIONS *From Chelmsford take A414 towards Maldon. After about 1½ miles, at The Bell Pub, turn right on to Well Lane. Follow the road for about ½ mile, turn left at T-junction and after about 1 mile, at the Bicknacre parish boundary sign, farm is signposted on left.*

It is generally thought that turkeys were first introduced to Europe by the Spanish explorer Cortez in the 16th century. He was supposed to have brought some birds back with him after conquering Mexico. These were the Mexican black birds from which our Norfolk Black turkey is descended (see The Happy Hog, page 246). One of the first references to them in this country comes from *The Four Books of Husbandry* written by Barnaby Googe in 1578. 'Turkey cocks we have not long had amongst us, for before the year of our Lord, 1530, they were not seen with us'.

The Cambridge Bronze turkey, on the other hand, is another wild species. A descendant of the North-American Bronze, it was probably brought over later. A very handsome bird, with its bronze feathers tinged with green, its meat has a good texture and a deep inherent flavour and, unlike the Norfolk Turkey, it has the advantage of a well-rounded plump breast. It has taken Derek Kelly and his son Paul 8 years to breed the Kelly Bronze to 'perfection'. Improved by selecting from various Bronze strains, they now have a bird with everything going for it: a full flavour, densely textured meat, a good fat cover (essential for moist meat), ample 'breast mass' and a slow maturer (for optimum flavour). It also matures to a range of sizes and this means that even if you order a smaller bird, it will have been grown for the same amount of time as a larger one and will have the same deep flavour.

The Kellys are both commercial breeders and growers; so not only do they supply growers all over the country with Bronze turkey poults (chicks), but they also grow somewhere in the region of 15,000 themselves. The Kellys grow to Traditional Farm Fresh Turkey Association standards (see Cottage Farms, page 133), so all their birds will be dry-plucked and hung for a minimum of 7 days. Weighing from 3.5-13.5 kg (8-30 lb), they are available fresh for Christmas and Easter. During the rest of the year you can buy frozen birds from the freezer cabinet in their office. They also run an information service to deal with enquiries for Kelly Bronzes all over the country; if *they* cannot supply you with a Bronze bird, they will put you in touch with a grower who can.

FINGRINGHOE   MAP 3

Clay Barn Orchard 🔲   QUINCES

Clay Barn, Fingringhoe, Colchester, Essex CO5 7AR

TEL *0206 735405* CONTACT *Charles Trollope* HOURS *Aug to Jan: dawn-dusk* DIRECTIONS *From Colchester, take B1025 towards Mersea. After about 5 miles, at The Langenhoe Lion, turn left on to Fingringhoe Road. Follow the road to T-junction and turn left. After about 1 mile, orchard is signposted on the right.*

Jane Grigson reflects in her *Fruit Book*, '(Quinces are) the fruit of love, marriage and fertility. In Spring on a warm day, if you sit in the lees of flowering quinces, you become quietly aware of a narcissus scent on the puffs of breeze. Very much the scent of the beginnings of love – its mildness goes unnoticed if you walk by without stopping.' She also quotes from a 10th-century Andalusian-Arabic poem about the quince by Shafer ben Utman al-Mushafi:

It is yellow in colour, as if it wore a daffodil
tunic, and it smells like musk, a penetrating smell.

It has the perfume of a loved woman and the same
hardness of heart, but it has the colour of the
impassioned and scrawny lover.

Its pallor is borrowed from my pallor; its smell
is my sweetheart's breath.

Quinces are more common to the Levant and South East Europe; 'Our weather, as opposed to their climate', says Charles Trollope, 'makes us marginal growers'. This does, however, give us one advantage: because of our relative coolness, quinces have a longer growing season. The result is a deeper-flavoured fruit with a glorious deep-pink flesh. The disadvantage is that a sharp drop in temperature can cause the quince to oxidize (turn the flesh brown). This is fine if you want them for juicing, but not so acceptable for cooking. The real problem is that you cannot always tell their condition just by looking at the skin.

The Trollopes grow 2½ acres quinces, which in a good year produce up to 12,200 kg (12 tons); and as they are immune to all the top-fruit diseases, they are only sprayed minimally against possible fungi. When they blossom in April, the Trollopes have several visitors who come to admire 'the narcissus scent. The furling twist of the bud, pink and white, opening into a globe of pale pink, ruffled with leaves'. Ripe from around 1st October to mid-November, the main varieties are Vranja and Pear Shaped. Each one has to be hand-picked as the skin is so easily marked with pin-point bruises. They are sold from a

QUINCES BAKED IN THE FRENCH STYLE
Coings au Four

Allowing 1 quince per person, peel and hollow out the cores of 6-8 quinces, being careful not to pierce through the bottom of the fruit. Sprinkle each one with lemon juice as you go. Stand the quinces in a buttered gratin dish.

Cream together 140 g (5 oz) caster sugar and scant 100 g (3½ oz) lightly salted or unsalted butter. Mix in 3 generous tablespoons of whipping or double cream and stuff the quinces with this mixture. Top each quince with a level tablespoon of sugar and bake at 190°C/375°F/gas 5 until the quinces are tender. Serve with cream and sugar.

Baked quince was Sir Isaac Newton's favourite pudding. (Adapted from *Jane Grigson's Fruit Book*)

covered table on the farm which is open all hours. Charles wishes his customers would not always plump for the biggest ones. 'It's perfectly understandable, but it's wrong. As they are so hard, it makes them a nightmare to cut'. Highly perfumed, quinces are almost impossible to eat raw, although Charles has some Jamaican customers who do, 'It's crazy, they're so acid that they dry your mouth up – but that doesn't seem to put them off'.

To prepare them, first you must wash off the grey down that covers the skin. As soon as you have cut, peeled and cored them, drop the pieces in lemon water to stop them from discolouring. Once cooked, they have a soft, slightly grained texture and taste of mellow fruity honey. They can be baked on their own or with apples, turned into jam or jelly (marmalade was originally made with quince), cooked with lamb (a Moroccan tradition), or steeped in alcohol for a liqueur. Luckily, the Trollopes usually have a pile of give-away recipe sheets with all sorts of ideas.

HAINAULT   MAP 3

Gramma's Concentrated Herbal Pepper Sauces
✉   HOT SAUCE

Unit 6, Acorn Centre, 29 Roebuck Road, Hainault Industrial Estate, Hainault, Essex IG6 3TU

TEL *081 501 3530* CONTACT *Dounne Alexander – mail order only*

Gramma's sauce is based on a Caribbean recipe. Although more of a paste than a pouring sauce, it follows in the same tradition of other hot sauces and can be eaten as a relish or used in cooking or to spice a hot toddy. Based on a recipe devised by Dounne's 'Gramma', a herbalist, it is a blend of fresh Caribbean hot peppers (namely Scotch bonnet), cider vinegar, sunflower oil, over 25 'secret' herbs and spices, sea salt and unrefined molasses (from cane sugar). Promoted both as a sauce and as 'an essential part of everyday health care', certain powers are attributed to the hot peppers, 'their antiseptic and anti-inflammatory properties (are) said to be extremely beneficial for a variety of common complaints, especially poor circulation, digestion, congestion, chills and breathing difficulties'.

Dounne started making Gramma's Sauces in 1987 from her council flat in London, but within 2 years had moved to a small industrial unit. Her energy and enthusiasm are incredible – proof, she claims, of her sauces' powers. They are now sold nation-wide in

> **GRAMMA'S HOT TODDY**
> (*serves 4*)
> Take 300 ml ($\frac{1}{2}$pt) of boiling water, $\frac{1}{2}$ teaspoon of Gramma's Pepper Sauce, the juice of 1 large lemon, 6 dessertspoons of honey, 1 dessertspoon of Caribbean rum, whisky or brandy and mix together and strain. Drink either hot or cold.

selected Asda, Tesco and Safeway supermarkets. Made in 4 strengths – mild, hot, extra-hot, and super-hot – if eaten on their own or used to spice butter or yoghurt, they have a pungent, fiery, peppery taste that warms, tickles and lingers in the mouth. Dounne suggests using a $\frac{1}{4}$-$\frac{1}{2}$ teaspoon of her sauce instead of pepper in a recipe; spreading it on pizzas, sandwiches, hot dogs or burgers, or mixing it into salad dressings, dips or marinades, or even spicing up a gravy. Be careful though – even the mildest is quite strong.

LAYER MARNEY   **MAP 3**

Marney Meats ✉ 🚜 ♟ RARE-BREED MEAT & VENISON

Layer Marney Tower, Layer Marney, Colchester, Essex CO5 9US

TEL *0206 330784* **CONTACT** *Nicholas Charrington* **HOURS** *Mon-Fri 9.00-17.00* **DIRECTIONS** *From Colchester, take B1022 towards Maldon. Follow the tourist signs for Layer Marney.*

Layer Marney is a glorious Tudor gatehouse set in park-land. Finished in 1525, it boasts a 24 m (80 ft) tower – the highest in England, with a commanding view of the county – decorated with ornate Italianate terracotta. It is open to the public at various times throughout the year. The small shop where the Charringtons sell their meat is in the house, but approached from the side.

Venison is farmed to British standard Prime Venison, slaughtered, hung for 7-10 days and butchered on site. Sold in a variety of cuts, including saddle, boned-and-rolled saddle, *médaillons*, haunch and haunch steak, they supply such top London restaurants as Launceston Place, Kensington Place, 190 Queensgate, and Odins. They also process burgers, sausages, pâtés, and smoked saddle and haunch.

Layer Marney, by way of being a rare-breed farm, also offers a range of rare-breed meats. As they are a small farm, not all the breeds are always available, but they welcome orders and promise to let you know when it has been slaughtered. All the animals are 'naturally reared', meaning that they grow at their own rate, are fed an antibiotic-free feed and kept outdoors most of the year.

Beef, hung for 3 weeks, is from Red Poll and the miniature Dexter; the latter is half the size of a normal cow, so produces half-size joints. Lamb, hung for a couple days, comes from the primitive Soay. It produces incredibly lean, dark-fleshed meat with a gamy taste. They also keep a few heavy-fleshed Portland which was reputed to be George IV's favourite lamb, because of its dense tangy flesh with a good covering of fat; and two good fleecy breeds – Lincoln Longwools and Norfolk Horns. Occasionally they also have mutton to sell as well. Their rare-breed pig is the Saddleback, with its fine black-and-white-striped back. A good fat breed, it produces medium-to-coarse-grained meat with a definite flavour and plenty of crisp crackling. They also sell kid from Golden Guernsey and Bagot goats butchered into legs, long loins (rack of goat) and diced shoulder.

In the shop the meat is mostly sold frozen, although you can buy it fresh by arrangement – and chefs insist on this. For mail order it is chilled.

The Maldon Crystal Salt Company in Maldon is the only remaining producer of sea salt in Britain. To explain their process: water is collected after a period of dry weather on the fortnightly high tides (known as spring tides) from the salt marshes around Blackwater Estuary. It is filtered, pumped into storage tanks and drawn off into salt pans that are mounted on an enclosed system of brick flues.

The water is brought to a 'galloping boiling' and as the impurities rise to the surface as lees (froth), they are skimmed off. The heat is then reduced and, as the water concentrates, crystals begin to appear on the surface. These form as tiny pyramid-like structures, unique to the Maldon process. As the crystals become heavier, they fill with liquid and sink to the bottom of the pan. After 15-16 hours, the pile of crystals reaches the surface of the liquid and the heating is stopped. The pans are cooled and 'drawn', the crystals are harvested by raking them to one side, then they are shovelled into drainage bins and finally into the salt store for further drying.

Maldon salt has a soft flaky crystal and a clean sharp taste, free of bitterness. The salt-works, unfortunately, are not open to the public, nor can you buy salt from them. It is, however, widely distributed throughout the country, so you should not have any trouble finding it. (Adapted from The Magic of Salt, issued by the Maldon Crystal Salt Company.)

SIBLE HEDINGHAM   MAP 3

Fuller's Dairy 🐄   DAIRY PRODUCTS

Brickwall Farm, Sible Hedingham, Halstead, Essex CO9 3RH

TEL *0787 60329* CONTACT *Jean Fuller* HOURS *Mon-Sat 9.00-17.30 Sun 9.30-12.30* DIRECTIONS *Farm is on the junction of A604 and A1017.*

For the last 2 years, I have judged a couple of classes at the Nantwich Cheese Show (held usually at the end of July). It is great fun – and serious hard work – tasting all those cheeses and when I've finished, I always nip over to sample the cream, yoghurt and butter entrants.

Fuller's Dairy always come up trumps, which is not surprising. Their unpasteurized cream – made from their own Jersey dairy herd – has a sparklingly pure and buttery quality with the merest hint of clover. Their live yoghurt, again made with their Jersey milk, has that same pureness. It comes as plain (full- or low-fat), thicker Greek-style (full-fat), and fruit in 8 bought-in flavours. My advice is to leave well alone, as these spoil the purity of the yoghurt. Far better, if you want a fruit yoghurt, to add your own chopped fresh fruit.

Butter, although not made by them, is packed by them on their farm. Produced by the Quality Milk Producers and made from the milk of various Jersey herds, it is a lightly salted, full-cream, golden-yellow butter. Rich, creamy and very yielding in texture (it is creamed to make it softer) it is most pleasant, but perhaps lacks the distinctiveness of other on-farm butters where only the milk of a single herd is used (see Berkley Farm Dairy, page 278).

From their farm-shop, Jean Fuller sells a variety of own-made curd cheese – low-, medium- and full-fat – that bear their distinctive pure, clean-tasting mark. You can also buy their unpasteurized (green top) milk, own-made truffles and fudge, and 14 different 'bought-in' flavours of ice-cream.

---

*When there is an 'r' in the month, **The Company Shed, 129 Coast Road, West Mersea** (tel 0206 382700) – literally, a converted oyster shed – always has 'laid Natives'. Richard Haward collects 3- to 4-year-old Native oysters in spring from the open Solent and brings them to the rich Mersea mud to fatten. Stocks of true Natives, although on the increase, are still depleted. At the start of the season in September, Richard's oysters are full and juicy with a sea-sweet bouquet.*

You can buy them to take away or – if you bring your own wine, lemon and bread – sit and eat them at the tables provided. Richard's wife Heather also sells fresh fish caught by local in-shore boats. Brill, herring, cod, dabs, pouting (a cross between whiting and cod), red gurnard and sprats were on offer one cold January day.

WRABNESS   MAP 3

The Priory Farm Shop ✉ 🚜   FRUIT CAKE

Priory Farm, Wrabness, Manningtree, Essex CO11 2UG

TEL *0255 880338* CONTACT *Edmund Swift* HOURS *Mon-Sat 9.00-17.30 Sun 10.00-13.00 (closed bank holidays)* DIRECTIONS *From Manningtree, take B1352 towards Harwich. After about 5 miles, farm-shop is on the left.*

Trading from an old Essex barn, Priory Farm Shop is well known for its own-made cakes. Best-seller is the traditional rich fruit cake made from a recipe that has been in Clare Swift's family for years. With an emphasis on quality ingredients, it contains Californian raisins, Australian sultanas and currants, unbleached self-raising white flour milled in Essex, unrefined Demerara sugar, slightly salted butter, fresh eggs, mixed peel and glacé cherries, rum and spices.

Clare has recently introduced a Special Rich Fruit Cake: richer and darker this also has chopped walnuts and muscovado sugar. All the cakes are made in various sizes: small round, weighing 900 g (2 lb);

large square and large round, weighing 1.8 kg (4 lb); and a 3.5 kg (8 lb) round. They are sold either plain, or neatly decorated with almonds and walnuts, with or without cherries. They are 'aged' for a couple of months before being sold and will keep for a year – longer, I'd have thought, provided you store them well wrapped in a cool, dry place.

They also make tea breads: 'plain', made with white flour and a generous quantity of vine fruits soaked in cold tea; 'honey', sweetened with a local honey; 'honey wholemeal'; 'sugar wholemeal'; and 'sugar-free wholemeal' that relies on the tea-soaked vine fruits to sweeten it. Then there is ginger cake, a crumbly shortbread, flapjacks and wholemeal rock cakes.

The shop also stocks own-grown vegetables: Brussels sprouts, calabrese, cauliflowers and some East Anglian produce, such as James White apple juice (see page 237), Stonham Hedgerow jams and chutneys (see page 244), Essex-made Cottage Cooking mustard relishes from The White House, Pembarsh (tel 0787 269342). These are runnier than most mustards and are a sweet blend of mustard seeds, honey and flavourings. (⊠ Fruit cakes only.)

GLOUCESTERSHIRE

CHURCHAM   MAP 2

Smart's Gloucester Cheeses ⊠ ▦
SINGLE & DOUBLE GLOUCESTER CHEESES

Old Ley Court, Chapel Lane, Churcham, Gloucestershire GL2 8AR

TEL *0452 750225*   CONTACT *Diana Smart*   HOURS *Mon-Thurs 8.30-18.30* DIRECTIONS *From Gloucester, take A40 towards Ross-on-Wye. Drive about 6 miles to Birdwood. Turn left into Chapel Lane immediately before Mobil garage. Drive on about $\frac{1}{2}$ mile and farm is signposted on the left.*

Opinions differ as to whether Single or Double Gloucester is the finer cheese. However, what everyone does agree is that both versions made by Diana Smart are excellent. There is a long tradition of Gloucester cheese for, as Patrick Rance points out in *The Great British Cheese Book*, '(it) is mentioned by name as early as 1594, which suggests that it was already travelling outside the county borders'.

It was not until the late 18th century that the 2 different Gloucesters evolved. Both are made from 2 meals (milkings), but the vital difference is that Double is a full milk cheese from 'either the cream from the overnight milk added to the whole morning milk, or ...the whole overnight milking ripened to start the whole morning milk when added to it.' Single, on the other hand, is made from skimmed overnight milk mixed in with the morning's milk.

However, just because Single Gloucester has a lower fat content (about 35%) than Double, you must not think it is a poorer cheese. A pale ivory cream, it is evocatively described by Michael Bateman in his comprehensive cheese directory complied for *The Independent on Sunday* as 'very mild, soft and delicate, like old-fashioned ice-cream'. There are various opinions as to why the cheeses were so named: one was that Double was always made as a larger cheese; another was because of its higher cream content.

Diana Smart makes each cheese once a week. She uses her own unpasteurized milk from a 45-strong herd, composed mainly of Holsteins although she is introducing Brown Swiss as their milk (similar in composition to the Gloucester Shorthorn) is so good for cheese-making. Single Gloucester is a slower and more difficult cheese to make: the curds are scalded at a lower temperature, then cut and turned at least 3 times to make tiny pieces before they are finally milled. Double Gloucester is made on similar lines to a Cheshire as the curds are cut into wedges and piled on top of the other and then turned. Both cheeses are pressed for 48 hours, during which period they are turned twice.

Single Gloucester is matured for anything from 3 to 12 weeks. Double is matured for a minimum of 3 months and it gets better the longer it is kept, which can be anything up to 8 months. Traditionally it has always been coloured (now using anatto) to make it a pale orange. It has a firmer texture and a deeper, more serious character with more 'bite'. As one sexist aficionado suggested, 'It's a masculine cheese, as it's one you have to take notice of, with plenty of zing'.

Both cheeses are made in 3.2-3.5 kg (7-8 lb) and 1.35-1.5 kg (3-3½ lb) truckles, with a small 675-900 g (1½-2 lb) truckle for Single Gloucester only available by mail order. On Tuesdays and Thursdays you can go and watch Diana and her son James making them. This is a slow all-day process, so it is best to avoid lunch-time as 'nothing much happens then'.

They also make their own unpasteurized double cream and yoghurt, and raise Tamworth, Gloucester Old Spot cross pigs that are whey-fed. These are cured for bacon (see Farmhouse Fresh Foods page 104) or hams. The latter are sold exclusively at Vivian's in Surrey (see page 251), where you can also buy their cheese.

CIRENCESTER   MAP 2

The Cotswold Gourmet ✉   RARE-BREED MEAT

PO Box 26, Cirencester, Gloucestershire GL7 5TJ

TEL *0285 860229*   **CONTACT** *Richard Lutwyche – mail order only*   **CARDS** *Access, Visa*

The Cotswold Gourmet sells rare-breed meat by mail order. Richard Lutwyche, who runs the business, has always been fascinated by rare breeds and felt that the selling and marketing of the end-product needed a push. However, unlike several other rare-breed producers (see Heal Farm, page 60, Paul Weaver page 271, and Layer Marney page 89), he does not farm himself. Instead he buys in animals on the hoof (ie live) from 20-25 (mostly) local farms, supervises the slaughtering, hanging, curing, butchering (carried out locally) and dispatching.

As Lawrence Alderson, executive director of the Rare Breeds Survival Trust explains, there are two important factors when it comes to the official classification of a rare breed: genetic characteristics and vulnerability. Genetic characteristics means that animal must be a distinct breed, a genuine part of our livestock heritage; vulnerability is if the continued survival of that animal is under threat. At the moment, vulnerability is assessed by the number of breeding females: for sheep the critical number is 1,500 ewes; for horses 1,000 mares; for cattle 750 cows; and for pigs and goats 500 sows and nannys. However, Lawrence is also pressing for the ratio of males to females, the number of units and the population trend to be taken into account.

You might think that it is slightly bizarre even to contemplate eating animals under threat, but unless a market and a positive and practical role – other than being kept in parks for visitors to gawk at – is found for them, they will surely disappear. Dissenters point out that often the reason they have become rare is because they are difficult to breed or slow-growing, or cannot be farmed intensively, or have a poor meat to carcass ratio – in other words they are not commercially viable. The newer 'improved' breeds, on the other hand, are far more efficient, therefore to try and market rare breeds is commercial suicide. But let us not forget one very important factor, their taste.

I do not know why, but most rare breeds do have a very distinctive taste. Try a Soay, it is lean and gamy, similar to venison but much richer; Tamworth pig is gutsier and meatier than most conventional breeds; and Gloucester beef is denser with a faint gelatinous texture. Even if the animals are fed on identical pastures, they still retain a different taste. Lawrence is also at loss to explain the reasons, as very little scientific research has been done in this area. Take primitive, or 'unselected' sheep as he would rather call them (eg Soay, Shetland, North Ronaldsay): there has been some initial work suggesting that they have a higher level of long-chain fatty acids and polyunsaturated fats. Now this might suggest they are better for you, but to what extent it affects their actual taste I am not sure. He also points out that their meat is finer-grained with a lower level of acidity and, when cooked, there is generally less moisture loss. It is a fascinating subject, and one I could speculate about for hours.

Cotswold Gourmet offers two services: own-delivery (within a radius of about 100 miles) of frozen half carcasses ready-butchered; and courier delivery of specific fresh cuts and joints, bone-in or boned, with or without stuffing, anywhere in the country. Beef is only from Old Gloucester, Pork comes from the Iron Age (a wild boar Tamworth cross and not a rare breed), Gloucestershire Old Spot, British Saddleback, Berkshire and Middle White (available as suckling pig only). Lamb is from Cotswold, Ryeland, Greyfaced, Dartmoor, Norfolk Horn, Shetland and Soay. Then there are sausages where breeds are specified, and smoked or unsmoked bacon and hams where they are not.

I have always felt that eating specific breeds adds a new dimension to meat. Try it for yourself and see.

The Bottle Green Drinks Company has recently moved to *Frogmarsh Mills, South Woodchester, nr Stroud, GL5 5ET (tel & fax 0453 872882)*. From their shop, they sell their elderflower and citrus cordials; pressés (ready-to-drink versions diluted with spring water and lightly carbonated); and Cotswold medium-dry cider made with cider apples from trees originally in Bulmer's orchards. They also sell wine made from seyval blanc, pinot noir and pinot blanc grapes grown in Jersey, that are pressed on the island with the juice shipped over to Gloucestershire for making and then sent back to Jersey for selling. A complicated process, as owner Kit Morris (ex Three Choirs Vineyards) cheerfully admits, but he likes it that way.

Their Elderflower cordial is made from wild flowers and during the season they have hordes of locals out picking for them by the bucket-load. They even issue them with picking instructions so the flowers arrive unbruised, without stalks and while still fresh (last year's going rate for a well-picked bucket was £2.50). The flowers, once picked over, are steeped in a sugar syrup, lightly crushed and pressed, and then filtered to get rid of any natural yeasts. The citrus cordial is made by the same process using oranges, lemons and limes instead. Both drinks are delightfully refreshing and make a welcome change from the usual run-of-the-mill squashes or fizzy drinks.

FILKINS MAP 2

Minola Smoked Products ✉ ⚖ SMOKED SALMON

Kencot Hill Farmhouse, Filkins, Lechlade, Gloucestershire GL7 3QY

TEL *0367 860391* FAX *0367 860544* CONTACT *Hugh Forestier-Walker* HOURS *Mon-Fri 8.00-17.30 Sat 9.30-17.30 Sun 10.00-12.00* CARDS *Access, Visa, Mastercard* DIRECTIONS *From Burford, take A361 towards Lechlade. After $3\frac{1}{2}$ miles, turn left at signpost for Minola on to a track. Follow track about $\frac{1}{4}$ mile to the airfield. Cross airfield and smokery is on the right.*

I have a sneaking suspicion that Hugh Forestier-Walker will smoke anything provided it stays still long enough. Look at his product list:

with over 30 items, you'll find smoked butter (apparently a great favourite with chefs for finishing a sauce), smoked cashew nuts, smoked prawns, smoked foie gras, smoked oysters (to spike up a beef and oyster pie) and even talk of smoked alligator. Is there is no end to his commitment to smoking? Although he must be admired for his dedication, I do think his discernment may be a little questionable.

For lovers of a strong smoke, however, Minola fits the bill. Using whole oak logs as Hugh considers 'sawdust too impure, particularly if it's from pine as the resin gets into it and can taint the food', they smoke in small wooden smoking houses with smoke-pots, holding the smouldering logs, in the centre. The heat causes the logs to release their tannins and acids, which will not only flavour the food but will cause it to lose moisture, inhibit bacteriological growth and thus preserve it. And Hugh is adamant that in spite of fridges, chilled cabinets and freezers, the keeping quality of smoked food is still important.

He is also proud of his ability to cold-smoke very slowly at a very low

*William Beeston is very hard to miss in Nailsworth. There is his shop **William's Kitchen** at **3 Fountain Street (tel 0453 832240, fax 0453 835950)**, his restaurant around the corner, and his catering company which travels as far afield as Liverpool and Plymouth.*

His long narrow shop comes as a bit of a surprise as the first thing that greets you is the huge marble slab brimming with fresh fish – not at all what you would expect in the middle of Gloucestershire. With 3 successful concerns to service, William – a fish fanatic – pulls it off, and by all accounts makes a profit as well. Throughout the week there is always a good selection including red mullet, undyed kippers, salmon, sea bass, Dover sole, chicken halibut and brill. For the weekends he gears up on a Thursday, adding yet more varieties and shellfish such as lobsters, crab, cockles, mussels and oysters; and he regularly makes up take-away plateaux de fruits de mer. He also sells some game, ducks, chicken, and Judy Goodman's geese (see page 282) at Christmas.

There is always a good choice of own-made soups and dishes. Try his robust fish soup with chunky fish pieces, made from a strong fish-and-shellfish stock flavoured with tomatoes, garlic and orange peel; or the potato and leek; the carrot and coriander; or the almond and watercress. William will happily cook any dish to order, but in the shop you are likely to find spicy beef with oranges and red wine, chicken breasts stuffed with smoked cheese and apricots in a cream sauce, a cheery paella, or salmon with an orange and lemon sauce.

The well-stocked shop also has a small selection of seasonal vegetables, such as local wild mushrooms, asparagus and artichokes. There are own-made marmalades and puddings (at Christmas they have their own puddings), local fruit cakes, white wines chosen with fish in mind, various breads, Richard Woodall's bacon (see page 46) and fresh pasta.

temperature (hence the smoked butter and foie gras). Chickens (deep-litter, maize-fed, locally reared birds) are wet-cured in brine for 24 hours, then cold-smoked for 24 hours and finished with a hot smoke to cook them through for a further $1\frac{1}{4}$ hours. Moist and succulent, they have a marked woody flavour that transforms an otherwise dull bird.

His smoked salmon is certainly a cut above the average. Salmon, farmed in Scotland, is dry-cured in Cheshire salt (and only salt) for 1 hour for every 450 g (1 lb) of salmon, and then cold-smoked for between 2-3 days. A rich orange-rose in colour, it has a firm texture, a good sheen, and a smoky taste pleasantly underpinned with a clean fresh taste of fish. It is sold either as whole sides; sides boned ready for slicing; sides long sliced, interleaved, and laid back on the skin; or sliced, interleaved in packs. Hugh sometimes also has wild salmon available and will smoke customers' fish for them.

While I was visiting his small portakabin shop by the smokehouses, a couple came in who had thought nothing of driving 30 miles to collect a pound of Hugh's smoked bacon. Spurred on by them, I was tempted and relished its meaty, woody flavour and firm but yielding texture. Apart from the unusual items I've already mentioned, they also smoke various cheeses, game birds, cod's roe, kippers, haddock and monkfish tails. Everything is sent either by first-class post or overnight carrier. During December, however, they will only process mail order for smoked salmon and gravlax.

GLOUCESTER   MAP 2

Workman & Meadows 🚌   ELVERS

Stalls 40 & 42, Eastgate Market, Gloucester, Gloucestershire GL1 1P4

TEL *0452 522257* **CONTACT** *Tim Meadows* **HOURS** *Mon-Thurs 8.30-17.00 Fri-Sat 8.00-17.00* **DIRECTIONS** *In covered market in town centre.*

Elvers have always fascinated me. Tom Stobart writes in *The Cooks Encyclopaedia*, 'Every spring, about March, baby eels (or elvers), tiny, worm-like animals only 6-8 cm ($2\frac{1}{4}$-$3\frac{1}{4}$ in) long and 2-3 mm ($\frac{1}{12}$-$\frac{1}{8}$ in) thick came wriggling up the rivers in a massive migration known as an eel-fare. The elvers pushed on into every tiny stream and even crossed fields to reach ponds and ditches'.

The life-cycle of the eel is a bit of a mystery. Its spawning ground is the Sargasso Sea and the silver (mature) eels return there, heading off in autumn. Every spring come the babies that have been carried by the currents over the Atlantic Ocean. In England, they are attracted by the huge outpourings of fresh water from the Severn and Parrot rivers into the Bristol Channel, and they wait off the coast to be carried up these rivers by the spring tides.

I was lucky enough to go elver catching on the Somerset levels. On a cold dark night, the banks of the Parrot were peppered with lone catchers, lit by the eerie light of oil lamps to attract the elvers. The excitement of netting a 'brood' was like panning for gold: tiny elvers glistened and shimmered, wriggling in their fine-gauge nets, and the value of the catch compares not unfavourably with the price of the metal.

That is the problem with eating elvers – they have become so expensive. Once they were a common seasonal delicacy: boiled and pressed into eel-cake or fried in bacon-fat. Most of them are now sold to the breeding stations for re-stocking eel farms on the Continent. Workman & Meadows, however, do sell elvers either live or frozen, along with a range of other fish from their stall in the busy (if disappointing) Gloucester Market. Michael Brown of Brown & Forrest (see page 223) also sometimes has a supply. Elvers are in season from about the end of February (depending on the spring tides) until mid-May. Sold by weight, you should be warned that 450 g (1 lb) can cost around the £20.00 mark; but a few do go a long way.

The simplest method the locals use for cooking is, I think, a little dull. Thoroughly washed in cold running water, they are boiled in lightly salted water until they turn opaque. I prefer to dust the washed elvers lightly in a seasoned flour and stir-fry them for a couple of minutes in a light olive oil along with a crushed garlic clove. Then they taste superb: mildly fishy, with a slight edge and a yielding crunchy texture.

*If visiting the charming town of Tetbury, do pop into **Tetbury Traditional Meats** at **31 Church Street (tel 0666 502892)**. A small butchers shop opposite the church, they have an interesting range of sausages including: pork, apple and cider; pork and cheese; ham & apricot; and a French-style Toulouse with a 97% meat content. There is also a Tetbury prosciutto, a dry-cured ham with a firm but yielding texture and a satisfying pig taste cut with salt. They sell a choice of dry-cured and maple-syrup-cured bacon, and some splendid-looking open-topped pies made with a flaky lard-based pastry. The fillings include pork, ham and apricot; and pork, ham and Stilton, covered with a layer of the melted cheese.*

Meat comes well hung and prepared: beef (from pure-bred or Hereford cross when available) is hung between 2-3 weeks; Gloucester leg of lamb for about a week, until the flesh is a deep red; and pork noisettes are well trimmed, neatly rolled and stuffed with chopped pork and apricots.

LECHLADE   MAP 2

The Flour Bag 🐷   BREADS

Burford Street, Lechlade, Gloucestershire GL7 3AP

TEL *0367 252322* CONTACT *Maurice Chaplais* HOURS *Mon-Sat 8.00-18.00*
DIRECTIONS *In town centre.*

Maurice Chaplais came to bread-making by a roundabout route, via hotel management. Happily ensconced in his small shop in Lechlade (which incidentally is the highest navigable point of the Thames), he now bakes an excellent range of breads, cakes and tarts every day.

The first thing he stresses is that he makes up all his own mixtures, there is not a bought-in pre-mix in sight. His flour is best quality: wholemeal comes from Shipton Mill (see page 100) and for his crusty French bread, he imports a milled flour from the Champagne country.

His range is always increasing, as Maurice is a man who loves new ideas and new flavours. His latest idea is an olive-oil-based chilli bread to serve with drinks. What else is on sale (and be warned, as he is a one-man band, the breads only start filling up the shelves at 9.00 and are not all in the shop until midday) are two superb old-fashioned country white loaves. Old-fashioned takes 16 hours to make; it has bulk rising and then a second rising in the tin. The other, Extra old-fashioned, is left to rise for 3 days in bulk, then rises again on the tray for 8 hours. To aid fermentation, the dough is made up with a small proportion of the previous batch's dough. Both breads have that splendid deep yeasty flavour and open but firm texture that only comes with a slow rising – the signs of a properly made bread.

Maurice also makes olive oil breads: mixed with about 10% extra virgin oil, there are sun-dried and olive versions. Both are richly dense and fruity, and liberally studded with chunky ingredients. His seed bread is something else: a 'secret' mixture of poppy, sesame, sunflower and millet seeds, malted oats, wheat flakes and – as he reluctantly told me – '4 different malt flours', it bounces with earthy punchy flavour. He also makes his own interpretation of the Jewish bread challah, only his is rich in butter and eggs and was more like a melt-in-the-mouth brioche. Maurice aims to please all his local customers, so there is a good mix of 'upmarket new and first-rate traditional baked lines'. In the latter category come diet-defying own-made doughnuts, oozing with raspberry jam, and possibly the best lardy cake I have ever eaten.

A good lardy cake should be studded with currants, made with a rich lard-based dough that is succulent and light but clean-tasting – an almost impossible combination to achieve. Maurice's does fit the bill: it is sumptuous, flaky and liberally fruity. Spread with apricot jam, this is a supremely indulgent sticky confection. As Dorothy Hartley in *Food in England* points out, '(lardy cakes) seem to crop up on the borders of the chalk line that runs across England from Wiltshire, through Oxfordshire to Cambridge', As the Flour Bag is on the Gloucestershire/Oxfordshire borders, it supports her assertion.

Maurice also makes mini treacle, Bakewell and pecan tarts, French apple flans, pear frangipanis, and apple and raisin Danish pastries. In his shop there is an extraordinary mixture of the best selection of olive oils in the county alongside a range of American products, 'here because I like to sell them'.

Ask any good baker and he is bound to say the right flour for the right bread is one of the secrets of baking. **Shipton Mill** ✉ at **Long Newnton, nr Tetbury GL8 8RP (tel 0666 505050, fax 0666 504666)** supply an amazing number of commercial bakers with their flours, so they must know what they are doing. Now you may have already seen in the shops their attractively designed retail organic (to Soil Association standards) range of wholemeal, strong white, and self-raising flours, but the good news is they will sell you their commercial range direct from the mill.

It includes such specialities as a coarse, gravelly soda bread flour which they actually export to Ireland; a ciabatta flour milled from a blend of hard American, Canadian and a little English wheats. With a coarser particle and a lower starch damage (which means the grain is split open less than usual, to make it less absorbent so the olive oil is not all soaked up), this is just the ticket for the open-textured, crusty bread. They also mill 4 different grades of rye flour: without wanting to go too deeply into the technicalities, rye flour differs in its bran and ash content, and the higher these are the more difficult it is to work. Apparently 'Unlike the Germans, we British rarely understand our ryes,' miller John Lister told me, which probably explains why I have such problems whenever I try to use the flour – I must be using the wrong one.

With over 30 different flours to choose from, you will probably find the right one to match your needs. If you ring up in advance and speak to John, not only will he advise you but he will also bag up a smaller weight than the normal 32 kg (5 stone) commercial sacks. I'd have thcught Shipton Mill a must for any avid home-baker.

MINSTERWORTH

MAP 2

Severn & Wye Smokery ✉ 🔲   SMOKED SALMON

Walmore Hill, Minsterworth, Gloucestershire GL2 8LA

TEL 0452 750 777 FAX 0452 750776 CONTACT *Richard Cook – telephone ahead*

Severn & Wye Smokery smoke 3 different grades of salmon: wild, conventionally farmed and Glenarm (see the feature on salmon on page 101). As far as I know they are the only company to smoke Glenarm salmon, and this is good news for anyone who does not like the texture of conventionally farmed salmon or disapproves of the effects of fish farming on the environment.

Severn & Wye dry-salt all their salmon and smoke it over oak chips in modern Maurer kilns. Conventionally farmed and Glenarm salmon are cured and always smoked fresh; wild salmon, caught by mainly rod-and-line fishermen from rivers in the south of England, is smoked fresh in season and during the rest of the year they use frozen stock.

Generally, wild salmon is far more difficult to smoke because of the variation in size, condition and oil content. None the less, theirs was firmly textured with a good bite and well-balanced and definite fish/salt flavour. Glenarm also had a firm texture and a full flavour, whereas the conventionally farmed salmon was much less interesting, with a milder sense of fish and a flabbier texture that broke up without resistance as you chewed it.

They smoke succulent Irish eels, with a rich woody finish, as well as herrings, trout; haddock. Their mackerel fillets come in natural, peppered, spiced and garlic flavours. The flavours are, in fact, a pre-mix – a sort of paste spread over the fish – and were disappointingly dull, as they did nothing to enhance the natural flavour of mackerel but only succeeded in subtracting from the juicy oiliness of the fish. They also hot-smoke chicken, poussin and duck breasts.

> " *Salmon farming is heading for a crisis. Fish are overcrowded, prone to disease and consequently fed antibiotics on a regular basis as a prophylactic measure; waters surrounding their cages are fast becoming polluted due to discharge of waste and chemicals; the market price is tumbling as there are just too many fish; and, to top it all, farmed salmon is often an inferior product, which can lack the complex taste and firm lean texture of its wild cousin.*
>
> *There is a way forward. Chicken farmers once flooded the market with cheap tasteless battery birds pumped full of chemicals. Then several decided to upgrade their standards in terms of feed and welfare conditions to produce free-range chickens. Salmon farmers also have this option and would do well to follow it, particularly as their farms are having such an adverse effect on the environment.*
>
> *Ghillie & Glen in Scotland and Glenarm in Northern Ireland have already led the way. Glenarm keep their fish in large enclosures with a stocking density of 12-14 kg per cubic metre (as opposed to 25-30 kg for conventional fish farms). This means there is more space for the fish to swim and, because they are not so crowded, the chances of disease and cross-infection are greatly reduced. Unlike most other farms, their cages are sited in open high-sea sites washed by the strong currents; not only do these tides clear out any accumulation of pollution but the fish are also forced to swim against them (it is estimated that Glenarm salmon can swim anything up to 9,000 miles a year – a distance similar to that travelled by wild salmon). Feed is also strictly monitored: the addition of hormones, antibiotics and Canthaxanthin (an artificial pigment for colouring the flesh 'salmon-pink') is banned.*
>
> *The result is fitter fish with better textured, leaner flesh that has improved eating qualities and is achieved at a far smaller cost to the environment. Surely this must be the future for salmon farming.* "

✕ The cooking at **The Marsh Goose Restaurant, High Street, Moreton-in-Marsh (tel 0608 52111)** wins 3 marks in 1993's Good Food Guide and is described as, 'distinct, fresh tastes; beautiful but not ostentatious; technically sound sauces; authentic flavours'. A fine recommendation. Next door is their food shop; and the glory of it is it sells terrines, pâtés, quiches and breads cooked by chef Sonya Kidney from the same restaurant kitchen. I tried a slice of a pretty and pungently flavoured chicken forcemeat terrine punched with spinach and herbs and studded with tongue and ham. Its originality and lingering subtleties could only have come from a first-rate kitchen. The shop also stocks a fair-priced selection of wines, jams, croissants, cheeses, coffees and olive oils. Provided you give enough notice, they will cook almost anything to take away – always in their own inimitable style.

NORTH CERNEY   **MAP 2**

Cerney Cheese ✉ ▯ ♟   GOATS' CHEESE

Cerney House, North Cerney, Cirencester, Gloucestershire GL7 7BX

TEL *0285 831300* **CONTACT** *Lady Angus* **HOURS** *Easter to Oct: Wed & Sat 14.00-18.00 (otherwise telephone ahead)* **DIRECTIONS** *From Cirencester, take A435 towards Cheltenham. After about 3½ miles, turn left at sign for Bagendon. Drive for ¼ mile and the house is signposted on the right.*

It's not every day that you drive up to a glorious Decimus Burton house and knock on an imposing double-fronted door to collect your cheese, but that is what is in store when you visit Cerney House. If you call on a Wednesday or Saturday afternoon from Easter right through to October, you may also have the added pleasure of wandering around the gardens and buying – from a shop in the tiny bothy – the goats'-milk cheese and fudge made by Marion Conisbee-Smith, as well as produce from the garden.

From the converted butler's pantry, Lady Angus – ably abetted by Marion – has been making an unpasteurized semi-soft goats'-milk cheese on a commercial basis for 3 years. Some of the milk comes from her own mixed herd of British Saanen, Anglo-Nubian and Golden Guernsey goats and the rest is bought in. The cheese, based on a Valençay recipe Lady Angus learnt to make while living in France, is made every day and takes 5 days to complete.

Full-cream milk is started and renneted and left to stand for 24 hours. Then the milk is ladled into cheese cloths and left to drain freely for another 24 hours; the curd is scooped into pyramid moulds, lightly pressed down to shape it, and left to drain for a further 24 hours. Next it is sprinkled with a mixture of salt and oak ash from France (giving it a speckly, stubbled coating) and left to stand for 24 hours. As the cheese absorbs the salt, it gives out more moisture. Finally it is turned out of the moulds, the remaining sides are lightly coated and it is put in the fridge to mature.

Sold in 225 g (8 oz) very French-looking pyramids, the cheese is young and very fresh with the merest hint of goat, if eaten at 5 days. As it matures, it develops a deeper, fuller taste. Lady Angus thinks it is at its best when matured for about a week; then it is creamy but smooth and dry with a pleasant cloyingness that clings to the roof of the mouth. It will keep for up to 28 days, by which time it is much stronger, harder and drier, 'definitely a cheese that needs a wine with it'.

And Also...

• Local carnivores Doug and Tessa Plowden swear by *Karen Mander's* beef for its 'old-fashioned intense flavour'. Sold from her magical grade-1 Stuart manor-house (open to the public, but check for times), it comes from grass-fed Herefords crossed either with Aberdeen Angus or Friesian. Slaughtered at 24 months, hung for 3 weeks and butchered locally, Karen will deliver the meat within the immediate area. She can be reached at Owlpen Manor, Dursley (tel 0453 860817).

• *Sarah & Richard Kelly* at Far Bank Farm, Horsley (tel 045383 5588) sell a range of organic produce (to Soil Association standards) from their farm in the hills near Nailsworth. Their chickens are excellent and they also produce potatoes; a range of vegetables; salads and herbs; and beef and pork.

• *The Organic Shop* in The Square, Stow-on-the-Wold (tel 0451 831004) has as good a selection of organic produce as you could ever hope to find. Their main criterion is if there is a market for a product and no organic example exists, they will stock a farm or locally made conventional alternative. Here you will find Rachel's Dairy range (see page 308), 15 different organic breads, organic meat from Pembrokeshire including 100% meat sausages, own-made pies, ready-meals, various vegetables, salads and herbs.

• A good farm-shop, conveniently situated on the A40 is *Over Farm Market* at Over (tel 0452 521014) with plenty of ready-picked seasonal fruit and vegetables and various jams, pickles and juices.

• Julie Raybould of *Farthing Fayre* at Farthings, Horsley, near Stroud (tel 0453 834937) produces a prettily packed range of chutneys, mustards, blackcurrant and redcurrant vinegars, and stuffed olives.

• *Cowcombe Farm Herbs* at Gipsy Lane, Chalford nr Stroud (tel 0285 760544) has a good selection of culinary, medicinal and decorative potted herbs. They also sell fresh or frozen goats' milk from their Golden Guernsey herd.

• *Preston Mill Trout Farm* at Preston Mill, nr Cirencester (tel 0285 653924) sells fresh trout, smoked trout, and a creamy smoked trout pâté made from a Katie Stewart recipe. In season they also have supplies of wild venison, mainly Fallow, culled from nearby Berkeley Park.

• *Selsley Herbs* is a charming shop at 4 George Street, Nailsworth (tel 0453 833118). They stock herbs grown from their own herb farm at Water Lane in Selsley, as well as dried herbs, herb chutneys, and herb mustards made by Highfield Preserves (see page 63).

• Brian Wither runs *Just Cheese*, a travelling market stall. Visit him all day Monday and Friday at Cirencester market, all day Tuesday at Minchinhampton or Saturday mornings only at Ledbury market. There is a good range of British on-farm cheeses, including local cheese-maker Charles Martell of Dymock's range of a pleasant Single Gloucester, marbled Double Berkeley, creamy Cloisters (all made with pasteurized Friesian milk) and Nuns of Caen, an unpasteurized sheep's-milk cheese.

• *House of Cheese* at 13 Church Street, Tetbury (tel 0666 502865) is run by Jenny Grant. Here you will find a good selection of ripened and matured British on-farm cheeses that vary according to the season. She also sells a buttery rich unpasteurized double cream.

• *Farmhouse Fresh Foods* at 61 Northgate Street, Gloucester (tel 0452 521784) dry-cure and sell bacon from Diana Smart's whey-fed Tamworth, Gloucester Old Spot cross pigs (see page 92). Cured in a mixture of salt, brown sugar and herbs, it has a full but mellow, sweetly tinged flavour and, because of the breed, it is a particularly fat bacon – sometimes the layer can run as deep as 10 cm (4 in). They also cure leaner bacon, ham and salt beef, and sell own-prepared Bath chaps, faggots and brawn.

• *Taynton Farm Shop* in the tiny village of Taynton (tel 0452 790220) sells own-reared ducks and various jams, pickles and cakes.

HAMPSHIRE

BLACKMOOR   MAP 2

The Blackmoor Nurseries & Apple Shop 🚜

APPLES & APPLE TREES

Blackmoor Estate, Blackmoor, Liss, Hampshire GU33 6BS

TEL *nursery: 0420 473576; shop: 0420 473782* FAX *0420 487813* CONTACT *nursery: Joy Walpole; shop: Lindy Moors* HOURS *(nursery) Nov to Mar : Sat 9.00-12.30; (shop) Tues-Sat 9.00-17.00* DIRECTIONS *From Greatham, take A325 towards Farnham. After about 1 mile, turn left signposted Blackmoor. Follow Blackmoor Apple Shop signs for about 1 mile to the estate.*

The Blackmoor Estate is home to Lord Selborne. A leading light in the agricultural world, he is also chairman of the Brogdale Horticultural

Trust (see page 129), so you would expect his fruit to be of the very best quality.

The nurseries are thought to be amongst the finest in the country. They supply trees to commercial growers, nurserymen, garden centres and – on Saturday mornings only – to amateur growers, the likes of you and me. Lord Selborne is a serious apple enthusiast and his private collection has some rare treasures. So as well as the modern commercial varieties you would hope to find some fine old varieties in his nursery. You will not be disappointed as, listed in the catalogue under the apt heading of Connoisseur's Choice, are some very choice trees.

There is my favourite Pitmaston Pineapple, with its tiny golden bell-shaped fruit, redolent with the aroma of pineapple; Court Pendu Plat, first described in 1613 and thought to be one of the oldest apples in cultivation, it has a curious flattened shape and a sweet luscious flavour; Devonshire Quarrenden, an 18th-century apple that is crisp to eat; Peasgood Nonesuch, raised by Mrs Peasgood in 1858 in Stamford, where the original tree is apparently still growing, is described as 'flesh tender, yellowish, of pleasant flavour and cooks frothily'; and the richly flavoured Cornish Gillyflower and Cornish Aromatic. As Blackmoor Nurseries grow both root-stock and bud trees, you can usually order the size to suit your garden – from dwarf to half-standard. They also have trained trees (espaliers, or fan-shaped, for growing against a wall) or family trees (one tree with different varieties grafted on). With so much choice, it is probably best to ring first to discuss your order.

Apart from apples, they have a good selection of pears, including the buttery Beurré Hardy, Glou Morceau, Louise Bonne of Jersey which boasts beautiful blossom and the meltingly fleshed Nouveau Poiteau. Plums are not forgotten, with amongst others Cambridge Gage and Shropshire Prune Damson, described as 'blue/black and rich flavour'. There are cherry, cob nut, fig, peach, apricot and nectarine trees as well. They also have a good selection of soft fruit bushes, and I was pleased to find the gooseberry Whinham's Industry with its large dark-red hairy berries that overflow with fruitiness.

From the shop, they sell about 20 – mostly commercial modern – varieties of apple, including Jupiter, Gala, Discovery, Katy, Jonagold, Cox's and Russet. Lord Selborne is also one of the largest apple growers, indeed many of the apples that find their way on to the supermarket shelves are grown at Blackmoor. They also sell pears and quinces (in season in October), as well as a selection of own-made cakes and jams from their fruit. Every year, usually on the second or third Sunday in October, there is a huge apple day when you can taste the different apples. It makes for a fun day out.

The Game Centre *at* **1 Petersfield Road, Greatham, nr Liss (tel 0420 538162)** *buys its game off the estates in the south of England. Before they opened their retail outlet last year, most of their game was exported so they tended not to go in for hanging for any length of time. Should you wish it, however, they will oblige. In season, game is sold fresh and oven-ready; out of season they have good supplies of it frozen. Expect to find partridge, occasional woodcock and snipe, wood pigeon (fresh all year round and sold as whole birds or breasts only), pheasants, saddle or haunch of hare, wild duck and venison. They make sausages from venison and, using the breast meat only, pheasant – both with a game content of 80%.*

BOROUGH BRIDGE MAP 2

West Lea Farm Shop WATERCRESS

Borough Bridge, Itchen Stoke, Alresford, Hampshire SO24 0QP

TEL *0962 732476* CONTACT *John Curtis* HOURS *Mon-Fri 10.00-16.30 Sat 10.00-16.00; May to Sept only: Sun 10.00-16.00* DIRECTIONS *From Alresford, take B3047 towards Winchester. After about ½ mile, shop is signposted on the right.*

Over the centuries much has been made of the healing properties of watercress; the Romans thought it helped them make bold decisions and, when mixed with vinegar, was used to treat mental illness. Culpepper, writing in the 16th century, advocated the bruised leaves or juice to free the face from blotches, spots and blemishes. In the 17th century it was used as a cure for hiccups or to get rid of freckles when applied externally.

Ideal growing conditions for watercress are neither too hot nor too cold. Gone are the days when it was in season only in the spring and autumn; modern growing techniques have seen to that. As Daphne MacCarthy states in her admirable *Food Focus*, a handbook of agricultural and horticultural produce from the United Kingdom, 'Watercress is now a year-round vegetable. Winter beds can be protected by plastic covers to guarantee supplies in frosty weather, and new seedling crops, marketed before they come into flower, ensure summer produce'. The main growing areas 'follow the chalk belt from Dorset and Wiltshire through Hampshire and the Home counties. Hampshire is the biggest production county. Pure water is essential for healthy watercress. It needs about 5-10 million litres per hectare per day. Most growers rely on water that rises from natural springs and bore-holes'.

John Curtis has several beds covering 4 acres, fed by both springs and artesian wells (bore-holes), the water is potable (of drinkable quality) and is regularly tested. Rich in minerals, particularly calcium and iron, it emerges from the ground at a temperature of 51°F (11°C) all year round. Watercress will only grow slightly above water level when the temperature is lower than that of the water, but well above water level when the air is warmer – hence the protection of the winter crop with plastic sheeting.

Watercress takes about 12 weeks from seeds to sale, and Jenny Woodham sells it picked daily in bunches from the farm-shop she runs in tandem with John. To keep it fresh, she suggests running it under a cool tap when you get it home, shaking off the water and storing it in a plastic bag in the fridge. Jenny also sells cartons of own-made watercress soup, Wild Blue pork (see below) sausages with watercress made especially for her, local honey, various cakes, pies, pâtés, vegetables and local produce, including Kingsclere Jersey ice-cream from Ramsdell near Basingstoke and bottles of Hazeley Down, the local spring water.

> ✉ As secretary of The British Sheep Dairying Association, Olivia Mills of **Brebilait Products, Wield Wood, nr Alresford, SO24 9RU (tel 0420 563151)** leads a busy life. Currently she is seeking a market for milk-fed lamb. Considered a delicacy in Spain, France and Greece, the baby lambs are exceptionally tender with a pale mild meat and are slaughtered before they are weaned, at around 30-35 days, to give a finished weight of around 4.5 kg (10 lb). A small leg should feed between 2 and 4 people, and Olivia plans to have some available from Christmas through to Easter; anyone interested should contact her. She still finds time between April and November to make Walda cheese from her Friesland and Friesland cross flock. Made in Gouda moulds, waxed and matured for between 3-6 months, it ripens to a texture similar to that of Emmental with a mild sweet flavour. A whole cheese weighs 2 kg ($4\frac{1}{2}$ lb) and Olivia also sells it vacuum-packed in cut pieces from 170 g (6 oz) upwards.

KING'S SOMBORNE   MAP 2

Sutherlands of Eldon ✉ ▦

WILD BLUE PORK & SAUSAGES

Upper Eldon Farm, King's Somborne, Hampshire SO20 6QN

TEL *0794 68158* CONTACT *Helen Sutherland – telephone ahead*

The Wild Blue pig, a cross between a wild boar and a Hampen Blue Gilt is farmed by Sam Olive and processed by Helen Sutherland. According to Helen, the advantages of this cross are numerous: it is cheaper to produce than wild boar as you get larger litters; the conformation of the carcass, more in line with the domestic pig, results in meatier cuts and joints; and the actual meat, while it is less gamy than wild boar, has a closer-grained texture than pork and a surprisingly good length of flavour.

The animals are reared extensively with stress – or rather the lack of it – an important factor: there are no farrowing crates and no teeth clipping or tail docking; the piglets are weaned at about 8 weeks when 'both sow and piglets are ready for it', they run free and feed on grass and roots supplemented with a specially formulated organic feed. Until recently the sows were kept 10 to a paddock, now the size of the herd has been reduced and there are only 4 in each paddock. As a result, Helen claims to have noticed a marked improvement in the eating qualities of the meat.

As a rule, all the meat is hung for 7 days. It can go for longer, up to 21 days when it acquires a deeper lingering resonance. 'The only disadvantage' Helen told me, 'is that the skin becomes very leathery and is no good for crackling at all'. The pork is sold in many ways: as whole legs, weighing about 6.8 kg (15 lb), or half legs at about 3.2 kg (7 lb); boned whole legs at 5.9 kg (13 lb) or half at 2.7 kg (6 lb); bone-in or boned loin joints or chops; loin steaks (eye of loin); tenderloin; belly; casserole meat (from the shoulder); and boned and rolled whole shoulder. Shoulder is the cut Helen likes above all for roasting as 'it's particularly sweet and succulent, with good intra-muscular fat'. In London both The Food Store at Harvey Nichols and Boucherie Lamartine sell Wild Blue pork or you can order it direct from the farm.

Helen processes Wild Blue into 80% meat content sausages, with rice and onion making up the balance, making them suitable for anyone with a gluten intolerance. These come in several flavours: salt & pepper, green peppercorn, honey & mustard, tomato & fennel, garlic and 100% meat. All the mixes are made up individually and she is more than happy to create a personal recipe for you with your favourite ingredients, provided you order a minimum of 9 kg (20 lb).

Anyone wanting to make their own pâtés, sausages and salamis should be interested to hear about the corn-fattened Wild Blue. Fed extra rations of 'corn flakes', their meat is of the same quality but they carry far more fat. Anyone who knows about *charcuterie* will tell you, it is both the quality and quantity of the fat that is so important. Top London chefs, Pierre Koffmann of Tante Claire, Simon Hopkinson of Bibendum and Mauro Bregoli of the Old Manor House (see opposite) all use it in their restaurants, so Sam and Helen must have got it right.

Chef-patron **Mauro Bregoli** *of* **Old Manor House, 21 Palmerston Street, Romsey (tel 0794 517353)** *uses Wild Blue pork from Sutherlands of Eldon to make glorious cotechino, coppa and salamis. The smoked sausages he serves with drinks in the bar.*

SHIRLEY   MAP 2

David Pirouet ✉ ☗   Clams

3 Redcar Street, Shirley, Southampton, Hampshire SO1 3NR

TEL 0703 788139   **CONTACT** David Pirouet   **HOURS** Tues-Sat 9.00-17.00
DIRECTIONS From Southampton, take Commercial Road towards Shirley,
signposted. Follow the road about ¼ mile to Shirley High Street. Shop is on
the right in the shopping precinct.

'Bivalves are creatures which live in double-hinged shells. They include
some of the most delicious of all seafood – oysters, scallops and clams',
writes Alan Davidson in *North Atlantic Seafood*. However, the name clam
can be confusing as it applies 'both in a general sense to a whole group
of bivalves and in a more restricted sense to certain species'.

Thus it is with a certain amount of trepidation that I tell you about
the American clam or, to give it its correct name, the Quahog (from the
Algonquin Indian name) or Hardshell clam. Native to North America
(although Alan Davidson says the truth is that most American species
exist in identical or similar form in Europe), it has established for itself –
via the kitchens of ocean liners – English colonies in Southampton
Water and Portsmouth Harbour. Ever since the 1930s, when the shells
were first chucked overboard, they have thrived there. From here on in,
my research fails me; I cannot honestly say for certain whether they still
grow naturally or are farmed and, although I hear tell of a clam farm off
the Isle of Wight, I have yet to track it down. I would welcome the
information. The thought of the clams settling so far from home is
rather cheery; they make a far more interesting and healthy import than
a Big Mac but, typically, we have embraced the hamburger with far
greater relish.

David Pirouet does sell native Hardshell clams. His are mostly grown
wild to the 'size of a lady's fist' and kept under ice to stay moist and cool.
Opening them can be rather hard work; it is far more difficult than an
oyster, although based on the same principle. I once read that the
solution is to pop them in the freezer for a couple of hours and thaw
them quickly; after that they will be in no condition to resist the
onslaught of your knife and will willingly give way. How you eat a
Hardshell depends on its size: little sweet tender ones (known as Little

---

✗ **Le Poussin** at **The Courtyard, Brookley Road, Brockenhurst**
(**tel 0590 23063**) is run by chef-patron Alex Aitken and his wife
Caroline. Alex places great emphasis on seasonal local produce in his
restaurant. In the late summer and early autumn he gathers wild
mushrooms from the New Forest; so you may well find local
chanterelle, brain fungus, chicken of the woods or wild oyster
mushroom on the menu.

Necks) can be eaten raw; the larger ones are best baked in their shell, cooked in a chowder or pasta sauce. With a firmer, more chewy texture than an oyster and a sweeter flavour, I think they are terrific.

David also sells *amandes de mer* (dog cockles) and *palourdes* (carpet-shell clams) imported from France. His wide range of fish comes from all over Britain and he also has a lobster *vivier* (tank) and will send lobsters willingly all over the country.

And Also...

• Food writer Susan Campbell recommends two butchers in the county. *The Hobler Butchery* at 28 Brockley Road, Brockenhurst (tel 0590 22145) supply Le Poussin with their meat and well-hung game. *S.W. Pickles & Sons* of 3 Fernhill Lane, New Milton (0425 614577), Susan describes as a traditional family butcher with well-hung game in season, interesting sausages and good English smoked bacon cut by hand.

• *David Bowtell* at Home Farm Shop, Home Farm, East Tisted, nr Alton (tel 0420 58418, fax 0420 587207) make their own sausages in 14 flavours, including a pork & Bramley, and a pork & Stilton. They butcher all their meat, and also sell poultry and on-farm cheeses.

• *Durleighmarsh Farm* at Rogate, nr Petersfield (tel 0730 821626) sells unpasteurized Jersey cream, pick-your-own soft fruit and, rather originally, pick-your-own herbs.

• For fresh and pickled quails' eggs and frozen quails, visit *Clements Farm*, Wheatley, Kingsley, nr Bordon (tel 0420 22485).

• *Chawton Park Farm* ⊠ at Chawton, Alton (tel 0420 83300) sell farmed Red deer hung for 10 days and butchered; they also sell haunch, which has been marinated in port and oak-smoked by Minola (see page 95), thinly sliced in 115 g (4 oz) vacuum packs. (⊠ Smoked goods only.)

• *Kimbridge Farm Shop* at Kimbridge, Romsey (tel 0794 340777, fax 0794 341295) are known for their well-sized fresh trout, which are mainly sold weighing 400-450 g (12-16 oz) or over 1.35 kg (3 lb). They also have it locally smoked over oak and sell Sutherlands of Eldon sausages (see page 107); a selection of British cheeses including Rosary, a fresh goats'-milk cheese made in Wiltshire; locally baked cakes and pies; and Kingsclere ice-cream.

• *Blackburne & Haynes* at Meadow Cottage Farm, Churt Road, Headley(tel 0428 712155, fax 0428 714001) make a Jersey ice-cream with a 15% fat content, a reduced-calorie ice-cream, a 'skimline' milk-ice and goats'- and sheep's-milk ice-cream.

HEREFORDSHIRE

September Dairy Products 🚜 🍦   ICE-CREAM

Newhouse Farm, Almeley, Kington, Herefordshire HR3 6LJ

TEL *0544 327561* **CONTACT** *Carey Glyn-Jones* **HOURS** *9.00-19.00*
DIRECTIONS *From Kington, take A4111 towards Eardisley. After about 3
miles, turn left at sign for Almeley. Follow signs for farm-shop for ³⁄₄ mile.
Shop is on the right.*

This small farm-shop, by the farmyard in front of the farmhouse,
operates on a rarely seen degree of trust. There is a bell that summons
Carey Glyn-Jones, but it is amazingly well hidden so most of the
customers help themselves and leave the money. For how much longer?
I can't help wondering.

In this glorious part of Herefordshire, with its ample rolling hills, it
looks as if time has stood still. So the Glyn-Joneses have had to keep one
step ahead of the pressures of farming. They still sell green-top
(unpasteurized) milk from their Friesian herd; a buttery unpasteurized
double cream; own free-range eggs; and, sporadically, pork and bacon
(cured by a butcher in Cinderford) from their whey-fed pigs.

They have also opted to add value to their milk and turn it into ice-
cream. Made in small batches with a fat content of 10-11% and an over-
run (added air) of about 50%, this is one of the very few ice-creams that
contains fresh eggs and no stabilizers or emulsifiers (see also Rocombe
Dairy page 65). The disadvantage is that it perhaps has a shorter life
than some 'after about 3 months, the texture does begin to deteriorate'
but this is, they feel, a small price to pay for a 'pure' ice-cream.

What of its taste? With a wide range of flavours, inevitably some taste
better than others, but the overall impression was one of a refreshing
milky flavour, unmuddied by gums and other 'unmentionable'
substances. Starting with the vanilla, it was quite sweet and faintly
tinged with the essence; coffee, made with an instant brew, was short
and sharp; cinnamon, gently flecked with ground-up sticks and lightly
sweetened with local honey, had a slightly dry flavour; both tayberry
and strawberry were actually made with the 'real' thing, fresh fruit
picked from a local fruit farm, and they were fresh and positively
buzzing with berries; the chocolate range (Choc Orange, Choc Mint and
Choc Ginger) was less successful, but this is not surprising if you insist
on using cocoa as the base.

Sold in individual, 1 and 4 litre (1³⁄₄ and 7 pt) tubs, September ice-
cream is well distributed within the county. You will find it at Hussey's
the Baker in Kington, the Harvest Store in Hereford and Monkton
Farmshop at Ocle Pychard. I suggest you make an effort to seek it out.

David & Sheila Jenkins *of* Green Acres Organic Growers, Green Acres, Dinmore (*tel* 056884 7045) *run a farm-shop full of organic (to Soil Association standards) produce. Vegetables and fruit are own-grown. When I visited in the late autumn I was taken with the display of winter squashes and marrows that included Vegetable Spaghetti, Buttercup and Little Gem. They also sell Desirée, Cara and Estima potatoes, onions, garlic, various cabbages, chilli peppers, green and ruby chard, fennel, various lettuces and salad leaves such as oak-leaf and mizuna, peppers and aubergines grown in poly-tunnels, fresh herbs cut from the garden, soft fruit, apples and plums including the plump juicy Yellow Egg. They also sell own organic beef and lamb. Pork and poultry come from Graig Farm (see page 00), bread is baked from organic grain by a baker in Dymock, and there are various jams and chutneys.*

CREDENHILL

MAP 2

L'Escargot Anglais ✉ 🚜

SNAILS

Credenhill Snail Farm, Credenhill, Herefordshire HR4 7DN

TEL & FAX *0432 760218* CONTACT *Anthony Vaughan* HOURS *May to Sept: 10.30-18.00; Oct to Apr: 10.30-17.00* DIRECTIONS *From Hereford, take A438 towards Brecon. After about $2\frac{1}{2}$ miles, turn right on to A480, signposted Credenhill. After about $2\frac{1}{2}$ miles, farm is signposted on the left.*

Credenhill Snail Farm rejoices under the title of the National Snail Farming Centre. This is possibly not as impressive as it sounds, as snail farming – after an initial burst of activity among farmers looking to diversify during the headier '80s – never really took off in Britain. Tony Vaughan lays claims to being one of our largest producers; he totals around 4 tons a year of the creatures, most of which are destined for the table. He also imports 4 tons a year, most of which are destined for breeding stock.

In Britain, and in fact throughout the world, most table snails are gathered from the wild rather than farmed. There is, however, good historic precedent for snail farms: the Romans, who knew how to cater for their every culinary need, set up *cochlearia*, special houses in which snails were fattened on a mixture of meal and wine. Tony farms his in a collection of barns and portakabins throughout the year, and in Summer they are outdoors in what looks suspiciously like cold-frames covered with wire-netting to stop them from escaping.

The best-known species of snail for eating is the large Roman or Burgundy snail (*Helix pomatia*). Contrary to popular belief the common Garden snail or *petits gris* (*H. apsera*) is also edible and it is these that Tony farms. By his own admission, snail farming is not very arduous; they have to be fed (on cereal meal) and watered, but otherwise there is not much else to do. He obviously has an affinity with them, claiming they 'have feelings of a sort, knock one around and it will hate you for ever more. If it's a small one it will get its own back, it will stop growing and then you can't eat it.'

Tony sells snails either live or as snail meat out of their shells (frozen, cooked and ready to be added to a sauce 'the equivalent of tinned but without brine'), or in a choice of three prepared dishes. All prepared on site, these are *à la Bourguignonne* (with garlic butter), Epicure (with port and chives) and *à la montagne noire* (with red wine and truffle juice).

If you visit Credenhill in the summer, an added thrill awaits you. Not only can you buy the snails but there is a 'Snail Trail' you can walk and guided tours so you can see for yourself the life-cycle of a snail. Without wanting to spoil your fun, I can tell you they are hermaphrodite and incredibly lazy.

> *The Hereford breed of cattle was developed from local stock in the late 18th and early 19th centuries by local farmers. Then they expected it to work in the yoke for 5 to 6 years, before selling it to graziers who would fatten it for the London market. It soon acquired a fine reputation for the eating quality of its meat, thought to be second only to the Aberdeen Angus. With a good conformation (build), plenty of intra-muscular flesh, and a dark fine-grained meat with a deep resonant flavour, this is the beef of Olde Englande. However, the Hereford has never given a very lean carcass; the fat distributes throughout the muscle, resulting in well-marbled meat. With the current trend for lean meat, the tendency nowadays is to cross the Hereford with a leaner Continental breed. Anyone who does not mind their meat laced with fat, and wants to try the flavour of the pure breed, should go to **Heggies** at **4 Yazor Road, Whitecross, Hereford (tel 0432 273300)** or **R. J. Moxley, 1 Winchester Avenue, Tupsley, Hereford (tel 0432 265351)**.*

PEMBRIDGE   MAP 2

Dunkertons Cider ✉ ⚒ ✿ ♟   CIDER & PERRY

Hays Head, Luntley, Pembridge, Leominster, Herefordshire HR6 9ED

TEL *05447 653* **CONTACT** *Susie Dunkerton* **HOURS** *Mon-Sat 10.00-18.00*
DIRECTIONS *From Leominster, take A44 towards Kington. After about 7 miles, turn left in the centre of Pembridge at The New Inn, signposted to cider mill. Follow the road for about 1 mile. Farm is signposted on the left.*

Dunkertons looks for all the world as if it had been styled for the pages of a glossy magazine as the perfect cider and perry farm. Overlooking picturesque orchards of ancient gnarled trees heavily laden with cider apples and pears, a lovingly restored half-timbered barn houses old presses, oak barrels and gallons of traditional cider. Their logo, a naked couple in a lush sunlit orchard, completes the rural scene.

Don't be fooled, however, the Dunkertons run a competitive business. Cider guru and author of *The Good Cider Guide*, David Kitton writes that '...purity, and indeed perfection, is what Susie and Ivor's cider and perry are all about. They specialize in high-quality brands, with full flavour and good strength, and take infinite care over the whole process. They handle their cider and perry with the same care as a wine, and indeed they do have much of the character of a light wine about them.'

Most of their cider is a blend of several well-known cider apple varieties, such as Foxwhelp, Brown Snout, Yarlington Mill or Strawberry Norman. But – and this is what makes their cider special – each variety of apple is pressed and fermented separately. Blending takes place later, continuing throughout the year, each blend varying according to the degree of tannin, sharpness and fermentation of the individual varieties.

While blending they also discovered that although most cider apples are too acid, too bitter or too sweet to be bottled singly, certain varieties do have sufficient balance, depth of character and flavour to stand up on their own. So they have developed Single Variety ciders made with: Breakwell's Seedling, a fresh fruity and medium-dry drink; Court Royal, which is medium-dry with a smoky tinge; and Kingston Black, a strong dry old-fashioned no-nonsense cider.

Because of the difficulty of obtaining some of the apples, the Dunkertons have been busy planting. The situation for perry pears is even more desperate; currently their fruity medium-dry perry that really tastes of pears is a blend of traditional varieties such as Redhorse, Merrylegs and Painted Lady (what wonderful if inappropriate names), but they have laid down avenues of Moorcroft and Thorne for the future. All their cider and perry come from unsprayed fruit and most of it qualifies for an organic (to Soil Association standards) symbol.

Blended varieties come as traditional dry, medium-dry, medium-sweet, and sweet in draught gallons, 575 ml (1 pt) stone jars, 1.1 litres (1 qt) stone jars and corked 1 litre (1¾ pt)

> Visit **The Cider Museum** ✉ at **Pomona Place, off Whitecross Road, Hereford, HR4 0LW (tel 0432 354207)** to find out how cider has been made through the ages. Distilled from the King Offa Distillery, installed in the museum in 1984, you can buy 40% proof 5-year-old Hereford Cider Brandy, and Hereford Cider Apple Liqueur, a blend of cider brandy and cider with 25% alcohol. They also sell Hereford Apple Aperitif, a blend of cider brandy and apple juice with an 18% alcohol strength, as well as Royal cider, made by distilling a 'hogshead' cask of cider and adding the resulting cider brandy to a second hogshead of cider.

bottles. The single varieties and perrys are sold in corked 1 litre bottles only. Still and strong, the ciders have an alcohol content up to 8%. They are finely tuned, old-fashioned, and have a long, lingering throaty taste to remind you of how ciders must have been when made by our forefathers.

> *Dinmore Farm Shop* ✉, *Queenswood Garden Centre, Wellington, Hereford, HR4 8BB (tel 0432 830032) presses its own apples for juice. They will send the juice anywhere in the country, either in mixed or single variety cases of Bramley for a sharp edge, Cox's & Bramley for a softer, sweeter flavour, vibrant Discovery, or Medium Sweet that changes with the season and is made from 'whatever apples at hand, blended with Bramley'. In total, they grow about 17 varieties of apples in their orchards, including Worcester Pearmain, known for its pear-drop flavour, Kidd's Orange, the nutty Egremont Russet and Cox's Orange Pippin.*

WEOBLEY   MAP 2

The Dairy House 🏆   DAIRY PRODUCTS

Whitehill Park, Weobley, Herefordshire HR4 8QE

TEL *0544 318815* CONTACT *Pru Lloyd* HOURS *Mon-Fri 8.30-16.00 Sat 9.00-13.00* DIRECTIONS *From Leominster, take A44 (becomes A4112) towards Sarnesfield. After about 7 miles turn left on to B4230, signposted Weobley. After 100 yards, turn left into the estate signposted Whitehill Park.*

Having started a business by making a soft cheese in the kitchen on her dairy farm appropriately called The Dairy House, Pru Lloyd has moved the operation into a unit on a small industrial estate. The location may have changed and the range expanded, but the quality – she assures me – has not.

Milk is delivered daily from a local Friesian herd and processed into a variety of produce. Starting with the soft cheeses, Pru still makes her first cheese, a medium-fat soft curd cheese with a fat content of 13% and now also makes a skimmed milk version with an incredibly low fat content of less than 2%. Both she describes as 'curd cheeses': the milk is started and renneted, the curds are hung up in cloths to drain and are shaped by hand into rounds. The results are fresh and delicately flavoured, but for fullness of flavour it goes without saying that (unless you are on a low-fat diet) the one to choose is the one with the higher fat content for its fine nutty creaminess. Pru also makes a fromage frais (6% fat content): for this she blends the curd cheese with milk for a runnier texture. She also makes various flavoured cheesecakes on bases of digestive biscuits and butter.

She also sells a range of cream: double, sour (30% fat content) and

Pullens Fruit Farm ✉ *at Ridgeway Cross, nr Malvern, WR13
5JN (tel 0886 880232) supply leading supermarket chains with
Elsanta and Honeoye strawberries. During the season you can buy them
direct from the farm-shop together with own-grown raspberries. They also
sell various apples, including the strawberry-fragrant Worcester Pearmain;
single variety apple juices from own-grown Cox's, Discovery and nutty
Egremont Russet; Conference, Comice and the red-flushed Bristol Cross
pear; dairy produce from Madresfield Dairy, and some own-grown
vegetables.*

crème fraîche (50-52% fat content). Using the same lactic culture and
process, the sour cream and crème fraîche have a sharpened flavour, a
slight lemon edge; the only difference is in the richness of taste. I
particularly liked her Greek-style yoghurt. Rich and mellow, with a
gentle tang, it had a smooth unctuousness that made me want to serve it
instead of cream – with its far lower fat content of 6-7%, it is probably
much better for you.

In the yoghurt line, Pru makes live low-fat (0.5%) plain and
flavoured ones. For some, like the damson, raspberry and strawberry,
she does use fresh fruit that she has picked; for the others, such as black
cherry, peach Melba, apricot, and pineapple, she buys in conserves. A
pity that, as so often they are over-sweet and drown the flavour of the
yoghurt. She also makes Bio ('the yoghurt of the '90s'), with the milder,
more digestible *acidophilous bifidus*. Generally I am no great yoghurt fan,
but her gentle version was very tempting.

Finally there is the butter. Made 'as and when there's surplus cream'
from 24-hour-ripened pasteurized full cream, it was charming. Fresh
and delicate, Pru generally makes it salted but, if you order in advance,
she can do it unsalted. Supplies are a little spasmodic for, as she says, 'If
I can sell the cream, why churn it into butter?' I see her point.

The Mousetrap Cheese Shop ✉ *has two branches in the county,
one at 3 School Lane, Leominster, HR6 8AA (tel 0568 615512),
the other at 1 Bewell Square, Hereford (tel 0432 353423). Owner Mark
Hindle, a one-time farmer, makes a point of selling on-farm British cheeses
from all over the county. Here you will find Hereford Hops (see page 286),
Llanboidy (see page 311), Cerney Ash (see page 102) and both Mary
Holbrook's (see page 9) and Robin Congdon's (see page 67) cheeses. He also
stocks Golden Guernsey cream, Elizabeth Botham's plum bread (see page
299) as 'it is great with cheese', Dorset Knobs (see page 76) and Stockan's
oatcakes (see page 345). There is also a small but well chosen range of
wines for drinking with cheese that includes Bodenham, a local vineyard.*

As well as making their own pies, pâtés, quiches and salads, **Barber & Manuel** in **Jubilee Buildings, Victoria Street, Leominster (tel 0568 613381)** sell a wide range of the county's products. Look out for The Dairy House range of products (see page 115), Dinmore apple juice (see page 115), Yan-tan-tethera Yoghurt (see page 326), Micarelli's fresh pasta made by an Italian, and pungent fruit sauces from Woodhouse Farm in 3 flavours: a sharp, nicely spiced Victoria plum, a tart damson and Scotch Bridget made from an old local apple variety.

WORMBRIDGE   MAP 2

Hereford Duck Company ✉ ▥ ♣   DUCKS

Trelough House, Wormbridge, Herefordshire HR2 9DH

TEL *098 121 767* CONTACT *Barry Clark – telephone ahead*

Developing a strain of a duck (or indeed any bird or animal) requires patience, enthusiasm and dedication, Barry Clark has them all in good measure. Eating several good ducks over several years in France spurred him on to experiment in England and, after a 4-year breeding programme, he felt he had arrived at the perfect product – the Trelough duck.

As its main bloodline, Barry took the Rouen, a large Normandy duck, 'But that takes about 7 months to mature which, in this country, doesn't make it commercially viable. So I bred it with various domestic birds for a quicker maturity and less fat but to keep its flavour and texture'. The result, the Trelough, takes about 10-12 weeks to mature, when it weighs between 1.8-2.3 kg (4-5 lb). It has a good meat-to-bone ratio, and is noticeably lean, 'unlike the Gressingham, another new strain, which can be quite fatty'. Other advantages are its good sized breast – about 225 g (8 oz) a side, and just what chefs want for a *magret* – and the fact that there is no difference in size and conformation between the male and female.

It also has an interesting flavour, the meat has a deep fruity resonance and a compact but pliable texture. Although, as Barry points out, this may be as much to do with the feed and the life-style as it is to do with the breed. This is why he insists on keeping complete control of its life-cycle. His ducks are reared extensively, able to run around in his orchards hoovering up the odd apple, and are fed an own-formulation mix of various grains, including wheat, barley and maize.

Understandably Barry is quite secretive about the breed, nor was he prepared to go into details about the feed, other than to say that the chick-feed does not contain a coccidiostat (to prevent intestinal disease) and he never gives them routine antibiotics, 'And I never lost a bird yet through ill-health. The only casualty was when a child smothered a duckling by mistake'. His breeding stock is kept in the gardens by his house and they run around under his collection of the rarest 'at-risk' apple trees in England. These (which include such romantic named trees as Fair Maid of Taunton) were given to him by the National Council for the Conservation of Plants and Gardens, and are duplicates of the collection given to Prince Charles for Highgrove. Barry is sure that eating the apples contributes to the ducks' flavour.

He also takes care about their

*You can stay the night at **Trelough House (tel 098 121 477)** on the edge of the Golden Valley, in the company of Barry, his wife Gay and their flock of Trelough Ducks. Breakfast includes their own free-range eggs, local bacon and sausages; and the five-course evening meal will, if you order it, feature duck.*

slaughtering. The birds are moved out of sight before their necks are dislocated to avoid distress to the remaining birds. The birds are then hung upside-down for between 24-48 hours and are never bled, 'as this diminishes the flavour'. Then they are dry-plucked and wax-dipped by machine. Ducks are sold oven-ready with giblets, or the breasts and surprisingly meaty legs are sold separately. He also sells frozen blocks of duck stock and packets of gizzards and hearts – the latter are splendid if pan-fried and added to a mixed leaf salad.

Production of the Trelough runs to about 15,000 a year, and Barry does plan to expand, 'This is a very special duck with a unique flavour – I think the best – and it is expensive; but everyone who's tried it comes back for more'. I did, and I must say I am inclined to agree.

And Also...

• From **Woonton Court**, Leysters, near Leominster (tel 056 887232), Mr and Mrs Thomas sell Golden Guernsey, a rich buttercup-yellow unpasteurized double cream and full-cream, green-top (unpasteurized) milk from their herd of 45 Guernsey cows.

• Anyone allergic to cow's milk will be interested in **Shepherds Ice-cream** at Cwm Farm, Peterchurch (tel 0981 550716). Made with sheep's milk, it comes in various flavours and has a very low fat content of 6%.

• Filtered through limestone rock of the Hereford Hills come 2 spring waters. Both can be bought direct from the source, either the **Berrington Pure Water Company**, Little Berrington Farm, Marden (tel 056 884 552) or **Hennerwood Oak Spring Water**, Hennerwood, Pencombe, nr Bromyard (tel 0885 400603).

• **Orleton Farm Shop** at Overton Farm, Orleton, nr Leominster (tel 0568 85750) sells Jacob Suffolk cross lamb, corn-fed Aylesbury ducks and chicken and geese and turkeys at Christmas.

• *Tavernors* ✉ at Yew Tree House, Lucton, nr Leominster (tel 0568 85384) sell wicker hampers packed with goodies from the county and will send them anywhere in Britain.

HERTFORDSHIRE

Littlefield Farm ▦   APPLES

Kinsbourne Green Lane, Harpenden, Hertfordshire AL5 3PF

TEL *0582 765027* CONTACT *Stephen Westley-Smith – telephone ahead*

A box of traditional apples makes a glorious present; but how about renting a tree? Littlefield Farm runs an enterprising rent-a-tree scheme, and it is so appealing I can't think why other orchards don't do it.

It works very simply: during blossom-time (usually the end of April to mid-May) you go to Littlefield, and stick a label with your name on a chosen tree. Then, when the apples are ripe, you go back to pick them. The prices vary according to the variety: this year James Grieve and Discovery cost £16.00; Spartan and Chivers Delight £17.00 and Cox's £20.00. Even if you have chosen a dud tree, you need not worry as they guarantee a minimum of 22.5 kg (50 lb) of apples to take home – easily eaten up by a family. If you select a late-season variety, Cox's or Chivers Delight, properly stored they will keep in a cool place right through to February.

An answering-machine gives information as to when the blossom is out and the apples are ready for picking; dates vary according to the weather and the variety. Picking week-ends are great fun: the farm lay on tea and coffee, wooden crates for picking and you can buy at cost boxes with cardboard layers in which to keep the apples. Any bruised or blemished apples can be juiced in the wooden apple press that is thoughtfully provided; and, if you freeze the juice, it will last all year.

The trees are in a fairly traditional orchard, planted about 5 to 7 m (15 to 20 ft) apart and pruned to the very manageable picking height of 2 m (6 ft). Spraying is kept to a minimum 'usually only at petal drop before the fruit is formed and only to beat the bugs,' Stephen Westley-Smith told me. As a result, in summer the orchard is filled with clouds of butterflies and colourful wild flowers. If you think this sounds one of the best present ideas you have heard, they also have gift tokens.

Ashwell Delicatessen ✉ 🚜   HAMS

Farrowby Farm, New Inn Road, Hinxworth,
Hertfordshire SG7 5EY

TEL *0462 733700* CONTACT *Nicholas Tracey-Williams* HOURS *Tues-Sat 9.00-17.00* CARDS *Access, Visa* DIRECTIONS *From Baldock, take A1 towards Biggleswade. After about 2 miles, turn right signposted Hinxworth. Farm is signposted immediately on the right.*

Nicholas Tracey-Williams produces two ranges of ham and bacon: Norfolk and Farrowby Farm. The former is cured from conventionally reared pigs that he buys in; the latter from his own free-range herd, reared to Conservation-grade standards. Hardy lean pigs, they live outdoors in arks running at 10 to the acre, are fed Conservation-grade feed and slaughtered at about 6 months. In fact, although Nicholas calls them Conservation-grade, officially he is not allowed to do so. The complication arises as all Conservation-grade animals have to be slaughtered at an approved slaughterhouse. As the nearest one to Nicholas is in Devon, not only would it be impractical, but also rather expensive.

Instead, the pigs are slaughtered in Northamptonshire and taken to Suffolk where both ranges are brine-cured for him in the same sweet cure made up with molasses. To be perfectly honest, I am not sure that I can detect a difference between the texture or taste of the conventionally reared Norfolk and the Conservation-grade Farrowby Farm. It is a pity, as I want to believe that a better-reared pig tastes better. As always, however, there are several other factors – such as the slaughtering, hanging, curing, etc – that affect its eating quality.

Both ranges of ham have a dense texture and a well-rounded flavour and are sold as boned half and whole hams in graded weights from 1.8-5.5 kg (4-12 lb). (There is whole leg on the bone for the Norfolk only.) On average, the Farrowby Farm pigs are slightly smaller and cost around 25-30% more per pound. They also sell a sweet-cure bacon and, from the Farrowby Farm range only, sausages with a 65% meat content.

LONDON COLNEY   MAP 3

Bowmans 🚜   YOGHURT & ICE-CREAM

Coursers Road, London Colney, St Albans,
Hertfordshire AL2 1BB

TEL *0727 822106* FAX *0272 826406* CONTACT *Bruce Luffman* HOURS *9.00-17.00* DIRECTIONS *Turn off M25 at junction 22 and follow signs for Bowmans for about $\frac{1}{2}$ mile.*

With their 380 Friesian cows kept in 3 dairy herds, Bowmans are the biggest milk producer in Hertfordshire. Everything they do seems to be large scale: their outdoor pig unit houses 250 sows (visitors can walk through its farrowing paddocks to see the sows and their piglets) and their busy farm-shop and restaurant covers an area of 6,000 square feet.

However, the scale of their enterprise has not affected the quality of their produce. From their milk they make a range of yoghurts, both low- and full-fat in plain and fruit flavours, and they claim to be the largest producer in this country of traditionally made Greek-style yoghurt. Made from full milk with an added Bulgaricus culture, it is set in buckets, then strained through Roquefort cheese bags to remove the

> You can pick up boxes of excellent freshly picked watercress from the farm gate at **Nine Wells Watercress Farm, Whitwell, nr Hitchin (tel 0438 871232)**. The nine wells are bore-holes dug to 75 m (250 ft) and they fill with a natural spring water used to water the watercress beds. Watercress has two harvests a year: spring, from February to June; and autumn, from September to December. Although, if the weather is mild, watercress can be cut throughout the year. Nine Wells propagate their own seeds; when they have germinated, they plant them out in the beds and it takes about 6 weeks to grow from seedlings. At the start of the harvest, their succulent dark-green-leaved watercress has a mild flavour that develops a peppery sharpness as the season progresses. Also sold from the gate are ungraded asparagus, or you can go and cut them from the field for yourself if you prefer.

whey 'for as long as needed for the right thickness'. Rich (it has a fat content of around 8%) and creamy, with a slight sharp aftertaste, it is satisfyingly thick with a vigorous flavour. Bowmans sell it direct to the public, as well as wholesaling it to processors for Tzatziki (yoghurt mixed with cucumber). Apparently, if you use a yoghurt that has been thickened by stabilization as opposed to straining, it falls apart when the cucumber is added and turns rather watery.

They also make ice-cream. Bruce Luffman wanted his to fit into the super-premium category; although it has no legal definition, it stands for an ice-cream with a high butterfat content (of over 16%), a low over-run (added air) for a dense creamy mix. 'So I had Häagen-Dazs taken apart at Reading University,' he told me with disarming honesty, 'to find out how it's made, what it contains and what's wrong with it. I wanted to do better'. Whether or not he has succeeded, I am not convinced. None the less, he makes a very agreeable, rich ice-cream. With a high fat content of $18\frac{1}{2}$% and an overrun of 40%, additions to Bruce's basic mix are eggs, double cream, 'about one-third of its weight is double cream... that means every third lick is cream' and, as a stabilizer, sodium alginate. 'Häagen-Dazs don't have one, but I think it needs it to improve the structure. Otherwise it melts too fast when on a cone.' Edwardian Vanilla is delightfully rich and creamy and, as a welcome change, restrainedly sweet; Velvet Chocolate also has a rich smoothness, but lacks the full vibrancy of Häagen-Dazs's really rich deep chocolate; and Plantation Coffee was most enjoyable, like cappuccino. Other flavours are Meadow Strawberry, Colonial Rum & Raisin, Autumn Hazelnut, Fruits of the Forest and a seasonal Christmas Pudding.

Now I know I keep banging on about it, but I really wish ice-cream manufacturers would not resort to buying in flavours from flavour-houses. Obviously it is easier for them, but they have a synthetic sameness and it just masks the flavour of the mix. If, like Bruce, you go to all the trouble of making a good mix, it seems a terrible waste then to buy in some of the flavours.

The farm-shop also has its own butchers. From there they also sell own-pork, hams and pies, lamb from Wales and pure Aberdeen Angus beef imported from Scotland.

And Also...

• *Gedi* at Plumridge Farm, Stagg Hill, Barnet (tel 081 449 0695, fax 081 449 1528) make 5 different pasteurized goats' cheeses. Widely distributed throughout the country – you may well have seen them with their distinctive red-striped label – you can also buy them straight from the farm. Try the charcoal-dusted Velde, the mild log-shaped Roubiliac or the mould-ripened Chavannes.

• *Graveley Hall Farm*, Church Meadows, Graveley runs an answer-phone number 0438 727709 during the season for the pick-your-own fruit. Here you can pick various strawberries, raspberries, loganberries, blackcurrants and juicy red Leveller gooseberries. They also have peas and broad beans.

• *Days of Ashwell*, 61 High Street, Ashwell (tel 0462 742202) are a no-nonsense local family baker with branches in Baldock and Royston. Their fruit cakes have a good local reputation and are often to be seen gracing local weddings and christenings.

ISLE OF MAN

DOUGLAS   MAP 7

George Devereau & Son ✉ ⛟   KIPPERS

33 Castle Street, Douglas, Isle of Man IM1 2EX

TEL *0624 673257* CONTACT *Peter Canipa* HOURS *May to Sept: Mon-Sat 8.00-17.30; Oct to April 8.30-17.00* DIRECTIONS *In town centre.*

Herrings swim around the coast of the British Isles, with the season starting in May off the Shetland Isles. An old map of the Ports and Seasons of the Herring Fishery shows them descending down the east coast as far south as Great Yarmouth and Lowestoft in October to December and on the west coast as far south as the Clyde ports in July to September.

Curiously it makes no mention of the Isle of Man, but Peter Canipa tells me the best herrings are caught off its shores between June and August, and while he still buys through to September he is 'not so fond of them'. A good herring for Peter's purposes, should have a high oil content; he likes them caught relatively early in the season when still feeding, as they are richer and sweeter and the quality is so much better.

On the principle that you cannot 'make a silk purse out of a sow's ear', he carefully selects herrings every morning at 6 am from the fish market or straight from the breakwater in Peel. Up until the '70s, George Devereau & Sons used to run their own boats but now Peter prefers to be able to make 'first choice' of the catch. The best herring come from Irish trawlers that fish in pairs, with 2 boats trawling one net so the fish are still in peak condition with no bruising or damage. The 'stunningly fresh' herrings are then transported a mere 400 yards to the factory in Mill Road, to be transformed into kippers. During the curing season you can also buy them straight from there, any time night or day.

To make kippers the herring are first split on a machine (at the height of the season they may deal with as many as 100,000 a day), then they are brined in salt for about 20 minutes. Although Peter employs a total of 48 staff, he still insists on smoking himself, 'I've been doing it for 40 years and it's only me doing it'. Rather reticent to pass on chapter and verse of how, how long and the temperature at which he smokes, he did explain that every fish can be different. It depends on its age, its condition, how it is broken down by the smoke, and even the outside temperature will affect it.

Unlike several other kipper curers, Peter only uses fresh herring. Others may use frozen herring and cure throughout the year, but he prefers to work them when fresh and freeze them cured and smoked for the rest of the year. 'They will keep in peak condition, as they are so rich in high-quality oil,' was his reasoning. Out of season he sells them defrosted, and these will last up to 10 days in a fridge; during the herring season, naturally, he sells them fresh.

With a 'cure for the palate rather than the eye' (it goes without saying that he uses no dyes or colourings), I tried a defrosted pair. Slightly on the smaller side, a pair weighs between 225-285 g (8-10 oz), they were extremely good: mellow, juicy and mildly sweet, they had a delicate flavour that merely hinted of kipper. As for cooking them, Peter heartily recommends a microwave '1½ minutes is spot on. All you are doing,' he explained, 'is heating it, it's already cooked in its own oil and as it is so rich, you don't need any fat. But if you don't have a microwave, then heat it in the oven set on tin foil.'

And Also...

On the basis that different people like different kippers, I feel duty-bound to mention *John Curtis* ✉, Manx Cold Storage Building, Mill Road, Peel (tel 0624 842715). His are saltier and more robust, and they are the ones served at breakfast in London's Connaught Hotel. He will supply orders of 3.2 kg (7 lb) and over by mail order.

ISLE OF WIGHT

Kingcob Garlic ✉ 🚜   GARLIC

Langbridge Farm Shop, Newchurch, Sandown,
Isle of Wight PO36 0NR

TEL *0983 865378* **FAX** *0983 862294* **CONTACT** *Colin Boswell* **HOURS** *Mon-Fri 9.00-17.00 Sat 10.00-16.00 Sun 10.00-13.00* **DIRECTIONS** *From Newport, take B3052 towards Sandown. After about 4 miles, turn left at The Fighting Cock pub cross-roads, signposted Newchurch. Follow the road through Newchurch and farm-shop is about 400 yards along on the left.*

I'm not criticizing, rather making an observation, when I say the Isle of Wight is a bit of a backwater. In the hinterland, away from the tourists, time seems to have stopped in the '50s: the roads are narrow B roads, and there are few, if any, housing estates and, until recently, no supermarkets. Life moves at a slower, more relaxed pace.

All the more surprising to find a garlic farm in the middle of the island, indeed Britain's largest grower (and importer) of this very un-English member of the onion family. 'Not so,' says Colin Boswell, 'surrounded by the sea, we have a micro-climate that gives perfectly good growing conditions'. On his 30 acres Colin produces about 100 tons a year of *ail rosé*, a French mountain garlic with a creamy white flesh and a silvery pale pink skin. With plump heads about 4-6 cm ($1\frac{1}{2}$-$2\frac{1}{4}$ in) round and about 12-15 cloves to the head, it has good keeping qualities and is richly juicy. I always thought that unless garlic was grown under the relentless sun of the Mediterranean it has no pungency. Again Colin put me right, 'At first, just after it's harvested, the garlic is quite mild. But as it dries out, its strength increases, so by November it is quite strong'. Harvesting takes place on and around July 5th, when the heads are lifted up and either laid in the fields or taken to a huge greenhouse to dry.

ROAST GARLIC

Simply take a few heads of garlic, brush them in olive oil and roast them in an oven preheated to 180°C/350°F/gas 4 for about 30 minutes. To extract the purée, slit the cloves with a knife and press them hard to squeeze it out. Serve as an accompaniment to roast lamb or simply spread on toast.

From the farm-shop, Colin sells it loose or neatly tied into plaits with 5, 10, 15 or 30 heads. He also sells smoked garlic: whole heads are cold-smoked over oak for between 2-4 days to give them an interesting smokiness that combines surprisingly well with the garlic's inherent aroma; and smoked garlic butter, made with minced smoked cloves mixed with salted butter. In season there are own-grown asparagus; potatoes, with Maris Baird as the first earlies on sale by the middle of April; sugar snap peas; and the most succulent of corns, the American Bicolor (with its yellow-and-white grains intermingling and a deep pile, when you bite into them the grains explode in your mouth with a satisfying sweetness). They stock various locally grown herbs and vegetables, wild-flower honey from the farm and, in autumn, huge pumpkins grown unaided by Hugo, Colin's 10-year-old son.

And Also...

• From *Island Mustard* ✉, Pelham House, 9 Bath Road, Cowes (tel 0983 291115) comes a range of mustards as well as Island Apple Chutney and Island Hunt Sauce, which is similar to Worcestershire Sauce but actually based on a family recipe.
• *Puffin Fisheries* at Saltern Wood Quay, Yarmouth (tel 0983 760090) are open 7 days a week in the summer to sell crabs and wet fish caught off the Isle of Wight.

KENT

ADISHAM   MAP 3

Wards of Adisham ✉ ▦   FUDGE

Little Bossington Farmhouse, Adisham, Canterbury,
Kent CT3 3LN

TEL *0227 720596* **CONTACT** *Ian Ward – telephone ahead*

Ian and Sally Ward have converted a small dairy into a fudge kitchen and almost every day in open pans they cook up a soft smooth and very unctuous fudge with a creamy fresh flavour. Theirs is a good old-fashioned recipe – the ingredients are sugar, butter and evaporated milk (easier to work with than cream) but no fondant. It was a particular favourite of the late Elizabeth David, who used to send off for a large box every Christmas. The range of flavours is pretty straightforward: vanilla made with essence, walnut using chopped nuts, ginger from crystallized ginger, coffee and chocolate from a Belgian chocolate. The quality is excellent. Packed in 225, 450 and 675 g ($\frac{1}{2}$, 1 and $1\frac{1}{2}$ lb) boxes, and 225 and 115g ($\frac{1}{2}$ and $\frac{1}{4}$ lb) bags, this is a fudge best eaten when fresh.

APPLEDORE   MAP 3

Appledore Salads 🔲   SALAD LEAVES

Park Hill, Appledore, Ashford, Kent TN26 2BJ

TEL *023383 201* CONTACT *Frances Smith – telephone ahead*

The chefs that Frances Smith supplies with her mixed leaves, edible
flowers and Japanese wineberries sound like a who's who of the food
world – Sally Clarke, John Burton Race and Stephen Bull to name but
three. She will, however, make up boxes or bags of salad leaves for us
mere home cooks, provided we give her plenty of warning and make
arrangements to have them collected (failing that you can buy a
selection of her produce at Villandry in Marylebone High Street,
London, see page 158).

Where to start with Frances? If you get her talking, she'll keep you
for hours as she is a total enthusiast. She is also a dedicated grower,
keen to experiment and to keep ahead of the trends, 'baby vegetables are
out of fashion now you can buy them at Marks & Spencer; possibly the
next new things are winter squashes or the hotter-tasting plain and curly
American salad mustards.'

In her numerous poly-tunnels, Frances concentrates on unusual
varieties, but she never sends out a list as they are always changing.
Apart from the usual range of leaves and herbs, when I visited her in the
late summer she was growing a selection that included: rocket; mizuna;
land and mega cress, with its larger peppery leaf; green and gold
summer purslane that has a hint of sorrel; curly leaf celery, 'a cracker of
a plant with its powerful flavour'; baby spinach; mouli pods; shungiku
(garland chrysanthemum) 'for a certain something'; all sorts of Italian
chicory, including the bitter pink and white-spotted Castelfranco; a tiny
and very juicy coquette frisée and strawberry spinach, with tiny spinach-
tasting leaves and small sweet nutty berries.

Frances will make up mixed bags according to your preference. All
you need do is toss them with a couple of Little Gem lettuces, a good nut
oil and a sprinkling of sea salt and you will have the salad of a lifetime.

BIDDENDEN   MAP 3

S.E. Lane 🚜   DAIRY PRODUCE

Whitehouse Farm, Three Chimneys, Biddenden,
Kent TN27 8LN

TEL *0580 291289* CONTACT *Michael Sargent* HOURS *8.00-18.00*
DIRECTIONS *From Biddenden, take A262 towards Tunbridge Wells. After*
about 1½ miles, turn right at The Three Chimneys Pub. Farm is about ¼
mile along on the left.

Like several other dairy farmers, the Sargents started 'adding value' to their milk about 5 years ago and now they keep back about 60% of the milk from their 95 Jersey cows to turn into cream, ice-cream and yoghurt. Their green top (unpasteurized) full-cream milk is rich and velvety with a hint of earthiness. It's a milk to die for – usually I would never dream of drinking milk by itself but, believe me, this I could drink by the jugful. The unpasteurized cream is equally stunning and slips down the throat, hinting of honeyed grass. Londoners should count themselves lucky that it is sold at Neal's Yard Dairy (see page 164).

Their ice-cream goes under the brand name of Winters Dairy Ices. It has a butterfat content of about 14% and, as it is made with Jersey milk, does have a buttery taste, even if it is a little on the sweet side (due perhaps to the inclusion of dextrose). Although the Sargents are toying with the idea of dropping the stabilizers, they haven't done so yet. So, as you can see from the label, it contains the usual range of guar, xanthus and locust bean gums. The cheaper flavours include: vanilla, made with a sickly vanilla bean essence; strawberry, using their own fruit topped up with a concentrate; a very sweet butterscotch; and chocolate made with cocoa powder that results in a disappointingly thin taste. They also do a 'luxury' range: rum & raisin; hazelnut and crème de cacao; whisky and ginger; chocolate, Grand Marnier and almond. These are far more heady, due no doubt to the bottles of liqueurs tipped into the mix.

In the shop, they also sell their own creamy stirred yoghurts, as well as soft fruit, the odd vegetable, field mushrooms as big as saucers in season, local honey, eggs, fudge, Duskin's (see page 131) and Biddenden Vineyard's apple juice.

BILTING   MAP 3

Perry Court Farm Shop 🛒 ☕   FRUIT & VEGETABLES

Perry Court, Bilting, Ashford, Kent TN25 4ES

TEL *0233 812408* CONTACT *Heidi Fermor* HOURS *9.00-18.00* DIRECTIONS *From Ashford, take A28 towards Canterbury. Farm-shop is on the right after about 4 miles.*

Perry Court is literally a huge barn of a shop, with a good selection of fruit and vegetables. Some are bought in but the rest are own-grown and, during the height of the picking season, they run an efficient answering-machine message service to let you know what is ripe. They really go out of their way to encourage their customers to try their fruit varieties, as they set up tasting tables with the fruit clearly marked – an essential service if you have never seen, let alone eaten, a particular variety. Throughout the year they sell the usual vegetables such as carrots, cabbages, cauliflowers, leeks and Wilja and Desirée potatoes grown on Romney Marsh. They also sell their own rhubarb, asparagus, sweetcorn, beans, peas, courgettes, garlic, squashes, PYO and ready-picked strawberries, raspberries, redcurrants, blackcurrants and gooseberries (Invicta, Careless and Levellers).

However, they really specialize in pears, plums and apples. They have a good range of pears: Williams Bon-Chrétien, Beth (like a Williams, but it does not go woolly), the buttery Beurré-Hardy, Conference, Doyenne du Comice, Comice, Packham's Triumph (similar to a Comice but with a tougher skin), Concorde and Gloumorceau (ideal for poaching). They also offer plenty of different plums: Czars, Opals, Early Rivers, a gloriously meaty Giant Prune, Belles, Victorias, Marjorie Seedlings and English Gages (in only its third fruiting year). At the moment they have 27 apple varieties running through the season. Discovery, Katy, James Grieve, Russet, Golden Smoothie (similar to Golden Delicious), Ida Red, Crown Gold are just a few and they promise another 40 to add to their list. These are the real traditional ones, mostly dating from the 18th century: D'Arcy Spice, Pitmaston Pineapple, Adam's Pearmain. Sadly, you will have to wait a couple of years before they are mature enough to pick.

They also have a chilled cabinet full of dairy produce, local jams, biscuits and sweets.

BOROUGH GREEN   MAP 3

Crowhurst Farm 🧺   CHERRIES

Crowhurst Farm, Crowhurst Lane, Borough Green, Sevenoaks, Kent TN15 8PE

TEL *0732 882905* CONTACT *Martin Leat* HOURS *mid-June to end-July: 9.30-20.00; Aug to Oct: 9.30-17.00* DIRECTIONS *From Wrotham Heath, take A25 into Borough Green. Turn left at main village cross-roads, signposted Crowhurst Farm. At roundabout, take first exit signposted Crowhurst Farm. Drive up the hill straight over the cross-roads and farm is about $1\frac{1}{4}$ miles along on the left.*

What makes Crowhurst Farm special is that it is one of the very few PYO outlets – if not the only one – with a large crop of cherries. The cherry industry has taken a bit of a dive in Britain. Our climate, with its late frosts, is not exactly conducive to cherry growing and, combined with plagues of starlings, makes us marginal growers. Ever since the restrictions were lifted on foreign imports about 10 years ago, we have not been able to compete on price, quantity and – in many cases – flavour.

Despite all this, the Leats have kept their cherries going and they have over 300 trees around their farm. Most of these are relatively old trees – they were planted in 1948 – which means that they are tall and bushy in good old-fashioned grassy orchards with splendid views over Kent. Picking from them can be hard work, but ladders, picking poles, buckets and plastic bags are provided. So if, unlike me, you don't suffer from vertigo you can nip up the ladder. Otherwise, with your feet firmly planted on *terra firma*, you lift the long pole with hooks and bag attached up to the tree, give it a sharp tug and the cherries simply fall into the bag. You do, however, need muscular arms!

The Leats are not too strong on what varieties they grow – nor are the trees marked – but you could try a few first until you find a cherry you like. Depending on the weather, the season starts around mid-June, with Early Rivers and the small pointy Merton Glory, then continues with the juicy Gaucher, Heart, Noir de Guben, and finishes early July with the white (really yellow, flushed with red) Napoleon and Florence.

> *Tony Redsell is one of the largest commercial cherry growers in Kent and, incidentally, walks away with most of the prizes for cherries at the Kent Fruit Show in July. Almost all his cherries go off to the wholesale market, but during the season from the end of June to the end of July you can buy direct from him at* **Homestall Farm, Boughton, nr Faversham (0227 751224)**. *He concentrates on the larger, firmer deep-red juicy modern varieties and these include Merchant, Stella, Colney, (white) Merla, Hertford and the smaller traditional Bradbourne Black. He is open 9.00-17.30 every day in season, but do ring first to check what is available.*

FAVERSHAM   MAP 3

Brogdale Horticultural Trust 🍴   FRUIT

Brogdale Farm, Faversham, Kent ME13 8XZ

TEL *0795 535286* **CONTACT** *Joy Wade* **HOURS** *Jan to Easter: Sat 11.00-17.00; Easter to Christmas: Wed-Sun 10.00-17.00; 12-23 Dec: Mon-Sun 11.00-17.00* **CARDS** *Access, Visa* **DIRECTIONS** *Turn off M2 at junction 6, signposted Faversham. Turn left off slip road down to T-junction. Turn left and, after about 500 yards, turn left into Brogdale Road. Follow the road over the motorway and, after about 1 mile, farm is signposted on the left.*

Brogdale Horticultural Trust is based at Brogdale Farm, the home of (probably) the world's largest collection of temperate fruits. 'Its purpose', the Director David Pennell told me, 'is to conserve the diversity of temperate fruits; to evaluate, develop and improve new varieties and to re-introduce the most appropriate varieties for today's commercial world'.

How the Trust came into being must number amongst one of the Ministry of Agriculture, Fisheries and Food's most serious mistakes. In those heady Thatcherite days, when every governmental department was turned into a 'cost centre', they wanted to grub up the collections and sell off the land. Howls of protest were raised, and after a fair amount of to-ing and fro-ing, the Duchy of Cornwall helped the newly formed trust with a mortgage to buy the land. Once the collections were safe, the trust set about making them accessible to the public.

If you think that visiting Brogdale might be a dry scientific experience, you couldn't be more wrong. For anyone at all interested in fruit, it is totally fascinating. There are 2,500 distinct apple varieties, 550 pears, 8 quinces and a few medlars, 350 plums, 220 cherries, 350 bush fruit (currants, gooseberries and blueberries), 42 cobnuts, 150 strawberries and 50 cane fruit (raspberries, blackberries and hybrid berries). Not only can you wander around by yourself on fruit trails through the orchards or go on guided walks but – as the fruit is picked – you can actually buy it in their shop. Believe me, you'll never want to eat a Golden Delicious again!

They also run open days for Summer Fruit and Apples (on the last apple day you could try any one of the 200 mid-season varieties) and there are always experts on hand to answer any questions, discuss the merits of particular varieties and identify particular plants or any fruit you care to bring from your garden. Of course none of this comes free – there is a small admission charge or £15.00 secures you admission as a Friend (along with other privileges, you receive their quixotic newsletter). It is a must for anybody who cares about one of the most important aspects of our culinary history.

---

*Romney Marsh lamb has a distinctive meaty flavour, with a dark close-grain-textured meat. The 'real thing', in season from July to October, comes from the Romney Marsh breed – a huge sturdy sheep with a heavy long-woolled fleece – and is born, grazed and fattened on the rich fertile Romney Marshland. **Archers of Westfield (0424 751030)** usually sell it. On the other hand, **J.C. Wickens of Winchelsea (0797 226287)** prefer a Romney Marsh Southdown cross as it produces a sweeter, finer-textured meat with a good vein of marbling running through it. They are reared specially for them by Frank Langrish, a local farmer whose animals graze on the remaining small amounts of traditional marsh pasture.*

IGHTHAM   MAP 3

Meg Game ✉ 🍲 ♣   COBNUTS

Oldbury Farmhouse, Ightham, Kent TN15 9DE

TEL *0732 882397* **CONTACT** *Meg Game* **HOURS** *last week Aug to mid-Oct: Sun 10.00-17.00* **DIRECTIONS** *From Borough Green, take A25 towards Sevenoaks. After about 1½ miles, turn right at The Cobtree Pub into Oldbury Lane. Follow the road for about ¼ mile to the top of the road, then turn a sharp right down the steep hill. House is on right at bottom of the hill.*

Cobnuts are a cultivated variety of hazelnut and, up until a century ago, cobnut plantations or 'plats' were a great feature of the Kentish countryside – extending over 7,000 acres. Now less than 250 acres remain, centred around the stony soil of the parishes of Ightham, Plaxtol and Maidstone. Unlike other nuts, cobnuts are eaten fresh, never dried. Their season starts towards the end of August – traditionally on St Philibert's Day, August 22nd – and lasts through to about the second week of October. For the first few weeks the husks and shells are still green and the kernel (nut) is white and crunchy. This is when I like to eat them, as they are rich and juicy and quite superb dipped into sea salt. Meg, however, prefers them later on when they have turned brown and are ripe, with a more pronounced nutty flavour.

In her 2-acre orchard, Meg grows 2 varieties without spraying: the Kentish Cob with its long kernel and the smaller, sweeter White Filbert. At the start of the season they have to be picked off the trees but as it progresses they are shaken off. Hence the Kentish question, 'Are the nuts shaking?' – meaning are they ripe. Ripe cobnuts can be kept until Christmas, provided you store them in a plastic bag in a cool place, preferably the fridge.

KINGSTON MAP 3

Duskin Farm 🖽 APPLE JUICE

The Ruffett, Duskin Farm, Covet Lane, Kingston, Canterbury, Kent CT4 6JS

TEL *0227 830194* CONTACT *Andrew Helbling – telephone ahead*

Duskin apple juice is different from almost all other apple juices as it is pressed from a single variety of apple rather than blended from the juice of several. This means you can really taste the flavour of the apple and, as Andrew Helbling usually has a hard core of about 6 varieties available, you can be sure of finding one to suit your palate.

As a guide, he divides his entire range into: sweet (russet, Worcester, Spartan); medium sweet (Ellison, Gala, Golden Delicious, Gloster, Ida Red; medium (Cox's, Fiesta, Jonagold, Laxton Superb, Melrose); medium sharp (Crispin, Discovery, Granny Smith, James Grieve); sharp (Bramley, Lord Derby). As some of the apple varieties are in quite short supply, he may run out quite early in the season. Andrew is very particular about his apples: some he grows himself and most of the rest are very definitely 'Kent' as opposed to 'Kentish', meaning from north and west of the Medway. A fine distinction!

The other major difference about Duskin juices is the production method. Andrew uses a slow labour-intensive method of macerating and cloth pressing the apples and then low-temperature (as opposed to flash) pasteurization to preserve as much of the aroma and flavour as possible. The result is a deeply fruity juice with a good length of flavour. Luckily the juices are widely distributed throughout the country, so if you want to try them ring Andrew to find your nearest stockist.

> Every August I look forward to the start of the Kentish Cobnut season and make a special journey to Kent to collect them. Since the formation of the marketing group Kentish Cobnuts they are now far more widely available, but serious aficionados still like to pick their own. Meg Game (see page 130), their publicity officer, only opens her orchard on Sundays, but other growers are open during the week.
>
> They are: **Pamela Jordan**, Silverhill Plantation, Dunks Green, nr Tonbridge (tel 0732 810745), **Brian Rudd**, Oast Cottage, Ightham (tel 0732 780764), **Mr Norman**, Oldbury House, Ightham (tel 0732 882320) and **Mrs Pazowski**, Hamptons Nurseries, Pillar Box Lane, Hadlow, nr Tonbridge (tel 0732 810633). **Mrs Jones**, Merrimans, Sandy Lane, Ivy Hatch, nr Sevenoaks (tel 0732 810884) sells ready-picked cobnuts from her gate.
>
> Please ring all of them first for opening times and availability. Remember that the season, although usually from the end of August to the second week of October, can vary depending on the weather.

MARDEN

MAP 3

H. E. Hall & Sons ✉ ☐ ♣ HOPSHOOTS

Little Mill Farm, Underling Lane, Marden, Kent TN12 9AT

TEL 0622 831448 **CONTACT** Peter Hall **HOURS** early-Apr to early-May – telephone ahead

Hopshoots or *jouets de blés* are tremendously popular in Belgium. In season from early April to early May, there the hops are grown in special blanching houses and the start of the season is eagerly anticipated. Young shoots, about the size of a finger, are boiled or steamed and eaten on their own with a hollandaise sauce or melted butter or cooked in an omelette. In Britain, however, the fashion has never really caught on.

As far as I know 'pikys' (Kentish dialect for vagabonds or generally low fellows) were the only people to eat them. Itinerant workers, they worked the hop gardens in the spring, twiddling the shoots, or bines, up the strings and pulling out the spare ones. Rather than discarding them, they would cook them over the camp fire. It is a pity that everyone else ignores them here, as hopshoots are very good indeed with their sharp, slightly bitter taste not unlike unblanched celery. Since the shoots are really no more than a by-product, selling them could help solve the depression in which most hop farmers find themselves.

Peter Hall is one hop farmer who does sell them. His come from his 15-acre hop garden, which is mostly conservation grade ($2\frac{1}{2}$ acres are Soil Association organic exclusively for the Caledonian Brewery), so you can be certain they are unsprayed. As his are grown outdoors rather than in the dark, they do have a pronounced, slightly astringent flavour which may be softened by first simmering them for 10-15 minutes.

Peter picks hopshoots only to order – they go limp quite quickly and have quite a short shelf-life – so do ring him first. He also sells asparagus from his gate, as well as various top-fruits all grown to either conservation or organic standards.

MATFIELD   MAP 3

Cottage Farms 🏠   TURKEY

Crundalls, Matfield, Tonbridge, Kent TN12 7EA

TEL 089272 2702   CONTACT David Browning – telephone ahead to order

David Browning is a founder-member of the Traditional Farmfresh Turkey Association and every Christmas he sells TFTA White turkeys direct from the farm. These birds are grown to very strict standards, with an emphasis on welfare and taste. Over the past few years they have steadily improved and are now certainly on a level with the French 'label rouge' birds.

Every TFTA turkey must be grown for a minimum of 18 weeks at a stocking density at or below that laid down by the Animal Welfare code, in naturally lit and ventilated buildings and fed a mainly cereal diet free of all antibiotics (unless prescribed by a vet) and growth promoters. Once slaughtered the birds must be dry-plucked and hung uneviscerated for 7-10 days to allow their flavour to develop. The actual breed of turkey is not specified, but they are either White or Bronze (see Kelly Turkey Farms, page 85).

Because of our curious new legislation dealing with the transportation of game birds and poultry, once a bird has been hung and eviscerated (drawn and cleaned) it can only be delivered direct to the consumer and within the immediate or adjoining area. Of course, there is nothing to stop you, the consumer, travelling miles to pick it up. (Butchers have their TFTA birds delivered uneviscerated so they get round the legislation that way.) However, as there are 28 growers producing around 73,000 birds (Christmas 1992), the chances are that there is a grower or butcher near you, so ring up the Traditional Farmfresh Turkey Association (0323 899802, fax 0323 899583) for details of your nearest stockist.

SHOREHAM   MAP 3

Sepham Farm Shop 🚜 ☕ ♟   FRUIT

Sepham Farm, Filston Lane, Shoreham, Kent TN14 5JT

TEL 0959 522774   CONTACT Nick Chard   HOURS 8.30-17.00   DIRECTIONS From Otford Duck Pond roundabout, turn into high street. Take the first turning on the right, opposite Fry's garage into Twitton Lane. Follow the lane and turn right at T-junction. Turn first right into farm.

Strange though it may seem to some, Sepham is my favourite pick-your-own in Kent and what appeals is its smallness, informality and position. Others may be far more efficient, have a wider range and better varieties, but none are as relaxed, peaceful and as uncommercial as here. Set in the Darenth Valley with its wide fertile meadows, Sepham is approached down a small lane past the oast house with its 3 roundels. To the west is 12 acres of chalk downland, co-managed with the Kent Trust for Nature Conservation. During the late spring and early summer it is ablaze with rare wild flowers.

John Fitton keeps his hives there and produces an early near-white honey that is a mixture of wild flowers, oil seed rape and cherry, plum and apple blossom. His later honey is richer and darker and comes from a far headier mixture of garden flowers, including chestnut, lime, clover and blackberry flowers. Both are on sale in the Sepham Farm Shop.

Nick's own vegetables start with rhubarb (in March) and asparagus (in April). The latter are sold ready-picked every day, but ungraded so you can rifle through and choose the size you want. It is, however, in soft- and top-fruit that Nick really specializes, choosing only varieties that he likes and making sure they are not sprayed once in fruit. You will find the lush Hapil and Elvira strawberries, Admiral, Glen Prosen, Malling Leo and Autumn Bliss raspberries that start around mid-July, with the later-cropping varieties carrying on till the first frost, sunberries, tayberries, redcurrants and blackcurrants and gooseberries. He has recently planted Van and Stella cherries, that usually fruit in the first 2 weeks of July, and has an interesting choice of plums including Reeves, Edward's and Greengage.

Apples were planted in 1986/7 and have grown to mature trees; amongst the varieties you can generally buy are Cox's, Bramley, Discovery, Vista Bella, Ribston Pippin, Pixie, Blenheim Orange and Merton Beauty. Throughout the year Nick also sells his own apple juice (a refreshing if dull and tight mixture of Cox's and Bramley), cider (made from the same blend), apple and raspberry and apple and blackberry juice mixtures, and locally grown potatoes and various bought-in vegetables.

STAPLEHURST   MAP 3

Iden Croft Herbs ✉ 🏷   HERBS

Frittenden Road, Staplehurst, Kent TN12 0DH

TEL *0580 891432* CONTACT *Rosemary Titterington* HOURS *Mar to end-Sept: Mon-Sat 9.00-17.00 Sun 11.00-17.00; Oct to Feb: Mon-Sat 9.00-17.00* CARDS *Access, Visa* DIRECTIONS *Drive through Staplehurst on A229 towards Hastings. On the outskirts of the village, turn left at the tourist signpost for Iden Croft Herbs on to Frittenden Road. After about 400 yards, at sign, turn right into the driveway.*

Rosemary Titterington has been growing herbs commercially for more than 20 years. During that time she has expanded her nursery and added a gift-shop and teashop, planted formal herb gardens, developed a wholesale business (now sold off) and started herb courses. Her mission is 'to encourage, educate and enthuse the public about herbs' and she does it to great effect. A determined, forthright and aptly named woman, her courses are great fun and informative. You learn about the history of the herbs as well as how to use them imaginatively, in a pesto or a coating for soft cheese for example.

During the summer, the nursery is packed with an exceptional collection of herb plants, both medicinal and culinary and the air is heady with their scents. Her mint collection is impressive – years ago I bought a large bush of Moroccan Mint (*Mentha spicata* 'Moroccan') from her and during the summer I crush the leaves for a refreshing, cleansing tea. Rosemary also grows edible flowers, such as heartsease, borage, nasturtium and pot marigold, and sells them in the summer together with trays of freshly picked herbs from her shop or she can send them by overnight delivery.

WHITSTABLE   MAP 3

Seasalter Shellfish ✉ ▥   OYSTERS

The Harbour, Whitstable, Kent CT5 1AB

TEL *0227 272003* **FAX** *0227 264829* **CONTACT** *Elaine Kirkaldie* **HOURS** *Mon-Fri 9.00-17.00 (closed bank holidays)* **CARDS** *Access, Visa* **DIRECTIONS** *In Whitstable, follow the signs for the harbour. Turn left opposite the car park into the second entrance for the harbour. Follow signs to Seasalter Shellfish on the end of East Quay.*

Whitstable was once famous for its Native oysters – the *Ostrea edulis*. Although, according to Alan Davidson in *North Atlantic Seafood*, Whitstable oysters were actually '...mostly re-laid seed oysters from Brittany and none the worse for that. However, Royal Whitstables, an appellation controlled by the Company of Free Fishers and Dredgers of Whitstable are genuine English Natives'. A fine but sadly academic distinction as nowadays most of what you buy at Whitstable are Pacific oysters – the *Crassostrea gigas*. I'm not sure that I'm either a sufficient connoisseur or I've eaten enough to tell the tastes apart but those who can say our Natives are smoother with a more delicate meat.

The demise of the Whitstable Native was due in part to over-fishing and to subsequent problems with disease. Seasalter Shellfish, a direct descendant of the old Seasalter & Ham Oyster Fishery Company with premises at Whitstable harbour since 1893, also runs a hatchery at Reculver in nearby Herne Bay for both Pacifics and Natives; so there is every sign that Natives will be farmed soon – possibly this September. Meanwhile you can buy their Pacifics farmed off the Pollard where once they dredged for Natives. Pacifics take about 3 years to mature and are sold either as medium – 80-100 g (3-3$\frac{1}{2}$ oz) or large – 100-120 g (3$\frac{1}{2}$-4 oz) – anything smaller gets put back in the sea. They are all passed through their purification tanks, packed in wooden tubs and sent anywhere in Britain by overnight courier.

Worth mentioning also are the Manila clams hatched by Seasalter. Heavy-shelled with a meaty, robust flesh they can also be bought at the door or sent by overnight courier. As they are quite large, allow about 50 clams per kilo (2$\frac{1}{4}$ lb).

The Royal Native Oyster Stores, The Horsebridge, Whitstable (0227 276856), *closed all day Monday, is now a fish restaurant that opens out on to the shingle beach. Specialities – not surprisingly – include Native oysters brought in by local fishermen, and farmed Pacifics; local lobsters; 'brown' shrimp; and a huge selection of simply cooked fresh fish mainly from Faversham and Whitstable boats.*

Ask to be taken down to the basement beneath the restaurant where the huge under-tidal tanks are housed. These are the original holding tanks for The Whitstable Oyster Fishery Company and they are fed by a pipe direct to the sea. Recently modified, they now hold the restaurant's stock of oysters and shellfish.

Opposite is a small wet fish shop run by the restaurant. It stocks a good selection of flat fish, including local slip soles, shellfish, own-smoked kippers, salmon and haddock, together with local hand-raked cockles in season from July to November. These are sold either fresh or cooked in vinegar, and there are a couple of tables and chairs in the shop where you can sit down and tuck in.

WROTHAM HEATH   MAP 3

Nepicar Farm ✉ 🏪   SHEEP'S-MILK CHEESE

Nepicar Farm, Wrotham Heath, Sevenoaks, Kent TN15 7SR

TEL *0732 883040* CONTACT *Harold Woolley* HOURS *mid-Mar to mid-Dec 11.00-17.00* DIRECTIONS *From Borough Green, take A25 towards West Malling. Farm is on left after about 1$\frac{1}{2}$ miles.*

Harold Woolley has been making sheep's-milk cheese since 1985. Recently he turned his farm into 'The Sheep Dairy Centre of the South East', so visitors can see a maternity unit and lamb nursery between mid-March and mid-May, an operational milking parlour from May to September, as well as plenty of friendly pigs, chickens, ducks, geese, turkey and rabbits for children to pet. Luckily all this tourist activity (100,000 visitors in 1992) has not put Harold off what I think he is best at – making cheese.

He originally started with Carolina, an unpasteurized hard-pressed cheese that claims to have been created from a recipe used by the Cistercian monks in the 12th century. Sold in small 450-675 g (1-1½ lb) or larger 2-2.7 kg (4½-6 lb) truckles, it is brined briefly and matured for about 60 days and has a good rounded sheep flavour. Cecilia is made in virtually the same way, except it is rubbed in salt and matured in oak barrels on a bed of hops for 6 weeks, resulting in a less intense cheese with a slight earthy sharpness. Both are interesting examples of sheep's-milk cheese suited to the average British palate (by that I mean the sheep flavour is not over-pronounced). Recently Harold has started making Nepicar – a pasteurized version of Cecilia without the hops. Although it is matured for 90 days, it lacks the guts and length of flavour of its unpasteurized cousins. However, anyone who objects to eating a raw milk cheese will find this a good alternative.

And Also...

• Venison (from mostly fallow deer), wild boar and freshwater crayfish are all available from **Wadhurst Park** at Morghew Farm, Tenterden (tel 0580 763158).
• **The Weald Smokery** ✉ (see page 256) have recently opened a shop at 2 Ely Court, Royal Victoria Place, Tunbridge Wells (tel 0892 519020).
• **The Wooden Spoon Preserving Company**, The New Oast, Coldharbour Farm, Wye (tel 0233 812251) produces various marmalades, jams (including High Dumpsie Dearie, a mixture of plum, pears and apples), fruit sauces, spiced fruit and chutneys. They are all made in small batches and 'stirred with a wooden spoon'.

LANCASHIRE

BLACKPOOL   MAP 6

The Coronation Rock Company 🏭   ROCK

11 Cherry Tree Road North, Blackpool, Lancashire FY4 4NY

TEL *0253 762366* CONTACT *Margaret Bell* HOURS *Mon-Thurs 10.00-15.00 Fri 10.00-14.00* DIRECTIONS *Turn off M55 at junction 4, At the roundabout, take the exit signposted A583. Follow the road for about ½ mile to the third set of traffic lights and turn left into Cherry Tree Road North. Unit is 150 yards along on the left.*

No seaside holiday in Britain is complete without a stick of rock. A gaudy confection of sugar, glucose, flavouring and colouring with a message running right the way through, it can ruin your teeth and sugar up your mouth – but it is irresistible.

Margaret Race in *The Story of Blackpool Rock* traces its origins back between 200 and 300 years, when sugar boiling was a cottage industry. 'In the 1700s a sugar boiler would have just a coke fire, a copper pan and a marble slab for his equipment and sugar, cream of tartar (no glucose then) flavouring and colouring for his ingredients. He would make the sweets in his kitchen, then either sell them in his own shop if he lived in a town or take them to market'. There is evidence that, in the early 1800s, sugar boilers were putting patterns and letters through sticks of rock, but it was miner turned sweet manufacturer, Ben Bullock from Burnley, who is credited with developing the craft. The first letters he ever put through rock were the title of a contemporary popular song, 'Whoa Emma'. However, after a trip to Blackpool in 1887 he hit on the idea of using the town's name.

Pink sticks of rock are still made in more or less the same way today. At the Coronation Rock Company you can watch the whole process from their viewing gallery. Sugar, glucose and water are heated in large copper pans to above 'crack' temperature (150°C/300°F), then poured out on water-cooled tables and folded into a manageable mass. Using vegetable dyes, some of it is dyed pink for the casing, some red for the lettering and some left undyed for the centre. The batch is then divided according to colour and cut with huge scissors. The uncoloured part is worked and pulled on a pulling machine until it is full of air and turns opaque white and soft; it is at this point that the flavouring (oil of peppermint) is added.

The red part is rolled into long flat red strips for the letters. These are built up by packing the spaces with white; eg to form a letter 'L' two pieces of red are put at right angles to each other and, to keep them in place, a white square-shaped roll is packed into the angle. After they are formed, the letters are laid together to spell out the word. Then the three parts of the rock: the middle white, the red letters and the pink casing have to be put together; some very complicated stretching and tucking takes place until the enormous ungainly 'lump' is ready for rolling, spinning and pulling into long thin 'strings'. These are then cut into the right length for sticks.

Rock is always at its best while still fresh. To test for this, gently knock one stick against another. If it sounds like shattering glass, it is fresh and will be crisp and crunchy; if it sounds like lead, then it is soft and soggy and bound to be stale as a result. The quality of the flavourings is important: Coronation, the oldest company still in business, use a good oil of peppermint for a clear, clean refreshing taste. They also make an imaginative range of multicoloured sticks and gaudy 'novelties', that include such flights of fancy as a breakfast plate of sausages, bacon and fried egg, fish fingers, chips and peas, doughnuts, jam tarts, Swiss rolls and eclairs. There seems no end to the flexibility of rock.

With a restaurant, a coffee shop and a food shop in the basement, **The Ramsbottom Victuallers** at **16-18 Market Place, Ramsbottom, nr Bury (tel 0706 825070)** is an interesting food complex. Run by Ros Hunter and her husband Chris Johnson, the shop was only opened a couple of years ago when Chris saw the change of direction away from expensive meals out to cooking at home and set about selling 'every ingredient Marcella Hazan et al writes in her recipes'. To prove the point he probably has one of the widest selections of estate-bottled olive oils (41 in total).

Apart from Parmesan he only sells British cheeses. These include: a soft 3-day-old unpasteurized goats' cheese made locally by Ann Holland; Heydale, made from sheep's milk at Heywood, an urban farm run by the local council; Bewcastle, a 3-week-old drained unpasteurized sheep's-milk cheese wrapped in vine leaves that maker Caroline Fairbairn of Thornby Moor Dairy also lightly smokes exclusively for Chris; and Mrs Kirkham's and Shorrock's 2-day-curd Lancashire. The latter is matured by Chris, he never sells it less than 12 months old, when it is 'interesting and strong, then it passes through a dumb, dead phase when I wouldn't dream of touching it until, at 24 months, it emerges intensely strong and creamy – it's just wonderful'.

He cures his own bresaola-style beef. Butchered by Chris himself, he then brines it in a sweet cure of sugar, molasses, juniper berries, salt and ale, and sends it up to The Old Smokehouse (see page 40) to be lightly smoked. On its return, Chris hangs it for 3-5 months and sells it sliced wafer-thin in both the shop and restaurant. He sells a good selection of localish produce, such as Burbush pies (see page 49), The Village Bakery (see page 44) bread, delivered fresh 3 times a week, Ancient Recipes (see page 47) pickles and chutneys; and Richard Woodall's (see page 46) ham and bacon. He likes to give his customers 'a bit of variety', so he is ever on the look out for new produce.

FARNWORTH   MAP 4

Morris's Gold Medal Black Pudding ✉ ⬛

BLACK PUDDING

120 Market Street, Farnworth, Bolton, Lancashire BL4 9AE

TEL 0204 71763 **CONTACT** Jack Morris **HOURS** Mon-Fri 8.00-17.00 (-12.30 Wed) Sat 8.00-14.00 **DIRECTIONS** In town centre, next to the market.

There seem to be as many different recipes for black pudding as there are weeks in the year, the only ingredient common to them all being pig's blood. From all over Northern France, Jane Grigson has collected for her *Charcuterie and French Pork Cookery* 13 recipes that include such diverse additions as chestnuts 'one of the most satisfactory *boudins noirs* I've ever bought', apples, parsley, chives or sage, spinach or spinach and white endive, *quatre-épices*, chard or beet leaves and cream. In Britain, we tend to a plainer heavier black pudding. This is because, as Jane Grigson points out, the French mix theirs with pork fat, onions and cream whereas we go for barley, flour and oatmeal.

As the name of his shop leads you to believe, Jack Morris has won several medals in this country for his puddings and they are very typically British. Dense and quite firm, they are made to a 'secret' recipe of pig's blood (although he does sometimes use ox) mixed with cereals, onions, herbs and spices in natural skins or intestines. More specific than that he would not be.

All his puddings are made out in the back of the shop, where he produces 2 versions: one heavily studded with diced pork fat, and a 'lean special' without. He can also be relied on to sell tripe, cow-heel, pork tasties (cooked belly of pork, a meatier version of 'scratchings') sold still warm first thing in the morning, and pig's nose that is eaten with vinegar and salt.

You either love or disdain black pudding, but among aficionados Jack Morris's is rated one of the best. ($\boxtimes$ Black pudding only.)

BLACK PUDDING WITH APPLE

Melt about 30 g (1 oz) of butter in a frying pan, add 2 cored and thinly sliced apples and fry them over a low heat. Slice a 450 g (1 lb) black pudding, add this to the pan and fry for 3-4 minutes on each side. Remove the black pudding and apple and keep warm.

Turn up the heat, pour in about 125 ml (4 fl oz) of dry cider and whisk in 15 g ($\frac{1}{2}$ oz) butter and 2 teaspoons of mustard. Stir together, scrape the pan thoroughly to deglaze and season.

Pour the sauce over the black pudding and apple to serve.

(Adapted from *10-minute Cuisine* by Henrietta Green & Marie-Pierre Moine.)

KIRKBY LONSDALE MAP 6

Sellet Hall Gardens $\boxtimes$ ⛏ ♣ HERBS

Sellet Hall, Kirkby Lonsdale, via Carnforth, Lancashire LA6 2QF

TEL *05242 71865* FAX *05242 72208* CONTACT *Judy Gray* HOURS *10.00-17.00 (gardens: Mar to Oct)* CARDS *Access, Visa* DIRECTIONS *Turn off M6 at junction 36, signposted Settle & Skipton. Take A65 towards Kirkby Lonsdale. After about 6 miles, turn right signposted Burton & Hutton Roof. Follow the tourist signs to the garden.*

Sellet Hall is set in a glorious undiscovered corner of Lancashire, in the foothills of the Dales in the Lune valley. Looking north from the gardens you can see Leck Fell, where the 'three counties stone' lies to mark the spot where Lancashire, Cumbria and North Yorkshire abut.

The Hall itself dates back to the 1500s. 'A yeoman's house' is how Judy Gray decidedly describes it; and a yeoman, halfway between a tenant and gentleman-farmer 'owned what he looked at'. The gardens, however, are entirely created by Judy and her husband George over the last 20 years. When you see them you will realize just how extraordinary this is as they look so established, so at one with the landscape that you think that, like the house, they must have been there for centuries. 'It is because we followed the old field patterns, using the 'copys' (the dry-stone walls that formed the enclosures for the animals) as our layout'. For a mere 70p, you can walk around them.

The herb garden, sheltered by towering yew hedges, is laid out in a formal style in the field where once a stock bull grazed. The herb nursery is around the back and it is here that Judy keeps her wide range of plants for sale. She has a good collection of unusual thymes, Silverdrift, compact white, caraway-scented and Lemon curd and she can also be relied on for a good stock of bistort. Also known as Passion Dock or Easter-Ledge, bistort grows wild in the hedgerows in the north. In spring its leaves and young shoots were boiled and eaten as a vegetable, or mixed with onion and pot barley to make Easter-Ledge pudding – a local and, I have to admit, rather dull speciality. Judy keeps 5 varieties: including wild, *superbum*, 'an improved flowering form' and Darjeeling red which she dismisses as 'incredibly bitter and far more useful as a skin tonic'.

She supplies local restaurants with a wide range of freshly cut culinary herbs, including rosemary, tarragon, chervil, dill and chives. Provided you give her notice, she will sell them straight from the garden. She also runs a tearoom and if you are as enchanted by the gardens as I am, you may feel tempted to rent one of their holiday cottages converted from a 16th-century tithe barn. (⊠ Plants only.)

MORECAMBE   MAP 6

James Baxter & Son ⊠ 🦞   POTTED SHRIMPS

Thornton Road, Morecambe, Lancashire LA4 5PB

TEL *0524 410 910* CONTACT *Bob Baxter* HOURS *Mon-Sat 9.00-17.30*
CARDS *Access, Visa, Mastercard* DIRECTIONS *In town centre.*

Bob Baxter has an endearing faith in the preservative qualities of his spiced butter: he is convinced that once sealed in it, his shrimps can be sent by post anywhere and everywhere in the world. They are...and, to date, with no ill effect.

All in all, butter is one of his great concerns. It is, he claims, his secret recipe for spicing it that makes his shrimps so piquant and the amount that his rivals put in that makes theirs not such good value. At pains to prove the point, he emerged from a freezer unit clutching several other pots; the shrimps had gone, but a layer of butter remained;

Of all the territorial (regional) cheeses, Lancashire is the softest, creamiest and most spreadable. Practically all of its makers are concentrated in the foothills of the Lancashire Moors between Preston, Chipping to the east and Garstang to the north. According to Malcolm Webster of Mendip Foods, this triangular area contains 9 cheese-makers: some are making it on-farm, others in a creamery.

Unlike the other cheeses, Lancashire – in its distinctive muslin bandage – is made with curds from 2 (and, in some dairies, 3) days. For my money, Ruth Kirkham's is the best Lancashire; she uses unpasteurized milk from her 40 Friesian cows and, in her small dairy, makes cheese 7 days a week, 52 weeks a year. To explain the process briefly: the evening and morning milk are mixed together, ripened (using only a minuscule amount of starter) and renneted. The curds are lightly scalded, cut, left to matt (bond) together, then scooped into tubs and lightly pressed for a couple of hours. They are turned out of the moulds, broken up by hand and divided into 2: one half is held over for the following day's cheese, the other is mixed with the curds from the previous day. The latter half is then milled, salted, put into moulds and lightly pressed for 2 days and left to mature for about 2-3 weeks, until it can be sold as 'Mild'.

One of the wonders of Lancashire is its subtle variations. At worst, it can admittedly be harsh, sharp and cloying; but at its best it is fragrantly rich, creamy with a lingering glow. According to Peter Gott (see below), some makers make 2 types: a softer, more mellow cheese that only has a small amount of starter; the other, made more quickly with more starter, is far more acid. 'I can't sell the acid cheese North of Preston, my customers won't touch it. They like it crumbly and buttery, so it leaves a smear on the knife'. Within the county there are strong allegiances to the makers, most customers specify their favourite maker by name; it is sold as Mild (from 1-4 weeks), Creamy (4-8 weeks), Tasty (8-16 weeks), and Strong (16 weeks upwards).

Unfortunately Ruth Kirkham does not sell direct from the farm, but her cheese (matured between 6-9 months) can be bought from **Peter Gott's Cheese & Bacon Stall, Unit 115-6 Barrow Market, Barrow-in-Furness (tel 0229 830956)**. He also sells Carron Lodge Creamy and Dewlay Creamy. Mrs Kirkham's can also be bought from Neal's Yard Dairy in London (see page 164), The Cheese Shop in Chester (see page 28).

Other good cheese-makers who sell direct are: **W.R. Shorrock & Sons** of **New House Farm, Ford Lane, Goosnargh (tel 0772 865250)** who make a 2- and a 3-day curd cheese; **Tom Barron** of **Ambrose Hall Farm, Woodplumpton (tel 0772 690480)** who make Mild, Cream, and Tasty Lancashire all with 2-day curd and best (full-cream) and whey-butter; **Carron Lodge** sells a high-acid, Creamy Mild, White Crumbly and Tasty from their shop **Annette's** at **16 Talbot Street, Chipping (tel 0995 640352)**. **Singleton Dairy** is a creamery but they have a small shop in the forecourt at **Mill Farm, Preston Road, Longridge (tel 0772 782112)**.

and, whereas his is never more than a few millimetres thick, theirs was at least 1 cm ($\frac{1}{2}$ in) deep.

Bob Baxter's family has been potting shrimps for over 100 years; he is the sixth generation. Once they ran their own boats, had a wet fish shop and employed a large staff, now he buys in his shrimps, sells them from his freezer centre and has Kathleen and Doreen potting out back in a small neat kitchen. The tiny brown shrimps are still harvested and processed in the same time-honoured way. Caught in the sandy estuaries of Morecambe Bay from the traditional 25-foot boats, they are cleaned and boiled at sea (cooking them in sea water was nearly banned by the EC on grounds of hygiene until Bob raised a rumpus); then they are peeled by the fishermen's wives and delivered to Bob's door within 36 hours of being caught.

Between them, Kathleen and Doreen make up around 500 pots a day. The shrimps are briefly stewed in the spiced butter, chilled off, packed into 50 or 200 g (2 or 7 oz) tubs, levelled off and sealed with a thin layer of butter. Moist, succulent and gently spiced (with, hazarding a guess, nutmeg and mace), they have a sweet fresh nuttiness. This is certainly a traditional British delicacy to savour.

---

*Lancashire is full of markets: some are in covered halls; others outside in the squares or streets. For my money **Preston Market** in **Market Hall, Earl Street (tel 0772 266048)** is the best for food. Look out for Michael Morris's stall, with a fine display of Welsh cakes, potato cakes, lacy oatcakes that look more like French crêpes and good old-fashioned crumpets. He also stocks Shorrock's Tasty and Dewlay's Mild Lancashire cheeses. From various other stalls you can buy black pudding, cow-heel, tripe and ladies' tripe (supposedly more refined, from the stomach), elder (from cow's udder), ham pestles (shanks) and all manner of 'goodies', some of which – I am ashamed to admit – I could not bring myself to try.*

PRESTWICH   MAP 4

The Swiss Cottage Patisserie ☖ BAGELS & CHALLAH

*118 Rectory Lane, Prestwich, Manchester, Lancashire
M25 5DA*

TEL 061 798 0897   **CONTACT** Jack Mauer   **HOURS** Tues-Thurs 8.30-17.00; Fri 7.30-14.30; Sun 7.30-14.00   **DIRECTIONS** From Manchester, take the A56 two miles two Prestwich. Turn right at the traffic lights into Scholes Lane. Take the first turning on the left into Haywood Road and the shop is 400 yards down on the right.

Jack Maurer is not my idea of a typical baker. Granted he does have that bleached-out-face-and-eyebrow look, an inevitable consequence of working night and day with flour; however, his hands are so soft, so delicate and so tiny they look as if they could not knead a single lump of dough, let alone plait one thousand 6-stranded challah loaves in 1 hour 27 minutes to win him the unofficial challah-plaiting world record.

To watch him work, swiftly and neatly folding cheesecake puffs, is magic. There in the middle of his busy bakery, surrounded by the banging and clattering of trays, the chattering of his workers and the calls from the shop out front for yet more bread or biscuits, he is an island of calmness.

Jack runs a strictly kosher (supervised by Beth Din) bakery that serves the large local Jewish population. As orthodox Jews cannot eat milk and meat together, he only uses vegetable margarine and vegetable oils to ensure that his breads are 'parev' (meaning neutral) so they can be eaten with both. Apart from challah, a rich festival bread traditionally eaten on the Sabbath, he bakes various other breads including a rye with caraway seeds, dark Russian rye (his grandparents were Russian) and a black rye bread. However, it was his bagels I found most interesting.

Although various food historains think the bagel originally came from Vienna in the 17th century, Evelyn Rose the Jewel food writer believes it can be traced back even earlier to the 15th century, and is a lineal descendant of 'pain échaudé' or boiled bread. The essential thing about these ring-shaped rolls is they are first boiled then baked to give them the creamy soft interior and crisp crust, not unlike French bread.

Jack makes his with flour, water, yeast, malt extract, salt and sugar (some bakers use egg). The dough, which has to be quite firm so it holds together, is shaped by machine, then it is submerged for a few seconds in boiling water until it swells up. Next it is drained, put on trays and baked in the oven. Some bagels can be incredibly hard-crusted and dry inside – but never Jack's. He prides himself on his bagels' chewiness and silky crusts, and makes something in the region of 9,000 every 2 days. They are sold plain or scattered with poppy or sesame seeds or kibbled onion, or even filled with cream cheese and smoked salmon.

While you are there, do try his moist, syrupy, lighty spiced ginger cake and his sweet-sour American-style cheesecake, which comes with different toppings but I think is best plain.

And Also...

• *Pugh's Piglets* ✉ of Bowgreave House Farm, Bowgreave, Garstang, nr Preston (tel 0995 602571, fax 0995 600126) market suckling pigs and will send them anywhere in Britain. Supplied head-on or head-off, boned or bone-in, they weigh anything from 3.5 kg (8 lb) up to as much as 10 kg (22 lb) when they are weaned. They come from various local farmers, hence there is a variety of breeds kept to differing welfare standards.
• Butcher *David Neave* of *Cockshouse Farm*, Ashworth, nr Rochdale

(tel 0706 526917) has on an irregular basis small amounts of well-hung beef, pork and lamb reared to Conservation grade to sell direct to the public.

• *Cowman's Famous Sausage Shop* ✉ at 13 Castle Street, Clitheroe (tel 0200 23842) sell about 54 different fresh sausages every day. With an average lean meat content of 75%, in a choice of medium- or coarse-textured, some are without any preservative and colouring. The Pork & walnut is even gluten-free. Other flavours include honey, pork & orange, beef & horseradish, wild boar and a mildly spiced turkey.

• Butcher *C.R. & J. Towers* at 70 Main Street, Hornby (tel 05242 21248) is a family concern. Father and one son raise the animals, while the other son runs the shop. Meat is well hung and butchered, and they make steak & kidney and meat & potato pies as well as juicy, well-peppered sausages, either plain or flavoured with leek or chives.

• Locals rave about Sissy Green's meat pies from *Ashworth Confectioners*, 30 Higher Deardon Gate, Haslingden (tel 0706 215099). Made with a crisp lard pastry and filled with a peppery minced beef, 'they stick to your ribs and keep you warm'. The old-fashioned shop also sells cracknells (sad cakes) made from rolled out and pricked left-over pastry.

LEICESTERSHIRE

BILLESDON MAP 4

Seldom Seen Farm ✉ 🛒 ⊖ ⚲ , GOOSE

Billesdon, Leicester, Leicestershire LE7 9FA

TEL *053755 742* **CONTACT** *Claire Symington* **HOURS** *June to mid-Sep: 10.00-20.00; 1-24 Dec 9.30-17.00* **DIRECTIONS** *From Leicester, take A47 towards Uppingham. After about 8 miles, turn left on to B6047, signposted Melton Mowbray. After about $\frac{1}{4}$ mile take first turning on the left at farm sign into a lane. After another $\frac{1}{4}$ mile, turn left again into farm drive.*

The view from Seldom Seen Farm is quite spectacular. From high up in the hills, on one side there is Billesdon Coplow and facing south on a clear day you can see over the county and just make out Rugby in the distance. On their secluded 207-acre mixed farm, set in glorious countryside, the Symingtons grow over 30 acres of fruit and vegetables. Some of it goes off to the wholesale market, but most is kept behind for pick-your-own or sold ready-picked from the farm-shop. The shop opens for 2 seasons in the year: for the summer's soft fruit; and for the whole of December leading up to Christmas.

In the summer season from the 10 acres of strawberries, you can choose from 4 different varieties: Elsanta, crisp smaller-fruited Honeoye,

Cambridge Favourite (which, when picked fully ripe, can be piercingly sweet), and large wedge-shaped Bogota. There are 5 acres planted with 6 varieties of raspberries to take you right through the season, ending with Autumn Bliss. They also grow tayberries, a hybrid berry bred from a cross between a blackberry and a raspberry; blackcurrants, redcurrants and – the prettiest of all – white currants; gooseberries; and Worcesterberries, a cross between gooseberries and blackcurrants, with soft juicy centres, that are splendid for jam-making or as a filling for a summer fruit pie. The Symingtons also grow their own early- and main-crop potatoes, broad beans and runner beans.

From their shop they sell their own honey collected from hives on the farm. A mixture of rape and raspberry blossom, it has a strong local following. Jams, chutneys, pickles and fruits made by a local friend, include well-fruited blackberry and raspberry vinegars. Trout, bought in from a local fish farm, are kept in a holding tank and killed, gutted and filleted to order. While you are waiting you could always tuck into the various cakes and biscuits that Claire bakes to serve in the tearoom. At Christmas the Symingtons do a roaring trade with their geese. This year, because of the demand, they have increased their flock size to 600. Free-ranging on grass and fed on own-grown potatoes and corn, their geese have a distinctive yellow flesh and a deep meaty flavour. Hung for 10 days and on sale from Michaelmas through to Christmas, they weigh anything between 3.5-6.8 kg (8-15 lb) and are all oven-ready complete with giblets and a chunk of their butter-yellow fat.

In November Claire also prepares a Three Bird Roast. A boned goose stuffed with a boned chicken stuffed with a boned pheasant. Hers differs from G.B. Geese's (see page 151) in that each bird is spread with a layer of pork stuffing made from a minced pork mixed with onions, breadcrumbs, orange rind and juice and chopped sage. Weighing between 4.5-5.5 kg (10-12 lb), it should feed about 14 guests; it is tremendously easy to carve, you just slice right through it like a loaf of bread, and it can be served either hot or cold. At Christmas they also sell pheasants, own-grown Bronze turkeys, frozen rare-breed (Shetland and Manx) lamb from a local farmer, Brussels sprouts on the stalk (so they remain fresh and firm throughout the holiday), pork and orange stuffing, as well as mince-pies, tarts and shortbread baked by Claire.

Walker & Son, with their main shop at 4 Cheapside, Leicester (tel 0533 625687) now have pork pie shops all over the county. Their pies are made in a state-of-the-art factory on an industrial estate on the edge of town. Despite modern machinery to chop the meat, press out the pastry and fill the moulds, their pies are more than passable. The meat is perhaps a little over-processed and over-peppered, and the pastry a trifle tough, but the pies are still a lot better than most. For anyone who wants to have a go at making their own hot-water crust, they also sell own-rendered lard.

MELTON MOWBRAY MAP 4

Ye Olde Pork Pie Shoppe ✉ 🏆

MELTON MOWBRAY PORK PIE & MELTON HUNT CAKE

10 Nottingham Street, Melton Mowbray, Leicestershire LE13 1NW

TEL *0664 62341* **CONTACT** *Stephen Hallam* **HOURS** *Mon-Sat 8.00-17.00* **DIRECTIONS** *In town centre.*

Dickinson and Morris's Ye Olde Pork Pie Shoppe is the oldest pork pie bakery in Melton Mowbray. Still trading from the original shop that was restored in October 1992 after a devastating fire, it also has the distinction of being the town's only producer of the 'real thing'.

A true Melton Mowbray pork pie is made with a hot-water paste of flour, lard, salt and water. The paste is hand-raised around a dolly (a cylindrical wooden block). As Stephen Hallam explains, 'You need a sure touch to raise the paste. If you press too hard, you'll cause it to stretch or split. Equally, the paste mustn't be too thick or uneven. However, doing it by hand – once you get it right – results in a far better pie than a piece of machinery can ever achieve.'

A Melton Mowbray pie also has a particularly distinctive shape. Unlike other pork pies with their straight-up-and-down sides and neatly tucked top, its top has wavy edges and bows and bulges like a pot belly. This is because it is hand-crimped and, baked without a hoop or tin, it is completely self supporting. Appearance is important, as Stephen says, 'Not only must it look right so you know it's authentic, but it also affects the way the filling cooks. We aim for a pie that's not just a rich pastry holding up a meat filling or a meaty filling enclosed in pastry – but a perfect marriage of the two'.

It goes without saying that the actual ingredients for the filling are also of prime importance. Pies have been baked in Melton Mowbray since the mid-18th century. Then they probably would have used meat from the Tamworth pig, a local breed fattened on whey, a by-product from Stilton the local cheese. Now Stephen uses good quality lean local pork, hand-chopped for a good texture. They always use fresh meat, unlike other pie-makers who often use cured. The filling may look an unappealing grey, but it has a far meatier and more vibrant taste. Once cooked, each pie is pricked to let the steam out and hand-filled with a proper jelly stock made from split pigs' trotters and bones – no commercially produced substitute or bought-in packets here.

The generous proportions of equal weights of meat to pastry ensure there is no scrimping. The pies are, as Stephen hopes, a satisfying combination of a rich crunchy pastry with a chunky textured moist clean-tasting filling, with a pricking peppery finish. Baked freshly every day in 450 and 900 g (1 and 2 lb) sizes, they can be sent by overnight courier for delivery mid-morning the next day.

The small shop is also the sole producer of the Melton Hunt cake. Apparently, in 1854 John Dickinson started making the cake for the members of the Melton Hunt as the custom was to have a slice at the Meet with a 'stirrup cup' or a glass of sherry before the off. Still using the same recipe, it makes for a good old-fashioned slightly crusty-topped cake that is certainly very fortifying – they probably needed it if they were hunting all day. Made with sultanas, currants, flour, sugar, butter, eggs, orange and lemon peel, cherries almonds and rum, it is sold as a 900 g (2 lb) cake or cut by weight from a block. They also produce various breads and biscuits and Christmas puddings.

And also...

• *David North*, 289 Station Road, Rothley (tel 0533 302263) runs a well-stocked shop with a good range of British cheeses, Ye Olde Pork Pie Shoppe pies (see page 147) and pies and dishes cooked by local ladies. Son Dominic trained with top *pâtissier* Michael Nadell and has returned to create his own mousses, *gâteaux* and cakes in the basement kitchen. Try his *tarte au citron* or French apple tart, made with fresh Bramleys.
• *J.E. Martin* ⊠, 4 Church Street, Market Harborough (tel 0858 462751, fax 0858 434544) stock around 36 varieties of seed potatoes many of them old-fashioned. Two earlies that connoisseurs go for are the pale yellow, floury fleshed Duke of York, ideally suited for baking; and the white Ulster Chieftain, with a pronounced earthiness, that roasts like a dream.

LINCOLNSHIRE

BELVOIR   MAP 5

Belvoir Fruit Farms ⊠ 🚜 ☕ 🌱   Fruit Cordials

Belvoir, Grantham, Lincolnshire NG32 1PB

TEL *0476 870286* CONTACT *Lord John Manners* HOURS *end-June to end-Aug 10.00-20.00* DIRECTIONS *From Grantham, take A52 towards Nottingham. After about 6½ miles, turn left off the Bottesford by-pass signposted Harby/Belvoir Castle. Drive 2 miles and then turn left at the cross-roads, signposted Belvoir Castle. After ½ mile, turn left into the fruit farm at the signpost.*

The 40-acre Belvoir Fruit Farms are in the fertile vale of Belvoir, overlooked by the spectacular Belvoir Castle. During the summer, about 5-6 acres are open to the public for pick-your-own and ready-picked fruit. Here you will find the usual soft fruit, such as strawberries, raspberries, blackcurrants, redcurrants, tayberries and gooseberries.

Castle apart, however, it is for their elegant fresh fruit cordials that Belvoir is best known. Made from fresh fruit, the range now includes blackcurrant, strawberry, raspberry, strawberry and raspberry mixed, lemon and bitter lemon. It all originally started with elderflower cordial, which Lord John Manners used to make on a small scale every summer in his kitchen for home consumption. When he saw that his entire store of bottles had been drunk by October, he realized he was on to a good thing.

The scale of the operation may have increased, but the method of production has remained virtually the same. Now he makes 100,000 bottles a year and has his own elderflower plantation on the estate. For the other fruits, whenever possible Lord John uses own-grown fruit. Elderflowers are picked by hand so as not to bruise them and, for the fullest possible bouquet, they are milled and pressed within 3 hours of picking. The juice is immediately filtered, mixed with sugar and bottled. Each of the fruit cordials contains the juice of nearly 900 g (2 lb) of fruit per bottle (with glucose to heighten the flavour further) and they have a startlingly strong fruity flavour. Lemon is made with the rind for that old-fashioned flavour and raspberry has a dash of lemon juice to lift the flavour of the fruit. Like – I suspect – Lord John, my favourite is still the original elderflower, with its muzzy-fuzzy, hazy taste that reminds me of ripe sweet summers.

Widely distributed throughout the country, you can also buy the cordials by mail order or from the fruit farm. When diluted with water, you will probably get about 20 glasses from the 74 cl (1$\frac{1}{4}$ pt) bottle.

CHAPEL ST LEONARDS

MAP 5

Thistledoons ✉ ▦

CARDOONS

Square Bays, Chapel St Leonards, Lincolnshire PE24 5TZ

TEL & FAX *0754 72396* CONTACT *Stephan Colback – telephone ahead in season (July to Christmas)*

'Cardoons, what are they?'... is most people's reaction when I mention the vegetable. If I then go on to explain that, although closely related to the globe artichoke, we eat their leaf stalks rather than the thistly heads, they invariably respond with a 'But surely they're not grown here?'

With a texture similar to celery and a sharp lemony taste rather like chicory, cardoons must rank as one of our great forgotten vegetables. They are grown here and, indeed, have been since Victorian times. Old cookery and gardening books are littered with references to them: *Cassell's Dictionary of Cookery* (1890) has at least 3 recipes and W. Taylor writing in *The Journal of Horticulture* in 1874 considers them an important crop, particularly 'where there is a French chef'.

Kate O'Meara owns and runs **Comestibles** ✉ at **82 Bailgate, Lincoln, LN1 3AR (tel 0522 520010)**. A well-stocked delicatessen, it makes a feature of its breads: the recipes are thought up by Kate and baked by a local baker. There are flavours like walnut and rye, rosemary and olive oil; but a prize for originality should be awarded to the Marmite bread. Looking rather like a Swiss roll, it is made with rolled-up brown and white dough lightly spread with Marmite. Tasting rather milder than I expected, but with a lasting tang, it could be rather interesting with a warming thick vegetable soup on a cold winter's night.

Kate stocks Derek Myer's Plum Bread (see page 153), juicy pork seasoned with sage sausages from Mountains in Boston, and a changing choice of Stiltons. The day I visited, there was a moist creamy Cropwell Bishop (see page 197) and a pappy and disappointing Long Clawson.

There are now two small cheese-makers in Lincolnshire and Kate sells both their cheeses. Janet Pauley of New York makes Easter Dawn: named after her first goat, it is sold as mild, matured for 2-3 months, or stronger, matured for 5-6 months. It is similar in style to a Havarti, but with a milder and mellower tang. Simon Jones of Ulceby Cross, near Louth makes Lincolnshire Poacher, an unpasteurized Cheddar-style cheese that has a good nuttiness and a splendid length of flavour. Relatively new to cheese-making, he only started last year, and his cheeses are best eaten while still quite young, at around 6 months.

Inevitably the French, Spanish and Italians value cardoons, they have hundreds of ways of cooking them, from braising to sautéing, frying and stewing. In Italy they are even eaten raw with *bagna cauda*, that glorious warm dip made with anchovies, garlic and olive oil. From September through to Christmas, the long pale ivory-green stalks, punctuated with leafy prickles and trimmed of their floppy silver-grey leaves, are tied up in overflowing bunches and sold on several market stalls. Venice, Bologna, Lyons and Rennes – wherever and whenever I see them, I snap them up and smuggle them home to serve to my unsuspecting friends.

Cardoons are quite time-consuming to grow. Each plant has to be blanched to remove its overwhelming bitterness. This is done early in the season by drawing the leaves together, tying them up in a bundle, and either wrapping the stalks in brown paper or banking them up with soil. If the Continentals can be bothered, why can't we?

But all is not lost… Almost single-handedly, Clarissa Dickson Wright (see Books for Cooks, page 163) has spearheaded a cardoon revival. About 4 years ago she persuaded friend Stephan Colback to grow them on his small-holding by the sea – ideal conditions with light sandy soil and frost-free climate. This autumn he produces his fourth commercial crop, although he is still experimenting with varieties. 'There are 5 Italian, one Spanish, a Giant American and a French. It's meant to have the best flavour, but it's most villainous thorn-wise. You have to wear gloves to handle it.'

Simple enough to prepare, you separate the heart and stalks, strip the stalks to get rid of any stringy fibres and prickles, and cut them into suitable lengths. Then parboil them in acidulated salted water for about 15 minutes, refresh in cold water and finally cook them by whatever method the recipe stipulates; a total cooking time of about 30-40 minutes is all you need.

Stephan will send freshly cut cardoons (stripped of their thorns) anywhere in the country. Last year I served them on Christmas day: they were splendid, tart and juicy, they set off the roast goose a treat.

---

*Lincolnshire sausages are traditionally made with quite coarsely chopped pork seasoned with sage. All over the county are various butchers who still make their own. F. C. Phipps (see page 154) make theirs with 90% meat and fresh sage and I can heartily recommend them. Michael Paske always buys his from **Cardy Tilley** at **Jomar, Honnington (tel 0400 50211)**. Others that have a good reputation are **Bycrofts** of **37 Wormgate, Boston (tel 0205 362625)** and **Parkinsons** of **6 West Street, Crowland (tel 0733 210233)**.*

CROXTON KERRIAL   MAP 5

G.B. Geese ✉ 🛒 ☕   GEESE

Lings View Farm, Croxton Kerrial, Grantham, Lincolnshire NG32 1QP

TEL *0476 870394*   CONTACT *Ann Botterill – telephone for details (end-Sept to 23rd Dec)*

Lings View Farm is mainly arable (growing winter wheat, beans and barley, spring oats, roots and kale) and grassland (stocked with ewes and lambs). As they have the grassland and their own feed, it made sense for the Botterills to diversify into geese about 5 years ago. Now they produce somewhere in the region of 2,000 birds for Michaelmas and Christmas. Rearing the birds must run in the family blood, as Ann Botterill is the sister of Judy Goodman (see page 282).

Bought in as day-old goslings from May onwards, once they are old enough they are let out to graze on the grassland. They are mainly fed own-grown wheat and oats, 'as the rest is grass, although they may have some potatoes'. This year the Botterills are trying a new bird, the Wessex goose: a Danish cross, it promises a smaller, lighter bird (something that, apparently, 'townies prefer') with a good meat-to-carcass ratio.

Killed on-farm at any age between 18-26 weeks, the geese are hung for 10 days and are sold from Michaelmas onwards as long-legged (plucked but undrawn), weighing from 5.5-10 kg (12-22 lb), or oven-ready weighing 4.5-6.3 kg (10-14 lb). The oven-ready birds, complete with giblets and a wodge of goose fat, come neatly trussed and dressed.

Once game is in season, Ann Botterill also sells a splendid boned goose stuffed with a boned chicken stuffed with a boned pheasant. Be warned, however, if you want one for Christmas you will have to order it during October or November and freeze it. From December onwards Ann is far too busy processing the orders even to think of preparing the birds as she tells me, 'it is very labour-intensive, and we just don't have the time'.

They also rear Bronze turkeys for Christmas and during the summer they are open for pick-your-own strawberries, raspberries and gooseberries.

HONINGTON   MAP 5

Michael Paske Farms ⊠ ▦   SEAKALE & ASPARAGUS

The Estate Office, Honington, Grantham, Lincolnshire NG32 2PG

TEL *0400 50449* FAX *0400 50204* CONTACT *Michael Paske – telephone ahead*

Seakale (*Crambe maritima*) is a native perennial vegetable found on coastal sands, shingle, rock and cliffs around the British Isles. For centuries its young shoots, naturally blanched by growing through the banks of sand and shingle, were gathered from the wild. Even the Romans were supposed to have eaten them, although it was not until the beginning of the 19th century that the plant was brought into cultivation.

Growing seakale proved a challenge to the gardeners of that time as, unless blanched, the tiny shoots are rather too bitter to eat. Shirley Hibberd writing in *Profitable Gardening* (1860) writes how, some time in December 'but not too soon, when the foot-stalks of the leaves have fairly separated themselves from the crown of the plants, heap over each a quarter of a peck of sea-sand or wood ashes...Then earth up the plants from a trench dug along the space between the rows exactly as if you were earthing up celery...The earth should be heaped up till it is about two feet above the crowns of the plants and then flattened down with the back of a spade, and the whole made very smooth and neat...In the spring when the shoots begin to push though, large cracks will be seen in the bank of mould, and a trial may be made with a trowel, as soon as they are supposed to be sufficiently advanced for cutting'.

Gardeners would time the planting to provide a succession of the delicate white shoots which were cut at a length of 15-23 cm (6-9 in). They could also be transplanted into forcing sheds and grown under specially made forcing pots. I discovered a fine example, an illustration of 'Pascall's Patent Sea-Kale Pot; a convenient means of indoor forcing'.

For a while, seakale was all the rage; but by the end of the last century, what with the difficulties of growing it and the expense of pots, manure and labour, it had fallen out of fashion. Anyway, by then demand was for headier, lusher and more exotic fruit and vegetables introduced from the tropics.

It is only in the past couple of years that seakale has become commercially available once again and we have the Paske family to thank. The wonderfully delicate flavour of the shoots was a great favourite of Mr Paske Senior but it was impossible to find. So he gathered seed heads from Dungeness and started to breed seakale selectively. The result is the Sauvage variety that, as its name implies, comes from wild stock.

His son Michael now cultivates 28 acres of seakale (he supplies Waitrose). He transplants the crowns into an inert compost in forcing sheds and harvests when the shoots are about 23.5 cm ($9\frac{1}{2}$ in) long. This year he plans to extend its season to start in early February right through to September.

> ### PREPARING SEAKALE
> Rinse the seakale well, as gritty particles can remain obstinately in the grooves. Trim off any earthy stalk. The young tender leaves can either be left on, or cut off and used in a salad. Re-tie the seakale into one or several bundles for cooking. Put them in boiling water on their side, and cover the pan. When the stalks are tender, drain the bundles well. Victorian cooks served them on folded napkins or pieces of toast to catch the last moisture, but this is unnecessary. Sauces that go with asparagus also go with seakale, from plain melted butter flavoured with lemon juice to a béchamel sauce with plenty of cream or a hollandaise. (From Jane Grigson's *Vegetables*)

Tender and juicy, the pale cream shoots of seakale look like small inner sticks of celery taken from the heart. Their taste is mild and dainty, similar to an asparagus but without the grassy sharpness. Michael sends seakale out in 500 g (1 lb 2 oz) trays or 5 kg (11 lb) boxes. If you want to try growing and forcing it yourself, he can also supply you with thongs (plants).

He also sends out asparagus, guaranteed harvested and posted the same day. This comes in either 1 or 5 kg ($2\frac{1}{4}$ or 11 lb) bundles, in three grades of size: the big fat jumbo (about 20 per kilo/$2\frac{1}{4}$ lb); selected (about 30 per kilo/$2\frac{1}{4}$ lb); and the thinner selected (about 40 per kilo/$2\frac{1}{4}$ lb).

HORNCASTLE   **MAP 5**

Derek Myers & Sons ✉ ♟

LINCOLNSHIRE PLUM BREAD

20 Bull Ring, Horncastle, Lincolnshire LN9 5HU

TEL *0507 522234* **CONTACT** *Richard Myers* **HOURS** *Mon-Sat 9.00-17.00 (-13.00 Wed)* **DIRECTIONS** *In town centre.*

Elizabeth David writes in her *English Bread and Yeast Cookery* that 'In no branch of English cookery is there a richer variety of recipes than in the making of cakes, scones and bread; it is of extraordinary interest to discover how large a proportion of these recipes is for yeast-leavened spice cakes and bread...in households where bread was no longer made, dough was bought from the baker and used as a basis in which to incorporate the dried fruit, butter or lard, sugar and spice. Other households, where there was no bread oven, or where the fuel to heat it was too expensive, managed things the other way round, and took their fruit and spices to the dough.'

From all over the country come variations of fruit bread recipes and, as she points out, 'when dealing with the old recipes it is sometimes difficult to make the modern distinction between bread and cake, proportions in the old formulas very often producing something between the two.' Richard Myers makes his plum bread according to his grandfather's recipe, and very good it is too. Ask anyone in Lincolnshire who makes the best plum bread in the county and they will invariably send you off to Horncastle.

His ingredients – plain flour, 3 different fats (lard and 2 shortenings), sultanas, currants, mixed peel, mixed spices, white and brown sugar, eggs, yeast, salt and water – are pretty straightforward and probably common to most plum breads. However, that from Richard Myers is streets ahead. Whether it is the blend of fats, the quality or quantity of fruit, or the fact that it is proved twice (once in the mixing bowl and then again in the tins), I really can't say. I do know that it is gloriously moist, rich and fruity, delicately hinting of spice, with a flaky texture and a clean aftertaste. So many others I tried are dry, stick in the throat or, worse still, leave an unfortunate coating of fat clinging to the palate.

With a shelf-life of 2 to 3 weeks, plum bread should be kept well wrapped in a cool place. Richard will post it anywhere in the country and prefers to send it out in batches of a minimum of 3 loaves. Try it, as he suggests, with a chunk of sharp cheese, and when it begins to dry out it can easily be revived by toasting.

MAREHAM-LE-FEN   MAP 5

F.C. Phipps ✉ 🦪   Lincolnshire Stuffed Chine

Osborne House, Mareham-Le-Fen, Boston, Lincolnshire PE22 7RW

TEL *0507 568235* **CONTACT** *Eric Phipps* **HOURS** *Mon-Fri 8.00-17.00 (-13.00 Wed) Sat 8.00-16.00* **DIRECTIONS** *From Boston, take B1183 towards Horncastle. At Revesby turn left on to A155, signposted Mareham-Le-Fen. Drive through the village and shop is on the left.*

Butcher Eric Phipps is a stickler for high standards. He buys meat on the hoof from local farms, slaughters it in his own impeccable slaughterhouse, hangs it and then from it prepares his own first-rate hams, sausages, pies and Lincolnshire stuffed chine.

Lincolnshire stuffed chine is a local speciality. The part of the pig used comes from the complete forequarters (fore-rib) and is butchered from the spine in the centre with 7.5-10 cm (3-4 in) of shoulder muscle still attached on either side. First it is cured for a fortnight in a brine based on an old recipe from Revesby Abbey made up from salt, saltpetre, sugar, black treacle, juniper berries and beer. It is then dry-cured in salt for another week. Once cured, it is cut at intervals at a right angle to the spine and the resulting pockets are ready for the stuffing.

Originally a springtime dish, according to Mr Phipps, 'all sorts of greenery was used for the stuffing – nettles, chives, sage, raspberry or blackcurrant leaves – I have come across recipes for them all. But it's best made with fresh chopped parsley and although some people do add a bit of sage, I like it best with only parsley. I use masses of it, some of my customers even bring some in for me and we barter. I give them some chine in return.' After being stuffed, the chine is then slowly cooked for hours, cooled and cut in thin slices across the bone.

It is certainly a local speciality worth preserving. It looks splendid – long slices of a rich pink meat studded with seams of deep green – and it tastes quite superb: pungent meat with a slightly gelatinous texture punched with mildly bitter herbs. Eaten cold with a strong mustard and a few drops of vinegar (one customer rather eccentrically eats his with vinegar sprinkled with brown sugar), Mr Phipps thinks it is the nearest English equivalent to the French *jambon persillé*.

Now you would think that a butcher as dedicated as Mr Phipps would get all the help and the encouragement he needs. His standards are high, his premises are immaculate and his commitment to local produce and local culinary traditions unquestionable. However, the reverse proved to be the case: an EC edict was issued (apparently) stating that the pig's spine had to be split right down the middle to avoid any possibility of disease, thus making the cut essential for stuffed chine illegal and putting its continuing production under threat.

Quite rightly, Mr Phipps was incensed. There was no need for it, as any infection can easily be detected at the 6th or 7th rib, where the chine is taken out. Already feeling swamped by petty regulations (every slaughterhouse now has to pay for a vet to stand by), he geared himself into action and – enlisting the help of his local MP – bombarded MAFF with protests. The result, you will be relieved to hear, was a total

Two other butchers in the county also sell their own Lincolnshire Stuffed Chine: A.W. Curtis have branches all over the country, with their main shop at 164 High Street, Lincoln (tel 0522 5272212), and Watkins & Son, 50 High Street, Grantham (tel 0476 63887).

climb-down by the Ministry. After months of to-ing and fro-ing and uncertainty, they have admitted to 'a mis-translation of the regulations' and Mr Phipps and his Lincolnshire stuffed chine are safe.

The whole episode is just another example of how EC bureaucracy is getting out of hand and MAFF's failure to address it is threatening the livelihood of so many of our small producers.

---

*In another life, before he became landlord of **The Red Lion Inn, Newton (tel 05297 256)**, Graham Watkin was a butcher. Now he combines both occupations successfully by curing and preparing a range of cold meats for his cold buffet. So, if you drop into his slightly over-modernized pub, you will be greeted with a fine display of salads, with own-cooked ham on the bone, crusty pies and the local speciality, Lincolnshire stuffed chine (see F.C. Phipps, page 154).*

STAMFORD   MAP 5

Les Fines Herbes ✉ 🏭

HERB JELLIES & VINEGARS, & GAME

8 St Mary's Hill, Stamford, Lincolnshire PE9 2DP

TEL 0780 57381 **CONTACT** Elinor Hawksley Beesley **HOURS** Mon-Sat 9.00-17.00 (-12.30 Thurs) **CARDS** Access, Visa **DIRECTIONS** In town centre.

At 8 St Mary's Hill is a gun-shop that doubles as a game dealer in autumn and winter. When it gets cooler, as you walk down the hill, you are bound to notice the game hanging outside the shop-front – and very Dickensian it looks. There is every sort of game, in fur or feather, from miles around: wild venison, red-legged and grey partridge, rabbits, hares, woodcock, the occasional snipe (this is not a good area for them), pheasant and pigeons, but no – definitely no – ducks.

Ducks are a sensitive issue. The shop is bang next to the river, where there are hundreds of ducks; and the children, after feeding them, would almost invariably burst into tears when they saw them hanging up, past all hope. So ducks are banned. However, if you want a mallard, widgeon, teal or diver (as mud-eaters, they are recommended for game pie only), you can get them from inside.

As if number 8 were not busy enough with guns and game, they also sell Les Fines Herbes range of herb jellies, vinegars, oils, mustards and seasonings. If you're wondering what the connection is, Elinor's husband is the gun-dealer and Elinor manufactures the herbal products from a cramped unit attached to the back of the shop.

The fruit, flower and herb vinegars come well presented in $\frac{1}{2}$ litre ($\frac{3}{4}$ pt) carafes, corked and wired like champagne. The base is distilled white malt vinegar and each one is made by soaking the fresh fruit, flower, or herb in the vinegar for several months. Some are more successful than others: rosemary was sharp and pungent; purple basil was mellow and delicately scented; raspberry had a mild fruity bouquet; and lavender a sweet floweriness. Her jellies, made with herbs, fruits or flowers, apple juice, sugar and vinegar are a semi-loose set with (mint excepting) no added colour. Rose petal had a strong fresh rosiness, lavender a warm headiness, elderflower a mere touch of muscat. The herb jellies, though, were less pleasing; they lacked a pungent freshness and were, perhaps, a little too sweet.

The salts are well flavoured. Hickory, imported from the USA, had that authentic woody flavour; gunpowder was hot and spicy; and garlic had a strong sweet flavour. Elinor also makes mustards in a range of flavours (Original Tewksbury, Spiced White Cambridge and Hot Black Lincolnshire) as well as spiced or herb-flavoured virgin olive oils. The range is plainly packed with charming labels that Elinor herself prints on an old-fashioned hand-operated printing press.

And Also...

• James Waterfield runs 2 mills in the county, *Five-Sailed Mill* in Alford and *The Maud Foster Mill* in Boston (tel 0205 352188). He supplies The South London Co-operative Bakery with their flour and pre-packs for Neal's Yard Wholefoods. You can also buy direct from the mills. His range includes a 100% wholemeal, 85% brown, untreated white flour, maize meal for polenta and a Dutch recipe pancake flour, which is mixed from wheat, buckwheat and rye flours and may be used for both pancakes and Yorkshire puddings.

• Using Lincolnshire carrots and flour from Maud Foster Mill, Barbara Battersby bakes a moist carrot cake at *Crossroads Cottage*, Eagle Road, Swinderby (tel 0522 868334). Sold throughout the area, you can also buy them at her stall in Newark Market on Wednesdays, Fridays and Saturdays.

• Relatively new to deer farming, Sheena Wesley sells assorted frozen cuts and joints of venison from her herd of Red deer at *Three Kings Farm*, Mareham Lane, Threekingham, near Sleaford (tel 0529 240555).

• *Special Edition Continental Chocolate* ⊠ Honeyholes Lane, Dunholme (tel 0673 860616) produce a range of moulded chocolates made with a German couverture. Particularly startling is the Lincoln Imp, with the proceeds going towards the fabric fund of Lincoln Cathedral.

LONDON

Choosing where a food lover should go in London is not easy – there are hundreds of shops, and everyone seems to have his or her favourite. As my *Food Lovers' Guide* is about British Food and British producers, I decided to leave out all the wonderful ethnic shops – be they Italian, Spanish, Greek, Chinese, Indian, Thai – on the grounds that they don't qualify (although I have to admit that the odd one has snuck in). I've tried to steer you through London's maze to places that are special or very good or just quixotic. As ever, if you think I've left any out please tell me. For more comprehensive guides you should read *Food Lovers' London* (no relation) by Jenny Linford and *The Gourmet's Guide to London* by Elaine Hallgarten and Linda Collister.

WI – WEST END

The kitchens at **Villandry, 89 Marylebone High Street (tel 071 487 3816, fax 071 486 1370)** produce wonderful pâtés and terrines, sweet and savoury tarts and quiches, pizzas, biscuits and cakes for sale or for eating in the restaurant at the back of the shop. They sell a small but perfectly formed collection of prize British produce. There is Richard Woodall's bacon (see page 46), Joyce Molyneux's Christmas puddings (see page 63), smoked chicken and duck from Johnny Cooke-Hurle (see page 80), cheeses supplied by Neal's Yard Dairy as well as their crème fraîche (see page 164), Wendy Brandon's jams and preserves (see page 305), bread from & Clarke's (see page 160) and Innes (see page 234), and vegetables and salads from Appledore Salads (see page 126).

There are food halls in 2 of London's top stores in W1, **Selfridges** ✉, **400 Oxford Street, W1A 1AB (tel 071 629 1234, fax 071 491 1880)** and **Fortnum & Mason** ✉, **181 Piccadilly, W1A 1ER (tel 071 734 8040)**. Fortnum & Mason has the edge on period atmosphere but – teas apart – it is a wasted opportunity. It could – indeed should – be a showcase for the best of British: instead you find block Cheddar, wet ham, solid pies and indifferent jams. However you ought to go once, if only to admire the fittings and giggle at the forbidding salesmen. Selfridges, on the other hand, is all white tiles, glass and chrome, but can be relied on for a wide range of interesting fresh and processed foods. They make an effort to encourage and stock British speciality food producers and, browsing their shelves and counters, you will come across some nice surprises. They even sell Rocombe Farm-fresh Ice-cream (see page 65).

✗ *Chef Gary Rhodes has built a fine reputation for his 'modern British' cooking at* **The Greenhouse, 27a Hay's Mews, Mayfair (tel 071 409 1017).** *If dining there is out of the question, then content yourself with jars of his chutneys – sultry green tomato or refreshing and light grape. At Christmas, you can try one of his rich fruity and subtly spiced puddings. Just pop into the restaurant to buy them.*

Around the corner **The Dorchester** ✉ *at* **53 Park Lane, W1A 2HJ (tel 071 629 8888)** *sells from its gift shop a Christmas hamper that includes chocolate truffles, Christmas pudding or cake, jars of prunes and apricots in syrup prepared under the supervision of chef Willi Elsner in the kitchens. Executive chef Vaughan Archer of the* **London Hilton on Park Lane, 22 Park Lane (tel 071 493 8000)** *is a dab hand at bottling and pickling, and you can buy the fruits of his labour in the foyer of the hotel, together with heart-shaped cookies or rose petal Valentine cake for St Valentine's day. Chef/patron Stephen Bull of* **Stephen Bull** ✉, **5-7 Blandford Street, W1H 3AA (tel 071 486 9696)** *prepares indulgent hampers for Christmas. Up to a point, he is prepared to vary the contents, as everything is made in the kitchens. Apart from champagne and bottles of wine, they contain jars of his own-made chutneys and relishes, marinated olives, freshly baked oatcakes to go with the cheese, lemon shortbread and a box of his chocolates. If you still can't book a table at* **Quaglino's, 16 Bury St, (tel 071 930 6767)** *console yourself with a box of dark or white chocolate truffles (containing glucose) made in the kitchen by chef Martin Webb and on sale in the shop.*

And Also...

• **Biggles** at 66 Marylebone Lane (tel 071 224 5937) makes sausages and only sausages – at last count the different varieties numbered 60. Some are pretty straightforward; others, such as Scottish mutton, barley and whiskey, sound a trifle eccentric.

• Fishmongers, **Richards** at 21 Brewer Street (tel 071 437 1358) have a good selection of wet fish and shellfish and do a roaring trade, so their fish can be relied on for freshness.

• **Wholefood** at 24 Paddington Street (tel 071 935 3924) with **Wholefood Butchers** down the road at number 31 Paddington Street (tel 071 486 1390) have a wide selection of organically produced (to the varying approved standards) fresh and processed foods, meat and poultry. They also have an interesting list of books on the subject of health and organic farming.

• In winter the shop-front of specialist game-dealer **R. Allen & Co** at 117 Mount Street, Mayfair (tel 071 499 5831) is decked out with fur and feather. Lamb, another speciality, is always English and hung for at least 1 week.

W4 – ACTON

For a tiny shop, **Mortimer & Bennett** ✉ at **33 Turnham Green Terrace, W4 1RG (tel 081 995 4145, fax 081 742 3068)** stocks an awful lot of interesting things. Dan Mortimer has organized a team of knowledgeable wild mushroom gatherers for the shop. Subject to the weather and the time of year, you can buy St George's mushrooms (traditionally found on April 23rd, St George's Day), parasols, giant puffballs, slippery Jack, penny bun, wood blewit, honey fungus and several more. When the frost kills off the mushrooms in this country, Dan and Di Bennett import them from abroad. They also sell a wide choice of breads from & Clarke's (see below) and Innes (see page 234), as well as the latter's salads, vegetables and cheese, La Fornaia *ciabatta* and French bread from Philippe Dadé, Fudges Bakery Dorset Cheddar wafers (see page 74), Duskin's apple juice (see page 131), Martin Pitt's eggs (see page 270), fresh pasta from Micarelli and Sabrizzi in Hereford, some interesting British cheeses including Harbourne and Beenleigh Blue (see page 67), and various cooked meats and pâtés.

W8 – KENSINGTON
& Clarke's 🏆   BREADS & TRUFFLES

122 Kensington Church Street, Notting Hill Gate, London W8 4BH

TEL *071 229 2190* **CONTACT** *Phillippa Grogan* **HOURS** *Mon-Fri 8.00-20.00 Sat 9.00-16.00* **CARDS** *Access, Visa, Mastercard*

Some of the liveliest food shops around the country are attached to a restaurant kitchen, and & Clarke's is no exception. Sally Clarke of Clarke's Restaurant fame opened the shop purely by chance, 'We bought the next-door premises to expand the restaurant into the basement. The shop space was designated for retail use only, so we thought 'let's use the shop to sell bread to the locals. A place to go to buy their daily loaf. Customers in the restaurant were always asking to buy bread or a box of our truffles – so why not'.

That was 5 years ago – the 'daily loaf' has burgeoned into a choice of 25, and they are now baked in an industrial unit alongside the Grand Union Canal but, Sally insists, 'are still the same as ever'. In various shapes and sizes, it is no ordinary loaf, but comes subtly mixed with different ingredients for variations of flavour, texture and colour. There is a cheery yellow cornbread; Cheddar from a milk, butter and cheese dough; apricot; hazelnut & raisins; sultana & sesame; green olive & herb; black olive; sun-dried tomato; walnut; buttermilk enriched with Normandy butter; pane Toscana with low salt, little yeast and 'no real flavour of its own so it's perfect for eating with strongly flavoured Italian food'; sour-dough; a 100% wholemeal that 'looks like a Hovis'. In the French line, there are *baguettes, ficelles*, plain and raisin & sugar brioche, and croissants.

Baker Didier Degaille uses a variety of flours, leaves the dough to rise twice and is very careful about how or when he adds the different ingredients to the bread. As Sally explained, 'In some cases you want the colour to leech – for example with the walnut bread, which goes a grey-brown; but for others, you don't. If you add the olives too soon, they get crushed; too late and their flavour doesn't permeate. So Didier will add them in two batches'. With a justified reputation for originality, I've long been a fan of & Clarke's bread. The texture is perhaps a little light, but the flavours are interesting and unexpected and it's fair to say that where they have led, others have followed.

Didier also makes the truffles at the unit. Deeply infused with bitter chocolate, they were originally made just for customers at the restaurant. Sally's recipe uses cream, eggs and chocolate, 'No butter as they've had enough during the meal'. Hand-rolled, hand-dipped and made in just the one flavour, 'plain – and the best', they are intense little bombs that fill the mouth with luscious richness. The restaurant kitchens still service the shop for the tarts, cakes, biscuits, pizzas and *focaccia* baked daily and brought up into the shop while still warm. They work on a 2-menu-a-week system, so if you want to order in advance you ring up to find out what is being cooked Monday to Wednesday or Thursday to Saturday. You will, however, always find packets of their nutty round and paper-thin oatmeal biscuits, ideal with cheese. From the kitchens also come an ever-varying choice of jams and pickles 'depending on the stress and strain of the kitchen and what's in season'. There is vivid red pepper purée, bottled onions, marmalade, pesto and olive paste or, at Christmas, a rumtopf (berries and apricots in alcohol). & Clarke's even make their own mustards: including Tewkesbury; stout; lemon & honey; and Roman, with pine-nuts and almonds.

They stock cheeses and yoghurts from Neal's Yard Dairy (see page 164), Innes cheese (see page 234), Duskin's apple juice (see page 131), vinegars from Womersley Crafts & Herbs (see page 301) and the occasional vegetable from Appledore Salads (see page 126), as well as an exceptionally good honey. In fact, everything is very good and appealingly displayed at & Clarke's; but then you would expect nothing less from a restaurateur as talented and meticulous as Sally Clarke.

W9 – LITTLE VENICE

The Realfood Store ⊠ at **14 Clifton Road, W9 1SS (tel & fax 071 266 1162)** offers a thoughtfully chosen range. They make a point of not selling anything with refined sugar, artificial colouring or flavours, but will sell anything they believe has been produced with integrity.

Consequently you will find Rocombe Farm Fresh Ice-cream (see page 65); Busses yoghurt from Sussex; cheeses from Neal's Yard Dairy (see page 164); Rachel's Dairy butter and cream (see page 308); Swaddles Green Farm meat (see page 219) to order; Wendy Brandon's jams, marmalades and preserves (see page 305); Packman Grey chutneys; various breads from &Clarke's (see page 160), Neal's Yard Bakery (see page 166) and a small German bakery in London; and fresh eggs and vegetables delivered by van from Devon and Cornwall.

Almost directly opposite is **Jefferson's Seafoods** at **17 Clifton Road (tel 071 266 0811)**. A plain smart shop, their fish is displayed on a bed of ice, so it is pert and fresh even on the hottest London summer day. They also cure their own mild gravlax with lashings of fresh dill.

W10 – LADBROKE GROVE

The Fresh Food Company ✉ and **The Fresh Fish Company** ✉ are both run by Thoby Young from **341A Ladbroke Grove, W10 6HA (tel & fax 081 969 0351)** as a delivery service throughout Britain. Thoby supplies fish from Cornwall in Catch of the Day or Prime Catch boxes (you can order specific fish but, I warn you, be specific otherwise you might be disappointed); Brogdale apples (see page 129); Wild Blue pork (see page 107); geese, turkeys and hams at Christmas; Colston Bassett Stilton (see page 195) and various teas, olive oils and other delicacies.

W11 – NOTTING HILL

C. Lidgate ✉ 🍖

110 Holland Park Avenue, Holland Park, London W11 4UA

TEL *071 727 8243* FAX *071 229 7160* CONTACT *David Lidgate* HOURS *Mon-Fri 7.30-18.00 Sat 7.30-17.00*

David Lidgate is the fourth generation in his family to run C. Lidgate, which first opened its doors in 1850. A man of vision, he leads the way in the butchery world; he was founding Chairman of the National Q Guild of Butchers ('Q' for quality) and his shop is regarded as the benchmark to which butchers aspire. What makes 'Lidgates' (as it is known) so unique – and here I should declare my interest, as it is my local butcher – is the attention to detail. The long narrow shop with its wooden front is satisfyingly 'old-fashioned', as are the standards of service. Customers wait patiently in a queue that often tumbles out into the street – last Christmas Eve it stretched right around the block; but no one seems to mind too much as it is worth the wait.

Scrupulous in his inspections of farms and slaughterhouses, David hand-picks and visits all his suppliers in his never-ending quest for the best possible quality meat. He sees quality as a chain in which every factor – from breed, feed, age of the beast and finish to the method of slaughter, conditions and age of hanging, and the art of butchering – must be taken into account. 'And every element in this chain must be right. It's no good buying organic meat if it's not well slaughtered or hung. For a good piece of meat everything must be right', he insists.

To that end, he buys grass-fed or organic lamb and beef, naturally and outdoor-reared pork free of antibiotics, growth promoters and animal residues. Poultry is free-range and reared slowly, and he was one of the first retail butchers to sell TFTA Bronze turkeys from Kelly Turkey Farms (see page 85). Meat is properly hung, lamb for about 7 days and beef for anything up to 3 weeks, and nothing is too much trouble, if you want a piece of meat specially butchered, boned or rolled, 'it's all part of the service'. More often than not, a small-scale bone for my small-scale dog is wrapped up in the parcel. After having been served so thoughtfully for all those years, it is natural that I should notice where other butchers fail. One thing that irritates me at other butchers is when, having bought a choice cut or finely shaved slices, they are bundled up in paper only to emerge squashed and bruised. This does not happen at Lidgates; everything is protected in a polystyrene tray and, although it means more packaging, the meat is the better for it.

Lidgates cook superb pies, sausages, sausage rolls, hams and quiches. They also bone and stuff with great expertise: try the noisettes of lamb, chicken breasts or chicken Kiev; and for ease of cooking there are always marinated cuts. In season, they sell game, ducks' and gulls' eggs; and they stock a fair selection of on-farm British cheeses, Martin Pitt eggs (see page 270), and various preserves and bottled sauces.

Neither a food producer nor food shop, **Books for Cooks** ⊠ at **4 Blenheim Crescent, W11 1NN (tel 071 221 1992)** is still a must for every food lover. It houses Britain's largest collection of food and wine books in print, with some useful second-hand ones for good measure. Managed by Clarissa Dickson Wright of cardoon fame (see Thistledoons, page 149), her encyclopaedic knowledge will unerringly guide you to the right book. There is almost nothing she cannot tell you about food, or any other subject come to that. The narrow shop is packed to the gunnels with books, it also serves lunches cooked to recipes from an ever-changing choice of cookery books, runs cookery classes in the kitchen upstairs, holds tastings and writers' signing sessions and is a font of food gossip. Drop in, you're almost bound to meet someone from the food world.

Under new management, **Tom's** at **226 Westbourne Grove (tel 071 221 8818)** looks as if it's on the up. There is plenty of own-cooked food-to-go, in the form of grilled vegetables, Puy lentil salad, grilled chicken with garlic and coriander; plus bought-in pizzas, *pissaladières* and individual tarts (the crab & fennel is excellent). Cheeses are mostly foreign, but you can buy bread from Innes (see page 234), fruit tarts from Michael Nadell (see page 173) and crème fraîche from Neal's Yard Dairy (see below).

And Also...

• Amongst the good own-made pâtés, terrines, *rillettes, soupe de poisson, pommes lyonnaise* and *pâtisserie* (their 'scrummy' *tartes brûlées* are particular favourites of my editor on this book, Lewis Esson), *Le Traiteur Français*, 142 Notting Hill Gate (tel 071 229 7185) also sells salad leaves from Innes (see page 234).

• On a Saturday, when the Portobello Market is in full swing, *Mr Christian's Delicatessen* at 11 Elgin Crescent (tel 071 229 0501, fax 071 221 1995) has a trestle table outside the shop laden with La Fornaia bread, smoked salmon & cream cheese bagels, *ciabatta* sarnies and hot coffee.

W12 – SHEPHERD'S BUSH

The Apple Man is Jonathan Pollitzer. From his shop at **114 Goldhawk Road (tel 081 749 9986)** he sells apples grown on his apple farm in Kent. During the year he has 14 varieties, including Laxton Superb, Ellison's Orange, Cox's, Spartan, Crispin, St Edmund and Egremont Russet, and James Grieve. The good news is that he also sells the small size at a bargain price, because no one seems to want them – I can't think why.

WC2 – COVENT GARDEN

Neal's Yard Dairy ✉ 🏬   ON-FARM CHEESES

17 Shorts Gardens, Covent Garden, London WC2H 9AT

TEL *071 379 7646* **FAX** *071 240 2442* **CONTACT** *Randolph Hodgson* **HOURS** *Mon-Sat 9.00-19.00 Sun 11.00-17.00* **CARDS** *Access, Visa, Mastercard, Eurocard, Switch*

As cheese enthusiasts in the '80s flocked to Patrick Rance's Wells Stores in Streatley (now closed), the '90s finds them at Neal's Yard Dairy. Run by Randolph Hodgson and Jane Scotter, it stocks a fine collection of on-farm cheeses gathered from, and only from, the British Isles.

A first visit has many a customer reeling with amazement at the variety of texture and taste of our indigenous cheeses – from a soft, ripe creamy Bonchester (see page 328) to a mature Mrs Kirkham's Lancashire (see page 142). Jane or Randolph only buy from the small-scale makers for whom cheese-making is still a craft; and, unlike most other cheese shops who use wholesalers, they always buys direct from the farm. This, Randolph feels, is terribly important; it enables him to build a relationship with the makers and so better understand their cheeses, to know when they are at their best and which to choose for a consistent quality. All this takes time, but then making or selling cheeses in peak condition is not something that can be hurried.

One of Randolph's great joys is the basement in their new shop (they have recently moved from Neal's Yard to Shorts Gardens around the corner). Stacked with something in the region of 900 cheeses, here he practises his alchemy: as an *affineur*, he ripens and matures the cheeses, bringing them to their peak in controlled conditions of temperature and humidity. It was Mrs Appleby, the supreme Cheshire-maker (see page 214) who first taught him the need of an *affineur*. Her cheeses are often sold too young without the chance to develop to their full potential, but Randolph will nurture them allowing them to flower fully. Not all cheese can – or indeed should – be ripened, but Randolph takes some that are traditionally eaten when young and transforms them to good effect. Try Chris Duckett's Caerphilly (see page 224): when young it is crumbly and sharp; when matured on by Randolph it acquires a subtle excellence – a deep firm richness – that is startling.

Almost all the cheeses sold at Neal's Yard are unpasteurized. 'When trying a new cheese, we try not to pre-judge them. Nor do we go looking for unpasteurized cheeses as such'. Randolph explained 'We select them on merit for texture and flavour. And it just so happens that the majority of the best cheeses are made with unpasteurized milk. It's because they have a greater depth of flavour – the same as the difference between stereo and mono. But that's not to say that there aren't any great pasteurized cheeses – a Colston Basset Stilton (see page 195) is one of the greats – or that all unpasteurized cheeses are good – some of them are terrible.' With around 60 cheeses in the shop made with cows', ewes' and goats' milk, Randolph numbers amongst his favourites, Mary Holbrook's goat (see page 9), Robin Congdon's Beenleigh Blue (see page 67) and the traditional territorials – the Lancashires, Cheshires, Cheddars, 'I still find it amazing that they can be so good when properly made. They don't compare with what most people eat. I get such a kick out of them'.

Years ago, cheeses were made at the Dairy when it was still in Neal's Yard. Now the cheese-making side has moved down to Ide Hill, near Sevenoaks, and is run by Charlie Westhead. From there he makes various soft unpasteurized cheeses: a light, markedly fresh fromage frais achieved by hanging the curds to drain then lightly whipping them; Wealden Round, a Coulommiers-style cheese layered with parsley and garlic, or chive, or tarragon, or spring onions, or black pepper & garlic; goats'-milk Perroche, a velvety fresh cheese with a delightful creamy texture and a delicate flavour of goat; thick crusty Greek-style and lighter low-fat yoghurts; and a proper crème fraîche made with rich double cream soured with a buttermilk starter. These, and the cheeses sold in the shop, are also wholesaled by Randolph. British cheeses are gaining popularity and admiration and this is due, in no small measure, to the sterling work of the entire team at Neal's Yard.

Neal's Yard was the brain-child of Nick Saunders; he developed the derelict warehouses around the triangular yard long before Covent Garden became the trendy place to hang out. At Number 6 is **Neal's Yard Bakery (tel 071 836 5199)** with a café upstairs. Bread baked on the premises is solid but good and includes a 100% wholemeal, a very cheesy cheese & herb, and three-seed. Just off the triangle is **Neal's Yard Wholefoods at 21-3 Shorts Gardens (tel 071 836 5151)**, with its amazing range of nuts, grains, pulses and seeds.

As you might expect from Priscilla and Antonio Carluccio's shop **Carluccio's, 28a Neal Street (tel 071 240 1487, fax 071 497 1361)** the accent is on Italian food and *funghi*. There is both fresh and dried pasta in various shapes and sizes, various freshly made sauces, ready-to-go meals appealingly presented in gleaming white dishes, salamis, sausages and Italian cheeses, own-made grissini that beat the packet kind hands-down, jars of pesto, preserved mushrooms and other Italian delights. Of course, there are also baskets of freshly picked wild mushrooms.

SW1 – KNIGHTSBRIDGE & BELGRAVIA

At first sight, the Food Halls at **Harrods** ✉, **Knightsbridge, SW1X 7XL (tel 071 730 1234)** take your breath away – there is just so much food. They claim to stock nearly 300 cheeses from all over the world, 130 breads, and goodness knows how many different cakes, hams, sausages, fresh fish or even smoked salmon. However, in spite of what Mr Fayed would like you to believe, not all of it is quite as top drawer as it could be.

You will, however, find some of our best British producers: cheeses are a strong point and the breads, in particular, are varied and interesting, although they do not specify the bakeries. Charcuterie tends to favour the foreign, but if you look carefully you will find some interesting British hams and pâtés. Food-to-go, in the form of canapés, sushi, pasta sauces, salads and pies, is of good quality and often imaginatively presented. Their fish display is famous; a work of food-montage-as-art, it is at times almost impossible to see for the hordes of tourists eager to be photographed beside it. If necessary, use your elbow power, as it would be a shame to miss the show. Game is nicely hung and dressed, as is the meat, with a choice of both traditional and

Continental butchering. English spring lamb at the start of the season is a real treat well worth the waiting.

You will be spoilt for choice at The Confectionary Hall, but I urge you to head for the **Gerard Ronay** counter. His chocolates may be among the most expensive, but they are very special indeed. Made with cream, butter and several different types of dark chocolate, they are truly innovative. Light in texture, but deep and long in piercing flavours, they come as intense silky confections of smoked lemon, raspberry, geranium, tea, red wine truffle, Calvados or gooseberry – to name but my favourites. Gerard does not sell direct, nor will he mail order; if you cannot get to Harrods, he can be contacted at 3 Warple Mews, Warple Way, W3 0RF (tel 081 743 0818) for details of other stockists around the country.

Harvey Nichols, Knightsbridge (tel 071 235 5000) opened their Julyan Wickham-designed food market, wine shop, restaurant and café last year. And what a stunning space it is, perched on the fifth floor of London's most stylish store. Much is made of their low-key design of own-label jams, preserves, teas and biscuits, but who actually makes for them, no one was prepared to reveal. Meat, wet fish and bread counters are very good, with an avowed policy to buy British as and when possible from the smaller producers. Less satisfactory are the cheese (too crowded) and deli (uninspired) counters, but I here tell that the management is working on them.

Paxton & Whitfield ✉, 93 Jermyn Street, SW1Y 6JE (tel 071 930 0259, fax 071 358 9556) have been cheese-mongers since 1797. With a shop-front that looks as if it has hardly changed in all those years, their cheese policy as explained by the relatively new proprietor Arthur Cunynghame 'is all-embracing, as we have block as well as farmhouse Cheddar – predominantly Mrs Montgomery's – and good natural artisan cheeses from here and the Continent'. Paxton & Whitfield has a reputation for well-kept Stilton: these tend to be selected from Cropwell Bishop (see page 197) which mature at an earlier age or the creamier Colston Bassett (see page 195). Although the business is based on 'sticking to the core of cheese', with Robin Congdon (see page 67) and John Curtis (see page 328) as two of Arthur's favourite British cheese-makers, they do sell various biscuits, including the suitably crested Duchy of Cornwall Originals, and York and Bradenham hams from Harris's (see page 292). They also run a monthly cheese club: members receive 4 cheeses a month, selected 'to ensure a variation of origin, texture, colour and flavour', as well as an efficient mail-order service.

Justin de Blank of **Justin de Blank**, at **42 Elizabeth Street, Belgravia (tel 071 730 0605)** has 'never pretended to run a Mother Earth British food shop', nor has he attempted to hide his preference for good French ingredients. Nevertheless, his own-made sausages are very British and very good, as are the fish-cakes, Parmesan shortbread and meringues ('made only with egg white and sugar', he proudly assured me). Justin has a reputation for discovering good indigenous products, then 'dropping them and moving on when the big boys take them up', and Miller Damsel wheat wafers must rate as one of his most successful discoveries. There are interesting plans in the pipeline to change the shop into 'an eatery', so you can buy and eat the cooked-on-the-premises food in the same place.

The last place you would probably think of buying an exceptionally light, fluffy and very creamy lemon curd is **The Lanesborough** at **Hyde Park Corner (tel 071 259 5599)**, one of London's newest and smartest hotels. However, head pastry chef Selwyn Stoby serves it at tea-time, or also sells it potted up in jars. He also sells his bitter-sweet Seville marmalade and Red Jam, made with equal amounts of strawberries and raspberries, and there are plans afoot to widen the choice, possibly even to include his vivid, refreshing orange-pink Pink Grapefruit marmalade. As everything is freshly made, to find out what is available and to place your order ring up and ask for the Conservatory desk.

And Also...

- *Rippon Cheese Stores* ✉ at 26 Upper Tachbrook Street, Pimlico (tel 071 931 0668, fax 071 828 2368) sell a wide range of on-farm and creamery-made cheese.
- *Boucherie Lamartine* ✉, 229 Ebury Street (tel 071 730 3037) is a very French-style *boucherie* with meat seam-butchered in the Continental manner. They also class themselves as *traiteur*, with pâtés, terrines and *pâtisserie* from the Roux brothers' kitchens.

SW3 – CHELSEA

From a *camionnette* (aka van – albeit a French one) parked in the courtyard of **Michelin House, 81 Fulham Road (tel 071 589 0864, fax 071 823 7148), Bibendum Crustacea** sell oysters (Native and Pacific), lobsters, langoustine, crabs, king and queenie scallops, prawns, brown shrimps, clams, whelks, winkles, cockles, mussels and Irish sea urchins. Quality and freshness are first class, as they are the same as served in both the Bibendum Restaurant and Oyster Bar. The small but stylish food department at **The Conran Shop (tel 071 589 7401)** in the same building stocks a wide range of Wendy Brandon's jams, marmalades and preserves (see page 305) as well as interesting imports and olive oils. Around the corner, **La Marée** at **76 Sloane Avenue (tel 071 589 8067)** has good wet fish.

Breakfast at **The Capital Hotel, Basil Street, Knightsbridge (tel 071 589 5171)** is a relaxed but stylish affair, with chef Philip Britten's gorgeously sharp marmalade containing the neatest slivers of peel I've ever seen and raspberry jam that comes packed with whole berries. Passers-by can buy them packed in glass preserving jars from the hotel.

And Also...

• Run by Chantal Cody, *Rococo Chocolates* ✉, 321 Kings Road, Chelsea (tel 071 352 5857) is well known for its witty chocolate novelties wrapped in garishly coloured silver foil. The jewellery collection is particularly decorative.
• Part of the St Quentin chain (there is a restaurant and a grill) *Les Specialités St Quentin*, 256 Brompton Road (tel 071 581 3511), with its own kitchens and pastry chefs, sells French-style breads and pastries, pâtés and a stunning *pièce montée* (French wedding cake made from a pyramid of choux buns) to order.
• From *Justin de Blank's Hygienic Bakery*, 46 Walton Street (tel 071 589 4734) you can buy a sturdy 100% wholemeal bread, as well as walnut, herb, cheese & onion, and olive breads.

SW4 – CLAPHAM

From her eponymous shop, **Pamela Price** at **26 The Pavement (tel 071 622 4051)** sells own-made salads and freezer meals, and a selection of well-chosen foods. Products to look out for are Rocombe Dairy ice-cream (see page 65), Richmond Park honey (see page 255), Womersley Hall vinegars (see page 301) and Gospel Green cheeses (see page 257).

SW7 – SOUTH KENSINGTON

Cheese-mongers **Jeroboams** ✉ at **24 Bute Street, South Kensington SW7 3EX (tel 071 225 2232)** and at **51 Elizabeth Street, SW1 (tel 071 823 5623)** have a wide selection of well-kept cheeses from Europe as well as the British Isles. The British lines include Mrs Appleby's Cheshire (see page 214), Caerphilly (see page 224), Colston Bassett Stilton (see page 195), Cornish Yarg (see page 38), Gospel Green (see page 257), Mendip Goat (see page 9), Spenwood (see page 14), Tala (see page 36) and Vulscombe (see page 56).

Fishmongers **John Nicholson** at **18 Bute Street (tel 071 584 3275)**, with a branch at **46 Devonshire Road, Chiswick W4 (tel 081 994 0809)**, smoke a variation on the traditional Finnan haddock. The backbone is removed before curing and the haddock is cold-smoked for a shorter time. Mild and nutty, with firm translucent flesh, it is best eaten raw.

SW8 – WANDSWORTH

Suppliers of excellent fruit and vegetables (some imported, some home-grown) to restaurateurs and caterers, **Hyams & Cockerton, 10 Southville, off the Wandsworth Road (tel 071 622 4349)** will supply the general public for special orders if you ring them in advance.

Condon Fishmongers at **363 Wandsworth Road, South Lambeth (tel 071 622 2934)** smoke salmon, haddock, cod's roe, mussels, mackerel, sprats, buckling (hot-smoked gutted and de-headed herring) in their traditional Edwardian brick smoke-house out back. They also have a good range of wet fish, and if you buy one of their fresh wild or farmed salmon or sea trout you can borrow one of the 18 fish kettles that Mr Condon thoughtfully keeps in stock.

For American-style loaf cakes, try **Ewing's Classic American Bakers** ✉ , **Unit 12, Sleaford Street, Nine Elms, SW8 5AB (tel 071 498 0550)**. Made with unbleached white flour, vegetable fat, fresh fruit and nuts, and a good deep chocolate, Scott Ewing bakes 10 different flavours, including date & walnut, cinnamon & maple, chocolate banana marble and their best seller carrot. The cakes weigh just over 900 g (2 lb) – American baking tin sizes are slightly different from ours – and will cut up into 12 generous slices.

SW11 – BATTERSEA

If you like your bread heavy and dense and made with organic (to Soil Association standards) flour, then the **South London Bakers Co-operative** at **219-221 Eversleigh Road (tel 071 228 1859)** is for you. They make 4 breads: a 100% stone-ground wholemeal with flour from Rushall Mill (see page 275), a 75% white, a wheat and rye, and a 4-grain (wheat, barley, oat and rye). They will sell direct from the bakery, deliver to you in London if your order warrants it; or if you ring them they can tell you your nearest stockist.

SW13 – BARNES

The Real Cheese Shop at **62 High Street, Barnes (081 878 6676)** with branches at **96a High Street, Wimbledon, SW19 (tel 081 947 0564)** and Morpeth in Northumberland (see page 195) has a nicely chosen range of British cheeses with, as you would expect, a fair selection of Northern cheeses, including Cotherstone and the range made by Mark Robertson of Redesdale Sheep Dairy (see page 192).

SW15 – ROEHAMPTON

Specializing in sausages, **St Marcus Fine Foods** ✉, **1 Rockingham Close, Roehampton, SW15 5RW (tel 081 878 1898)** is run by a proprietor who rejoices in the unlikely name of Emory St. Marcus. He makes *biltong* (that South African curiosity of strips of salted dried meat) and, also from South Africa, *Boerewors* (spiced fresh beef sausages). Sausages from nearer home include Lyonnais Truffles, a pork-based sausage with truffles, pistachio and brandy; and Wild Boar flavoured with herbs, white wine, vodka and 'exotic nuts'. As a member of the Aberdeen Angus Cattle Society, he is licensed to sell pure Aberdeen Angus beef, and he has also been known to sell ostrich steaks properly hung for a minimum of 2 weeks.

SW16 – STREATHAM

Lesley Chamberlain, author of *The Food and Cooking of Eastern Europe*, first introduced me to **Korona Delicatessen** ✉, **58 Streatham High Road, SW16 1BZ (tel 081 769 6647)**. A sound Polish deli, I have sneaked it into my list as every London food lover should know that it is a source of wild mushrooms gathered by knowing Poles from secret spots in Guildford and Wimbledon Common. There are necklaces of dried fungi threaded on string hanging by the till, jars of own-made mixed pickled mushrooms, earthy and pungent in vinegar. They make their own *pierogi*, or 'savoury pasta pockets' as Lesley calls them, stuffed with wild mushrooms and cabbage, cheese and potato, or meat, to be eaten with butter or *smetana*, a silky soured cream which they sell in cartons. As you'd expect, there were countless smoked sausages: boiling rings, slicing sausage, liver sausage, and farmer's sausage with a 100% meat content. They also sell a mild sauerkraut, made with white wine and caraway, and sour-dough bread from Kolos (see page 289).

SW18 – WANDSWORTH

Sara Jayne ✉   CHOCOLATE TRUFFLES

517 Old York Road, Wandsworth, London SW18 1TS

TEL *081 874 8500* FAX *081 874 8575* CONTACT *Sara Jayne – mail order only*

Sara Jayne's day job is running the Académie Culinaire, the association for Britain's serious chefs. However, evenings (and, at Christmas-time, nights too) find her making the most sublime of truffles. Unlike her rivals, Sara is avid to tell you how as she has had so much help and advice from the likes of the Roux brothers and John Huber, Senior Pastry Lecturer at Thames Valley College; she feels it is only proper and correct to pass it on.

The secrets of a truffle are the components of the ganache (centre) and the quality of the chocolate and the flavourings. Now every *chocolatier* has his or her way of making a ganache – some use butter and cream, some just butter, others use eggs and cream, or eggs and butter. Sara makes hers with just whipping cream and, of course, chocolate. She can see no advantage in using any other fats, as their flavour detracts from the purity and strength of the chocolate. So whipping cream it is and for every 575 ml (1 pt) of it she uses 900 g (2 lb) of best dark bitter couverture with a high cocoa solids content. The cream is gently heated in a saucepan, the chocolate broken up in pieces, added and generally fussed and stirred over until it is melted. Then it is left to cool and briefly whisked for lightness (again some *chocolatiers*, particularly the Belgians, will whisk their ganache for a long time as they like their truffles very light and airy). Next come the flavourings, and I have seen Sara pour into the ganache literally cupfuls of Tia Maria, or champagne, or Calvados, or brandy (apparently a rough brandy works better than a smooth old Cognac); there's no stinting with the flavourings here.

Then the truffles are either rolled out by hand or piped into her Venus Nipples. Some are rolled in cocoa powder or chopped nuts, others hand-dipped into yet more chocolate to give them a glossy hard coat and a delightful contrast of textures – the hard chocolate cracks as you bite into the truffle, giving way to a rich soft yielding centre. Like Sara's nature, but not – I hasten to add – her figure, the truffles are generous in every way. Lavish in size, these are at least three-bite chocolates, full in flavour and deeply rich and creamy. I could go on eating them for ever.

N1 – ISLINGTON

Pâtissier **Michael Nadell** supplies several top shops and restaurants from his pastry kitchen at **Units 4 & 5, Angel House, 9 White Lion Street (tel 071 833 2461)**. He will supply you directly if you order in advance and are prepared to collect your order. Particularly proud of his *Frutti à la Vanille* (a confection of sponge sandwiched with raspberry jam, vanilla mousse and available fruit), he also makes buttery croissants, chocolate indulgences, brioches, *clafoutis*, *truffe au chocolat*, glistening *tartes aux pommes* and *aux poires* and much, much more.

Jean-Baptiste Reynaud used to run Leith's – Prue Leith's restaurant in Notting Hill Gate. Now he owns **Victoria Plum, 30 Duncan Street, The Angel (tel 071 278 7515)** where he bakes good cakes, tarts and pastries. He also serves teas and coffees, as well as catering for private parties.

An articulate obliging gentleman, Steve Hatt of **Steve Hatt, 88-90 Essex Road (tel 071 226 3963)** seems to be every London-based cookery writer's favourite fishmonger. I'm not sure exactly why, other than that he does have a good range of fish and shellfish; it is good and fresh and he does buy knowingly.

N5 – HIGHBURY

With a shop at **7 Highbury Park (tel 071 226 2425) Frank Godfrey** is one of the few London butchers licensed to sell pure-bred Aberdeen Angus beef.

N10 – MUSWELL HILL

If you live in London and would like to have organic (to Soil Association standards) beef, pork or lamb delivered to your door on a Thursday or Friday, contact **Meat Matters** at **67 Woodland Rise (tel 081 442 0658)**. They also supply organic chicken, sausages and beefburgers (made from organic meat and dry-cured bacon).

NW1 – CAMDEN TOWN

I have Elaine Hallgarten and Linda Collister to thank for pointing me in the direction of **The Austrian Sausage Centre** at **10A Belmont Street (tel 071 267 3601, fax 071 482 4965)**. It both makes and imports a whole range of Austrian/German/Polish sausages that, unlike ours, are round, heavy and full. They can be divided into 3 categories: Bruhwurst, Rohwurst and Kochwurst. Bruhwurst are fresh, scalded sausages, with Frankfurters or Bratwurst as everyone's favourites. Rohwurst, cured, air-dried and/or smoked, are keeping sausages: usually made from finely minced pork, spare-rib bacon or beef, they are eaten sliced or sometimes spread on bread, if they are soft enough. Kochwurst, translates as 'cooked sausage' and that is exactly what they are: boiled or steamed liver sausages, or black and white puddings. If you are keen on 'foreign' sausages, you should go pay this place a visit.

Friend, Carol Ingram runs a very stylish B&B in Primrose Hill and buys her bread for breakfast from **Lou's Bakery** at **8 Ferdinand Street (tel 071 284 4644)**. She raves about the Four-seed.

NW3 – HAMPSTEAD

Ring **The English Cheesecake Co. (tel 071 586 3236)** in the morning to order a 15 or 20 cm (6 or 8 in) cheesecake and they will deliver within the Central London area by the next day. The base is made with crushed digestive biscuits and the baked filling from medium-fat curd cheese, eggs, sugar and vanilla essence. It is dense and quite sweet, and comes topped with sour cream.

NW5 – KENTISH TOWN

Bob Birchenall of **B&M Seafoods** at **258 Kentish Town Road, NW5 2AA (tel 071 485 0346)** is an ex-fisherman from Devon and most of the fish still comes from boats belonging to family and friends; and, as food writer Richard Ehrlich says, 'It's the best in town.'

Recently he also took over **Pure Meat Direct** ✉, the mail ordering side of the Pure Meat Company which reared meat to Conservation grade, following a strict animal welfare code and farming the land on a basis of low chemical input. Bob now runs a butchery from the same premises and sends Conservation-grade meat all over the country. In fact some of the meat is actually produced to organic (Soil Association approved) standards, but as the Soil Association standards are even stricter than Conservation-grade no one should mind too much about the confusion. If you do want to try Conservation-grade meat, at the moment the only place you can buy it is from Asda Stores. Meanwhile Pure Meat Direct sells a comprehensive range of meat, nicely butchered, including the Three-bird and Five-bird Roasts, and Eldon Blue pork (see page 107).

NW6 – SWISS COTTAGE

According to columnist and critic Nigella Lawson, 'there are fancier chocolates in fancier boxes, but those made by **Ackerman's** ✉, **9 Goldhurst Terrace, Swiss Cottage, NW6 3HX (tel 071 624 2742)** are the best. You may have eaten them unwittingly, for rumour has it that they come swathed in other famous labels. Truffles are infused with Irish whiskey and coffee, with marc de Champagne or rum, Cointreau, and Cognac. There are rose and violet creams, dark dense disks of bittermints, thin and brittle wafers of chocolate made by hand, and compelling cherries soaked in brandy for 2 years, thinly dipped in fondant and dipped again in chocolate so dark it's black.'

Gourmet Away at **3 Goldhurst Terrace (tel 071 625 8525)** specializes in freshly cooked oven-ready meals, conveniently packed in microwave-proof packs.

NW8 – ST JOHN'S WOOD

Panzer Delicatessen ✉, **13-19 Circus Road, St John's Wood, NW8 6PB (tel 071 722 8596)** is *the* place to buy smoked salmon in North-west London. Not only is there a choice of grades and quality, but to watch Alec carve it by hand with such ease and precision is to watch a true craftsman at work.

E1 – SPITALFIELDS

Elizabeth Taylor runs the **Organic Food Market** at the **Old Fruit & Veg Market, Spitalfields, Brushfields Street** on Sundays from 9.00-15.00. Stall-holders vary from week to week, but for further details she or John Cassidy can be contacted at **Organic Food Markets, 18th Floor, 2 Fore Street, EC2 (tel 071 625 8056)**.

Reputed to be the best in town, **The Bagel Bake** at **159 Brick Lane (tel 071 729 0616)** churns them out 24 hours a day, as they never close. Buy them plain or split and filled with smoked salmon and cream cheese or salt beef. While you're there, try the rye bread.

E2 – BETHNAL GREEN

Loaves and Fishes ✉ ▦

IRISH SODA BREAD

The Irish Brown Bread Company, Unit 3, Parmiter Industrial Estate, Parmiter Street, Bethnal Green, London E2 9HZ

TEL *081 983 0316* **CONTACT** *Margaret Joyce* **HOURS** *Mon-Fri 8.00-18.00*

'In Ireland', writes Clare Connery in *In an Irish Country Kitchen*, 'the traditional breads were designed to suit both the ingredients and the cooking facilities which were available. Owing to the country's climatic conditions, a soft wheat was grown, which was not suitable for making the yeast breads so popular in other countries. As a result Irish breads developed from using a soft wheat flour and the popular milk of the time, buttermilk, which raised or leavened the dough along with bicarbonate of soda...The soda, when mixed with the acids in the buttermilk, acts as a raising agent...The art of making soda bread is to handle the dough quickly and gently and to cook it at a high temperature. In fact the less you do to it, the better the bread'.

Originally from Galway, Margaret Joyce has always made Irish soda bread, but only started baking it commercially last September. It took her a good year's intensive research and baking before she felt she had got it right. Soda bread can be made with white or brown flour, or a mixture of the two in varying proportions; Margaret chose to use a 100% stone-ground flour. Finding the correct flour was a problem, she must have tried at least 40 before she struck on the right one. The difference, as she explained, 'is that flours here are too processed. Even if it's stone-ground, it has too much of the kernel ground down'. So she imports a flour from Ireland that fits her specifications as it is nuttier with more oil in the grain, resulting in a more moist bread. The supply of buttermilk proved to be another problem and it also is imported from Ireland.

Armed with the 'correct' ingredients, Margaret makes it by mixing the flour, buttermilk and bread soda together and baking it for 'a good hour'. The result is a good crusted loaf with a moist, dense – almost cakey – interior and warm nutty flavour that an Irish friend of mine pronounced, 'as good as any you'll find in Ireland'. Margaret has recently launched an Irish Fruit and Nut Soda, made with a slightly lighter soda mix but plenty of sultanas, raisins and almonds lightly spiced with cinnamon and nutmeg.

E9 – HACKNEY

One of the last salmon smokers left in London's East End is **H. Forman & Son** ✉, **6 Queen's Yard, Whitepost Lane, Hackney Wick, E9 5EN (tel 081 985 0378, fax 081 985 0180)**. Salmon with a London-smoke is traditionally milder-flavoured than that from Scotland and has a smoother silken texture. Mr Forman is very guarded about how it is achieved; all he would tell me is that two types of salt are used for the dry-salting, that less salt is used during the curing (which can take anything from 12 to 14 hours) and the fish are smoked for 4-8 hours, depending on their weight, over 'mainly oak'. They smoke both wild (frozen for use throughout the year) and farmed Scottish salmon, and 'in an emergency' the occasional farmed Norwegian salmon, and send it in slices as 450 g (1 lb) packs, 675 g ($1\frac{1}{2}$ lb) pre-sliced sides and 900 g (2 lb) whole sides.

E14 – DOCKLANDS

Billingsgate Fish Market, Trafalgar Way, Docklands (tel 071 987 1118, fax 071 987 0258) trades on Tuesday to Saturday from 5.00-8.30 and on Sundays (for a limited of selection of shellfish only) from 7.30-8.30. Primarily a wholesale fish market, the public are welcome, but not all of the 60-odd fish merchants will sell to you. Even if they will, be prepared to buy in quantity; you can buy a single whole lobster or salmon, but wet fish is generally sold by the stone, i.e. 6.4 kg (14 pounds).

EC4 – CITY

Ann Goberdhan at a wine bar called **The Wine Barrel** ✉, **13 St Brides Street, EC4A 4AS (tel 071 353 4500)** makes an unusual wine-based root vegetable chutney. Available as Original, or matured for at least a year as Vintage with port, or Reserve with extra spices, it has an interesting crunchy texture and a relatively punchy flavour.

SE10 – GREENWICH

O'Hagan's Sausage Shop 🍖   SAUSAGES

192 Trafalgar Road, Greenwich, London SE10 9TZ

TEL *081 858 2833*   CONTACT *Bill O'Hagan*   HOURS *Mon 8.30-16.00 Tues-Sat 8.30-17.30*

When it comes to sausages, there is no end to the inventiveness of Bill O'Hagan. He likes to think of them as 'designer' sausages. 'They're special. Exactly what you'd expect from a proper sausage, but usually don't get. Mine are made with real skins, natural seasonings, proper cuts of fresh meat and are hand-linked,' he told me proudly, 'nothing but the best'. With a meat content that varies between 75 and 100%, depending on the sausage, he only resorts to bread and rusk 'when necessary to bind the ingredients together – but never to bulk up'. It goes without saying that no offal, trimmings or any of the other unmentionable nasties such as MRM ('mechanically recovered meat') come anywhere near Bill's sausages.

As a sausage fanatic, Bill is forever on the look-out for new ideas and flavours. While researching in the Samuel Pepys Library in Cambridge, he came across Samuel Pepys' favourite sausage – made with pork and spinach. Other more exotic flights of fancy are Champagne Cocktails of pork, pink champagne, bread, free-range eggs and black mushrooms; there is even a smoked salmon sausage. Pork & Cabbage is a splendid mix of pork, red cabbage, apples and cider; Italian Summer sausage, a spicy blend of pork, green peppers, wine and chilli; Forum is 100% lamb with fresh coriander; and Tio Pepe comes as pork with green olives and sherry. The more traditional ones – Cumberland in one long link, a herby Oxford, Lincolnshire with sage – are not forgotten either. At last count there were somewhere in the range of 50 varieties, but not all of them are available fresh all the time; although you should be able to find them in the freezer.

Bill is very particular about how his sausages should be cooked, 'Treat our sausages with respect – cook them slowly and gently. As we only use natural skins, don't prick them and don't let them go too brown. Bake them in the oven on a slightly greased dish for 35-40 minutes at 180°C/350°F/gas 4'.

MERSEYSIDE

LIVERPOOL MAP 4

Croxteth Hall and Country Park 🍄 MUSHROOMS

Liverpool, Merseyside L12 0HB

TEL *051 228 5311* CONTACT *Ted Jackson* HOURS *Easter to end-Sept: 11.00-17.00* DIRECTIONS *From A580 Liverpool Ring Road, follow signs to Croxteth Hall.*

Croxteth Hall and Country Park, a 500-acre estate, was conveyed to the city of Liverpool in 1973 after the death of the seventh Earl of Sefton. Surrounded by modern housing estates, it is an oasis of calm and enchantment just outside the city centre.

For a food lover, its main attraction is the 2-acre Victorian walled garden full of curiosities. Look out for the flued walls that were built before glass-houses were fashionable and worked on a similar principle to a radiator. Constructed with hollow sections that conducted heat from fired boilers, once heated the wall was able to protect and nurture the more tender plants. Trained against them and free-standing in the garden are fruit trees as fans, espaliers, double-trunked espaliers, cordons and double cordons or goblets pruned to grow to all points of the compass. There is a fine example of a peach house, with several different varieties of peaches, nectarines and a Black Hamburg vine. There is also a large wooden melon pit sadly empty of melons, although there are plans to restore it to its original use. The Heritage Seed garden under the aegis of the HDRA (see page 265) produces some long-forgotten varieties of vegetables and, in the modern plot, you will find the more common ones.

In the far corner is the brick Edwardian mushroom house restored in 1984. The late Keith Chilton, estate manager at Croxteth, described its workings in The Royal Horticultural Society's magazine *The Garden*, 'The house is equipped with 4-inch thick hot-water pipes to provide heating for mushroom production during the winter months while a boarded double roof helps to maintain an even temperature all year round. The cropping beds are supported on an ornamental cast-iron framework with slate foundations and fronts. These are arranged in double tiers on each side of the wide central pathway of York stone and there is ample space between the bottom shelves in which to force early season vegetables such as chicory and rhubarb. Not surprisingly perhaps, a mushroom house built to grace the prestigious kitchen garden of the Earls of Sefton had to be the deluxe model of its day, so it was slightly larger than the standard version with several ornamental embellishments'.

When you visit, and I do urge you to go, you will see on one side of the house a display of the stages of mushroom growing in Edwardian times, and on the other mushrooms being grown using modern materials and techniques. It provides a fascinating insight into the world of mushrooms and is particularly interesting as generally, because of the required controlled environment, the public are never allowed into a mushroom house, so it is rare to see them grown. Afterwards you can taste the fruits of Croxteth, as all the produce is on sale from the gift shop.

MUSHROOM CAVIAR

Heat 1 tablespoon of olive oil in a sauté pan and cook 1 chopped onion until soft.

Whizz 350 g (12 oz) mushrooms in a food processor until very finely chopped.

Add to the pan, season and cook over a low heat for about 8 minutes, until the mushrooms are soft and creamy-textured.

remove the pan from the heat, stir in the juice of 1/2 lemon, 3 tablespoons of sour cream and chives, adjust the seasoning and chill for a couple of hours.

NORFOLK

W. D. Oram 🔳   ASPARAGUS

Old Hall Farm, Attlebridge, Norwich, Norfolk NR9 5TQ

TEL *0603 867317* CONTACT *Diane Oram* HOURS *end-Apr to mid-June: Mon-Fri 9.30-18.00 Sat-Sun 9.30-17.00* DIRECTIONS *From Norwich, take A1067 towards Fakenham. Pass through Taverham and, after about 1 mile at signpost to farm, turn left on to a rough road.*

Don't be surprised if, during asparagus season, you see a queue stretching from the Oram's garage right down the driveway. It is known as the place to buy asparagus. In fact, the Orams have only been growing for 5 years, but in that time they have firmly established their reputation for succulent spears. Their beds cover 4 acres of well-drained sandy soil on a south-facing slope, and everything is cut by hand on a daily basis and sold direct to the public – so it is exceptionally fresh.

The asparagus is also graded by hand. Everything they sell as grade 1 is tightly budded, with no hint of seed and no bending. Within this grade, they also separate the asparagus into short-thin, short-fat, short-medium, long-thin, long-fat and long-medium, so you can choose exactly the size and shape you want. They also sort for a grade 2 – a sort of mixed bag – that does work out a lot cheaper, but then not all the stalks are perfect. It can be good value as Mrs Oram reckons that for every 900 g (2 lb) you buy you'll probably get 450 g (1 lb) of the good stuff. Finally there is soup sprue, ie the pencil-thin asparagus or sprue that could also be starting to seed slightly but, as the name suggests, is exactly what you need for soup.

Cley Smokehouse ✉ 🔳   SMOKED FISH

Cley, Holt, Norfolk NR25 7RF

TEL *0263 740282* CONTACT *Mike Rhodes* HOURS *Apr to end-Oct: 9.00-18.00 Nov to end-Mar 9.00-17.00* DIRECTIONS *In the village.*

Cley-next-the-Sea is serious picture postcard land – a jumble of weather-board houses hugging a narrow high street. Among the tea and pottery shops, you'll find the Smokehouse. The shop is small and dark with a large refrigerated counter filled with fish products (Cley only sells fish). However, the actual smoking is all done in the back in a large brick smoke-chimney.

Everything is cold-smoked over oak sawdust and no dyes whatsoever are used. If there is a damp off-shore wind, the kippers can stay in the chimney for as long as 48 hours before they are ready, although 18 hours is the more usual time. This may be herring country, but the Rhodes find the local long-shore fish too small for curing so they tend to use frozen Norwegian ones. These are cleaned and cured and threaded on 'speats' for bloaters or split, cured and hung on tenterhooks for kippers. Their kippers are quite robust and Carla Phillips of The Moorings Restaurant (see below) describes the bloaters as 'quite beautiful'. I adored their cod's roe: round, plump and a shiny pale-orange, they were succulent and grainy textured with a good salty smoky taste. They also smoke wild salmon, mostly from the River Tay.

On sale in the shop, but not available by mail order, are a buttery and lightly spiced crab pâté, potted shrimps made from brown shrimps caught in the Wash, a sweet pickle herring made with meaty fillets that tasted a little on the sharp side, and a fresh herring roe pâté that was surprisingly smooth but could have been a little creamier. Do look out for the whitebait. It is caught in nets by a local fisherman off Blakeney Point and frozen within the hour. They often have it in bags in the freezer. ([m]Mail order between October and May only)

> ✗ **The Moorings Restaurant, Wells-next-the-Sea (tel 0328 710949)** is a snug restaurant just off the harbour. As you might hope, fresh locally caught fish is always on the menu and Bernard and Carla Phillips go out of their way to use local suppliers and growers. Carla holds forth in the kitchen, constantly changing the menu to fit the seasons and available produce, while Bernard runs front-of-house.

CROMER   MAP 5

Richard & Julie Davies ✗   CRABS

7 Garden Street, Cromer, Norfolk NR7 9HN

TEL *0263 512727* CONTACT *Julie Davies* HOURS *mid-Mar to mid-Oct: 8.30-17.30; mid-Oct to mid-Mar: Tues-Sat 8.30-17.30 (-13.00 Weds)* DIRECTIONS *In town centre.*

Cromer crabs have a certain reputation for being the best in Britain. If you ask the locals they will tell you that although smaller than Yorkshire or Cornwall crabs, theirs are definitely much meatier and sweeter. However, they probably will not be able to tell you why, although one plausible explanation is that the crabs feed on the particularly plankton-rich and clean chalk shelf near Cromer – a sort of leftover of the cliffs that have plunged into the sea.

Mr and Mrs Davies specialize in Cromer crabs. With their son, they run two small boats that work around the chalk shelf between March and September, when the sea warms up. They also run a larger boat catching off Wells-next-the-Sea that can supply them all year round. As

Mrs Davies admits, however, 'Crabs from there are probably larger and not quite as sweet'.

Their crabs are cooked daily; first they are submerged in cold fresh water and when they are sufficiently sleepy, they are scrubbed and plunged into boiling water and then scrubbed again. If they are wide awake when cooked they 'shoot off their claws', and that would never do. Mrs Davies has several girls at the back of the shop dressing the crabs and there are various ways of presenting them, although she favours separating the white and dark meat 'so you can see exactly what you're getting'.

They are very good – sparklingly flavoured, succulently fleshed and very rich indeed. The Davies sell both whole and dressed crabs and are happy to give you a bag of ice to keep them chilled on the way home. They also sell lobsters, King's Lynn shrimps, local herrings, smoked fish from Cley and a selection of fresh fish usually bought from Lowestoft.

You could also pop down the road to 10 Brook Street and buy a dressed crab from Buster an ex-fisherman who sells them from a chilled display hanging out of his front window. His is a much easier life now he no longer puts to sea but as he says, 'I spend more time picking over the crabs than I ever did catching them'.

From Cley to Brancaster is one coast where you can find plenty of good fresh fish and shellfish. There are several Pacific oyster farmers but possibly only 2 – **Christine Mullis, nr Brancaster (tel 0485 210652)** *and* **Andrew Athill, Morston (tel 0263 740306)** *– sell direct to the public. Christine should be telephoned first, but to visit Andrew turn off at the sign in the village of Morston, down a windy lane to his house on the coast and buy them straight out of the water. Margaret and Stephen Bocking run* **The Fish Shed, Brancaster Staithe (0485 210532)** *with another branch in Wells. There is also the splendid shop* **Gurneys, Burnham Market (tel 0328 738967)** *and their roadside hut in Brancaster. During the season, from May to September, you will always find bunches of freshly picked samphire (sea asparagus), crabs, lobsters, local brown shrimps and mussels. Both concerns also stock good fresh fish, such as grey mullet, Dover sole and local herring. There seems to be a fair bit of good-natured rivalry as to whose fish-cakes and potted crab are best.*

KING'S LYNN   MAP 5

Melanie Knibbs 🛒   JAMS & PRESERVES

St Nicholas, Bevis Way, King's Lynn, Norfolk PE30 3AG

TEL *0553 674703* CONTACT *Melanie Knibbs* HOURS *Thurs am at Fakenham Market; Sat at Swaffham Market* DIRECTIONS *Markets in town centres.*

Melanie Knibbs is one of the few commercial jam-makers whose produce can truly be described as home-made. She still makes it in her kitchen exactly as she did 12 years ago when she first went into business. It is not that home-made jam is necessarily better than commercially made jam, but the chances are that it may be.

Melanie makes hers in small 5.5 kg (12 lb) batches – she usually has 3 pans on the go – to keep a tight control on the quality, and prefers to boil the jams hard to get a set rather than add any commercial pectin. She makes 5 varieties of marmalades: a tart Seville; a rich Old English with dark sugar; a light Grapefruit; Trinity, a 3-fruit sweeter version, and a Ginger that she describes as 'pretty hot because people who like ginger like it that way'.

Melanie also produces jams that contain nothing but the fruit and sugar. There is Strawberry, Raspberry, Victoria Plum, Blackcurrant, Gooseberry, Damson, Blackberry & Apple, and Apricot. They are the good old-fashioned strong-flavoured jams with plenty of satisfying pieces of fruit. Melanie's chutneys are also very popular locally, as are the fruit jellies: Redcurrant, Gooseberry and Quince. These may not win prizes for their sparkling translucence, but they taste jolly good.

She also bakes an 18 cm (7 in) fruit cake, 'an everyday cake but richer than a Dundee' and Victoria Sponges, as well as various biscuits, shortbread and flapjacks that you can nibble at as you wander around the market stalls. With the exception of the lemon curd everything is made with vegetable products and that includes the mincemeat she sells at Christmas.

LETHERINGSETT   MAP 5

Letheringsett Watermill ✉ 🏪   FLOUR & BREAD

Riverside Road, Holt, Letheringsett, Norfolk NR25 7YD

TEL *0263 713153* CONTACT *Michael Thurlow* HOURS *Tues-Fri 9.00-13.00 & 14.00-17.00* DIRECTIONS *From Holt, take A148 towards Fakenham. After about 1 mile, follow the Watermill tourist signs to the left.*

Letheringsett Watermill is a forbidding red-brick building 4 storeys high. Set in its centre is the huge iron waterwheel constructed in 1802. This is powered by the river Glaven, with the water flow controlled by the lifting or lowering of external sluice gates. Most afternoons (except Mondays and Saturdays) from Whitsun to the end of August between 2.00 and 4.30, Michael Thurlow the miller gives formal demonstrations. At other times he is almost always on hand to chat to anyone who is interested.

On entering the mill, the first thing that you see is the shop. Frankly, it is a bit of a jumble, with pet foods predominating. That should not put you off, however, as the flour, according to Linda Collister in *The Bread Book*, is particularly good. The 100% stone-ground Conservation Grade flour is milled from Alexandria wheat. This is a pre-war variety that, as Linda says, 'has the best taste in the country. It's sweet, nutty, more intensely flavoured and, unlike many other wholemeal flours, it's never bitter. Michael grinds his quite coarse, but he's also happy to grind to your specifications. You can stick your hand underneath as the flour falls and, if you don't like the feel, he'll adjust it for you.' He also mills a softer French variety, Flanders, imported from France. This bakes up into a lighter-textured product, well suited for pastry and French bread.

Michael also sells fresh bread made with his own flour by a baker in Sherringham on a daily basis. It has a strong nutty taste but is surprisingly soft and light for a 100% loaf – possibly too much so.

On the way out, do stop and look over the vegetable stand. It is run by the villagers of Thornage Hall, the local Camphill Trust, and the produce is all grown to Demeter standards. There is the usual selection of seasonal produce, but it is topped up every day and it is satisfying to know your money is supporting a worthwhile cause.

Burnham Market is one of Norfolk's prettiest villages, with a large lozenge-shaped green and some very good shops. There is an interesting wine merchant, an excellent fishmonger and the bright and breezy **Humble Pie (tel 0328 738581)** *run by Sue Elston. The shop 'is here to make life easy for everyone. I sell prepared food from the freezer – casseroles, fish pies and the like – for people who don't like to cook and all sorts of ingredients – fiddly things like pine kernels and sun-dried tomatoes – for people who do'.*

There is a small but enviable cheese counter with about 30 cheeses that ring the changes throughout the year. Certain to find several British on-farm ones I noticed a large truckle of Keen's Cheddar (see page 229) and well-ripened Bonchester (see page 328). To go with the cheese, Sue sells bread made to her own recipes by a local baker. There is a 'chunk' honey complete with a section of comb from Wells, Broadland bacon from Norwich, a good selection of Melanie Knibbs preserves (see page 182), and raised pies by The Gingham Pantry of Fakenham.

Sue has a willing team of local ladies who bake shortbread, rock cakes, and traditional sponges with fillings of chocolate, coffee with walnut, and buttercream with jam. These are usually sold out by lunchtime. Then there are own-made salads and pâtés, interesting jars of own-pickled mushrooms, layered olives and preserved clementines. At Christmas, Sue sells own-made pudding and rich fruit cake.

With a stock that changes constantly, the shop is too small to have everything all the time. Sue admits it is a relief, as she would get bored if it was always the same, 'And if I get bored, then so will my customers'. A pleasant change from shopping in supermarkets, where the policy is everything has to be in supply every day of the year.

Bryan Pickering ✉ 🏭   SAUSAGES

30 The Street, Old Costessey, Norwich, Norfolk NR8 5DB

TEL 0603 742002 **CONTACT** Bryan Pickering **CARDS** Visa **HOURS** Mon-Sat
7.30-17.30 **DIRECTIONS** From Norwich, take A1074 (A47) towards King's
Lynn. Past Norwich ring road, turn right at second lights, signposted Old
Costessey. Turn right at The White Hart pub. Shop is 200 yards on right.

Bryan Pickering is, by his own admission, 'obsessed by what you can do
with meat', particularly as he thinks the day is not far off when most of
us will no longer be able to afford primary cuts. Unlike many of his
colleagues, he travels for inspiration. When he came back from the
United States he introduced soft hamburgers and he also tends to
Continental or 'seam' butchering, where there is far less wastage. All his
meat is well hung and from known local farmers.

There is, however, little in the shop in its raw natural state as he is far
more interested in 'servicing the consumer' by selling prepared end-
products. So there are pâtés and cooked cold cuts aplenty, including
natural, Virginia roast, German-style and Swiss peppered hams, as well
as roast beef, haslet, and ready-seasoned joints. 'Gourmet Specials' are
marinated and/or stuffed cuts, like pepper pork steaks and steak-burger
with Gouda cheese. The range is impressive, if a little overwhelming. So
I was happier focusing on Bryan's true obsession – sausages.

He makes around 52 varieties, although you are not likely to find
them on sale at one time. Everything is prepared in his processing rooms
at the back where he proudly showed me his expensive Continental
bowl-chop machine. This processes meat in 18 kg (40 lb) batches and
has the advantage of 'bringing out the natural binding in meat by its
chopping action'. Although Bryan claims his sausages have a good
texture, soft and flexible, I find them a little too finely minced.

They do have a high meat content – around 95% – made from good
cuts 'you can't hide inferior meat as the sausage will cook wrong'. He
uses natural skins (except collagen for the frankfurters) and small
amounts of preservatives. Look out for the regional sausages – I
particularly enjoyed Oxfordshire with fresh lemon, marjoram, sage and
thyme, Somerset with a hearty blend of pork and cider, and Yorkshire
with its pleasant aftertaste of cloves.

The Royal Fruit Farms 🍎   APPLES

Sandringham, King's Lynn, Norfolk P31 6EN

TEL 0553 772675 **CONTACT** Mr Benefer **HOURS** mid-September to about 3rd
week Oct: Mon-Sat 9.00-17.00 Sun 10.00-17.00 **DIRECTIONS** From King's
Lynn, take A149 to Hunstanton. Follow signs off to the right to fruit farm.

The thought of eating the very same apples as the Queen is immensely appealing although, as Freddie Benefer the Fruit Farm manager points out, 'People may come for the first time because it is The Royal Fruit Farm but they come back a second time because they get a bargain'. According to Mr Benefer, growing apples in Norfolk has certain advantages as 'you may not get the tonnes that you would in Kent but you get a much harder-textured and crisp Cox from the chalky soil'.

There are 60 acres of orchards about 2 miles from Sandringham House – but no, you won't see either the Queen picking-her-own or the House. Nor are you likely to see Prince Charles, as this is one orchard that must go against the grain because the apples are conventionally grown (a polite way of saying sprayed) and, unlike his rare collection at Highgrove, only commercial varieties are cultivated. The PYO season starts around the middle of September, but do check ahead by ringing the estate office during working hours (see above) or Mr Benefer on 0485 541128 after office hours.

For the first week there are Worcester Pearmain; Laxton's Fortune for the second; Cox's for the third, and Cox's and Bramley for the fourth. It is very much pick-your-own – and you will be given a smart heavy-duty plastic bag for your fruit – with no tree out of arm's reach. They do, however, sell Howgate Wonder bagged in 9 kg (20 lb) bags from the back of a trailer. During the height of the soft-fruit season you can also pick strawberries and raspberries.

> *During daylight hours between August and mid-October, you are unlikely to find Peter Jordan, landlord of the **Lord Nelson** pub, **Burnham Market** (tel 0328 738321), much in evidence. He's far more likely to be pursuing his passion for wild mushrooms. Do drop in anyway and try some of their wild mushroom dishes. There's wild mushroom soup, chicken stuffed with wild mushrooms and ramekins of baked wild mushrooms in butter. The quality of the cooking may be a bit erratic but the mushrooms are magnificent.*

STARSTON   MAP 5

Susan Moore Dairy Products 🛒 DAIRY PRODUCE

Cranes Watering Farm Shop, Rushall Road, Starston, Harleston, Norfolk IP20 9NE

TEL *0379 852387* CONTACT *Susan Moore* HOURS *June to end-Aug: Mon-Fri 9.00-17.30 Sat 9.00-17.00 Sun 9.30-12.30; Sept to end-May: Tues, Wed and Fri 9.00-17.30 Sat 9.00-17.00 Sun 9.30-12.30* DIRECTIONS *From Pulham Market, take B1134 towards Harleston. Follow the road through Starston and turn right immediately after crossing the bridge. Follow the road about ½ mile to cross-roads. Turn right and dairy is immediately on the left.*

Apart from the shop, the Moore's farm is also open to the public, so you can wander around and even inspect their 100-strong herd of Guernsey and Jersey cows. Most of the milk goes to the Milk Marketing Board, but some is kept back to be sold in their farm-shop either as fresh (pasteurized or unpasteurized) full cream, semi-skimmed or skimmed, or as a rich buttery double cream that is also either treated or untreated. If there is any cream left at the end of the week, Mrs Moore churns it into a well-ripened, full-flavoured (salted or unsalted) butter that makes the visit worthwhile. In her neat little dairy in the barn behind the shop, she also processes the milk into ice-cream, soft cheeses, yoghurt, clotted cream and a sharp, loose-textured lemon curd.

The ice-cream is mixed in 100-litre (176-pint) batches, then left overnight to age. With a 60% over-run (incorporated air), the ingredients are pretty straightforward – cream, milk, sugar and eggs – and it has a variable fat content of 12-15%. Although Mrs Moore has dispensed with emulsifiers, she still sees fit to add stabilizers (a mixture of the 4 gums, xanthus, carageen, locust bean and guar). Elizabethan Vanilla excepted, however, she does use real ingredients and fresh local fruit for the flavourings. Rum and Raisin is made with 'a bottle of rum and a few packets of raisins' and has a good alcoholic flavour; Gooseberry Fool contains real gooseberries simmered in sugar and is gloriously rich and fruity; Autumn Glory, a mixture of poached blackberries and apples, is unfortunately dull as the apple taste just does not come through.

I do like all her soft cheeses, however. There's a rich full-cream cheese – plain or with garlic and fresh herbs – and an unpasteurized full-milk cheese. Simply made, it is moulded and drained for a couple of days, so the texture is not unlike a young Coulommiers and comes either as plain, rolled in herbs, topped with walnuts or decorated with bay leaves. Although not stunning examples with complex tastes, they none the less have a lively freshness.

WYMONDHAM   MAP 5

Merv's Hot Bread Kitchen 🍞   NORFOLK KNOBS

38 Market Place, Wymondham, Norfolk NR17 0JU

TEL *0953 607118* **CONTACT** *Merv Ayers* **HOURS** *Mon-Sat 8.00-17.30*
DIRECTIONS *In town centre.*

From the outside, Merv's looks like any other ordinary high-street bakery, but twice a week it is a hot-bed of activity when Mr Ashworth comes in to bake Norfolk Knobs or, as they are known locally, 'hollow biscuits'. Mr Ashworth is actually semi-retired (he used to run the Ashworth's chain) and, as far as I know, he is the only person in the county still baking Knobs.

Similar to rusks in texture, Knobs look like pale-gold doorknobs and are puffed up with 'spent' sides that give a slightly crushed look.

Thought to have originated in the Low Countries, they are made from a dough of flour, fat, salt, yeast and sugar. The secret is to mix the dough with cold water to stop it rising too quickly, then to turn and fold it to get the hollowness. It is cut by hand and baked in a hot oven, left to cool and then finally dried out in a cool oven.

To eat a Knob, either bite into it whole or twist it gently and you will find it breaks in half, revealing the hollow centre. With a slightly sweet taste, the crunchy crust gives way to a crisp centre that dissolves in a burst of bubbles in your mouth. Traditionally spread with butter and served with jam or cheese, they are sold in packets of 12 and will keep for about 3 months.

And Also...

• Well known for his modern British cooking, David Adlard of *Adlard's Restaurant*, 79 Upper St Giles Street, Norwich (tel 0603 633522) now prepares take-away food. Every dish is ready for a final home-cook (even vegetables are peeled and diced) and – within reason – anything can be ordered, provided David has at least 3 days' notice.

• *Pri Emma* ✉, The Loke, Ipswich Road, Newton Flotman, nr Norwich (tel 0508 470768) grow their herbs in glass-houses and supply them pre-cut by mail order all year round.

• Royal Food freaks can buy meat from *R.F. & J. Scoles*, Dersingham (tel 0485 540309), the Royal butcher and game dealer (their sweet-cure ham is, by all accounts, very good); and fish, smoked salmon and caviar from the thrice-warranted *W.F. Sproston* ✉, Barnham, nr Thetford (tel 0842 890230).

• Pressed on-farm medium-sweet apple juice, made from Crispin, and a good selection of old varieties of apple trees can be found at *Ranworth Farms*, The Old House, Ranworth (tel 060549 722).

NORTHAMPTONSHIRE

DAVENTRY   MAP 4

The Nuns of Daventry ✉ ▤   TRUFFLES

The Convent of our Lady of the Passion Monastery,
4 Badby Road West, Daventry, Northamptonshire NN11 4NH

TEL 0327 702569   **CONTACT** *Sister Jane Anne – telephone ahead*

You may well have heard of the Nuns of Daventry. They made the front pages when, at the height of the salmonella scare, they were forced to slaughter their hens. 'We came a cropper' is how Sister Jane Anne remembers it. Undaunted they have since turned their talents to chocolate-making, a seemingly less controversial occupation. This was relatively easily accomplished as 'one of the sisters has a Belgian cousin, a fine *chocolatier* who came over to teach us how to make truffles'.

In case you are wondering how or why the Nuns of Daventry should follow such a commercial pursuit, and particularly one that is so obviously bound up with gratifying the pleasures, Sister Jane Anne explained. 'We belong to the Order of Passionist Nuns, a small contemplative order founded to postulate prayer. We make the chocolates to support our prayer life'. Fair enough – but working with all that alcohol? Still I didn't feel I could press the point.

Sister Jane Anne, aided by 2 other sisters, makes truffles about 4 days a week in their own kitchen in a converted stable, while 'trying to maintain a prayerful silence'. As a toddler, I was briefly taught by the nuns and to this day retain a memory of their forceful presence, so I find it jolly hard to be totally objective about their chocolates. I'd far rather leave it by describing them as 'interesting'. If pushed I would have to say that, although the truffle centres were rich, smoothly light and lavished with alcohol (champagne, rum, Grand Marnier, malt whisky, Drambuie, Irish Mist or Tia Maria), they were marred by too thick and too sweet a coating of chocolate. In effect it drowned the subtlety of the ganache and created too great a contrast of textures. Packed in 115, 225 and 450 g ($\frac{1}{4}$, $\frac{1}{2}$ and 1 lb) boxes, it is reassuring to know they are made with the best motives in mind.

And Also...

- **Essentially English** at 10b West Street, Oundle (tel 08322 74396) has twice been chosen as Midlands and East Anglia Deli of the Year by The Delicatessen and Fine Food Association. Worth noting are the hams cured in Cambridgeshire and the wide range of jams, pickles, chutneys and mustards.
- Locals know to buy Brixworth pâté from **Chambers Butchers**, 105 Northampton Road, Brixworth (tel 0604 880226). A rich chicken liver and pork pâté, it is liberally doused in sherry. They also produce a meaty bacon, dry-cured with a little sugar.
- **Ark Farm Sheep Dairy** at Tiffield, Towcester (0327 50202) makes yoghurt and ice-cream from the milk of the farm's sheep; some milk is sent off to Shepherd's Purse (see page 290) in Yorkshire to be made into cheese which is also available at the dairy. They also sell their own lamb, slaughtered at anything from 13 weeks to 6 months, lamb-burgers and lamb sausages.
- Spiced Beef is the speciality of **Wakefield Farm Shop**, Potterspury, nr Towcester (tel 0327 33493). Beef, marinated for a week in black treacle,

mace, allspice and garlic is poached and sold as whole joints or sliced.

• *Hill Farm Herbs* ✉ at Park Walk, Brigstock (tel 0536 373694, fax 0536 373246) have a wide range of culinary herb plants, scented geraniums and herb seeds. They have put together a 'Herbs for Cooking' collection of 10 plants that includes chives, fennel and sorrel and 6 packs of annuals – sweet basil, borage, chervil, coriander, dill and Italian (flat-leaf) parsley.

NORTHUMBERLAND

ALNWICK   MAP 6

Robertson's Prime 🏆   GAME

Unit 1B, Willowtree Industrial Estate, Alnwick, Northumberland NE66 2PF

TEL *0665 604386*   **CONTACT** *Ian Robertson*   **HOURS** *Mon-Sat 9.00-17.00*
DIRECTIONS *From the A1 travelling north, turn off at the first sign for Alnwick. Follow the road to the Shell garage, take the first turning on the right, signposted Willowtree Industrial Estate. Shop is 100 yards along on the right.*

Surrounded as he is with some of the best shoots and grouse moors in the country, you would expect Ian Robertson to have first-class game in his shop on an industrial estate just outside Alnwick. He does not disappoint.

Grouse (mainly from Alnwick Moor, the Duke of Northumberland's shoot and the Lillburne estates) arrives straight from the shoots and is hung for about 7 days. The condition varies, 'depending on who shoots, it can be peppered with shot,' Ian told me, far too discreet to name names. After about 2 months into the season, he 'freezes them up' because, extraordinarily enough, 'they're not too popular round here, people think they're too heathery'.

Also from the local estates come hare, mallard, teal, snipe, widgeon, rabbits, pheasant and wild pigeons. Everything is hung, racked, plucked and chilled out in the back and sold oven-ready. There is a tremendous range of wild venison (Ian would not dream of selling farmed) from Roe, Fallow, Sikka and Red deer that is hung and butchered into a range of cuts including saddle, haunch, boned and rolled haunch, double loin chops from the Roe deer, shoulder and steaks. A local butcher makes up venison sausages with herbs and (as the meat is so lean) pork fat. Ian also sells a game pie mix of 60% venison, 10% hare, 10% pheasant, 10% pigeon and 10% rabbit, depending on the season and supply.

He also prides himself on his fish that he collects himself, straight off the boats (mainly from Amble). Sometimes he gets codling from the cobles (flat-bottomed in-shore boats), but he can generally be relied on for cod, haddock, lemon and Dover sole, monkfish, live crabs and turbot (he does a roaring trade with the Chinese restaurants in Newcastle). Lobster he supplies to order as he has no tanks and, from Scotland, he gets Loch Fyne kippers, fresh scallops and smoked salmon.

CRASTER   MAP 6

L. Robson & Sons ✉ 🐟   CRASTER KIPPERS

Haven Hill, Craster, Alnwick, Northumberland NE66 3TR

TEL *0665 576223* CONTACT *Alan Robson* HOURS *Mon-Fri 9.00-12.00 & 13.00-17.00 Sat 9.00-12.00* DIRECTIONS *In village centre, by the harbour.*

Craster kippers have been famous for generations. Still smoked in the same way in the same towering smoke-houses built in 1856, the taste is probably exactly as it was all those years ago.

Nowadays, however, few herrings are caught off the Northumberland coast; instead they are brought in 'wherever decent herring are landed, last year they came from the West coast of Scotland, landed at Ayr or Tarbet or from Fraserburgh and Peterhead on the East coast'. The season, when the fish are at their plumpest and oiliest, can start as early as mid-May and lasts until September. After that, herrings start to spawn and get rather thin. Mr Robson uses fresh herrings almost exclusively (he will cure frozen Norwegian fish out of season, but only for special orders for certain shops – he never sends them out to his postal customers). All the curing is done during the summer months, the rest of the time he busies himself smoking salmon. As he never freezes his kippers, this is the only period they are available.

In the 'good old days', herring lassies would split and gut the herrings by hand, now it is done by machine. The herrings are washed, brined for about 20 minutes, and taken to the 'trows' (boxes) over which tenter-sticks are suspended. The herrings are hooked on the line of tenterhooks on the tenter-sticks, carried into the smokehouse and strung up row upon row into the rafters. Fires of white-wood covered with oak sawdust are lit and the herrings are gently cooked, as the smoke wafts up to the ceiling and out through the shutters, worked by rope pulls.

The sight of a smoke-house, its chambers packed with fish, is never to be forgotten. The walls, shiny black and sticky with tar, are a contrasting foil to the regimented lines of glistening mahogany-brown

> 🐟 *Further up the coast,* **Swallow Fish** ✉ *at* **2 South Street, Seahouses, NE68 7RP (tel 0665 721052)** *also have excellent kippers smoked over oak in their traditional smoke-holes. Lightly smoked, they are meaty and juicy.*

fish stretching as far as the eye can soar. A warm woody aroma fills the air as the slow gentle process of smoking carries on. At their busiest in the height of the season, Robson can smoke anything up to 6,000 a day, and depending on the weather they may stay in the smoke-house for as long as 14 hours.

Mr Robson reckons on his kippers weighing about three to the 450 g (1 lb). As for cooking them, he follows the late local squire Sir John Craster's method of jugging them in boiling water for 5 minutes. Failing that you could pop into the Robson's restaurant and treat yourself to a kipper tea – kippers, brown bread and butter and a pot of tea. Just what's needed after a good blow, walking along the coast.

In contrast to the picturesque town, **The Corbridge Larder** ✉ at **Hill Street, Corbridge, NE45 5AA (tel 0434 632948)** is a stylish modern shop and owner Richard Burt runs it with great flair. Immensely proud of his stack of Duskin's apple juice (see page 00) imported all the way from Kent, he generally does buy as locally as possible. Here I discovered thick, deep and heavily fruited Tarset Valley marmalade made with black treacle; a charming range of aromatic jams, including a peach & apricot conserve; and melissa bee honey from a small local honey-maker. There are local and Yorkshire Dale cheeses, bacon and sausages from Richard Woodall (see page 00), The Village Bakery Bread (see page 00) and, last but by no means least, the best Border tart I have tasted to date. Made exclusively for him by a Mrs Archer, the crisp and buttery pastry case was lined with a light vanilla sauce and piled with buttery raisins, sultanas and currants – it was artery-clogging heaven. Richard has a local team cooking for him, including a Pakistani family based in Newcastle who make, so he told me, the best samosas west of Karachi.

ELSDON   MAP 6

Redesdale Sheep Dairy ✉ 🛒 ♣   CHEESE

Soppitt Farm, Elsdon, Otterburn, Northumberland NE19 1AF

TEL *0830 20506* FAX *0830 20796* CONTACT *Mark Robertson* HOURS *Apr 1 to end-Oct: 10.00-18.00; Nov to Mar 31: Mon-Fri 10.00-14.00 Sat & Sun 10.00-18.00* CARDS *Access, Visa* DIRECTIONS *From Otterburn, take B6341 towards Elsdon. After about 2¼ miles, dairy is signposted on the left.*

Sheltered on a hill overlooking the Ride Valley in the glorious open moorlands of Northumberland's Southern Uplands, Soppit Farm is a glorious spot. From here Mark Robertson, makes 5 different cheeses, and there is a riding centre and activity and riding holidays

Mark stopped milking a few years ago to concentrate on cheese-making, simply 'because I enjoy it the most'. Now he buys in cows' milk from 2 local farms, goats' from 'a variety of county ladies and sheep's from the Sheep Milk Producers Association'. All of it is pasteurized before use.

He has fairly forceful opinions about the current state of the cheese-making industry, which is not altogether surprising as he seems to have suffered from the over-zealous ministrations of his local Environmental Health Officer. Apparently (and I do stress apparently, as I have only heard Mark's side of the argument) the EHO will not let Mark's cheeses touch wood while maturing, on the grounds that it is a health hazard. This was a problem, as his shelves are made of wood and to replace them would cost a lot of money. The solution Mark hit on was to vacuum-pack them; but he does not like it as the cheeses do not form a rind and 'Anyway I didn't go into cheese-making to spend my time putting things into paper bags'.

It is a very curious state of affairs: all over the country cheese-makers are maturing their cheeses on wood without any problem or possible danger, so why should one EHO object? When it comes down to it, the implementation of our food legislation is inconsistent: and some of the legal requirements are inappropriate, unrealistic, unnecessary and so expensive that, if implemented, they would force small producers to shut down. MAFF may make noises about supporting the smaller specialist food producer but, in fact, does little to help them. Surely what needs to happen is for the legislators, the enforcers of the legislation, the food producers and the consumers to get together in order to discuss what is necessary, realistic, achievable and appropriate. Then, and only then, we will have sensible legislation that will not endanger our small producers.

But back to Mark's cheeses...if I'm being perfectly honest I do think that possibly as a result of not being allowed to mature naturally some suffer from a lack of heightened flavour. On the other hand, it may be that, when I sampled them on the farm, they were still a little too young. Northumberland, made with cows' milk and based on a Gouda-style recipe, was smooth and compact with a decent length of flavour: this he makes as plain or flavoured with chives or pepper, or garlic or nettles, and he also sells a smoked version. Coquetdale, also from cows' milk, is a semi-hard dome-shaped cheese based on a French Tomme and matured for 5 weeks; a little salty, it has a pleasant mild tang. 'Real' Wensleydale, from a mixture of cows' and sheep's-milk, was by Mark's admission, 'a little variable – last month's had been rather blue', and it was quite sharp and acidic. His sheep's milk cheese, Redesdale, is hard-pressed and matured for about 8 weeks; dry and quite crumbly, it had a good 'kick'. Finally goats'-milk Elsdon is matured for 6 weeks to give it a mild but pronounced taste of goat.

All the cheeses can be bought from the shop, with a café attached which also sells a small selection of local jams and marmalades. Mail-order customers will be interested to know Mark puts together a Northumberland Cheeseboard so you can compare all his cheeses.

> Alongside eggs, vegetables and fruit, **North Acomb Farm Shop, North Acomb Farm, Stocksfield (tel 0661 843181)** sell green-top (unpasteurized) milk, own-made butter and cream from their Friesian herd. They also have a wide range of own-made fresh or frozen ready-cooked meals, including Lancashire hot-pot and salmon poached in a court-bouillon with parsley sauce. They make their own pasties and sausages, cure their own bacon and hams and, at Christmas, have turkeys and geese.

ROSEDEN   **MAP 6**

Roseden Farm Shop 🚜   FRESH MEAT & BAKED GOODS

Roseden, Wooperton, Alnwick, Northumberland NE66 4XU

TEL 06687 271   **CONTACT** Anne Walton   **HOURS** Tues-Sun 10.00-17.00 (closed Sun mid-Oct to Easter)   **CARDS** Access, Visa, Mastercard, Switch **DIRECTIONS** From Powburn, take A697 towards Wooler. After about $4\frac{1}{2}$ miles, turn left at sign for Roseden. Farm-shop is about $\frac{1}{4}$ mile on the right.

Anne Walton runs a very jolly farm-shop, with a teashop attached that 2 nights a week is open for dinner. 'It's a lot of hard work, a 20-hour rather than a 12-hour job. In spite of that, before I opened the shop I was 2 stone lighter.'

Anne obviously enjoys food, she has even written *Farmhouse Cookery*, a book of her own recipes, and most everything she sells is own-grown and own-made. Meat mainly comes from the farm: Aberdeen Angus-cross beef is hung for 10-14 days and boasts a good covering of fat; their own lamb is grass-fed Suffolk cross and her son, a hill farmer, supplies Blackie lamb from his heather-fed flock on the moors. Free-range pork, chicken, ducks and, at Christmas, traditional farm-fresh turkeys and free-range geese are all bought in locally. These are either sold fresh, frozen or turned into a wide and varying range of ready-cooked dishes, 'anything from lasagne to chicken pie'. Anne also makes her own pâtés and pork sausages, lightly seasoned with herbs, and has just started dry-curing bacon.

A keen baker, she always has plenty of scones, fruit pies, fruit cakes, meringues, tea loaves and Border tarts in her shop, together with a fair range of own-made jams, pickles and lemon curd. At Christmas she also makes puddings, cakes, mince pies, mincemeat and brandy butter. She will, if you ask, actually make butter in her Kenwood mixer. Using a local cream, she beats it until it comes together, washes it and hand pats it in a matter of minutes. As you can imagine, it is rather rich, creamy and clean-tasting; 'something,' Anne suggests, 'to do with the local pure spring water'. Her philosophy is 'to cater for what people want, putting the very best ingredients in, to get the very best out'.

And Also...

• Near Chester's Roman Fort on Hadrian's Wall, *Hexham Herbs* at The Chesters Walled Garden, Chollerford, Hexham (tel 0434 681483) has a Roman garden, showing – they claim – the herb varieties the Romans grew in Britain. They also sell a wide variety of modern culinary herb plants and, if you want cut herbs, they will pick them while you wait.

• The 19th-century water-powered corn mill at *Heatherslaw Corn Mill*, Ford Forge, Cornhill-on-Tweed (0890 820338) grinds very slowly indeed to produce wholemeal and an 80% extraction flours. From the shop you can also buy, made from their own flour, a Tweed bannock – similar to the Selkirk bannock (see page 330) but with wholemeal flour.

• *J. Bryson & Son* of Market Place, Wooler are good old-fashioned bakers; so old-fashioned in fact, they don't have a telephone. Mr Bryson still bakes oatcakes, plain or fruit girdle scones, treacly sticky parkin and granny (tea) loaf.

• Up the road at 50 High Street, Wooler (tel 0668 81700), *The Good Life Shop* ✉ stocks local cheeses, including Bonchester (see page 328) and Redesdale Dairy's (see page 192). There is a good range of oatmeal from Edington Mills, including pinhead, fine, medium and porridge oats, plus a good local Jersey cream and butter.

• Robert Handyside runs his *Real Cheese Shops* with great enthusiasm. With a branch in Barnes (see page 171), Wimbledon and at 6 Oldgate, Morpeth (tel 0670 505555), you are bound to find a good choice of well-matured local on-farm cheeses.

• My friends Mark and Stella Wrightson insisted I stopped at their local butcher, *John Robinson* at Great Smeaton (tel 0609 81213) to view the meat. Beef hung for around 3 weeks, with a good rim of yellow fat, was meltingly tender; brisket and tongue are soundly pickled for at least 2 months and, in season, they have lamb off the moors.

NOTTINGHAMSHIRE

COLSTON BASSETT   MAP 4

Colston Bassett & District Dairy ✉ 🎲 CHEESE

Harby Lane, Colston Bassett, Nottinghamshire NG12 3FN

TEL *0949 81322* **FAX** *0949 81132* **CONTACT** *Ernie Wagstaff* **HOURS** *Mon-Fri 9.00-12.30 & 13.30-16.00 Sat 9.00-11.30* **DIRECTIONS** *From Leicester, take A46 towards Newark. Turn right at sign for Colston Bassett about 3 miles after roundabout junction with the A606. Follow road for about 2$\frac{3}{4}$ miles through the village. Dairy is on the right as you leave village.*

Stilton is known as 'the King of English cheeses'. Sandy Carr, in the useful *Mitchell Beazley Pocket Cheese Book*, describes it as 'velvety, close-textured, unpressed with a pale ivory paste grading to amber at the edges and marbled with greenish-blue veins. The rind is dry, crusty, greyish brown and slightly wrinkled, with white powdery patches. The flavour ranges from mild with a sharp edge when young, to rich and tangy when mature'.

Currently Stilton is the only British cheese to be legally protected along similar lines to the French Appellation Contrôlée or Label Rouge schemes. Its legal definition, given the backing of a High Court judgement in 1969, is as follows: 'Stilton is a blue or white cheese made from full-cream milk, with no applied pressure, forming its own crust or coat and made in cylindrical form, the milk coming from English dairy herds in the district of Melton Mowbray and surrounding areas falling within the counties of Leicestershire (now including Rutland), Derbyshire and Nottinghamshire'. As Patrick Rance in *The Great British Cheese Book* so rightly points out, however, the judgement came too late to exclude pasteurization – a practice that all except the Colston Bassett Dairy had already adopted.

Fours years ago Colston Bassett Dairy, under pressure caused by the listeria scare, was also forced to pasteurize. Now no unpas-teurized Stilton is made. The people at Colston Bassett Dairy claim their cheese is as good as ever – better, even, as it has more consistency. Well, they would, wouldn't they? Connoisseurs would probably disagree, claiming it has lost some of its rich complexity and depth. Nevertheless, it is generally thought that theirs is the most interesting Stilton.

A small dairy, they make between 60-100 cheeses a day (about 4% of the total Stilton output) from the milk of 5 farms within the area (the farthest-flung being a mere $2\frac{1}{2}$ miles away). The cheeses are still turned by hand – every day for the first 20 days, then 3 times a week until they are pierced to encourage the veining. Theirs is a rich, buttery, relatively soft cheese with a mellow, deep flavour that lingers in the mouth. When buying Stilton, always look for evenly distributed veins, a good blueing and a good contrast between the paste and veins.

Although you may be tempted to buy a small 450 g (1 lb) truckle, it is not necessarily a good idea. Their flavour is not nearly so highly developed because – as they dry out far more quickly –

NO-COOK STILTON AND ROCKET SAUCE WITH PASTA

In a food processor, whizz 85 g (3 oz) Stilton, a handful of rocket leaves (reserving a few whole ones) and a 150 ml ($\frac{1}{4}$ pt) carton of single cream to a thickish paste. Mix into the cooked and drained pasta. Snip over the remaining rocket leaves and season with freshly ground black pepper. (Adapted from *10-minute Cuisine* by Henrietta Green & Marie-Pierre Moine).

they mature much younger. It is far better to buy a piece cut off a large cheese. Keep Stilton in a cool place, preferably a larder; if you don't have one, a fridge will do. Wrap the cheese in a lightly moistened cloth to stop it from drying out, but always remember to unwrap and leave it at room temperature a good couple of hours before you eat it.

> *Several Stilton cheese-makers sell their cheese direct to the public. Also in the county is **Cropwell Bishop Creamery, Cropwell Bishop (0602 892350)**. Others out of the county include **Webster's Dairy, Main Street, Saxelbye, nr Melton Mowbray, Leicestershire (tel 0664 812223)** and **J.M. Nutall of Dove Dairy**, who also run **The Olde Cheese Shop, Market Place, Hartington, Derbyshire (tel 0298 84496)**.*

CROPWELL BUTLER   MAP **4**

Mrs Elizabeth King 🏭🚚   PORK PIES

Hardigate Road, Cropwell Butler, Nottinghamshire NG12 3AG
TEL *0602 332252* **CONTACT** *Ian Hartland* **HOURS** *Mon-Fri 9.00-17.00 Sat 9.00-12.30 Thurs at Bingham Market* **DIRECTIONS** *From Newark, take A46 towards Leicester. Turn left about 1 mile after junction with A52 at sign for Cropwell Butler. Turn right at signpost for shop. Market in town centre.*

In 1853 Mrs Elizabeth King first set up her business in Lister Gate, Nottingham making sausages and pork pies. After 2 years she was so successful that she moved to larger premises in Beastmarket Hill where, incidentally, her next-door neighbour was a Mr John Player the tobacconist. The company passed through various hands until it ended up as a part of Pork Farms – a huge food conglomerate. When Kenneth Parr their managing director retired 10 years ago, he bought back the business because he felt technology had taken over and compromised quality. He wanted to go back to making pies as good as they had been when he was a lad. Whether they are or not, obviously I cannot tell. They are, however, made with great care and, for what it is worth, have won the Melton Mowbray Pork Pie Championship (always held on the last Tuesday before Christmas) 3 times.

The hand-raised pies are made from 'coarsely chopped pork shoulder, salt and pepper – full stop' and a boiling pastry of flour, water, lard and salt. They are sold frozen, with the aim of ensuring that they are always eaten at peak freshness. The pies are in 450 g, 675 g, 1.35 and 2.3 kg (1, 1½, 3, and 5 lb) sizes and come with detailed and remarkably clear baking instructions, together with a little sack of jelly for you to pour in as the pie cools. They also make frozen sausages with a meat content 'towards 90%' and collagen skins, sausage bombs (sausage-meat wrapped in pastry), Eccles cakes and ready-frozen pastry.

Mrs Potter's Perfect Pork ✉ 🚚 ▦

PORK PRODUCTS

The Manor House, Langford, Newark on Trent, Nottinghamshire NG23 7RW

TEL *0636 611156* CONTACT *Trudy Potter – telephone ahead* HOURS *Wed &*
Fri 9.00-16.00 at Newark Market; Sat 8.30-15.00 at Southwell Market
DIRECTIONS *Market in town centres.*

Trudy Potter's land is on the site of a declared ancient monument. Once
a medieval village, it was razed to the ground in the 16th century, when
the villagers refused to pay their tithes. Now her animals graze there
contentedly, and Trudy – although she does not farm to any officially
recognized standards – practises a high degree of animal welfare. Her
pigs are free-range in the true sense of the word, as they are both reared
and fattened outdoors. She has banished all inhumane husbandry
practices, namely farrowing pens, teeth clipping, tail cutting, castration
and early weaning. Her pigs live in family groups and are fed on a locally
grown mixture containing milled barley, beans and vegetable waste.
Farrowing sows also get milk from their Jersey cow; they still milk by
hand. The foundation of her pig herd is the rare-breed Gloucester Old
Spot, because 'it's good for pork and bacon and it is remarkably docile'.

Apart from fresh pork, they are processed into a wide range of
sausages that she is always adding to as she cannot resist experimenting
or making up new flavours when someone asks. When I visited I found
original sage (their first recipe); plain pork; smoked bacon and tomato;
tomato, basil and chilli; red pepper, mushroom and onion (with garlic,
chilli and ginger); rosemary and garlic; and sour cherry, chives and
honey. Containing 80% meat, they are made from shoulder and belly,
with either wholemeal rusk or oatmeal, packed in natural casings and
have a wholesome coarse texture. A.W. Curtis of Lincoln (see page 155)
cure her ham and bacon for her. She sells Wiltshire-cure bacon and in
summer she sells Wiltshire-cure hams, and a few dry-cure hams in
winter. The latter, cured for 6 weeks in salt, saltpetre and brown sugar,
has a well-rounded flavour which is nicely balanced with a hint of
sweetness.

On Trudy's market stall you will also usually find pigs' fry (a mixture
of pigs' offal that should include trimmed liver, heart, kidney,
sweetbread, brain, tongue and skirt, mesentery or frill) which in this
area is traditionally eaten with boiled onions and greens. There are also
'real' free-range eggs from her maize-fed mixed flock of Marans that lay a
rich dark brown egg, Rhode Islands and Light Sussex, with their
enchanting speckled egg. In season she also has lamb from her own
Suffolks, and occasionally grass-fed beef from her own herd, which has
been hung for a minimum of 3 weeks.

The Country Victualler ✉ HAMS

Winkburn Hall, Newark, Nottinghamshire NG22 8PQ

TEL *0636 86465* FAX *0636 86717* CARDS *Access, Visa, Mastercard*
CONTACT *Richard Craven-Smith-Milnes – mail order only*

Although the major part of the Country Victualler's business is
wholesale (they supply Fortnum & Mason, Harrods, Selfridges and
Partridges of Sloane Street, London), they do sell a small range direct to
the public by mail order. Top of their list is the Alderton ham. Injected
(to speed up the process) and wet-cured for 2 days in brine flavoured
with brown sugar, the hams are steam-cooked for 4 hours, then dressed
in a lavish coat of marmalade and baked for a further 4 hours. Sold as
whole hams on the bone in two sizes, large at least 5.85 kg (13 lb) and
small at least 5 kg (11 lb), they have a thick, glossy marmalade glaze and
are mild and moist with a pliant texture and a tangy edge.

At Christmas they also sell puddings. These are generally made in
sizeable batches – a mix will make one hundred 900 g (2 lb) puddings
or the equivalent – and they are well matured. This produces a very dark
shiny solid pudding. This is not surprising as, apart from the usual vine
fruits, apples, mixed peel, nuts, brandy, rum, spices etc, it also contains
suet, breadcrumbs, eggs and flour. They will also post you 2 of their
pâtés: Terrine de Campagne, a coarse pork pâté with a hint of nutmeg,
and the gutsier Wild Boar with Juniper Berries.

Spring Farm Shop 🛒 WIDE RANGE OF FARM PRODUCE

The Moor, Trowell, Nottinghamshire NG9 3PQ

TEL *0602 282076* CONTACT *Barbara Haynes* HOURS *Mon, Tues & Thurs
9.00-17.00 Fri 9.00-18.00 Sat 8.30-17.00* DIRECTIONS *From Nottingham,
take A609 towards Ilkeston. Immediately after crossing over the A6002,
turn right at signpost for Spring Farm and follow the lane for ½ mile.*

Perched on the side of a hill, Spring Farm Shop has a bird's-eye view
over Nottingham; beyond it lies the open country. There Barbara Haynes
makes all her own jams, pickles and chutneys. Stacked in the farmhouse
dresser you will find a meaty apricot jam complete with kernels, wild
plum and damson jams, a tart rhubarb chutney, beetroot relish, fruity
marmalades, pickled onions and eggs, raspberry vinegar, and a beetroot
relish. The family help with the poultry. Foxes are a problem so the
chickens are barn-reared, but hung for around 4 days to give them a
fuller flavour. They sell hen, duck and goose eggs (from February to
May), and, at Christmas, their own-grown turkeys, geese and ducks and
Barbara's puddings.

Throughout the year there is a selection of own-grown vegetables and soft fruit including peas, runner beans, courgettes, marrow, broad beans, shallots, freshly cut Webb's lettuce, bunched beetroot still with their tops, 'ordinary' and cherry tomatoes, gooseberries, damsons and Victoria plums. Potatoes are a speciality and they grow Desirée and Wilja. These have a local reputation for a particularly fine flavour due, as Barbara explained, to the seam of limestone that runs all the way from Worksop and ends on their top fields.

> *Set in the lush vale of Belvoir is **Langar Hall, Langar (tel 0949 60559)**, a plain-fronted house built in 1830 with a tranquil sunken water garden. Imogen Skirving has converted her family home into a cosy and relaxed country hotel where you (and your dog) will feel unbelievably welcome and cosseted.*
>
> *The chefs place an emphasis on local produce and while I tucked into a tender and well-hung braised pheasant with apples, my dog Violet was royally fed left-over fillet tails. Enjoy a refreshing Belvoir Cocktail Royale made with sparkling white wine and strawberry cordial (see Belvoir Fruit Farms, page 148) and make sure you leave room for a slice of Colston Bassett Stilton, collected from the dairy a mile down the road. There is always one on the go and they usually get through a whole cheese every week.*

And also....

• **Cheese Cuisine**, 10 Saracen's Head Yard, Newark (tel 0636 703313), with another branch 10 miles away at 14 Market Street, Bingham (tel 0949 837409), sells a good selection of British cheeses, including Colston Bassett Stilton, as well as locally made Thaymar Ice-cream.

OXFORDSHIRE

BANBURY   MAP 2

R.S. Malcolm ✉ 📷   BANBURY CAKES

41 High Street, Banbury, Oxfordshire OX16 8LA

TEL *0295 257724* CONTACT *Raymond Malcolm* HOURS *Mon-Fri 9.00-17.30 Sat 8.30-17.00* DIRECTIONS *In town centre.*

According to Florence White in *Good Things in England*, Banbury cakes, Eccles cakes (from Lancashire) and Coventry Godcakes (given to godchildren by their godparents on their birthday) 'all belong to the same class. They consist of pastry, short or puff as the case may be, round as in the case of Eccles, at Coventry taking the form of an isosceles triangle, and at Banbury made into the oval shape of a rather wide shuttle. Each and all are filled with a special mixture partaking of the character of the mincemeat we put in pies at Christmas time.'

Banbury – and indeed all the cakes Florence White lists above – are really small pies or covered tarts. There are various theories as to how they came into being, but what seems clear is that they are variations on a theme, each taking its name after the town or region where they were first made. Good ones, as far as I'm concerned, should have a light crisp pastry case that is positively crammed with a moist filling. It's so disappointing when bakers skimp on the filling – and so many of them do – as it makes for a very dull dry cake indeed.

Raymond Malcolm, you will pleased to hear, does not fail us with his Banbury cakes. They are generously stuffed with an oozing mincemeat of butter, brown sugar, currants, sultanas and mixed peel, all subtly flavoured with rose water, rum and lemon essence and nutmeg. For once, the fruits are not over-chopped, so it has a chunky texture, studded with whole vine fruits. The pastry, rich and flaky, comes sprinkled with icing sugar; so when, as Malcolm suggests, you gently heat the cake in the oven before eating, it crispens to a crunchy, sweet coating that explodes as you bite into it.

Raymond sends Banbury cakes all over the world; but you can also buy them freshly made at his shop, along with a range of breads, cakes, pies and slices, or direct from his bakery around the corner at 53 Middleton Road, which has a tiny shop attached.

ELSFIELD MAP 2

The Oxford Pick Your Own Farm 🚜 🍲

ASPARAGUS & MANGE-TOUT PEAS

Elsfield, Oxford, Oxfordshire OX3 9UW

TEL *0865 351561 (Information service 0865 358873)* FAX *0865 351463* CONTACT *Peter Clarke* HOURS *June to end-Oct 9.30-19.00; Nov to end-May 9.30-17.00* DIRECTIONS *From Eynsham, take A40 towards Wheatley. Turn left at sign for Elsfield. Drive through village and turn left on to B4027. After ½ mile farm is signposted on the left.*

It was Raymond Blanc who first told me about Peter Clarke and his pick-your own farm. Raymond's obsessions with the best possible quality, the freshest and tiniest vegetables are well known and now he has sumptuous kitchen gardens at his heavenly restaurant Le Manoir aux Quat' Saisons that are dedicated to his every need. In the early days, however, when he had a mere shop-of-a-restaurant in Oxford itself he relied on Peter Clarke. Every morning, Raymond and his band of sous-chefs would be out there picking baby produce, with Peter anxiously waiting for the top chef's approval.

Peter has to be unique: he is the only pick-your-own farmer I have ever come across who actually wants his customers to pick baby produce. 'Not many do,' he told me resignedly, 'as most people go for size. They're quicker and easier to pick but smaller vegetables have a greater intensity of flavour, are far sweeter and, of course, need far less and gentler cooking.' He sells ready-picked as well, but prefers customers to pick (or dig) their own and runs an answering machine service to tell you what is ready.

Apart from the more usual vegetables, he also grows globe artichokes in season in June and July; baby round carrots; bright yellow courgettes, tasting of honey when picked at finger-size; ivory-coloured patty-pan squashes that best steamed or gently stewed in butter; baby sweetcorn; Florence fennel; mange-tout peas that you nip off while the pods are so young they are almost transparent; plain and ruby spinach and yes, you can pick the 'pousses' or baby leaves; green or purple kohlrabi, best for eating raw, grated in salads when the size of a golf ball; and pak-choi, a mildly flavoured succulent Chinese leafy Brassica. In the dig-your-own line (forks are provided), there are various potatoes, including the much-favoured Pink Fir Apple; leeks for pulling when ribbon-thin; Jerusalem artichokes, and celeriac.

There is also a good selection of strawberries and raspberries, with varieties chosen for taste and to last through the season: redcurrants, blackcurrants and white currants; various apples starting with Vistabella, 'whose main claim to fame is that it's the first of the earlies'; plums, starting with Early Rivers running through to the newer varieties, Excalibur and Avalon; and Conference and Williams pears.

As well as ready-picked produce, the shop sells Lady Wills' Guernsey cream (see page 15) in the soft fruit season, locally baked cakes and biscuits, a fair selection of Chatsworth's long-shelf-life produce (see page 52) and, at Christmas, free-range turkeys, geese and ducks.

---

*The Apple Centre on **Witney Road, Kingston Bagpuize, nr Abingdon (tel 0865 820183)** sells a wide variety of produce. Soft fruit, various vegetables and locally made cakes are bought in; but the apples and pears are all own-grown. Varieties available include Williams, the small round Merton Pride, Conference, Comice and Concorde pears; Discovery, Worcester Pearmain, Jersey Mackintosh, Fiesta, Golden Delicious and the similar Crispin and Greensleeves, Jonagold, Rubinette, Cox's Orange Pippin, Queen Cox's, Katy, Melrose, Ida Red, Lobo, Spartan and Orléans Reinette – 17 varieties of apples in total. They also have own-grown asparagus in 2 grades, sprue and a 'good mixed grade', and sell potatoes from early Maris Bard running through to maincrop Wilja, Marfona and Desirée.*

Rodney Whitworth ✉ ▦   EWES'-MILK CHEESE

Abbey Farm, Goosey, Faringdon, Oxfordshire SN7 8PA

TEL *0367 718060* CONTACT *Rodney Whitworth – telephone ahead*

In case you think British sheep's-milk cheeses are a new fad, I must point out they have been made here for centuries. Wensleydale (see page 298) was originally a ewes'-milk cheese made by the monks; Lanark Blue (see page 361) follows a revived 16th-century recipe; and Leafield and Tubney follow an age-old tradition. The farms of Goosey, a peaceful hamlet in south-west Oxfordshire and home to Rodney Whitworth, supplied Abingdon Abbey in the 12th century with '28 ponders of ewes' cheese a year, each weighing 252 lb'.

It is rather satisfying that history has come full circle and now cheese is made again at Abbey Farm. Even if the cheeses have an impeccable lineage and have won prizes at the Bath and West and the Bakewell cheese shows, life for Rodney is no rural idyll. Working as a one-man band, the hours are long, the work tough and Rodney feels particularly strongly that in comparison to the help his fellow cheese-makers receive in France, he is seriously disadvantaged. The French, notorious cheese-lovers, relish diversity and the authorities go out of their way to encourage the makers; here the reverse is true.

Undaunted he carries on, although last year he was forced to give up his 100 Friesland sheep flock as 'milking and making was just too much' and now buys in milk from a friend in Stratford-upon-Avon. Rodney started making on a regular commercial basis about 2 years ago and produces 3 cheeses in all: Leafield and Tubney, both unpasteurized; and pasteurized Oxford Buttons, soft fresh rounds made with full-cream milk and sold at about 5 days.

Leafield is a more complex cheese, both in how it is made and in its taste. The curds are cut, scalded and pitched into 2.25 kg ($4\frac{1}{2}$ lb) moulds, then it is lightly pressed for 12 hours, brined for 12-24 hours and left to dry for 2-3 days. At this point it is painted with a plastic coating and matured from anything between $1\frac{1}{2}$ to 4 months. I tried it when relatively mature and enjoyed its well-developed taste, which is similar to a Gruyère – although its texture could not have been more different as it is hard and quite dry with a grittiness, similar to a Parmesan. Sometimes Rodney makes Leafield flavoured with rosemary to give it a vague woody herbiness that balances the cheese's inherent saltiness.

Tubney is initially made in the same way as Leafield, but then it is moulded into 300 g ($10\frac{1}{2}$ oz) Dutch Gouda moulds to end up 'the size and shape of a cricket ball'. Matured for about 6-8 weeks, it is a milder and less brittle cheese; occasionally Rodney takes a batch to Minola (see page 95) to have them smoked. The result is not altogether successful, I think, as it seizes the cheese – giving it a slightly acrid aftertaste. But then, as I freely admit, I am no great fan of smoked cheese.

Rodney's cheeses are sold at The Oxford Cheese Shop in the covered market, Wells Stores in Abingdon (see page 206), and Rippon Cheese Stores (see page 168) and Harrods in London (see page 166).

---

*Locals rave about the bread from **The Old Farmhouse Bakery, Steventon, nr Abingdon (tel 0235 831230)**. Their philosophy is to produce bread as it is baked at home, and it is done in a 1930s brick oven in an old barn converted from a cart-shed, using flour from various local millers. The 30-odd breads are made up from the 14 different flours on hand: white flour is always unbleached, as 'customers like it that way' and most breads are left to prove twice. Thursday is 'organic' day, when organic breads are made. Otherwise, choose one of their unusually flavoured breads: such as walnut plait, made with a mixture of 3 flours (with wholemeal predominating), fresh walnuts and a pinch of curry powder to spice it up; tomato and basil with fresh tomatoes; pecan, bay and olive; or a strong cheese and onion with English Cheddar. They also make a remarkably sticky gingerbread, open fruit flans and butter croissants. There is a small cheese counter in the shop, selling on-farm cheeses, and they also sell own-made frozen pastry.*

SHRIVENHAM   MAP 2

The HOF Shop of Eastbrook Farm ✉ 🏠 ⚘
BEEF, HAMS & SAUSAGES

50 High Street, Shrivenham, Oxfordshire SN6 8AA

TEL 0793 782211 **CONTACT** Helen Browning **HOURS** Mon 9.00-16.00 Tues-Thurs 8.00-17.00 Fri 8.00-18.00 Sat 8.00-14.00 **DIRECTIONS** *From Swindon, take A420 towards Oxford. After about 4 miles, turn right after the railway bridge at sign for Shrivenham. Follow the road 1 mile to village and shop is signposted on the left.*

BEST ORGANIC PRODUCE

Helen Browning is one of the most commercially successful of all organic farmers in Britain. Her detractors might say that she had an easier start than most as she took over the family farm, Eastbrook Farm in Bishopstone, Wiltshire, covering 1,350 acres of prime downland. To give Helen her due, however, it was she who had the vision and tenacity to convert it to Soil Association standards.

She views organic farming as a challenge, 'similar to an athlete running full steam without the boost of any drugs. It may not be the easiest option, but it's a system that does work and the only feasible way of farming.' She also believes that the produce must be competitive price-wise and easily accessible to the public. The net result is that she now runs two butcher's shops (in Shrivenham and in Mortimer's, Northbrook Street, Newbury) and an efficient mail order service.

Altogether she employs 5 traditional butchers, including Tony from the now defunct Pork Shop in Swindon (and anyone who used to shop there must remember their exquisite crisp pork scratchings). The beef is excellent, firm-textured and with a well-developed taste and a good length of flavour. It comes from her mixed herd of Angus, Hereford and various Continental breeds and is hung for a minimum of 14 days. The lamb is reared on the downland clover pastures, which gives it a pleasant hazy taste. The pork is Saddleback Landrace cross raised on a fully outdoor organic system, so you can be sure that – unlike some free-range pork – it is not brought indoors to be fattened.

The HOF Shop also cure hams and bacon and they make their own sausages using only the 'real' fresh ingredients. There is a chunky gutsy Cumberland, with a good whiff of spices; cider and apple; plain pork; beer and garlic; Welsh leek, Beef and Guinness. The only complaint is that their texture is a little too pasty, as if the meat has been over-pounded rather than minced. They also sell additive-free, free-range chickens and eggs (organic poultry is still hard to come by due to the shortage of organic chick-feed and grain).

A thoroughly professional organization, this is one of the few organic operations I have visited that offers consistency and volume of produce.

STANTON ST JOHN   MAP 2

Rectory Farm 🚜 🥘   ASPARAGUS

Stanton St John, Oxford, Oxfordshire OX9 1HF

TEL *0865 351214* **CONTACT** *Richard Stanley* **HOURS** *Tues-Thurs 14.00-18.00 Fri 10.00-18.00 Sat-Sun 9.30-13.00.* **DIRECTIONS** *From A40 Headington roundabout in Oxford, take exit signposted Stanton St John. Follow signs 1½ miles towards the village. PYO site is signposted.*

Most growers sell ready-picked asparagus as the thought of hordes of customers trampling over their beds fills them with horror. Richard Stanley is one grower who is all for picking-your-own, 'In fact there is very little damage anyone can do; the top of the crowns (the actual plants) are buried in about 6 inches of soil, so the worst that can happen is a few spears will be snapped off.'

Asparagus has a relatively short eating-season: depending on the weather, it starts around the end of April and lasts through to mid-June. The part we eat is the spear (shoot); when left uncut, its tips open and it develops into a fern. Although the crown carries on throwing spears until late summer, they should not be cut after mid-June as it is through the ferns the plant obtains its food and energy. If you keep cutting, the crown does not get a chance to build up its strength for the following year.

In Britain, because of our dubious climate we are marginal growers.

Some areas, like California or Peru, even manage 2 seasons a year: 1 in spring, another in autumn. Wherever you are, however, asparagus can be quite tricky. If it is too hot, the tips open before you have a chance to pick them; if it is too cold, the season is very short and you have to balance up quantity of spears against giving the crowns a chance to photosynthesize.

The difference in the various varieties of asparagus is more a question of performance and size of spears than in taste. Richard grows both French and Dutch varieties in 10 acres of coarse Oxfordshire sand; 'perfect soil conditions; but if there's a wind, it blows the soil up like a dust cloud. Combine that with rain and you can get sand in the asparagus – but it's nothing a good soak won't cure.'

Arriving at the farm, you can drive along the bumpy track down to the fields where people are picking the serried rows of wavy green spears. There is always someone from the farm to show you how, but if in doubt Richard does have printed leaflets. 'The best way is to snap an asparagus off by hand at ground level or about $\frac{1}{2}$ inch above the ground, so there is no woody bit of stem.'

Some people prefer the sharper, more acidulated taste of 'French-style' white asparagus. Actually it is the same variety just grown in a different way, in trenches or banked soil to exclude the light (ie blanched). Although Richard does not trench his asparagus, you are welcome to pick them when you see the tip just breaking through the soil; although shorter, they will be blanched. 'All you do is burrow down, like a rabbit, with a long knife and cut them off a few inches down.'

So what are the advantages of picking-your-own? Your asparagus will be super-fresh, straight-from-the-field (but to be fair most ready-picked ones are picked and sold the same day), you can choose your own, and if a day-out is what you are after then this could be it. Remember to

It's good to know that **Wells Stores** ✉ at **29 Stert Street, Abingdon, OX14 3SF (tel 0235 535978)** is up and running again. The original Wells Stores was in Streatley, run by Patrick Rance, the British cheese guru. It was he who single-handedly put on-farm cheeses on the map and did more to encourage small cheese-makers than anyone else. When he retired to France it was left to Randolph Hodgson (see Neal's Yard Dairy, page 164) to carry on the good work. Hughie, Patrick's son, meanwhile ran Streatley and opened another store in Abingdon. However, Hughie's heart was not in it and both shops closed, until Gill Draycott, a former employee at Abingdon, bought this one. Now in Gill's safe hands, it is run on similar lines with a commitment to British cheese in general and small unpasteurized on-farm cheeses in particular. There is a good choice of British territorials and French cheese, delivered once a week from France, and Gill does some of her own ripening in the cold store out back.

bring along a knife for burrowing, gloves to protect your hands, a scarf if it is blowy, and a chill-box to keep the asparagus fresh. If all this sounds daunting, Richard does sell ready-picked asparagus, graded into 3 qualities – with an extra class of rejects for soup-making.

Later on in the season he also has ready-picked and pick-your-own vegetables and soft fruit. Strawberries are grown for taste, 'I can be more ambitious with varieties. They're not going to supermarkets, so you don't have to be able to play football with them. I grow Elvira, Korona with a good sweet flavour, Tamara, Pegasus and the late Pandora.' Raspberries are the pale Glen Moy, Malling Admiral, the best-flavoured Leo, dark-fleshed Augusta and the late Autumn Bliss; and there are gooseberries, redcurrants, blackcurrants, white currants, tayberries and sunberries.

> ### ROAST ASPARAGUS
>
> One of the easiest ways of cooking asparagus stalks is to roast them. Simply brush a roasting pan with a little olive oil, spread the asparagus over the bottom, brush them with a little more olive oil and scatter some sea salt on top. Put in an oven pre-heated to 180°C/ 350°F/ gas 4 for about 10-15 minutes, depending on how thick they are. Serve with lemon juice.

WHITCHURCH-ON-THAMES   MAP 2

The Old Dairy Farm Shop 🛒 ✒ ♟

ORGANIC BEEF & CREAM

Path Hill Farm, Whitchurch-on-Thames, Reading, Oxfordshire RG8 7RE

TEL *0734 842392* **CONTACT** *Elizabeth Rose* **HOURS** *Wed-Sat 10.00-17.00*
DIRECTIONS *From Reading, take A329 about 3 miles into Pangbourne. Turn right at The George Hotel on to B471, cross the toll bridge and follow the road to Whitchurch-on-Thames. Take the first turning on the right into Hardwick High Street, just opposite a shop on the left called Heron Pictures. Follow the road out of the village and up Path Hill. At the top, turn right into the farm lane just opposite the sharp left bend in the road. Follow the lane and shop is in front of you.*

As its name implies, the farm-shop at Path Hill Farm is converted from the old dairy. The farm is part of the 1,000-acre Hardwick Estate and Elizabeth, married to the owner Sir Julian Rose, positively encourages visitors to walk around the 600 acres of woodlands, 'provided they keep to the paths'. She even has maps of the walkways in the shop.

Julian is a stalwart member of the Soil Association and has sat on the Council for years; so not surprisingly the farm is farmed to Soil Association approved organic standards and most of the produce Elizabeth sells in the shop is own-grown and organic. Beef comes mainly from their suckler (allowed to wean naturally) mixed beef herd of Aberdeen Angus, North Devon, and Charolais (although they sometimes sell sucklers from the dairy herd). The calves are reared on their mothers' milk for the first 6 months to give them a good start, then fed on grass, cereal and silage, and slaughtered at anything between 2-3 years. Hung for about 3 weeks, this is beef at its best: well-grained and juicy with a deep meaty taste and a superb length of flavour, it demands to be noticed. Lamb, grazed on their organic pastures, is hung for 2 weeks and again has that glorious full flavour.

Chickens and – at Christmas-time – turkeys are also first class. I must point out here, however, that they cannot be sold as certified organic because of a mere although to the Soil Association important technicality. The Roses buy in chicks and poults (day-old turkeys) that are not fed organic chick-feed as it is difficult to buy and its cost is prohibitive. So, although they are reared in optimum organic conditions, are truly free-ranging (see the turkeys out in the fields scratching around for nettles), they do not qualify for the symbol. I only wish other producers would be as scrupulous. Pork is bought in from the HOF Shop (see page 204); hams cured for them at Minola (see page 95) and they make their own sausages. These come as chipolatas with 82% meat content in 2 flavours: mild, with nutmeg and sage; spicy, with coriander and ginger; or plump English country, with 99% meat content and

*The pork and chive sausage from butcher **John Walton** at **Steeple Aston (tel 0869 40222)** was the Guardian's champion sausage in 1992. Variously described by the judges as 'Very meaty... Great flavour', 'Juicy, Well-rounded flavour', 'Perfumed', 'Fatty, good texture', Nicholas Soames, the Food Minister, was the only person not fulsome in his praise. He pronounced that it 'smelt better than it tasted', which only goes to prove that you can't please all the people all the time. In fact John's family have been butchers since the late 18th century although, unlike many in his trade, he has kept up and moved with the times. Meat is all bought locally on the hoof from local farms or at market. He hangs his lamb and beef for 14 days, and pork for about a week. He takes pride in preparing and curing tongue, salt beef, pickled brisket and silverside. Sausages are made on the premises, with an average meat content of 84%, although as he is at pains to explain, 'It's the quality of the meat that really matters. It should have a good balance of fat and lean, with plenty of shoulder thrown in for good measure. Then the texture's important – good and chunky – natural casings must be used.' Surprisingly, he does not make up his flavourings or use fresh herbs; everything comes in packets as a pre-mix. In the shop you will find the prize-winning pork and chive, pork and garlic, Lincolnshire, pork and honey, pork and venison, mildly spiced, and hot spicy.*

flavoured with sage and thyme.

The shop has only been open for about 18 months and, at the moment, there is not enough volume to justify stocking every meat fresh every week. Elizabeth has devised a system that works quite efficiently: there is a big blackboard in the shop giving a timetable of what will be in fresh and when, giving everyone plenty of notice and the opportunity to order. If you are after a particular meat, it is best to check first; failing that you can always buy from the well-stocked freezer. During the season there is also game, venison, pheasant, and wild rabbit from the estate and the farm manager's wife makes a hearty rabbit pie well flavoured with celery and carrots.

Rich buttery unpasteurized cream from the Guernsey herd is another must. At one time Julian used to drive up to London and deliver it to the door of the Bibendum restaurant as chef Simon Hopkinson would use nothing else, but time and distance soon made it uneconomical so the only restaurants he now supplies are the Beetle & Wedge at Moulsford and The Royal Oak at Yattendon. Then there are own eggs; organic flour (grown on the estate and milled at Berkley Mills); bread from their flour and oats, baked by a local baker; a selection of own-grown vegetables, including Pink Fir Apple potatoes, various lettuces, shallots, garlic, red onions, carrots and Swiss chard; and own honey.

With plans to widen the range of bought-in organic products, Elizabeth and Julian's commitment to Soil Association standards and a reasonable pricing policy is beyond doubt.

And Also...

• *Shaken Oak Products* ✉ at Shaken Oak Farm, Hailey, nr Witney (tel 0993 868 398) produce a range of handmade hot, medium and mild coarse-grain mustards.

• Set in glorious countryside on the Mapledurham Estate, *Mapledurham Watermill* (tel 0734 723350) is the last working corn and grist mill on the river Thames. There has been a mill on the site since Saxon times. They mill and sell 100% and 81% stone-ground flours; and the machinery is still only powered by the river.

• Butcher *M. Newitt & Sons* at 10 High Street, Thame (tel 0844 212103, fax 0844 217715) is well known for the quality of his meat, the standard of butchering and dressing, the unusual sausages (he has recently introduced 3 new pork flavours: with walnuts, chives, and apricots), and his interest in wild boar. He buys in whole carcasses from Barrow Boar (see page 228), sells various cuts and even makes a wild boar and sherry sausage.

• For excellent free-range Bronze turkeys and geese at Christmas-time, order from *Homewood Partners* ✉, Peach Croft Farm, Radley, nr Abingdon (tel 0235 520094, fax 0235 522688). During the rest of the year they have own-grown soft fruit, potatoes, various vegetables and bags of maincrop potatoes.

• Food writer Ruth Ward highly recommends wholefood shop *Frugal Foods* at 17 West St Helen's Street, Abingdon (tel 0235 522239). Flours and cereals are sold loose and, at Christmas, if you leave your cake and pudding recipes with them, they will weigh out the individual ingredients for you.

• *Hambleden Herbs* ✉ at Hambleden, nr Henley-on-Thames, RG9 6SX (tel 0491 571598, fax 0491 574102) supply – by mail order only – a comprehensive range of dried medicinal and culinary organic (to Soil Association standards) herbs. They also blend some rather interesting teas, including sharp and refreshing Lemon Heaven (a mixture of lemon balm, lemongrass, lemon thyme, lemon verbena, lemon peel and hibiscus), and a punchy Red Mix (made with hibiscus, rosehip, elderflower, orange peel and marigold flowers).

• *Grove Farms (Harwell)* at Milton Hill, nr Abingdon (tel 0235 831575) sell both pick-your-own and a wider choice of ready-picked apples, pears, strawberries, raspberries and plums. If you enjoy unusual plums, try to time a visit for some time in September when the golden-yellow Warwickshire Drooper is ripe. Large, extra-sweet and juicy, it is an old-fashioned variety that lasts a mere day or so. They also have about 18 different ready-picked cherries, starting in June with the densely black sweet Early Rivers through to the meaty Stella in mid- to late-July.

• *Richard Bartlett* (tel 0865 890180) worked for Raymond Blanc for 5 years, helping establish his impressive (and immensely productive) kitchen gardens at Le Manoir. Now he runs his own small business and supplies several local restaurants with an eclectic range of salad crops from all over the world. Apart from rocket, red and green salad bowl, there is the winter-hardy Greek cress, mitzuba (Japanese parsley), purple flowering choy-sum, edible chrysanthemums (for the succulent leaves) and an over-wintered Grumolo chicory.

RUTLAND

THISTLETON   MAP 4

The Herb Nursery 🛒   FRESH HERBS

Grange Farm, Thistleton, Rutland LE15 7RE

TEL *0572 767658* **CONTACT** *Peter Bench* **HOURS** *9.00-18.00* **DIRECTIONS**
From Stamford, take A1 towards Grantham. After about 11 miles, take the Oakham exit, turn right signposted Thistleton and follow signs to village. Herb Farm is in village on the right.

SCENTED SUGAR

Pick a few of the best unblemished leaves from a heavily perfumed scented leaf geranium. Place one on the bottom of a clean dry jar with a tight-fitting lid, tip in some caster sugar and cover with another leaf. Carry on until the jar is full. Close tightly and leave for a couple of months until the sugar is infused with the leaves' volatile oils. Use to sprinkle over soft fruit.

The Herb Nursery is surrounded by flat open countryside. Once inside the stone courtyard surrounded by old barns and the Bench's cottage, however, you feel totally sheltered. Here they grow a wide range of culinary herbs with scented leaf geraniums (pelargoniums), a special feature. Comparatively easy to look after – you let them dry-out thoroughly, then soak them in water – they are a particular favourite. My flat is filled with them; they provide a welcome touch of green all year and scent the rooms with their spicy subtlety every time you brush against the leaves. Moreover, if you are still not convinced of their wonderfulness, the leaves can be used to flavour food (see Les Fines Herbes, page 156).

Peter Bench grows well over 50 varieties. Atomic Snowflake looks splendid with its green and cream foliage, but it loses hands-down to the sharp lemon scent of Lemon Fancy or Mabel Grey. Mint addicts will probably prefer Tomentosum with its downy leaf, Chocolate Peppermint, with its leaves striped with chocolate-brown, or the truly overpowering Peppermint. I spent nearly all day trying to make up my mind, and it is a tribute to Peter's patience that he did not once seem the slightest bit ruffled.

Apart from the potted herbs in the courtyard, Peter grows most varieties of cutting herbs, including parsley, chives, tarragon, chervil, etc. These are sold by weight and cut to order. He supplies nearby Hambleton Hall and other restaurants in the area. He also supplies them with edible flowers, such as marigolds, nasturtiums and borage, and he is more than happy to make up orders, provided you give him a bit of notice.

The **Ram Jam Inn, Stretton (tel 0780 410776)** is a road-side café on the A1 between Stamford and Grantham. Open daily between 7.00-23.00, it is run by Tim Hart of Hambleton Hall fame. No ordinary motorway stop, the food is excellent. Try the meaty Lincolnshire sausages made by Culpin, the butchers in Uppingham, served with a generous helping of their tangy onion marmalade.

SHROPSHIRE

Blackhurst of Shropshire ✉ 🛎   SMOKED FOOD

Drawwell, Clive, Shrewsbury, Shropshire SY4 3JN

TEL *093 928329* CONTACT *Jim Blackhurst* HOURS *9.00-18.00* DIRECTIONS
*From Shrewsbury, take A49 towards Whitchurch. Follow the road about 10
miles into Preston Brockhurst and turn left at sign for Clive. Follow the road
$1\frac{1}{2}$ miles into Clive and take the first turning left in the village at sign for
Drawwell. Smokery is 100 yards along on the right, opposite the church.*

Clive's parish church has a commanding position on the slopes of
Grinshill Hill. Restored by the Bibby family in Victorian times, it is a
local landmark; as you approach the village, the spire-topped tower
draws you in like a beacon. In its shadows lies the Blackhurst smokery.

Jim Blackhurst spent a fair amount of time in Scandinavia, where he
learned to smoke. As a result, the style of smoking is heavier, 'Not for
metropolitan tastes,' says his wife Frances obviously on the defensive.
Country dwellers, however, seem to approve as 'half the county dines
out on our produce' and they boast customers from as far afield as
Staffordshire and Cheshire.

Smoking is done every day in 2 small smoking cabinets over oak
chips, flavoured at times with different aromatic woods. Their products
are certainly gutsy, but not overly so for a mere urban palate: imported
corn-fed chicken, cold-smoked for 36 hours then roasted to cook it
through, is succulent with a well-married taste of salt and smoke;
pheasant from a local shoot, cured in salt and brown sugar and smoked

---

> 🚌 *Be warned, once you start talking to **Arthur Hollins** of*
> **Fordhall Farm** ✉, **Market Drayton, TF9 3PR (tel 0630
> 638255)** *he will keep you at it for hours. Totally at one with his land
> (and there have been Hollins there since the 15th century), farming is
> his consuming passion. An ardent and early member of the Soil
> Association, his ideas are probably best described as 'radical'. When I
> visited him, he insisted on showing me an extraordinary Heath
> Robinson machine he has developed to replace the plough; he believes
> ploughing is harmful to the land, it causes soil infertility and erosion
> and the useful insects are killed when churned up and exposed to
> sunlight. But back to his produce, which he sells either from the farm,
> or by mail order or from his stall at Altrincham Organic market (see
> page 28). As well as fresh beef, pork and lamb, there are chickens
> weighing from 1.8-4 kg (4-9 lb) which are good, strong and immensely
> well-flavoured birds.*

---

over oak mixed with apple-wood, is fairly gamy but has a pleasant sweet haziness; and their hot-smoked trout, farmed over the borders at Glynceiriog near Chirk, had a welcome bite to it.

They also smoke imported corn-fed guinea fowl; Barbary duck breasts for between 8-10 hours to ensure they have a dense smokiness; poussin; quail; and haunch of farmed venison, sold thinly sliced. Farmed salmon from Scotland is cured and cold-smoked, or cured with fresh dill for gravlax – and here the Scandinavian influence is discernible as theirs is far more full-bodied than most.

The Blackhursts also have some 'prepared to order' products: whole duck boned and stuffed with pork, brandy and herbs based on a Nicola Cox recipe; smoked salmon terrine, a creamy mousse wrapped in slices of salmon; and smoked salmon, smoked trout and ducks' liver pâtés. (⊠ Smoked products only.)

PREES GREEN   MAP 4

Dalesman's Ice Cream 🏆   ICE-CREAM

Cruckmoor Farm, Prees Green, Whitchurch, Shropshire SY13 2BS

TEL *0948 840217* **CONTACT** *Andrew Fawcett* **HOURS** *Easter to mid-Sept: Thurs-Sun 10.30-17.30* **DIRECTIONS** *From Whitchurch, take A49 towards Shrewsbury. After about 5½ miles, go over the by-pass and turn left just after The Thames Valley Egg Depot on the left corner. Farm is 600 yards along on the left.*

Dalesman's ice-cream is a marriage of several cultures. Andrew Fawcett hails from Yorkshire (hence the name Dalesman) and he is helped by a German uncle married to an Italian. The uncle has been making ice-cream for 40 years and it was his know-how that gave Andrew a head start.

Cruckmoor is still very much a family farm run by Andrew, his brother and father, with the milk for the ice-cream coming from their 120 Friesian herd. There are two unusual things about Dalesman's ice-cream – its ingredients and its texture. Made from own-milk, sugar, cream and fresh eggs, it does contain an emulsifier/stabilizer in the form of sodium alginate/guar gum. Surprisingly however (and unlike almost every other ice-cream), it does not contain any skimmed milk powder: having worked out their own mix to suit their old-fashioned Italian ice-cream maker, it is just not needed.

The over-run (added air) is also exceptionally low, between 20-25%; as a result this is one ice-cream with a very heavy, dense texture. The overall impression is one of a deep richness, an ice-cream that you can 'bite' into, with plenty of substance – you either love or hate it. Rather misleadingly, its actual fat content ranges between 4 and 7%, but this is because it is gauged on the ice-cream's liquid state and Dalesman's is far thicker than most. So, if it were to have a usual over-run, its fat content would rise to the more normal range of 10-14%.

They make a range of 9 flavours. Some, namely hazelnut, pistachio, mint and toffee, are bought in from an Italian flavour-house; others are own-made and much the better for it. Try as they may, flavour-houses can never exactly reproduce the flavours and I only wish more ice-cream producers would leave well alone. Vanilla is made with ground-up pods and you can see the little black speckles which, believe it or not, actually put some people off. I loved it: buttery and not over-sweet, it was laced with a true musk rather than a synthetic syrupiness. Banana is again made with the 'real' thing, mashed fruit, and again it had the true taste; chocolate, from a dark Belgian couverture, was rich and strong-bodied. Andrew also makes raspberry and strawberry fruit-ices with egg white, sugar and fruit purée; more of a sorbet than an ice-cream, they were refreshing and fruity – if a little too heavily sugared for my taste.

A friendly place (my dog Violet was even offered her own cornet), Andrew sells his ice-cream, along with cream teas and other snacks from a converted cow 'shippon' (cattle shed) and, if the weather is warm enough, you can sit outside in the farmyard sampling the flavours. From the café they sell cornets as well as 1 & 4 litre ($1\frac{3}{4}$ & 7 pt) packs, so remember to bring a freezer bag along with you.

WESTON   MAP 4

Appleby's of Hawkstone 🔲   CHESHIRE CHEESE

Hawkstone Abbey Farm, Weston, Shrewsbury, Shropshire S74 5LE

TEL *0948 840387* CONTACT *Edward Appleby – telephone ahead*

Although not actually in the county of Cheshire, the Applebys make a very fine Cheshire. The special flavour of this territorial cheese, according to John Arlott, is due to the soil of Cheshire, which contains rich deposits of salts. The Appleby's land – not far from the county border – is, they assured me, imbued with the correct minerals.

Mrs Appleby is still in charge of the cheese-making. Taught by her family, she was brought up making cheese a mere 4 miles away until she married and moved lock, stock and barrel in 1940 to Hawkstone Abbey Farm. Here, unlike anywhere else I visited, the cheese-making room is attached to the main house; you enter it straight from the hall that was once the farmhouse kitchen. It must be a bit of a mixed blessing, as Mrs Appleby can never ever really get away from her work. Not that she seems to mind, in fact she positively relishes it as Cheshire is her pride and joy.

John Arlott wrote that, in 1939, there were about 400 farmhouses turning out some 6,000 tons of Cheshire cheese a year, almost all of it a pale orange, coloured with anatto. Now there are a mere handful, with

*George Morley's mother was a Marsh of Marsh & Baxter (one of the great producers of York ham). When George left the family company, he started **Dukeshill Ham** ✉, **Deuxhill, Bridgnorth, WV16 6AF (tel 074 635519)** which specializes in York ham 'the smoked salmon of the meat trade'. He buys in legs of pork with a good fat cover as 'for curing, it's important they're not hyper lean' and dry-cures them for 3 weeks in salt and saltpetre, brushing off and changing the cure 3 times. Then the hams are hung to mature for about 12 weeks until ready; they may be kept longer but, according to George, their taste will not change much after that although their texture becomes denser. Sold uncooked or cooked, on-the-bone (he will bone them raw, but is reluctant to do so because they will not cook so well) and as hams (rather than by actual weight) with a guaranteed minimum weight of 3 kg (6½ lb) for half a ham, 5 kg (11 lb) for a small and 6.3 kg (14 lb) for a whole large one. Definitely not a ham for the faint-hearted, these have a markedly deep robust flavour that is far stronger than the milder Wiltshire-cure hams which George also sells.*

the Appleby's the only one to make a cloth-bound unpasteurized version. They make it 6 days a week with their own milk from their Friesian Holstein-cross herd, and they also make it a lot slower than most. Cheshire has a reputation for being quite a sharp acidic cheese due, in part, to the amount of starter used. The Applebys use far less – about 0.5% as opposed to as much as 5% by others. This means the acidity level in the milk takes far longer to rise, but the result – a richer, buttery, more mellow cheese – makes it worth it.

Cheshire cheese is well known for its loose, crumbly texture and this is achieved by cutting the curds, then breaking them by hand and finally – when all the whey is drained off – milling them. The downside is that it is notoriously difficult to store as it is prone to cracking (which is how it blues naturally) or drying out. The Applebys wrap theirs in calico, then smear it with a bought-in edible paste (originally flour and water) and mature it for at least 6 weeks, but possibly up to 10. (Randolph Hodgson at Neal's Yard Dairy (see page 00), will mature it on for as long as 12 months.) Sold in truckles, ranging from 1.25-22.5 kg (2¾-50 lb), it is a delight: moist, sharp and cut with a subtle saltiness that lingers on the palate. One of the oldest cheeses this country boasts, it was I believe mentioned by name in the Domesday Book. I only hope the Applebys will carry on the great tradition.

Mrs Appleby also makes a mellow Double Gloucester and soft, mild-salted whey-butter that is still churned by hand every day in the wooden butter churn.

> 🚋 Friday is the best day to visit **Shrewsbury Covered Market**. Karen Ross (see page 304) is there selling her cheeses, there are a few market gardeners selling their own-grown vegetables and fruit and a couple of stalls with eggs, poultry and game. **Cook and Carve** at **Unit 12-13 in The Market Hall (tel 0743 231358)** have a permanent stall, where you will find Maynard's bacon, sausages and ham (see below); Herbert's Particular, a locally produced mild but nicely balanced whole-grain mustard, and sharp richly spiced Herbert's Spiced Kumquats; locally made brawn and haslet; as well as own-cooked turkey and ham.

WESTON-UNDER-REDCASTLE

MAP 4

Maynard's Farm Bacon 🏆

BACON & HAM

The Hough, Weston-under-Redcastle, Shrewsbury, Shropshire SY4 5LR

TEL *0948 840252* **CONTACT** *Maynard Davies* **HOURS** *Tues-Sun 9.00-17.30* **DIRECTIONS** *From Shrewsbury take A49, towards Whitchurch. Farm-shop is on the left, after about 12 miles.*

I've had the pleasure of breakfasting with Maynard Davies in his snug dining-room with a warm crackling open fire. It was no cosy occasion this; with him, me and a cast of thousands recording Radio 4's *On Your Farm*. If you're wondering, yes we do eat breakfast while we're chatting and, yes, although the programme is not live, we do record it early in the morning at breakfast-time. Two things stick in my mind about that morning, the quality of the bacon and Maynard's complete dedication to his bacon.

He is a fanatic. Of the school that believes if you do one thing really well you should stay with it, he concentrates on what he knows – producing as good a product as he can. Pigs, reared to Conservation-grade standards are bought in from a local farmer, 'You've got to know where they come from, the age, breed, feed, if they're swill pigs; and for curing for bacon or ham, it's even more important.'

Curing is done in his converted barns behind the shop, where he prepares an extraordinarily wide range of bacons, each differently cured for a different flavour. There is Traditional, dry-salted with an iodine-free salt, 'so it won't weep in the pan', with a good biting texture and a well-developed earthy flavour; Shropshire, dry-cured for longer to give it a slightly harsher, saltier taste; Welsh, cured in a mixture of salt and saltpetre, is softer textured; County, the mildest of them all, is brined with sugar; Honey, brined in an English honey has a shy sweet flavour; English Gold, cured in a treacle brine, has a thicker richer flavour; and Staffordshire Black, easily recognizable by its dark rind, is cured in black treacle for an even thicker, soupier taste. Not everything is in the shop all the time, but each cure comes as a choice of cut from the middle and back (streaky) and as green (unsmoked) or smoked over apple-wood.

Maynard also produces 5 different sausages with natural skins that he fills with lean shoulder meat. These include Shropshire with a 100% meat content, mildly seasoned with salt and pepper; a more heavily seasoned Cambridge; and Lincoln, flavoured with dried sage. Then there are his dry-cured hams; he works them relatively fast as the actual process from curing to maturation takes him about 4 months. The range includes York, dry-cured in salt and saltpetre; and a sweeter, softer Honey ham. If passing, do stop at Maynard's; if you like good old-fashioned bacon, you will not be disappointed.

WROCKWARDINE   MAP 4

The Wrekin Honey Shop ✉ 🏺   HONEY

The Avenue, Wrockwardine, Shropshire TF6 5DG

TEL *0952 254894* **CONTACT** *Ralph Palmer* **HOURS** *Tues-Sun 9.00-18.30* **DIRECTIONS** *Turn off M54 at junction 7, signposted Wellington. Follow the slip road and turn right signposted Wrockwardine. Follow the road about ¹⁄₂ mile into the village. Shop is by the church.*

I have a horror of bees. I'm hyper-allergic to the creatures and, if stung, have to inject myself otherwise I'd be a 'goner'. So it says a lot about Ralph Palmer's enthusiasm and calm gentle air that, even though I was surrounded by those (to me) terrifying insects, I sat still listening to his every word as he waxed on about the glories of his honey.

He runs a tiny shop on the edge of the village, full of all things connected with bees. As well as honey and bee-keeping equipment, you will find candles, teapots and trays decorated with buzzing bees as well as a few of the county's products. A bee-keeper for 20 years, Ralph keeps something in the region of 300 hives based on The Wrekin, an extinct volcano and one of the oldest hills in England. During the spring and summer, he moves his hives all around the county, as not only does he practise migratory bee-keeping in an attempt to obtain the distinctive flavour of a single flower honey, but also the farmers need his bees to pollinate their crops.

As bees travel about 3 miles in any direction, Ralph cannot label his honey as coming from a specific blossom or flower; unless it can be guaranteed. When I visited they were not named as such, but I gather this has changed. Either way he is usually on hand to talk you through the different flavours and there are always plenty of open jars for you to taste. One of the first honeys of the season is pale oilseed rape: not one of my favourites this, I find it bland, sickly sweet and hinting of cabbage. Far more enjoyable are a charmingly light general hedgerow; or a deep aromatic wild flower; clover with a dense lingering aftertaste; a vividly fruity raspberry; or a thick and unctuous broad bean. Depending on where his hives have been placed, you may well find a tingling lime or, if they have been up on the ridge near Stretton, a deep rich heather honey.

Unlike large-scale honey producers, Ralph never flash-heats his to dissolve the crystals and keep it liquid. The very process, he says destroys the enzymes and sugar and reduces the immediacy of the honey's flavour. This does mean that some will crystallize, but honey can always be easily liquefied by gently heating it in a *bain-marie*.

> **T.O. Williams of Wem** ⊠ at **17 High Street, Wem, SY4 5AA (tel 0939 232552)**, *with a branch at Shawbury, make a point of selling local cheeses. Here you will find Cheshire from Appleby's (see page 214), Hares (see page 25) and Windsors, last year's winner at the Nantwich Cheese Show.*

And Also...

• *Franklin's Cider Farm* at The Cliffs, Little Hereford, nr Ludlow (tel 0584 810488) makes cider, scrumpy and a dry and fruity sweet perry from Taynton Squash, Barland, Blakeney Red, Moorcroft and Yellow Huffcap – all traditional perry pears.

• Mike and Julia Thomas of *Stoke Manor*, Stoke-on-Tern, nr Market Drayton (tel 0630 84222) supply most of the local hotels and restaurants with farmed crayfish (see also Whistley Crayfish, page 75). Weighing between 55-85 g (2-3 oz) each and in season from about May to October, they will sell them direct from the farm provided you give them notice.

• Run by Ginny Mayall, *Pimhill Organic Centre and Farm Shop* at Lea Hall, Harmer Hill, nr Shrewsbury (tel 0939 290342) has been battening down the hatches. They have moved back to their original small shop, but still sell frozen organic (to Soil Association standards) meat, own-flour, and bread baked from their flour by T.O. Williams and Bloomers of Wem. I welcome reports on how they have changed.

• *C.G. Sadd* ⊠ of Dorrington (tel 07437 18215) dry-cure hams in salt, saltpetre and brown sugar, then mature them for up to 12 months for a strong meaty flavour and sell them smoked or unsmoked, raw or cooked, on or off the bone. They also cure for bacon.

• *Ellesmere Road Organic Nursery*, Cockshutt, nr Ellesmere (tel 0939 270270) grows a wide range of produce to Soil Association standards. These include strawberries, raspberries, broad beans, tomatoes, cucumber and stunningly sweet hot-house melons that are ripe during July and August.

• *Greenfields Country Store* and PYO is just outside Telford at Station Road, Donnington (tel 0952 677345). The store is packed with local produce and, in season, there is plenty of soft fruit and vegetables to pick.

• Buying asparagus from *Golding Hall*, Pitchford nr Shrewsbury (tel 0694 731204) is an experience. On your way to the 4 acres of asparagus fields, you saunter past the gabled Tudor Hall with a later red-bricked facade that belies its true age. From about the beginning of May through to mid-June you can pick-your-own asparagus. Baskets, knives and a demonstration are provided, but bring your own gloves. If you prefer, you can telephone ahead to order your asparagus ready-picked.

• *Meadow View Quail* ⊠ of Meadow View Farm, Church Lane, Whixall, nr Whitchurch (tel 0948 880300) sells fresh and smoked (to order) quails' eggs as well as jars of pickled eggs and smoked pickled eggs. Pickled sherry eggs are promised for this Christmas and, if you want fresh quail, they will supply them (but the catch is you will have to pluck, clean and dress them yourself).

• *The Hollies Farmshop*, Welshampton, nr Ellesmere (tel 0948 75253) specializes in a wide range of own-made jams, marmalades, pickles and chutneys. Mrs Thomson claims to be 'excellent with spices' and to prove her point makes an Iranian-style pickled aubergine and a red-and-yellow-pepper jelly.

SOMERSET

BUCKLAND ST MARY

MAP 2

Swaddles Green Farm ⊠ 🚜 🌿   ORGANIC MEAT

Swaddles Green Farm, Hare Lane, Buckland St Mary, Chard, Somerset TA20 3JR

TEL *0460 234387*   **FAX** *0460 234591*   **CARDS** *Access, Visa*   **CONTACT** *Charlotte Reynolds*   **HOURS** *Thurs-Fri 10.00-18.00 Sat 10.00-13.00* **DIRECTIONS** *From Ilminster, take A358 towards Taunton. After about $2\frac{1}{2}$ miles, turn left at sign for Broadway. Drive through Broadway and, after about $1\frac{1}{2}$ miles, signpost for farm-shop is on right.*

Swaddles Green Farm, a 35-acre holding in the Blackdown Hills, has been farmed by Charlotte and Bill Reynolds since 1987. All the meat and poultry they sell conforms to the Organic Farmers and Growers Association, approved by UKROFS (the United Kingdom Register of Organic Food Standards). Recently they have converted an old flint barn into a cold store, chilled cutting rooms and poultry processing units in 'an attempt to keep well ahead of all anticipated EC regulations'. Although as Bill wryly points out, 'You have to be a pretty talented mind reader to anticipate the vagaries of the Brussels bureaucrat'.

They sell lamb, pork, poultry and beef. Although they do not farm the entire range themselves (due to the size of their holding, they have to buy in from other approved organic farms), everything is hung and butchered there. Beef, however, is mostly from their own herd. Raised as single-sucklers (left to wean naturally), they are fed on grass and hay, supplemented with turnips and barley. Slaughtered at a minimum age of 2 years to ensure a full rounded flavour, the beef has a tender texture, partly no doubt because it is always hung for 3 weeks. I was also impressed by the quality of their mince. There are 3 grades: everyday – from flank, bits of brisket and trimmings; lean – from chuck, clod and sticking (the top end of the rump); and ground steak – from the top rump and steak trimmings. Before he joined Swaddles Green, butcher Graham was of the 'traditional' school, a polite way of saying that he subscribed to the view that mince was no more than 'a receptacle for the junk'. They have, however, swiftly won him round.

Lamb comes from a Friesland milking sheep crossed with a Suffolk ram, because they believe it has good eating qualities. Their pigs – reared near Okehampton and on the Quantocks – are a mixture of various old rare breeds, such as Saddlebacks, Berkshire, Gloucester Old Spots and Tamworths for a fuller, deeper flavour. All the normal cuts are sold but shoulders are invariably used for sausages with a 95% meat content. These are chunky, satisfying robust versions, that come as: plain; herb; garlic (made with fresh garlic for a change); tomato and chilli; tomato, basil and garlic, and red wine. The range of *charcuterie*, however, was far less pleasing: *jambon cru* was dry, over-salted and over-smoked and a couple of the pâtés I tasted were a little grainy and unsubtle. They also prepare chunky faggots (made from liver, lights and heart) and various pies and freezer meals.

For Christmas they grow Bronze turkeys. Dry-plucked and hung for 7-10 days, they weigh between 5-10 kg (11-22 lb) and of these I have heard good reports. Chickens are available all year round. Reared on an organic cereal mix with a fair amount of lucerne, their flesh is a glossy yellow. Killed at about 10 weeks, they normally weigh between 1.35-2.3 kg (3-5 lb), although at Christmas and Easter they welcome special orders for larger birds that can weigh anything up to 3.75 kg ($8\frac{1}{2}$ lb). Bill does a weekly run to London for a door-to-door delivery service.

CHEWTON MENDIP   MAP 2

Chewton Dairy Farms ✉ ☎

CHEDDAR CHEESE & BUTTER

Priory Farm, Chewton Mendip, nr Bath, Somerset BA3 4NT

TEL *0761 241666* CONTACT *Nigel Pooley* HOURS *Mon-Sat 9.00-16.30; Sun 10.00-16.30* DIRECTIONS *From Bath, take A39 towards Wells. Follow signposts to dairy.*

Although I do not rank their Cheddar as one of the 'greats', it is still better than several I have tried. They make traditional cloth-bound cheeses using pasteurized milk from the 5 tenanted farms on Lord Chewton's estate. Sold as mild (matured for 6 months), mature (9-12 months) and extra-mature (over 12 months), it has a firm texture and a sharp flavour that mellows and fills out as it ages. Sainsbury's own-label farmhouse extra-mature is, I believe, supplied by them. The dairies are worth visiting if for no other reason than to see Cheddar being made. They have a viewing gallery where, if you can spare the time, you can stay to watch the whole process or just drop in for a few minutes. There is also a shop where you can buy their cheese and whey-butter with its pronounced cheesy flavour, own-made jams and various other English cheeses.

A few traditional Cheddar cheese-makers will sell direct to the public either from the dairy or a small shop. These include: **Mrs Montgomery** ✉, **Manor Farm, North Cadbury, nr Yeovil, BA22 7DW (tel 0963 40243)** *who makes a fine classic unpasteurized cheese and nicely ripened whey-butter;* **H.G. Green, Newton Farm, Pennard, nr Glastonbury (tel 0458 834414)**, *their pasteurized Cheddar is a fine nutty cheese;* **Times Past Cheese Dairy** ✉, **The Wireworks Estate, Bristol Road, Bridgewater, TA6 4AP (tel 0278 445339)** *make both unpasteurized and pasteurized cheeses; and* **Cricket Malherbie Farms, Stowey Court, Nether Stowey, nr Bridgewater (tel 0278 732084)** *who sell both traditional and block cheeses and whey-butter. See also Denhay Farms (page 71), D.M. Keen & Sons (page 229); and Chewton Dairy Farms (page 220).*

CREECH ST MICHAEL MAP 2

Charlton Orchards ✉ 🛒 APPLES

Charlton Road, Creech St Michael, Taunton, Somerset TA3 5PF

TEL *0823 412979* **CONTACT** *Robin Small* **HOURS** *mid-Aug to end-Mar: Mon-Fri 15.30-18.00 Sat-Sun 10.00-17.00* **DIRECTIONS** *At exit 24 of M5, take A38 towards Taunton. Follow the road for about 3 miles, turn left on to A361, direction Glastonbury. After about ¾ mile, turn left at sign for Charlton Road (No Through Road). Orchard is 1 mile down road on the left.*

Unlike many other commercial apple orchards where 'yield per tree, regularity of cropping and uniformity of fruit size' are the major preoccupations, June and Robin Small choose their varieties for their flavour and texture. 'We only grow them if they are really good to eat'. Grown under an 'integrated pest management system' (meaning they do not blanket spray trees, but monitor them closely and only spray when necessary), they have over 15 varieties and are always adding to them.

The apple season starts in mid-August with the lightly strawberry-flavoured Discovery and moves on to Katy, Merton and Fortune in September. Next come late-season apples (varieties ripening for eating in October to December) including the nutty Cox's, the orange-and-red-cheeked Lord Lambourne and one of my great favourites, the creamy-white-fleshed, slightly russeted, sweet and intensely aromatic Orléans Reinette – the ideal Christmas apple. They grow a few extra-late season apples (for eating in December to March) like Winston, Gloster 69 and the firm juicy Suntan with plenty of acidity. To add to these, they are putting in Claygate Pearmain, originally found in Claygate in 1822, with its rich nuttiness and refreshing zest, and Ashmead's Kernel, an old variety, famous for its 'pear-drop' taste.

All their apples are kept in cold storage until ready, and are sold from their grading shed by the pound or in 4.5 and 9 kg (10 and 20 lb) trays. There are 'always apples for tasting so visitors can try the varieties and see what is in season'. The Smalls also mail out a 2.7 kg (6 lb) Traditional English Apple box of either Cox's, Suntan or Orléans Reinette (or a mixture of the 3). A superb Christmas present – one year I gave a box each to all my friends and they have not stopped talking about it since – each apple is hand-wrapped in tissue, so not only do they look pretty but they also keep a lot longer.

With several orchards in the county, there are 2 more worthy of special mention. **West Bradley Orchards, nr Glastonbury (tel 0458 50227)** has special PYO week-ends in September (telephone for dates). Here you will find a good variety of apples, including Charles Ross and the aniseed-tasting Kidd's Orange. Earlier in the year they also sell Early Rivers and Marjorie Seedling plums, pears such as Concorde, Conference, Comice and Beth, greengages (provided the frost does not get to them); and, only very occasionally, apricots (if the badgers do not get to them first, the squirrels will). They also sell their own apple juice, the blend depending on what varieties are available. **Stawell Fruit Farm, Stawell, nr Bridgewater (tel 0278 722732)** grow 25 varieties of apple in their orchards sheltered in a fold of the Polden Hills on the edge of Sedgemoor. Their PYO season usually starts in the second week of August and runs through until mid-October, and the orchards are open from 11.00-17.00 on Wednesdays to Sundays only. They grow 2 early cookers, Grenadier and George Neal, and the later Bramley. Amongst their eaters are the early Scarlet Pimpernel and Discovery, Worcester Pearmain, Cherry Cox (a Cox clone with a dark red flush), Greensleeves and Fiesta in mid-September. Later on come Ida Red, Laxton Superb and Ashmead's Kernel. They also sell their own cloudy juice pressed for them. Made primarily from Cox's and Bramley, with other varieties added, it has a full fresh fruity flavour with a pleasing sweetness.

CURRY RIVEL

MAP 2

French's Escargots 🔲

SNAILS

Beechfield Farm, Curry Rivel, Langport, Somerset TA10 ONP

TEL *0458 252246* FAX *0458 253072* CONTACT Nicola French – *telephone ahead*

The British have never embraced snails with quite the same enthusiasm as the French. In the West Country, where they are known as 'wallfish' (because they float along walls – imagine), they are supposed to be a local delicacy. I have yet to meet a local who indulges. There must be a demand, however, because Nicola French farms them there. Admittedly most of her customers are local restaurants, but she is more than happy to sell them directly to the public.

Her snails are superior garden snails, *'petit gris'*, the variety favoured by the French. Reared outdoors in poly-tunnels between April and September and fed on mixed greens growing in the tunnels, they are then brought indoors into a barn to hibernate. Available throughout the year, Nicola needs at least 24 hours notice to collect an order. The advantage of buying snails from her is that they are so fresh they are still alive; the disadvantage is the lengthy preparation this incurs.

Actually, it is not that difficult. Once you have collected the snails (and do remember to take a box with a tight-fitting lid otherwise they will escape all over the car), the first thing is to kill them. This is achieved simply enough by plunging them in boiling water. Once cooled down, they have to be hoicked out of their shells. Again, a simple enough operation provided you have a skewer and a strong wrist-flicking action. Then they have to be thoroughly washed under cold running water until it runs clear. Finally they must be gently simmered (too high a heat and they turn rubbery) for about 1 hour, preferably in a *court-bouillon* made with water, cider or wine, bay leaves, onion, carrot, mixed herbs, salt and pepper. At last they are ready to be stuffed back in their shells and baked in garlic butter or whatever you fancy.

HAMBRIDGE

MAP 2

Brown & Forrest ✉ 🔲

SMOKED EEL

The Smokery, Bowdens Farm, Hambridge,
Somerset TA10 0DR

TEL *0458 251520* FAX *0458 253475* CARDS Access, Visa, Mastercard, Eurocard CONTACT Michael Brown – *telephone ahead*

The natural habitats of the Common or Freshwater Eel are rivers, ponds and lakes, but it is able to survive both in and out of water. In the autumn – when mature – eels turn silver and this is the best time to trap them, while they are plump and juicy with rich succulent flesh. To avoid damaging them, they are caught in racks straddled across the rivers as they swim downstream on their way to the sea, beginning their extraordinary exhausting journey to their breeding grounds in the Sargasso Sea. Because of our current problem of pollution, it is vital that eels come from clean, unpolluted water.

Michael Brown collects his from all over the country – from the pure sweet black water of Lake Llangorse in Brecon, the upper sources of the chalk streams of the river Itchen near Winchester, Test near Whitchurch, Nadder near Hindon, and locally. Then Michael freezes them as 'it's the most efficient and painless method of killing them'. It also means that he has a supply of eels in prime condition throughout the year. Hot-smoked over beech-wood to cook them right through, they are sold as whole eels, usually weighing about 900 g (2 lb), and in 225 g (8 oz) and 450 g (1 lb) packs of neatly cut fillets. With a full meaty flavour and a soft, slightly gelatinous texture, Michael recommends eating them simply seasoned with freshly ground black pepper and a squeeze of lemon to cut their richness. Occasionally, Michael has a supply of elvers (see Workman & Meadows, page 97).

He also smokes wild Scottish salmon and hot- or cold-smokes trout. The cold-smoked trout is cured in a mixture of salt, brown sugar and whisky that results in a mild sweet flavour.

> *On top of the Mendips is serious snail country. Between May and August, **The Miner's Arms, Priddy (tel 0749 870217)** is awash with fine specimens gathered by the locals. Frozen to ensure a year-round supply, they are served baked with a herb butter without a trace of garlic.*

HEATH HOUSE   MAP 2

R.A. Duckett & Co   CAERPHILLY

Walnut Tree Farm, Heath House, Wedmore,
Somerset BS28 4UJ

TEL *0934 712218* CONTACT *Chris Duckett – telephone ahead*

Caerphilly, although thought of as a Welsh cheese, has a tradition of being made in Somerset and this is the third generation of Ducketts to produce it. Chris's mother still remembers when cheeses were taken to market at Highbridge and sent by rail to Wales. During the last century, the size of the rural population in Wales shrank due to growing industrialization. However, as it was such a favourite of the miners, demand for Caerphilly increased. As not enough milk was produced in Wales to fulfil the demand, the farmers on the other side of the Bristol Channel saw the opportunity and swiftly went for it. Already producing Cheddar, the idea of adding Caerphilly to the list suited them as it is a quick cheese to make with a fast turnover. Cheddar takes at least 6 months to mature, but Caerphilly is ready within 5 days.

Chris, his brother Phil and their mother make Caerphilly every day with unpasteurized milk from their herd of 120 Friesians. Using the night and morning milk, it is started and renneted (using a vegetarian rennet). From then they have to work very fast as the whole process takes a mere 2 hours. The junket is cut in 3 directions, stirred for 45 minutes and quickly drained until the whey has settled. The curds are then piled in a 'semicone' and stacked at one end of the vat, cut with hand-knives into 2.5 cm (1 in) cubes, salted and – if making the chive-flavoured Wedmore – the dried herbs are added.

Finally they fill the traditional Caerphilly moulds (made from metal) which have a cap or rim at the top, making the cheese instantly recognizable by its distinctive curved shape. The Ducketts still use them (several farmers have gone over to more convenient straight-sided plastic moulds) and they also still use their magnificent, ornately decorated, cast-iron upright cheese presses dating from 1866. The cheeses are lightly pressed for about 18 hours, depending on their size – they produce 3.5-4 kg (8-9 lb), 1.8-2.3 kg (4-5 lb) and 900g-1.35 kg (2-3 lb) rounds – then brined for 24 hours and kept until about 4-5 days old. Eaten when young, Caerphilly is moist and crumbly with a sharp, fresh lemony flavour punched with salt.

Unlike most other Caerphilly, however, these can also be successfully aged. Randolph Hodgson of Neal's Yard Dairy (see page 164) matures them for 2-3 months, until they acquire a richness and a nutty mellowness. James Aldridge, a self-appointed artisan cheese maturer, washes the rinds and bathes them in wine from Kent. The result is Tornegus, similar in texture to a Pont L'Evêque, but with a cleaner, sharper flavour. Chris usually keeps back a young plain and a Wedmore to sell from the farm to his local customers. As by-products from the whey, he also makes a rich, sharp clotted cream and, at the end of the week, churns that into a ravishing butter.

KILMERSDON   MAP 2

R.T. Herbs ▟   HERBS

Orange Farm, Kilmersdon, Bath, Somerset BA3 5TD

TEL *0761 435470* **CONTACT** *Richard Taylor* **HOURS** *9.00-18.00*
DIRECTIONS *In village centre.*

Crammed into a long narrow strip is one of the most magical herb gardens you are ever likely to find. It is a quiet gentle place and the only noise you are likely to hear is the constant fluttering of pigeons as they fly back and forth into their loft in the middle of the gardens. Richard and his wife Alice, who incidentally doubles up as the village's sub-postmistress, grow a wide range of culinary herbs as well as some splendid herbaceous perennials.

Virtually all the plants are grown by propagation and look very healthy specimens indeed. Apart from the usual culinary herbs, you will find some interesting varieties: pineapple sage; prostrate rosemary which grows flat to the ground; garlic-flavoured chives; wild celery; silver-grey buddleia mint; and Buckler's sorrel, with its small heart-shaped, sour-flavoured leaf that is splendid mixed into a salad.

There are some plants with edible flowers, such as violas, violets and mallows, and the odd old-fashioned vegetable, like Alexanders, cardoon, Good King Henry and sea holly. The latter's roots, Alice assured me, can be candied, although she confessed she has had neither the time nor inclination to try it.

> Phil Vickery, the chef at the **Castle Hotel, Taunton (tel 0823 272671)** together with Kit Chapman the owner/manager make a point of focusing on local produce. The style is traditional-with-a-twist. On the menu last November was a Baked Crab Tart with Hollandaise Sauce; a hearty and richly sauced Braised Beef with Chestnuts, Celery and Port; a selection of cheeses (invariably Mrs Montgomery's Cheddar, see page 221) with Home-made Walnut Bread and then Bread and Butter Pudding with cream to finish. Ever keen to promote their local producers, they print names and addresses on the menu.

KINGSBURY EPISCOPI

MAP 2

The Somerset Cider Brandy Company ✉ 🍶
CIDER & CIDER BRANDY

Burrow Hill, Kingsbury Episcopi, Martock, Somerset TA12 5BU

TEL *0460 40782* **CONTACT** *Julian Temperley* **HOURS** *Mon-Sat 9.00-17.30* **DIRECTIONS** *From Langport, follow road towards Muchleney into Kingsbury Episcopi. At village, follow the Hambridge Road past The Rusty Axe pub. Cider farm is ½ mile along on left.*

According to David Kitton, author of *The Good Cider Guide* who you would expect to know about these things, 'Julian Temperley is something of a politician in the world of traditional cider. He is an enthusiastic advocate for the supremacy of Somerset, stoutly maintaining that his county grows the finest apples and consequently produces the best results'. Getting a cider right means 'getting the orchard right and his (Julian's) 140 acres are a careful selection of some 10,000 trees, mostly Somerset varieties such as Dabinett, Porter's Perfection, Yarlington Mill, Chisel Jersey, Somerset Red Streak and, of course, the famous Kingston Black.'

Julian despairs of other counties, foreign apples and – worse still –

chemical concoctions of the mass producers. His cider is made in a wooden slatted cider house that has been in use for well over 100 years, fermented in oak vats and sold from wooden barrels. Visitors are positively encouraged to sample before buying.

Somerset Royal Cider Brandy, however, is the fulfilment of a dream. Cider Brandy (similar to Calvados) had not been distilled in England for several hundred years, until the mid-1980s, when Hereford Cider Museum was granted a licence. In 1989 Julian Temperley was awarded the first commercial one, although thanks to the vagaries of HM Customs and Excise, the distillery has to be sited 2 miles away and is not visitable. Somerset Royal Cider Brandy can, however, be tasted and bought at Burrow Hill. Aged for 3 years in oak barrels and with a fine spicy bouquet and a fresh apply palate, it slips down the throat like a dream – with plenty of kick. Made from a variety of apples, including Royal Somerset, with a bottled alcohol strength of 42%, each year produces a different vintage. To mark the years Julian commissions artists to illustrate the labels. In 1991 it was Dame Elizabeth Frink. In 1992 Patrick Reynties. (⊠ Somerset Royal Cider Brandy only.)

Phil Bowditch, 7 Bath Place, Taunton (tel 0823 253500) is *the fishmonger in Taunton. His shop is very cool, with white tiles, plants in baskets and simple uncluttered displays of fish bedded in crushed ice and surrounded by seaweed. The fish is first rate, with freshness a priority – exactly what you would expect from a fishmonger who meets the exacting standards of Shaun Hill at Gidleigh Park.*

Mostly Phil buys from Brixham Market and from his own 2 boats. There is never a huge display in the shop, but if you are after a particular species do ask as he keeps a larger selection out at the back. In summer you could be tempted by gleaming wild salmon caught in the West Country from the rivers Exe, Dart and Teign (Phil reckons that Teign salmon is best); stiff silvery sea-bass; or the cheaper alternative of black bream; and big-shelled, fat-fit-to-busting mussels from Barnstable in North Devon with a flavour 'way out on their own'.

PAWLETT   MAP 2

Barnard & Gooding Dairies 🏠   ICE-CREAM

Keward Farm, River Road, Pawlett, Somerset TA6 4SE

TEL 0278 685173 **FAX** 0278 684664 **CONTACT** *Jim Barnard* **HOURS** *Mon-Fri 9.00-17.00 Sat 9.00-12.00* **DIRECTIONS** *From Bridgewater, take A38 towards Bristol. After about 2 miles, turn left just before the Pawlett Manor nightclub. Follow the road past the post office, turn first left into Gaunts Road and turn first left again into River Road. Turn second left into dairy.*

Barnard & Gooding is a farm-based dairy with its own pasteurizing, bottling and ice-cream plants. They run several local milk-rounds and the milk for all their products – fresh milk, single, double, whipping and clotted cream and ice-cream – comes from their own Friesian herd that graze on the lush pastures bordering the Pawlett Hams. Dr Jim Barnard is a trained scientist who once worked at Scotland Yard. His background actually helped him for, as he told me, 'against the advice of ice-cream experts who said that chemicals were necessary, it helped me to develop a pure "natural" ice-cream that contains no artificial anything'.

The ice-cream is made with their milk and double cream, sugar, egg yolk, dried skimmed milk and carob bean gum. Extracted from the seed of the carob tree, carob bean gum is a natural ingredient, but that does not necessarily make it good. Used here as a stabilizer 'to maintain its (the ice-cream's) rich texture', it does, in fact, give it a slightly gummy taste. A pity that, as otherwise their ice-cream would be very good indeed. With a fat content 'heading for 16%' and an over-run (added air) of 30%, it is creamy and fresh tasting. Banana, 'to which we simply add fresh bananas,' had a musky lingering flavour; Coffee was nicely intense; Cointreau & Ginger, a mixture of the liqueur and orange zest, was perhaps a little sweet for my taste. Vanilla, always a good test for quality, had a buttery creaminess; Chocolate Chip and Chocolate were a little dull, but then I like them oozing with the stuff; and the Strawberry, replete with pips, was made with frozen strawberries and essence of strawberries dissolved in alcohol. Doesn't sound too natural to me.

At Christmas they also make a Christmas Pudding ice-cream which, when I tasted on site, was incredibly moreish. However, several months later a sample arrived for *The Farming Week* Christmas programme (we were broadcasting a farmer's Christmas meal) and this was far thinner and lacked the original spice and punch. It is only fair to say at this point that Barnard & Gooding ice-cream is far better than most; it is just when it is so nearly right I get very picky.

Nigel Dauncey is one of the country's biggest dealers in wild boar. With over 50 breeding sows, his troop (herd) is pure-bred (as opposed to cross-bred with pigs) from French, German and Polish stock. Raised outdoors, they graze on grass, seeds or whatever they find and are fed a mixed feed of root crops, sugar beet, fodder beet and potatoes. Slaughtered at about 18 months for a full flavour, the carcasses are hung for about 2 weeks and sold whole, or butchered into specific joints such as loin, loin chops, boned-out haunch, and diced shoulder. They may also be turned into meaty and rather powerful sausages. Wild boar meat – a dark rich red in colour – is rather robust and pungent, with a dense texture. Details from **Barrow Boar** ✉ , **Fosters Farm, South Barrow, nr Yeovil, BA22 7LN (tel 0963 40315)**.

D.M. Keen & Sons 🏠   CHEDDAR CHEESE

Moorhayes Farm, Verrington Lane, Wincanton,
Somerset BA9 8JR

TEL *0963 32286* CONTACT *Stephen Keen – telephone ahead*

Moorhayes Farm is situated in the sheltered countryside between the Blackmore Vale and Mere Downs. Stone brash and clays underlay the soil on which their 160 Friesian cows graze and the Keen family use all the milk to make a superb – probably the best – traditional unpasteurized Farmhouse Cheddar cheese. In 1990 they built a new state-of-the-art dairy with a 1,000-gallon vat but, I am delighted to say, cheese-maker Jack Parsons still makes traditional farmhouse Cheddar in the time-honoured way.

To explain the lengthy process as simply as possible: once the milk has been started and renneted, it coagulates and forms a junket which is cut by knives to separate it into curds and whey. These are then 'scalded' at a temperature of 40-41°C (104-106°F) until the desired acidity level is reached. The whey is drained off and the curds cool, then they are cut into large rectangular pieces ready for 'cheddaring'. This is done by hand and is incredibly hard work as the curds are stacked and re-stacked and turned to assist the draining of the whey. It continues until the whey runs clean and the level of acidity is right. Next the curds are milled, salted and finally shovelled into cloth-lined moulds, ready for pressing.

Initially pressed for 24 hours, they are then grease-bandaged (wrapped in a muslin cloth dipped in lard) to help form the rind on the cheese. A rind allows a cheese to breathe as it matures, but prevents mould penetration. The cheeses are stored and turned until ready to eat, which for a mild cheese could be as little as 9 months and for an extra-mature one as long as 20 months.

The Keen's Cheddar is quite marvellous. I tried a wedge cut from a 16-month truckle – golden yellow, quite firm and dry, it cut 'clean' and had a nutty rich well-balanced flavour with the merest hint of salt and a 'kick' in the throat. They do make small truckles weighing about 675 g ($1\frac{1}{2}$ lb), but these never seem to develop the same length and complexity of flavours. If visiting, do not forget to try their creamy whey-butter with an acid catch and the thick, unctuous pasteurized double cream. Quite rightly, the family has resisted pressure to pasteurize the milk.

As far as I know, only 2 farms exclusively make unpasteurized Farmhouse Cheddar – here at Moorhayes and Mrs Montgomery at Manor Farm, North Cadbury (see page 221). Until recently, most of the supermarkets (somewhat misguidedly) insisted on pasteurized cheese and it still remains a controversial issue. For a small on-farm maker using their own milk or milk from known sources, it should not be necessary, particularly if the milk is carefully handled and scrupulous hygiene is practised from milking right through to the storing.

The best argument against pasteurization I ever read, comes from *Cheese* (4 vols) by Dr J.G. Davis, 'Raw milk cheese nearly always has a fuller flavour than pasteurized milk cheese. Such a need (of pasteurization) would indicate careless methods of production for which there is no excuse...The commonest danger...is the assumption by less well-informed workers that pasteurization will make dirty milk clean, and eliminate all troubles of bacterial origin'.

> " *When used to describe any product, the term 'farmhouse' conjures up a certain image. We expect (or rather hope, as most of us are aware how much the word is abused and mis-used) that the food is 'traditionally' made on a farm and 'wholesome' (another word to conjure with).*
>
> *Let us look at the Farmhouse Cheddar Cheese scheme run by The Milk Marketing Board in conjunction with Mendip Foods Ltd, wholesalers, marketers and distributors. In order to use the distinctive black, yellow and white Farmhouse logo, the cheese must be made 'on a farm' by a registered milk producer; must include a proportion of milk from that farm with the balance coming from identifiable farms; must be made by traditional 'in-vat' methods; must be graded by the MMB and achieve a superfine or fine grade; and must be sold via Mendip Foods Ltd.*
>
> *So far, so good. But does it go far enough? What it does not stipulate is the shape and maturation of the cheese. A traditional Farmhouse Cheddar – as far as I am concerned – is cylindrical, clothbound, rinded and matured for a minimum of 10 months. Several Farmhouse Cheddar-makers, however, also produce 'block' cheese. Made in exactly the same way up to the point of pressing, it is pressed in cloth-lined rectangular moulds, turned out, wrapped in plastic film and packed in wooden slats to ripen for only 6 months. Unlike the cylindrical cheeses, this does not breathe and loose moisture and it matures a lot faster.*
>
> *As such, I have nothing against block farmhouse – one was even voted Supreme Champion at The Bath & West Cheese Show in 1992 – although in terms of texture and taste, it is denser and generally far less interesting. Currently both traditional cylindrical and block versions are marketed as the same cheese, but Cheddar cheese-makers ought to be obliged to distinguish between the two. They are not the same cheese as they are not matured to the same traditional recipe. The reputation and future of Traditional Farmhouse Cheddar will be undermined unless the situation is clarified.* "

And also....

• For lean duck with plenty of breast meat, a good meat-to-carcass ratio and a good strong taste, try oven-ready Gressingham, a mallard hybrid, from **Burrow Products**, Higher Burrow Farm, Timberscombe, nr Minehead (tel 0643 841427).

• Gill Durman of **Somerset Ducks** ✉, North Newton, nr Bridgewater (tel 0278 662656) bones, stuffs and cooks whole ducks or turns them into sausages, pies, and pâtés.

• Mostly blue cheese is made at **Exmoor Blue Cheese** ✉, Willett Farm, Lydeard St Lawrence (tel 09847 328). The range covers an unpressed 'spreadable' hard and a soft 'similar to a Bleu d'Auvergne' in goats', sheep's and cows' milk.

• Juicy heads of unsprayed garlic, sold loose or in plaits, can be bought straight from **Somerset Garlic**, Bradfields Farm, Bradford-on-Tone, nr Taunton (tel 0823 461260).

• When in the country, Caroline Waldegrave, Principal of Leith's School of Food & Wine, buys her bread freshly baked by **The Post Office**, Bathway, Chewton Mendip (tel 0761 241325).

• If you like *cidre bouché* (sparkling mellow Normandy cider), the nearest English equivalents I have found are medium Bullfinch and dry Goldfinch from **Sheppy's Cider** ✉, Three Bridges, Bradford-on-Tone, nr Taunton (tel 0823 461233).

STAFFORDSHIRE

ACTON   MAP 4

Staffordshire Organic Cheese ✉ ▦ ✐

STAFFORDSHIRE CHEESE

New House Farm, Acton, Newcastle, Staffordshire ST5 4EE

TEL *0782 680366* **CONTACT** *Betty Deaville – telephone ahead*

Michael and Betty Deaville have been farming organically to Soil Association standards since 1975, but it was not until 1984 that they decided to make cheese using unpasteurized milk from their Ayrshire herd.

As Staffordshire has no history of cheese-making, there was no local traditional recipe so Betty opted instead for a Cheddar-style recipe. Unlike a Cheddar, hers is a fast-maturing cheese ready for eating at 2 months and quite strong by 6 months. The only explanation Betty could offer for this was the fact she uses a vegetarian rennet; but, as several Cheddar-makers do use a vegetarian rennet, I was not convinced.

No matter, her cheese is still interesting. When eaten young – at about 3 months – it is moist and buttery with a mild grassy tang. As it matures it hardens slightly and develops a deeper resonance and a more punchy kick. Betty also makes 3 flavoured versions: mixed herbs, made with dried herbs that were far too overpowering; chives, fresh from the garden that gave it a mild, light touch; and wild garlic gathered from the local woods that lend a 'certain pungency'. If you like garlic-flavoured cheese, you will enjoy this one.

The cheeses are sold as 1.35, 9 or 18 kg (3, 20, or 40 lb) cloth-bound truckles. Betty, although sadly no longer running her farm-shop, keeps supplies of her cheeses for anyone who cares to visit.

Essington Fruit Farm at **Bognop Road, Essington nr Wolverhampton (tel 0902 735 724)** *has a very wide range of pick-your-own and ready-picked fruit and vegetables. Strawberries start the season in June and carry through to September with the autumn-fruiting Ostara. There are also raspberries, tayberries, gooseberries, redcurrants and blackcurrants, blueberries in an acidified bed, and marionberries – a cross between an American black raspberry and a blackberry. In the vegetable line, they grow a good range of Brassicas, including various cabbages, sprouts on the stem, cauliflowers, broccoli and borecole (curly kale). There are also spinach, beetroots, carrots, onions, shallots, peas, sugar snap peas, broad beans, French beans, runner beans, leeks and sweetcorn. Potatoes are not forgotten as they grow over 10 varieties, starting with the early Maris Bard through to Wilja, Cara and the red Stemster.*

BURSLEM MAP 4

High Lane Oatcakes ✉ 🏭 STAFFORDSHIRE OATCAKES

599 High Lane, Burslem, Stoke-on-Trent,
Staffordshire ST6 7EP

TEL *0782 810180* **CONTACT** *Roy Gavin* **HOURS** *Tues 13.00-17.30 Thurs-Sat 7.00-18.00 Sun 7.00-12.00* **CARDS** *Access, Visa* **DIRECTIONS** *From Hanley, take Town Road towards Chell. After about 2 miles, go straight across the Smallthorne roundabout. Follow the road about $\frac{3}{4}$ mile and shop is signposted on the left.*

Quite how and why Staffordshire oatcakes came into being seems lost in the mists of time. William Pitt, in a paper on the agriculture of Staffordshire in 1796, mentions 'oat-bread, which is eaten in considerable quantities in the north of the county, and in the Potteries', but there are few other early references.

From 19th century records, however, a clearer picture emerges: I quote from the treatise 'Oatbread in North Staffordshire' given to me by

Roy Gavin. 'It was rare for the normal village baker to make them. Typically the maker was an elderly widow who earned her living making a few dozen each day on an iron bake-stone over a stick fire on the kitchen range, hanging them to cool on a rack or over a chair back, and selling them around the village from a basket'. Men took over the trade as it progressed, setting up shops in the front rooms of other people's houses and, if the site was good enough 'adjacent to a group of potbanks', business would thrive. Allison Uttley, in *Recipes from an Old Farmhouse*, remembers that although she adored oatcakes 'they were never made at home, for the oatcake man came every fortnight, walking across the hills on mountain paths with his large basket of oatcakes on his arm'.

Staffordshire oatcakes are quite different from the Scottish ones in that they are made with fine oatmeal, white flour and yeast, baked on hot plates and have a texture similar to a pancake rather than a biscuit. Roy Gavin makes about 5,000 a day from his oatcake shop. Large gas-fired bake-stones (griddles) are kept permanently warm and larded and a hopper moves back and forth dropping on the mixture. They bubble up, flatten out and, with a flick of the wrist, are turned over. Racked to dry, they are then ready for eating. On the griddle, Roy also cooks either plain or fruit pikelets that are similar to crumpets.

Quite chewy, Staffordshire oatcakes have a soft pliable texture and a slightly sharp flavour that comes, no doubt, from the oatmeal. The size of a plate and only a few millimetres thick, they are best eaten when warm and can be easily reheated in the oven, under a grill or in a microwave. It was nearly 200 years ago when William Pitt wrote they are 'scarcely known in the south' – and things haven't changed. It is a pity, as their flavour and versatility are appealing. Try them plain, spread with butter or honey, served stacked on a warm plate for breakfast, or wrap them around cheese, sausages or any savoury filling you care to name.

> *In the Potteries, where the oatcakes are sometimes called 'Potteries Popadums' or 'Clay Suzettes', there are several makers.* **The Oatcakery** ✉ *at* **3 High Street, Biddulph, ST8 6AW (tel 0782 517649)** *is also recommended – reports on others please.*

RUSHTON SPENCER   MAP 4

Moorlands Cheesemakers ✉ ▤   GOATS' CHEESE

Blackwood Hill, Rushton Spencer, Macclesfield, Cheshire SK11 0RU

TEL 0260 226336 **CONTACT** *Mary Gregory – telephone ahead* **CARDS** *Access, Visa*

Moorlands Cheesemakers is a borderline case. The farm, set in the stunning countryside on the edge of the Peak District, is in Staffordshire while the postal address is in Cheshire. Mary Gregory suffers from no such identity crisis, she is a cheese-maker through and through. Until recently she kept her own goats, but gave them up as they could not produce enough volume of milk; now she buys in milk and pasteurizes it to make her cheeses. She makes 3 different types. Moorlands Original, a soft moulded cheese with a mild flavour, comes as plain, coated with crushed peppercorns or herbs, in 90 g or 1 kg (3 oz or $2\frac{1}{4}$ lb) rounds. Blackwood, made with a mould culture imported from France, is left to ripen for about 3 weeks to develop a bluish grey 'skin' with a soft creamy white interior: 'As it's not pierced,' Mary explained, 'it never blues inside, but if you leave it in the warm, it should ooze like a ripe Camembert'. Rushmoor, made in 1 kg ($2\frac{1}{4}$ lb) truckles, is hard-pressed for about 4 days and matured for a month; it too has the hallmark of all Mary's cheeses – a good consistent texture but a mild (some might say bland) almost imperceptible goatiness.

Mary is a competent cheese-maker; she supplies a whole range of cheese-making equipment by mail order and runs cheese-making courses to prove it. Anyone can apply, and in the one-day course you learn the basics of making curd cheese, soft moulded cheese and hard cheese. Now cheese-making is a craft, and obviously cannot be taught or learnt in 1 day. However, these days are a start and, under Mary's tutelage, they offer an interesting insight into the glorious world of cheese. ($\boxtimes$ Cheese-making equipment only.)

STATFOLD   MAP 4

Innes $\boxtimes$ ▦   Sour-dough Bread & Goats' Cheese

Highfields, Statfold, Tamworth, Staffordshire B79 0AQ

TEL *0827 830097* FAX *0827 830628* CONTACT *Andy Bakewell – telephone ahead*

Hugh Lillingston is a man with a vision, and the guts and determination to see it through. He took over a farm on the family estate in 1986 with the sole intention of producing from it a whole range of quality food. 'That's where the future – if there is any future – for agriculture lies. We were buying in from the Continent all these "fancy" foods that we could as easily make here. So that's what I set out to do'.

From the farm he runs 2 separate but complementary businesses: the bakery and the dairy. Baker Hannah Bennett was sent off to train in France, to learn how to make a true sour-dough bread. Now she bakes the 'real thing' with flour, salt and water and nothing else – no yeast, no sour-dough starter, no nothing. Made over a 5-day period: on the first day flour and water are mixed together in a bucket and left to rise over 24 hours; the next day the mixture is split in half and then doubled up

Rosemary Barnes runs **The Old Stables** at **Packington Moor Farm** ✉, **Lichfield, WS14 9QA (tel 0543 481 223)** *from a converted barn. Most of what is sold is either grown on the farm or cooked in the barn; there are pick-your-own or ready-picked gooseberries, raspberries, redcurrants and blackcurrants, and a few varieties of strawberries – Elsanta, Totem (a good freezing variety) and the Cambridge Favourite. You can buy bunches of their own herbs, including sage, parsley, thyme, chives and mint; bags of their main-crop Romano or Wilja potatoes and 'Barney Bakers', which are washed, scrubbed and ready for the oven; local apples; peas and beans; onions and other root crops, such as turnips and swedes; cabbages and excellent creamy cauliflowers. They also sell a limited supply of their own lamb, fresh pork and bacon, ham and sausages processed from their own pigs by Rosemary's father, a butcher who lives nearby. At Christmas they rear a few turkeys, geese, ducks and cockerels that can weigh as much as 5.4 kg (12 lb). With a bakery on the premises using – whenever possible – the Barnes' own flour, they bake farmhouse bread, scones, feathery light Victoria sponge cakes filled with lemon, chocolate or coffee buttercream, sponge slices, biscuits, Dundee fruit cake, sausage rolls and savoury quiches. They also do a wide range of dishes, pies and casseroles baked to order. Own-made jams – including gooseberry, strawberry, raspberry, damson, rhubarb & ginger, and redcurrant jelly – are all made with their own fruit. They also sell 2 local ice-creams from Park Lane Dairies and Needwood.*

with new flour and water; and so it continues doubling up each day so that from 1 bucket you get 16. On the last day the dough is hand-kneaded, mixed with the nuts or whatever (see below), left for between 4-8 hours for a final rise, then baked off.

Sour-dough is made by a natural fermentation of the flour and was how bread used to be made before yeast was available. Very few bakers in this country make it using the 5-day process (most use a sour-dough starter and leave it for anything between 12-30 hours). Apart from it being an obviously lengthy process, you also need the correct environment to encourage the flour to ferment. 'It took us about 9 months before we had the right yeasts and bacteria floating about in the air', explained Hugh, 'but once you get going, the dough sours consistently'. The result is a dense, very solid bread, a thick – almost teeth-breaking – crust and a glorious tingling, mildly smoky flavour with a mild sour aftertaste which is similar – but much less marked – to a well made, properly brewed bitter. Innes sour-dough comes as a huge 2 kg (4½ lb) loaf 'the mother of them all', that is put in huge wicker baskets for its final rise so that the air can circulate all around it. The 800 g (1¾ lb) loaves are either plain or *pain aux noix* (mixed with hazelnuts, walnuts and raisins); and 400 g (14 oz) loaves are also plain or flavoured with olives, sun-dried tomatoes & mustard seed, walnuts, and sultanas & walnuts.

All the bread is baked in an igloo-shaped wood-burning stone oven that Hugh brought back from St Tropez and re-built stone by stone on the farm. Believed to be over 200 years old, each stone was carved with its number and, to make assembling easier, even the keystone had a key carved in it. To give a good flavour, mostly pine is burnt in the oven; once the fire dies down, the embers are raked to the back and the large breads are put straight on the stone floor, the smaller ones have to stay in their tins, otherwise they would collapse while baking. Unique to this country, Innes bread has an extraordinarily good shelf-life; if kept wrapped up and in a cool place, it should last a good 10 days.

BAKED GOAT'S CHEESE

Simply take one semi-mature Button on a slice of Innes sourdough and place in an oven preheated to 200°C/400°F/gas 6 for approximately 15 minutes. When golden brown, dribble with olive oil and a pinch of oregano and serve immediately.

To go with the bread are the goats' cheeses. These are made by cheese-maker Stella Bennett using unpasteurized milk from the Saanen and Toggenburg herd. She makes 2 types; a fresh light and fluffy curd that is drained in muslin bags and sold in 150 and 200 g (5½ and 7 oz) pots; and a round moulded cheese that is sold fresh at 3 days, semi-mature at 3-5 days and mature at 5-14 days. With a smooth texture, a startlingly pure taste and the mildest hint of goat that develops as the cheese matures, it is sold in 3 different sizes when fresh: Button, the smallest, weighs 40 g (1½ oz), Clifton 150 g (5½ oz) and Bosworth 350 g (12 oz). As the cheeses age, however, they shrink in size and weight.

You can also buy organically grown (to Soil Association standards) vegetables and salads from the walled vegetable garden nearby. And there are plans afoot to start using Friesian cows' milk for a full-cream ripened (lactic) butter and curd cheese. For my money, Innes is a farm with a future.

And Also...

• Keith Stevens, agricultural journalist and part-time farmer, grows a good variety of soft fruit at his 20-acre smallholding *Acton Trussell Fruit Farm*, Acton Trussell (tel 0785 661833). For sale either as ready-picked or pick-your-own are tayberries; blackcurrants; a wide range of strawberries, including Cambridge Favourite, large-fruited but insipidly flavoured Hapil, sweet Gorella, Elsanta, and good-for-freezing Totem; Careless gooseberries; and Glen Clover and Admiral raspberries. The season lasts from about 15th June to the beginning of August. For Christmas he rears free-range geese.

• **Park Lane Dairy** at Manor House, Ashley, nr Market Drayton (tel 0630 673284) makes ice-cream with a 12% fat content in various flavours including rum & raisin (with raisins soaked overnight in rum), Christmas pudding, and raspberry, strawberry and blackcurrant made from frozen fruit. They also serve teas from the farm.

SUFFOLK

ASHBOCKING   MAP 5

James White Apple Juice & Cider Company

APPLE JUICE

The Farm Shop, Helmingham Road, Ashbocking,
Suffolk IP6 9JS

TEL *0473 890202* FAX *0473 890020* CONTACT *Lawrence Mallinson* HOURS *Mon-Sat 9.00-17.00 Sun 10.00-16.00* DIRECTIONS *From Ipswich, take B1077 towards Debenham. After about 7 miles, farm-shop is on the left.*

Proper on-farm apple juices are made with fresh apples. This is the basic and important difference between them and most cartons of apple juices on sale in supermarkets. Whatever they may say about 'pure' or 'no added ingredients', look again carefully. More often than not they are made up from apple concentrates, usually with added sugar. James White's apple juices, needless to say, are made from fresh English apples and – apart from Vitamin C to stop the juice from turning brown – nothing else.

Unlike most on-farm juices, they are filtered completely clear, and are sold in rather sophisticated clear glass bottles. Pressed by variety – Bramley, Cox's and Russet – each one has a distinctive flavour. Bramley is dry and crisp and with, borrowing from wine-speak, 'a thin nose'; Cox's is far fuller, with a deep fruity bouquet that hints of nuts; and Russet is superbly rich with a flowery sweetness that, as Lawrence suggests, 'is best drunk with a dessert or cheese or as an indulgence on its own'.

They also produce cider vinegar and a range of ciders made with cooking and eating apples. According to David Kitton in the *Good Cider Directory*, this is an accepted East Anglian tradition as West Country cider fruit was regarded as 'too bitter'. Suffolk Cider, which is naturally fermented to over 8% alcohol and matured in oak for at least 5 months, has a crisp dry flavour; October Gold, matured for 8 months and then blended with apple juice, is fuller-bodied and fruitier; and Cider Royale, a mixture for mulling, is made with cider, cinnamon, ginger and cloves.

✖ *The Leaping Hare Café, Wyken Hall, Stanton, nr Bury St Edmunds (tel 0359 50240) is a real treat. Run by Carla Carlisle, who did a stint at Chez Panisse in California and now successfully recreates their Almond Tart in Suffolk, it is in a stylish barn conversion with a vineyard attached. You can sip their Chardonnay, Auxerrois and Kernling wines while tucking into California-style food.*

Try their onion tart, or own-smoked (using vine-trimmings) chicken or salmon fish-cakes lightly flavoured with leeks and chillies and served with a sorrel sauce. During the summer there is an emphasis on fish from Lowestoft and salads and vegetables from the garden.

Open from 1st May through to the end of September – on Thursdays and Sundays only – they also organize wine dinners and concerts and open for Christmas shopping and meals in November and December.

CREETING ST MARY · **MAP 5**

Alder Carr Farm Shop 🚜 ⬤

FARM PRODUCE & ICE-CREAM

Alder Carr Farm, Creeting St. Mary, Ipswich, Suffolk IP6 8LX

TEL 0449 720820 **CONTACT** *Joan Hardingham* **HOURS** *Jan to Apr: telephone ahead; end-Apr to end-Aug: 9.30-17.30 Mon-Sat 9.30-17.00; Sept to Christmas: Tues-Sat 9.30-17.00; Sun 10.00-16.00* **DIRECTIONS** *Drive into Needham Market on B1113 towards Stowmarket. Pass the church and turn right at sign for Creeting into Hawksmill Street. Follow the road for $\frac{1}{4}$ mile past the mill and over the bridge. Farm-shop is on the right.*

There is nothing fancy-looking about Alder Carr Farm Shop – it is an honest-to-goodness farm-shop with good honest produce. Most of what is sold is own-grown, starting with asparagus in May (incidentally they supply Marks & Spencer). This is sold graded by size – jumbo, medium and sprue – and condition: grade 1, tightly budded; grade 2, open; and bent, where the bud may be tightly closed but the shape is, well, bent. Then they move on to various soft fruits, such as strawberries, raspberries; redcurrants – Red Lake with its small berries full of flavour and Jonkheer van Tets with its relatively tasteless but huge berries; gooseberries like Leveller, Invicta and the glorious dusty-red Whinham's Industry that eat like plums; loganberries and tayberries – in fact all the usual soft fruit.

What is more unusual is their range of potatoes: the early white waxy-fleshed Maris Bard; Pentland Javelin which is good for boiling; Costello; firm fleshed Wilja; red-skinned Desirée, a good all-rounder; soft-textured Cara for baking; maincrop Maris Piper, excellent for mash; Linzer Delikates which are small waxy potatoes that are ideal for salads. The Hardinghams also grow a good selection of lettuces, including iceberg, butterheads, cos, Little Gems, lollo rosso, as well as escarole

(Batavian) and curly endive. They also provide a colourful collection of both decorative and edible squashes: Hamburg parsley (a mild root vegetable that looks like a small parsnip for adding to soups and stews); spinach; celeriac; and Brussels sprouts sold on stalks, so you can keep them outside and pick them off as you need them for extra freshness.

Joan makes a good selection of jams from their own fruit – greengage, tayberry, strawberry, rhubarb – and the most heavenly fruit ice-cream. Actually it is more like frozen mousse and it is made by whipping the cream and stirring in the fruit. No flavourings, no stabilizers, no emulsifiers, no anything is added – it is so rich, so tempting and, for a change, so pure. Unfortunately, however, it is only sold from the farm-shop.

From their wall-lined freezer and fridge cabinets, they also sell sausages and Suffolk sweet-cure bacon from Creasey in Peasenhall (which, I am sorry to say, is not a patch on Mr Jerrey's, see page 241), Susan Moore's butter and soft cheeses (see page 186) and excellent full buttery Jersey cream from C.E. & V.A. Ayers at Red Lion Farm, Levington (tel 0473 659692).

LITTLE CORNARD   MAP 5

Sawyers Seeds ✉ 🛒 🌿   FRESH HERBS

Sawyers Farm, Little Cornard, Sudbury, Suffolk CO10 0NY

TEL *0787 228498* FAX *0787 227258* CONTACT *John Stevens* HOURS *Sat 9.00-17.00* CARDS *Access, Visa, Mastercard* DIRECTIONS *Telephone ahead.*

Caroline and John Stevens were the founders of Suffolk Herbs. A superb nursery, it quickly built up a reputation for first-class herbs and wild flowers, as well as unusual herb, wildflower and vegetable seeds. In December 1991 they sold the retail/mail order side of the seed-packet business to E.W. King (see page 85) who kept the name Suffolk Herbs. This left the Stevens, now trading as Sawyers Seeds, free to concentrate on growing herbs and wildflowers for seed production and as stock plants.

On Saturdays, you can still buy their organic herbs (grown to Organic Farmers & Growers standards). These include such novelties as anise hyssop with its mauve flowering spikes and anise-flavoured leaves; the long flat-leaved garlic (Chinese) chives with a flavour that is half garlic and half onion; Greek oregano 'the true fiery aroma of Greek cooking'; Italian giant leaf parsley, with its strong flavour and huge leaves; and mountain mint, a North American wild herb with a clear, clean taste of peppermint.

When visiting, if you have the time, do go to Great Cornard Country Park, 3 miles down the road. There is a stunning 10-acre flowering hay meadow seeded by the Stevens. A model of its type, in spring and early summer it is ablaze with a hodge-podge of wildflowers.

> Newmarket is famous for 2 things – racehorses and sausages. Not being a racing man, I can't say anything about the horses, except I hope they're better than the sausages. For years Newmarket has traded on the reputation of its coarse sausages flavoured with 'a secret blend of ingredients'. It is totally unjustifiable as, I have to tell you, they are worse than average. With fierce rivalry as to whose is the authentic sausage, they are made by 3 butchers in the town: the royal-warranted **Musks**, now de-camped from the High Street to **1 The Rookery (tel 0638 661824)**; **F. Holloway & Son, Market Street (tel 0638 662515)**, and **The Pork Shop, Wellington Street (tel 0638 662418)**. With a declared minimum 65% meat content, Musk's were wet, soft and bland, excessively bready, finely chopped and burst their skins when grilled. F. Holloway's (76% meat content) had a coarser texture and marginally better flavour but were, perhaps, not of the first order of freshness. The Pork Shop's (80% meat content) had a fine-to-medium chop, were remarkably pink, dry-textured and had a strong peppery taste. I rest my case.

ORFORD

MAP 5

Butley Orford Oysterage ✉ 🔨   SMOKED FISH

Market Hill, Orford, Woodbridge, Suffolk IP12 2LH

TEL 0394 450277 CONTACT William Pinney HOURS Mon-Sat 9.00-17.00 (-13.00 Tues) Sun 11.00-16.00 DIRECTIONS In village centre.

For good fresh or smoked fish, Butley's is the place to go. The Oysterage Restaurant serves simply prepared fish in unpretentious but friendly surroundings. The accent is on own-smoked fish and oysters (see below), with daily specialities chalked up on a blackboard. It is open daily during the tourist season for lunch and supper (check for times out of season). After a satisfying lunch, the best thing to do is to work it off by walking to the romantic ruined castle on top of the hill.

The shop also sells fresh and smoked fish, and oysters. Fresh fish is caught by Bill Pinney, who runs 2 boats off the coast. Food writer Colin Spencer, who lives locally, says it can be relied on for being extremely fresh. Pacific oysters, plump and juicy with a strong whiff of the sea, are farmed from their own beds in Butley Creek. Colin buys them in an extra-large size (ordered in advance) and grills them in their shells mixed with butter, chopped parsley and garlic, then coated with breadcrumbs. Fish is smoked over oak logs in their smoke-house down by the creek. There is a choice of farmed Scottish or wild Irish smoked salmon.

I treated myself to a few slices of the latter to take to lunch with Colin Spencer and Claire Clifton. We were seriously impressed as it was excellent. Lightly cured, mild, lean and easy textured, it was like biting into butter (with just a slight edge as your teeth met) and slipped down the throat with resounding waves. They also smoke trout; a chubby cod's roe with a strong sense of salt; kippers; bloaters; chewy, densely flavoured sprats; juicy mackerel, and fat eels caught in the local dikes and ditches. Incidentally, if you are wondering, they are related but no longer connected to Pinney's smoked salmon of Scotland.

ORFORD   MAP 5

Richardson's Smokehouse ✉ ♜

SMOKED MEAT & GAME

The Old Smokehouse, Bakers Lane, Orford, Suffolk IP12 2LH

TEL *0394 450103* **CONTACT** *Steve Richardson* **HOURS** *Apr to end-Oct: 10.00-18.00; Nov to Mar: 10.00-15.00* **DIRECTIONS** *Off Market Hill.*

I have Claire Clifton, food writer and ace-shopper, to thank for introducing me to Richardson's. Unless you know about them, in the rush to get to the better-known Butley's (see page 240) they are easy to miss down the lane. Although the family have lived in Orford for generations, Steve left the village and only came back in 1983. Then he set about resurrecting the old blackened lean-to smoke-house. Divided into 2, it looks a bit ramshackle but it works a treat.

One side, with the boiler (fired with oak logs), is for hot-smoking and the smoke is vented through to the other compartment for a longer cooler smoke. Pigeon has a light woody haze and whole chickens, brined for 6 hours and then smoked for a mere half day, are soft-fleshed with a musky flavour. Prawns were amazingly succulent and the wild duck and pheasant looked tempting.

Unusually for a smoker, Steve is interested in building and creating subtlety of flavours. For him, it is more than 'adding value' to food with a uniform smoke – he knows and cares about tastes. For the first time I actually enjoyed smoked cheese. Normally I find it unpleasantly acrid and hard. Anyway cheese, one of life's great joys, should not be messed around with. Steve's was different: a mature Cheddar, for instance, was lifted and enhanced by a delicate woodiness.

I was also impressed by the fish-cakes. Made from own-smoked Alaskan salmon and mixed with potatoes and marjoram, they were satisfyingly rough and chunky in texture, bulging and well flavoured with fish cunningly spiked with lemon.

PEASENHALL   MAP 5

Emmett's Stores ✉ ♜

SUFFOLK HAM

Peasenhall, Saxmundham, Suffolk IP17 2HJ

TEL *072879 250* **CONTACT** *Nigel Jerrey* **HOURS** *Mon-Sat 8.30-13.00 & 14.00-17.30 (-17.00 Sat)* **DIRECTIONS** *In village centre.*

Emmett's store is actually the village supermarket, newsagent, post office and haberdasher all rolled into one. The only give-away that something special might be going on is the huge royal warrant (granted by HRH the Queen Mum) plastered over the front door. Inside, amongst the jumble of woolly socks, copies of *Woman's Own*, cat food, processed peas and the like, is one of the best hams and bacons you will find in this country.

Quite how and why Mr Jerrey Sr (now handed down to Mr Jerrey Jr) started making their Suffolk-cure ham has never been fully explained – it is enough that they do. The traditional Suffolk cure is made with black treacle, sugar, salt and stout (one recipe I found also added vinegar, but this was the only time I have seen it suggested) and he also produces a lighter Suffolk cider-pickled ham using James White cider (see page 237) instead of stout. Both hams are made in the same way in the back yard behind the stores. Mr Jerrey buys in pork, 'mostly' as he puts it, 'from happy pigs because it is important to some customers, but I can't guarantee it'. Curiously enough 'one in every 200 hams won't take a pickle'. Although not exactly sure why this is, Mr Jerrey has a few ideas but at the moment, he is not letting on.

First he brines the pork in salt, saltpetre and water, then pickles them in either cure for about 3-4 weeks. Next they are gently smoked for about 5 days in the smoke-holes over oak sawdust. Finally they are hung for at least a month to mature. Sold vacuum-packed either as whole hams weighing 6.3-8 kg (14-18 lb) or half hams weighing 3.5-4.5 kg (8-10 lb), they have a rich deep blackish-brown skin. The taste is unique; these are strongly flavoured hams with a biting texture – the Suffolk sweet pickle is sweet, punchy and very meaty; the cider-cure lighter, even sweeter with a hint of fruit.

Also worth trying is the sweet-pickled bacon; again it has a good firm texture with a sweet smoky flavour but not overly so. Beware of pale imitations. I tried one competitor's bacon and it was quite disgusting – cloyingly flavoured with a sweet-sour aftertaste, it spluttered and shrank away merrily in the pan. Mr Jerrey's is one of the best in the county.

To cook his hams, Mr Jerrey recommends soaking them overnight in water, then sealing them in a large piece of foil with about 5 cm (2 in) of cider and baking them in an oven preheated to 180°C/350°F/gas 4 for about 25 minutes to the 450 g (1 lb).

SOUTHWOLD MAP 5

John's Fish Shop 🐟 BLOATERS, KIPPERS & FRESH FISH

5 East Street, Southwold, Suffolk IP18 6EH

TEL *0502 724253* CONTACT *John Huggins* HOURS *Tues-Sat 9.00-17.00 (-13.00 Wed mid-Sept to Whitsun)* DIRECTIONS *In town centre.*

Southwold, home to Adnams Brewery, The Swan and The Crown Hotels, is a very special seaside town. It may welcome tourists, but it

Suffolk Larder ✉, **17 The Thoroughfare, Woodbridge, IP12 1AA (tel 0394 386676)** is a small and original shop. Run by Tony Constantine-Smith and his wife, Sue. Most of what they sell is either made by them – or exclusively for them – to recipes they have developed.

First off is a crumbly, moist Suffolk Cyder (sic) Cake made with eggs, sugar, butter, flour, sultanas, raisins and, of course, Suffolk Cyder (from James White, see page 237). Then there is Suffolk spiced lamb: whole boned-out leg of lamb cured in a rosemary-flavoured salt and hot-smoked until the meat is a deep-pink right the way through, it has a grassy nuance. They also sell interesting bacon, particularly the sweet pickle which has vinegar added to the brine for a sharp flavour.

They make their own flavoured vinegars using cider vinegar as a base: elderberry; a muscat-tinged elderflower; a fruity blackcurrant; strawberry; raspberry, and redcurrant. Then there are the mustards, based on a Sole Bay (Southwold) recipe: Master's Own, with green peppercorns; pungent Boatyard, with paprika and black peppercorns; mild Sweet Honey; and a hot and strong Horseradish.

There's a fair range of cheeses with a British bias: unpasteurized Cheddar from Times Past (see page 221); various Dale cheeses and a mild, clean, fresh-tasting, hard-pressed goats' cheese made at nearby Otley College of Agriculture. Suffolk Larder runs an efficient mail order service for most of the items mentioned.

shows little signs of pandering to them. It resolutely carries on with its bustling daily life, refusing to allow jangling arcades, tatty promenade illuminations or noisy dodgems.

The only concession fishmonger John Higgins makes to the summer influx of visitors is to stay open all day on Wednesdays. Otherwise – summer and winter – it is business as usual at his bright, white-tiled shop in a side street leading down to the promenade. With a well-earned local reputation, he sells a range of wet fish and a serious selection of herrings, fresh and variously cured and smoked.

I visited him in the autumn, when the local long-shore herrings are in season. 'Stiff alive', their skins hued with the colours of the rainbow, they had been caught within 1 mile of shore and specially selected by John. Whenever possible, he buys herring weighing about 285 g (10 oz), 'the best size to eat' and caught in drift nets. 'You can tell because they still have their scales on; trawled herrings are usually bruised and battered'. They are sold whole or as fillets. He also sells a choice of fresh herring roe: the hard and darker roe from the female and the softer milky male roe called milt. Herring, I must admit, has never been a favourite fish of mine, but John's were sweet and clean-tasting; the roe were glorious and popped in my mouth like tiny bubbles.

He also sells kippers, bloaters, buckling and red herring. With the help of John and an old booklet published by the defunct Herring Industry Board, I will try and explain the differences. Kippers are gutted, split down the middle, hung open, salted for about $\frac{1}{2}$ hour and smoked for about 18 hours both inside and out. Bloaters – the name comes from the Swedish *blota* meaning to steep or soak – are gutted but unsplit, steeped in salt for about 4 hours then smoked for about 18 hours. As the smoke is filtered through the skin, they have a mellower, milder flavour. Buckling are decapitated and gutted, but left closed, salted for a couple of hours and then hot-smoked for about 1 hour. They have a pleasing soft and delicate taste. Red herring – now here's a curiosity, probably more for their bright tandoori-pink colour than actually eating – are tough and very concentrated in flavour, rather like eating a fish 'jerky'. Locally known as 'high dries' because they are hung so high in the smoke-house, they are left unsplit, salted for 1 week and smoked for 6. Apparently a red herring will keep for a year. John sells them complete with several old recipes for preparing them (they have to be soaked before cooking). To be perfectly honest, however, I think they have a harsh taste unsuited to modern palates.

During the summer, when local herrings are not in season he buys them from Scotland and he also sells local samphire and Norfolk crabs.

STONHAM ASPAL   MAP 5

Stonham Hedgerow Products 🝆

JAMS & PRESERVES

Stonham Barns, Stonham Aspal, Stowmarket, Suffolk IP14 6AT

TEL *0449 711755* FAX *0449 711174* CARDS *Access, Visa* CONTACT *Kathy Neuteboom* HOURS *10.00-17.30* DIRECTIONS *From Stowmarket, take A1120 towards Yoxford. Drive through Stonham Aspal and, after about 1 mile, turn right into Stonham Barns.*

A large gleaming glass-house, Stonham Barns is a garden centre. Tucked away behind the coffee-shop, Kathy makes her jams. The reason for this unusual arrangement lies with her father, the well-respected apple grower Dan Neuteboom. It was his land and his development, so it was natural that space be found for Kathy. Jams are her passion and she has very firm ideas about how they should be made: 'I want to stick to basic principles like using real whole fruit and chopping it by hand – too much machinery only bruises it. A good raw cane natural sugar – ours is from Mauritius. It may make the jam darker and give it a definite taste but I – and my customers – like it that way'.

Jams are made on a small(ish) scale, 'mostly in 9-13.5 kg (20-30 lb) batches, although we do have a 45-kg (100-lb) boiler for easy-preparation jams like strawberry. The home-made feel is important and we want to keep it that way. We started out like Cartwright & Butler (an

East Anglian company now out of business) but they went and opened a large factory and where's the "home-made" gone? I don't want that to happen to us'. Fruit is bought from local growers when the quality and price are right, then frozen and used accordingly throughout the year. Jams are made with fruit, cane sugar and – although Kathy goes for a slack set – she does add pectin.

With a sugar content of 'anything between 60-66%' the wide range includes: greengage; Mixed Fruit (apple, strawberry, blackberry and loganberry); a reddish Gooseberry brimming with whole fruit; a nutty-flavoured Apricot made with fruit imported from Cyprus and whole kernels; a sharp Apple & Ginger 'made with my father's Bramleys – he'd never forgive me if I used anyone else's'; and Sunberry that 'looks like a raspberry but tastes more like a blackberry'.

There are also several 'reasonably clear' jellies, such as crab apple, quince, redcurrant, and morello cherry 'from fruit grown here that take hours to stone', as well as various marmalades and chutneys, including a novel Uncooked Fruit, made by soaking raw chopped bananas, apples, onions, sultanas, raisins and currants in vinegar overnight with salt and spices. I found it a little harsh. I much preferred Suffolk Chutney, a powerful blend of cooked apple and black treacle, seasoned with mustard and curry powder.

Kathy also makes reduced-sugar jams, legally known as 'conserves' as they have a sugar content between 40-45%. Unfortunately in order to achieve a set, Kathy is forced to add extra pectin and, particularly in the case of the strawberry, this is evident. Undaunted, she is working on a 'no-sugar' range, more of a fruit spread. I wish her luck.

SWEFFLING   MAP 5

Cornucopia Produce 🔲   OYSTER MUSHROOMS

Sweffling Lodge, Sweffling, Saxmundham, Suffolk IP17 2BG

TEL *0728 78570* CONTACT *Mary Kennedy – telephone ahead*

Restaurateur and shop-owner Antonio Carluccio (see page 166) writes in his *A Passion for Mushrooms*: 'Named after the oyster because of its shape and its greyish-blue colour *Pleurotus ostreatus* is one of the few mushrooms that have been found suitable for cultivation. The domestic version of the oyster mushroom can be found in supermarkets, although I prefer the wild version, which has a stronger taste'. Obviously not their greatest fan, he continues, 'They are not superior mushrooms in the culinary sense – they do not have an outstanding flavour – but they are versatile when cooked fresh, and their availability in cultivation makes them useful for adding that extra mushroomy something to a dish'.

Grower Mary Kennedy agrees that most oyster mushrooms are lacking in flavour, although this need not be the case, 'I describe myself as a patient grower – I grow at a slower rate at a lower temperature without forcing the spores. This makes for a better mushroom with a firmer texture and a better distributed taste. If it's too hot and too humid, the mushrooms are soft, vapid and tasteless.' Mary has been growing commercially for the last 2 years with her spawning sheds on site by the house and her fruiting sheds at the other side of the village. She now supplies local restaurants like The Swan and The Crown in Southwold, Hintlesham Hall and Robert Mabey's Brasserie in Sudbury.

Although there is virtually no difference in taste, oyster mushrooms come in 4 colours: grey, brown (the least successful as it turns black immediately it is cooked), pink with a mild peppery flavour, and yellow that should only be cooked for a second otherwise it looses its colour. They have a cycle of about 6-8 weeks and Mary picks and sells them in clusters to keep them fresher for longer (supermarkets tend to cut them into individual mushrooms). They are refrigerated before being dispatched and she reckons they will keep fresh for about a week, if wrapped in a bag in the fridge. She also grows brown caps with a more intense flavour similar to that of the field mushroom. They vary in size and have been known to be as big in diameter as 30 cm (12 in), but that is quite rare as the usual size is around 12.5 cm (5 in).

In her huge back garden, she also grows various culinary herbs, with basil a speciality. She has 14 varieties of the herb, including cinnamon, fine, opal (purple), lemon, sweet and holy – and all sorts of other 'unusual things' like leaves and herbs for a *mesclun* (a Provençal mixed leaf salad of rocket, chervil, different lettuces and sometimes endives); or salad burnet with its gentle cucumber taste. These she grows more because she really enjoys doing so than for commercial reasons, but she will sell them in unwashed mixed bunches to anyone who is interested.

WOODBRIDGE   MAP 5

The Happy Hog ✉ 🔳

FREE-RANGE PORK & NORFOLK BLACK TURKEYS

Kyson Hill, Woodbridge, Suffolk IP12 4DN

TEL *0394 383922* CONTACT *Sarah Pinfold – telephone ahead*

Sarah Pinfold's happy hogs are, from what I could see, really happy. These Large Black, Large White cross (Blue & White) pigs are kept outdoors to rummage away and are fed an antibiotic-free diet. Their meat (loin chops, shoulder and boned leg) is firm-textured and fully flavoured, with a covering of skin that makes a crisp crackling. Bacon is cured and smoked for them by Mr Jerrey at Emmett Stores (see page 241).

For Christmas, Sarah grows Norfolk Black turkeys. Once the traditional breed of the area, their popularity declined because they are slow developers, lack the plump breasts we seem to think important and have an off-putting (to some) designer-stubble or black pitting in their skin caused by the tiny feather stumps that are almost impossible to pull out. Their flavour is so distinctive, however, that it seriously outweighs these so-called disadvantages. Sarah buys them in as day-old chicks. As soon as they are old enough they are turned out into the fields, although they are locked up at night 'because of foxes'. They are fed grain supplemented with fruit, wild berries, greens and nettles until suitably fattened at about 25 weeks. Killed on site, they are dry-plucked while still warm 'to keep their bloom and it's easier to pull out those tough feathers', and hung uneviscerated for 10-14 days. Hen birds weigh between 4.5-6.8 kg (10-15 lb) and stags 7.2-10.5 kg (16-24 lb).

On my recommendation, Sheila Dillon of Radio 4's *Food Programme* ordered one for Thanksgiving. She pronounced it 'a very fine-looking bird, well dressed and finished and particularly moist and tasty'. She was also rather touched by an accompanying note – Sarah wrote that she was mortified as the turkey had wandered into a patch of brambles and scratched its skin and, as it was early in the season, no replacement was possible. Let us hope it had, at the very least, had a good time foraging. Sarah sends her turkeys all over the country by chilled transport. Locals know to come and collect them on Christmas Eve, when there is a glass of mulled wine and some sausage rolls (made with Happy Hog sausages) waiting.

In summer, from about the second week in June to the first week in September, Sarah collects samphire from around the estuary of the river Debden 'right out by my back yard'. Careful not to pull up the roots, she picks it over, washes it and sells it in bunches weighing 115-170 g (4-6 oz). (✉ Turkeys and samphire only.)

SAMPHIRE

Samphire (Marsh Samphire or Glasswort) grows on the south-east and west coasts of England, coastal areas of Wales and the west coasts of Scotland. An annual, it is found on open sandy mud in salt marshes and tradition says that it is ready for picking on the longest day right through to the end of August, the healthiest specimens being those which have been washed by every tide. To prepare samphire, wash it thoroughly and either boil it in shallow unsalted water for 8-10 minutes, or steam it until relatively soft. Serve nice and hot with melted butter and pepper. (From *Wild Food* by Roger Phillips.)

YOXFORD MAP 5

Garden of Suffolk Preserves 🗒 JAMS & PRESERVES

Yoxford Place, Yoxford, Saxmundham, Suffolk IP17 3HY

TEL *072877 343* CONTACT *Mary Holmes – telephone ahead*

BEST JAMS & PRESERVES

Housed in her rambling Georgian house, Mary Holmes's jam factory is really a domestic kitchen converted from an old pantry. Here

Mary and two helpers, 'just make jam all the time' – something in the order of 36,000 kg (80,000 lb) a year. Made in 9 kg (20 lb) batches, all she uses is fruit, sugar and pectin. Sugar is always 'ordinary granulated as preserving sugar is, I think, a con. Pectin, I add in varying amounts; it cuts down the boiling time required for a set, so I get a stronger-flavoured jam with a better colour'. Fruit, the most important ingredient, is something else Mary is picky about it, 'I only use whole fruit. And it's the best – nothing over-ripe as it won't set. I buy direct from growers and use as much as possible – about one-third – fresh. The rest I freeze and draw on throughout the year'.

Her jam is made with the minimum of equipment, 'We're not even mechanized yet, everything is stoned by hand, we use a jug and people for filling the jars, and then screw on the hot lids immediately. Turn the jars upside down for 5 minutes to sterilize the air, then turn them back up – and you've got a partial vacuum.'

What makes Mary's jam unique is the time and trouble she goes to with her varieties. Her father grew all sorts of different plums and she was brought up in a household where 'just "plum" jam wasn't good enough'. Taking this to heart, every year she produces a range of 8 named varietal plum jams, each with a distinctive flavour, colour and consistency. Ariel is a shy yellow with a light taste, hinting of peaches; Cherry (Mirabelle) a yellowy-red, is quite sharp and acid; rich-red Bullace (wild plum) is meaty; Victoria is paler, with a creamy texture and a cheery taste; Greengage is an inviting green, but sadly little intensity of fruit; purple-red Czar is seriously pungent, with an almost chocolatey flavour; Early Rivers is densely purple, with a flowery fragrance; and Damson, a deeply dark purple, was contrastingly light in taste. Imagine the fun I had tasting them. She also makes strawberry, raspberry, tayberry, loganberry, a strong green gooseberry jam that really does taste of the fruit, morello cherry, blueberry, and mulberry with fruit 'supplied by a little old lady who picks them for me'.

Her jellies are sparklingly clear and unusually flavoured: there is Gooseberry & Elderflower with a muscat fragrance; Quince; Medlar; Japonica (a pea-green scented fruit, 'the size of an apple and as hard as nails'); Spiced Hedgerow (made with hedgerow fruits 'and Christmas cake spices'); and English Black Grape (with grapes from Mary's garden). There is also a range of marmalades, including a treacly Seville, Coarse-cut Seville, Orange, Lemon & Grapefruit, and Lime; as well as original preserves, which include Fig (from dried fruit) and a sharp thick Cranberry. Also worth a mention is Mary's tart Lemon Curd.

And also....

- At *The Post Office, Moulton*, nr Newmarket (tel 0638 750242), Jeanie Marcel cooks bought-in hams in a special cooker based on the old-fashioned hay box. Hams are brought to the boil, then left in the water for about 15 hours to cook right through. Sold as whole hams on the bone, boned-out halves, or sliced, they are finished either in an orange and brown sugar glaze or with a coating of breadcrumbs.

• The tiny fish shop of **Brown & May**, 7a Broad Street, Eye (tel 0379 870181) is full of own-smoked salmon, samphire in season, and a good selection of wet fish.

• **The Cheese Shop**, 74 Beccles Road, Oulton Broads (tel 0502 564664) has a deserved reputation for selling an interesting selection of British and Continental cheeses.

• Simon Wooster both mills the flour and bakes the bread at **Bardwell Mill Bakery**, Bardwell, nr Bury St Edmunds (tel 0359 52094). Sadly, the windmill lost its sails in the great storm a couple of years ago, so now it is powered by electricity. With an interest in Continental-style breads, Simon's *ciabatta* with olives and sun-dried tomatoes is worth the detour.

• One of the best butchers in the county is **David Rolfe**, Walsham-le-Willows (tel 0359 259225). Meat is well hung, sausages are plump and meaty and their Suffolk ham, back and streaky bacon cured in molasses, brown sugar and ale, are all first rate.

• During the summer you can buy fresh fish from the fish-sheds on the shore at Aldeburgh. Sold by the fishermen, the quality and freshness can be excellent. Food writer Colin Spencer also buys from **Harveys**, 115 High Street (tel 0728 452145) who offer the advantages of a year-round supply – their fish comes mainly from Lowestoft – and a far wider range that includes Cromer crabs, samphire and fresh brown shrimps, provided 'the French haven't snapped them up first'.

SURREY

CHESSINGTON   MAP 3

The Game Larder ✉ 🏆   GAME

Rushett Farm, Chessington, Surrey KT9 2NQ

TEL 0372 749000 **CONTACT** *Fraser Ashley Bach* **HOURS** *Mon-Sat 10.00-18.00 Sun 10.30-16.00* **DIRECTIONS** *Turn off A3 on to A243, signposted Chessington World of Adventure. Follow the road past Chessington on the right and go straight over the traffic lights. Farm is signposted about ½ mile along on the left.*

The Game Larder buy their pheasant from local shoots, 'But preferably not from a syndicate shoot,' Fraser's husband Charles Ashley Bach explained, 'they rent out the right to shoot on a per-day basis; more often than not the members are inexperienced. And the chances are that the birds will be peppered with shot'. Now I've never been shooting (it's not that I have any objection, it is just I've never been asked) but I still know enough by listening to the Archers about the trouble George Barford has with syndicate members to know that this makes sense. 'And,' Charles went on to tell me, 'a high-flying bird makes the best eating, it'll be better reared, better exercised and better shot – a bad shot is likely to miss it altogether if it's that high in the sky'.

The birds are collected and hung in a chilled game cart, so they cool down immediately; this means they can be hung longer without acquiring those green, bitter overtones. They hang game to order, depending on the time of the season it is usually around the 5- to 7-day mark. Sometimes they get a request for birds to be hung as long as 3 weeks, 'which is fine, provided the game is carefully handled from the start'. In season the game is fresh, but for the rest of the year they can be relied on to have frozen supplies. Apart from pheasants, they sell red-legged partridges and the finer-textured grey (English), Roe and Fallow deer (stalked mainly in the South of England), woodcock, various wild ducks, hare, pigeon and rabbit. They also stock wild boar from Nigel Dauncey (see page 228) and bison (which apparently tastes like a slightly sweet beef). They sometimes also have own-grown fresh herbs and garlic, duck and pheasant eggs and various game pies.

Secretts of **Hurst Farm, Chapel Lane, Milford** *runs a* **PYO** *(tel 0483 426543) and a* **farm-shop** *(tel 0483 426789). In the former you can pick 10 different strawberry varieties spread over the season: raspberries, white currants, blackcurrants and redcurrants, tayberries, gooseberries, lollo rosso, Little Gem, oak leaf, four seasons and Webb's lettuces, baby carrots, sweetcorn and broad and runner beans. In the farm-shop you can buy their ready-picked fruit and vegetables, including several different potatoes and a good range of on-farm cheeses.*

EGHAM   MAP 3

Green Landscape Nurseries 🔲 ♨   TOMATOES

Hurst Lane, Egham, Surrey TW20 8QJ

TEL *0784 435545* **CONTACT** *Mario Mingoia* **HOURS** *mid-June to end-Oct: 6.00-20.00* **DIRECTIONS** *From Egham, follow road across the railway line towards Virginia Water. After about 50 yards, take the last exit off the roundabout signposted Virginia Water. Follow the road about 1 mile to the next roundabout and drive straight across, signposted Virginia Water. After about ½ mile, take the first turning on the left after the Great Fosters Hotel, into Hurst Lane. Farm is signposted on the left.*

> **Vivian's** ✉ at **2 Worple Way, Richmond TW10 6DF (tel 081 940 3600, fax 081 332 1276)** is, *for my money, one of the country's more interesting food shops. One of its delights is the range that restaurateur Stephen Bull cooks exclusively for them. Supplies can be a bit spasmodic if he is too busy in his restaurants. Look out for his superb terrine of duck confit, with bite-size pieces of confit set in jelly studded with vegetables and wrapped in lightly blanched cabbage leaves; or the omelette terrine consisting of cunning layers of paper-thin omelettes with spinach and sweet pepper stuffed between. The brill, red mullet and artichoke terrine wrapped in seaweed looks almost too pretty to eat; the spinach and ricotta parfait is light and airy and very subtly flavoured. Stephen also prepares jars of* cassoulet *and a white bean* garbure, *sticky pecan pies and various chutneys and relishes including a crisp and zesty pickled fennel and orange. Vivian's also sell on-farm British cheeses, including Bonchester and Teviotdale (see page 328), Smart's Single and Double Gloucester Cheeses (see page 92), and a choice of Keen's (see page 229) and Mrs Montgomery's (see page 221) Cheddar and Cropwell Bishop Stilton (see page 197). There is a rich, meaty and very fat ham from Diana Smart's whey-fed Tamworth, Gloucester Old Spot cross, Bowmans ice-cream (see page 120) and Richmond Park honey (see page 255).*

If you live in or around London and want to buy your vegetables from the same source as restaurants like Quaglino's, The River Café, Cecconi's, The Ivy, Le Caprice and many more, then you had better go and visit Mario Mingoia at Green Landscape Nurseries who imports out of season and grows-his-own in season.

As his name suggests, Mario is of Italian origin – actually he is half-Sicilian, half-cockney; but, as most of his seeds come from Italy, his produce definitely has an Italian accent. Grown mostly under glass, with no sprays or artificial fertilizers ('only horse manure'), you will find cardoons, *rucola d'orta* (a deep-green rocket with a hot peppery flavour) as ready-picked only, green and Valeriana radicchio, green and white baby *zucchini* (courgettes) – and, of course, their flowers for stuffing – fat green yellow and red peppers, glossy and plump deep-purple aubergines, both large and baby cucumbers, and an unusual range of beans that includes *cornetti gialli* (yellow French beans) and runner beans. For podding and eating either fresh or dried, there are borlotti beans, which cookery writer Anna del Conte describes in her *Gastronomy of Italy* as, 'pale pink with red speckles, they are best in soups and stews because of their creamy consistency'; and cannellini 'a white bean best sautéed or in salads'. It is these very beans that are used for a classic *tonno e fagioli*, or bean, tuna and red onion salad.

Last, but by no means least, are Mario's tomatoes. Anna swears they are 'the best grown in the country – so sweet and juicy'. He grows 6 varieties: the round Shirley, sugar-sweet Cherry, Beefsteak, the capsicum-shaped juicy Canadian that tastes like 'none has tasted before' and 2 different-sized San Marzano plum tomatoes, large for cooking and piccolo for salads. He also has a good range of fresh herbs and this year he is experimenting with growing artichokes.

EGHAM   MAP 3

Wentworth Exotic Mushrooms ✉ 🍴

OYSTER MUSHROOMS

1 Hurst Lane, Egham, Surrey TW20 8QJ

TEL *0344 842795* FAX *0344 845002* CONTACT *Peter Hawton* HOURS *9.30-17.00* DIRECTIONS *As above.*

Peter Hawton is one of the largest oyster mushroom growers in this country. His sheds may look a bit ramshackle, with plastic sheets flapping about and huge rubbish bags overflowing with compost; but ignore it and focus on the mushrooms. There they are, poking through the slashes in the bags at all angles, clustered in colonies of dusty pink, pale canary yellow, pearly grey and the palest of pale-browns, looking for all the world like flattened frilly fans.

Of course, you can now buy oyster mushrooms with reasonable ease (Peter supplies the likes of Sainsbury), but there is something quite satisfying about growing-your-own. To this end, Peter sells grow-bags of composted straw inoculated with the fungus strain of either the grey (*ostreatus pleurotus*), yellow (*cornucopiae pleurotus*), pink (*samoneostramineus pleurotus*) or 2 different but similar tasting browns (*sajor caju or pulmonarius pleurotus*). Unlike the common cultivated mushroom (*agaricus bisporus*), oyster mushrooms thrive on daylight; the ideal place to keep the bag is in a warm and humid bathroom or kitchen. You cut slits about 2.5 cm (1 in) long, no more than 6 evenly spaced over the bag, then sit back and wait. After about 10 days, the mushrooms should start to appear. From then on they should be lightly sprayed with water every day.

It takes a few days for the mushrooms to reach a pickable size, but the larger you leave them to grow the smaller the overall yield. On average, each bag produces between 10-15% of its weight in

---

> ✗ *So one story goes,* **Maids of Honour**, *the delicate tartlets made with curd cheese set in rough-puff pastry, got their name from Henry VIII. On inspecting the kitchens at Richmond Palace, he saw a group of Maids of Honour eating the tarts; he liked them and the name stuck. Another story is that as the tarts emerge from the oven the filling bobs in a curtsy, like any good maid. The only place to try them is* **The Original Maids of Honour Shop, 288 Kew Road, Kew Gardens** *(tel 081 940 2752).*

mushrooms; as a bag weighs 5 kg (11 lb), you can expect about 500-750 g (1-1$\frac{3}{4}$ lb) of mushrooms. If you pick the first flush when quite small, you may well get another 2 or 3 flushes appearing, with approximately 10 days between each one. The difference in taste between the varieties is minimal: pink is mildly peppery in flavour, and yellow is probably best eaten raw as it looses its colour if cooked for more than a second.

> *Priory Farm, Nutfield, nr Redhill (tel 0737 822603, fax 0737 823568) has something for everyone. There is a nature trail, coarse fishing on two well-stocked lakes which promise carp up to 8 kg (18 lb), tea gardens, children's play area, plant centre, farm-shop and pick-your-own. As well as the usual soft fruit and vegetables, from late June through to early July, you can pick-your-own cherries; the season starts with Merchant early black and ends with large black Colney with Merton Glory early white, Merpet, Mermat, dark and juicy Van, Stella, Sunburst and Lapins fitting in between.*

GUILDFORD   MAP 3

Montgomery Moore ✉ 🏭   CHOCOLATES

17 Tunsgate, Guildford, Surrey GU1 3QT

TEL & FAX *0483 451620* **CONTACT** *Sheila Torrance* **HOURS** *Mon-Fri 10.00-17.30 Sat 9.00-18.00* **CARDS** *Access, Visa, Mastercard* **DIRECTIONS** *In town centre.*

Montgomery Moore only opened their smart oak-fronted shop just off Guildford High Street last year; but they have already acquired a reputation for their hand-made chocolates. So often chocolates are 'thin' and over-sweet. This is partly because the quality of the couverture is poor, with a low cocoa solids content, so sugar is added to compensate; and partly because we expect our chocolates to have a long shelf-life, so sugar is used a preservative.

Sheila Torrance and David Hunt set out to produce a better class of chocolates, definitely ones that 'are not too sweet'. To this end they use a couverture with a high cocoa solids content and relatively un-sweet fillings. They are made daily and the whole premises are air-conditioned to maintain a cool constant temperature. Like several *chocolatiers* I have come across, David was reluctant to go into too much detail about his recipes. Making good chocolates is a highly competitive craft, where so much depends on the proportion of ingredients, balance of the flavours, texture and finish. Given – as in Montgomery Moore's case – that good ingredients are used (fresh cream, 'real' alcohol, butter rather than a vegetable fat and, of course, a good couverture), it is those 'secrets' that make all the difference.

Truffles, made with a ganache of cream, chocolate and 'the tiniest bit

> **John Patrick Coles** of **Upper Ridgeway Farm, Thursley, Godalming (tel 0428 604508)** is known locally as the 'Strawberry King' for the superb flavour of his fruit. Varieties, chosen for flavour 'rather than ease of growing or travelling', are sold ready-picked from the barn. For the first 3 to 4 weeks of the season, you can buy the pointy Cambridge Vigour, with its biting sweet 5-star flavour, with Elvira and Honeoye as 2 other earlies. Then come Elsanta and Pegasus, followed by Bogota, Pandora and the Italian Marmalada.

of butter' (that much I did manage to extract from David) and flavoured with raspberry, rum, brandy, whisky, coffee, Champagne, pear or Cointreau, are fresh and creamy with a clean aftertaste. They are quite dense as, unlike the Belgian ones, the filling is not whipped. Tea chocolates, a ganache infused with Earl Grey, Lapsang Souchong, Mango or Passion, are rather unusual; I tried the Earl Grey and it had a subtle flavour with the merest hint of the smoky brew. David likes to focus on textures; as a result there is a dark hazelnut cluster with a rich praline; *feuilletines* with a crunchy filling lined with thin pallets of chocolate, and coffee & walnut marzipan with minuscule chips of walnuts. They also sell jars of spoonable chocolate sauce that comes as plain or laden with Cointreau, cognac or rum.

This Christmas promises (for display purposes only) a chocolate Nativity scene, complete with crib, ox, shepherds, Virgin Mary and Joseph; it sounds too heavenly. You will be able to buy boxed sets of the Three Kings and a good range of novelties as well as their chocolates in various selections, starting from 60 g (2 oz).

> One of the better kept secrets I have uncovered is that you can buy fruit grown in **The Royal Horticultural Society's Garden** at **Wisley, Woking (tel 0483 224234)**. You don't need to be a member nor do you have to pay an entrance fee as the produce hut is sited outside the gardens. The drawback is that no one is prepared to tell you what the varieties are and when they are in season. I usually visit in late October when I'm certain to find several unusual apple varieties. I've never made it in summer, but I hear that the soft fruit is excellent.

SHERE   MAP 3

Old Scotland Farmhouse Cheese ✉ 🏠 CHEESE

Staple Lane, Shere, Guildford, Surrey GU5 9TE

TEL 0483 222526 CONTACT Pat Vigar HOURS 14.00-18.00 DIRECTIONS From Guildford, take A246 towards Leatherhead. After about 5 miles, turn right signposted Shere. Follow the road about $\frac{1}{2}$ mile up the hill.

Several years ago I tried a superbly subtle Cheddar-style cheese from Sussex called Castle Hill. It was stunning – flowery and mellow with a gentle nuttiness. Then, due in part to an over-zealous Environmental Health Officer, suddenly it was no more. Admittedly cheeses do come and go – particularly as the life of any small cheese-maker is rigorous and they often lose heart – but Castle Hill was a gem. I mourned its departure.

The good news is that it is being made again under the guise of Old Scotland Farmhouse: the same recipe; the same equipment; the same guiding hand of David Doble, the original maker; but a different herd grazing in different pastures. Pat Vigar, its maker, told me 'If anything, the cheese is slightly creamier due, no doubt, to the differences of the milk. And David used both morning and evening milk, whereas I only use the morning milk'. The other variation is that Pat's winter cheeses are straw-pale and creamy (the cows are silage-fed); whereas the summer cheeses (when the cows are grazing on the pastures) are sunshine yellow, slightly drier and more intense.

Made with the unpasteurized milk of their Friesian herd 5 days a week, Old Scotland is pressed for 2 days and then matured for about 3 months. With a close texture and a well-formed natural rind, Pat sells whole cheeses weighing approximately 4 kg (9 lb), half cheeses, truckles weighing 1.8 kg (4 lb) and mini-truckles at 550 g ($1\frac{1}{4}$ lb). What is so surprising is that such a comparatively young cheese can have such a rich, deep and complex flavour.

Fiona Dickson ✉, *although she lives at* **Didlington Manor, Didlington, Thetford, Norfolk IP26 5AT (tel 0284 828300)** *keeps hives in Richmond Park for Richmond Park Honey. Sold in 225 and 450 g ($\frac{1}{2}$ and 1 lb) jars, its flavour varies from year to year depending on the weather. Sometimes 'it's limy and light, other times it's darker and more heathery, and sometimes there's a bit of hawthorn thrown in'. Whatever the dominant flavour, it is sure to be good as it was the winner of the Light Honey class in last year's National Honey Show. For the first time this year, she will be collecting honey from her hives in Windsor Great Park.*

And Also...

- For one of the best selection of real American foods – Hershey choc-fudge topping, Aunt Jemima Cornbread Mix, Libby's pumpkin *et al* – try **Anton's Delicatessen** ✉, 101 Hare Lane, Claygate (tel 0372 462306).
- *at Home Catering*, 40 High Street, Cobham (tel 0932 862026) sell from their shop ready-cooked dishes, cheeses, pastries, flavoured vinegars and marinated olives. Within the area, they also deliver whole meals to your home.

- Loseley yoghurt is still made at Loseley Park, even if the ice-cream is not. You can, however, buy it – along with their cream, sorbets, own-baked bread, cakes, jams and Robert Bowden's pork produced on the estate – from *Loseley Park Farm Shop*, Loseley Park, nr Guildford (tel 0483 304440).

- More reports please on *The Belgian Patisserie*, 72 Walton Road, East Molesey (tel 081 979 8123). With another shop at 86-88 High Street, Dorking (0306 880998), I'm told they are as good as any you'll find in Belgium.

- If you believe that the sign of a good fishmonger is a queue of Japanese customers, then *Jarvis & Sons*, 56 Coombe Road, Norbiton (tel 081 546 0989, fax 081 943 0470) must be excellent. Their fish is extra-fresh and they will fillet away for you – even preparing the fish for sushi.

SUSSEX

FLIMWELL   MAP 3

The Weald Smokery ✉ 🏭

SMOKED DUCK & CHICKEN

Mount Farm, Hawkhurst Road, Flimwell, Sussex TN5 7QL

TEL *058087 601* **CONTACT** *Andrew Wickham* **HOURS** *Mon-Sat 9.00-18.00 Easter to end-Oct: Sun 10.00-18.00* **CARDS** *Visa, Mastercard* **DIRECTIONS** *From Flimwell, take A268 towards Hawkhurst. Smokery is first property on the left.*

The Weald Smokery was originally started by a German and, although it is now run by a thoroughly English couple, his influence lingers on. The first, and most obvious, sign of a Teutonic legacy is a curious 'sculpture' clanking in the wind outside the shop: it is a larger-than-life eel, trout and salmon, suspended over a bonfire made out of heavy Germanic wrought iron.

Inside the log cabin shop has a *'gemütlich'* feel and even the smoked products have that distinctive strong Germanic smoke taste. This is because, as Andrew explained, he was taught to cure and smoke by the now departed owner. They have 3 kilns: 2 in metal for hot-smoking; and a third made out of brick with a separate duct to pipe in the smoke from a separate source that is used exclusively for cold-smoking.

The Wickhams use oak logs that smoulder rather than burn, giving them better temperature control so they can smoke for a longer period of time without over-cooking the food. The result – a powerful woody flavour – is particularly obvious in the trout and locally made Toulouse-style sausages. The salmon, farmed in Argyll then dry-cured in salt for

SMOKED CHICKEN SKIN SALAD

To use up the skins from smoked chicken, simply pop them under a hot grill for a couple of minutes until they are crisp. Then chop them and toss them in a salad of sliced avocado mixed with watercress and dress with a creamy vinaigrette.

15 hours and smoked for 1-2 days (which struck me as quite a long time), has a buttery texture even if it is slightly overpowered by the pronounced smoke.

The *magret* of duck was far mor subtle; brined with herbs and bay leaves then briefly hot-smoked, it had a good gamy flavour and a biting texture. Their boneless breasts of chicken – sold in packs of 2 – were sweet and moist and certainly perked up what was possibly an otherwise dull bird. All their produce comes vacuum-packed and is sold in the shop, along with a well-chosen range of on-farm British and French cheeses, wines, jams, pickles, sauces and mustards.

> **The Horsham Cheese Shop** at **20 Carfax, Horsham (tel 0403 254272)** can be relied on to stock a good choice of local cheeses from their 250-odd selection. Here you will find Gospel Green (see below), Tornegus (Caerphilly washed in Kentish wine and matured by James Aldridge), Old Scotland Farmhouse and, on an exclusive basis, a garlic version of that cheese (see page 254), Rumbold made locally by the Gibbs (0403 88404) from their Guernsey milk, and the little waxed Chabis from Nut Knowle Farm. They also sell own-made pasta, pesto sauce, crisp cheese straws and bread.

GOSPEL GREEN   MAP 3

Gospel Green Cheese ✉ 🖼 ♟
CYDER & GOSPEL GREEN CHEESE

Gospel Green Cottage, Gospel Green, Haslemere, Sussex GU27 3BH

TEL *0428 654120* CONTACT *James Lane – telephone ahead*

The hamlet and the cheese of Gospel Green are imbued with history. It was on the Green that, in Wesleyan times, itinerant preachers spread the Gospel. Cheese-makers James and Cathy Lane live opposite in an old timbered house, easily recognized by the topiary in the front garden, which purports to be a Victorian fertility symbol. The cheese is also made with equipment that dates back to Victorian times: a water-jacketed curd bin, a curd knife and fork, and sturdy cheese-presses. This is not for any sentimental reasons, rather that James bought them in a farm sale; he had always promised himself and the previous owner that one day he would make cheese, so when he saw them he snapped them up.

The equipment has done him proud, as he has now been making for 7 years. Using the unpasteurized milk from his father's Friesian herd, he makes a buttery and fruity hard-pressed cheese that is notable for its mildly grassy flavour. Made in small batches in a 400-litre (90-gallon) vat, the cheese is a bit of a hybrid, 'I don't know how to bracket it,' James told me, 'it's not as hard-pressed as a Cheddar, but it does have a high butterfat content of around 55%. The curds are cut, milled, then broken up by hand, similar to both a Cheshire and Caerphilly'.

Its texture changes with the time of year; the cows calve in August and the earlier cheeses, made in September through to Christmas (and sold after 3 months) tend to be softer, crumblier and creamier. As the season progresses, the cheeses turn out to be firmer and harder, with a deeper fuller flavour and colour. Made in 900 g, 1.8 and 3.2 kg (2, 4, and 7 lb) truckles, they are interesting any time of the year.

Recently the Lanes have started making cider, or 'cyder' as they call it. A blend of two-thirds eating apples and one-third cookers, including the Norman Mère de Menage but 'definitely no bitter-sweets (cider apples)', the juice is stored in oak whisky barrels. After 6 months, when it has completed its first fermentation, it is racked, blended in an active champagne yeast solution with cane sugar, bottled in full strength champagne bottles and stored for a minimum of 10 months. During that time a second fermentation takes place, and then – following the traditional Champagne method – the *remuage* takes place. This is a highly skilled process whereby the bottles are turned so the sediment falls on to the cap. It is then frozen for removal and, finally, the cider is given a *dosage* of cider and cane sugar to top it up and make it *brut*, or dry, in Champagne terms. The result is highly successful: a sophisticated, very French, evenly balanced, dry cider with a lingering apple flavour almost – but not quite – as satisfying as Champagne.

SLINDON

MAP 3

C. R. Upton

PUMPKINS & SQUASHES

Pumpkin Cottage, 4 Top Road, Slindon, Sussex BN18 ORP

TEL 0243 65219 CONTACT *C. R. Upton* HOURS *mid-July to end-Oct: 9.00-19.00* DIRECTIONS *From Fontwell, take A29 towards Watersfield. Follow the road and turn left signposted Slindon. Follow the road through Slindon to the top of the hill, past The Newburgh Arms. The house is about 30 yards along on the left.*

Whenever I visit Mr Upton I always think of Jane Grigson's introduction to pumpkins in her *Vegetable Book*. She wrote that one of the best sights in autumn 'is a pile of pumpkins in a farmyard, tumbled in giant profusion against the round strawsacks. Colours go from greenish white and green, through yellow and ochre, to the most intense orange. sometimes the colour is mottled or spotted or streaked. The shapes are as varied as the colour'. She must have had Mr Upton in mind, because there they all are, stacked on straw, crammed in wheelbarrows, hanging from the rafters, and piled on the roof – seemingly hundreds of different pumpkins and squashes.

In fact, Mr Upton grows about 30 varieties of pumpkins and 30 varieties of squashes revelling in such glorious names as Pink Banana, Hungarian Mammoth, Funny Faces (pumpkins) or Golden Nugget, Sweet Dumpling, Crookneck or Turk's Turban (squashes). The difference between a pumpkin and a squash – both members of the cucumber family – becomes even more complicated to explain when you realize that there are summer squashes (*Cucurbita pepo*) and winter squashes (*C. maxima*) and the same name may well be used for different varieties. Suffice to say that some have hard skin, others are soft and pliable to touch; some are huge (Mr Upton's record-breaker topped the scales at 27kg/60 lb), others tiny; some are soft-fleshed and custardy, others incredibly stringy or pappy; some are stuffed with seeds, others have virtually none. Luckily Mrs Upton, by way of being a keen cook, has written the booklet 'Pumpkins, Squashes and Things... and How to Cook Them' and is usually on hand to guide you through the cornucopia.

The awful truth is – and Mr Upton will probably never forgive me for saying so – that apart from a few of the tiny sweet and nutty summer squashes, such as patty pans, I find that most of them taste the same. However, for a truly vibrantly colourful display, them a visit.

MRS UPTON'S PUMPKIN MARMALADE

Makes about 1.8 kg (4 lb)

900 g (2 lb) pumpkin or winter squash (weighed after removing skin and seeds)

900 g (2 lb) granulated sugar
2 oranges

Cut the pumpkin or squash into small cubes and mix with the sugar in a large bowl.

Slice the oranges thinly, cut the slices roughly into quarters and, in a separate bowl, cover with 250 ml (8 fl oz) water.

Leave both bowls to stand for 24 hours, stirring the pumpkin occasionally.

Next day, put the oranges and water in a large saucepan and bring to the boil. Add the pumpkin and sugar and bring gently back to the boil, stirring to dissolve the sugar. Boil until the mixture is thick and syrupy, about 30 minutes.

Pour into sterilized jars and seal.

(Adapted from *Eat Your Greens* by Sophie Grigson)

Holmbush Wild Boar Company ✉ at Holmbush Farm Shop, Faygate, Horsham, RH12 4SE (tel 0293 851674) sells whole carcasses and butchered cuts of boar slaughtered at any age between 12-18 months. They also sell whole suckler boar for roasting on a spit, and boars' heads and trotters on special request. The boars are wet-cured and cold-smoked by Minola (see page 95) for a moist ham, streaky bacon and lardons. Cut from the saddle, these have a generous layer of back fat and are splendid for using in a terrine. Port-cured ham is a speciality: the haunch or loin is cured for about 2 weeks in a port- and herb-flavoured brine, cold-smoked for about 3 months over oak logs, sliced very finely and packed into 115 g (4 oz) packs with about 150 slices per 450g (1lb). Sausages, well spiced with green and pink peppercorns and with an 80% meat content, are available both smoked and unsmoked.

WHITESMITH   MAP 3

Kevin & Alison Blunt ▯▯   GOATS' CHEESE

Greenacres Farm, Whitesmith, Lewes, Sussex BN8 6JA

TEL *0825 872380* CONTACT *Mr Kevin Blunt – telephone ahead*

Texture for a soft cheese is all important; it should neither be too dense nor too thin. I've always thought really well-made ones have that intense smooth velvetiness made up of layer upon layer of thick pile: and this is where the skill of a cheese-maker comes into play. Obviously all the factors have to be right – milk, acidity level, temperature, hygiene, humidity – but it is how the curds are handled that make a soft cheese stand out.

Kevin and Alison Blunt have been making unpasteurized goats' cheese for over 4 years and they continue to go from strength to strength. Milk from their Toggenburg and British Saanen flock is turned into Golden Cross, Chabis and Laughton Log (aka Greenacre) – 3 differently shaped and sized cheeses, but made from the same recipe. The recipe they use is that for a Saint-Maure, a soft creamy goats' cheese from Touraine. A mixture of evening and morning milk is started, renneted, injected with a penicillin culture and left to ripen for 24 hours. The curds are cut and gently ladled into the different moulds: Golden Cross comes as a 225 g (½ lb) log, Laughton Log weighs 900 g (2 lb) and Chabis, a 85 g (3 oz) truncated cone. These are then left to

Conveniently situated on the Cowdray Estate so they serve their game, Ye Olde White Horse at Eastbourne, nr Midhurst (tel 0730 813521) also serve fresh crab from Selsey, and Gospel Green cheeses and cyder (see page 257).

drain for 24 hours.

The following day, they are carefully unmoulded, drained, put into the drying room for a day, then salted by hand. After a couple of days, they are removed to a maturing room kept at a constant temperature of 10°C (50°F). At this point the techniques for the cheeses differ: Chabis, creamy with a fresh floweriness, is eaten while still quite young; Golden Cross and Laughton Log, on the other hand, are rubbed in charcoal and left to mature for up to 2 weeks. Rubbing a cheese in charcoal encourages the penicillin to grow; so, after a few days, the mould starts to develop and forms a furry coating on the outside.

The Blunts sell their cheese at about 2 weeks, but it is at its best when eaten between 4-5 weeks. By then it has developed a smooth white coating and an unctuous rich creamy interior, with a light sweetness balanced by a hint of lemon. From the farm they also sell goats' milk, yoghurt and free-range eggs.

The Weald & Downland Open Air Museum, Lurgashall Mill, Singleton, nr Chichester, PO18 OEU (tel 0243 63348) is a fascinating place to visit. With the aim 'to save threatened buildings, and exhibit them in such a way as to help visitors appreciate the rich heritage of historic buildings in the region', it offers an insight into rural life of days long since gone. Occasionally you may see the old Lurgashall water-mill in action, and from the shop you can buy their coarsely stone-ground 100% flour from English wheat.

And Also...

• As well as selling on-farm cheeses, eggs, cream, own-made jams and marmalades, cakes, pies and meat, *Middle Farm Shop*, Middle Farm, Firle, nr Lewes (tel 0323 811411) is also home to the English Farm Cider Centre. As such it houses the largest collection of farmhouse ciders and perries in the country.

• *Old Spot Farm Shop* ✉ at Piltdown, nr Uckfield, TN22 3XN (tel 0825 723920) sells own-reared free-range pork, mostly from old breeds. They also cure ham and bacon, produce about 20 different sausages (including an Orchard Pork with fresh apples and cinnamon), and hand-raised Sussex pork, pork & turkey, and game pies.

• I have heard good reports about the smoked Sussex silver eel from *Dalton's Natural Food Centre*, Barnham Road, Eastergate (tel 0243 543 543) and they also sell and smoke game...more details please.

• *Knightsbridge Farm*, Hellingly (tel 0435 32574) sell thick unpasteurized Jersey cream from their own herd. They also make ice-cream with a 9% fat content in 10 flavours.

• *Bartley Mill* ✉, Bells Yew Green, nr Frant (tel 0892 890372) is a charming water-mill on the river Winn. Here you can buy a range of the usual organic (to Organic Farmers & Growers standards) flours, as well as some specials that include Abbots Fancy (with sesame and sunflower seeds) and Pride of the Mill (with Korean ginseng and peach flavour). They also sell Fudges biscuits (see page 74).

• *Dounhurst Farm* at Skiff Lane, Wisborough Green (tel 0403 77209) sells a cloudy apple juice; neither too sweet nor too sharp, it is a blend of Cox's and Bramley apples.

• *Ann Knowles of Burstye Soays*, Burstye Farm, Lindfield, nr Haywards Heath (tel 0444 483376) keeps Soay lamb, a small almost deer-like sheep with lean, gamy meat. She has a small amount available (mainly between October to December) as boned and rolled saddle or boned leg and shoulder.

• Local cookery writer Rosemary Moon recommends 2 producers in the county: *Jenny Ferris of Malthouse Cottage Farm* ✉, Malthouse Lane, Ashington, nr Pulborough (tel 0903 892456) for her full-fat pressed cheese Burndell, made with organic goats' milk; and butcher *Gary Young of R.G. Young & Son* at Sussex Cottage, Petworth Road, Chiddingfold (tel 0428 683434) for his sausages.

• Haloumi and Feta are just two of the sheep's-milk products made by *Sussex High Weald Dairy* ✉, Putlands Farm, Duddleswell, Uckfield (tel 0825 712647, fax 0825 768410). The others are Duddleswell, a hard-pressed cheese; Sussex Slipcote, a soft cheese; low-fat soft cheese dips, and fromage frais, ricotta and yoghurt.

• By all accounts – and I would welcome reports – *Slindon Bakery* at The Old Bakery, Slindon (tel 0243 65369) bake interesting breads in their pre-war brick-lined, wood-fired oven. Apart from wholemeal, there is Irish soda bread, properly made with buttermilk, and sun-dried tomato, olive and cheese breads. Milk bread has a dough made up with 3-parts milk to 1-part water.

WARWICKSHIRE

HARBURY   MAP 4

Take Two Cooks 🔳   PATISSERIE

Rosello, Harbury, Leamington Spa, Warwickshire CV33 9JD

TEL *0926 612417* CONTACT *Caroline Iacaruso – telephone ahead*

If Meg Rivers (see page 00) is Warwickshire's best fruit cake-maker, then Take Two Cooks is its Continental counterpart.

Run by a husband and wife team, Caroline organizes while Pino cooks. His pedigree is impressive; he trained in the kitchens of the

Belgian ambassador to Rome in the '60s, then moved on to Nyffenaggars, the *pâtisserie* in Lausanne. From there to London, where he worked first as second chef to the Italian ambassador, then for Princess Margaret and he catered the private parties for the likes of the Prince Michaels (as *Hello!* would have it) and the Thyssens, cooking his fifth wedding breakfast – but enough of this name-dropping.

Quite how and why they ended up in Harbury 5 years ago is another story. Suffice to say, working from their large kitchen (and would you believe that, apart from large fridges and 2 ovens, his equipment is probably no different from yours or mine), Pino not only still carries on the private catering but also makes Continental-style cakes and pastries. Everything is cooked to order, goes out the same day and is made with fresh ingredients bought as locally as possibly. Cheese for the airy *truffe de fromage* comes from the nearby Ram's Hall Dairy, and fruit for the open flans from a local farm-shop.

The range is extensive and, if asked, Pino will make almost anything in any size: *croquembouche, gâteau St Honoré, bavarois, Sachertorte* to die for, a rich-beyond-dreams chocolate truffle cake, *Paris-Brest,* a sharp lemon tart, open apple flan, millefeuille, roulades...I could go on and on, but before I stop I must mention the meltingly rich Yule log; it is an interesting change from the ubiquitous Christmas fruit cake.

Paxton & Whitfield, formerly **Langmans Cheese Shop, 13 Wood Street, Stratford-upon-Avon (tel 0789 415544)** *stock Cerney cheese (see page 102), Smart's Double Gloucester (see page 92), and Charles Martell's Single Gloucester sold at about 3 weeks old. Mrs Montgomery's Cheddar is aged for 12-18 months, but Ruth Kirkham's Lancashire (see page 142) is sold fairly young at 2 months. They also stock Bonchester (see page 328), the full range of Robin Congdon's blue cheeses (see page 67), Dorset Blue Vinney (see page 77).*

MIDDLE TYSOE   **MAP 4**

Meg Rivers Cakes ✉ ⚖   FRUIT CAKES

Middle Tysoe, Warwickshire CV35 0SE

TEL *0295 688101* **CONTACT** *Meg Dorman* **HOURS** *Mon-Sat 10.00-16.00* **CARDS** *Access, Visa, Amex* **DIRECTIONS** *From Stratford-upon-Avon, take A422 towards Banbury. After about 8 miles, turn right just before the Edgehill escarpment signposted Tysoe. Follow the road about 2 miles into Middle Tysoe and shop is signposted on the left.*

The small one-storey converted outbuilding that houses Meg Rivers' shop and bakery is set at right angles to the quiet main street of Middle Tysoe. A gleaming whitewashed front, colourfully planted hanging baskets, a mounted shop sign creaking gently in the breeze and a large window set the scene. Inside, the tiny shop is charmingly laid out; an old pine dresser displays the cakes, tucked under the table are pine chairs for customers to sit on while considering which of Meg Dorman's 30 fruit cakes to choose. The pity of it is that very few – hardly any – of Meg's 10,000-odd customers ever see the shop; they order their cakes by post.

With, on average, a 75% take-up from her well-designed catalogues – a figure many larger companies envy – she runs one of the most successful small mail-order businesses in the country. If you order a cake on Monday, Meg guarantees it will be there for the weekend. As a treat for yourself, or as a present for a friend, you can join her Cake Club; every member receives a different cake for the first weekend of every other month.

Her cakes are made with the very best natural ingredients: raw sugar, organic flour, free-range eggs and English butter, 'If I use alcohol – rum, brandy or kirsch – that's what I pour in. I don't use any nasty essences. Unbleached white flour is organically produced and the dried fruits are the best money can buy'. Baking powder has been banished, 'you don't need it if you cream the butter properly'. Although it may sound a contradiction, Meg places an emphasis on healthy eating, 'Some, like the apricot & nut or fig & fruit, contain no added sugar; they don't need it; the natural sugars in the fruit make them sweet enough'. Others have minimal or no added fat.

Meg's cakes vary with the seasons. During the summer there are lighter fruit cakes: cherry cake made with cherries soaked in kirsch, or an old-fashioned seed cake with caraway seeds soaked in lemon juice and orange and lemon peel. There are sporting cakes: for summer, a cricket cake tinged with Cointreau, a sailing cake doused in rum and packed with walnuts, cashews, hazelnuts, almonds and Brazil nuts. In winter there is a rich dark rugby cake, soaked in stout, and a huntsman's cake made from an old Cotswold recipe; Easter produces a Simnel cake; winter, a choice of rich fruit cakes with or without alcohol. Her Christmas cake is spectacular: a confection of vine fruits, nuts, mixed peel and spices laced in brandy. All of them come carefully decorated on top with whole nuts or fruit, tied up in a band or ribbon and well packed for safe transport.

What I particularly like about the cakes is their 'wholesomeness', their clarity of flavours and freshness. Generously packed with fruit or nuts, they are rich but not overly so, sweet without cloying the palate and dense without being too heavy. Meg and her staff bake something in the region of 15,000 cakes a year. As she started the business baking at home on an Aga helped by the vicar's wife, she is determined to carry on with the 'home-made feel' – everything is still done in small batches and by hand. Meg modestly claims, 'There's no great secret to making a good cake. All you need is a sound recipe and first-class ingredients'.

Ryton Organic Gardens ✉ ♟ ♣   SEEDS

Ryton-on-Dunsmore, Coventry, Warwickshire CV8 3LG

TEL *0203 303517* FAX *0203 639229* CONTACT *Jackie Gear* HOURS *10.00-17.00* DIRECTIONS *From Coventry, take A45 towards the M45. After about 5 miles, turn left on to B4029 signposted Ryton Organic Gardens. Gardens are 200 yards along on the right.*

There's an awful lot going on at Ryton Gardens. As the National Centre for Organic Gardening it is also the headquarters for the Henry Doubleday Research Association and, as such, promotes, advises, runs courses and carries out research for organic gardening. If you think that sounds dull, think again. Their 10-acre gardens are a pleasure to wander around, as well as a source of great interest. Divided into areas for soft fruit, top fruit, vegetables growing in beds, no-dig vegetable garden, weed control, composting and soil fertility, herbs, and many others, there is much to enjoy as well as to learn. For anyone interested in growing without chemicals, this is the place to visit.

Jackie Gear, Executive Director of the HDRA (you may have seen her and husband Alan, Chief Executive of the HDRA on Channel 4's *Muck and Magic*), runs the shop and café. The café serves wholesome salads, soups and meals from organic (to Soil Association standards) produce, while the shop sells a wide selection of organic produce.

Another vital aspect is the Heritage Seed Library run by Doctor Jeremy Cherfas. As he explains, 'For any vegetable or fruit seed to be sold in this country, it has to be registered on the national list. Now that costs a lot of money, about £200 per variety, and you'd have to sell a lot of seed to make it worthwhile for the seed merchants. Some varieties, although popular with gardeners, are just not commercially viable. The merchants can't afford to register them and so they are dropped. The danger is these varieties will just disappear forever. To prevent this, we have established a seed library – a genetic bank to keep them going. We need to preserve these seeds; they represent diversity, a range of tastes, colours, textures, sizes and shapes. Some could prove to be the best source of resistance to pests and diseases; others to be more fertile than modern varieties that only work when force-fed with fertilizers and propped up with chemicals. And there's taste – the fullness of flavour from old-fashioned varieties isn't something we can afford to lose'.

At Ryton, there is a Seed Library Garden dedicated to these endangered vegetables and occasionally there are tastings of the different varieties. Anyone can join the Heritage Seed Programme, it costs £12.00 a year (£6.00 for existing members of the HDRA). Membership entitles you, amongst other things, to a choice of seeds from 5 varieties to grow in your garden. When I asked Jeremy for his choice, he came up with the Crimson-flowered broad bean, with blood red flowers, that 'tastes so good'; white Belgian carrot that is actually a white carrot; 2 extra-ordinary-sounding beans – Brown Soldier dwarf French, and Red and White 'excellent for drying'; and asparagus kale, 'you eat the tender white shoots as they push up through the soil'.

There are many, many more. Remember Cottager's kale, or Black-seeded Simpson lettuce (a cut-and-come-again lettuce with charming puckered leaves), or the potato onion? You can no longer buy the seeds but, thankfully, Jeremy has them in his library. He would love to hear from you if you grow a threatened vegetable and welcomes the seeds.

And Also...

• **Wellesbourne Water Mill** at Mill Farm, Kineton Road, Wellesbourne (tel 0789 470237) mill organic (to Soil Association standards) and conventionally grown wheat for wholemeal and 81% unbleached white flour. Own-made cakes are served in the tearoom and sold from the shop.
• **Fosse Way Honey** ✉, Northcote, Deppers Bridge, nr Leamington Spa (tel 0926 612322) run 350 hives. They sell a light flowery honey, a deep rich and strong ling heather (the hives are taken up to the Peak District National Park in Derbyshire in late summer) or a mixture of the two.
• **Quality Quail** at Home Farm, Bourton-on-Dunsmore, Rugby (tel 0926 632298) sell fresh, pickled or brined quails' eggs and, to order, fresh or frozen dressed quail weighing around 170-200 g (6-7 oz).
• **Holly Bush Farm Country Centre** at Astely, Nuneaton (tel 0676 41364) runs a PYO that includes marionberries (a loganberry raspberry cross) and woosterberries (a gooseberry raspberry cross). They also run a bakery, butchery and deli counter.

WEST MIDLANDS

EARLSWOOD   MAP 4

Fowler's Forest Dairy ✉ ▦   LITTLE DERBY CHEESE

Small Lane, Earlswood, Solihull, West Midlands B94 5EL

TEL *0564 62329* **CONTACT** *Pat Fowler – telephone ahead*

The 'Little' of Little Derby means that it is made out of the county. Within the county of Derbyshire, as far as Pat Fowler can tell, no one is making the cheese on-farm. Although the Fowlers have been making it on and off since the mid nineteenth century and claim to be the oldest cheese-making family in England, they only started making it again at Forest Dairy about 5 years ago, and it took Pat '3 years to get into my stride'. Derby cheese has a chequered history; it was known as a poor man's Cheddar as, apparently, poor Cheddar was often passed off as Derby. As for Sage Derby, Pat's theory is that the herb was added 'to cover off flavours. In the 1800s, milk from around there was of a poor quality and the cheeses suffered'.

Above all, Derby has a reputation for mildness. Ambrose Heath, in his *English Cheeses of the North*, was obviously no great fan as he describes it as 'the least strongly flavoured of cheese...and its mildness has caused it to be described as acceptable for both everyday lunch and for the epicure's dinner; a claim which in the second case seems to me to be exaggerated'. Closely textured, or as Pat prefers to call it 'close knit', not unlike Edam, she makes hers with the pasteurized milk of their Friesian Holstein herd in both block and traditional wheels. Lightly pressed with a soft golden rind, Pat washes the cheese in red wine and matures the wheels for 7 months. In fact Mr Heath does the cheese down unnecessarily, as a slice cut from a wheel has a creamy texture and a soft mellow tang. This may come as a surprise if you are used to eating creamery-made Derby – which is almost universally tasteless as it is sold when far too young.

And Also...

• For a good selection of on-farm cheeses, visit **Paxton & Whitfield** (formerly Langmans) at 3 Manor Walk, Solihull (tel 021 705 2535).
• If the thought of knocking at the convent door to buy the Nuns of Daventry truffles (see page 188) daunts you, you can buy them from **Southfield Farm Shop**, Kenilworth Road, Balsall Common, nr Coventry (tel 0676 532212).

WILTSHIRE

ALDBOURNE   **MAP 2**

Baydon Hill Farm Cheeses ✉ ▦   CHEESE

Eventide, Baydon Hill Farm, Aldbourne, Wiltshire SN8 2DJ

TEL *0672 40677* **CONTACT** *Mrs Jo Hale – telephone ahead*

Cheese-making once flourished in Wiltshire, although it has been lost for the last hundred years. According to John Arlott writing in *English Cheeses of the South and West*, the saying 'as different as chalk and cheese' comes from there. He explains '(It) went on "chalk is church and cheese is chapel". This referred to the division of the county between sheep-rearing on the chalk downs as opposed to the dairy farming and cheese-making in the valleys, plus the adherence of the Downsmen to the Church of England in the face of the spread of Methodism through the valley communities.'

Jo Hale has revived an old North Wiltshire recipe that is best described as a cross between a Double Gloucester and Cheddar. It was originally made with sheep's milk until the Black Death when, for some inexplicable reason, cows' milk took over. Jo Hale now makes the 2 cheeses: one from sheep's milk and the other with a mixture of Friesian and Guernsey cows' milk. A hard-pressed cheese, it is made into 1.8 kg (4 lb) truckles or 450 g (1 lb) rounds or 'loaves' as they were traditionally known. It is then matured for 5-6 months.

Cookery writer Philippa Davenport and I tasted them together and we both agreed that the better cheese is cut from the truckles as the rounds tend to be rather dry and do not develop much flavour. The cows'-milk cheese was creamy, almost paste-like, with a mild flavour. The sheep's-milk cheese was denser, drier with a stronger 'animally' taste and this we found more interesting as it had plenty of character. It is, however, a cheese that needs careful keeping as if left to get too warm it sweats profusely and becomes very hard and overpowering.

BROMHAM   MAP 2

Sandridge Farmhouse Bacon ✉ 🚜

BACON & HAMS

Sandridge Farm, Bromham, Chippenham, Wiltshire SN15 2JL

TEL *0380 850304* **CONTACT** *Roger Keen* **HOURS** *Mon-Sat 9.00-17.30* **DIRECTIONS** *From Chippenham, take A4 towards Devizes. Turn right on to A342, direction Devizes. After about 7 miles, turn right at sign for Melksham. Follow road for 2 miles and turn left at sign for Bromham. Farm is 150 yards along the right.*

All the bacon products from Sandridge Farm come from Roger Keen's own pigs. So if you do not mind getting a bit muddy, you can wander around the fields and see the pigs snuffling around outdoors. In winter they are brought indoors and kept in straw yards (Roger Keen claims the wet land causes the sows considerable discomfort). Throughout the year they are fed on pig rations from mostly home-grown cereal without any artificial hormones, routine growth promoters or antibiotic feed additives. Roger used to supply bacon pigs to the local Harris bacon factory, so he must know how to finish a bacon pig. When it closed down several years ago he also started to process the meat.

He now sells a wide range of Village Hams (so called as each one is named after a local village). The strong-bodied, heavily salted and darkly fleshed Brunham takes about 8 months to mature, as first it is dry-cured then steeped in molasses flavoured with juniper berries – it is certainly not a ham for the faint-hearted. Trubridge is what Roger Keen describes as a York Ham (see Harris-Leeming Bar, page 292) although it is, in fact, briefly dry-cured only. For Devyses he uses the local brew – Wadworth's 6X – and the result is a robust, slightly hoppy ham (fine if you like beer). Chipnam is a Wiltshire-cure ham, which means that it is brined rather than dry-cured, and Golden Rind is the smoked version. He also prepares an Apple-cure bacon which has a pleasant sweet flavour, and both smoked and unsmoked (green) Wiltshire-cure bacon.

VINAIGRETTE

To make a strong vinaigrette to accompany Bath Chaps: mix 5 tablespoons of a good extra virgin olive oil with 1 tablespoon of white wine vinegar and a teaspoon of French mustard. Then finely chop a small bunch of parsley, about 1 teaspoon of drained capers and a couple of gherkins. Stir these into the vinaigrette and season with salt and pepper. Remember to go easy on the salt as Bath Chaps can already be quite salty.

His sausages I did not rate, but his Bath Chaps were splendid. These come from the fleshy part of the pig's jaw, the jowl, although I have read that the lower cheek and tongue can sometimes be used. It is salt-cured, cooked, boned and then rolled to look like a miniature ham. Usually eaten cold and sometimes coated in breadcrumbs, it can be a little fatty, so it is best served with a strong sharp vinaigrette.

CHISBURY   MAP 2

Louisa Maskell 🔲 ♟   PICKLES & SAUCES

31-2 Lower Horsehall Hill Cottages, Chisbury, Marlborough, Wiltshire SN8 3HX

TEL *0672 870639* CONTACT *Louisa Maskell – telephone ahead*

At the edge of Savernake Forest, tucked down at the end of a leafy track in an enchanting, idyllic cottage, you will find Louisa Maskell cooking her 'wild foods'. However, do not even attempt to visit her without first phoning for explicit directions as you are bound to get lost (I did). Anyway she does not like to be disturbed.

Louisa is a real food find. A naturally inventive cook with an intuitive sense of flavour, she also is passionate about using local ingredients. From spring to autumn you may come across her loaded down with baskets filled with flowers, fungi, nuts and berries gathered from the forest. Her fruit cheeses (really more thick pastes) vary with the seasons, but they are always made with English fruit locally grown, or even grown in her own garden. Last year she made Rhubarb with Ginger, Elderflower with Gooseberry, Elderberry with Apple and Damson with kernels. The latter was a shiny ruby-red confection which was tart (Louisa by her own admission does not like sweet things) and bursting with ripe fruitiness. It was so good that you could hoover it up on its own, or with slices of fresh goats' cheese.

She pickles walnuts from her own trees. First the green walnuts are pricked, soaked in brine and left to dry until they turn black in our so-called sun. Then they are stored in a spiced vinegar for 2 months, until they emerge with a flowery taste spiced with a hint of

> ### PICKLED WALNUT GRAVY
>
> To make a rich gravy to go with roast beef: simply mash a couple of pickled walnuts in the roasting pan and stir them in with the meat juices. Add some stock, a glassful of red wine and slowly bring to boiling point. Serve with the meat.

cloves. Fighting back the invasion of pesto, Louisa has come up with a British answer – Savernake nut and herb pastes. Again these vary according to the season, but you might try a piquant green sauce made with parsley, elderberry capers and ground hazelnuts, wild forest mushrooms in oil, or even one made with her pickled green walnuts. Everything is charmingly presented, tied up in brown paper – yet another example of Louisa's great style and flair.

CLENCH COMMON   MAP 2

Martin Pitt 🔲   FREE-RANGE EGGS

Levetts Farm, Clench Common, Marlborough, Wiltshire SN8 4DS

TEL *0672 512035* CONTACT *Martin Pitt* HOURS *Mon-Fri 8.30-17.30 Sat 8.30-12.00* DIRECTIONS *From Marlborough, take A345 towards Upavon. The farm is just before Clench Common on the right.*

'Free-range' can be very loosely interpreted, but when it comes to eggs it does, in fact, have an EC legal definition. The hens must have continuous access to open-air runs during the day and most of these should be mainly covered with vegetation. Inside the hen-house, the birds must be kept at no more than 25 per square metre (giving each the space of an A4 sheet of paper) with perches allowing 15 cm per hen.

Martin Pitt, however, is an egg farmer who thinks the EC definitions are not stringent enough. What they do not control is the feed – most farmers add antibiotics and chemical colorants (or at best natural ones) to turn the yolks the sunshine yellow we have come to expect. Martin Pitt adds nothing. He feeds them a home-grown mix that includes wheat, barley, soya bean oil, limestone, ground oyster shells (for the shells of their eggs) and maize (for the yolks). He also refuses to buy chicks that have been de-beaked – farmers usually burn off the tips to stop the hens from attacking each other. Martin Pitt believes this only happens if they are given an imbalanced diet and are housed in poorly ventilated buildings with too many birds crammed in. Anyway, as he points out, 'if they are de-beaked, they won't be able to grub for food or pick at the grass. It defeats one of the objects of "free-range"'.

His are molly-coddled hens, kept at one-third of the usual stocking density in small separately housed flocks of 1,800. In the EC regulations there is no restriction on flock sizes – some flocks are as large as 20,000 birds crammed into one building – which means they would waddle miles just to get to the runs. Even if they bothered to make the journey, because of the EC lack of control of the number and size of exits, the hens rarely venture out. It is made far too difficult for them.

Martin Pitt's hen-houses are specially designed airy barns with huge doors running the length of the buildings and his hens do go outdoors. They lay their eggs in the 'potty' system he designed himself, which provides them with space and comfort. His eggs may come more expensive than most, but you are guaranteed that they come from sleek happy hens (visitors are welcome to inspect the hen-houses). They taste remarkably good and, because of his unique collecting and date-laying stamping procedure, are also remarkably fresh. Widely distributed throughout the south of England, you can also buy them from the farm.

Gloucester-cure ham is a new one for me and I discovered it at **Chesterton Farm** ✉, **Chesterton Lane, Cirencester GL7 6JP (tel 0285 653003)**. *It is actually similar to a dry-cured Bradenham, with a meaty, yielding texture and a cutting 'pig' taste. Its only disadvantage is that it can be a little dry, especially if sliced. This can be easily overcome by either asking them to cut it thicker or by buying a half or whole ham and carving as needed. (✉ Hams only.)*

CORSHAM

MAP 2

P & S Weaver Beef 🛻 ⚘ GLOUCESTER BEEF

New Farm, Lacock Road, Corsham, Wiltshire SN13 9QJ

TEL 0249 730678 **CONTACT** *Paul Weaver – telephone ahead*

Gloucester cattle are officially classed as a 'rare breed', which means that they are under threat of extinction. So it may seem a little odd that Paul Weaver rears them for meat but, as he points out, unless he breeds them and markets their beef to create a demand their future survival cannot be ensured. The Shorthorn Gloucester is a dark reddish-mahogany and easily recognized by its distinctive broad white stripe (or finching) running down its back, rump, tail and underparts. Although classed as dual-purpose, it was primarily thought of as a dairy breed; its milk has very small fat globules that made it suitable for the making of Double Gloucester cheese (see Smarts, page 92). They also have much narrower hind-quarters than traditional beef stock and, as this is where the valuable eating cuts are, selling them for meat is – to put it mildly – a challenge.

Paul Weaver, however, maintains that 'their flavour knocks spots off Continental breeds'. Bred to Conservation grade, Paul feeds them on his own grass and hay and mixes his own feed. The cattle are slaughtered at about 2 years, hung for 2-3 weeks and then butchered traditionally. As demand is a little inconsistent, Paul freezes the meat. This is a pity, particularly as I do not think he takes enough care in preparing it for the freezer (my rib bone-in showed signs of ice on the actual flesh).

However, he does supply three local butchers: Jesse Smith of Tetbury (tel 0666 502730); Andrew Smith of Bathwick Hill, Bath (tel 0225 466654) and R. Artingstall of Marshfield (tel 0225 891304), so you may have better luck there. As for its eating quality, it was certainly different. Generously marbled with fat, it had a rich creamy texture (one dissenter thought it almost gelatinous) with the eye as tender as butter, but far chewier outer meat. Not as full-bodied as pure-breed Angus, it none the less had an interesting deep taste with a good length of flavour.

HEYTESBURY   MAP 2

The Real Meat Company ✉ Fresh Meat & Poultry

East Hill Farm, Heytesbury, Warminster, Wiltshire BA12 0HR

TEL 0985 40501 **FAX** 0985 40231 **CONTACT** *Richard Guy – mail order only*
CARDS *Access, Visa, Mastercard, Switch*

The Real Meat Company, run by Richard Guy, produces meat to its own welfare and dietary codes, and I quote 'Diet prohibits all growth promoters and all pre-emptive medication regimes. Welfare codes provide highest practical welfare considerations. Both (are) independently monitored by the University of Bristol Veterinary School run by Professor John Webster'. Codes are available for public scrutiny and farms are visitable by prior arrangement (see opposite).

In spite of this, however, it is only fair to point out that a certain controversy surrounds The Real Meat Company's welfare codes – namely their use of farrowing crates and teeth clipping. Their sows are restrained in a small restricted space for a period prior to birth, during birth and until weaning; and their piglets' teeth are clipped soon after birth. The Real Meat Company argues that these are 'practical welfare considerations', done in the best interest of the sow and her litter. Unless the sow is confined, she is likely to roll over and squash her piglets, and unless their teeth are clipped, they will bite the sow's teats and each other. Other 'alternative' meat producers, however, claim that these practices are not welfare-friendly. They distress the pigs and they are unnecessary in well-planned alternative systems.

These finer points of animal welfare are often quite difficult for us layfolk to grasp, but it is important that we do try to get to grips with them. If we are prepared to pay the price premium that this meat commands, we must have a full confidence and understanding of what we are buying. The other consideration is, of course, taste. Again most 'alternative' producers make the claim that because their animals are reared extensively and fed a well-balanced additive-free diet, they have a better taste and texture. As I have mentioned, however, the eating quality of meat depends on a continuous chain that includes many factors: breed, feed, age, slaughtering, hanging, butchering. Each of these factors – and no particular one – is vital to the end result.

Having said all this, I have eaten meat and poultry from The Real Meat Company over the years and have been impressed. With their overnight courier service and their Real Meat retail shops in London, Carshalton Beeches, Bath and Poole, plus other butchers who sell it alongside their conventionally reared meat, they do have a comprehensive distribution. Their standards are certainly superior to some, but my conscience prevents me recommending them wholeheartedly.

> **❝** *Most meat we eat in this country is 'intensively' produced. By that I mean by a highly efficient farming system where the major considerations are maximum output in minimum time at as low a price as possible. Increasingly we, the general public, have become concerned about certain practices, such as the use of drugs – animals are fed them prophylactically (preventitively) on a daily basis; the housing – too often they are kept in restricted spaces where, for example, pigs are permanently stalled and crated, chickens are reared in permanent artificial light with no access to the open air etc. The list is endless.*
>
> *For those of us who are concerned, there are several 'alternative' producers who farm extensively with the animals' welfare as a prime consideration. Some belong to trustworthy organizations, namely the Soil Association, Demeter, Organic Farmers & Growers, and the Guild of Conservation Farmers, all of whom have established standards, published codes of practice and independent monitoring. Some farm independently of these organizations and they may be genuine. Others promise a lot, but deliver little. Offering no more than a half-way house, their extravagant claims for animal husbandry – when compared with the MAFF code of practices – do not stand up. It is, unfortunately, easy enough to mislead us. One supermarket chain, for example, boasts of 'outdoor reared pigs'; what they do not mention is that these very same pigs are finished indoors for the last 6-8 weeks of their lives.*
>
> *What is needed is a legal definition of the criteria for animal-welfare/alternative producers. If these criteria existed, we would all be able to compare each farming system, to ask the right questions and to check the details. Then, and only then, would we be sure that the meat conforms to its claims. We would know we are buying the genuine article and not being fobbed off with welfare tokenism.* **❞**

LEIGH   MAP 2

Brocken Dairy Goats   GOATS' CHEESE

Brookside Farm, Swan Lane, Leigh, nr Cricklade,
Wiltshire SN6 6RD

TEL *0285 861257* CONTACT *Mrs A. Storrar – telephone ahead*

It was Colin White, former chef/patron of Whites at nearby Cricklade
who discovered these cheeses. Now running the kitchens at Woolley
Grange, he is one of many British chefs to make a point of using home-
grown produce whenever possible, and Mrs Storrar's fresh goats' cheese
– 'a creamy delicate round' – is a particular favourite. Although she had
always been interested in cheese, Mrs Storrar came to cheese-making
very late in life. 'It's a small retirement hobby that has got slightly out of
hand.' Now she keeps 6 Anglo-Nubian milking goats, because 'their milk
has more character' and makes cheese 3 times a week.

   Her method is simple enough. Once the starter and vegetarian rennet
have been added to the fresh unpasteurized milk, she ladles it into small
moulds, leaves them to drain, salts and drains them again on mats and
then wraps and freezes them – the whole process taking between 5-6
days, 'depending on the weather'. Each cheese weighs around 115 g (4
oz) and has a rich moist texture and mild flavour, best described as
goaty but not overly so. Surprisingly, the cheese does not seem to be
affected by freezing. Sometimes Mrs Storrar makes a hard-pressed
cheese, matured for 6-8 weeks, which has a crumbly texture and a taste
that hints of walnuts – but it is not always available.

MERE   MAP 2

Mere Fish Farm   COLD-SMOKED TROUT

Ivymead, Mere, Warminster, Wiltshire BA12 6EN

TEL *0747 860461* CONTACT *Janet & Chris Wood* HOURS *Mon-Fri 9.00-*
17.30 Sat 9.00-12.00 DIRECTIONS *In Mere town centre, pass the public car*
park on your right and, after about 50 yards, turn right into Water Street.
Then turn first left into Ivymead and, ignoring the bend in the road, drive
straight on. Follow the track to the Fish Farm.

There are several fish farms in the area: Mere, Farleigh Hungerford, near
Trowbridge and Longbridge Deverill near Warminster to name but 3.
Mere Fish Farm, however, deserves a special mention. As you drive
through the small town, passing Robin Yapp the excellent wine
merchant on your left, turn down the small lane crowded with assorted
bungalows and through on to an unmade track. You still will not see any
sign for the farm but do not give up. Past assorted ducks and geese
grazing in the field, over a couple of planks serving as an excuse for a
bridge covering a clear running chalk stream and there is the simple hut

that serves as the shop. Even then you may not be sure if this is the right place as the welcome can be curt, to say the least, and service a little haphazard. Do persevere, as their cold-smoked trout is worth it.

Cold-smoked trout looks like smoked salmon, and is prepared in exactly the same way. The trout is cured, smoked for several hours over a cold smoke – Mere Farm use beech-wood – then thinly sliced and vacuumed into 225 g (8 oz) and 450 g (1 lb) packs or whole sides to order. What Mere Farm do to make theirs so special, I cannot imagine, but it is delicate, finely textured and moist. As local aficionado Michael Murphy says, 'It's like eating smoked salmon but paying trout prices'. Also available are hot-smoked trout, an excellent trout pâté and fresh trout in a range of sizes.

RUSHALL   MAP 2

Rushall Mill ✉ 🏭 ✏   FLOUR, GRAINS & BREAD

Rushall, Pewsey, Wiltshire SN9 6EB

TEL *0980 630335* CONTACT *Barry Wookey* HOURS *Mon-Fri 8.00-12.30 & 13.30-16.00 Sat 8.00-10.00* DIRECTIONS *From Pewsey, take A345 towards Marlborough. Drive through Rushall and turn right at the first cross-roads. Follow the road for about 250 yards and Mill is on the left.*

Rushall wholemeal flour is milled from wheat farmed to Soil Association standards on Rushall Farm. All the wheat they grow there is from 'hard or strong' varieties, meaning they have a hard grain with a high protein content. As the more protein the flour contains the more gluten there will be in the dough, it makes a flour suited to bread-making. The 100% wholemeal flour is produced in a no-nonsense, seriously charmless – but extremely efficient – modern agricultural building powered by electricity (not for them an olde worlde tumble-down mill). They do, however, use millstones, thus ensuring all the goodness of the flour is retained. The flour is sold in huge 25 kg (55 lb) sacks, and in 12.5 and 1.5 kg ($27\frac{1}{2}$ and $3\frac{1}{2}$ lb) bags. For anyone who is determined to grind their own flour, whole wheat is available in 25 kg (55 lb) sacks. Rushall has also installed a pearling machine, so they sell pearl barley processed from their own barley.

Every Tuesday and Friday are baking days at the mill, and David Fuller the miller also doubles up as baker. He comes from a long line of bakers (his father ran a bakery at Upavon) and all his breads are made with yeast rather than any of 'those commercial rising agents or improvers'. His is certainly a solid bread, with a pleasant earthy taste and, unlike several 100% wholemeal breads, it does not sit heavy on the stomach. He also bakes astonishingly light scones, crisp and very strong garlic croutons, a sultana loaf stuffed with fruit, and a sticky malt loaf.

However, unless you have a rottweiler, it may be advisable to ignore the organic dog biscuits aka Wookey's Woofs. Violet, my greedy (and fat) Yorkshire terrier, will eat almost anything, but even she had to admit defeat when confronted by them. 'Hard' does not even begin to describe them (apparently they are twice-, possibly even thrice-baked) and she nearly cracked her front teeth. I even tried soaking them in a bowl of water to soften them – all they did was float to the top.

Anyone who is making a special trip should order their bread by phone in advance (they have a 24-hour answering machine) as it can sell out very quickly.

RUSHALL'S WHOLEMEAL BREAD

1.5 kg (3 lb) Rushall Wholemeal flour	1½ tsp sugar
25 g (¾ oz) salt	1½ tbsp vegetable oil, plus more for greasing
85 g (3 oz) yeast	850 ml (1½ pt) warm water

Preheat the oven to 450°F/ 230°C/gas 8 and grease some loaf or roll tins

Place the flour and salt in a large bowl and mix well. Add the yeast, sugar and oil to the warm water. Mix well until dissolved.

Make a well in centre of flour and add the yeast mixture. Mix well and turn the dough on to a lightly floured board. Knead for about 5 minutes.

Divide into shapes as required and leave to rise until doubled in size (only requires one rise).

Bake for 30 minutes for bread, 20 minutes for rolls.

(Reproduced by kind permission of Rushall Mill.)

SHERSTON   MAP 2

The Wiltshire Tracklement Company ✉
MUSTARD

The Dairy Farm, Pinkney Park, Sherston, Malmesbury, Wiltshire SN16 0NX

TEL 0666 840851   FAX 0666 840022   CONTACT William Tullberg – mail order only

'Mustard should never up and hit you on the forefront of your palate. Initially it gives a mild sensation, then creeps back increasing as it goes' is how William Tullberg, a large jocular man, defines a good mustard. Mustard has been made for centuries in England and William has been in the mustard business for a mere 23 years. Still making it more or less by hand in the traditional way, he started off with a recipe found in a John Evelyn diary and is one of the very few to grind his own seeds.

To explain the process briefly, first he mills or grinds the seeds – usually a mixture of locally grown white (*Brassica alba*) and black (*Brassica nigra*)

mustards – to crush them. For a smooth mustard he may have to grind them up to 4 times. Then he mixes them with water, wine and cider vinegar, beer, honey, spices or herbs – again it depends on the mustard he is making – and leaves them to stand in huge drums for around 14 days. The weather plays a part: the colder it is, the longer it takes for the seeds to absorb the liquid. William can, however, tell instantly as he stirs them with a huge paddle, 'It's just a question of feel and smell'.

The strength of a mustard depends on the mix of seeds, how finely they are ground and the quality of the vinegar and the spices. William uses the best possible for his range of 8 coarse-ground and 8 smooth mustards. For Tarragon he mixes in frozen French tarragon to give it that sharp distinctive flavour; Full Strength is robust and gently tickles your throat; Devizes Beer, made with Wadworth's 6X, is full and creamy, and Green Peppercorn delightfully piquant.

William also makes other 'tracklements' (a Lincolnshire word for meat accompaniments) – jellies, sauces and condiments – and they are all first-rate. As they have just moved down the road to larger premises, you can no longer pop into their shop to sample and buy direct from them. They do now, however, have national distribution, so you can probably find Wiltshire Tracklements throughout the country – failing that they do offer a mail-order service.

Mackintosh of Marlborough, 42A High Street, Marlborough (tel 0672 514069) is run by Nigel Mackintosh, an ex-employee of Justin de Blank (see page 169). His policy is to stock unusual hand-made products made from small and, whenever possible, local producers. Here is a shop after my own heart, as it stocks most of my favourite products from the county – and more.

You will find Berkeley Farm Dairy cream and butter (see page 278), Louisa Maskell's fruit cheeses (see page 269), Rushall's bread (see page 275) – delivered on Fridays only, a superbly fruity well-balanced apple juice made by Peter Pitman of Pewsey, Hotshop's sparklingly fresh-tasting unusual pickles and chutneys, cold- and hot-smoked trout from Mere Fish Farm (see page 274), worthy rich fruit cakes and chocolate, coffee and Victoria sponges baked by local ex-W. I. ladies. They also have HOF Shop (see page 204) free-range eggs and Rosary log, a very mild crumbly textured pasteurized goats' cheese made near Salisbury.

From outside the county come Ackerman's truffles (see page 175), Alderton Ham (see page 199), a full range of Wendy Brandon Preserves (see page 305), a good choice of mostly unpasteurized farmhouse and territorial British cheeses, and James Baxter's potted shrimps (see page 141). Nigel also sells a range of own-prepared foods, either fresh or frozen pâtés, roulades, main dishes, puddings and canapés – including crumbly and sharply cheesy Parmesan shortbreads. These are an idea he 'borrowed' from Justin, but are none the worse for that.

Berkeley Farm Dairy 🔲   BUTTER & DAIRY PRODUCE

Berkeley Farm, Wroughton, Swindon, Wiltshire SN4 9AQ

TEL *0793 812228*   **CONTACT** *Mrs Gosling*   **HOURS** *Mon-Sat 8.00-17.00 (-14.00 Sun)*   **DIRECTIONS** *From Swindon Old Town, take A4361 towards Avebury. After about $1\frac{1}{2}$ miles you reach Wroughton. Dairy is on the left.*

The Goslings run a mixed arable farm with a 100-strong Guernsey herd. Their milk supplies their own 7 local milk-rounds, or you can buy the produce straight from the dairy. All their milk is pasteurized and sold as Channel Island or Gold Top (with a minimum 4.9% fat content), semi-skimmed (1.5-1.8% fat) and skimmed (less than 0.3%). The skim is then either sold as cream or churned into butter. Most dairies double-pasteurize their cream (the milk is pasteurized, passed through the skimmer and the skim is then re-pasteurized) resulting in a 'dead-tasting' cream with a slightly plastic smell. Theirs is very definitely only pasteurized once and, although purists may say even this kills off some of its flavour, it is still rich with a thick buttery taste.

Mrs Gosling makes full-cream butter that really is made with full cream as opposed to whey cream (see Ducketts, page 224). It is unbelievably creamy, with a thick heavy spread, and an extraordinary bright orange in colour in the spring, when the cows have just gone out to grass. She makes it twice a week in her small 18-litre (4-gallon) wooden churn using cream that has been ripened (aged) for 3 days. Once it has turned a scrambled egg consistency, she washes it to get rid of the buttermilk, works or kneads it by hand (lightly salting it if required), weighs it into 250 g ($8\frac{1}{2}$ oz) pieces, shapes them with her wooden butter pats and wraps them in butter paper.

Not only was I pleased to find a traditionally made full-cream butter – once tasted it is never forgotten – but I was also delighted to hear that Mrs Gosling actually enjoys making it. This is probably just as well as there are plenty of eager customers as well as rumours of a royal one in Gloucestershire.

And also...

- At the **Front Room Pâtisserie**, 5 Market Hill, Calne (tel 0249 817401) Tina and Michael Phoenix bake cakes, tarts and pastries. Some have a Continental bias, like apple strudel, *Bienenstich*, and croissants. Others, such as frangipani, lemon and treacle tarts, and a substantial apple crumble cake, are more traditional.
- The **Nadder Catering Food Shop** ✉, 4 North Street, Wilton (tel 0722 744707) specializes in prepared take-away food in 'creamy Cordon Bleu' style. At Christmas the shop is crammed with food-for-presents, including flavoured oils, mustards, a range of spices prettily wrapped in

their distinctive blue-and-white ribbon, as well as own-made mince pies, stuffings and royal-iced Christmas cakes.

• **Fjordling Smokehouses** ✉, Dunstable Farm, Pitton Road, West Winterslow, nr Salisbury (tel 0980 862689) smoke a whole range of meat, poultry and fish.

• Own fresh quails' eggs and frozen bought-in quail are available from **Sherston Quail**, Homeview, Tetbury Road, Sherston (tel 0666 840303).

• The shop at **Lackham College**, Lacock, nr Chippenham (tel 0249 443111) often sells fruit and vegetables grown by the students and staff.

WORCESTERSHIRE

BROADWAY   MAP 4

Kite's Nest Farm 🚜 🌾 ♟   BEEF

Kite's Nest Farm, Broadway, Worcestershire WR12 7JT

TEL *0386 853320* CONTACT *Rosamund Young – telephone ahead*

For the crème de la crème of organic (to Soil Association standards) beef, you cannot do better than the Young family. Perched on the edge of the Cotswold escarpment, before it plunges into the Vale of Evesham, their farm is a role-model for organic methods.

It was in 1966 that Mr and Mrs Young Sr first had their doubts about the then current agricultural methods, particularly the contents of animal feed and the destruction of the environment. After discussions with like-minded people, they determined to farm organically. Their contented cattle are now fed exclusively on own-grown organic feed, and as a side-benefit, their meadows and hedgerows are seeded with rare wildflowers and populated with birds – rarely seen elsewhere.

Son Richard, one time chairman of the Soil Association's livestock committee, was, as such, responsible for implementing its standards. The standards he practises at Kite's Nest are even more extreme – some say too extreme, and question whether they are practical and realistic (let alone commercially viable) for the modern world. They are, however, what he and his family chooses and no one can question their commitment.

Their herd of mixed cattle (primarily Lincoln Red and Welsh Black with a sprinkling of Hereford, Shorthorn and Charolais) are reared on a single-suckler system, with the calves feeding from their mothers for at least a year. They are allowed to stay in family groups throughout their lives; if you wander around the farm you will see small groups of a mother, her children and grandchildren. They are free to go out or stay in the barns as they choose; any time of night or day the gates are always

" To farm organically means no chemical fertilizers and pesticides; rotation of nitrogen-giving plants with arable or vegetable crops; conserving the environment; and, in the case of animals, following the regulations of feed, housing, welfare and veterinary treatment. Patrick Holden of the Soil Association defines organic farming as 'a sustainable management system involving rotation, careful and sensitive management of crops and livestock and a commitment to long-term soil fertility and environment. It aims to work with nature rather than dominate it, to avoid pollution, to enhance the soil and to maintain and develop its fertility'.

The organic movement has attracted an ever-increasing amount of interest over the last few years. Some people herald it as the salvation of agriculture; others dismiss it as impractical, uncommercial – no more than a muddled attempt to turn the clock back. However, organic farming has not turned its back on all of modern technology; it may ban the use of toxic sprays and drugs, but it welcomes the advantages of scientific research – plant breeding, increase in yields, more efficient crop rotation and modern machinery.

What most people possibly do not realize is that to farm organically is more than just holding to a philosophy. It means following a farming system with legally binding standards written by the EC and implemented in this country by the United Kingdom Registrar for Organic Farming (UKROF), a government regulatory body in conjunction with the Soil Association and Organic Farmers and Growers. If farmers or growers do not adhere to these standards, have not registered and not been inspected by any one of these groups, they are breaking the law if they use the word 'organic' to describe their produce.

They may try to convince you otherwise. They may say their grain 'is nearly organic – after all we don't spray' or their livestock 'is almost organic – it grazes on land that hasn't been touched for years and we don't give them drugs' or 'we do farm organically, but we do it in our own way'. There is no such thing as 'nearly' or 'almost' or 'doing it our own way'. Either the regulations are fully complied with and the produce is organic; or if they are not, the produce is not – end of argument.

Whether you agree or disagree with its principles, or whether or not you think it holds the key to solving our agricultural problems is not the issue here. What is at stake is the consumers' right to protection. If we choose to buy organic food, then we must have the confidence we are buying the genuine article rather than a pale imitation. It has a legal definition; the sooner it is understood and legally enforced, the better it will be for everyone. Anyone interested in finding out more about the organic movement can write to The Soil Association, 86 Colston Street, Bristol BS1 5BB (tel 0272 290661). "

open. As daughter Rosamund says, 'Our cattle are completely free from stress, they're never cold or miserable, can exercise whenever they feel like it on a variety of grazings, both young and old grasses. Their environment, welfare, medication and feed are of prime importance. They are incredibly healthy, rarely – almost never – falling ill, as I believe they even practise their own herbal medicine. We're a fanatic family. We mightn't live well, but our animals certainly do.'

If an animal falls ill, in spite of what you may have heard, the Soil Association does, in fact, allow the use of drugs; what is banned is their prophylactic (ie preventative) use. Also, once the animal has been treated, a suitable period of withdrawal must be enforced before the animal is allowed to return to the herd and its meat or milk sold.

Rosamund believes that the way in which their animals are reared, contributes enormously to the eating quality of the meat. When I tried the beef, I found it to have a resisting texture, but great depth of flavour, a subtle richness with an underlying gentle grassiness. What was really extraordinary was how long it kept its flavour as I slowly chewed; all too often, flavour evaporates after the first bite and you are left chewing the culinary equivalent of cotton wool.

Slaughtered as humanely as possible at around about 24 months, their 30-odd carcasses a year are hung for about 14 days, then butchered into traditional cuts ('nothing fancy or exotic') and sold from the farm. Here, you can also buy organic flour from their corn in 1.5 kg (3½ lb) bags. In keeping with their philosophy, prices are also kept low

GREAT WITLEY   MAP 4

Abberley Deer & Wild Boar Farm 📫 🏢
WILD BOAR & VENISON

West Lodge, Stanford Road, Great Witley, Worcestershire WR6 6JG

TEL *0299 896704* CONTACT *Ian and Tracy Ballard – telephone ahead*

Keen active members of the British Wild Boar Association, the Ballards are very particular that the lineage of their herd is stressed; theirs are pure-bred wild boar (*Sus scropha*) from a mixture of French and Danish strains. Anyone knowing anything about the history of wild boar farming in this country, will understand just how important this is.

When the BWBA was set up in September 1989, and I was there at its inaugural meeting, there were heated discussions about the definition of 'wild boar'. Did 'wild' refer to how it was kept or its parentage? Some farmers kept pure wild boar, others crossed theirs with the domestic pig and wanted to sell it as the 'real thing', but did it qualify? The conundrum has now been resolved; domestic pig blood lines have been banished and only registered pure-bred wild boar is allowed by the BWBA. If you want to be certain you are buying the 'real thing' you should ask whether it is registered stock or you can write to the British Wild Boar Association, 30 Fenn Road, Milton, Cambridgeshire CB4 6AD (with a sae) for a list of their approved farmers. Pure-bred wild boar has different eating qualities from a cross-breed: the meat is darker, leaner and finer-grained, and it has a fuller, gamier flavour.

As breeding stock, the Ballards keep 15 sows and 3 boars. The sows farrow on average 3 times in 2 years, so they probably have around 90 young. Kept outdoors in huge paddocks, they graze on the grass with a feed supplement of potatoes, fodder beet in winter and a boar 'muesli' mixed with molasses. Slaughtered between 12-15 months when they are at their most succulent (they can also supply suckling boar killed at about 7 months), boar are hung for about 10-14 days and butchered into haunches, saddles

> ## WILD BOAR BURGERS
>
> These hamburgers remind me of eating wild boar in Tuscany where there is a tradition of flavouring it with fennel seed to add an edge to the meat.
>
> Mince 450 g (1 lb) lean wild boar meat from the shoulder or loin with 55 g (2 oz) of wild boar or pork back fat. Mix in 3 tablespoons of breadcrumbs, 2 tablespoons of fresh cream, 2 tablespoons of fennel seeds, a small pinch each of ground cloves and nutmeg and season with sea salt and freshly ground black pepper. If you prefer, whizz all the ingredients together in a food processor.
>
> Shape the mixture into smallish hamburgers in the palm of your hands and grill them for about 5-7 minutes on each side. (Adapted from Patricia Lousada's *Game Cookery*.)

and shoulders (boned and rolled), or turned into a medium-textured gutsy sausage with an 80% meat content flavoured with sage.

They also farm Red deer that are also kept outdoor in paddocks (but different ones from the boar). As with the boar, the Ballards do all the slaughtering (their deer are shot), hanging and butchering of their venison, and both are available frozen all year or fresh at specific times.

GREAT WITLEY   MAP 4

Goodman's Geese ✉ ▦ ♟ ⛑

GEESE, ASPARAGUS & SOFT FRUIT

Walsgrove Farm, Great Witley, Worcester, Worcestershire WR6 6JJ

TEL *0299 896272* **CONTACT** *Judy Goodman* **HOURS** *May to end-July: 9.00-17.00 – Sept 23 to Dec 23 telephone ahead for geese* **DIRECTIONS** *From Worcester, take A443 about 12 miles into Great Witley. Turn left on to B4203 at sign for Bromyard. After about 100 yards, take the first turning on the left and farm is ¼ mile along on the right.*

Judy Goodman is possibly the largest free-range goose producer in Britain, this year she promises around 2,500 over the Christmas period. The farm, nestling in the Abberley Hills, is run by her husband and his brother and covers 500 acres in total. For the geese they have set aside 50 acres of good grass.

During the summer and autumn you can watch them waddling around picking away contentedly; then suddenly, and for no apparent reason, they will come together in a whoosh of white, flapping and cackling as if the world was coming to an end – they are wonderfully powerful birds. Judy buys them in as day-old goslings and they peck at the grass, supplemented with a compound feed of minerals, vitamins, wheat and barley made up to Judy's specifications.

They are slaughtered by dislocation of the neck (the approved way) at any age between 22-28 weeks, hung for about 10 days, dry-plucked and eviscerated, and sold oven-ready weighing between 4.5-5.85 kg (10-13 lb). Orders can be placed at any time from August onwards and, such is the demand, she has been known to sell out quite early in the season. With some geese ready by September 23rd (for Michaelmas) through to December 23rd, Judy will send them by overnight transport anywhere in Britain, or they can be collected from the farm.

For a couple of years now I have had geese from Judy for Christmas. They are magnificent meaty birds with moist deeply resonant flesh. Carefully plucked for an unbruised and unbroken skin, they are beautifully presented, trussed with string to make stuffing easier. They also come with a full complement of giblets, a chunk of goose fat and a bunch of fresh herbs. What is particularly striking about Judy's birds is their finish; unlike some other geese, they have a good meat-to-bone ratio – a 4.5 kg (10 lb) goose is ample for 6 greedy eaters – as they are comparatively lean. When cooked, some geese swim in fat and shrink to almost half their size; not so Judy's.

The excellence of her birds is, as Judy explains, 'A question of good management. First the breed and quality of goslings must be right, I choose a Legarth cross. It's a large meaty bird from Denmark and I always buy them from the same trusty source. And you have to look after them; feed them well, take care they're never frightened or frustrated. And we only kill them when they're mature, you get better, deeper-flavoured meat. We don't try to bring them on too fast, if we did, they'd only turn to fat.' Whatever Judy does, as far as I'm concerned, she certainly does it right.

Starting in May, from the pack-house Judy sells ready-picked asparagus in 3 grades: sprue, choice and jumbo. Following on from mid-June through to the end of July, she also has pick-your-own or ready-picked strawberries, raspberries and tayberries. (✉ Geese only.)

KEMPSEY MAP 4

Ansteys of Worcester 🚜 CHEESE

Broomhall Farm, Kempsey, Worcester, Worcestershire
WR5 2NT

TEL & FAX *0905 820232* CONTACT *Alyson Anstey* HOURS *Mon-Sat 9.00-15.00* DIRECTIONS *From Worcester, take A38 towards Gloucester. After about 1 mile, turn left, signposted Hatfield. Dairy is 200 yards on the right.*

Worcestershire has no territorial cheese nor any great cheese history. Patrick Rance in his *The Great British Cheese Book* points out that it was noted 'as a producer of butter for Birmingham and consequently also of a skimmed-milk cheese called "two meals" or "seconds"'. Colin and Alyson Anstey, looking for ways to add value to the milk from their Friesian herd, set about creating one.

Both self-taught cheese-makers, they learnt through trail and error, including, as Colin freely admits, 'a fair degree of mistakes'. Now, after 5 years of making cheese 5 days a week in their 500-litre (880-gallon) vat, they are confident they have it right. The cheese the Ansteys 'invented' is the Old Worcester White; Colin describes it as a cross between a Cheddar and a Cheshire. Indeed it does have a Cheshire's open crumbly texture, but it is firmer and drier; and although it does have a mellow tang, it does not have much of a Cheddar's resonant tang.

The significant thing about how it is made is that the curds are 'snapped' or broken up by hand. The only other time I have ever seen this done is when I watched Suzanne Stirke make her Wensleydale (see page 298). Believe me, that was exhausting enough. The reason for hand-milling, in Colin's case, is to arrive at the open texture without creating too moist a cheese. To ensure the dryness and firmness, Old Worcester is pressed for 24 hours, wrapped in a calico bandage and pressed for a further 24 hours and matured up to 3 months.

Keen to capitalize on whatever local associations they could find, the Ansteys have also developed a Worcestershire Sauce cheese. Made in the same way as Old Worcester, the sauce is added as the cheese is 'snapped'. The result is a pale ivory cheese mottled with chestnut brown (a similar effect to a Sage Derby) and although sold younger at about 6 weeks, it does have a certain punch. They also make a Double Worcester which, coloured with anatto, is actually made in more or less the same way as a Double Gloucester. The cheeses, made in 450 g and 2.7-3.5 kg (1 and 6-8 lb) truckles, can be bought from the tiny farm-shop.

NEWNHAM BRIDGE MAP 4

Newnham Mill 📖 🌾 🌳 STONE-GROUND FLOUR

Newnham Bridge, Tenbury Wells, Worcestershire WR15 8JE
TEL *058479 494* CONTACT *Robert Higginson – telephone ahead*

An enchanting red-brick mill tucked down the bottom of a track, Newnham Mill dates from around the 1700s and, like most of the old country watermills, it has been altered several times over the centuries. In its lifetime not only has it ground flour and livestock feed for all the surrounding farms but it has also driven a water pump, a saw-bench and a cider press.

Restored during the 1970s, now it is used exclusively for the production of flour, ground on the French burr millstones. According to Robert Higginson these stones, cut from fresh-water quartz, were imported as crude lumps and made into millstones here by shaping the pieces and binding them with wire hoops. Making them was the millstone manufacturer's skill; dressing them that of the millwright.

Miller Robert concentrates on strong flour with a high gluten content for bread-making which he supplies mainly to local bakers. According to Robert it is a myth that we do not grow strong wheat in Britain; it is just a case of choosing the right varieties. He uses mainly local wheat, topped up with imported strong wheat from Canada. He produces 2 ranges: one conventional, the other organic (to Soil Association standards). Both have a strong wholemeal; a strong brown, an 81% extraction with the coarse bran removed; a strong unbleached white; and a strong malted 3-grain, a blend of brown flour, rye meal, malted barley flour and malted wheat flakes. He also produces stone-ground white flour, an organic self-raising brown, organic bran and organic rye meal.

T. H. Checketts in *Main Road, Ombersley (tel 0905 620284)* *is one of a dying breed – a traditional butcher. So many factors (supermarkets, EC regulations, changing social and dietary habits) contrive to make the butcher's lot a hard one, but Tony Checketts is determined to carry on. He buys meat locally and still slaughters and hangs it himself, 'the only way to keep complete control of the quality'. Beef comes mostly from heifers, 'because of their marked tenderness,' and he favours a Hereford Friesian cross 'as it takes a lot of beating'. Hung for 'a good 14 days, a special piece will go to 21 days and in practice, most everything is', it eats succulently and richly. A rib comes highly recommended by food writer Philippa Davenport as, 'the most vibrantly flavoured I've had in years'. Lamb, mostly Charolais or Suffolk cross is well-marbled and finished and is hung for a week to 10 days. Pork has a 'pearly' finish and Mr Checketts processes his own tongues; hams; dry-cured bacon (which won a gold medal at the Smithfield Show); and Cumberland, pork, and pork & beef sausages. He also sells haggis, another more unusual white pudding made with leeks, groats, flour and pork fat by a small producer in Worcester; farmed venison; wild duck; hare; pheasant; and, at Christmas, fresh cockerels weighing up to 4.5 kg (10 lb) and hung for 10 days; Judy Goodman's geese (see page 282), and Bronze turkeys.*

MAP **4**

Malvern Cheesewrights ✉ 📭   CHEESE

Manor House, Malvern Road, Lower Wick, Worcester,
Worcestershire WR2 4BS

TEL *0905 748255* FAX *0905 748106* CONTACT *Nicholas Hodgetts* HOURS
Mon-Sat 9.00-18.00 (-20.00 Fri) DIRECTIONS *From Worcester, take*
A44/A49 towards Leominster and Ledbury. Shop is 200 yards before the
intersection of the roads, on the left.

The Malvern Cheesewrights is run by Nick Hodgetts. As linchpin of the
whole operation, not only does he actually make an interesting and
varied range of cheeses but he also acts as sales co-ordinator for the
cheeses of its members (see Richard Rogers, page 287, and Fowlers,
page 266) as well as his own.

Nick rents his premises from Bennetts, a milk-bottling dairy, and you
can buy his cheeses from their large supermarket out front. His milk is
delivered directly to him; and to ensure it has the quality and
characteristics he needs for cheese-making, it all comes from single
herds. For Guernster, he uses a Channel Island milk (Jersey and
Guernsey mixed) from Sandwell Priory, home to one of the few
remaining herds run by Benedictine monks. A lightly pressed cheese,
matured for around 14 weeks, it has a creamy, rich flavour with a
buttery texture.

Hereford Hops, made with local unpasteurized Friesian milk, is a
Gloucester-type cheese, but it is pressed for 48 hours then coated in
hops and left to mature for anything between 6-10 weeks. The result is a
smooth buttery cheese with a mild lemon astringency. Single Worcester,
a Single Gloucester-type cheese, is made with the same milk, 'but
skimmed in the old farmhouse way', as Nick explained. 'Once it has
settled and the cream has risen to the top, I just skim it off and use it in
Hereford Hops. The remaining milk I use for the Worcester.' Moist, mild
and delicately spiced, Nick also makes it with red peppers exclusively
for Harrods, who sell it under the name of Millers.

All Nick's cheeses have a rich butteriness about them. This he puts
down in part to the quality of the milk, and in part to the particular way
he makes them. He tends to scald the curd at a relatively higher
temperature than most, as is the case for Bedwardine which is also from
Friesian milk. A melting, rich cheese similar to a Port Salut, but with a
far gutsier, more complex punch; the curds, once scalded are washed
through with water, pressed briefly for 5 hours, brined for about 12
hours and then left to mature for about 5-6 weeks until a pliable rind
develops.

Symonds Yat, made from goats' milk, is pressed for longer (24 hours)
and at a much greater pressure. Short and crumbly, it has a nicely
developed punch of goat. Nick's favourite cheese is Malvern, made from

unpasteurized ewes' milk, which is not altogether surprising as he was a dairy sheep farmer and now buys in the Friesland milk from the very flocks he helped establish. Made in a similar way to a Manchego, pressed for anything between 36-48 hours and only lightly salted, it is sold while still comparatively young at anything between 3-5 months. I can quite see why Nick likes it, with a texture that cuts like butter and a well-rounded soft sweetness with a hint of a nuttiness, it is a cheese over which to linger.

> **Richard Rogers** of **Little Lightwood Farm, Cotheridge, nr Worcester (tel 0905 333236)** *lives ½ a mile from Elgar's birthplace, so it seems only proper and correct that he should name one of his cheeses after the famous composer. The other, Severn Sisters, takes its name from the river running in his valley, a tributary of the river Severn. Both of Richard's cheeses are unpasteurized, made with vegetarian rennet and are distributed by the Malvern Cheesewrights (see page 286). Elgar, in 1.8 kg (4 lb) truckles, is a semi-hard rich and creamy cheese. Reports please on how they are shaping up.*

And Also....

• In her kitchen behind the post office, postmistress *Sue Coley* makes piccalilli, green bean, tomato and beetroot chutneys. Made regularly throughout the year with fresh ingredients, they can be bought direct from Abberley Post Office, Abberley (tel 0299 896213)

• *Mrs Scott of Newhouse Farm* ✉, Lower Rochford, nr Tenbury Wells (tel 058 479400) has 7 acres of plum orchards, more than she can cope with. So she is perfectly happy for visitors to picnic under the old trees and fill up their baskets with the different varieties that include Purple Pershore, Prolific and Victorias. Using damsons and damazines (a large damson) and sugar, she makes a deep ruby-red purée and sells it in 250 and 500 g (8½ oz and 1 lb 2 oz) tubs, frozen or fresh in season.

• Dr Carol Field of *Teme Valley Honey Farm* ✉ at Bath House, Sutton, nr Tenbury Wells (tel 0584 810424) is often called upon as a honey judge at local shows, so her own product must be up to scratch. She describes most of what she sells as Mixed blossom; a medium-to-light honey with a gentle floweriness. Occasionally she has lime and – if she takes her hives to the Welsh moors – thick heather honeys.

• *Just Pies* of Unit 4, Hanley Workshops, Hanley Swan (tel 0684 310958) make good old-fashioned meat pies. These include a meaty steak and kidney in red wine; beef in beer with Banks' best bitter; lamb & orange; pork in cider, with chopped prunes, apricots and the local Norbury's Black Bull cider. Anne Savage, a home economics teacher, cooks everything herself, even her own-made shortcrust pastry.

YORKSHIRE

Ampleforth Abbey Apples 🚜 ⚓   APPLES

Ampleforth Abbey, Ampleforth, Yorkshire YO6 4HA

TEL *0439 3485* **CONTACT** *Stuart Murfitt* **HOURS** *Sept to Apr: 8.00-17.00*
DIRECTIONS *From Oswalkirk, take the Ampleforth Road towards Coxwold.*
After about 1 mile, orchard is signposted on the left.

Although Ampleforth Abbey Orchards now boasts 58 varieties of apples
on 2,500 trees, it started with 5 Bramley trees and 1 Grenadier. The
reason Ampleforth has an orchard at all was explained by its present
keeper and apple-enthusiast, Stuart Murfitt. Apparently, several years
ago an asthmatic priest was advised by his doctor to get out in the fresh
air and take some exercise, his solution was to plant the apple trees.

Now Stuart, ably abetted by 3 or 4 novice priests – but only during
picking time – has been tending the orchards for the last 5 years. 'I
prune and keep them tidy, Mother Nature does the rest', he told me
rather sanguinely, 'This being quite far north and not that well sheltered,
late frosts can knock us back'. Last year he lost a third of his cookers,
but if he gets past mid-May without mishap, he reckons he is home and
dry. The risks may be greater, 'As a rule of thumb we're about 14-21
days behind Kent,' but the advantage of growing apples this far north is
that it produces more intense and deeper-flavoured fruit. For apples and
most temperate fruit, it is warm days and cool nights that make ideal
growing conditions; too warm a day will bring on the fruit too fast,
whereas a cold night – provided, of course, it is frost-free – can only
intensify the flavour.

The apples are kept in large wooden boxes in a narrow dark barn that
serves as the orchard's store. As it is not refrigerated, the varieties have
been chosen with their natural keeping qualities in mind. Most of them
are late- and extra-late-season varieties; this means that, although picked
in September to early October, they are ready for eating only from late
October through to the New Year (or even later) to provide a succession
of fruit throughout the late autumn and winter. 'Earlies are eaten
directly off the tree, the others we store off and mature like wine'.
Stuart's favourite is the early Red Gravenstein, which he describes as
'firm, crisp and juicy, it lasts well. Early on it's got a good smack to it,
then it mellows out'. Another splendid and rare early is Irish Peach, with
its greenish-white flesh tinged with red and its aromatic flavour.
Unusual late apples include the yellow-skinned Belle de Boskoop, the
irregularly shaped and briskly juicy King's Acre Pippin, Ribston Pippin
with its original tree at Ribston Hall in nearby Knaresborough, and the
acid Lane's Prince Albert.

With fruit to sample and an honesty box for leaving money when Stuart is not around, Ampleforth is a relaxed and informal orchard to visit. Up until now the Abbey has subsidized its existence, but Stuart has given himself 10 years in which to produce a crop that will pay its way. He wants to keep the old-fashioned varieties going, but it may prove to be a battle. Let's wish him luck.

BRADFORD   MAP 4

Kolos Bakery ✉ ▦   SOUR-DOUGH BREAD

128-132 Parkside Road, Bradford, Yorkshire BD5 8EH

TEL *0274 729958* **CONTACT** *Jaroslaw Prytulak* **HOURS** *Mon-Fri 7.00-18.00 Sat 7.00-13.00* **DIRECTIONS** *Turn off the M606 at the last exit, signposted Bradford. Follow the slip-road to the roundabout and turn right off the roundabout towards The Rooley pub. Turn left immediately after the pub into Parkway Road. Follow the road about $\frac{1}{4}$ mile to a T-junction and turn left. Bakery is signposted about 500 yards on the left.*

When Ivan Prytulak bought an existing bakery in Bradford in 1961, it seemed logical to name it Kolos (Ukrainian for an ear of wheat) after the bakery in Stanislaviw where he served his apprenticeship before the Second World War. As Bradford had one of the largest Ukrainian communities in the United Kingdom, it also made sense to carry on making the rye breads he had been taught to make.

Kolos is now run by Ivan's 3 sons, and what was once a corner shop has grown into a large wholesale bakery. It still services the local community as throughout the day the door bell rings and another customer pops in to buy bread; but it also distributes it around the country. They do make white and brown wheat bread, Vienna bread, French sticks, tea-cakes and baps, but it is for the sour-dough rye breads that I sought them out. These come as Ukrainian rye, a comparatively light bread with a mix of 50% rye and 50 % wheat and according to Jaroslaw 'best for the English taste'; Bauernbrot, a German-style rye with 70% rye and 30% wheat, is closer-textured; Estonian, with 80% rye, is closer still; and Bavarian, with 100% rye, positively verges on the solid.

All the breads are made with the same sour-dough starter kept in a huge bin in the bakery that goes on and on for years provided you feed it with flour. The bread, left to rise once, is knocked back and rises again 'like nature intended', in order to develop its flavour. When tasting, none of them had a very pronounced sourness, although the higher the rye flour content the more marked it became. Rather they were moist, slightly sweet and delightfully dense, the sign of a good solid rye. As they have a good keeping quality, Jaroslaw is more than happy to post loaves, should you wish it and be prepared to pay for it. Ukrainians, according to Jaroslaw, are notoriously tight and they never will.

✉ *Suddenly there seem to be several Dale cheeses. On closer inspection, some are using the old Dale recipes with milk from the Dale; others are probably no more than using the name. In fact, several makers think that Dale cheese recipes are remarkably similar and it is the characteristics of the milk from the Dale that counts. We have already dealt with Wensleydale (see page 298), then there is Ribblesdale made by Iain Hill at **Ashes Farm, Horton-in-Ribblesdale, Settle, BD24 0JB (tel 0729 860231)** high in the Pennines. Cheese was once made in this dale, but it had long since disappeared when Iain started in 1982. Instead, he chose to follow a Wensleydale-style recipe and produces pasteurized cows'-, sheep's- and goats'-milk cheese. David Reed of **The Swaledale Cheese Company** at **Mercury Road, Richmond, DL10 4TQ (tel 0748 824932)** makes Swaledale, which was originally made by the monks with ewes' milk. David makes 2 versions: 1 with pasteurized ewes' milk; the other with pasteurized cows' milk for a buttery, almost spreadable, cheese similar to a Tomme de Savoie. **Shepherd's Purse, Leachfield Grange, Newsham, Thirsk, YO7 4DL (tel 0845 587220)** make various ewes'-milk cheeses. Their range includes what they choose to call The Original Farmhouse Wensleydale; it is made with ewes' milk, but the dairy and the milk are from outside the Dale; Herriot is matured on for 3 months; Yorkshire Blue is its blued version; and Olde York, a wax-coated Coulommiers-style cheese – flavoured with chives, green peppercorns, or garlic & parsley – that strikes me as a poorly drained cheese. Shepherd's Purse also make Ashdale, a goats'-milk cheese, for Town Head Farm and Wharfedale and Brymoor, 2 Guernsey-milk cheeses, for Brian Moore (tel 0677 60337).*

DANBY MAP 6

Botton Village Foods 🗫 🍴   CHEESES

The Camphill Village Trust, Danby, Whitby, Yorkshire YO21 2NJ

TEL *0287 661270* **FAX** *0287 660888* **CONTACT** *Paul Abel* **HOURS** *Mon-Fri 9.00-12.00 14.00-17.30* **DIRECTIONS** *From Middlesbrough, take A171 towards Guisborough. After about 12 miles, turn right signposted Castleton/Danby. Follow the road about 5 miles and turn right, signposted Botton Village. Follow the road about 3 miles to the end of Danby Dale into the village. The Trust is in the village.*

The drive through the sparsely inhabited North Yorkshire Moors to Botton Village is spectacular and when you arrive the first impression is of a busy thriving community set in isolated countryside. With 5 farms, a bakery, dairy and food centre, as well as craft workshops and a printing press, Botton Village is one of many of The Camphill

Communities in Britain. Established by Dr Karl Koënig, their purpose is many-stranded; primarily it is to work with the mentally handicapped to give them a life, an occupation and a purpose in a community where everyone, according to their ability, contributes what they can towards the well-being of their fellows. To this end, co-workers (trained staff or volunteers) run the workshops – helped by villagers – with the goal of producing good products (to Bio-dynamic standards).

The creamery, using unpasteurized milk from the village's Ayrshire and Shorthorn herd, makes Botton. This hard-pressed Cheddar-style cheese, matured for 3-4 months, has a short, sharp flavour that develops a deep tang as it warms in the mouth. It comes as plain or flavoured with chives, or marjoram and basil. Then there is Danby Dale, a compact, slightly too salty curd cheese drained in moulds, brined and then waxed into 300 g ($10\frac{1}{2}$ oz) rounds; and they also make a vibrant curd cheese using a starter but no rennet, then they hang up the soured milk in cheese-cloths to drain.

From the bakery workshop comes a hearty choice of breads and biscuits made from either their own or bought-in (to Soil Association standards) grain. These include a splendid herb & cheese loaf (using Botton cheese), bread rolls – or buns as they are called in this part of the world – made with two-thirds wholemeal and one-third white flour; and a substantial tea bread. The Food Centre produces a range of fruity jams, some made with their own fruit and others from bought-in fruit: there is a deep and very fruity blackberry, a well spiced rhubarb & ginger, and a nutty damson; thick-cut orange marmalade made with raw cane sugar and no added pectin for a sharp, slack-set preserve. There are also cordials made in the fruit press that come in apple, blackcurrant, redcurrant and strawberry flavours; a thick mayonnaise made from their whole free-range eggs and olive and sunflower oil; and a cloudy apple juice.

Indeed, the products are good; but more, much more than that, the dedication of the co-workers and the enthusiasm of the villagers made visiting Botton Village a memorable experience.

Butcher **Derek Fox** ✉ *at* **25 Market Place, Malton, YO17 0LP (tel 0653 600338)** *is proud of his Yorkshire Pots for Christmas. They are actually a series of boned-out birds and game, spread with stuffing, laid one within the other and then rolled up. Starting from the outside and working in, the pot is made from duck, chicken, pheasant, partridge and venison wrapped around the birds' livers. In fact, he will make more or less any combination a customer asks for, 'if they don't like pheasant, we'll put in a guinea fowl or swap the duck for a turkey'. The boning and assembly is done by his daughter Melanie and they are prepared in advance and frozen; for mail order they are packed in ice and sent while still frozen, although he will prepare them to arrive fresh for Christmas as a special order.*

In spite of the stories you may have heard about how York hams were smoked over oak chippings while the Minster was being built; do not believe a word. York ham is a green (unsmoked) ham. In fact it is dry-cured in salt, saltpetre and brown sugar for a month, then hung up to age for 'at least 4 months' by Harris-Leeming Bar, 'up to a year' at G. Scott or 'between 1-2 years' at Radford's. Only legs that carry a certain amount of fat are suitable for a York-cure; if they are too lean, not only will the ham lack flavour but its texture will be 'like wood'. A well-cured and well-aged York ham has a firm, dry and resilient texture, a mild but obvious flavour of pig cut with a gentle saltiness and a sharply pink colour. Buy them from **Harris-Leeming Bar** ✉, **Leases Road, Leeming Bar, Northallerton, DL7 9AW (tel 0677 422661, fax 0677424986)** – *who also produce the black-skinned Bradenham ham, which is dry-cured for 2 weeks, marinated for a month in molasses, juniper berries and various spices, then hung for 10 weeks to mature –* or **George Scott** ✉, **81 Low Petergate, York, Y01 2HY (tel 0904 622972),** *or the first-class* **Radford's Butchers** ✉ *at* **81 Coach Road, Sleights, nr Whitby, Y022 5EH (tel 0947 810229)** *who have recently developed the Admiral Ham that is first dry-cured, then marinated in Guinness and molasses 'for quite a long time' and finally hung for 4-6 months.* ✉ *All three offer mail order.*

EAST AYTON   MAP 6

Sneaton Dale Honey Farm ✉ 🐝   HONEY

The Honey Farm, 1 Race Course Road, East Ayton, Scarborough, Yorkshire YO13 9HT

TEL 0723 864001 **FAX** 0947 820618 **CONTACT** Steve Ryan **HOURS** 9.30-17.00 **CARDS** Access, Visa, Mastercard, Eurocard **DIRECTIONS** From Scarborough, take A170 towards East Ayton. Follow the road about 3 miles and farm is signposted on the left.

Philippe Marcheray writes in *L'Homme et l'Abeille* (Man & Bee) that 1 kg ($2\frac{1}{2}$ lb) of honey represents a vast amount of labour. It takes bees between 20,000 and 100,000 journeys to bring a single 1 litre ($1\frac{3}{4}$ pts) of nectar back to the hive and 5 litres (8 pts) of nectar make 1 litre ($1\frac{3}{4}$ pts) of honey.

Upstairs in the Sneaton Dale Honey Farm, the curious workings of the bee will be made clearer with the various exhibits explaining their comings and goings. There are even 18 very busy wild bee colonies securely enclosed, I was glad to notice, under a thick layer of glass; but I didn't linger too long as bees and I do not agree. However, it has never prevented me from taking an interest in their honey.

Downstairs is the shop where they sell the honey from the 960 hives Steve Ryan manages. I visited last autumn when they were still 'sat on the moor waiting to come down' for, like all good bee-keepers, Steve moves his hives around the countryside within a 30-mile circuit. The season starts in April, when the bees go to the fields for the flower honey, 'It's 50% rape and beans with dandelion, hawthorn and hedgerow flowers thrown in'. On the 1st of July, 'everything goes to borage. Fishers, the seed merchants in Cranswick have 5,000 acres planted and on a hot summer's day it looks beautiful with the blue flowers and the bees working around them'. The legal requirement for a honey to be called mono-floral (single flower) is that it must contain 92% of that flower's pollen. As a bee can travel up to 3 miles in any direction, it means a pretty large area is necessary; but 'borage' is how the summer's honey is labelled and borage is what it is. A mild fruity, relatively thin honey, it is remarkable for a distinctive lemon tang that sharpens its flavour.

After they are sated with borage, the bees go up to the moors to work on the heather. The more common Bell heather honey is usually mixed in with the summer flowers, but the heather honey from the ling (*Calluna vulgaris*) is very special indeed. Gelatinous in texture and full of air bubbles, it is thick with a deep, dark flavour and very definitely sold separately. Thus the year's cycle, when the hives come down from the moors, is completed. By the way, health freaks might be interested to know that Sneaton Dale is one of the few producers of propolis (bee glue) which is claimed to be a natural antibiotic.

HAREWOOD   **MAP 6**

M. L. & R. C. Snowden 🏠 🥣

SALADS & BABY VEGETABLES

Wharfedale Grange, Harewood, Yorkshire LS17 9LW

TEL 0532 886320 **FAX** 0532 886206 **CONTACT** Richard Snowden **HOURS** Jul to Aug 14: 9.00-18.00; rest of year – telephone ahead **DIRECTIONS** From Harewood take A61 towards Harrogate. Follow the road about 1 mile over the river Wharfe bridge and farm is signposted about $\frac{1}{4}$ mile on the left.

During July and the beginning of August (although some years it is earlier) Wharfedale Grange is open for pick-your-own soft fruit and 'normal vegetables that don't frighten the English'. So you'll find various strawberries, raspberries, tayberries, blackcurrants and redcurrants, broad beans, peas, onions, spinach, courgettes and calabrese – to mention but a few.

During the rest of the year Richard Snowden grows a superb collection of vegetables and salads he describes as Fine Garnishing Vegetables. In fact, he does have them displayed on his stall during the PYO season, but he is always amazed at the lack of interest shown by his 'native' customers, 'The foreigners will snap them all up but even if I were to force them down their throats, the British will hardly touch them'. A pity that, as they are missing out on great flavours and textures, but when it comes to food Richard is the first to admit, 'we are poorly educated and deeply conservative'. As a result most of his trade is with hotels, restaurants or the wholesale market in Leeds but, provided you ring in advance, he will supply any open-minded shopper and, with a series of poly-tunnels, he can be relied on for a good year-round supply.

Ingredients for a salad are one of his specialities: as well as the various coloured lettuces, chicories, purslane, corn salad and rocket, you will find baby spinach, radish pods that are picked when the radishes are left to go to seed and have a mild peppery flavour and a crisp biteable texture, and (new this year) *Perilla fruitescens* with its leaves of deep rich purple and a taste described by Richard 'like a sweet nettle'. Baby vegetables are another speciality and you can buy baby almost anything, from carrots and cabbages to golden beetroot, turnips and baby courgettes – but ordinary-sized courgette flowers. In winter Richard also grows Hamburg parsley, a much neglected root vegetable that looks like a parsnip but tastes like a deeply aromatic parsley. An original grower, Richard is a vegetable fanatic; if he senses that you share his passion, he can talk for hours.

Harry Ramsden's at **White Cross, Guiseley (tel 0943 879531)** *is famous throughout the world for his fish and chips. They are good, but not good enough to justify his staggering yearly turnover of 120,000 kg (264,000 lb) haddock, 3,700 litres (6,500 pints) of vinegar, 300,000 kg (660,000 lb) of potatoes and 360,000 tea bags.*

HARROGATE MAP 6

Bettys and Taylors by Post ✉ 🏷 & Bettys Café Tea Rooms BREAD & CAKES

1 Parliament Street, Harrogate, Yorkshire HG1 2QU

TEL *(by Post)* 0423 531211 *(Tea Room)* 0423 502746 FAX 0423 565191
CONTACT *Ian Jackson* HOURS 9.00-21.00 CARDS *Access, Visa* DIRECTIONS
In town centre.

In Yorkshire, Bettys is an institution and whether it's for a cup of coffee and a Fat Rascal (a cross between a rock cake and a scone, that hails from the moors) or just a loaf of wholemeal bread, who can resist popping in? Betty's first café tearoom was opened in Harrogate in 1919 by Frederick Belmont, a Swiss confectioner. Still very much a family firm, there are now branches at 188 High Street, Northallerton (tel 0609 775154); 36, The Grove, Ilkley (tel 0943 608029); and at 6-8 St Helen's Square, York (tel 0904 659142), with its art-deco interior modelled on the *Queen Mary* and fine stained-glass picture-windows.

Everything is baked in their central bakery and whisked around the county to the shops in the Bettys vans; standards are kept high by using the best ingredients (butter, fresh cream, unbleached white flour) and working by hand in small batches on a daily basis to ensure peak freshness. The range is a comfortable balance of traditional – parkin (sticky squares of a dense spiced cake made with black treacle for Bonfire Night), rich Yorkshire curd tarts, pikelets, Yule loaf (a fruity tea cake from Rippon), Yorkshire tea loaf (similar to Yule loaf but with the addition of spices and mixed peel), comforting egg and cress sandwiches, and feather-light baps – and Continental – rich Sachertorte, vanilla slice (aka *millefeuille*), Venetian Festival cake (a heavenly confection of sponge soaked in apricot brandy, sandwiched together with apricot jam, coated in an almond and apricot icing, scorched in the oven to brown and topped with dried figs, prunes or apricots), an authentic *panforte di Siena*, plain and pesto *ciabatta*, and wreaths of mixed olive, rosemary and sun-dried tomato bread.

If you cannot go in person, the next best thing is to order from Bettys and Taylors by Post. Offering a selection of goodies from the huge range in the shops, at Easter there is Simnel cake and fancily decorated chocolate eggs; at Christmas there are dark puddings, rich fruit cakes steeped in sherry, a Swiss Lebkuchen (gingerbread) chalet and an array of chocolate novelties. All through the year, there are fine teas and coffees (Bettys now own Taylors of Harrogate, the tea and coffee merchants) and fruit cakes in tins. Each weighing 700 g (1 lb 10 oz), these include Earl Grey (with vine fruit soaked in the bergamot-rich tea), a darker Old Perculier (with its malty flavour as this time the sultanas, raisins, currants and cherries are steeped in the Yorkshire stout), and Sloe Gin (with glacé apricots, plums, cherries and a good measure of sloe gin).

HEALEY   MAP 6

Rosebud Preserves ✉ 🚚 ▦   JAMS & CHUTNEYS

Rosebud Farm, Healey, Ripon, Yorkshire HG4 4LH

TEL *0765 689174* **FAX** *0765 689174* **CONTACT** *Elspeth Biltoft* **HOURS** *9.00-18.00: Masham Market Wed, Sat & Bank Holiday Mons; Middleham Market Suns only Easter to end September (weather permitting)* **DIRECTIONS** *Markets in town centres.*

Elspeth is a Yorkshire girl at heart. Having travelled the world, she has finally settled to make jams in Healey just south of Wensleydale – a Dale down from Swaledale where she was born.

A very exacting jam-, jelly- and chutney-maker, Elspeth claims to be no food technologist but with the help of good ingredients and a refractometer (sugar measurer) she achieves clarity and freshness of flavour, the hallmarks of well-made preserves. Her 'secret' is to cook no more than 120 jars of jam or jelly at a boiling 'then it sets within half an hour; after that the flavour has gone'. This she achieves without pectin; it is not that she has anything against it as such, 'but why use it when you don't need it?'.

Using a light golden granular sugar, lemon juice and plenty of fruit, she describes her jams as 'honest products with a soft set, but I and my customers like it that way'. Strawberry is classified as an extra-jam (with a fruit- content of over 65%) but 'in fact they're all pretty high in fruit and relatively low in sugar. Rhubarb & ginger, rhubarb & orange and apricot & almond actually fit into the reduced-sugar category'. Low sugar or not, the apricot & almond is stunning; sharp, meaty and intensely fruity it is punched with slivers of whole almonds which Elspeth buys in from California as whole and unpeeled; then she gets the 'girls' to peel and blanch them, 'they're so much brighter-flavoured than buying them in ready-peeled and blanched'. Damson, sharpened with a touch of lemon, was full of body and made in the good old-fashioned way with the stones thrown in for good measure.

Jellies have a sparkling translucence and an unusual – and welcome – sharpness that comes from adding Bramley apple. Chutneys and pickles are made using a light Muscovado sugar, fresh spices, malt vinegar and sea salt. Elspeth divides them into 2 distinct categories: of a traditional British bent, such as Spiced Plum, Green Tomato; or from India and the Far East with a spicier, headier base. Malay Vegetable Pickle fits into the latter category: a powerful blend of roasted peanuts and toasted sesame seeds with crunchy pieces of carrots, cucumbers and cauliflowers punched with fresh chillies and garlic, it is remarkable for its crisp texture and mild hotness that creeps up on you unaware. They are all matured in the jar for at least a month to allow the flavours to meld together, and they certainly do improve with keeping.

Elspeth was born a jam- and chutney-maker, and her enjoyment is immediately evident. She actually prefers selling to the public which is why on fine days you will find her at the local markets. 'I can meet my customers and find out exactly what they like. Then I know I'm doing it right if they come back next week for another pot'.

> *Before the Second World War, there were 147 Wensleydale-makers in Wensleydale – now there are 3.* **Wensleydale Creamery, Gayle Lane, Hawes (tel 0969 667664, fax 0969 667638)** *have re-opened to make their pasteurized cheese after a successful management buy-out. A furore erupted last year when Dairy Crest tried to shut the creamery down and move the cheese-making from Upper Wensleydale to Lancashire, but its future is now secure.* **Fountains Dairy** *at* **Kirkby Malzeard (tel 0765 658212)** *also make a pasteurized version. And, of course, there is Fortmayne Dairy (see page 298).*

> ✗ The bar at **The Fox & Hounds** in **Carthorpe, nr Bedale (tel 0845 567433)** is well stocked with jars of chutneys, jams and marmalade made by the landlord's daughter, Helen Fitzgerald.

MELTHAM   MAP 4

R. & J. Lodge ✉ 📠   MEAT PIES

Greens End Road, Meltham, Huddersfield, Yorkshire HD7 3NW

TEL 0484 850571 **CONTACT** Raymond Lodge **HOURS** Tues-Fri 8.30-17.00 (-13.30 Wed) Sat 8.30-12.30 **DIRECTIONS** From Holmfirth, take A635 towards Manchester. After about $1\frac{1}{2}$ miles, turn right just after The Ford Inn signposted Meltham. Follow the road about $1\frac{1}{2}$ miles into the village centre and turn left just after the church, into Greens End Road. Shop is immediately on the left.

Even in these health-conscious days, pies prove tremendously popular. Around the Huddersfield area, Raymond Lodge seems to have cornered the market. A one-time butcher, he now dedicates his time to hand-raised pies or, as he puts it, '26 years down the road and a lot of hard graft behind me'.

As with all specialities, it is not only how they are made but the quality of the ingredients that counts. Raymond makes his own hot-water crust with lard 'melted not too hot 'cos it would make pastry too hard', leaves it to rest overnight, then hand-raises it around a wooden die (mould). Whereas several makers use left-overs or scraps for the fillings, Raymond will have none of that. His pork pie is made with freshly minced shoulder; turkey, ham & cranberry has good chunks of both meats; game is a coarse mix of rabbit, hare, pigeon, mallard, venison and wild boar stewed in red wine; and Fidget, traditionally a harvest pie, contains pork cut from the shoulder, ham, sage and onion stuffing topped with slices of apples. New to me are the wild boar, blackberry & mushroom and the vegetarian, containing potatoes, carrots, peas, tomatoes, sweetcorn, garlic, basil and cheese, and using a pastry made with vegetable shortening.

Raymond does produce a range of machine-moulded 115 g (4 oz) pies, but all the larger pies, weighing from 285 g (10 oz) to 1.8 kg (4 lb) are 'stand' pies, meaning they stand up by themselves and are baked without hoops or tins 'because that's always how I've made them'. The tops are hand-crimped, baked in the oven and washed in an egg glaze for a golden finish. Once cooled, they are pierced and filled with Raymond's 'gravy'; this he makes in a huge saucepan from 'pigs' feet, tails, bones, rind, ribs – anything to boil off for a jelly' to give them a moist succulence.

> Village Craft Flours at Thorpe Mill, Grewelthorpe, Ripon (tel 0765 658534) supply Elizabeth Botham with their flour. A small mill on the edge of the Yorkshire Dales, they set up business in 1985 after renovating an old grinding machine. They stone-grind about 18 different types of flour, including various strong wheats for bread-making and softer ones for cake-making.

NEWTON-LE-WILLOWS   MAP 6

Fortmayne Farm Dairy ✉ ▦   WENSLEYDALE

Fortmayne Cottage, Newton-le-Willows, Bedale, Yorkshire DL8 1SL

TEL *0677 50660* CONTACT *Suzanne Stirke – telephone ahead*

I have good news. Farmhouse Wensleydale is being made in a farmhouse in Lower Wensleydale and, in the capable hands of Suzanne Stirke, is thriving. Now I realize some people might not find this as exciting as I do; but if we are to preserve our culinary heritage and all its richness and diversity, then small-scale makers working in the 'traditional' way must be fostered and encouraged. I certainly wouldn't presume to say that Suzanne's Wensleydale is consistently better than those made in the creameries, but it is more interesting and a better example of the cheese that our forefathers once ate.

Wensleydale is thought to go back as early as the time of the Norman Conquest. As the story has it, Norman soldiers stationed up North complained bitterly about the food and King William persuaded his uncle, the Abbot of Savigny, to send over some monks to make cheese. The first monastery was built in Fors, in Upper Wensleydale, but they soon moved to Jervaulx in Lower Wensleydale, where the weather was more clement and the natives less hostile. The cheese they made used ewes' milk like a Roquefort and would blue naturally; quite how and why it changed from ewes' to cows' milk, no one is too sure.

After the dissolution of the monasteries, it was the farmers' wives who made the cheese. And so they carried on, although their numbers slowly diminished with the formation of the creameries, until the Second World War. What then brought farmhouse production to an abrupt halt was the edict that all milk available for cheese should be brought into factories and turned into hard cheese with a maximum moisture content of 40% – unachievable with Wensleydale. Somehow, after the war, only the creameries started making it again and it was thought to be lost from the farmhouses for ever.

Suzanne has only been making for the last 5 years and deliberately set out to achieve the same pre-war moist cheese. She makes it with unpasteurized milk from the next-door Friesian herd, in a small 225-litre (50-gallon) vat. 'A simple cheese to make', the milk is started and renneted for about an hour, the curds are cut and stirred with a ladle, left to sit in the whey for an hour, then the whey takes about an hour to drain away. The curds are then cut into blocks, turned and then broken up by hand and salted at the same time. It is immensely hard work, I felt exhausted just watching Suzanne, so goodness knows how tired she must have been. The curds are milled, packed into cloth-lined moulds and turned; the following day they are turned and lightly weighted for 24 hours, turned again, washed in salt and water and bandaged.

Made in 450, 900 g and 2.3 kg (1, 2 and 5 lb) cheeses, it is eaten young (when only 2 weeks) or it can be kept to about 5 weeks for a deeper-flavoured, slightly drier cheese. I tried it when still young and was delighted by its moist butteriness and its loose crumbly texture. When I remarked on the taste, that hints of honey, Suzanne was thrilled, 'It's what I was always told that a proper Wensleydale should taste like, and that's what I set out to make'. Believe me, she has succeeded.

> As far as I could find out, the only bakers in Yorkshire who still make their own curd for their Yorkshire Curd Tarts are **Castlegate Cafe & Cake Shop** in **Helmsley (tel 0439 70304)**. They are so popular that by the time I got there, sadly, they were sold out.

Elizabeth Botham & Sons ✉ 🏭
WHITBY GINGERBREAD

35-39 Skinner Street, Whitby, Yorkshire YO21 3AH

TEL *0947 602823* CONTACT *Mike Jarman* HOURS *Mon-Sat 8.30-17.30 (closed Mons from October to May)* CARDS *Access, Visa* DIRECTIONS *In town centre.*

Established in 1865, Elizabeth Botham still dispenses morning coffees and afternoon teas with light luncheons in between, served by suitably starched waitresses. 'We like to keep to tradition. We are still a family firm with Mrs Botham's grandson our chairman and her great-grandchildren directors'. Michael Jarman told me as we chattered over morning coffee and biscuits in the chandelier-lit upstairs dining room, surrounded by Whitby's more leisured matrons.

Downstairs is the spacious wooden-panelled shop, stocked with 200 lines baked at a central bakery that also supplies branches in downtown Baxtergate and Sleight. In all the shops you will find a range of the more usual breads as 'Whitby is not ready for olive oil bread yet' made with flour milled at Grewelthorpe (see opposite). There are hand-raised pork pies, various cakes, biscuits and a well-spiced buttery Yorkshire curd tart made with 'a mixture of cows' and – if we can get it – goats' curd from a Greek Orthodox convent in North Yorkshire. Supplies can be difficult, particularly as one of the nuns has been ill, but a monk has been sent to help out'.

You'd have thought with all these goings-on, trade at Elizabeth Botham has boomed consistently, but they went through difficult times; tearooms went out of fashion and the tourist trade slumped. In order to keep going and the bakery busy, they sensibly developed a wholesale/mail order range that is also sold in the shops. This features Whitby Gingerbread, a local speciality that, unlike most British gingerbread, is baked as a firm loaf. Closely textured, with a mild whiff of ginger, it is dry rather than treacly and is traditionally eaten cut into thin slices, spread liberally with butter and topped with one of the Dale cheeses. Originally it was made in 1.8 kg (4 lb) blocks, then cut into 4 or sold by weight; now it is made in 450 g (1 lb) loaves but is still baked in January and matured on until Christmas to allow the sugars to break down. Plum Bread, a relatively new product to them, is made in the best Lincolnshire tradition (see Derek Myers & Sons page 153), with lard and oodles of fruit. It has a spicy bloom, a dense texture and (in spite of the lard), a clean aftertaste. They also sell crisp, crunchy biscuits; Shah ginger biscuits feature Jamaican ginger, as does chocolate chip & ginger, and there is also a plain tea biscuit.

WHITBY   MAP 6

Fortunes 🍵   KIPPERS

22 Henrietta Street, Whitby, Yorkshire YO22 4DW

TEL *0947 601659*   CONTACT *Bill Fortune*   HOURS *Mon-Fri 9.00-16.00 Sat 9.00-15.30; June to end Sept: Sun 9.00-12.00*   DIRECTIONS *East of the town centre near the 199 steps.*

Walking up the steep narrow cobbled street, lined with a row of two-up, two-down narrow seamen's cottages is like walking back in history. Apart from the television aerials, everything looks the perfect period piece. As I turned the corner, the full pungency of smoke and kippers wafting down from Fortunes hit me on the nose.

Fortunes has not changed much, if at all. It is a ramshackle set of buildings, smoke-houses blackened with smoke and tar, with old signs dating to who-knows-when hanging up in the front shed that serves as a shop – Bill Fortune is obviously not one for 'improvements'. Like the surroundings, the curing of the kippers has not changed either. 'I do them the same as I've always done and it goes back to my great, great-granddad – 4 generations. I don't know any other way except what my Granddad taught me and his taught him'. The only change is that the herrings now come from Iceland; 'it's 20 years since we caught herring here', and the boats lying idle in Whitby harbour testify to that.

Salted for 40 minutes and smoked over a mixture of hard and soft woods from anything from 16 to 30 hours, depending on the weather ('it can get right windy up here'), the kippers are sold in pairs (as 'we've always sold them in pairs') and they were certainly the cheapest I've bought yet. Mildly cured but evenly and strongly smoked, they had pleasant but not over-strong sharpness. I am sorry to disappoint you, but if you want Bill's kippers 'you'll have to come for them, everyone in town does' as there was no way I could persuade him to mail order them. After all, his Granddad never did, so why should he?

> *You'll pass **R.J. Noble** at **113, Church Street, Whitby (tel 0947 601555)** on the way up from Fortunes. Their factory and curing shed are out on the promontory under the shadow of Count Dracula's ruin; but they only sell direct from the shop. They have kippers as well and smoked salmon, cod, haddock, ling (which was a bit dull) and wolf-fish (currently out-of-stock). Baked herrings are a speciality, although they perhaps lacked the punch of a spice or two, and they can also be relied on for crabs and lobsters in season.*

WOMERSLEY   **MAP 4**

Womersley Crafts & Herbs ✉ 🗲 ♣
FRUIT & HERB VINEGARS

Womersley Hall, Womersley, Doncaster, Yorkshire DN6 9BH

TEL 0977 620294 **CONTACT** Martin Parsons **HOURS** Jan to mid-Mar: Sun 14.00-17.00; mid-Mar to 10 Dec: Sat 10.30-18.00 Sun 12.00-18.00; 11 Dec to Christmas Eve: Mon-Fri 14.00-17.00 Sat 10.30-18.00 Sun 12.00-18.00 **DIRECTIONS** In village centre.

Every so often I discover a product of such startling wonderfulness that it makes worthwhile all those thousands of lonely miles that I and Violet, my faithful terrier, travel. In a shop packed with dried flowers, herb pillows, herb teas, aromatherapy oils, candles, own-grown fruit and vegetables, and goodness knows what else, I found Martin and Aline Parsons' fruit vinegars.

Now you should know there are fruit vinegars, and there are Womersley fruit vinegars; and the difference is like trying to compare an industrially made balsamic vinegar with a traditionally made one. Basically you can't – they are as different as chalk and cheese. Most of our fruit vinegars are really no more than fruit infused in a vinegar; Martin, however, prepares his using the proper time-honoured process. First he soaks the fruit for a few days in a non-brewed condiment, leaves it to strain overnight through a sieve ('the finer the better, but no way should you force it through'), then he cooks it gently with sugar, leaves it to cool and finally sieves and sieves it time after time. The result is like a bitter-sweet syrup or cordial, mellow and full-bodied, with all the richness and the ripe sweetness of the fruit balanced with the mildest hint of acidity.

Using mostly own-grown fruit for blackberry, loganberry, mulberry, raspberry and golden raspberry (a limpid, clear golden liquid), Martin succeeds in giving each one its own true flavour. These are serious vinegars: cook with them, using them in soups and stews, for deglazing a pan, or transform a salad with them (recently I liberally dressed a hastily rustled-up tuna and bean salad out of tins for food writers Susan Campbell and Claire Clifton with mulberry vinegar – they went into raptures). I honestly cannot praise them high enough.

If this is not enough, Martin also makes superb French tarragon and Dark Opal basil herb vinegars. Using a different but equally time-consuming process, he first makes a herb mash (or, as he calls it, 'pesto'), soaks it in a little scalded vinegar, then strains it to produce a clear herb concentrate. This is then added drop by drop to a bottle of vinegar; and it is the power of the concentrate that gives the deep intensity of the herb. Loosely set herb and flower jellies are also touched with the same intensity: a heady flowery lavender, a mild fragrant geranium, a startling Lemon Verbena are just some of the 11 flavours he produces.

Then there are his mellow, meaty pickled walnuts, and one extraordinary curiosity, a set honey, from hives kept on his land, that has a deep mint flavour. Neither he nor the beekeeper could explain how this has came about; but if Martin still has any left, snap it up. Last year, a few favoured friends received vinegars for Christmas – they are still raving, and begging for more. What better recommendation could you need?

And Also...

• The hand-raised pork pies from both *T. Appleton & Sons*, 6 Market Place, Ripon (tel 0765 603198) and J. B. Cockburn, Market Place, Bedale (tel 0677 422126) come highly recommended as having a 'meaty, slightly spicy finish, and good crisp pastry'.

• Good marzipan depends on the quality and quantity of ground almonds; at *Shepcote Distributors* ✉ of 5 Albion Street, Driffield (tel 0377 42537, fax 0377 42539) both are good and high. Try their boxes of miniature soft marzipan fruits; they look uncannily like the real thing.

• When in Scarborough, the place to go is *Bonnet's* ✉ at 38-40 Huntriss Row, (tel 0723 361033) for tea, coffee or their hand-dipped soft-centred chocolates – including lily of the valley – and truffles.

• For a good choice of local cheese, visit *The Cheeseboard* at 1 Commercial Street, Harrogate (tel 0423 508837).

• *Albert Hirst*, with a stall in the Barnsley Meat and Fish market (tel 0226 284851), sells his English-style black pudding.

• *Wensleydale Wild Boar Breeders* ✉ of Manor Farm, Thornton Steward, Ripon (tel 0677 60239) not only sell jointed fresh wild boar but also liver for adding to pâtés and terrines, and dry-cured and oak-smoked haunch.

• **White's Butchers** at Morton-on-Swale, Northallerton (tel 0609 772855) still buy from the Northallerton auctions and slaughter and hang their own meat. For what it's worth, their pork sausage won first prize last year at the Northallerton and District Butchers' Association.

• Unfortunately I missed out on **The Smithy Farmshop**, Baldersby, Thirsk (tel 0765 640676), but their list sounds so intriguing that they are worth at least a mention. They offer Dexter beef, Berkshire pork, Sunrise chicken 'locally reared in open-fronted barns and dry-plucked', Richard Woodall's bacon (see page 46), Slack's sausages (see page 49), Rosebud preserves (see page 295), Pepper Arden game pies and lots more. Reports please.

• Whitby Jet is well known, but have you ever tried Whitby Jet cheese? Made at **Littlebeck Dairies** ✉, Moorside Farm, Littlebeck, nr Whitby (tel 0947 810823) with pasteurized sheep's milk, it is a mild semi-hard cheese sold in a black wax coating.

• Filey is a charming seaside resort with several B&B's hugging the crescent-shaped bay. Salmon caught in Filey Bay is a local treat; in season between May and the end of August, you can find it at fishmongers **H.G. Lovitt** in Filey (tel 0723 512370) along with cod and dabs caught from the cobble boats.

• Amidst the endless rows of Epicure tins you will, if you look hard, find some good local products at **Lewis & Cooper**, 92 High Street, Northallerton (tel 0609 772880, fax 0609 777933).

• For well-hung and well-butchered farmed venison, smoked venison and venison sausages, try **Round Green Deer Farm** ✉, Worsbrough, Barnsley (tel 0226 205577, fax 0226 281294).

Wales

DYFED

Little Acorn Products ✉ 🚐   CHEESE

Mesen Fach Farm, Bethania, Llanon, Dyfed SY23 5NL

TEL *0974 821 348* **CONTACT** *Karen Ross* **HOURS** *Fri-Sat 8.00-17.00 at Shrewsbury Market*

Karen Ross and her husband Don started cheese-making as 'purists' and, while they still make 'purist' cheeses, regretfully their non-purist cheeses have proved to be far greater commercial successes. Dealing with these first – and very briefly – they are of the milled variety (see also Abergavenny Fine Food, page 320) and rejoice under such historically inspired names as Merlin's Sandwich (Cheddar with horseradish and chives in a central layer) or Monks of Strata Florida Malt Whisky (Cheddar with malt whisky and toasted oatmeal). Honestly, even writing about them distresses me as I think they are a travesty.

Leaving them behind, thankfully – and I probably ought to point out that although I usually pride myself on being reasonably diplomatic while sampling most people's products, the Ross's knew exactly how I felt – let us move on to their 'purist' cheeses. These are all made with the unpasteurized milk of the Friesland dairy sheep flock and are what I consider to be 'real' cheese. Acorn is not unlike a Wensleydale and, in the good old days, Wensleydale was made with sheep's milk. A semi-hard, lightly pressed cheese, it can be eaten young (but not as young as a Wensleydale), at 6 weeks, but Karen thinks it is at its best at 3-4 months. She cut me a slice from a 7-week cheese and I could see that it would develop nicely as, although still quite sharp, there was an underlying nuttiness that, given time, would surely strengthen. Skirrid is made to a Caerphilly recipe, is harder pressed and brined with mead before maturing. Mild with a gentle sweetness, it is perfectly pleasant but lacks much in the way of follow-through. The star of the show is Lady Llanover; a compact cheese, it is pressed harder for a denser, drier texture, then bathed in saffron for about a month and matured on for 7-8 months. When well aged (and I have tried it younger and it does not compare) it is an admirable cheese with the powerful tang and crisp pungency of a Manchego.

The Salad Shop in **Great Darkgate Street, Aberystwyth (tel 0970 61 5791)** is a great shop. Run by husband-and-wife team David and Barbara Frost, either you can buy salads made freshly each day by Barbara or lettuces, salad leaves and vegetables grown by David for making-your-own. Lettuces include Little Gems, cos, lollo rosso and biondo and salad bowl. There are bunches of radishes, escarole and broad leaf endive, frisée, lamb's lettuce, oak leaf, rocket, claytonia, mizuna and all sorts of other Chinese leaves, various herbs, nasturtium leaves and flowers and marigold and borage flowers as well. They make a 'saladini' mix: what it includes will depend on the time of the year, but it may well have various chicories, such as sugar loaf, chioggia treviso or radicchio. Other produce includes mini and ridge cucumbers, baby spinach leaves, sorrel, Swiss and ruby chard, yellow and green courgettes with their flowers, Pink Fir Apple and Charlotte potatoes (both good for salads), as well as Estima and Desirée. There is also an interesting choice of onions, including spring, Japanese bunching, Welsh, tree and red-skinned. Barbara also makes herb-flavoured vinegars from elderflower, tarragon, borage, raspberry, green and purple basil, sage and rosemary which she dismisses as 'far too medicinal but OK with game'.

BONCATH   MAP 7

Wendy Brandon ✉ ▦   PRESERVES

Felin Wen, Boncath, Dyfed SA37 OJR

TEL *0239 841568* **FAX** *0239 841746* **CONTACT** *Wendy Brandon* **HOURS** *Mon-Fri 9.00-17.00* **CARDS** *Access, Visa* **DIRECTIONS** *From Newcastle Emlyn, take A484 towards Cenarth. Follow the road about 2½ miles and turn left on to the B4332, signposted Boncath. Follow the road into Boncath and turn left at the cross-roads signposted Bwlchygroes. Jam factory is on the right at the bottom of the hill.*

Having completed her move from Sussex to Felin Wen (White Mill), Wendy Brandon has got back into her stride. She started preserve-making relatively late in life: 'Anything to get out of teaching, I even tried selling insurance'. Luckily for us, that was not a success, so preserve-making it was, kicking off with the 'Green-label' range – standing for no salt and no added sugar – the first customers were enlightened health-food shops. Making them takes twice as long as her other preserves as, instead of sugar, Wendy adds concentrated apple juice. 'It takes longer to evaporate and longer to reach a set. They have a much more concentrated flavour as they are all fruit and juice – nothing else, a 100% fruit content. And for every kilo of preserve there's about 1½ kilos of fruit'. Marmalades in this range tend to be darker in colour and pack a powerful punch. There are 7 different combinations, including a sultry orange made with sweet oranges, orange hotted up with ginger, and a sharp tangy lemon and grapefruit. Wendy also makes Green-label fruit sauces and there is a rich smooth, buttery Spiced apple and an equally smooth Plum perked up with mint. Her chutneys are dense and well spiced: Peach & Lemon has a full-blown fruitiness; and Kashmiri apple a pungent blend of spices.

'Orange-label' marmalades are made with a mixture of cane sugar and concentrated apple juice. Bursting with fruit, my favourites included Orange with molasses and rum, a clear clean grapefruit, and grapefruit with elderflower for a hazy tinge. 'Red-Label' are traditional preserves (ie made with sugar) and although Wendy by her own admission 'can't get excited about jams as I'm more of a marmalade and chutney specialist', she still makes good ones. There is a Plum & crab apple with walnut, Gooseberry with elderflower and good old-fashioned Raspberry or Strawberry with a few redcurrants 'to help the set and sharpen the flavour'. Jellies in this range include a Violet currant, a sparkling blue-black mixture of redcurrants and blackcurrants; and to prove her interest in marmalades there is a shell-pink Pink grapefruit marmalade with Campari and a piercing Lime marmalade with tequila.

What I like about Wendy is her open-minded approach and inventiveness, she is always game to try new ideas, combinations or even different methods. When I came back from Bologna a couple of years ago, I was laden with preserves I had been given by the wife of a wine grower. This lady's pantry, with its rows of stacked glass jars in a cool stone-walled room with high vaulted ceilings, was enviable; and the Italian produce delightful and so different in style of making from ours. I gave Wendy the mostarda di frutta and now her version of that is featured in her 'Blue-label' (international) range. Wendy's is thicker in texture than the traditional Italian sweet-sharp syrup they eat with boiled meats, but none the less interesting. I also particularly like the Spring Onion pickle and her sweet and crunchy Pickled Turnips, subtly flavoured with honey, ginger, soy sauce and star anise.

Everything is made in small batches, so it receives her careful attention and only fresh (frozen out of season) fruit and vegetables, good quality spices and cider vinegars are used. Commercial pectin is banned, 'usually we don't need it...but if we do, I'll make my own using apple cores!'. There is nothing synthetic about Wendy's preserves.

> For a dry-salted Welsh bacon, cured from the whole middle and rolled up in the round, try butcher **D. I. J. Davies, Tregaron** (**tel 0974 298565**) or **Albert Rees, Market Precinct, Carmarthen** (**tel 0267 231204**), who also produces a deeply salty dry-salted Carmarthen ham.

While Caerphilly cheese is made by several creameries ('dairy-speak' for factories), there are only a few cheese-makers still making it on-farm. A relatively simple cheese to make, each maker has his or her particular foibles. In general, however, it is a crumbly, quite sharp cheese that at its best will have a clean butteriness with a hint of sweet grass. Out of the county – and indeed out of Wales altogether – is R. A. Duckett (see page 224), but for Caerphilly made in Dyfed try **Thelma Adams** *of* **Caws Cenarth** ✉ *at* **Fferm Glyneithinog, Pontseli, Boncath, SA37 0LH (tel 0239 710432)**. *She makes an unpasteurized moist creamy Caerphilly that hints of lemon in 400 g (14 oz) rounds and 2.7 and 4 kg (6 and 9 lb) wheels, matured for a minimum of 3 weeks. There are also smoked and fresh herb versions and if you are interested you can watch Thelma making it in the dairy.* **Felin Gernos** ✉ *at* **Maesllyn, Llandyssul, SA44 5NB (tel 023 985 8951)** *make a much faster-maturing cheese from bought in unpasteurized Friesian milk. It is sharper and more acidic and can be eaten as young as 6 days. Caws Nantybwla is made at* **Nantybwla** ✉, **College Road, Carmarthen, SA31 3QS (tel 0267 237905)** *from unpasteurized Holstein milk. Matured for a minimum of 4 weeks, it is quite sharp but has a pleasant underlying richness, although it can on occasions be quite dry and crumbly. I have just heard Teifi Cheese (see page 310) have started making a Caerphilly as well; by all accounts it is a stunning example of the cheese.*

CASTLE MORRIS MAP 7

Llangloffan Farmhouse Cheese ✉ 🚜 CHEESE

Llangloffan Farm, Castle Morris, Haverfordwest, Dyfed SA62 5ET

TEL 03485 241 **CONTACT** Leon Downey **HOURS** Mon-Sat 9.00-17.00 **DIRECTIONS** *From Fishguard, take A487 towards St Davids. Follow the road about 4 miles and turn left, signposted Llangloffan Farmhouse Cheese. Follow the road about 2 miles and farm is signposted on the left.*

One time viola player with the Hallé Orchestra, Leon Downey now performs most days on a round cheese vat. Join him in his dairy any morning on a Monday, Wednesday, Thursday and Saturday in April or October or between Monday and Saturday from May to September to see him making cheese. The audience may be smaller and the ovation quieter, but he finds it just as satisfying.

Llangloffan is a farmhouse cheese in every sense of the word. Made on-farm with the unpasteurized milk from their 20-strong Jersey herd, the cows graze on permanent ley pastures for a rich milk that transforms into a full grassy cheese with great depth. Cheese-making starts up some time in March when the cows go out, and lasts through to December when the cows come in. Leon only makes cheese when the cows are on grass and never when they are kept inside and fed on silage as he believes it taints the milk. The best of all cheeses come from the September milk and these he selects for keeping until Christmas and the following year. Llangloffan he describes as 'an old-fashioned creamy Cheshire', and the curds are broken down in a similar way. Pressed for 2 days, it can be eaten at 8 weeks when still mild or matured for up to 6 months, when it becomes far more deeply flavoured. A cheese with a good resonance, quite dry and crumbly but with a buttery flavour, Leon makes it both plain and flavoured with chives and garlic and coloured red using anatto. You can buy it from the farm-shop, along with Little Acorn cheeses (see page 304), Merlin Goats' cheese made by Roy Patema near Aberystwyth and Rachel's Dairy products (see below).

For the last couple of years Leon's cheese has not carried the organic symbol although he still farms to organic standards. Ever outspoken, he told me it was because he does not agree 'with the Soil Association's viewpoint'. This refers to the vast quantities of organic milk being transformed into 2 pasteurized cheeses – Pencarreg and a Cheddar made by Dougal Campbell. For Leon, pasteurizing is a travesty and it goes against the grain of the organic movement. Whether you agree or disagree, I sure you will agree he makes a fine cheese.

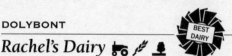

DOLYBONT MAP 7

Rachel's Dairy BUTTER & YOGHURT

Brynllys Farm, Dolybont, Borth, Dyfed SY24 5LZ

TEL *0970 625805* **FAX** *0970 626591* **CONTACT** *Rachel Rowlands* **HOURS** *Sat & Sun 10.00-17.00 Mon-Fri telephone ahead; July 1 to Sept 1 only: 10.00-17.00 every day* **DIRECTIONS** *From Borth, take B4353 towards Llandre. Follow road about 2 miles and turn left, signposted Dolybont. Follow road about ¼ mile and take first turning on left at farm sign.*

Rachel and Gareth Rowlands have come a long way in the last 10 years. From a small on-farm dairy to a gleaming processing unit on Aberystwyth's industrial estate; from selling to a small group of local customers and health-food shops to supplying Sainsbury. All this they have achieved without compromising either their principles or their products. They started as organic (to Soil Association standards) dairy farmers 'And on this we will never change,' Gareth assured me.

Originally it was only their own milk that made the cream, butter and yoghurt; now they buy in somewhere in the region 300,000 litres (528,000 pints) a year although the unpasteurized cream and butter still come from the milk of their 75-strong Guernsey herd. Now you can buy their products all over Britain, but it is still worth visiting the farm (the industrial unit is off-limits to the general public), if for no other reason than to enjoy the planned walk and to admire the view. As well as for the dairy products, the farm-shop is open for own-grown organic vegetables and honey.

Butter, and its by-product buttermilk, is still made on the farm with the Guernsey milk. Rachel's butter is a lactic butter; this means that once the milk is separated, the cream is ripened with a lactic culture for about 3 days to give it a sharper but creamy taste with a good depth. Most butter made in Britain is, in fact, sweet cream butter, that is to say it is made with cream that has usually been aged or rested but never cultured. Rachel, however,

YOGHURT CAKE

Cream 170 g / 6 oz butter with 170 g / 6 oz sugar and beat in 2 eggs, one at a time. Stir in the grated zest of 1 lemon and 250 ml / 8 fl oz yoghurt. Sift in 225 g / 8 oz plain flour, 2 tsp baking powder, $\frac{1}{2}$ tsp bicarbonate of soda and a pinch of salt and beat until smooth. Turn into a well-greased baking tin and bake in an oven preheated to 180°C / 350°F / gas 4 for about 35 minutes. (Adapted from a recipe leaflet by Brynllys Farmhouse.)

has chosen to follow the French style of butter-making. Her butter is always churned in a wooden churn; according to Rachel, this is vital 'other materials will just not do – only wood enriches the flavour and won't taint the butter'. Once the butter granules are formed and have come together like clusters of grapes, it is washed again and again until the water runs clear; then, if required, salt is added. Finally it is patted by hand into neat blocks with wooden butter pats and wrapped in butter paper for sale. Their butter is one of life's great treats; creamy with a gentle tartness, it is delicate but rich and immensely satisfying.

The rest of their range has moved to Aberystwyth. Here their live Greek-style yoghurt is made cultured with *Lactobacillus bulgaricus* and *Lactobacillus acidophilous* and *Bifidus*. Rachel kindly showed me around the unit. Their products are still as clean-tasting, creamy and as sharp and refreshing as ever. They also make a live very-low-fat and a live whole-milk yoghurt, as either natural or fruit-flavoured. Unlike most other flavoured yoghurts, theirs are made with 'real' fruit that they boil up with sugar as opposed to fruit concentrates or various confections dreamt up by obliging flavour-houses. My objection to the manufactured sort is they muddy up the yoghurt, cloying its natural acidity with a sickly sweet, synthetic flavour. Try Rachel's Dairy yoghurt and you will notice how good a fruit flavour can be.

Rennet-free cottage cheese is made with a lactic curd; left to set and drained in cheese bags, the texture depends on the time of the year. When, in summer, the milk comes from grass-fed cows, it is smoother and looser; in winter, when they change over to silage, it becomes firmer. Mass-produced cottage cheese just does not compare; but then Rachel's Dairy is in a class of its own. It is a fine example of how a small company can expand and gear up to mass production, while still making first-class products. If they can do it, why can't the others?

LLANDYSUL   MAP 7

Teifi Cheese ✉ 🚜 🚚   CHEESE

Glynhynod Farm, Ffostrasol, Llandysul, Dyfed SA44 5JY

TEL *0239 851528* **CONTACT** *John Savage* **HOURS** *9.00-18.00 (Carmarthen Market: Wed, Fri & Sat 9.00-16.00; Spitalfields Market: Sun 9.00-13.00)* **DIRECTIONS** *From Llandysul, take A486 towards New Quay. Follow the road about 11 miles and turn left, signposted Teifi Cheese, on to a dead-end road. After about ¾ mile, farm is signposted on the left.*

When John Savage met Patrice in Holland, he showed immense good sense by marrying her and bringing her back to Wales. For not only was she charming but also an inspired cheese-maker, having been taught by the reputable Mrs Vermeer of Brabant. Thus Teifi – a Gouda-style cheese – was born. Using her neighbours' unpasteurized Friesian milk, Patrice makes cheese 5 or 6 days a week in a traditional vat she imported from Holland. It is round, with an inner lining of stainless steel and an outer casing of teak wood. The wood looks rather homely in a dairy but while working the curd for a Gouda you need a relatively high temperature and the wood provides good insulation.

Patrice makes her own starter every day; using a packet would be a far easier option 'but it doesn't give such a good flavour'. Instead she propagates on a daily basis; working to a similar principle as for a sourdough starter, she adds a little fresh milk to the 'mother starter', incubates it for 24 hours for the next day's cheese, and repeats the process. The starter she adds to the milk, heats it slowly and adds the rennet. After it has set for about 30 minutes, the curds are cut 'to the size of a pea', roughly one-third of the whey is drained off and the curds are washed in warm water. Then it is stirred, more of the whey is drained off, stirred again and left for 30 minutes to ripen; the curds are ladled into moulds, pressed for about 21/2 hours, then turned out and rested for about 16 hours. The cheese is then brined from 8 hours to 4 days, depending on the size, and matured from 4 weeks to 1 year.

Sold in 450 and 900 g and 3.5 kg (1, 2 and 8 lb) truckles and 7-9 and 11.3 kg (16-20 and 25 lb) wheels, it is a buttery, dense and smooth cheese with a light sweetness when young. The longer it is matured, the more it develops its toffee-like flavour. Patrice also makes the smaller cheeses flavoured with garlic, garlic & onion, celery, nettle, sweet pepper, chives, seaweed, mustard and cumin seed. They also keep a small Jersey herd exclusively for their cream, butter and soft cheese.

🚜 *Penbryn cheese, made with organic (to Soil Association standards) milk from a Friesian and Ayrshire herd and matured for 2½ months, is another Gouda-style cheese. Buy it straight from **Ty Hen, Sarnau, Llandysul (tel 0239 810347)**, overlooking Cardigan Bay, or in various cheese shops in Wales.*

Llanboidy Cheesemakers 🚜   LLANBOIDY CHEESE

Cilowen Uchaf, Login, Whitland, Dyfed SA34 OTJ

TEL *0994 448 303* CONTACT *Sue Jones – telephone ahead*

What makes Llanboidy cheese so unusual is that it is made with the milk from the rare-breed Red Poll cattle. An amalgamation of the Suffolk Dun and two Norfolk breeds (one horned, the other polled), the Red Poll was registered as a breed in 1856. Breeders were proud of its milking performance and Lord Rothschild, who kept a herd at Tring, published milking records in 1903 which showed that in terms of quantity and quality of milk it came between the Jersey and the Shorthorn. Incidentally, all that remains of the original Norfolk breed is a stuffed bull's head in the Colman's Mustard shop in Norwich; it was the model for their trademark.

Sue Jones, with her 40-odd cows, runs one of the few milking herds left in Britain. Their milk is ideal for cheese-making, as 'the ratio of protein to fat is well balanced and the molecules of fat are small so that the cheese is smooth, even in texture and easy to digest'. She makes the cheese to an old Dunlop recipe, using unpasteurized morning and evening's milk. It is heated, started, renneted, the curds are cut, milled, packed into 4.5 kg (10 lb) wheels and pressed for about 36 hours. Then it is dry-salted and matured for anything from 2 to 11 months. The piece I tried was fairly young, with a mild tang but a rich buttery flavour lightly overlaid with herbs. Sue also makes Llanboidy with added laver bread from the Gower Peninsula; this hastens the maturity and gives it a crisp saltiness.

Y Felin ✉ 🏭   FLOUR

Mill Street, St Dogmaels, Cardigan, Dyfed SA43 3DY

TEL *0239 613999* CONTACT *Michael Hall* HOURS *Easter to end-Sept: 10.30-5.30; Oct to Easter: Mon-Fri 10.30-17.30* DIRECTIONS *From Cardigan, take A487 towards Fishguard. Cross the bridge and take the first turning on the right. Follow the road about ½ mile and take the second turning on the left, signposted Felin Mill. After about 50 yards, shop is on the left.*

Tucked away in a little back street, with a stream running through the back garden, is Y Felin, which means 'the mill'. Michael Hill restored it himself in 1980 and it once served as the mill for the adjacent Abbey of St Dogmaels.

Michael is Chairman of the Traditional Cornmiller's Guild and a great believer in milling the old-fashioned way, with millstones powered by water. His is an overshot mill meaning the water goes over the mill wheel and, for those in the know, it would also indicate it is powered by a small stream. Obviously a small stream only turns the stones slowly, but this has its advantages, 'if you mill at a slow speed, it spreads the wheat germ through the flour'. Michael tends to mill his flour reasonably finely, although he will grind it coarser on demand. 'The coarser the flour, he explained, 'the less water it absorbs, so the less the gluten has been broken down. This, in turn, tends to a finer, better loaf'.

Y Felin has three sets of stones: two sets of French burr stones for wheat and rye, and one granite set from Derbyshire for oatmeal. Michael currently mills 100% wholemeal flour, unbleached white to an 85% extraction, rye flour and occasionally barley flour. He has his own lean-to kiln and malts his own wheat flakes by wetting the grain, leaving it to sprout for a week, then putting it in the kiln for about 24 hours, turning it occasionally. These are added to his nutty 'granary type' flour that has a wholemeal base with rye flour, malted wheat flakes, malted grain and malt flour. He also blends a seed and herb flour; again it has a wholemeal base but to it are added sunflower, poppy, sesame and millet seeds as well as sage and thyme. He sells bread baked a bakery with his own flour in Cardigan and an Irish soda bread mix brought in from Ireland.

Ever keen to extol the virtues of Welsh produce, cookery writer Gilli Davies put me in touch with **Neville Pugh** *at* **Hayston Hall, Johnston, Haverfordwest (tel 0437 890143)**. *He rears pure-breed Welsh Black Mountain sheep and Welsh Black cattle – both with superb eating qualities. Quantities are small and he prefers it if you buy whole lambs and made-up boxes of beef. I am told they are worth it. By the way, the meat is butchered by Postmaster Martin Davies at* **The Post Office & Butcher shop, Merlins Bridge, Haverfordwest (tel 0437 762521)** *who doubles up as a butcher.*

WEST WILLIAMSTON   MAP 7

Carew Oysters ✉ 🔲 ☗   OYSTERS

Tything Barn, West Williamston, Kilgetty, Dyfed SA68 OTN

TEL *0646 651452*   **CONTACT** *Joe Folder*   **HOURS** *Mon-Sat 8.00-18.00 Sun 9.00-13.00* **CARDS** *Visa, Mastercard* **DIRECTIONS** *From Carew, take A4075 towards Canastan Bridge. Cross the old bridge in Carew and take the first turning on the left at sign for the picnic site. Follow the road about 1 mile and oystery is on the left.*

After you have bought the oysters, wander down to the river Carew. The view is magical as on the far bank stand the ruins of the Norman Carew Castle in all its glory. You are welcome to picnic there, but Joe Folder takes great pains to point out that, in summer, the land at the back by the inlet lagoon (where they harden off the seed or spats), is let to naturists. If the thought embarrasses you, stay by the banks – the view is better there anyway.

Jo farms his Pacific oysters fairly high up in the estuary of the river Carew, about 20 miles from the sea; as a result they tend to be sweeter and less salty than most. One side of the river is limestone, the other is sandstone, 'It's brackish waters here, rich in plankton. And there's a big tidal range, with plenty of power so plenty of silt is deposited right where the oysters are. They really do feed well and we have a good oyster as they feed off a good range of plankton'. As a result his oysters are plump with massive shells, 'We only sell them in one size, the equivalent to 3's and they are purified and pressure-washed inside and out so they reach the customer clean'.

Available all year round, for mail order customers Joe dry-packs them in polystyrene and sends them out between Tuesday and Friday by overnight delivery so you should receive them within 24 hours of placing your order. In order to get their full velvety richness, however, I can't help thinking you would be better off enjoying them by the banks of the Carew.

> With huge slate counters and windows overlooking the estuary of the river Aeron, **The Fish on the Quay** at **Cadwgan Place, Aberaeron (tel 0545 571294)** has a good range of seafood. Sewin comes from the river, live cockles or cooked cockle meat from Penclawdd (see page 316); some of the fish is caught off Newquay and the rest is ferried down from the west coast of Scotland. Expect to find brill, cod, codling, whiting, huss, turbot, plaice, crabs, lobster, whelks from the bay, rock prawns (big shrimps) and fresh or jellied eels that they prepare themselves. All the fish are displayed whole and filleted to order so you can see exactly how fresh they are.

And Also...

• **Pemberton's Victorian Chocolates** ✉ at Bronyscawen Farm, Llanboidy (tel 0994 448768) offers a chocolate experience. During the season, from May to October, you can watch chocolate demonstrations, drink hot chocolate and eat chocolate Welsh cakes in the chocolate parlour as well as buy the chocolates from the chocolate shop.
• **Quail World**, Glenydd, Penrhiwllan, Llandysul (tel 0559 370105) sells quails' eggs and oven-ready birds.
• **Popty Bach-y-Wlad** (the name means 'little baker in the countryside') at Court Farm, Pentrecourt, Llandysul (tel 0559 362335) bake Welsh cakes, Teisen Lap (Welsh plate cake) and various buns, cakes and breads. Buy them in Carmarthen Market on Wednesdays and Saturdays

or direct from the bakery.

• **Rhydlewis Trout Farm**, Rhydlewis, Llandysul (tel 0239 851224) are open for trout fishing and sell own-smoked trout and smoked salmon.

• **Jones the Fish** at 2 Terrace Road, Aberystwyth (tel 0970 623891) can be relied on for a good choice of fish.

• With most of their shellfish exported, you can buy Native oysters, crawfish, lobsters, crabs, cockles and winkles direct from **Oneida Fish Viviers**, Brunel Quay, Neyland (tel 0646 600220, fax 0646 602240)

• By all accounts, the Seville marmalade and raspberry jam made and sold by **Penbontbren Farm Hotel**, Glynarthen, nr Cardigan (tel 0239 810248) are very good; they also produce a coarse-grain mustard.

• If you're on holiday in the area and do not want to cook, try **Cottage Caterers** at Min-yr-Afon, Jordanston Bridge, Castle Morris (03485 296) for their food-to-go.

GLAMORGAN

CARDIFF   MAP 7

Gorno's Charcuterie 📧 📪   SALAMI

30 Tudor Street, Riverside, Cardiff, Glamorgan CF1 8RH

TEL *0222 372782*   CONTACT *Franco Gorno*   HOURS *Mon-Sat 8.00-17.30*
DIRECTIONS *In city centre, near the Empire Pool.*

It was several years ago in Cardiff's covered market that I first heard of Gorno's Charcuterie; there on a butcher's stall among the more traditional meats, tripe and blood sausages was a packet of round, fat and Italian-looking fresh sausages. I surreptitiously peered at the label, made a note of the address and hot-footed it over to Franco. I could not believe it, in the middle of Cardiff was a proper Italian *salumeria*.

Franco hails from the Po Valley in Lombardy and it follows that his repertoire should include these regional specialities. For a quick explanation of how a lad from Lombardy ended up in Cardiff, I should tell you that at the age of 23, having already worked several years for his butcher uncle, he answered an ad for steel workers in Port Talbot. Food was his first love and he soon returned to the kitchens, and later on to Italy briefly to brush up on his butchering, until finally he opened his own shop in 1979. This is where you will find him, ably abetted by his son Andy, curing pork from Porthcawl and the West Country into a myriad Italian delights.

His range can be divided into fresh products for cooking (*salumi freschi da cuocere*), matured products ready to eat (*salumi stragionati*) and cooked pork products (*salumi cotti*). For everything, he uses free-range pork, 'I need large pigs with a good layer of fat so I have a good size joint for salting. Today's pigs are generally too lean'. Boars will not do as they have too strong a flavour, so he prefers gilts or sows. Delivered as whole sides, Franco hangs them for 3-4 days to firm up the flesh, then butchers them into the various joints and the magical process of curing begins. He makes *Milano* or *luganica*, a single coil of thin, fresh and lightly spiced sausages; *cotechino* the fat boiling sausage; *pancetta affumicata*, dry-salted matured and smoked belly of pork; and *Rosetta Lombarda*, Lombardy rosette made with coarsely chopped shoulder of lightly cured pork, pistachios, spices, herbs, garlic and white wine, wrapped in caul. To cook it, you poach it gently for about 1½ hours and traditionally serve it with polenta and spinach.

Franco makes authentic salamis by chopping or mincing the various cuts of pork to whatever the required texture, salting it, then adding the spices and stuffing the skins for curing. Lombardo is spiked with black pepper, Calabrese a fiery mix of chilli and fennel seed, Napoli comes lightly smoked and the finer-textured Milano is suitably mild. He prepares his own *prosciutto crudo*, a cured raw ham that is meaty and succulent with a well-defined flavour, *coppa* cured from the loin, and *Lonza piccante* or *al pepe nero* where the centre of the pork loin is cured in wine, brandy, spices and either hot chillies or black pepper for biting slices of tender meat. Smoked pepperoni is very popular on pizzas and he also makes pork *rillettes*, black and white pudding and an excellent British style dry-cured bacon.

FELINDRE   MAP 7

Pencoed Organic Growers ▨ ✒

SALADS & VEGETABLES

Felindre, Pencoed, Glamorgan CF35 5HU

TEL *0656 861956* CONTACT *John Roberts – telephone ahead*

Pencoed are small but interesting growers; they sell from their barn and, during the week, prefer it if you ring up and give 24 hours' notice for an order. Then they will leave the order out for you and you leave the money. On Fridays and Saturdays, there is usually someone around.

With 5 poly-tunnels and 'a bit of glass', they grow organically (to Soil Association standards) such vegetables as curly kale, cabbages, chunky French and runner beans, broccoli, bell (small and round) courgettes, a sweet Cherry Sita tomato, and various herbs 'but nothing very exciting – only basil, coriander, dill, thyme, sage, rosemary and chives' that they sell in bunches. Their salads and salad leaves are exciting; lettuces include green and red lollo, green and red oak leaf, Four Seasons and a red-tinged Butterhead. In peak season, there will be at least 10 different leaves and they do vary according to the times of year. When I visited in late autumn, I nibbled several Oriental greens, such as mizuna, the spoon-shaped leaves of tatsoi with their gelatinous texture, crisp komatsuna with a clear sharp bite, a mustardy amsoi and the milder Gai-choy that would give any salad a 'bit of pep'. In the European line, they grow rocket, radicchio, Claytonia and corn salad.

One point worth making is that, up until recently, John Roberts was prepared to sell them as mixed prepared bags. Due to our new legislation this is no longer possible as, in order to carry on offering the service, he would have to invest in separate packing rooms, washing facilities, chilled rooms, etc, etc... I can see the sense of this if you are dealing on a large scale and the prepared leaves may be travelling hundreds of miles before they reach a shop, but to stop John – who works on a small scale and deals directly with his customers – seems to be crazy. It is yet another example of how our legislation is hampering the good work of the small producers.

GWERNFRWDD   MAP 7

Lynch Cockle Factory 🔳 ♣   PENCLAWDD COCKLES

Marsh Road, Gwernfrwdd, Penclawdd, Glamorgan SA4 3HY
TEL *0792 850033* CONTACT *Brian Jones – telephone ahead*

'Who'd be a cockle gatherer on a cold windy day?' asks Gilli Davies cookery writer and presenter of the TV series *Tastes of Wales*, 'dashing down to scrape the sand-flats as the tide goes out and expose those tasty molluscs'. All along the coast of the Gower Peninsula, with its wide open

> *Like so many of our regional products, the cockle industry is under threat. It is not enough that they have been gathered since Roman times and eaten without a break since then. Apparently the powers-that-be deem the small family-shared cockle factories scattered along the coast to be unhygienic and not up to EC standards. They want spanking new state-of-the-art factories that require a huge investment. Surely it is unnecessary, the system works very well as it is, the sweet meaty cockles are always fresh; so why should anyone interfere? Anyway cockle gatherers are notoriously independent and are loath to come together in a big unit. It also begs the question of whether or not the returns on such a large investment would justify it (the rumoured figure along the coast was £65,000). Currently there are 3 factories in Penclawdd itself, another in Llandridion and there is* **Penclawdd Cockles** *at* **1 Osborne Place Llanmorlais (tel 0792 850826)**. *As well as cockle meat, laver bread and mussels in season, they sometimes sell cockles in their shells. These need a lot of rinsing to get rid of the sand, but are splendid for a pasta sauce or soup. Times of opening for all the cockle factories vary with the seasons and tides – but for how much longer?*

expanses of flat sands running down to the sea, cockles are still gathered daily.

Gilli tells of meeting Selwyn Jones, who has been collecting for the past 50 years using no more than a cockle rake, a crescent-shaped cockle knife for scraping and a sieve as his tools. His haul is brought back to the family cockle factory, where they are boiled and sold as cockle meat in the markets and fish stalls. Sometimes mussels are gathered and sometimes the seaweed laver that is boiled up until it breaks down to a sticky, salty mass of laver bread. It is a tough life, but luckily for us there still are people who are prepared to work the sands. Brian Jones is one such gatherer and he has heavily invested in the cockling industry and built an EC-approved factory right by the sands so he can boil them up in optimum conditions – long may he continue.

> *Swansea Market, Oxford Street, Swansea (tel 0792 654296)* is set in a light airy and utterly charmless market hall; but the food you find here is interesting. Unlike any other market I visited, room is made for 'casuals' – growers, mostly from the Gower Peninsula, who come to town and set up on wooden benches or tables to sell their wares. There are freshly cut cauliflowers, bunches of carrots, beetroots dug up that day and still with their tops on, earthy potatoes and bunches of herbs. Nearby are the bakery stalls where cosy ladies cook up Welsh cakes and pancakes on griddles and fish stalls piled high with Penclawdd cockles (see opposite), gooey green-brown fresh laver bread and the inevitable crab sticks. You can buy Thayer's clotted cream, inspect Nancy Morgan's stack of freshly baked breads and cakes from Tuckers in the corner, or buy a leg of Welsh lamb wrapped in caul fat. As markets go in Britain, it is one of the best. *Cardiff's Central Market, St Mary Street (tel 0222 822670),* on the other hand, may look more picturesque, but the food is perhaps not as varied. J. T. Morgan sells mountain lamb and some lean-looking, well-trimmed lamb shanks (last winter's craze), lamb & mint sausages and an old-fashioned curiosity – freshly cooked pressed chitterlings. J. T. Evans does a good line in dry-salt bacon and Ashton's the fishmonger sells a varied range of wet fish, all sorts of clams, freshly boiled crabs and, naturally, fresh laver bread.

PETERSTON-SUPER-ELY   MAP 7

Ices from the Fruit Garden 🚜 🍐 ICE-CREAM & FRUIT

Groes Faen Road, Peterston-super-Ely, Cardiff, Glamorgan CF5 6NE

TEL 0446 760358 **CONTACT** Linda George **HOURS** May to beg-Aug: 9.00-20.00 **DIRECTIONS** On the outskirts of the village, AA signposted on the Groe's Faen Road

Linda George runs about $5\frac{1}{2}$ acres of pick-your-own and ready-picked fruit and asparagus. Grown in half an acre, the asparagus kicks off the season: sold as ready-picked and graded into sprue, cooking and mixed, it lasts through to mid-June. Describing her land as 'top grade loam on a south-facing well-drained site and well suited to soft fruit' she grows Elsanta strawberries and other varieties that 'vary enormously from year to year'; Red Lake redcurrants; a green cooking gooseberry that 'ripens to dessert quality' and the red Whinham's Industry; and a big juicy cultivated blackberry. Raspberries proved a disaster as Linda lost the lot, so – forced to fill in with hybrid berries – she now grows tayberries, tummelberries (a raspberry-blackberry cross that is bigger than a tayberry but perhaps lacks its flavour), and jostaberries (a blackcurrant-gooseberry cross that 'makes gorgeous jam').

Using her strawberries, Linda started making ice-cream with 'originally just strawberries and cream'. When it was purely for the visitors to the farm, that really was all it contained, more or less. The business grew, however, and Linda built an ice-cream parlour and started wholesaling around the county. The pity is that she now adds emulsifier E471 and sodium alginate as a stabilizer. I am not suggesting that there is anything inherently wrong with them, it is just that they, so to speak, 'gum up the works'. Where once there was an ice-cream with a clean pure and vibrant flavour, it now has a marginally muddied taste. Sold in 0.5 litres (16 fl oz), in the quite the most chic packaging I've seen, the basic mix contains whole milk, double cream, skimmed milk powder, pasteurized egg yolks and the above-mentioned emulsifier and stabilizer. The fat content is around 14% and the over-run (added air) varies from 50% upwards. Flavours include strawberry, gooseberry fool (made with her own gooseberries), and crème brûlée. She also makes 3 fruit sorbets, again using her own fruit: strawberry, blackcurrant and summer fruits – a mix of tayberries, redcurrants and blackcurrants with blackberry liqueur. Here the flavours were far fresher, if a little sweet.

ST FAGANS   MAP 7

Derwen Bakehouse 🍶 🍴   BARA BRITH

Welsh Folk Museum, St Fagans, Cardiff, Glamorgan CF5 6XB

TEL *0222 569441* CONTACT *Chris Aston* HOURS *10.00-17.00; Nov to Mar: Mon-Sat only* DIRECTIONS *Turn off the M4 at Junction 33 and follow signposts for the Welsh Folk Museum.*

Bara brith from a museum – surely some mistake? You might think that if you have never been there, and if you have not you should. The Welsh Folk museum is a huge open-air museum with the stated aim 'to show how many of the people of Wales lived, worked and spent their leisure time over the last four hundred years'. To this end they have moved thirty original buildings from all over the principality and carefully re-erected and furnished them in period style. There is a 1610 farmhouse from Gower, painted red as it was thought the colour protected the house against evil spirits; a working corn-mill with flour for sale; a circular pigsty complete with pig; a toll house; a cock-pit; and a saddler's workshop, a smithy, a pottery and a tannery with the appropriate working craftsmen.

Derwen Bakehouse, built in 1900, comes from Thespian Street in Aberystwyth where it was the main bake-house or 'commune' (after 'communal

Also at the Welsh Folk Museum, the Gwalia was a valley store from Ogmore Vale, Mid Glamorgan. Now reconstructed in the museum's grounds, it is laid out exactly as it was at the beginning of this century when it flourished. From here, among the string, buckets and tin baths, you can buy a small selection of Welsh foods – various on-farm cheeses, a well-salted Welsh butter, a harshly cured bacon and flavoured vinegars and herb jellies.

oven'). In those days housewives would prepare the dough at home, bring it to the wood-fired ovens for baking and pay the baker for cooking it. Chris Aston has been installed as the baker and runs it as a shop, using the original brick-wall oven that she fires with silver birch and ash 'as whatever wood you put in makes a difference'. In the tiny cramped shop you can watch her at work, mixing the dough using all the old equipment – wooden dough bins and paddles – and working to traditional recipes, and then buy the bread.

She makes a nutty dense wholemeal bread, apple bread puffs, slices of apple baked like a turnover in slices of bread for a crisp finish and an interesting contrast of textures; light and cheesy cheese puffs, and Bara brith. Literally translated, this means 'speckled bread' and is a yeast-based dough with eggs and butter liberally scattered with mixed peel and raisins. I have to tell you that out of the several I tried as I travelled through Wales, Chris's is far and away the best. Rich, moist and chewy, with a mild fragrance of honey, it was wonderfully fresh as you can buy it straight from the oven if you time your visit right. At different times, she bakes the range of traditional Welsh cakes and breads.

*Shopping in Cowbridge, nr Cardiff, is a pleasure. Visit **Tony Holtam** at **50A High Street** (tel 0446 772230) for fresh sewin from the Tewy and a good selection of locally grown vegetables. Next door is **Glyn T. Jenkins** ✉, **50 High Street, CF7 7AH** (tel 0446 773545) who sells Welsh farmhouse cheese, Welsh butter, bacon, Zest Food's sauces for pasta. He also makes his own fresh pasta and stocks a range of Franco Gorno's products (see page 314), Sid Aston's bread baked in a wood-fired oven and lots more.*

And Also...

- Reports please on the chocolates and fudge made by Sue Lowman from *Truffles* ⊠, 4-5 Church Street, Llantwit Major (tel 0446 792954).
- *Charles Sadler* at 8 Royal Buildings, Penarth, Cardiff (tel 0222 709100) sells fish, cockles, farmed Welsh oysters, laver bread, game and poultry, including TFTA Bronze turkeys at Christmas (see page 133).
- Butcher *Colin Davies* at 7 The Precinct, Killay, Swansea (tel 0792 290114) sells Welsh lamb, Welsh lamb pastrami and Welsh lamb sausages with garlic.

GWENT

ABERGAVENNY   MAP 7

Abergavenny Fine Foods ⊠ 🏭   CHEESE

4 Castle Meadows Park, Abergavenny, Gwent NP7 7RZ

TEL *0873 850001* **FAX** *0873 850002* **CONTACT** *Melanie Bowman* **HOURS** *Mon-Fri 9.00-17.00* **CARDS** *Access, Visa, Mastercard* **DIRECTIONS** *From Abergavenny, take A40 towards Brecon. At the first roundabout outside Abergavenny, take the first exit off the roundabout and unit is 400 yards on the right.*

Tony Craske started Abergavenny Fine Foods several years ago with a soft goats' cheese called Pantysgawn made on-farm with milk from his own herd in the Brecon Beacons National Park. In the ensuing years, he built up the business developing his own and 'added-value' cheeses and wholesaling other makers' on-farm Welsh cheeses so they became more accessible both in and out of the principality. Finally he moved the whole operation to an industrial unit just outside Abergavenny which is where he functions today.

Tony's own cheeses are what I would call middle-of-the-road; by that I mean they are produced thoroughly professionally with an enviable consistency, but they perhaps lack the character and depth of those made on a smaller-scale operation. Pantysgawn is still made, but now with bought-in pasteurized milk; soft with a smooth consistency and a mild, bland taste, it comes as natural, herb, garlic with chives, and citrus pepper. Chevelles, developed from Pantysgawn for grilling, baking or frying, is the same cheese rolled in breadcrumbs. Glamorgan Sausages, based on the traditional recipe of a cheese rather than a meat sausage, are a salty mixture of Cheddar and Caerphilly with leek and spices rolled in breadcrumbs. St David's is a washed-rind cheese that Tony developed in conjunction with the Welsh Development Agency; made with bought-in pasteurized cows' milk to a Chaumes-style recipe, it is a competent cheese that does not scale the peaks but then never dips into the troughs.

Both St Illtyd and Y-Fenni are milled cheeses, and I find this new-found enthusiasm for them rather disturbing. In effect, they are (usually) block cheeses that are milled to break them down, mixed with a variety of flavours – in this case Welsh wine, garlic & herbs and Welsh ale & whole-grain mustard, and then re-assembled for a smooth spreadable texture. To my mind they are not cheese in the true sense of the word: they are not made like a cheese, rather they are put together. The flavours are added rather late in the day and tend to dominate, and they have no real texture. Ever the marketing man, however, Tony has seen the opportunity and the cheeses must be popular or he would not make them.

Upper Pant Farm Traditional Meats ✉ *of* **Upper Pant Farm, Llandewi, Rhydderch NP7 9TL (tel 0873 858091)** *do not run a mail-order service as such but organize group deliveries as far afield as London, Cardiff, Bristol and Oxford. Raised to a welfare-friendly system, beef comes from the traditional British breeds, either Aberdeen Angus or Hereford, crossed with the Continental Limousin and Blonde d'Aquitaine because, as Chris Wardle told me, 'we want flavour and size'. Taste is all-important: beef is grass-fed, slaughtered at 2-3 years for a deep, mature flavour and hung for at least 2 weeks; lamb is from Suffolk cross Texel and slaughtered at any age from 4-8 months to ensure an even supply from June to February, and hung for about a week; pork from a Welsh Duroc cross is free-range and slaughtered at 4 months. Sold in the various traditional cuts, Chris is more than happy to discuss the order and if you want the more unusual 'bits and pieces', like trotters or brisket of beef, he will try to supply you.*

COEDKERNEW   MAP 7

Berryhill Farm 🚜   FRUIT & VEGETABLES

Coedkernew, Newport, Gwent NP1 9UD

TEL *0633 680 827* **CONTACT** *Robert Peel* **HOURS** *May to Aug: 9.30-19.00; Sept-23 Dec: Tues-Sun 9.30-17.00* **DIRECTIONS** *Turn off M4 at junction 28. Follow the slip road to the roundabout and take the exit signposted Castleton/A48. Follow the road about $2\frac{1}{4}$ miles and farm is signposted on the left.*

You would expect Robert Peel, one-time chairman of the Farm Shop and Pick-Your-Own Association to run a professional operation – and you will not be disappointed. Fruit and vegetables are the mainstay of the business, but they also sell cream to go with the soft fruit, and Mrs Peel's cakes and chutneys. There is also a tearoom open from Thursday to Sunday to refresh you while picking during the PYO season.

Apples are ever-popular and Robert is increasing his orchard to 10 acres. Sold as pick-your-own, during harvesting from August to October, and ready-picked, the varieties include Bramley, Discovery, Katy, Greensleeves, Royal Gala, Elstar, Crown Gold (a red clone of Jonagold), Gala, Spartan, Flanders Cox's and Queen Cox's. From Charlton Orchards (see page 221), they buy in Orléans Reinette, Ashmead's Kernel and Suntan, a cross between a Cox's and a Court Pendu Plat. There is a good range of plums, including Sanctus Hubertus, a black early that crops in July with a luscious sweetness; Marjorie Seedling, ripe in late August early September; Reeves Seedling, round and golden and very lush; Victoria and Czar. Cooking gooseberries are Invicta, but they also grow Lord Derby, a large juicy dark red dessert gooseberry. There are strawberries, raspberries, redcurrants and blackcurrants, and sunberries (elongated berries that are a blackberry-raspberry cross) as well as fragrant tayberries and tummelberries. The vegetable season starts at the end of April with ready-picked asparagus, moves on to broad, French and runner beans, dependable Shirley tomatoes and sweetcorn, and finishes with a good display of winter squashes, including butternut, ponca, table ace and sweet dumpling.

For Christmas, Fiona Peel bakes a traditional fruit cake with flour, brown sugar, vegetable margarine, eggs, dried fruits, glacé cherries, toasted blanched almonds, treacle, spices and brandy. Sold as plain, with marzipan or with marzipan and icing, it comes as a 15 and 22.5 cm (6 and 9 in) round or 22.5 cm (9 in) square and can be ordered in advance. During the rest of the year she bakes fruit pies, tarte Normande, coffee, chocolate, lemon and vanilla sponges with buttercream, cider and fruit wholemeal cake, Bramley apple or blackcurrant cake and honey cake.

*Downstairs in **Vin Sullivan Stores** ⊠ at **4 Frogmore Street, Abergavenny NP7 5AE (tel 0873 856989)** is an impressive array of ethnic tins and preparations. Upstairs is an equally impressive choice of fresh fish. Here you will find brill, turbot, lemon sole, pollack, plaice, flounder, mackerel and a regular supply of sewin (sea or salmon trout. They also sell fresh laver bread from Swansea and game from local shoots.*

And Also...

• **Brookes Dairy Co** at Panta Farm, Devauden (tel 02915 786) make ice-cream with a 12% fat content with milk from their Friesian herd. Flavours include a sweet vanilla and a sophisticated Orange & Cointreau with finely grated orange, and ginger.

• *G. & P. Roser*, Coleford Road, Tutshill, nr Chepstow (tel 0291 622063) is more than an ordinary butcher. They bake their own bread, make their own pies, and dry-cure bacon. They also sell local game, wild salmon from the rivers Severn and Wye, lamb from their own flock of Jacob sheep and a full-cream farmhouse butter from Netherend Dairy in Woolaston, nr Lydney (tel 0594 529484).

• *Jereboams Delicatessen* at 11 St Mary Street, Chepstow (tel 0291 622386) has a good range of cooked meats and pâtés; breads baked by North Bakery in Chepstow include a sesame-seed plait; various Welsh cheeses, such as Teifi (see page 310) and Llanboidy (see page 311); and their own-made rich Chocolat Saint-Emilion pudding and macaroons in brandy.

• Delicatessen **W. S. Baldock** at 18-22 The Provision Market, High Street, Newport (tel 0633 257312) stock a good selection of Welsh cheeses, including Teifi (see page 310) and Pencarreg, tins of laver bread and Franco Gorno's charcuterie (see page 314).

GWYNEDD

MAP 7

Future Foods ✉   RARE SEEDS & PLANTS

3 Tai Madog, Stablau, Llanrug, Gwynedd LL55 3PH

TEL *0286 870606* CONTACT *Owen Smith – mail order only*

'*Cadw dy ardd, ceidw dy ardd dithau*' (look after your garden and your garden will look after you) is how Future Foods start their catalogue, and what an interesting and informative catalogue it is too. With the aim 'to make available and promote rare and unusual crop plants', they will supply you with seeds, tubers, plants, mushroom spawns or even starter cultures for fermented foods. The collection has been built up slowly over the years by Owen Smith, 'through a network of vegetable enthusiasts' and with help from the Seed Savers' Exchange in the USA. Some are Owen's own seeds, others are imported, but none are chemically treated and the tubers and plants he grows himself.

The choice is truly unusual – several plants I've never even heard of. One, *Huauzontli Chenopodium berlanderi* belongs to the beet family: it is 'a Mexican annual cultivated for its mild-flavoured leaves, which are traditionally eaten fried with onions or in salads. They produce large quantities of seeds which can be ground to make flour for tortillas or as a millet substitute and it has been suggested as a potential new grain. In cold weather the leaves turn red'. I can't wait to try it. Another is beetberry (and I suspect it is similar to, if not the same as, the

> **The Fridge** at **Port Penrhyn, Bangor (tel 0248 351814)** on the quay, has a splendid display of fresh fish bought from local boats or markets. At various times in the year you will find sea bass, Dover and lemon sole, turbot, grey mullet, monkfish, squid, herring and mackerel. Wild salmon is caught by hook and line locally, oysters are farmed in the Menai Straits, and scallops come from the Irish Sea by the Isle of Man. Also in Port Penryhn is **Myti Mussels (tel 0248 354878)** mussel farmers in the Menai Straits. Here the mussels are bottom-cultured (grown on lathes on the sea bed), for a plump juicy mussel with a clean smooth shell as there are no barnacles on the bottom of the sea bed.

strawberry spinach raved about by Frances Smith of Appledore Salads, page 126), with 'numerous sweet red fruits in the leaf axils which taste rather like bland mulberries...and leaves (that) can also be eaten like spinach'.

There are packets of seeds for Asparagus pea; or salad mallow with its light green crinkly leaves, for stir-frying or chopping into a salad; or Autumn olive, 'a dense deciduous shrub...the small fragrant flowers are followed by bright red berries which look and taste similar to redcurrants. They make good jams and jellies and can also be left to shrivel into sweet raisins.' Other interesting fruits include dewberries, thimbleberries, Japanese wineberries and salmonberries. There are cloves of Elephant garlic 'actually a bulbing leek'; spawns imported from France for Wood Blewit, Shaggy Cap, Shiitake and various species of the oyster mushroom. Owen assured me you can grow them successfully, 'As it's a question of scale. Commercial growers might not be able to succeed, but I recently had a letter from a customer who has hundreds in a mulched comfrey bed'. Kits of yoghurt starter cultures, that look 'like bits of cauliflower', make Bulgarian Kefir yoghurts; and there is also a 'Tunnel Hill' sour-dough culture that 'comes from friends in North California and is noted for its reliability'. If you are looking for the unusual edible, I'm sure you will not be disappointed.

> **Blas ar Fwyd** ✉ **25 Heol yr Orsaf, Llanrwst, LL26 0BT (tel 0492 640215)** is one of Gilli Davies's favourite food shops in Wales. With their kitchen at the heart of the business, practically everything they sell is own-made, using as much local produce as possible. They make their own jams, chutneys, pasta, game pies, cure salt beef and bresaola, press tongue and run a busy outside catering service. There are plenty of Welsh cheeses, well ripened in their maturing rooms and they even make an unpasteurized goats' cheese similar to a crottin.

And Also...

• **Conwy Valley Fisheries** ✉, Glyn Isa, Rowen, Conwy (tel 0492 650063) have a fly-fishing lake stocked with trout from 550 g to 3.5 kg (11/2 to 8 lb). From the farm-shop they sell fresh and own-smoked trout and salmon, fish pâtés and a few Welsh foods. If you catch a fish, they will smoke it for you. (✉ Smoked salmon and trout only.)

• As well as seeing the displays of fish at **Anglesey Sea Zoo** at Brynsiencyn, Anglesey (tel 0248 430411), visitors can buy Pacific oysters farmed by the curator in the Menai Straits.

• Gilli Davies, presenter of BBC Wales' *Tastes of Wales* recommends **Edwards of Conwy**, High Sreet, Conwy (tel 0492 592443) for their lamb and beef from pure-bred Welsh black that they buy direct from the farms.

POWYS

DOLAU   MAP 7

Graig Farm Meat 🚜 🌿   CHICKEN & MEAT

Graig Farm, Dolau, Llandrindod Wells, Powys LD1 5TL

TEL *0597 851 655* **FAX** *0597 851 655* **CONTACT** *Bob Kennard* **HOURS** *Mon-Sat 9.00-18.00 Sun telephone ahead* **DIRECTIONS** *From Knighton, take A488 towards Llandrindod Wells. Follow the road about 10 miles and farm is signposted on the left.*

Graig Farm sells both Organic (to Soil Association standards) and additive-free meat. Beef, pork, lamb and mutton (from any sheep over 2 years old) are bought in from various local farmers within Wales who are all registered members of the Soil Association. Slaughtered, hung and 'rough butchered' at Lentwardine slaughterhouse, the meat comes to the farm for final butchering or processing into sausages made with rolled organic oats, spring water, herbs, spices and seasonings.

Poultry and wild boar (reared in Radnor) are additive-free. This Bob Kennard describes as a compromise for practical reasons as to be able to call them organic they must be fed organic grain. The quantity of grain needed is not always available and he feels it would make the cost of the end-product prohibitive – at current prices an organic chicken would cost £2.00 per 450 g (1 lb). Instead he feeds them conventionally grown grain, guarantees that the meat is from animals which have not been given any routine drugs, growth promoters or meat and bone meal and, in matters of welfare follows the standards set by the Soil Association.

Chickens, bought in as day-old, are kept in small groups of 250 because Bob explained, 'they can develop and maintain a "pecking" order, so bullying and feather pecking and general stress are avoided'. Fed on a ration of wheat, soya, fishmeal, vitamins and minerals, they are kept in naturally lit airy barns, at 'a stocking density of under five birds per square metre – nearly five times the space of a bird in an intensive broiler system'. They cannot be classified as free-range as they do not have constant access to the outdoors; but in good weather (a rare occurrence I'd have thought in this neck of the woods) the barn doors are opened and the birds are free to roam outdoors.

Now, I have visited several broiler chicken units and, believe me, it is a deeply distressing experience. Seemingly thousands of birds are crammed into huge artificially and constantly lit barns, the noise level is disturbingly high and the stench of ammonia overpowering. Here the birds appeared far more at ease. Most broiler birds are slaughtered at around 50 days; Bob slaughters his on-farm at 63-77 days to allow them to mature, then hangs them for about 8 days for an even fuller flavour. I bought a chicken and took it off for supper with friend and cookery writer Elizabeth Luard. I did no more than lightly brush it with olive oil, stuff the cavity with a sprig or two of rosemary and roast it. We both pronounced it as one of the more 'interesting' chickens we had eaten in a long time, as the flesh actually had texture and a depth of flavour that did not disappear after a first chew.

At Christmas they rear a modern hybrid turkey to similar standards and they also have the occasional cockerel. They buy in additive-free goat and also sell wild rabbit shot on their farm and on other local farms, as well as Fallow and Roe deer culled from local forests.

> ✉ *Fresh venison from farmed Red deer is available from the* **Welsh Venison Centre, Middlewood Farm, Bwlch, Brecon, LD3 7HQ (tel 0874 730 246, fax 0874 730566)** *in various butchered cuts or in slices cut from the haunch, marinated with orange and juniper and hot-smoked over oak.*

LLANBISTER   MAP 7

Yan-tan-tethera 🎲   SHEEP'S-MILK YOGHURT

Llugwy Farm, Llanbister Road, Powys LD1 5UT

TEL *054781 641* CONTACT *Belinda Scadding – telephone ahead*

It strikes me that to start a new food business in the current economic and legislation-ridden climate, is either bold or foolhardy – and I can't decide which. Strictly speaking, Belinda Scadding has not just started up, rather she has moved across the border from Hereford; but it is tantamount to the same thing as her dairy had to be built from scratch and she has to deal with a new set of officials.

Using the milk from her 36-strong Friesland dairy sheep herd, Belinda makes an excellent yoghurt. I am not the greatest fan of yoghurt; all too often it is sharp to the point of acidity, thin and dull. Yan-tan-tethera is in another class, as it is rich and creamy with a refreshing but nicely rounded tang. Named after the old Celtic shepherds' way of counting sheep (it means 'one-two-three'), Belinda makes her yoghurt twice a week in her spick-and-span dairy in 12.5-litre (22-pint) batches. A starter is added to milk, it is incubated in pots for 2-4 hours and left to set, with a satisfyingly thick crust forming on the top. 'The milk is naturally rich. In the spring the fat content is around 6%, but it can go as high as $8\frac{1}{2}$% and we ride on the back of its flavour.'

Belinda currently makes a basic pasteurized soft cheese that is hung up in cheese cloths to drain, then salted and rolled out in little balls by hand and sealed in glass jars with extra-virgin olive oil and sea salt. With a firm texture and a light creamy flavour, like the yoghurt they had all of the sheep's-milk's richness but none of its 'animaly' overtone. She will make a fresh soft cheese to order and, from June to Christmas, sells her Friesland wether (male) lambs when they are about 18 months old. 'As they are a good old-fashioned dairy sheep, they don't carry much fat and they are lean when slaughtered with a terrific flavour', she assured me. Sold as either whole carcasses or in butchered joints, frozen or fresh to order, 'if you hit the right time', the meat is a deep dark red, similar in colour to venison.

As soon as the cheese-store is built, Belinda plans to make a hard cheese 'half-way between a Caerphilly and Cheddar'. Having tasted her current products, I have every confidence that it will be good, and I have a hunch that Belinda is a food producer to watch.

And Also...

• For freshwater Signal crayfish, contact **Brook Mill Farm**, Brook Mill, Mochdre, Newtown (tel 06866 24679).

• Look out for honey by **Jennings Beekeepers**, Cwmbrain, Llanbister (tel 0597 83294). Flavours vary from year to year, but you may well find a dark Hawthorne, a delicate Willowherb or a flowery mixed blossom.

• **Edward Hamer** at Plyn Limon House, Llanidloes (tel 0686 412209) specializes in pure- and cross-bred Welsh mountain lamb. Lambs come from the pastures within a 25-mile radius, are slaughtered in their own abattoirs and are processed into any one of the 90 different cuts of which they boast. The season starts in May with the spring lambs born in January and runs on right through to the following January, with the pure-breeds coming into season around July and August. They also sell properly hung pure-bred Welsh Black beef.

Scotland

BORDERS

Easter Weens Enterprises 🔳   BONCHESTER CHEESE

Bonchester Bridge, Hawick, Roxburghshire, Borders TD9 8JQ

TEL *045 086 635*   CONTACT *John Curtis*   HOURS *Apr to Christmas Eve: 8.00-18.00*   DIRECTIONS *From Hawick, take A6088 towards Bonchester Bridge. Follow the road about 7 miles to village. At war memorial junction, turn left on to B6357 towards Jedburgh. After 1 mile, farm is signposted on right.*

John Curtis has been making cheese for over 12 years and during that time he has built a fine reputation. As Randolph Hodgson of Neal's Yard Dairy (see page 164) says, 'John is one of the best. It's the care and attention he pays to every detail, from the management of his herd to the making of his cheeses. And it's reflected in the quality'.

How John ended up in the Borders with 18 Jersey cows is a rumbustious story that involves Thames barges, working as a second mate on a coasting vessel, pyo and selling his motorbike to pay for 2 cows to produce the cream to sell with the fruit. When John realized that off-season he had all that cream and no one to buy it, he decided to make cheese. Resorting to a self-sufficiency manual, he hit on a recipe for a Camembert that involved breaking off a chunk, liquidizing it with warm water, adding it to the milk overnight and the following day – hey presto, there were curds. 'It was,' he told me, giggling, 'a bit of a hitty-missy affair – but it did work. And we made it like that for about a year'. With masterly understatement, he continued, 'We've moved on since then.'

It was Janet Gallway from the then West of Scotland Agriculture College who first taught him how to make a Camembert-style cheese properly. He now makes it every morning using unpasteurized Jersey milk: first John adds the mould, *penicillium candidum* and a starter, leaves the milk to stand for about $1\frac{1}{2}$ hours, adds the rennet, leaves it for another hour, then he cuts the curds with a curd knife, tips them into moulds and, after lunch, the moulds are turned. Next day the cheeses are moved into the brining room and brined briefly, left to stand and drain, turned and so remain for about 4 days. Then they are moved into the maturing room to develop a flossy white coat and their flowery flavour.

When John sends them out, either as 100 or 285 g ($3\frac{1}{2}$ or 10 oz) rounds, the interior is still firm. It is best eaten when soft and creamy, with the centre oozing in a run of custard yellow cream. If you keep a Bonchester at room temperature it runs within a couple of days; in a cold fridge it can take up to 2 months. It is a sublime cheese, deep and rich as good as any French mould-ripened ones but with a flavour of its own. John also makes Teviotdale, which he describes as 'the equivalent of four Bonchesters in one, weighing about $2\frac{1}{2}$ pounds'. Made in the same way as a Bonchester, the only difference is that it is lightly pressed. 'This changes its character as it's a drier cheese, it remains harder and won't run when it's ripe'. None the less it still has that flowery creaminess – a hallmark of John's cheeses – if with a more intense and deeper flavour. Belle d'Ecosse is a smaller and lighter pressed version; similar to a Vignotte it does go soft and creamy, but it too will not run. 'It's a question of pressing; the more pressure you apply, the more moisture you take out and the harder the cheese is. If you press too dry, it won't ripen; if it's not dry enough, it ripens too quickly'.

Making cheese is an exacting craft and John is the first to admit he's made a lot of mistakes on the way. He has, however, come far since he whizzed up cheese in the liquidizer and long may he flourish.

ECKFORD   MAP 8

The Teviot Game Fare Smokery ✉ 🏭

SMOKED EELS & FISH

Kirkbank House, Eckford, Kelso, Roxburghshire, Borders TD5 8LE

TEL & FAX *08355 253* CONTACT *Denis Wilson* HOURS *Apr to Sept: Mon-Sat 10.00-16.30 Sun 11.00-16.00; Oct to Mar: Mon-Sat 10.00-16.30* DIRECTIONS *From Kelso, take A698 towards Jedburgh. Follow the road for about 4 miles and smokery is signposted on the right.*

Housed in an 18th-century coaching house, Teviot Game Fare Smokery is a small family business that concentrates on smoking local produce. Eel is a speciality, and the Wilson's son is the officially recommended eel-catcher for the river Tweed. He catches them in their prime in the autumn, when plump and silver as they go downstream for their long slog back to the Sargasso Sea to breed. Because the waters are colder this far north, the eels take comparatively longer to grow; for a good size for smoking, they are usually about 12 years upwards. Once caught, they are 'starved' in the river for a couple of weeks, then lightly brined, cold-smoked over oak chips for 6-7 hours, then hot-smoked for about 3 hours to 'cook' them right through. A whole gutted eel generally weighs around 450 g (1 lb); the largest they have ever caught weighed 3.5 kg (8 lb). Buttery and moist, they sell them filleted in 115 g (4 oz) packs or whole 'as connoisseurs prefer them that way'.

Trout comes from a local trout farm and is smoked in the same way as the eels. As a rule I try to avoid it farmed as, either fresh or smoked, it is an insipid fish. Theirs were a delight: moist with a good body and texture, and a light smoke that served to heighten the flavour of the fish; by comparison, with its harsh saltiness, the hand-sliced smoked salmon was a disappointment. Denis Wilson's approach is 'to smoke for a long time – very slowly. It's the essence of a good flavour'. Pheasants from local shoots are hung for about 4 days to develop a flavour, then brined for a good day, cold-smoked for 24 hours, and finally briefly hot-smoked; and wood pigeon is subjected to a similar treatment. In summer they cure gravlax but, interestingly, use fennel from the garden rather than the more usual dill. They also make 115 g ($^1/_4$ lb) pots of pâtés, using their smoked produce and mixing it with cream and yoghurt, marinated herrings and marmalade. In Kelso, you can buy their smoked produce from the Teviot Fish Shop opposite the old post office.

With *Jethart Snails* from Jedburgh, *Hawick Balls* from Hawick, *Berwick Cockles* from Berwick and *Gala Soor Plums* from Galashiels, the Borders are strong on sweets. **Millers** ⊠ *at* **10 High Street, Jedburgh, TD8 6AG (tel 0835 62252)** *have been making Jethart Snails ever since they were shown how by a French Napoleonic prisoner of war. Sugar boiled with mint essence is hand-pulled into long thin strands and twisted round until it looks like a brown snail.* **Hills of Hawick** ⊠, **16 Commercial Road, Hawick TD9 7AQ (tel 0450 73869, fax 0450 371139)** *first made Hawick Balls, a brittle buttery mint sweet, at the turn of the century. Now they also produce the startling green sharp-tasting Soor Plums and red-and-white-striped Berwick Cockles, that may look like humbugs but have a softer, chewier texture achieved by 'knocking' the heated sugar to introduce air, then leaving the finished sweets to 'grain' for a creamy texture.*

GALASHIELS   MAP 8

Alex Dalgetty & Sons ⊠ ⚖   SELKIRK BANNOCKS

6 Bank Street, Galashiels, Borders TD1 1N7

TEL *0896 2508* **CONTACT** *Bill Murray* **HOURS** *Mon-Sat 7.30-17.00*
DIRECTIONS *In town centre.*

The *Concise Oxford Dictionary* describes a bannock as 'Scotch or N. Eng home-made loaf usu. unleavened, flat, & round or oval'. The Selkirk bannock, however, is a different beast – it is a rich yeasted fruit loaf shaped like a round cob.

History has it first made by a Robbie Douglas in his bakery in Selkirk Market Place in 1859. Queen Victoria, on visiting Sir Walter Scott's granddaughter at Abbotsford in 1867, refused the sumptuous spread in favour of a slice of Selkirk bannock – no producer could hope for a better endorsement. Alexander Dalgetty, a canny Scot, worked for the bakery in Selkirk and, on leaving to start his own business in Galashiels, took the recipe with him. Today his great-grandchildren run the bakery and still make the Selkirk bannock following the original recipe.

Heavily fruited with sultanas, and only sultanas – some recipes call for mixed peel, but Bill Murray claims they are no more than a recent addition – the yeast-based dough is made with strong unbleached flour, sugar, salt and enriched with butter and a little vegetable fat. (I did question Bill about the authenticity of the vegetable fat as I would have thought that it was more likely to contain lard; but he was adamant that vegetable fat was what it was and what it always has been.) Once risen, the dough is hand-shaped, glazed with an egg for a light shiny crust and baked. The result is a plain and 'sensible' open-textured bread. Liberally studded with raisins it is, I think, best in thin slices and toasted.

With another shop in Galashiels attached to the bakery at 21 Island Street and a branch in the High Street in Melrose, they also sell Scotch (Black) bun. Although it, too, is made with a butter-enriched yeast dough, its texture is far more like a dense dark cake; round in shape, it is far more exotic in taste as it is packed with sultanas and currants and lightly spiced. Traditionally Scotch bun is wrapped in a thin layer of the plain dough (set aside before any fruit is added) which, when baked, forms a thin golden brown crust. From the shops you can also buy a good range of oven and hot-plate scones and, at weekends only, light and satisfying potato and cheese & potato scones.

> *Other bakers in the area producing a good Selkirk Bannock are* **Houston Bakers** ✉**, 16 Bourtree Place, Hawick, TD9 9HW (tel 0450 370075)** *and* **R.T. Hossack** ✉ *at* **50 Horsemarket, Kelso, TD5 7AE (tel 0573 224139)** *with branches in Melrose, Coldstream and Selkirk. Using a 100% wholemeal stone-ground flour from Heatherslaw Mill (see page 195), they also make a Tweed bannock with a denser texture.*

STICHILL   MAP 8

Stichill Jerseys ✉ ▦   STICHILL CHEESE

Garden Cottage Farm, Stichill, Kelso, Borders TD5 7TL

TEL *0573 470 263* **CONTACT** *Brenda Leddy – telephone ahead*

From the milk of her 25-strong Jersey herd, Brenda Ledy produces an interesting range of unpasteurized cheeses. Stichill Soft is a rich, full-fat cheese with a good body and clean creamy flavour. Brenda makes it simply by draining the curds in muslin, mixing them with salt and sometimes fresh garlic or chives or mixed herbs and then shaping the curds into rolls or 55 g (2 oz) rounds. These are then rolled in chopped nuts or peppercorns or oatmeal or indeed 'anything I can lay my hands on that goes with cheese'.

Brenda's pressed cheeses, Stichill and Kelsae are unusual in that the former is made without a starter and the latter has Brenda's own-made yoghurt as a starter; other than that they are made in almost the same way. Stichill, Brenda describes as similar to a Cheshire, but as it is made with Jersey milk it is richer and creamier. Kelsae (the original name for nearby Kelso) she describes as akin to Wensleydale, but 'with more taste'. Again because of its richer milk, it is far creamier in both texture and taste. Brenda also makes butter with her Jersey milk; first it is heat-treated, ripened for a couple of days and then whipped up in her Kenwood chef. It is actually a simple enough way to make butter, provided you do not over-work it and wash it thoroughly several times to squeeze out the buttermilk.

The massive walls of Traquair, a royal hunting lodge, have in their time housed many a Scottish and English king. When Mary Queen of Scots visited in 1566 they were already brewing their own ale and in 1739 a 900-litre (200-gallon) copper was installed in the brew-house beneath the chapel. For over 200 years the copper mash tun (vat), open coolers, fermenters and wooden stirring paddles lay idle until, in 1965, the 20th Laird re-started brewing. Now the business is in the capable hands of his charming daughter Catherine Maxwell Stuart and at **Traquair House** ✉, **Innerleithen, EH44 6PW (tel 0896 830323)** *you can visit the house and get lost in the maze as well as buy the ale and own-made cakes and mustard that all contain the old-fashioned brew. (✉ Minimum quantity one case of ale).*

And Also...

• Once a net salmon fisherman on the river Tweed, **Mr Fairbairn** ✉ of Rose Cottage, Birgham, nr Kelso (tel 0890 830 250) now smokes salmon. Mostly he smokes privately caught fish (customers drop it in on their way down south), but he does smoke both bought farmed and wild salmon for 'a middle of the road' smoke.

• From a small bakery beneath the house, Helen Drummond of **Shirra Bakery** ✉, 14 Market Place, Selkirk (tel 0750 20690) bakes a buttery shortbread in 5 flavours: original, brown sugar, brandy, chocolate chip and almond.

• **Eden Plants** at Cliftonhill Farm, Ednam, Kelso (tel 0573 225028) sell bunches of freshly cut asparagus in season from May to June and asparagus crowns (plants). If you book in for B&B, they will cook asparagus for supper.

- **Border Berries** at Rutherford Farm, Kelso (tel 0835 23763) have good PYO and ready-picked strawberries and raspberries.
- Set in a courtyard with a smoke-house and processing room, **John Waddell & Son** at Mason's Wynd, Eyemouth (tel 0890 750392) sells fish off the day boats from Eyemouth Market, and lobster and dressed crab from Burgon. They smoke Finnan haddock and, in summer, herrings and sea-caught wild salmon.
- **David Palmer** ✉ at 3 High Street, Jedburgh (tel 0835 63276) was haggis champion of Scotland from 1984-6. Since then he's slipped down the ladder, but still regularly features in the top 12. Made with all the usual unmentionables (liver, heart, lungs, etc), he claims his haggis has a high meat content. Sold in 675-900 g (11/2-2 lb) rounds in plastic skins, he can make them with natural skins, in any size up to 2.7 kg (6 lb), or as a long thin slicing or horseshoe-shaped haggis.
- **Clarke's of Loch Ewe** ✉, Home Place, Coldstream (tel 0890 883153, fax 0890 883534) produces whisky truffles and marchpane (marzipan) cubes, made with almonds and white cane sugar covered in chocolate.
- The fish at fishmonger **Dan Ross**, 19 Northgate, Peebles (0721 720108) comes from Aberdeen's fish market.
- **Liddy Hall** at **Hundalee Cottars Farm** ✉, by Jedburgh (tel 0835 62064) makes a range of goats'-milk products, including ice-cream, hard and soft cheeses, and Greek-style and ordinary yoghurts.

DUMFRIES & GALLOWAY

BEESWING   MAP 8

Loch Arthur Creamery ✉ 🔳 🌾 🌳   CHEESE

Camphill Village Trust, Beeswing, Dumfries, Dumfries & Galloway DG2 8JQ

TEL *038 776 296* **CONTACT** *Barry Graham* **HOURS** *Mon-Fri 9.00-17.30 Sat-Sun telephone ahead* **DIRECTIONS** *From Dumfries, take A711 towards Beeswing. Follow the road about 4 miles into the village and take the first turning on the left past the church. After about 30 yards, Camphill Trust is signposted on the left.*

Loch Arthur Creamery is part of Loch Arthur Community and belongs to the Camphill Village Trust (see Botton Village Foods, page 290). The community's estate covers over 500 acres, with the loch in the centre of an impressive landscape. The land, primarily farmland, is farmed to organic (Soil Association) and Demeter (biodynamic) standards and they keep cows and sheep and grow vegetables. As well as the dairy, they run a small bakery and a weavery.

Barry Graham, assisted by community members, makes Loch Arthur Farmhouse cheese from organic unpasteurized milk from their Ayrshire herd. Made along similar lines to a Cheddar, the curds are cut and 'cheddared', stacked, re-stacked and turned to assist the draining of the whey until the whey runs clean and the level of acidity is right. Then they are packed in 9 kg (20 lb) moulds, pressed for a total of about 2 days and matured for around 7 months. Quite a firm dry cheese, it comes as plain or flavoured with mixed herbs or caraway. Described evocatively by cheese-writer Juliet Harbutt as having 'a full-bodied creamy finish...there is a spicy tang of young celery', it won first prize in its class at the 1991 & 1992 Royal Highland Show and the 1993 Bakewell Show.

The dairy also makes a 'live' yoghurt, a smooth and creamy quark, a full-fat lactic curd cheese and Crannog, a soft cheese simply made from 'scooping off the Cheddar curds early on', straining them and coating the finished cheese in wax; this comes either as plain or mixed with fresh herbs.

The Moffat Toffee Shop ✉, High Street, Moffat, DG10 9DW (tel 0683 20032) is one of the biggest sweetie shops in the country. Out in the back they still make toffee based on the 'secret' recipe of Mr Blair Blacklock's great-grandmother. The only details I could glean are that, in batches of 35 kg (75 lb), he boils up brown and white sugar with liquid glucose to 155°C/310°F (in sugar boiling terms, a temperature somewhere between 'hard crack' and 'caramel'). It is poured on to a slab and pulled on a pulling machine to aerate it, thus giving it a lighter, chewier texture and a lighter colour. Then it is cut, wrapped in its darker brown casing and popped into 225 and 450 g (½ and 1 lb) tins, decorated in the local black-and-white Shepherd's tartan. Crunchy, with a sharp, slightly lemony centre and a treacly coating, it is fresh teeth-clogging toffee.

CARSLUITH   MAP 8

The Galloway Smokehouse ✉ 🏭

SMOKED SALMON & VENISON

Carsluith, Newton Stewart, Dumfries & Galloway DG8 7DN

TEL 0671 82354   CONTACT *Allan Watson*   HOURS *9.00-17.30*   DIRECTIONS *From Newton Stewart, take A75 towards Carsluith. Follow road about 8 miles into the village centre and smokery is signposted on the left.*

It never ceases to amaze me just how different smoked salmon can taste from one smoke-house to another. On reflection, I suppose I ought not to be that surprised as there are so many variables involved – the condition of the raw product, the ingredients of the cure, for how long it is cured, the temperature of the smoke, the length of time it is smoked – each and every factor does ultimately affect the eating quality of the end-product.

Allan Watson opts for a serious smoke: his salmon has a deep strong flavour of wood underlined with a pronounced sweetness. This he achieves by curing either wild or farmed salmon in salt with 'dark syrup and dark rum' for an undisclosed length of time. Smoking is carried out at a temperature- and humidity-controlled kiln over whisky-impregnated oak sawdust from Grant's Distillery for an incredible 36 hours. As he says, he does not like the normal 'acceptable bland' smoked salmon, so obviously he has chosen to produce something decidedly different.

Venison from wild Roe deer is also subjected to a long smoke, apparently it lasts 3 days in the kiln once it has been brined (again for an undisclosed length of time) in the dark syrup and dark rum brine. Chickens and Barbary duck breasts also have the same flavoured brine; duck is smoked for 2 days, chicken a mere 6 hours. In fact Mr Watson will seemingly smoke anything from lobster, crab and prawns to eel and hard-boiled eggs. Salmon, however, is his speciality, and if you like one with a strong smoke, I suggest you try it.

PORTPATRICK   MAP 8

The Colfin Smokehouse ✉ 🏠   SMOKED FOOD

Portpatrick, Wigtownshire, Dumfries & Galloway DG9 9BN

TEL & FAX *0776 82622* **CONTACT** *Scott Baillie* **HOURS** *Mon-Sat 9.00-17.00 Sun 10.00-15.00* **CARDS** *Access, Visa, Mastercard* **DIRECTIONS** *From Lochans, take A77 towards Portpatrick. Follow the road about 2 miles and turn left at sign for the smokehouse. After about 100 yards, smokery is signposted on the left.*

The original purpose of smoking food was to preserve it. Since the introduction of canning and refrigeration, however, it has become redundant as a method of preservation. Now it is no more than a means of introducing a variety of flavours to food and, as a result, smoking has become a far more subtle craft. Gone are the harsh salty cures needed to extract the moisture from food or the heavy deep smokes to dry and/or cook it.

The Colfin Smokehouse are innovative curers; whereas most traditional smokers favour a dry salt cure for salmon, they cure both the wild netted in Luce Bay and the farmed salmon in a salt brine flavoured with brown sugar, dark rum, juniper berries, black peppercorns and bay leaves for about 15 hours. In fact they use the same flavour of brine for the Clyde herrings bought from Ayr Market and the farmed trout.

Venison (sometimes wild, sometimes farmed), mussels, chicken and pheasant, on the other hand, are brined in a salt solution flavoured with brown sugar and a hint of garlic. For the actual smoking, they use oak chips and sawdust (often from sherry casks), and for an extra woodiness lay juniper berries on top.

Salmon, once cured, is then dried by blowing warm air over the fish for a few hours and finally cold-smoked for between 12-14 hours. The result is a slightly 'kippered' texture, a mild-to-medium smoke with a just discernible sweetness. Kippers are a pale nut brown in colour but deeply woody in taste, and the chicken is sweet, soft and succulent.

FIFE

AUCHTERMUCHTY MAP 8

Fletchers of Auchtermuchty ✉ 🚜 ♦

FARMED VENISON

Reediehill Farm, Auchtermuchty, Fife KY14 7HS

TEL *0337 28369* FAX *0337 27001* CONTACT *Nichola Fletcher – telephone ahead* CARDS *Access, Visa, Mastercard, Eurocard*

'We're in the fertile Howe of Fife where the Ochils peter out,' is how Nichola Fletcher likes to describe the setting of Reediehill Farm. Then she explains that Auchtermuchty is the Pictish for hill (*auchter*) of the wild pig (*muchty*) and tells of how the kings and queens of Scotland hunted for them on her land from Falkland Palace. Wild pig is now replaced with farmed deer (although the Fletchers did briefly flirt with wild boar farming) but the spirit lives on.

Fletcher's is a founder member of the quality assurance scheme British Prime Venison run by the British Deer Farmers Association. If you buy venison with a BPV mark it is a guarantee it comes from farmed deer less than 27 months old, that is fed on natural feedstuffs with no growth promoters, and is slaughtered, hung and butchered in approved premises. The obvious question to ask Nichola is what she thinks are the advantages of farmed over wild venison: 'reliability and consistency – it's not variable. As it's under 27 months, you know for certain the meat is going to be tender as opposed to wild venison that can be any age. Also, our deer are clean shot, we take a rifle to them in the field – so there's no stress. And we all know just how much stress can affect the texture of meat'.

But what about taste? A tricky one that as we all probably want to believe that a wild deer roaming with all of Nature's glorious bounty to feed on will have a better flavour. Nichola was quick to dispel that illusion. 'As far as tests and taste panels go, no discernible difference has been found between the two. And our deer are better fed and sheltered, some are housed in winter because of our ghastly weather – they can go out, but they never do. It's infinitely preferable to the lot of the wild deer that can starve or die of exposure when the weather gets rough'.

Nichola's deer are Red deer: the other species in this country are the Roe that is about one-quarter of the size of the Red, and the Fallow that comes half-way between the two. The only difference in eating quality, as far as Nichola is concerned, is the tighter grain of the meat of the smaller species. In summer her deer graze extensively on the grassy paddocks and rough hills of the farm; in winter they are fed hay or silage supplemented with potatoes and carrots. The young stock get a special ration of barley to build them up. All her meat is hung for between 2-3 weeks as a carcass, a point she wishes to stress as she is very dismissive of dealers who hang their meat jointed and vacuum-packed as it does not have the desired effect. It is butchered into shoulder on or off the bone, haunch (leg) on or off the bone, saddle, escalope (knuckle steaks), topside or silverside steaks, médaillons (sirloin steaks), whole fillets, chops (cutlets), casserole (chopped shoulder), stew (chopped shin) and 'veniburgers'. She also makes venison sausages, a firm rich venison haggis from meat mixed with the lights and oatmeal, spiced venison parcels and a smooth venison liver pâté.

The haunch is also cured for about 3 days in a salt, pepper, red wine, wine vinegar and root ginger brine, hung to dry for another day then sent off for hot- or cold-smoking. When cold-smoked, it has a mildly gamy, mellow flavour with a soft pliable texture. From the shop you can also buy Nichola's strongly flavoured Wild Rowan jelly, splendid with venison, and copies of her two cookery books that, not surprisingly, are about venison and game. For details of other members of the quality assurance scheme British Prime Venison run by the British Deer Farmers Association, contact John Elliot, 6 Pound Cottages, Streatley, Reading RG8 9JH (tel 0491 872275).

NEWBURGH   **MAP 8**

Ian Miller's Organic Meat ✉ 🚜 / ORGANIC MEAT

Jamesfield Farm, by Newburgh, Fife KY14 6EW

TEL *0738 85498* FAX *0738 85741* CONTACT *Ian Miller* HOURS *Fri 13.00-16.00 Sat-Sun 10.00-16.00* CARDS *Access, Visa, Mastercard* DIRECTIONS *From Abernethy, take A913 towards Newburgh. After about 1 mile, turn left at sign for the Organic Shop. Follow the road $\frac{1}{2}$ mile and shop is on right.*

Although Ian Miller is now totally committed to organic (to Soil Association standards) farming, it has not always been the case. He tells of the time when 'as a young headstrong lad aged 20, I rowed with my father as I wanted to pile more chemicals on the land. Land is precious',

he told me, 'and must be handed on to the next generation more fertile –
that was not the way to achieve it'. The statement stuck in Ian's mind
and over the next 20 years he saw a serious deterioration in the soil until
he realized he must change his method of farming. It is a great source of
satisfaction to him that he saw the error of his ways in time to tell his
father before he died. Converting – and indeed farming – to organic
standards is not an easy option. When Ian wanted to convert about 8
years ago he went around to the agricultural colleges and to his horror
found 'not a paragraph of information. I was out in limbo land'. In fact,
it is marginally easier now, and Ian's own farm was the subject of a 2-
year study carried out by the Agricultural College of Edinburgh
University and funded by Safeway.

It is for his meat and vegetables that Ian is fast building a reputation;
especially the quality of his beef, with its layer of yellow fat and pleasing
marbling, the attention to detail and the personal service. In fact, Ian
does not produce all the beef he sells as some is bought in from about 6
other Highland organic farmers; but in order to offer a consistency of
standards, he makes notes for all his mail-order customers of their likes
and dislikes, the farm from which the meat comes and the cross-breed,
'so I always stick to the same'. The beef is Aberdeen Angus crossed
either with Hereford or Shorthorn; raised as suckler herds and weaned
at around 6 months to give them a good start, it is slaughtered between
18-24 months for a deep length of flavour. The carcasses come to Ian
and he hangs them for about 14 days and then butchers them into
conventional cuts 'or any cut the customer wants provided we can get
the terminology right'.

Terminology being, according to Ian, a bit of a problem as the names
of the cuts change from one place to another; what he calls 'popeseye'
we down South call rump and his 'salmon cut' is our best-end silverside.
Organic lamb from traditional grey or black-face breeds also presents the
same butchering problem. In Scotland leg is 'gigot', but once you come
to grips with this matter of language, ordering is easy and delivery no
problem 'as it leaves us at 17.00 one day, it's with our customers no later
than 17.00 the next'. He also sells free-range pork and traditionally
cured bacon by MacDonald's of Pitlochry, and free-range chickens.
From the farm-shop, he also sells own-grown vegetables (Ian is probably
the largest organic vegetable grower in Scotland): these include
cauliflower, carrots, onions, broccoli, turnips, parsnips, various potatoes
(such as Cara, Pentland Squire and Maris Piper), Little Gem, lollo rosso,
lollo biondo, Iceberg lettuces and curly endive.

And Also...

- Haggis from *Gronbachs* ✉, 198 & 202 High Street, Cowdenbeath
(tel 0383 510906) is rated highly by those who know. Reports please.

- *Fisher & Donaldson* at 21 Crossgate, Cupar (tel 0334 52551), with branches at 13 Church Street, St Andrews and 12 Whitehall Street, Dundee, have a huge range of breads and cakes. Traditionalists go for their oatmeal shortbread and Abernethy biscuits.
- *Flower of May Apiaries*, 17 Hill Crescent, Cupar (tel 0334 55461) sell fruity flower and rich heather honeys.
- *St Andrews Delicatessen*, Mercat Wynd, Market Street, St Andrews (tel 0334 76444), boasts at least 26 different Scottish cheeses. These include Isle of Mull Cheddar, Dunloppe (see page 362), Dunsyre Blue (see page 361) and smoked cheese from MacDonald's Smoked Produce (see page 350).

GRAMPIAN

DINNET   MAP 8

Deeside Smoked Salmon ✉ 🍴   SMOKED SALMON

Headinch House, Dinnet, Aboyne, Aberdeenshire, Grampian AB34 5NY

TEL *03398 85304* CONTACT *Fergus and Shona Cumming – telephone ahead*

One morning while staying with friends in the wilds of Shropshire, a side of smoked salmon dropped through the letterbox. Eager, and far too greedy to wait, we sliced a little for a luxurious breakfast with scrambled eggs, it was buttery and mild and quite delightful. When I asked Emily, my hostess, from where had it come, her reply was short and to the point, 'From my brother Fergus who is a gillie by day and smokes salmon at night'.

Fergus Cumming may by now be familiar to readers of Michael Raffael's excellent columns in the *Sunday Telegraph*. He too discovered the glories of Fergus's smoked salmon and wrote about it at great length. What makes it so unique is Fergus's deep and serious understanding of the nature of the salmon and how, operating on a tiny scale, he is able to adjust and tailor his curing and smoking to suit each and every fish. He smokes both farmed and wild salmon; the latter is either netted at sea and bought in Aberdeen or caught in the river and bought wherever possible 'but definitely no dodgy (a polite way of saying poached) stuff'. Those caught at sea, Fergus notices, can sometimes be softer than a river fish; it tends to have harder, tougher muscles 'no doubt from fighting the currents as it swims up stream'. A wild salmon can also be richer in oil 'sometimes it just oozes oil in the kiln', whereas a farmed fish is drier but fatter with reserves of fat around its belly. Then again it is so variable but, as Fergus says, 'one thing is certain, if you start with a good fish you will end up with a good smoked one'.

The fish are salted in a pure dried vacuum salt; similar to a table salt this, he feels, is the best for salting. Interestingly, he notices that frozen fish take a cure far more quickly, 'possibly because they've lost some moisture in the freezing'. The whole sides are cold-smoked over oak chips and will stay there for anything from 6 to 8 hours, or sometimes even longer. He sells them as whole unsliced sides, which are particularly popular with anglers and foreigners on holiday.

Highland Venison ✉, *Grantown-on-Spey, Morayshire, PH26 3NA (tel 0479 2255, fax 0479 3055) is a co-operative of 90 estates in the Grampian and Highlands and will supply – by mail order only – packs of venison from wild Red deer. These come as an 'Introductory Pack', of four 200-225 g (7-8 oz) venison steaks and two 450 g (1 lb) portions of diced venison, or a 'Connoisseur's pack' of two 900g (2 lb) rolled haunch roasts, twelve 200-225 g (7-8 oz) venison steaks and six 450 g (1 lb) portions of diced venison. Wild venison, they claim, has a better taste because it is heather-fed and if it is handled properly the age of the deer is irrelevant. The carcasses are 'gralloched' (eviscerated) by the stalkers on the hill, then taken down to the estate's larders where a spreader is put into the chest cavity to improve the circulation of the air and cool the carcass down. It is taken by refrigerated transport to the butchering unit, inspected, cut into prime cuts, vacuum-packed and aged in the bag for about 4 days.*

FORRES   MAP 8

MacBeth's ✉ 🏆   HIGHLAND BEEF

20 High Street, Forres, Morayshire, Grampian IV36 0DB
TEL *0309 672254* **FAX** *034389 404* **CONTACT** *Susan Gibson* **HOURS** *Mon & Wed 9.00-13.00; Tues, Thurs, Fri & Sat 9.00-17.00* **CARDS** *Access, Visa* **DIRECTIONS** *In town centre, near to the floral gardens.*

Lovers of good beef know and respect Aberdeen Angus, but according to Michael Gibson 'Highland beef from pure-bred Highland cattle has the slight edge. It's leaner with a little more flavour'. Not that you or I or, as Michael politely puts it, 'over 90% of the population' could probably tell the difference. Just like connoisseurs can tell their malt whiskies, however, I'd like to think I can tell my beefs apart'.

Michael specializes in Scottish native breeds of cattle. He has a 500-strong herd of pure-bred Aberdeen Angus, pure-bred Beef Shorthorn, Aberdeen Angus-Shorthorn cross and pure-bred Highland Cattle. Not for him the Continental Limousin or Charolais that have a lot to answer for when it comes to comparison with the flavour of most home-bred

> A visit to **Gordon & MacPhail** ✉ at **58-60 South Street, Elgin, Morayshire, IV30 1JY (tel 0343 545110, fax 0343 540155)** cannot fail to delight every whisky lover. Their 'own-label' bottlings are in 6 groups: rare old whiskies (malts distilled in the '60s, '50s, '40s and even the '30's); single malts aged for 8-40 years; connoisseur's choice (leading examples of the regional characteristics with bottling between 10 and 35 years); vatted malt whiskies (blends of malt whiskies from different distilleries, said sometimes to be superior to the individual malts they contain); blended whiskies; and whisky liqueur.

beef. He unashamedly concentrates on 100% beef breeds and rears them for slaughtering at the right weight for butchering and at the right maturity for eating. Finishing an animal is a skilled business; for Michael the essence is to get the right degree of marbling through the meat as this is essential for the flavour. 'Marbling is a function of maturity. Until an animal reaches a certain age, it won't lay any significant marbling down unless you are grossly overfeeding it. And if you have pushed it, the meat will be lighter in colour, it may be tender but it will be bland like cardboard. But a properly reared animal will have close textured firm meat with a fine marbling for flavour'.

Only steers (castrated males) are sent for slaughter for 2 good reasons. The first is practical: his heifers are sold for breeding stock; the second has more to do with eating quality 'as, dare I say, like most females, they put fat on in the wrong places and their meat tends to be flabbier and looser'. His steers are slaughtered at a minimum of 24 months; once taken to the slaughterhouse, he insists they are rested for 18 hours prior to slaughter to reduce 'dark cutting'. This, as Michael explains, comes when the animal is stressed as it releases adrenalin into the muscles to tense them. The net result is tougher darkened meat which, no matter how long you hang it, will never tenderize. All his beef is hung for 7 days at the slaughterhouse, then transferred to his state-of-the-art shop in the small village of Forres. The forequarters (for mince, sausages and the like) are processed immediately, prime cuts from the hind sirloin are hung for another 10 days and 'it is hung on the bone, essential to draw out the flavour of the bone'.

About 70% of his business is with the catering trade. In London the likes of Rowley Leigh at Kensington Place and Bruno Loubet at The Four Seasons at the Inn on the Park use his meat, and it is sometimes on sale at Boucherie Lamartine in Ebury Street. You can go in and buy from his shop – they also sell lamb from black-faced sheep, game, sausages, black pudding and haggis – but you will not see meat on display; everything, even the mince, is cut to order by his staff, or 'technicians', as he likes to call them. 'We butcher every which way, in traditional cuts or Continental seaming and we'll send whatever you want. If you just want a fillet, we'll send you a fillet'. As for which of the breeds you should choose, in fact most of his customers do not specify; but if you want to, Michael will be delighted to accommodate you, provided you are prepared to wait if necessary. The difference, as he has already said, is minimal but when pushed he describes Highland as bigger with more flavour, Aberdeen Angus as richer and slightly fattier 'with not quite the edge', and Shorthorn as somewhere between the two. As far as I'm concerned they were all superb, deep rich and with the resonance of properly reared and hung beef.

MONTGARRIE   MAP 8

A. MacDonald & Son ✉ 🔨   OATMEAL

Montgarrie Mill, Montgarrie, Alford, Aberdeenshire,
Grampian AB33 8AP

TEL *09755 62209* **FAX** *09755 62295* **CONTACT** *Donald MacDonald* **HOURS** *Mon-Fri 7.00-17.00 Sat 7.00-12.00* **DIRECTIONS** *From Tillyfourie, take A944 towards Alford. Follow the road about 4 miles into the centre of Alford and turn right just before the Spar shop. Follow the road about 1 mile to the Montgarrie Post Office on the right-hand side of the road. Turn left opposite the post office and, after about 100 yards, mill is on the left.*

A while ago I received a straight to-the-point letter from a Dr Evelyn Gavin of Peterculter recommending, 'as a first-class food the oatmeal produced by MacDonald & Son. This is one of the few products still produced by the traditional methods – the oats kiln-dried, which is essential to produce flavour, and stone-ground which is essential for the right texture and avoidance of metal contact...Almost all the traditional oatmeal mills have now sadly gone out of existence. This is why the Montgarrie Mills are unique. People in this part of the world who appreciate oatmeal will use no other brand. It is fresh, fragrant, wholesome, tasty, good enough to eat raw, a sprinkling over cooked dishes'.

What more can I add? Perhaps to tell you that the MacDonalds have owned and run Montgarrie Mills since 1894. For the most part the oats come from the North-East corner of Scotland and first they are dried (conditioned) down to a 15% moisture to ensure they keep fresh and 'sweet'. Then they are laid out to dry down to a $4\frac{1}{2}$% moisture content on the flat kiln floor made of perforated mild steel sheets with a furnace fired by smokeless anthracite coal 6m (24 ft) below. The oats are turned by hand shovel so they dry evenly, and slowly the temperature is increased until, after 4 hours, it has reached 88°C (190°F) and the oats are toasted to give them that rich nutty flavour.

Stored until needed, they are screened to remove any extraneous matter and put through the shelling stones to remove the husk from the kernel; then they are ground into 6 different cuts or grades: superfine, fine (no $3\frac{1}{2}$), medium (no 4), medium/rough (no $4\frac{1}{2}$), rough (no 5) and pinhead (which is the kernel cut in half with any floury meal sifted out). Sold from the mill door in 0.5, 1, 1.5, 3, and 6 kg (1, $2\frac{1}{4}$, $3\frac{1}{2}$, $6\frac{1}{2}$ and 13 lb) polythene packs these are the real thing. As Dr Gavin writes, 'It is essential that oatmeal used for porridge should be full-flavoured, as it loses a little in flavour in the cooking; given most of the poor meal on the market it is not surprising that many people reject it or cover it with sugar. Porridge made with real oatmeal requires only salt'.

And Also...

• *Mr McKenzie's Biscuits* ✉, 41 Main Street, Turriff (tel 0888 62425) bakes a well-spiced Scotch black bun as a 900 g-1.25 kg ($2-2\frac{1}{2}$ lb) square enclosed in pastry or cut 450 g (1 lb) slabs, as well as an all-butter shortbread.

• Sweeties from *Dee Valley Confectioners* ✉, Station Square, Ballater (tel 03397 55499) include clove rock, bullseyes, brandy balls and tablet.

• Ballindalloch is an unpasteurized hard goats' cheese matured for 4 to 5 months from *Highland Goat Products* ✉, Corglass Farm, Ballindalloch AB37 9BS (tel 0807 500269).

HIGHLANDS
& ISLANDS

ACHILTIBUIE   MAP 8

Summer Isles Foods ✉ 🏭 🎣   SALMON & KIPPERS

Achiltibuie, Ullapool, Ross-shire, Highlands & Islands IV26 2YG

(Mail order address: Summer Isles Foods, 19-22 Industrial Estate, Alness, Ross-shire, Highland & Islands IV17 0XS) **TEL** *085 482 353* **FAX** *085 482 335 (Mail order: tel 0349 884341, fax 0349 884074)* **CONTACT** *Keith Dunbar* **HOURS** *Mon-Fri 9.30-17.00* **CARDS** *Access, Visa* **DIRECTIONS** *From Ullapool, take A835 towards Ledmore. Follow the road about 10 miles and turn left signposted Achiltibuie on to a single track road. Follow the road about 12 miles to the second junction and turn right, signposted Summer Isles. Smoke-house is on the left after about 2 miles, just before The Fuaran pub.*

As you wind down the single track to Achiltibuie, you just have to stop to take in the view – it is stupendous. Scattered in clumps and stretching out towards the horizon are the Summer Isles, that look for all the world like huge sleeping prehistoric animals with rounded hump backs. If you are lucky – and I was – you will catch your first sight just before the sun sinks into the sea; the dying rays cast golden paths over the water and bathe the bay in a warm glow. Imagine what it must be like to be Keith Dunbar and go to work every morning with a view like this. He has been at Achiltibuie for nearly 16 years and never gets tired of it.

From what must be the smoke-house with one of the best views, and incidentally one of the most tortuous to get to, Keith smokes a range of fish and his partner-in-smoke the Alness Smokehouse does the meat, game and mail order. One of his specialities is salmon: he uses mainly farmed fish and cures them in a sweet brine of salt, rum, molasses and boiled-up juniper berries for about 8 hours. Opinions seem to be divided as to whether a dry-salt or brine cure is the more effective: Keith prefers a brine as he feels it offers him more control and a greater subtlety of flavours. The salmon is smoked for about 20 hours over oak sawdust from sherry casks from the Invergordon Distillery and the result is a mellow rich fish with that melt-in-the-mouth texture.

The other speciality is kippers that have proved so popular that he now runs a kipper club: a subscription secures you 2 pairs of fine plump kippers – a pair weighs around 40 g (14 oz) – every month. Keith buys Scottish herrings 'when the quality is right and the fat content is high enough', with a catching season between June to September. Brined in salt for about 30 minutes, then smoked for between 18 and 24 hours, his are juicy with plenty of punch. He also smokes eel, queen scallops and mussels, and cures gravlax.

> Fish merchants **Andy Race** ✉ at **The Harbour, Port of Mallaig, PH41 4PX (tel 0687 2626, fax 0687 2060)** sell a range of both fresh and own-smoked fish, and about 99% is landed in the port. There seems no end to the fish they smoke (over a mixture of oak, peat, pine and beech); the range includes Mallaig herrings slowly smoked for about 24 hours; whole lemon soles smoked on the bone; lobster either as meat or in the shell; Dublin Bay Prawns (aka Norwegian lobsters, aka langoustines); turbot; halibut; cod; monkfish; prawns; sprats; dogfish; whelks and Finnan haddock.

BALMUCHY   MAP 8

Clokie's Sea Vegetables ✉   SEAWEED

Pitkerrie, Balmuchy, Fearn, Ross-shire, Highlands & Islands IV20 1TN

TEL *086287 272* CONTACT *Julian Clokie – mail order only*

Julian Clokie, a Master of Science in Biology, now earns his keep collecting (or 'ranching', as he would have it) seaweed. Seaweeds are his passion and, if he would have his way, we would all eat a lot more of them. To him, it is utterly illogical that only those who live around the Pacific indulge – the Welsh and their laver bread apart. Apparently, though, the French have seen fit to encourage the seaweed industry around Brittany where there are about 8 government- or bank-funded companies. When I told him of my trip there and how I had alighted on seaweed-flavoured croutons – and very good they were too – he visibly brightened.

Ranching seaweed is, in fact, a skilled job; to get it right is far more complicated then just nipping down to the seashore with bucket and wellies. 'Each seaweed has a picking season of 2-4 weeks. You must pick it just before it is fertile and before it has built up its tannin-like content, a sort of anti-fouling chemical that puts off the predators while it releases its myriad spores. The problem is there is no immediate difference in its appearance as to whether it is fertile or not. So picking comes down to a compromise between size and fertility'. As if that was bad enough, there is the problem of where to pick it; it should be at the meristem (the growing part of the seaweed); but cunning little thing that it is, the meristem is apparently not where you would think it ought to be.

Yet another complication is the flavour. This can vary for the same variety from bay to bay and, worse still, within the same bay – as 'whether it's on the headland or point or by the rocks makes a huge difference'. You can quite realize why Julian likes to keep his favoured spots a secret. As for the varieties, they rejoice in such names as dabberlocks, so called because it looks like the hair (locks) of a mermaid (dabber); grockle; sugar ware (ware is the old Scottish word for sea-weed); finger ware presumably because the ware are finger-shaped; sloke (wild nori); dulse (from the old Gaelic duileasg), autumn dulse and dead man's thongs. The seaweeds are dried in a single-pass recirculating drying oven (and Julian insisted I mentioned it) that gives a fairly low heat to preserve the flavour; then wrapped in 50 g (2 oz) packs to give a reconstituted weight that, depending on the seaweed, varies from 400 to 750 g (14 oz to $1\frac{3}{4}$ lb).

Apart from the odd small collector of dulse, Julian is the only commercial supplier in Britain. In his attempt to convert our palates, he ranches from Inverness to Skye.

✉ *Tods of Orkney, 25 Northend Road, Stromness, Orkney, KW16 3AS (tel 0856 850873) have recently taken over Gardens and Stockans but still make the same quality of oatcakes. Made with oatmeal, salt, vegetable oils, a tiny amount of sugar and, occasionally, wheat flour, they produce a range of 6 different types. These include: thin – about 3 mm ($\frac{1}{8}$ in); thick – about 7-8 mm ($\frac{1}{4}$ in); wholemeal & honey; cheese, flavoured with a dried cheese powder; large rounds and small cocktail-size oatcakes.*

The Boardhouse Mill ✉ 🏠 ♣   BEREMEAL

Birsay, Orkney, Highlands & Islands KW17 2LY

TEL 0408 633 278 **CONTACT** Fergus Morrison – telephone ahead

'Beremeal', Fergus Morrison told me, 'is Neolithic barley'. With a great flourish, he traced its origins back to Mesopotamia, via King Alfred and his burnt beremeal cakes, and Orkney where he is the only grower and miller of the grain. Beremeal has a reputation for its earthy taste and as Fergus says, 'it's much better than ordinary barley and far less bland'. It was widely grown in Scotland and used for bere bannocks until about the mid 19th century, although it still remains popular in Orkney. As I have never tried the bere bannocks, I must rely on Scottish cookery writer Catherine Brown's opinion; she pronounced them 'earthy' and 'distinctive'.

Fergus grows beremeal, 'as it's genetically pure, it behaves like wild grass. I use untreated seed, never spray the grain. It grows quickly and just bosses out the weed'. After harvesting, it has to be dried in the kiln fired by the chaff from the previous load; the moisture content is taken down to around 8% for a 'nutty, smoky taste'. It is then ground between three pairs of water driven stones. The first set removes the awn or 'spiky bit' and the grain is cleaned and aspirated; then it is coarsely ground, and lastly ground finely.

Now based on the mainland, Fergus also runs Golspie Mill in Golspie, Sutherland KW10 6RA (tel 0408 633 278). Here he produces peasemeal from Lincolnshire peas. First they are roasted, then ground to a flour which is used for brose, thickening soups or baking breads. (✉ Golspie Mill only.)

> ## BEREMEAL BANNOCKS
> *(old method)*
>
> Put 300 ml ($\frac{1}{2}$ pt) of milk into a pan with a pinch of salt and 30 g (1 oz) or more of butter. Bring to the boil and stir in quickly enough beremeal – about 115 g (4 oz) – to make a pliable dough. Turn out on a floured board, roll out thinly, cut into rounds the size of a meat plate. Bake on a hot girdle (griddle), turning once, on a rather sharp fire. Eat hot. (Adapted from *The Scots Kitchen* by F. Marian McNeill.)

Mermaid Fish Supplies ✉ 🏠   SMOKED SALMON

Clachan, Locheport, Lochmaddy, North Uist, Highlands & Islands PA82 5ET

TEL 08764 209 **FAX** 08764 323 **CONTACT** George Jackson **HOURS** Mon-Sat 8.00-18.00 **CARDS** Access, Visa, Mastercard **DIRECTIONS** On the west side of the island, near Clachan Corner.

Both Derek Cooper, who – as presenter of Radio 4's *Food Programme* – needs no introduction, and cookery writer Catherine Brown have been extremely helpful guiding me to the best Scotland has to offer. Both of them recommended George Jackson for his smoked salmon.

What makes George's salmon unique is how he smokes it. On North Uist, there is no wood, so he uses peat instead. Using farmed salmon from the smaller local farms that, according to George, 'produce good fish unlike the large farms', he dry-cures it then smokes it in his kiln, which is really 'more of a box with drawers underneath for the burning peat and a fan at the back to circulate the air. And as it's so damp here, humidity is a problem'. Peat burns hot and, unlike wood, does not smoulder, so cold-smoking could prove difficult; somehow George manages it – but that is his secret.

The result is quite distinctive; the salmon acquires a gentle smoky haze unlike any other, as it is soft and gentle with none of the fierceness often associated with a strong smoke. Sold as whole or sliced sides or as sliced packets, George also smokes fillets of cod, whiting and haddock.

North Isles Shellfish at **Crowness Crescent, Hatston Industrial Estate, Kirkwall, Orkney** (tel 0856 876161) *sell live lobsters, brown and velvet crabs, dived scallops and razor fish, known locally as 'spoot ebb'. Raw or lightly grilled or fried, they have the texture of squid but the taste of a scallop.*

CONON BRIDGE   MAP 8

Struan Apiaries ✉ 🔢   HONEY

Burnside Lane, Conon Bridge, Ross-shire, Highlands & Islands IV7 8EX

TEL & FAX *0349 61427* **CONTACT** *Hamish Robertson* **HOURS** *Mon-Fri 9.00-18.00* **CARDS** *Access, Visa* **DIRECTIONS** *In the village centre, opposite the post office.*

One of the more flattering descriptions the Romans granted us was 'the Isle of Honey'. In those days our countryside was naturally forested and buzzed with colonies of wild black bees, a strain most suited to the climate as they are very hardy indeed. It is not, however, the strain of bees that affects the taste of the honey but the nectar – the strain only influences how hard the bees work. Different flowers produce different nectars that vary considerably in composition of quantity and types of sugar and other trace elements. The characteristics of honey – its taste, aroma and colour – depend on the nectar from which it comes.

The best and most expensive honey is mono-floral (single flower) that is made predominantly, and legally – according to Hamish Robertson – with a content of no less than 75%, of the nectar of the flowers of a single species. At its most superb, it has a unique flavour and aroma. It can be quite delicate or quite strong, depending on the flower. Like an estate-bottled wine, it should have plenty of distinctive character that varies from to year according to the climate. Poly-floral (many flower) honey is produced from several different species of flowers from within an area; and blended honey comes from different flowers and places mixed together by a honey packer, resulting in a bland undistinguished product that generally lacks character and vitality.

Struan Honey produce a range of mono-floral honey in 45 g ($1\frac{1}{2}$ oz) jars. They run about 400 hives themselves with a few local beekeepers working with them. They shift their hives about several times during the season to be near the different blossoms and flowers. Even then, bee-keepers can be thwarted, as bees can in theory buzz off as far as three miles in any direction. In practice, Hamish Robertson told me, 'Nature sorts itself out rather well. It produces a high density of flowers from particular crops at particular times of the year and the bees work the flowers to a maximum of one crop'. To emphasize the flavour further from that particular flower, Hamish extracts the honey from the combs each time he moves the hives and changes the combs.

Thus they produce a raspberry honey made around the fields of the local fruit farm that is delicately fruity and pale-white; an oil-seed rape that I usually find bland and over-sweet, but here had a surprising depth; a pert clover; a flowery, almost port-wine-coloured bell heather; and a powerful thixotropic (jelly-like) ling heather. From the woods of 2 local estates, Foulis and Castle Leod come a sycamore and chestnut honey, with a good nutty flavour; a deep rich lime (from the estates) and, at certain times of the year, the Scottish blossom which contains a large proportion of willow herb for a particularly delicate aroma.

These are all delightful honeys worth savouring, the only drawback being Struan's irritating ordering system. At the moment, apart from heather and blossom, they sell their honeys as random selections; this means that you cannot choose your flavours nor will you be guaranteed to receive every flavour even if you order all the selections. A pity that, and I do wish they would do something about it.

While in theory anything can be smoked, in practice it is not always worthwhile. Smoked scallops I hesitate to recommend unreservedly as I find smoking masks rather than enhances their sweet succulence – none the less try them for yourself. Set in half shells and sold as smoked king, queen or princess scallops from **Benesther Shellfish, Duncans, Deerness, Orkney, KW17 2QH (tel 0856 74 267, fax 0856 74 214)**. *They also produce smoked salmon, Orkney whisky smoked salmon with the sides 'rubbed with Orkney's famous Highland Park Malt whisky during the smoking process', smoked salmon sausage, and smoked oysters and mussels.*

The Shetland Smokehouse ✉ ▦   SMOKED SALMON

Skeld, Shetland, Highlands & Islands ZE2 9NS

TEL *059586 251* **FAX** *059586 203* **CONTACT** *Debbie Hammond* **HOURS** *Mon-Fri 7.30-16.30* **CARDS** *Access, Visa* **DIRECTIONS** *On the west side of the mainland.*

When writing *The Salmon Cookbook*, Tessa Hayward was lucky enough to spend time researching on Shetland. When I asked her whose smoked salmon she liked the best, she recommended The Shetland Smokehouse 'for hitting the right strength, neither too mild nor too strong'. They process salmon farmed to the Shetland Salmon Farmers' Association which issues, and here I quote Tessa, 'its own directives, which often, especially with regard to the use of chemicals, go well beyond the government's requirements. For instance, if, for any reason, antibiotics have been prescribed, a statutory period must elapse before the fish can be harvested. In Shetland this period is lengthened and then sample fish are tested and passed by Shetland Seafood Quality Control as residue-free and suitable for harvesting'. Equally if the fish are treated with chemicals to eliminate sea-lice 'similar safety precautions are adopted'.

Incidentally Tessa assures me that if any fish have been contaminated by the recent spillage from the oil-tanker Braer, there is no way they would be passed after being tested for chemicals and pollutants nor would the SSFA risk their reputation by allowing them to be sold. So, assured of a quality farmed salmon, The Shetland Smokehouse dry-cure it for about 6-12 hours and then smoke it over oak for about the same time for a moderate smoke. They also hot-smoke salmon by a time-consuming process of changing the temperature in their modern kiln 3 times; the first smoke dries out the fish, the temperature is raised to 'seal' it and finally, at an even higher temperature, to 'cook' it. They smoke herrings for kippers, cold-smoke fillets of cod and haddock, and hot-smoke mackerel.

Highland Fine Cheeses ✉ ▦ ♟
CROWDIE & CABOC CHEESE

Knockbreck, Tain, Ross-shire, Highlands & Islands IV19 1LZ

TEL *0862 892034* **CONTACT** *Susannah Stone* **HOURS** *Mon-Fri 9.30-17.00*
DIRECTIONS *Follow Tain high-street north past the Royal Hotel and take the second right at the St Duthus Hotel into Shore road. Follow the road and turn left at the bottom of the hill opposite the tractor garage. Follow the road along the high wall until you come to the sign for the farm.*

Susannah Stone is one of the great talkers of the cheese world. She can chatter away for hours about her cheeses, completely intriguing you as she sets their historical context; but she tells you very little about how she makes them. This is done for good reason, as Caboc – a chieftain's cheese enjoyed by Susannah's ancestors – is a fiercely guarded secret. Sublimely rich (as it is made with double cream) and rolled in toasted pinhead oatmeal, it comes from the Western Isles and lays claim to be one of Scotland's oldest cheeses. No one but Susannah knows how to make it and as she says firmly, 'they don't need to'. With a beady eye for the future, she has willed 'the funny old recipe from my grandmother for my sons to read when I die'.

About Crowdie ('*gruth*' in Gaelic), she is marginally more forthcoming. It is an old Highland cheese 'and only made in the Highlands and Islands, and it's so darn simple – only cooked curd that's citrusy tasting'. In the old days, Susannah told me, it was made by the crofters; they left a bowl of whole fresh milk to sour by the windowsill or near the stove, at some point skimming it to remove the cream. Once the milk had thickened, it was heated on the stove 'until scrambled, tipped in to muslin, drained, mashed with a fork with, if they could afford it, a little cream and mostly it was eaten fresh. Susannah makes her Highland Crowdie more or less the same way – minus the cream as hers is a low-fat cheese.

Gruth Dhu (black Crowdie) is Crowdie mixed with double cream and rolled in toasted pinhead oats and black pepper; Hramsa, sold in pots, is Crowdie mixed with double cream and the 'all-healing herb', wild garlic and white and red pepper; Galic is Hramsa rolled in crumbled and flaked hazlenuts and almonds that by Susannah's admission, 'are not very authentic.'; Highland soft, in spite of its name, is a soft full-fat lowland cheese from Ayrshire. All her cheeses are made with pasteurized cows' milk from 'three nearby chosen farms' and all are made with a natural lactic acid rather than rennet. 'It's the key to their flavour, their fresh, sharp, lemony taste – rennet would kill that off. And it isn't original anyway'...and Susannah would never agree to that.

And Also...

* *Poyntzfield Herb Nursery* ✉, Black Isle, by Dingwall (tel 03818 352) has a wide range of culinary herb plants and seeds including Japanese horseradish and rock samphire.
* Wine writer Andrew Jefford describes the Silver Birch wine from *Highland Wineries* ✉, Moniack Castle, Kirkhill, Inverness (tel 0463 83283) as 'haunting but mildly oppressive'. Try it or any of their other country wines and preserves.
* *Macdonald's Smoked Produce* ✉, Glenuig, Lochailort (tel 068 77 266) smokes 'everything but cigarettes'. Apart from the usual fish, their extensive list features alligator (apparently it tastes a bit like a cross

between pork and haddock), tuna, red snapper and even ostrich.

• *Peerie Smokehouses* ✉, right on the end of the pier at The Harbour, Nairn (tel 0667 53750) cure salmon in salt and whisky and smoke it in a 100-year-old kiln for a mere 5 hours. They also smoke mussels, prawns, trout and customers' own venison and pheasant to order.

• *Letterfinlay Game Services* ✉, The Boathouse, Letterfinlay, Spean Bridge (tel 0397 712626, fax 0397 712510) supply hung and smoked game. They also smoke Aberdeen Silverside brined to 'a secret recipe' and cold-smoked over whole oak logs.

• *Rothie Murchus Fish Farm Shop* ✉, Rothie Murchus, Aviemore (tel 0479 810703) sell own-farmed red deer, and fresh and smoked trout from the fish farm behind the shop.

• *Orkney Seafoods* ✉, 10-12 Ayre Road, Kirkwall, Orkney (tel 085687 2173) smoke farmed salmon over beech and elder-wood and sell live lobsters caught around the Orkneys.

• *Orkney Seafayre* ✉, Marsdene, Grimbister, Orkney (tel 0856 76 544) farm Pacific oysters deep in the Bay of Firth.

• Reports please on *West Highland Dairy* ✉, Achmore, Stromeferry, nr Kyle (tel 0599 87203).

LOTHIAN

EDINBURGH   MAP 8

Macsween ✉ 🏆   HAGGIS

130 Bruntsfield Place, Edinburgh, Lothian EH10 4ES

TEL *031 229 1216* FAX *031 229 9102* CONTACT *John Macsween* HOURS *Mon-Fri 8.00-17.30 (-13.00 Wed) Sat 8.00-16.30* CARDS *Access, Visa, Mastercard* DIRECTIONS *About 1½ miles from the town centre.*

'Every country is celebrated for some culinary preparation,' writes Mistress Margaret Dods in *Cook and Housewife's Manual* in 1829, 'Accordingly the Spanish olio, the Italian macaroni, the French ragout, the Turkish pillau, and, though last not least, in our good love, the Scotch haggis, differing essentially as they do, are, nevertheless, all equally good after their kind. We give precedence to the "Great chieftain of the pudding race"'.

For the past 40 years, John Macsween has been making the Great Chieftain and although I lay claim to no great expertise in the matter, his are far and away the best I've tasted. In that time his methods and ingredients have barely changed, although he has made the odd adjustment at the suggestion of his customers. Here may I suggest that if you are squeamish you hastily turn the page.

Mr Macsween's haggises are made with sheep's pluck – the lung, heart and liver. Now I've come across recipes that include minced meat of sheep's head, leg of mutton, beef marrow and ox liver, but that – according to him – is not on. The proportion of liver is, however, a question of debate as, 'if you add too much, it's overpowering. We only use a very little liver. The pluck is cooked and minced and is mixed with beef body back fat, which in Mr MacSween's view is infinitely preferable to the more normal suet as 'it doesn't cook out keeps the meat moist and gives a much cleaner taste'. Next comes oatmeal from the Borders in 2 grists, pinhead and medium, 'over the years we've changed the proportions as we want to keep the texture moist but crumbly, so it doesn't stick together'. Then onions are added 'dried as it is easier, otherwise we'd have to peel 140 pounds a day', followed by seasoning 'we make up ourselves as its purer, we know what's in it and anyway it's cheaper' of salt, black and white pepper, nutmeg, mace and coriander and finally a little 'gravy' from the boiling meat.

Everything is mixed together, put into a hopper, with the 'bung' (the bovine equivalent of an appendix) fixed around the nozzle. 'We only use natural casings. For a haggis between $\frac{1}{2}$ to 5 lb we use the bungs, for the sizes upwards to 18 pounds we use the sheep's bag that's also called stomach or paunch'. The haggises are filled in a long link and clipped with a metal clip, 'in the old days we used string and I can honestly say that is the only difference in how we make them now'. The links of haggis are put back in the hot water and gently cooked for about 45 minutes or until the required inner temperature is reached (and it's the hot water that makes the skin contract so they assume the shape of a tight round ball). Left to cool, they are ready for dispatch.

All you need to do is to wrap them in foil (in case you allow it to boil and the skin bursts) and gently simmer it for about 45 minutes per 450 g (1 lb), then it's ready. Moist, crumbly and spoonable – if you can slice a hot haggis there is something badly wrong with its texture – it has a mild meatiness and a rich nuttiness and a noticeably clean aftertaste (so many I've tried cloy the mouth). Incidentally as Mr Macsween believes that eating haggis is a ritual, he caters for vegetarians with a haggis containing black kidney beans, lentils, swedes, onions, carrots and mushrooms, in case they should feel left out on Burns' Night.

Butchers **A. Crombie & Son** ✉, **97-101 Broughton Street, Edinburgh, EH1 3RZ (tel 031 556 7643)** *make about 22 different sausages. Using pork from what they class as 'welfare pigs', they produce a special Pork, an Italian-style flavoured with aniseed and fennel, Northumbrian leek, Pork & orange (with grated zest), Spicy cajun and Toulouse with red wine, garlic & parsley. Wild venison from the Balmoral Estate and pork 'for a bit of moistness' are turned into venison sausages, and they also are well known for their haggis.*

The Shortbread House of Edinburgh ✉

SHORTBREAD

14 New Broompark, Edinburgh, Lothian EH5 1RS

TEL *031 552 0381* FAX *031 552 0027* CONTACT *Anthony Laing – mail order only*

Inevitably there are good and bad shortbreads in Scotland. F. Marian McNeill writes in *The Scots Kitchen* in 1929 that for the finest quality shortbread the ingredients are flour, rice flour, butter and caster sugar and, 'Only the best materials must be used. The flour should be dried and sieved. The butter... should be squeezed free of all water. The sugar should be fine caster sugar. Two other things are essential for success – the careful blending of the ingredients and careful firing.'

The Shortbread House makes on a commercial scale, but they are careful to keep to the old formula. Their ingredients are white flour, rice flour for 'thickening and firming up the mix so it's not too crumbly', extra fine sugar and butter which is, as Anthony Laing rightly points out, is 'the most crucial ingredient'. It goes without saying that it must be fresh (and I have tasted several shortbreads that leave a nasty rancid aftertaste). Surprisingly, he favours New Zealand butter as it is 'richer and more mature'; apparently too pale and too young a butter is no good for shortbread. He also adds a good quality vegetable shortening to lighten the mix and to ensure the biscuits remain moist. Anthony knows of no other bakeries who do this and, although it may not be strictly adhering to the McNeill rules, it works. Above all others I tried, theirs is light, delicately crumbly, rich and superbly buttery.

They are sold in 190 g ($6\frac{3}{4}$ oz) packets or distinctive dark blue and gold 500 g (1 lb 2 oz) tins, as hand-cut fingers, round biscuits, or 'petticoat tails' (fan-shaped). F. Marian McNeill has 2 possible explanations for this name. 'An English traveller in Scotland...states... that "petticoat tails" is a corruption of the French *petites gatelles* (sic)... though we rather think (it) has its origin in the shape of the cakes, which is exactly that of the bell-hoop petticoats...' They also make stem ginger shortbread, Oaties (sweet biscuits with grated coconut), and a spiced Dundee cake.

George Campbell & Sons ✉ ▦

SMOKED SALMON

The Smokehouse, West Harbour Road, Granton, Edinburgh, Lothian EH5 1RF

TEL *031 552 0376* FAX *031 551 1149* CONTACT *Iain Campbell* HOURS *Mon-Fri 7.00-16.00 Sat 8.00-11.00* CARDS *Visa, Amex* DIRECTIONS *Just off Granton Square.*

About 90% of the produce is own-grown or own-made at **Knowes Farm Shop** ✉, *by East Linton, Dunbar, EH42 1XJ* *(tel 0620 860010)*. *Cauliflower, calabrese and main-crop potatoes (Maris Piper and Pentland Squire) are grown on a field scale, but on a smaller scale especially for the shop they grow unsprayed vegetables and customers can ask to have them picked at baby-size. These include carrots, parsnips, courgettes, various cabbages and dwarf French beans. There about 15 different fresh herbs, radicchio and Iceberg lettuce, and potatoes include the ideal chipper, Golden Wonder, Pink Fir Apple and Scotland's favourite roaster Kerr's Pink. They also make marmalade, a range of Hedgerow Harvest jams, jellies and chutneys, herb vinegars, ready-meals and 8 different frozen soups. In season they sell local soft fruit and asparagus with own-made cartons of hollandaise sauce.*

A family business, George Campbell & Sons was established in 1872; they were granted a Royal Warrant in 1968 and now supply Holyrood House with fish and poultry when the Firm are in residence. Although they have closed their Edinburgh shop, you can still buy from the factory.

Their list of game is comprehensive and it comes from shoots all over Scotland. Apart from grouse in season from August 12th to December 10th, and pheasant from October 1 to February 1, it very rarely includes ptarmigan from August 12 to December 10th and capercaillie from October 1 to January 31st. These last two birds are both members of the grouse family, but thought to be inferior in eating quality to the Red or Scottish grouse (usually just known as grouse). Snipe is available from August 12 to January 31 and woodcock from September 1 to January 31. Although the latter's season starts in August, they are plumper and better for the table by the beginning of September when they have fattened up.

They also sell an amazing range of whole and filleted fresh fish, with varieties varying according to the season. Smoked salmon is available throughout the year from Scottish farmed salmon; smoked over oak chips it has a rich smoky flavour and comes as whole, trimmed or pre-sliced sides, weighing between 675 g-1.5 kg (1½-3½ lb) or sliced 115-450 g (4 oz-1 lb) packs. (✉ Smoked salmon only.)

And Also...

• *Henderson's Farm Shop* at 92 Hanover Street, Edinburgh (tel 031 225 6694) is wholly vegetarian. They sell organic fruit, vegetables and salads, own-made marmalade and lemon curd, cheeses made with vegetarian rennet, a good range of breads and cakes, and oatcakes baked in their own bakery.

• *Rowland's* ✉, 42 Howe Street, Edinburgh (tel 031 225 3711) keeps a few on-farm Scottish cheeses at a time, including Bonchester (see page 328), Lanark (see page 361) and Stichill (see page 331). They make their own terrines, pâtés and salads and ready-meals.

• *George Armstrong*, 80 Raeburn Place, Edinburgh (tel 031 315 2033) has a good display of wet fish and shellfish and in the smoke-house at the back smokes salmon, both wild and farmed, trout and scallops.

• Delicatessen *Victor Hugo* ✉ at 26-27 Melville Terrace, Edinburgh (tel 031 667 1827) stocks at least a dozen different rye breads and a good selection of on-farm British cheeses.

Valvona & Crolla ✉, *19 Elm Row, Edinburgh, EH7 4AA (tel 031 556 6066, fax 031 556 1668) is the Italian deli of the North. As well as Parmesan, salamis, fresh pasta and one of the best selection of Italian wines and olive oils, expect to find good indigenous produce. British on-farm cheeses include Bonchester (see page 328), Lanark Blue (see page 361), Stichill (see page 331), Isle of Mull Cheddar, Cornish Yarg (see page 38) and Clifton from Innes (see page 234). There is Bresaola-style Aberdeen Angus beef from Champney's of Linlithgow, fresh herbs and vanilla and strawberry ice-cream from Luca's of Mussleburgh. Very much a family shop, all the relations go out on tutored mushroom forays and bring back chanterelles and porcini (ceps) to sell in the shop and they organize wine tastings and cookery demonstrations throughout the year. During the Festival this year, they promise a special 'sing-song' celebrating the joys and pitfalls of Scottish/Italian life.*

STRATHCLYDE

BENDERLOCH   **MAP 8**

Scottish Shellfish ✉   SHELLFISH

Lochnell Estate, Old Farm Court Yard, Benderloch, by Oban, Argyllshire, Strathclyde PA37 1QV

TEL *0631 72 350* **FAX** *0631 72 581* **CONTACT** *George Burton – mail order only*

Shellfish farming is relatively new to the West Coast of Scotland; it includes the growing of oysters, mussels and scallops. Unlike salmon farming, shellfish farming causes virtually no pollution of the sea lochs as very few – if any – chemicals are used, the stocking densities are lower, the shellfish feed naturally and expel little waste.

Mussels are cultivated by rope culture: hairy ropes are suspended from rafts or long lines, the spats (mussel larvae) attach themselves to the ropes, feed on plankton and are harvested when about 2 years old. According to George Burton the advantage of a farmed over a 'wild' mussel is that it has a better meat-to-shell ratio. One of the reasons for this is that their mussels are submerged in water the whole time, so they grow quicker and only produce a light thin shell. Unlike wild mussels, with their deep purple and black shells, farmed mussels are the colour of a tiger's eye, dark brown flecked with gold. Sold live with their bibus (beard) attached as, George maintains, if it is pulled out it kills them, they are in season from June to March.

Scallop farming is only marginally more complex. The scallop spats are caught in spat collectors, they attach themselves to the sides of the nets and as their shell begins to grow, they drop off into the bottom of the collector. If they were left to grow naturally, they would settle on the sea-bed; instead they are transferred to lantern nets suspended in the water and, apart from protecting them from predators and thinning them out after about 2 years, they need little more attention. Again, according to George, there are several advantages of buying a farmed scallop: firstly it has a known age – scallops are usually around 5 years when harvested, whereas a dived or dredged scallop can be anything up to 20 years old and quite tough at that; the texture of a farmed scallop's muscle (the white meat we eat) tends to be finer as, so the theory goes, it has not had to fight for its survival; also, because it is suspended in mid-water which is far richer in plankton and algae than the sea-bed, it has a higher meat content. Farmed scallops come as Kings, with a top flat and bottom concave shell and a muscle measuring about 5 cm (2 in) in diameter; Queens are smaller with both shells concave and their white meat is sweeter and about the size of a new 10p piece; and Princesses are immature Queens with a muscle the size of a new 5p piece. In season from December to September, if you are particularly

---

Taylor's of Waterside Bakery ✉, **Waterside Street, Strathaven, ML10 6AW (tel 0357 21260)** *bakes an interesting range of thoroughly traditional Scottish cakes, biscuits, breads and scones, plus a couple of 'novelty' ones. Traditional lines include a buttery shortbread, oatcakes baked freshly at least once a week, gingerbread, a firm honey bread, Scotch bun made with butter as 'it's not necessary to use vegetable fats'. From the hot-plate, there are drop scones, pancakes, crumpets, and thin triangular potato scones made with mashed potato. Apart from the more usual breads, there is an Oatie loaf made with white flour and flaked oats; a round white Crusty cut into 4 peaks that were supposed to be 4 church spires to frighten away the Devil; an Italian loaf flavoured with olive oil, Scottish Cheddar, fresh onion, garlic and black olives; a tomato & herb loaf made from olive oil, tomato paste, mixed herbs, garlic and a smidgen of cheese. (✉ Shortbread and black bun only.)*

---

fond of the coral, the best time to buy them is between February to April when at their plumpest.

Farmed Pacific oysters (see Loch Fyne Oysters, page 00) are available all year round. Graded by size in 70-80 g ($2\frac{1}{2}$-$2\frac{3}{4}$ oz), 80-95 g ($2\frac{3}{4}$-$3\frac{1}{4}$ oz) and 'regal', anything upwards from 95 g ($3\frac{1}{4}$ oz) and sometimes so big that it is a 'knife and fork job'. Oysters are sold purified and unpurified (some growers pass their oysters through UV tanks for about 48 hours, and keep them in aerated holding tanks until sold); the net result can be a loss of flavour. It should not be necessary as virtually all Scottish Shellfish oysters are grown in grade A (tops for purity) waters; the only exceptions are those farmed at Seil Island, but they are transferred to grade A waters for a month's clean-up before sale.

Now Scottish Shellfish exists as a marketing co-operative for 20 shellfish growers. If you order from them, they will supply shellfish grown to the Association of Scottish Shellfish Growers standards that take into account husbandry practice, shapes and sizes of the shellfish and the current legislation, and they guarantee to deliver to you within 24 hours of harvesting. Their members stretch from Loch Laxford, south of Cape Wrath, to as far south as Loch Tarbet in South Argyll; some farming in sea lochs, others in oceanic sites. It follows therefore that there may be a variation of flavour and, particularly in the case of the oysters, in saltiness. They will, however, supply you with produce from a particular farm. They also supply langoustines creel-caught from Lochs Linnie and Leven and dived scallops.

> **Creelers** ✉ at **The Home Farm, Brodick, Isle of Arran KA27 8DD (tel 0770 302810)** *are a seafood restaurant and shop. Tim and Fran James run their own boat out of Arran and buy from markets. You are likely to find, on the menu or in the shop, cod, monkfish, hake or haddock. They also have oysters, langoustines, Queen scallops and mussels. Lobsters and crabs are kept live in a tank or 'in the sea as we're so close' and they cure and cold-smoke trout and salmon and make a gravlax. (✉ Smoked fish only.)*

CAIRNDOW   MAP 8

Loch Fyne Smokehouse ✉ 🏪 ♣
OYSTERS & SMOKED SALMON

Clachan Farm, Ardkinglas, Cairndow, Argyllshire, Strathclyde PA26 8BH

TEL *04996 217* **FAX** *04996 234* **CONTACT** *Andy Lane or Johnny Noble* **HOURS** *Easter to end-Oct: 9.00-19.00; Nov to Easter: 9.00-17.00* **CARDS** *Access, Visa* **DIRECTIONS** *From Cairndow, take A83 towards Inveraray. Follow the road about 2 miles and shop is signposted on the right.*

At the head of Loch Fyne is Clachan Farm. With a view down the loch as far as the eye can see, it is a perfect place to stop for oysters and a glass of wine in the oyster bar or to buy them from the shop to take-away. The waters of Loch Fyne are rich in plankton; hence the fame of the fat, juicy and oily herring for Loch Fyne kippers. 'It was only 6 years ago' so Andy Lane told me 'that the basking sharks disappeared. It wasn't that they no longer liked the waters, but that one man from Ardrossan decimated the lot with a harpoon gun'. Last year there were sightings and, with bated breath, everyone around the loch is waiting to see whether they will come back. Obviously the pull of the rich waters is too strong for them to ignore.

Herring catching was banned 8 years ago in the Loch as stocks were decimated. Now it is allowed again 'but the trouble is the open season starts too soon in June when the stocks are young and scraggy. It's far too early as they haven't fattened up yet'. The best time is between August and November, when they are caught down loch, heading out to sea, between Campbeltown and Tarbet. Loch Fyne Smokehouse cure and smoke them, supplementing their stock with Minch herring. 'But we say so, which is more than some'. As Andy says rightly, because of their fine reputation, 'people try to pass off any old herring as a Loch Fyne'. He has even heard of curers resorting to using Norwegian, or worse still, Canadian fish.

The advantage of farming oysters in Loch Fyne is the richness of the feed. They buy in spats and lay them in sacks on racks on the shore. Depending whether the tides are spring or neap, they will be out of the water for 4 – 8 hours 'It does them good not to be covered continuously, as they learn to close properly and how to survive in air – essential, if like us, they are sent around the world'. Oyster farming strikes me as not being too arduous, as all you have to do is lay them down and leave them to grow, 'There's more to it than that' Andy insists, 'You constantly have to grade them out, otherwise the smaller ones will suffer, and you have to turn the bags to kill off the seaweed', Loch Fyne oysters take about 2 summers to reach their proper size. Hamish, a 14-year-old veteran oyster currently tips the scales at a massive 625g (1 lb 6 oz) and the similarly aged Mick the Mussel weighs 180 g (6¾ oz).

Apart from herring, Loch Fyne Smokehouse cure farmed salmon in salt and soft brown sugar for about 4-6 hours, then cold-smoke it for 4-8 hours. Many people, myself included, compare theirs to the famous London-smoke (see Formans page 176) as, at its best, it does have that yielding, mild texture and soft buttery flavour. They also smoke mussels, cod's roe, trout, and cure gravlax, as well as a new addition discovered through an accident with an over-heated kiln, Bradhan rost (Gaelic for roast salmon) – ie hot-smoked. From the shop you can also buy creel-caught langoustines, velvet crabs, Finnan haddies, scallops and clams – and once you stop, you will have to be very strong-minded not to indulge at the oyster bar.

> **The Cheese & Wine Shop** ✉, **112 George Street, Oban,
> PA34 5NN (tel 0631 64409)** *is a good shop to while away the
> hour if waiting for the ferry over to Mull. They stock over 100 malt
> whiskies, lots of Scottish cheeses with a new one to me called
> Cairnsmore Ewes' Milk and plenty of smoked local produce including
> the inevitable smoked salmon, venison and trout.*

> *Andrew Abrahams runs* **Isle of Colonsay Oysters** ✉ *and* **Isle of
> Colonsay Apiaries** ✉ *from* **The Strand, Isle of Colonsay, PA61
> 7YR (tel 09512 365)**. *Oysters are farmed Pacific, and honey is
> collected from hives scattered around the isle. The honey comes as a
> thick butterscotch-coloured Wildflower, with a light almost lemon
> fragrance, and Heather is thicker, darker with a powerful, lingering
> flavour.*

CARLUKE   MAP 8

Ramsay of Carluke 🐷   AYRSHIRE BACON

22 Mount Stewart Street, Carluke, Lanarkshire, Strathclyde
ML8 5ED

TEL 0555 772277 **FAX** 0555 750686 **CONTACT** *Andrew Ramsay* **HOURS**
Mon-Fri 8.00-16.30 Sat 8.00-12.30 **DIRECTIONS** *From Bogside, take A73
into the centre of Carluke. Take the first turning on the right after The
Crown Hotel into Mount Stewart Street. After about 100 yards, shop is
signposted on the right.*

Ramsay of Carluke are members of the National Q Guild of Butchers,
the group of Britain's top butchers. Their meat is perfectly good, but it is
perhaps for their Ayrshire-cure bacon that they are best known. Ayrshire
is similar to a Wiltshire cure in that both are brine cures but, and this is
the significant difference, for an Ayrshire cure the pig is skinned, the fat
trimmed to a layer about 1-2.5 cm ($\frac{1}{2}$-1 in) thick, and the side boned
before curing.

Using Large White-Landrace cross farm pigs with 'no hormones, no
injections and no boars because of possible taint – but not free-range,' as
Andrew Ramsay thinks they are tasteless, Ramsay slaughter and skin the
pigs themselves, split them down the middle into full sides of the gigot
(leg), middle and fore, bone them out and trim them. The sides are
pickled (cured) for about 2 days in a solution of salt, water, saltpetre
and sodium nitrate, then stacked to drain for up to 2 weeks. Andrew's
family have been curing for the last 150 years and as he stresses, 'the
water content of our bacon when we sell it is 0%'.

The bacon sides are either smoked by them over hardwood chips for
about 6 hours for a mild finish or left green; then they are cut up into

Ayrshire gigot, sold mostly as gammon steaks; Ayrshire fore, sliced as bacon; and Ayrshire middle, rolled up whole and sold in the round surrounded by a circle of gleaming fat, or separated into back and streaky rashers. It may have slightly more fat than mass-processed bacon, but its full-bodied taste cannot be compared. With the resilient texture of proper 'old-fashioned' bacon, cooking it is a pleasure; it does not spit or shrink, nor does it leave an unfortunate pool of scum in the pan – always a sign of a badly cured bacon or one that has been pumped up with polyphosphates. The Scottish Gourmet (see below) will send it to you anywhere in the country, or if you live in London you can buy it at Justin de Blank's (see page 169).

The Scottish Gourmet ✉, **Thistle Mill, Station Road, Biggar, ML12 6LP (tel 0899 21001, fax 0899 20456)** *is a mail-order food club. Anyone can join for an annual subscription of £9.95 and, for that, they receive 12 monthly newsletters, recipes and an order form. Food divides into 2 categories: ready-food, cooked by chef Bernard Alessi, delivered chilled for you to reheat and assemble; or raw ingredients that you can cook. The selection changes each month; looking at the catalogue for last May, I discovered 80/- (shilling) Pancakes that arrive as 6 pancakes with, packed separately, a filling of Aberdeen Angus ground steak cooked with 80/- Ale from Edinburgh's Caledonian Brewery and blended with butter and mace. Other regional delights were Scapa Flan made with smoked salmon and smoked scallops 'brought up by divers from the perilous Scapa Flow' and Caledonian Collops, 'oblong slices of venison cut from the haunch...in a gravy of Moniack blaeberry wine and Pentland heather honey with mushrooms, onions and the traditional addition of pickled walnuts'. It sounds interesting but, as I'm not a member, I can't tell you what it tastes like. On the ingredients front you can order Ramsay's of Carluke Ayrshire-cure bacon (see page 359), wild boar steaks, Loch Fyne kippers and marinated wild venison from Johnny Rutherford of Burnside. They also send out smoked salmon (May's was chosen from Michael and Karen Leng of Alba Foods), cheeses from Ann Dorward cheeses (see page 362) and Susannah Stone (see page 349), and cakes from Hossacks (see page 331), Houstons (see page 331) and Goodfellow & Steven (see page 367) and lots more. They always make a point of emphasizing the names and locations of all their producers, so you will know the pedigree of the food. On the other hand, another mail-order food service* **Highland & Island Food Company** ✉, **Ferngrove Fine Foods, Ferngrove, Kilmun, PA23 8SB (tel 036984 334 fax 036984 424),** *don't. They have a wide selection, but smoked salmon is smoked salmon, oatcakes are oatcakes; with no further details other than weight, packaging and price.*

H. J. Errington & Co ✉ ⊞ ♟   LANARK CHEESE

Braehead Farm, Walston, Ogscastle, Carnwath, Lanarkshire,
Strathclyde ML11 8NF

TEL & FAX *089 981 257* **CONTACT** *Humphrey Errington* **HOURS** *Mon-Fri*
7.00-16.00 **DIRECTIONS** *From Carnwath, take A721 towards Peebles. After*
about 3 miles, turn left signposted Walston. After about ¼ mile, go straight
over the cross-roads and farm is signposted about 300 yards on the right.

The 'First Statistical Account of Scotland', a detailed assessment of the
state of the countryside prepared in the 1790s, mentions the sheep's-
milk cheese made in the parish of Dunsyre. Further research by
Humphrey Errington revealed that there was a tradition all over the
Upper Tweed and Clyde Valleys of using sheep's milk for cheese that
blued spontaneously. Cheese-making died out with the Industrial
Revolution, but it seemed only natural to Humphrey, when he and his
family moved to the 300-m (1,000-ft) plateau between the valleys, to
attempt to revive the craft. He deliberately set out to recreate the same
style of cheese. Like John Curtis (see page 328), Humphrey was greatly
helped by Janet Galloway, a dairy technologist who had worked in
Roquefort, and they were both struck by the similarity between the
cheeses. Thus Lanark Blue evolved using the unpasteurized milk from
his 400-strong Friesland dairy flock crossed with the hardier Gray Face.

The essential difference between Lanark Blue (and Roquefort) and a
Stilton (and most of our other Blue territorials) is that whereas a Stilton
is left to mature and form a crust and is pierced only after several weeks
to encourage blueing, Lanark Blue is brined and rubbed in salt and
pierced within a few days of making. It results in a creamy but sharp
blue cheese with a far crumblier texture and a lingering aftertaste. Using
the same recipe, Humphrey also makes Dunsyre Blue – with a rich, silky
sweet flavour – from the unpasteurized milk of a neighbouring Ayrshire
herd collected daily by tractor.

The actual process of making both cheeses is 'surprisingly simple';
the milk is started, inoculated with *penicillium rocquefortii*, then a
vegetarian rennet is added. The curd is cut 'and we hardly stir it',
drained, packed into 3 kg (6½ lb) moulds and left to settle naturally over
4 days. The cheeses are brine-dipped, rubbed all over with salt and then
pierced when about 6 days old. They go to the maturing room for about
3 months, where they are turned every day and, at some point, wrapped
in foil to discourage surface mould. Humphrey also produces
Humphrey's Revenge, 'a serious cheese, it's creamy soft and very strong'.
It comes from Dunsyre that 'I take on for about a year. It only works
with the October and November cheeses, and I've never discovered
why'. None the less it has many 'private fans' and is sold at a few select
shops including Valvona & Crolla in Edinburgh (see page 355).

> ⬛ **Star Continental Bakery** ✉, *158 Fore Street, Scotstoun,*
> *Glasgow, G14 OAE (tel 041 959 7307) sell their Polish,*
> *Italian and Kosher (under the supervision of Beth Din) breads direct*
> *from the bakery. Banaura, a 'health bread' made from 100%*
> *wholemeal, has a certain reputation in the West of Scotland for keeping*
> *one regular. Reports on it and the rest of their range please.*

STEWARTON MAP 8

Ann Dorward ▦ DUNLOPPE CHEESE

West Clerkland Farm, Stewarton, Ayrshire, Strathclyde
KA3 5LP

TEL *0560 482494* **CONTACT** *Ann Dorward – telephone ahead*

Ann Dorwood has been making cheese 'seriously' for about 4 years now. She makes 3 pasteurized cheeses from more or less the same recipe with the 3 milks – cows', goats' and sheep's. Swinzie (named after a nearby burn or stream), hard-pressed and matured for 6 months, is made with the milk from her Friesland flock of sheep; Bonnet (also the local name for Stewarton) is made with a mixture of own and bought-in goats' milk and matured for 3-4 months; and Dunloppe (spelled the old way), is made with 'black and white' (Friesian) milk bought in from one farm.

Dunlop was thought to be the first 'sweet-milk' or full-cream hard cheese made in Scotland. It originated in the parish of Dunlop in Ayrshire due to the cheese-making skills of a Barbara Gilmour. Stories tell of how she came from Ireland with the recipe and settled in Dunlop in 1688 to make cheese; but as Patrick Rance rightly points out Ireland was not renowned for its cheese-making. It was far more likely she was exiled from England, where she had learnt to make the cheese in the first place, to Ireland only finally to settle in Scotland. Be that as it may, it was she who first made the cheese. Dunlop is often compared with Cheddar and is made to a very similar recipe, although it is softer-textured and lacks Cheddar's 'bite'. Ann matures her Dunloppe for about 6 months for a mild, creamy and relatively close-textured cheese. ✉ For mail order information see Scottish Gourmet (page 360).

TAYNUILT MAP 8

Inverawe Smokehouses ✉ ⬛ BOTARGO

Taynuilt, Argyll, Strathclyde PA35 1HN

TEL *08662 446* **FAX** *08662 274* **CONTACT** *Robert Campbell-Preston* **HOURS** *9.00-18.30* **CARDS** *Access, Visa, Mastercard* **DIRECTIONS** *From Crianlarich, take A85 towards Oban. Drive through Dalmally and after about 10 miles, just before Taynuilt, turn right at the signpost for the smokery.*

If you stand on tippy-toes, you can just see Loch Etive through the trees from Inverawe Smokehouses. In the brackish waters of the loch trout are farmed and in the smoke-house Robert Campbell-Preston smokes them and extracts their eggs for botargo.

To call it botargo, from the Arab *batarkhah* or *batarekh* is misleading; strictly speaking, as Tom Stobart writes in *The Cook's Encyclopaedia*, that is the salted, pressed, dried female roe of either the tuna or the Striped Grey Mullet. Robert's trout version is cured rather than dried and left unpressed. The idea occurred to him while visiting a food fair in Germany; there he saw the Scandinavians displaying cured and unpressed salmon eggs. Salmon eggs though, were out of the question as in Scotland it is illegal even to handle them. This is, as Robert told me, because salmon roe makes the best bait ever; apparently if you make a 'mush' with the roe and throw it in the river, you'll attract every male fish within miles – a poacher's idea of heaven. As he was already handling the trouts' roe when gutting the fish and 'just chucking them out', it occurred to him to try using trouts' eggs.

Only roe between October and December can be used, just before the fish start breeding; if you leave it later when they are breeding between January and March, the roe is hard and tastes 'foul and bitter'. What Robert does is to extract the roe from the fish and griddle the eggs out from the membrane; he cleans them, matures them overnight in salt, then pots them in 55 g (2 oz) glass jars ready for sale. The roes can be frozen in the membrane for the rest of the year without affecting their taste or texture. It sounds simple enough, but it took him 3 years to get the technique right and he reckons he is still learning. I love his botargo, little (they are smaller than salmon eggs) bright orange balls that pop in your mouth with a mild saltiness and a delicate taste of fish; they are a poor man's caviar, but far more interesting than the ubiquitous lumpfish roe. I use them on canapés or even with a pasta sauce of sour cream and fresh chopped dill, just spooning a few on top.

Apart from the trout, Inverawe also smoke wild and fresh salmon, eel from Loch Awe, and herring from the North Sea for Inverawe kippers. Using a series of brick smoke-houses, they smoke on the Pinney principle – in fact, Robert was taught by Mr Pinney of Orford (see Butley's, page 240) – of burning oak logs on the floor of the smoke-house with the fish suspended around it. They also sell venison, Argyll ham, beef and duck smoked by Roy Forsyth at Spean Bridge.

And Also...

• Fishmongers *Alex S. Walker* of 7 Park Place, Biggar (tel 0899 20243) buy their wet fish from the market at Newhaven on the Forth. Salmon cured in brown sugar and Drambuie is smoked for 3 nights – and only the nights – and they also produce a traditional undyed Finnan haddock.

• *Scales & Tails* at 455a Great Western Road, Glasgow (tel 041 339 4288) sells a good selection of wet fish and shellfish displayed on a large bed of ice. *Roots & Fruits* (tel 041 334 3530), their shop next door, sometimes has locally picked chanterelles and a few of the more unusual apple varieties in season.

• As the name suggests, *Das Brot*, 51 Hyndland Street, Partick, Glasgow (tel 041 334 8234) specializes in German-style breads and cakes. They bake about 15 different rye sour-dough breads, rye biscuits, Black Forest gâteau and cheesecake. Reports please.

• *Argyll Smoked Products* ✉, Eilean Beag, North Connel, Oban (tel 063 171 597) smoke duck, quail, chicken, wild boar and guinea fowl as well as salmon, kippers from Mallaig herrings, squid and trout.

• *Butchers James McIntyre* ✉ at 74 Montague Street, Rothesay (tel 0700 503672) make their own haggis and black and white puddings and a spiced suet pudding with plenty of fruit.

• *Tobermory Fish Farm* ✉ at Main Street, Tobermory, Isle of Mull (tel 0688 2120, fax 0688 2140) cure farmed trout and salmon in salt, herbs and spices, cold-smoke them over local wood, and send them as whole or sliced sides or in 115, 225 and 450 g (4, 8 oz and 1lb) packs.

• *Ritchies of Rothesay* ✉ at 111 Montague Street and 37 Watergate, Isle of Bute (tel 0700 505414) have a reputation for good fish as well as kippers, smoked salmon and salmon fish-cakes.

TAYSIDE

ABERFELDY   MAP 8

Aberfeldy Water Mill ✉ 🏪 ✒   OATMEAL

Mill Street, Aberfeldy, Tayside PH15 2BG

TEL *0887 820803* CONTACT *Tom Rodger* HOURS *Easter to end-Oct: Mon-Sat 10.00-17.30 Sun 12.00-17.30* DIRECTIONS *From Ballinluig, take A827 about 10 miles into the centre of Aberfeldy. Follow the road through the square and over the bridge. Take the first turning on the right after the bridge into Mill Street. Mill is signposted on the right.*

'Oats,' writes André Simon in his *Concise Encyclopaedia of Gastronomy* 'are the seeds of the cereal *Avena* which was already being cultivated in the days of Pliny. Oats will grow in colder and wetter climates and on poorer soils than any of the other cereals; also in hotter climates than either wheat or rye'.

Aberfeldy Water Mill, built in 1825 and restored by Tom Rodger in 1987, buy in their oats locally and only from organic (Soil Association approved) farmers because Tom thinks, 'the flavour is slightly better and

OATMEAL BREAD

Take 225 g (1/2 lb) of flour, 225 g (1/2 lb) oatmeal, 1 tsp salt, 1 tsp baking soda, 1 tsp cream of tartar, 300 ml (10 fl oz) buttermilk. Soak the oatmeal in the buttermilk for 2 hours, then add the flour mixed with the other dry ingredients, knead lightly, from into a loaf and bake in a hot oven (230°C/450°F/gas 8) for 30-40 minutes. (Adapted from André Simon's *Concise Encyclopaedia of Gastronomy*.)

it gives me peace of mind'. The oats arrive while still fresh and damp with a moisture content of around 14%; first they are dried in the kiln to take their moisture level down to around 5%. 'It's this that enhances the flavour and makes them nutty'. The next stage is to dress the oats to remove the weeds and any immature grains, which is done in a machine with varying sized sieves.

Then they are cracked by one se of millstones to remove their shells or husks, which are particularly hard and generally discarded, although André Simon writes of 'a sort of porridge called Sowens (q.v.) made from the husks'. The shells are blown off and the shelled oats are known as groats, 'A groat is an oat that has lost its coat' is the rhyme Tom repeats to the school children he shows around his mill. Finally the oats are ground in the other set of millstones into 3 grades: fine, 'a bit coarser than wheat flour' for a gruel or bannocks; medium for oatcakes, parkin and porridge; and coarse for a 'chewier porridge'. Sold in 500 g, 1 and 1.5 kg (1 lb 2 oz, $2\frac{1}{4}$ and $3\frac{1}{2}$ lb) bags, Tom claims his oats are so dry, they will keep for up to 12 months if stored properly.

*With so much to see at **Scone Palace, Perth (tel 0738 52308, fax 0738 52588)**, you may well miss the produce shop; but the preserves and marmalades are worth seeking out. Sold under the label of The Countess of Mansfield's Preserves. Damsons, for a meaty chutney, come from the Countess's garden in Shropshire, Garden pickle is made with fresh carrots, onions and apples and Spiced apricot & walnut is particularly well balanced. They also make a Seville orange marmalade, sold plain for traditionalists with a good cutting bite, or flavoured with whisky.*

ARBROATH   MAP 8

R. R. Spink & Sons ✉ ⚖   ARBROATH SMOKIES

33-35 Seagate, Arbroath, Angus, Tayside DD11 1BJ

TEL 0241 72023 **FAX** 0241 75663 **CONTACT** Bob Spink **HOURS** Mon 14.00-17.00 Tues-Fri 9.00-17.30 Sat 9.00-17.00 **DIRECTIONS** In town centre, near the harbour.

Scotland has always derived a large proportion of its income from the sea; fishing was once a major industry, with the more recent bonuses of oil and gas. For centuries fishing was concentrated around the East Coast as, although it had few natural harbours, the North Sea offered a seemingly inexhaustible supply of fish and the markets of the larger cities in the South were relatively easily accessible.

The fishermen lived in close communities scattered along the coastline. It was the womenfolk who dealt with the catch; they, rather than the men, would haggle over prices and developed crude ways of preserving fish so as to prolong the life of the haul. It was not until the 14th century that a Dutchman William Beukelsz found the answer to long-term preservation – dry-salting. He decreed that fish must be fresh; packed to exclude as much air as possible and that no liquid should be added. Thus the moment a catch was hauled aboard, all fish not destined to be sold as fresh were gutted, split, rinsed, layered in barrels and tightly packed with coarse salt. Prior to that fish had been wind-dried ('blawn') or sun-dried ('rizzar'd' or 'tiled') to make a flat, heavy-textured, chewy piece of fish that was possibly none too appetizing; Curious though it may sound, I have heard it suggested that it was often used as a bread substitute.

Haddock, like so many white fish, is at its best when caught from the cooler Northern waters when its flesh is denser, fatter and cleaner tasting. With a lower oil content than salmon, mackerel or herring, it has poorer keeping qualities. So, determinedly, the Scots continued

With numerous salmon smokers all over Scotland, **Dunkeld Smoked Salmon, Springwells Smokehouse, Brae Street, Dunkeld, Perthshire, PH8 0BA (tel 0350 727639, fax 0350 728760)** comes highly recommended. In the estuary of the river Tay, between Perth and Dundee, salmon are still commercially netted; and, as the smoke-house is but a short walk from the banks of the river, it is only natural they should specialize in wild Tay salmon. David and Wendy Louden claim the best of all salmon is caught early in the season, while newly in fresh water; once the salmon enter the river they stop feeding. They buy from the netters during July and August, when the price drops but before the fish are out of condition, 'with little flesh – just skin and roe'. They blast-freeze their stock to last throughout the year, cure them traditionally in dry salt for about 24 hours, and smoke them over oak sawdust and chips made from old whisky barrels 'to give them a bit of spirit' for 16-18 hours at about 26°C (79°F). The result is a mild smoke with a melt-in-the-mouth texture, either as whole unsliced or hand-sliced sides from 675 g (1½ lb) or hand- or machine-sliced packs from 115 g (4 oz). They offer an efficient service for anglers, even offering to collect their fish if they are too busy to leave the river banks.

refining the methods of preserving – 'reisted' (smoke-dried) became more popular as did 'spelding' (a method from the fishing village Collieston where haddock was split and dried on the rocks). From these methods evolved Arbroath Smokies.

Haddock is gutted and cleaned but not split open and the heads are removed; then they are dry-salted for around 2 hours, depending on the size and age of the fish. This is done both to reduce the moisture content of the flesh and to harden the skin to stop it from splitting open when the fierce heat is applied. The fish are tied by the tail into pairs of equal size, brushed and washed to get rid of the salt, draped over triangular wooden sticks and left to dry for a further 5 hours so that the skin hardens even further. Smoking originally took place in a half barrel (a whisky one, no doubt) dug into the ground, but now a brick pit dug 1 m (3 ft) deep is used. A hardwood log fire (usually oak or beech) is lit and, as the flames roar and rise above the pit, they are doused and the fish is immediately suspended above the fierce embers on its sticks. The pit is then covered with a hessian sheet and the fish are hot-smoked for about 45 minutes to lock in the flavour while, the theory is, the bone running up the centre retains the moisture. Pale gold, they are extraordinarily juicy and the fish flakes easily into satisfying chunks with a salty mellow taste. They also smoke salmon and sell wet-fish from the shop.

> *The raspberries of Blairgowrie have a reputation for their fine taste, but whether it is because of the climate or the limy soil no one seems too sure. Sadly, several of the growers are going out of business because of the competition from the Eastern European countries. Within the area you can still pick-your-own at **Bankhead** of **Kinloch, Meigle (tel 082 84265)** who has 6 acres of Glen Clover, Glen Moy and Glen Prosen raspberries, as well as Elsanta strawberries, redcurrants, blackcurrants and white currants and gooseberries; and at **Stiellsmuir Farm, Rosemount (tel 0250 872237)**. Picking starts around the second week of July, but it is wise to telephone ahead to check.*

BROUGHTY FERRY   **MAP 8**

Goodfellow & Steven ✉ 🦐   DUNDEE FRUIT CAKE

81-83 Gray Street, Broughty Ferry, Dundee, Tayside DD5 2BQ

TEL *0382 730181* **FAX** *0382 736041* **CONTACT** *David Goodfellow* **HOURS** *Mon-Sat 8.00-17.00* **DIRECTIONS** *From Dundee, take A930 towards Broughty Ferry. Follow road about 3 miles to the cross-roads, with The Occidental pub on the left. Turn right into Church Street. Take first turning on left into Brook Street. Follow road to centre of Broughty Ferry and turn right just before The Royal Arch pub into Gray Street. Shop is on right.*

What curious times – food-wise – these are in which we live. On one hand MAFF introduces legislation that renders it difficult for small-scale speciality food producers even to stay in business; on the other, MAFF is looking at introducing schemes to protect our products along the lines of the French Appellation Contrôlée d'Origine. The about-to-be-introduced schemes are currently rather cumbersomely entitled 'Protection of Geographical Names and Designation of Origin' and 'Products of Specific Character'. If accepted, it will mean traditional food/recipes will be protected and if – as in, say, Bakewell Pudding – they are named after a place, they will only be allowed to use that name if they are actually made in that place. So far, so good; but I believe it is only worth the paper it is written on if the food/recipe is authentic and uses the 'proper' ingredients, and if making it in a particular place affects the eating qualities of the end-product – for example, in the case of Wensleydale cheese where the milk should come from within the dale.

Dundee cakes are another matter. No two people can agree on what is a true Dundee cake – whether it should or should not contain sultanas and/or currants, glacé cherries, treacle, spices, whole or nibbed almonds, candied mixed or just orange peel, sherry or brandy or no alcohol at all. Even its origin is under dispute; it has been suggested that it is a descendent of Dundee gingerbread cake rather than, as I had always thought, an invention by Keillers because they needed some way of

The late Captain Donald MacLean was the potato enthusiast. His knowledge of potatoes knew no bounds and he loved them for their flavour, texture and colour. When I was working at the British Harvest restaurant, he came to see me, proudly sporting red, white and blue potatoes for a patriotic potato salad. However, in spite of both our pleas, we never were able to persuade the chef to put it on the menu. Captain Donald is much missed, but his widow carries on the good work and will supply tubers for a potato lover, in limited numbers as availability is scarce. The list is divided into Exhibition packs (varieties suitable for the show bench), Eelworm Resistant packs (varieties showing resistance to Potato Cyst Nematode), Museum Collection packs (older varieties of historic interest), Quality Eating packs, Quality Eating Individual Varieties, Salad and Gourmet Varieties, and Scarce and Unusual Varieties. Look out for such treasures as Cornes de Bique, an early main-crop with long thin white tubers; Pride of Bute, a long-shaped blue potato; the black-skinned Shetland Black and the blue-skinned and blue-fleshed Salad Blue. For details of the list and how to order, send a s.a.e. to **Mrs M. MacLean** ✉, **Dornock Farm, Crieff, Perthshire, PH7 3QN** *(tel 0764 652472). She also has 2 information leaflets available, Fact Sheet on 'Special Properties of Potato Varieties', revised 1990 (50p), and 'Growing Potatoes for Exhibition', 1987 (30p).*

using up the excess orange peel from their marmalade-making. However the original Mr Goodfellow, David's grandfather, knew the Keillers and believed the recipe did come from them.

That recipe is still used 'more or less', with various 'adjustments' for the fats (vegetable margarine instead of butter) and other ingredients; thus theirs contains plain white flour, eggs (pasteurized, not fresh), vegetable margarine and golden shortening, Primrose sugar (a golden brown bakers' sugar half-way between Demerara and white, that apparently has the advantage of 'not clagging'), sultanas, candied orange peel and 'Black Jack' (burnt sugar) to give it its deep gingerbread colour. Apparently a Dundee cake should not be too heavily fruited 'if it is, it's not a proper Dundee', so the Goodfellows mix in one-third fruit in proportion to the rest of the ingredients. On top there must be split almonds, turned to a golden brown, as they are put in place before the cake is baked. As for the taste, it is lighter and plainer than a fruit cake, with the barest hint of orange. The Goodfellows bake theirs straight in 750 g (1¾ lb) tins and seal them while still hot to create a vacuum; that way, unopened, they can last up to 2 years, although the Dundee is a cake that does not benefit from ageing and is best eaten fresh, straight out of the oven. It is an interesting cake but, on current standards, not one that would – or should – qualify for the Government's Protection of Geographical Names and Designation of Origin.

KINLOCH RANNOCH   MAP 8

Rannoch Smokery ✉   SMOKED WILD VENISON

Kinloch Rannoch, by Pitlochry, Perthshire, Tayside PH16 5QD
TEL *0882 632344* FAX *0882 632441* CONTACT *Leo Barclay – mail order only.*

With a smokery in the Highlands, Leo Barclay concentrates on smoking local produce. Wild Red deer shot on the surrounding estates comes to him via Highland Venison (see page 340) to ensure it is in good condition. He hangs it for about a week to develop the flavour as he found that if he let it go for longer, his customers would sometimes complain about a 'really gamy taste'. Leo butchers the haunch (leg) into the 3 main cuts – silverside, topside and thick flank for 'decent slices of meat from the three main muscles'. These he brines in a mixture of Muscovado sugar, salt and 'other secret ingredients' for about 3 days, then hangs them to dry for about 48 hours. Both these processes are done at a controlled temperature, which Leo considers 'really counts for the flavour and texture'.

Next comes the smoking, which takes about 3 days. He favours a heavy cold-smoke and uses oak chips from whisky barrels. Finally the venison is thinly sliced and vacuum packed in 100 or 250 g (¼ or ½ lb) packs, either as plain or marinated in olive oil and herbs. I have tried both, and both have an obvious gaminess lifted by a salty smoke; if I had to choose I would go for the marinated version, for its softer texture and its flavour enhanced by the herbs. They also make an interestingly meaty but comparatively mild smoked venison pâté with pork, cream, butter, red wine, spices and garlic, that is sold in pasteurized tubs weighing 115 g or 1 kg (4 oz or 2¼ lb); and throughout the year they hot-smoke pheasant and sell it vacuum-packed as whole birds or as two drumsticks or two breasts. Between August and January they also hot-smoke grouse and are planning to market properly hung Scottish Blackface lamb.

And Also...

• With the aim 'to provide good food with traditional flavour', *The Strathmore Larder* ✉, Cowford, Menmuir, Brechin (tel 0356 660238, fax 0356 660214) cure ham and bacon from their own or bought-in free-range pigs. From their shop, they also sell wild boar, venison, Scottish cheese, mustards, honey and preserves.

• The Association of Deer Management Groups highly recommend wild venison from *Joseph Mitchell* of 2 Woodside Road, Letham, by Forfar (tel 0307 818 220), butchered into saddle, haunch or shoulder. Reports please.

• *Scotherbs* ✉, Waterybutts, Grange, Errol (tel 0821 642228, fax 0821 642523) grow herbs both outside and in poly-tunnels. Some, such as lemon grass, sorrel or coriander, are available all year; others, like sweet cicely and garlic chives, are seasonal. They also grow a good range of edible flowers.

• *Gowrie Growers* at Kingswell, 12 Holding Road, Longforgan (tel 0826 22620) grow soft fruit and vegetables to sell in their farm-shop. I hear tell that courgette flowers are on sale between July and September, as well as a selection of interesting lettuces.

• *Keracher* ✉, 168 South Street, Perth (0738 38454) keep a vivier tank for their lobsters. Everything else is fresh, as it is packed on ice, and they also smoke a wide range of fish.

• The *Ingle Smokehouse* ✉ at Units 2&3, North Muirton Industrial Estate, Arran Place, Perth (tel 0738 30121) make 500 g (1 lb 2 oz) truckles of unpasteurized Cheddar-style cheese from bought-in Friesian milk, mature them for 3 months and smoke over oak chips from old whisky barrels for about 4 hours.

• Look out for washed-rind St Andrews (a soft pasteurized cows'-milk cheese), Ettrick (similar in appearance to an Edam) and Scottish Brie and Camembert, and the various cream cheese logs rolled in oatmeal or peppercorns made by *Howgate Dairy Foods*, Camperdown Creamery, Faraday Street, Dundee (tel 0382 811622, fax 0382 89993).

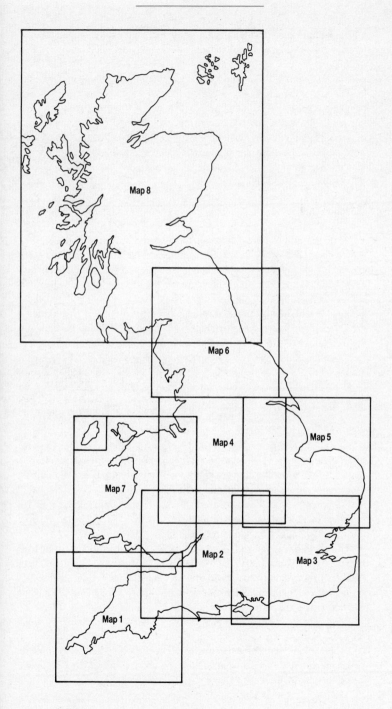

MAP 1

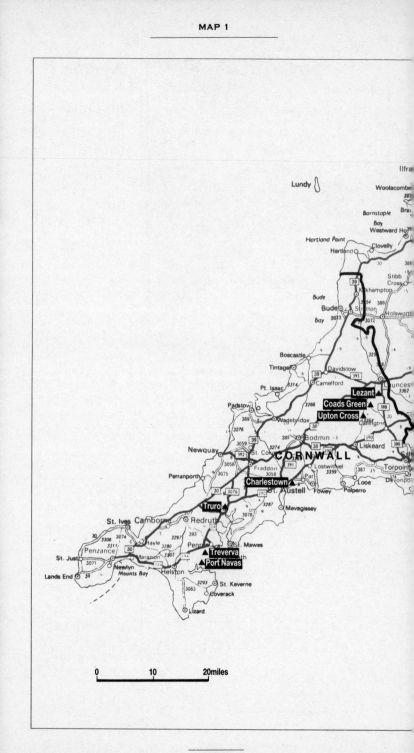

MAP 1

MAP 1

*England –
Devon &
Cornwall*

Cornwall
(see pages 30-40)
Devon
(see pages 55-70)

MAP 2

MAP 2

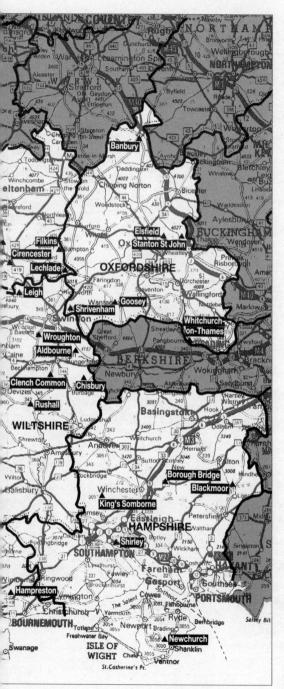

MAP 2

England – South-west

Avon
  (see pages 8-11)
Dorset
  (see pages 70-80)
Gloucestershire
  (see pages 92-104)
Hampshire
  (see pages 104-110)
Herefordshire
  (see pages 111-118)
Isle of Wight
  (see pages 124-125)
Oxfordshire
  (see pages 200-210)
Somerset
  (see pages 219-231)
Wiltshire
  (see pages 267-279)

MAP 3

MAP 3

MAP 3

England – South-east

MAP 4

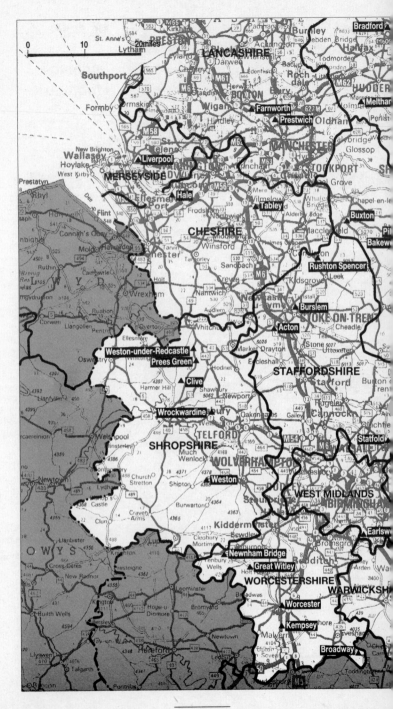

MAP 4

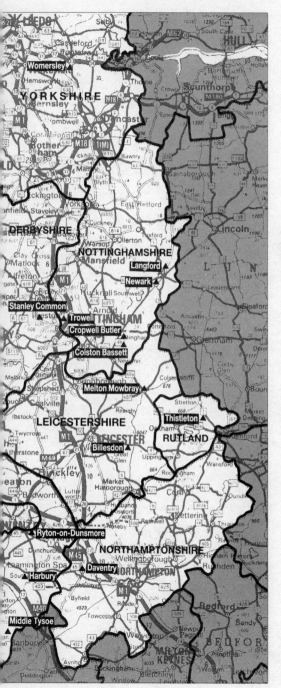

MAP 4

England – Midlands & North-west

Cheshire
  (see pages 24-28)
Derbyshire
  (see pages 50-55)
Lancashire (South)
  (see pages 137-145)
Leicestershire
  (see pages 145-148)
Merseyside
  (see pages 178-179)
Northamptonshire
  (see pages 188-190)
Nottinghamshire
  (see pages 195-200)
Rutland
  (see pages 210-211)
Shropshire
  (see pages 212-219)
Staffordshire
  (see pages 231-237)
Warwickshire
  (see pages 262-266)
West Midlands
  (see pages 266-267)
Worcestershire
  (see pages 279-287)
Yorkshire (South)
  (see pages 288-303)

MAP 5

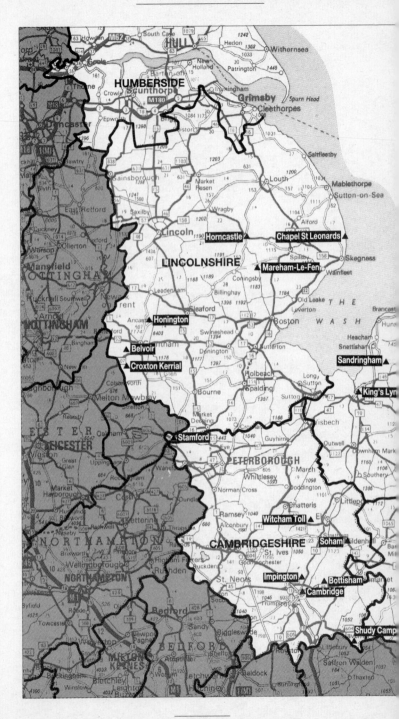

MAP 5

MAP 5

England – East

Cambridgeshire
  (see pages 17-24)
Lincolnshire
  (see pages 148-157)
Norfolk
  (see pages 180-188)
Suffolk
  (see pages 237-249)

0   10   20miles

MAP 6

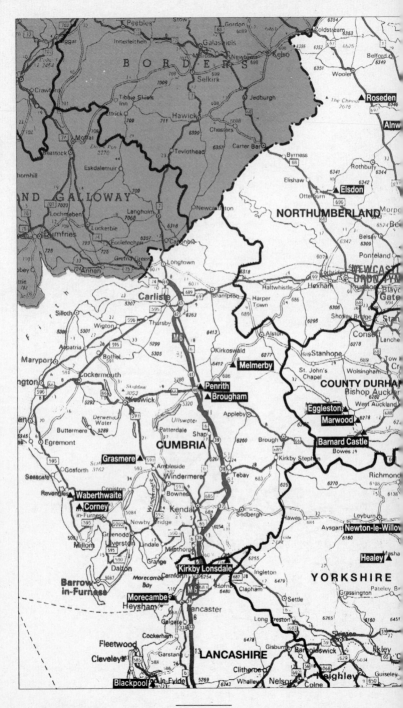

MAP 6

MAP 6

England – North

Cleveland
(see page 29)
Cumbria
(see pages 40-50)
Durham
(see pages 80-83)
Lancashire (North)
(see pages 137-145)
Northumberland
(see pages 190-195)
Yorkshire (North)
(see pages 288-303)

MAP 7

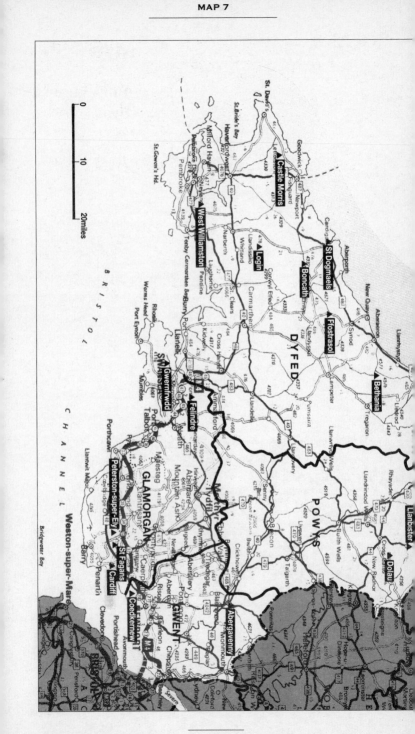

MAP 7

MAP 7

Wales &
Isle of Man

Wales
Dyfed
  (see pages 304-314)
Glamorgan
  (see pages 314-320)
Gwent
  (see pages 320-323)
Gwynedd
  (see pages 323-325)
Powys
  (see pages 325-327)

Isle of Man
  (see pages 122-123)

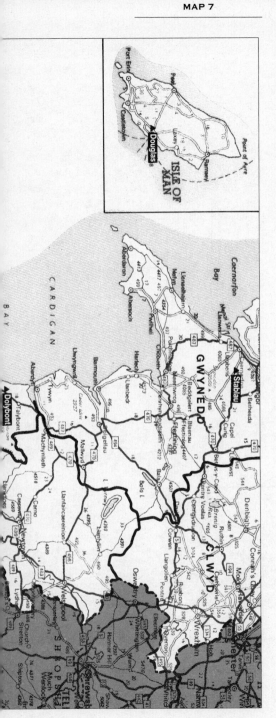

MAP 8

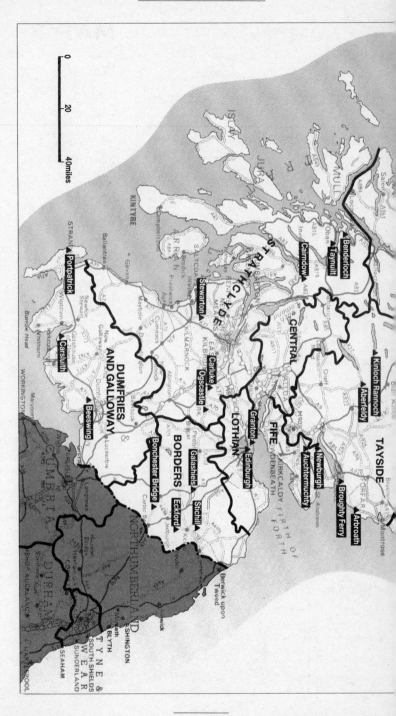

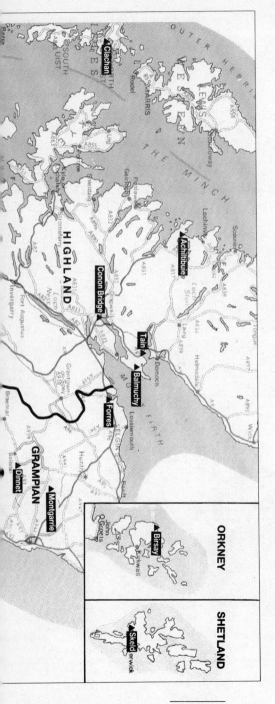

MAP 8

MAP 8

Scotland

PRODUCER INDEX

Numerals in bold indicate main entry.

Numerals in bold indicate main entry.

Numerals in bold indicate main entry.

Numerals in bold indicate main entry.

Numerals in bold indicate main entry.

PRODUCT INDEX

ACKNOWLEDGEMENTS

I owe many people a big thank-you for their help and support in making it possible for me to write my *Food Lovers' Guide to Britain*.

The Rural Development Commission for their generous financial support and their help in the initial stages of research, and I would particularly like to single out George Gray, the former Vice-Chairman for his encouragement, Suzanne Webber of BBC Books and Sheila Dillon of Radio 4's *Food Programme* for agreeing to the project in the first place and guiding me through it; Lewis Esson for his editorial prowess; Jessica Mitchell for retaining a stunning good humour against all odds; the designer David Robinson; Khadija Manjlai and Caroline Plaisted at BBC Books for all their efforts, and Teresa Wickham of Safeway plc for her generous help and enthusiasm.

So many people – food writers, friends and strangers – have made contributions, had me to stay, given me details of their favourite suppliers or allowed me to quote from their books, they are too numerous to list in their entirety, but I would like to single out the following: Michael Bateman, Bill & Carol Brown, Catherine Brown, Susan Campbell, Moppet Cooke-Hurle, Claire Clifton, Anna del Conte, Derek Cooper, Philippa Davenport, Alan Davidson, Gilli Davies, Jossie Dimbleby, Clarissa Dickson Wright, Tim Finney, Matthew Fort, Jim Gooding, George & Judy Gray, Sophie Grigson, Juliet Harbutt, Valentina Harris, Julian Hartnoll, Tessa Hayward, Marie Helly, Andrew Hewson, Virginia Ironside, Tom Jaine, Michelle Kurland, Emily & Bobby Jones, Jack Lang, Nigella Lawson, Elizabeth Luard, Mary Kennedy, Dee McQuillan, Marie-Pierre Moine, Rosemary Moon, Jenny & Christopher Newall, Martina & John Nicolls, Bernard & Carla Phillips, Tessa and Doug Plowden, Michael Raffael, Patrick Rance, Robin Robb, Jill Slotover, Jessica Strang, Keith & Penny Turner, Caroline Waldegrave, Ruth Ward, Ruby Wax, Sarah Woodward, Mark & Stella Wrightson, Juliet Wrightson, all the hundreds of Radio 4's *Food Programme* listeners who sent in their recommendations, all the producers I visited and telephoned for their time and patience, and last but no means least my dog Violet – a faithful travelling companion.

BIBLIOGRAPHY

The following publications have proved invaluable in the compilation of this book and are recommended as further reading:

John Arlott *English Cheeses of the South & West* G. G. Harrap; Tom Carter *The Victorian Garden* Bell & Hyman 1984; Antonio Carluccio *A Passion for Mushrooms* Pavilion 1990; *Cassell's Dictionary of Cookery* 1890; Clare Connery *In an Irish Kitchen* Weidenfeld & Nicolson 1992; Anna del Conte *Gastronomy of Italy* Bantam Press 1987; Elizabeth David *Spices, Salt and Aromatics in the English Kitchen* Penguin Books 1970; Elizabeth David *English Bread and Yeast Cookery* Allen Lane 1977; Dr J. G. Davis *Cheese* 4 vols Churchill Livingstone 1965-76; Mistress Margaret Dods *Cook & Housewife's Manual* Oliver & Boyd 1829; Alan Davidson *North Atlantic Seafood* Macmillan 1979; Jane Grigson *Charcuterie and French Pork Cookery* Michael Joseph 1967; Jane Grigson's *Fruit Book* Michael Joseph 1982; Jane Grigson's *Vegetable Book* Michael Joseph 1978; Sophie Grigson *Eat Your Greens* Network Books 1993; Henrietta Green & Marie-Pierre Moine *10-minute Cuisine* Conran Octopus 1991; N. H. Grubb *Cherries* Crosby Lockwood & Son 1949; *A Guide to the Finest Cheeses of Britain & Ireland* The Specialist Cheesemaker's Association 1992; Theodora FitzGibbon *The Food of the Western World* Hutchinson 1976; Stephen Hall & Juliet Clutton-Brock *Two Hundred Years of British Farm Livestock* British Museum Press 1989; Dorothy Hartley *Food in England* Macdonald 1954; Tessa Hayward *The Salmon Cookbook* Ebury 1992; Ambrose Heath *English Cheeses of the North* G. C. Harrap; David Kitton *The Good Cider Guide* Alma Books 1990; Patricia Lousada *Game Cookery* John Murray 1989; F. Marian McNeill *The Scots Kitchen* Blackie & Son 1929; *The Mitchell Beazley Pocket Cheese Book* Mitchell Beazley 1992; Joan Morgan & Alison Richards *A Paradise out of a Common Field* Random Century 1990; *The Oxford Book of Food Plants* Oxford University Press 1969; Roger Phillips *Wild Food* Pan Books 1983; Margaret Race *A Story of Blackpool Rock*; Patrick Rance *The Great Cheese Book* Macmillan 1982; André L. Simon *A Concise Encyclopaedia of Gastronomy* Allen Lane 1983; Tom Stobart *The Cook's Encyclopaedia* B. T. Batsford 1980; H. V. Taylor *The Apples of England* Crosby Lockwood & Son 1945; Maguelonne Toussaint-Samat *History of Food* Blackwell 1992; *The Vegetable Finder* The Henry Doubleday Research Association 1993; Florence White *Good Things in England* Jonathan Cape 1968; Ralph Whitlock *Dorset Farming* Dovecot Press 1982.